ADVERSARIAL LEGALISM

ADVERSARIAL LEGALISM

The American Way of Law

SECOND EDITION

ROBERT A. KAGAN

Harvard University Press

Cambridge, Massachusetts
London, England

2019

First printing

Library of Congress Cataloging-in-Publication Data
Names: Kagan, Robert A., author.
Title: Adversarial legalism : the American way of law / Robert A. Kagan.
Description: Second edition. | Cambridge, Massachusetts : Harvard University
Press, 2019. | Includes bibliographical references and index.
Identifiers: LCCN 2019010206 | ISBN 9780674238367 (alk. paper)
Subjects: LCSH: Adversary system (Law)–United States. |
Justice, Administration of–United States. | Law–Political aspects.
Classification: LCC KF384 .K34 2019 | DDC 347.73–dc23
LC record available at https://lccn.loc.gov/2019010206

To Elsie and to Susan

Contents

———

Preface to the Second Edition

In 2001, when *Adversarial Legalism* was published, I never imagined that the book would deserve or need a second edition. After all, it repeatedly asserted that adversarial legalism is "the American way of law," so deeply embedded in the country's political structure and culture that it would be highly resistant to significant change. Well, live and learn. In October 2012 my recidivist coauthor and friend Neil Gunningham invited me to give a lecture on adversarial legalism at Australian National University. I decided to focus on adversarial legalism and the American legal system in the first decade or so of the twenty-first century. Surveying that period, I was most struck by a political development: the determined effort of politically conservative activists, lawyers, judges, and Republican Party leaders to *curtail or transform* adversarial legalism. In my talk, therefore, I asked: "How much has the legal system actually been changed? Is adversarial legalism quite as entrenched as I had thought?"

Later, I wondered if my lecture in Australia might be the basis for an Afterword appended to a second printing of *Adversarial Legalism*. When asked about that possibility, Harvard University Press editor Kathleen McDermott suggested that I include such an Afterword in a more thoroughgoing revision of the book as whole. So here we are. In this edition I have tried to update the original version, weaving into it subsequent scholarship and selected legal developments that enhance or alter the first edition's portrait of the American legal system. Most significant in that regard, as in my first impression, are the changes that have flowed from what Steven Teles (2008) labeled "the conservative legal movement" and from the growing political power, over the last two decades, of a more ideologically conservative, more antistatist Republican Party. Many of those legal changes are inserted throughout this volume, although there are separate discussions of the conservative legal changes at the end of Chapter 9 and in the Afterword. The latter chapter wholly replaces the conclusion chapter of the first edition. Otherwise, this edition retains the same structure, basic

ideas, and substance as the original—although I have made additions, dele-
tions, and editorial changes on virtually every page.

Many of those changes reflect a significant adjustment of the book's perspective, to explain which I need to turn briefly to the book's first chapters. Chapter 1, as its title promises, outlines the concept of adversarial
legalism—a mode of legal policy-implementation and dispute resolution that
differs from alternatives such as bureaucratic legalism, expert judgment,
and negotiation. Chapter 1 also presents evidence that adversarial legalism
is a far more prominent feature of governance in the United States than it
is in other economically advanced democracies. Chapter 2 then addresses
some consequences of America's reliance on adversarial legalism, illustrating both its positive and its negative effects on governance, dispute resolution, and the pursuit of justice. In the original edition, the chapter then
says that the rest of the book, as it moves through different areas of law and
governance, devotes more space to the downside of adversarial legalism,
to its costs, devoting less space to the benefits that it generates. Why that
gloomy choice? Because, I wrote, "If we are to retain the system's virtues, it
is important to understand and hence to tame its vices." My hopes, I wrote
at several points in that edition, were for reforms that would strive to strike
that delicate balance, such as reforms that paired constraints on adversarial
legalism with innovative institutions that would do a better job of providing
justice and ensuring governmental and corporate accountability—or reforms
that ensure that adversarial legalism's strengths in performing those functions
would not be significantly impaired.

In contrast, the legal changes wrought by Republican political leaders
and judges in the early twenty-first century generally have not seemed cali-
brated to strike that balance, at least in my view. The conservative changes,
often designed to deter legally unfounded, costly litigation and excessively
legalistic government regulation, usually strike me as one-sided, aimed at
simply stopping litigation and protecting corporate interests, with little concern for how much those changes also block meritorious lawsuits and regulatory requirements. Nor do the conservative legal changes deal with those
adverse consequences by providing any alternative mode of doing justice
and preventing harm. With those thoughts in mind, this edition, even as it
retains the first edition's account of adversarial legalism's unfortunate consequences, shaves some of the sharper edges off that analysis and more
often speaks of adversarial legalism's virtues.

Among those virtues is that adversarial legalism empowers citizens,
lawyers, and judges to mount legal challenges to the arbitrary or unlawful
exercise of government authority. That capacity has become both more
prominent and more essential in recent years—years in which intensely partisan Republican politicians in many states have taken measures to suppress
or dilute Democratic votes; in which President Trump's fervently antiregula-

tion appointees to top positions in regulatory agencies, in repealing existing rules and issuing new ones, have disregarded established procedures and cast aside traditions of rational, evidence-based deliberation; and in which the president himself has shown little regard for constitutional norms, the rule of law, professionalism, and individual rights. The Trump administration's actions have triggered an upsurge in adversarial legalism: waves of lawsuits by politically liberal state attorneys general and nongovernmental organizations challenging the constitutionality or legality of inadequately justified executive orders and administrative policy changes. Repeatedly, lower court federal judges have upheld those challenges, blocking or forcing amendments of some of the most harsh or blatantly illegal presidential and administrative initiatives. Thus adversarial legalism has reaffirmed its worth as an essential bulwark for the rule of law itself in troubled political times.

The barrage of policy-oriented lawsuits against the Trump administration, as noted in the Afterword, echo those initiated, in a similarly collaborative manner, by politically conservative state attorneys general during the preceding Obama administration. That parallelism foreshadows this edition's answer to one of my initial questions, "Is adversarial legalism quite as entrenched as I had thought?" The answer is "yes." True, as the Afterword spells out, the conservative legal attack has impeded and diminished some kinds of litigation. But other kinds of litigation have increased. That is because adversarial legalism's basic legal structures and traditions remain in place, used by conservatives as well as liberals to advance their values and interests.

One final introductory point: *Adversarial Legalism* originally emerged, at least in part, from my experience in teaching undergraduate students, in teaching Ph.D. students who may have had little prior background in law, and in teaching foreign law school graduates who were just learning about the American legal system. I tried in the original edition, therefore, to make the book accessible to nonexperts, indeed to nonlawyers. I conceived it as a work of political science and sociolegal studies that could serve as an empirically-grounded introduction to the American legal system, one that would help lawyers and legal scholars from other countries, as well as any reader, to see how the ostensible irrationalities and frustrating inefficiencies of the American legal system—and its virtues as well—flow from fundamental features of the American *political* system. Hoping this second edition will be similarly useful, I have tried to retain or improve that accessibility.

While working on this second edition, I continued to receive valuable support from the Center for the Study of Law & Society at the University of California, Berkeley and from Berkeley Law. After shifting my residence, first in part and then fully, to Cambridge, Massachusetts, first the Department of Government at Harvard University and then Harvard Law

School's Center for East Asian Studies offered me visiting scholar status, which gave me access to Harvard's superb library system. I received invaluable advice from a great many scholars. Among them are Dan Kelemen and others who attended a talk that Kim Scheppele invited me to give at Princeton's program in Law and Public Affairs. In March 2017, the Center for Law & Society at Berkeley organized a seminar in which I received important insights from Stephen Burbank, Peter Schuck, Paul Pierson, Shep Melnick (on whose scholarship I have leaned very heavily in this book), Sean Farhang (the same), and my ever-insightful Berkeley friend and colleague, Gene Bardach. In April 2018, Timothy Lytton organized a wonderful book workshop at Georgia State Law School at which I profited greatly from a close reading and constructive criticism from Jeb Barnes, Cary Coglianese, Sean Farhang, Daniel Ho, Robert Howard, Amalia Kessler, Tim Lytton himself, Nicholas Parillo, Edward Rubin, Peter Schuck, Amy Steigerwalt, Steven Sugarman, and David Vogel. Mary Jo Bane, after carefully reading a draft of Chapter 8, brought me up to date on research concerning social justice in the United States; Henry Hecht did the same with respect to civil justice in Chapter 6. Tom Burke and Jeb Barnes's introduction to *Varieties of Legal Order* (2018) gave me new insight into the concept of adversarial legalism; and the manuscript was improved by access to the fine chapters in that volume by Shep Melnick, Francis Bignami and Dan Kelemen, Michael McCann and Bill Haltom, Cary Coglianese, Malcolm Feeley, Neil Gunningham, and Kathie Hendley.

A decade ago, I was blessed by a new love—my wife, Dr. Susan Barron, who has given me a vibrant new life and extended family. Notwithstanding the many hours I have spent at my desk, preparing this new edition, Susan has been unwavering in giving me love, support, and large doses of commonsense advice, for which I have been and will continue to be immensely grateful. I am equally grateful for the love and the regular injections of joi de vivre I get from my daughter, Elsie, her husband Carl, and their children, Jasper, Lex, and Willa.

Preface to the First Edition

On the evening of December 12, 2000, Americans by the millions—and for all I know, millions of people around the world—watched their television sets for the announcement of a decision by the Supreme Court of the United States. After weeks of postelection litigation concerning the proper counting of ballots in the state of Florida, the court's ruling could determine whether the Democratic Party's candidate for president, Vice President Albert Gore, or the Republican Party's candidate, Texas Governor George W. Bush, would be declared the victor. A few days earlier, on December 8, a decision by the Supreme Court of Florida left Bush ahead, or so it appeared, by fewer than 200 votes (out of some 4.8 million in the state). The Florida court, however, had ordered a manual review of thousands of ballots to determine whether votes for president had not been recorded by Florida's voting machines. The Bush campaign organization, fearing that the recount would propel Gore into the presidency, had appealed to the U.S. Supreme Court. On December 9, a bitterly divided Supreme Court accepted the case and ordered a temporary stop to the manual recount, dashing spirits in the Gore camp. On December 11, the Court heard oral arguments. But there was no consensus among legal experts about how the Court, which traditionally had deferred to state courts in the interpretation of state electoral law, would actually decide.

Finally, late in the evening of December 12, the Court's ruling was distributed to waiting journalists, who struggled to decode a cryptic per curiam opinion, four dissenting opinions, and one concurrence. The Court, it was clear, had vacated the Florida Supreme Court's ruling by a seven-to-two margin, employing an unprecedented "equal protection clause" argument. But it also held that the recount could proceed if the Florida courts would issue uniform statewide standards for counting disputed ballots. Then it gradually dawned on the television reporters, and hence on the waiting viewers, that by a five-to-four vote, the Supreme Court had interpreted Florida law to impose an inalterable December 12 deadline for the

XIV   PREFACE TO THE FIRST EDITION

certification of Florida's electoral votes. That deadline made the belatedly permitted recount impossible. The next day, Gore conceded. By a one-vote majority, the five most politically conservative justices had enabled Bush to gain the presidency.

To many foreign observers, it may have seemed simultaneously remarkable and typical that the political contest for the American presidency had triggered an explosion of litigation—fourteen separate lawsuits, numerous appeals, and two U.S. Supreme Court reviews, the second of which, by blocking the counting of the disputed ballots, had determined the winner. As an earlier foreign observer, Alexis de Tocqueville (1835: 290), had written, "Scarcely any political question arises in the United States that is not resolved, sooner or later, into a judicial question." Yet even de Tocqueville would have been astonished by the nature of the postelection litigation in 2000—so sprawling, so resistant to legal finality, so legally unpredictable, so combative in its intensity. A complex set of legal rules and institutions designed to contain the passions and opportunism of politics became a partisan battleground itself.

In the weeks following the November 7 election, with the Florida result still in doubt, both political parties unleashed the dogs of law. Squadrons of Democratic and Republican lawyers were deployed, speed-reading the details of Florida's election laws, performing prodigies of brief-writing, meeting legal losses in one forum with an appeal or a new lawsuit in another. As the statutory date for the Florida's selection of electors approached, Democratic lawyers frantically prodded election officials and judges to count disputed votes or ballots. Republican lawyers argued that there was no legal justification or no time to keep counting, successfully delaying manual counts several times. As often occurs in American litigation, the outcome was shaped more by the delays and opportunity costs of extended adversarial legal processes than by authoritative legal judgments about the just result.

To observers from other constitutional democracies, where judges generally are selected through professional, less overtly political mechanisms, it must also have been remarkable that the American judges seemed to be such creatures of politics. As the hydra-headed litigation moved from court to court, journalists pointed out the political party background and connections of particular judges, as if those, and not the law, were likely to shape the court's decision. Indeed, it turned out that the Florida Supreme Court, composed of appointees of a Democratic governor, made two crucial and controversial decisions that favored Gore. The U.S. Supreme Court, made up predominantly of judges appointed by Republican presidents, vacated those decisions, employing legal arguments that surprised (or dismayed) most constitutional scholars. Yet it was not certain ex ante that the judges' political backgrounds would entirely predict their decisions. Generally, American judges are motivated not only by their political philosophies but also by the desire to maintain a reputation for legal craftsmanship and to protect the perceived legitimacy of the courts. Sometimes a judge's individual political views matter a great deal, but sometimes they don't. The Florida Supreme Court decided in Gore's favor in two appeals but against him in several others. A U.S. Court of Appeals, with a majority of Republican judges, rejected a Bush appeal that sought to block the handcounting of ballots—although the predominantly Republican U.S. Supreme Court, in a separate suit, effectively did just that (with two politically moderate Republican judges dissenting). It is this shifting balance of political and legal factors, combined with the staggering complexity of contemporary American law, that makes a high level of *unpredictability* such a distinctive feature of adjudication in the United States—not just in the election litigation but in general.

Nevertheless, in *this* set of cases, the judges' political leanings seemed to be the deciding factor. Legal scholars, like the public at large, ended up viewing the propriety of each Florida and U.S. Supreme Court decision through sharply divergent partisan lenses, just as the high court itself divided along moderate-conservative lines. Tossed about by these turbulent political waves, the very notion of legal objectivity, already weakened by years of "legal realism," "critical legal studies," and an increasingly partisan judicial selection process, seemed close to death. In a December 11, 2000, public opinion poll, a majority of respondents (53 percent) said they believed the Supreme Court's decision to stay the Florida manual recount was based on politics rather than law (34 percent).

The postelection legal battle thus exemplified and intensified America's ambivalence about law and litigation. On one hand, the litigation underscored the nation's fundamental respect for the rule of law and the authority of courts. Just as President Richard Nixon in the Watergate tapes case had bowed to a Supreme Court decision that he knew would doom his ability to remain in office, Vice President Gore, while stating he strongly disagreed with the Court's December 12 decision, was quick to add that he accepted its authority. Throughout the litigation Bush and Gore supporters mounted loud demonstrations outside the key courthouses, but there seemed to be a reservoir of faith and pride that somber legal argument and constitutional procedures, not mobs or raw political power, ultimately would settle the various disputes and produce a smooth transfer of power. On the other hand, many citizens expressed annoyance that dueling lawyers had taken over the selection of the president. Others (including, perhaps, a majority of U.S. Supreme Court justices) worried that the litigation and counterlitigation would spiral out of control, generating not legal finality but a constitutional crisis. The Bush campaign organization found it politically acceptable and even desirable to repeatedly denounce the Florida Supreme Court's attempt to reconcile ostensibly conflicting statutory provisions as "changing the rules after the election was over." Not only the courts but the rule of law itself had become politically contested territory—and not for the first time in American history.

In many respects, therefore, the protracted courthouse struggle following the 2000 election, for all its uniqueness, did typify the American political system, which persistently venerates courts and the rule of law but just as persistently derides the rule of lawyers, judges, and legal excess. "Adversarial legalism," as I call the rambunctious, peculiarly American style of law and legal decision-making exhibited in late 2000, has become a common phenomenon in the life of the nation. It recurs in everyday American processes of criminal and civil litigation, and in American methods of regulating police and schools and businesses, of compensating accident victims, and of holding governmental officials accountable.

The elements that fostered adversarial legalism in the 2000 election endgame, this book argues, affect almost every sphere of governmental and economic activity. They include adjudicatory systems that give lawyers for the competing parties a very large and creative role in gathering evidence, formulating legal arguments, and influencing decisions—and hence foster an especially entrepreneurial and aggressive legal profession; a politically selected, somewhat unpredictable, and uniquely powerful judiciary; a fragmented governmental and court system (which often enables losers in one forum to seek a different decision in another); and a system of governmental administration that is more decentralized, more responsive to democratic political pressures, and more generally distrusted than the national bureaucracies and court systems of, say, Western European countries.

Reflecting that combination of decentralization, politicization, and distrust, Florida's election laws were so complex because the legislature periodically had promulgated new, more specific rules to regulate the state's politically selected county election boards. The electoral decisions of Florida's secretary of state had been made legally subject to review by courts because she, like her predecessors, was a partisan political official (in this case, a co-chair of Bush's Florida campaign organization) rather than an apolitical, professional bureaucrat. Some U.S. Supreme Court justices voted to stop the manual recount because they indicated that they did not trust Florida election officials or trial judges to conduct the recount in a neutral, consistent, and professional manner. These distrustful attitudes toward a decentralized, politically permeable governmental structure do not affect elections alone. They permeate American politics and governance, making adversarial legalism a pervasive feature of American life.

The passions that trigger adversarial legalism, with its hopes for justice and fears of costly legal excess, usually are not (as in the *Bush v. Gore* legal saga) national in scope and attention. Rather, they are local and familiar. They arise in the course of everyday criminal prosecutions, personal injury lawsuits, and disputes over land use. They emerge from environmental controversies, from conflicts between regulatory officials and businesses, between commercial enterprises, and between employees and employers. That is the terrain that this book traverses, exploring the ways in which American adversarial legalism differs from law and governance in other economically advanced democracies, examining why that is the case, and describing its consequences, both positive and negative.

As best I can piece it together, the idea for this book arose during a fellowship I was granted by the Netherlands Institute for Advanced Study in the Social and Behavioral Sciences (NIAS) in 1987. Month after month, I was immersed in discussions of the Dutch and other European legal processes with Erhard Blankenburg, Kees Groenendyk, Albert Klijn, and other sociolegal scholars—conversations in which we explored what was different about American legal culture, methods of regulation, and modes of adjudication, and why those differences arose and persist.

I also used the NIAS fellowship to begin a comparative study of seaports and intermodal transportation. My goal was to compare Dutch and U.S. legal and regulatory processes in resolving cargo damage claims, promoting safety, managing labor relations, fostering technological innovation, and protecting the environment. In this book one can find traces of my interviews in and around the Port of Rotterdam with regulatory officials, labor unionists, port officials, lawyers, shipping line and terminal managers, marine insurance companies, and freight forwarders. Their day-to-day experiences underscored some distinctive aspects of American legal and regulatory processes, particularly their higher costs, heavier penalties, and greater levels of uncertainty.

In the years that followed, I gathered sociolegal studies that compare particular legal and regulatory processes in the United States with similar processes in other economically advanced democracies. These studies, summarized in Table 1 in Chapter 1 and referred to throughout this volume, all seemed to tell the same story: American legal and regulatory regimes, compared to their counterparts in other countries, generally are characterized by more detailed and prescriptive legal rules, more litigation, more costly forms of legal contestation, more fearsome legal penalties, more political conflict, and higher levels of legal malleability and uncertainty.

My research on seaports also led to a detailed case study of the legal and regulatory struggles surrounding the efforts of the Port of Oakland, California, to dredge its harbors. To me, the Port of Oakland story epitomized the way in which adversarial legal struggle has become an ever-present propensity of American governance, often with highly disruptive, inefficient, and unjust consequences. When Martin Levin of Brandeis University invited me to write a paper for a conference on American public policy, I sought to link the Port of Oakland story (discussed in Chapters 2 and 10 of this book) to a broader account of American law and regulation. My work on that paper was supported by the Center for Advanced Study in the Social and Behavioral Sciences in Stanford, California. In the paper, subsequently published in the *Journal for Public Policy and Management* and in a volume edited by Levin and Marc Landy, I conjured up the concept of adversarial legalism to distinguish American legal processes from the more hierarchical, less participatory methods of regulation and adjudication used in other countries. In writing that paper, I also came to see more clearly how American adversarial legalism springs from fundamental features of American politics, particularly the propensity to distrust and fragment governmental authority—even as government is asked to become more active in providing justice and reducing risk. At my urging, Kenneth Hanf of Erasmus University and Yoshinobu Kitamura of Yokohama University wrote conference papers comparing the Oakland experience with parallel regulatory processes in the ports of Rotterdam and Kobe, respectively, and their research further highlighted the uniqueness of American adversarial legalism.

I am grateful to Professor Herbert McClosky for urging me to turn my initial article into a book, to Aida Donald of Harvard University Press for additional encouragement, and to a year as visiting professor at the College of Law, Ohio State University, during which I was able to conduct additional research about the role of American lawyers, judges, and legal scholars in fostering adversarial legalism. In 1995–1998 I was given the opportunity to undertake a research project that used the cross-national experience of selected multinational corporations to compare legal and regulatory regimes in the United States with parallel regimes in other economically advanced democracies. The project produced ten detailed case studies, gathered in *Regulatory Encounters: Multinational Corporations and American Adversarial Legalism* (2000). I am grateful to the case study authors, Lee Axelrad, John Dwyer, Kirsten Engel, Holly Welles, Kazumasu Aoki, John Cioffi, Lori Johnson, Martine Kraus, Laura Beth Nielsen, Charles Ruhlin, Deepak Somaya, Tatsuya Fujie, Marius Aalders, Richard Brooks, and Alan Marco. Their efforts provided findings and analyses that filled important gaps in the comparative literature and that I rely on at several points in this book.

My work on the manuscript benefited greatly from the support of Berkeley's Center for the Study of Law and Society and its staff, particularly Rod Watanabe and Margo Rodriguez. I received superb research assistance from outstanding graduate students, including Todd Lochner, Lori Johnson, Linus Masuredis, Brendon Swedlow, Sara Rushing, and especially Jeb Barnes, who not only found facts and summarized literature but also constantly pushed me to sharpen my arguments. The experience of teaching hundreds of Berkeley students over the last decade has also been immensely valuable, forcing me to view the American legal system afresh each year and to focus on its many strengths as well as its disturbing qualities.

So many valued and able academic colleagues have read and commented on various draft chapters of *Adversarial Legalism* that I fear that I will fail to mention everyone who provided important corrections or encouragement or both. Among the most prominent in my mind today are Sandy Muir, Eugene Bardach, David Vogel, Malcolm Feeley, Tom Burke, Albert Klijn, Harry Scheiber, Lawrence M. Friedman, David Kirp, Margaret Weir, David Johnson, Peter Schuck, William Pizzi, Bud Bynack, and David Levine. There are many more scholars whose careful research and thoughtful analyses provided the bulk of the information in this book; their names are in the list of references at the end.

Most important to me have been those whose love and patience have sustained and strengthened me, even as I withdrew into my study on far too many evenings—Betsy, my caring, lovely, and ever-insightful wife, and my wonderful and amazing daughter Elsie.

ADVERSARIAL LEGALISM

PART I

ADVERSARIAL LEGALISM

Contours, Consequences, Causes

CHAPTER ONE

The Concept of Adversarial Legalism

In contemporary democracies law is inescapable. It is essential for maintaining order in rapidly changing societies, regulating political processes, and making economic markets work well. When bad things happen and attract media attention, political leaders respond by enacting reform laws, promulgating new regulations, and intensifying legal enforcement. Different nations, however, make and implement law somewhat differently. Compared to other economically advanced democracies, the United States more often relies on courts, lawyers, legal threats, and legal contestation in making and implementing public policies, in compensating accident victims, in striving to hold governmental officials accountable, and in regulating economic behavior. American laws generally are more detailed, complicated, and prescriptive. American methods of litigating and adjudicating legal disputes are more adversarial and more costly. Legal penalties in the United States, on average, are more severe. And overall, American economic and political life is more deeply pervaded by litigation (or the threat of it) and by political controversy about the judiciary and legal processes.

To encapsulate some of these distinctive qualities of governance and legal process in the United States, I use the shorthand term "adversarial legalism," defined as policymaking, policy implementation, and dispute resolution by means of party-and-lawyer-dominated legal contestation. Adversarial legalism contrasts with governance and dispute resolution that rely instead on other methods—bureaucratic administration, discretionary judgment by experts or political authorities, informal negotiation or mediation, and the judge-dominated style of litigation common in many other countries. While the United States employs these other methods too, they operate in the shadow of the legal structures of adversarial legalism. And adversarial legalism is far more prominent in the United States than in other economically advanced democracies.

American adversarial legalism has both positive and negative effects. Viewed in cross-national comparison, the legal system of the United States is especially open to new kinds of justice claims and political movements. American judiciaries are particularly flexible and creative. American lawyers, litigation, and courts serve as powerful (even if not always complete) checks against official intolerance, corruption and arbitrariness, as protectors of essential individual rights, and as deterrents to corporate heedlessness. Adversarial legalism provides a channel for addressing serious social problems or injustices that legislatures neglect or are too politically deadlocked to resolve. In so doing, adversarial legalism enhances the political legitimacy of the system of government as a whole.

At the same time, however, adversarial legalism is an inefficient and costly method of governance and dispute resolution. The complexity, expense, and unpredictability of its processes often deter the assertion of meritorious legal claims and compel the compromise of meritorious defenses, alienating many citizens from the law itself. Adversarial legalism often inspires legal defensiveness and contentiousness, clogging up the processes of governance, business, and other spheres of activity. By making courts politically powerful, it makes the judiciary a focus of partisan political conflict, which tends to make the law more malleable and less predictable.

Do the negative aspects of American adversarial legalism outweigh its positive features? To pose the question in such global terms is problematic. There is no way to count up and compare all the costs and benefits that a gigantic, multifaceted legal system sends rippling through economic, political, and communal life. And even if one could make such a calculation, the question would remain: Compared to what? That is, would alternative ways of governance and dispute resolution yield higher aggregate benefits and lower social costs—or not? That question too defies any easy answer, at least at that sweeping, system-wide level of analysis.

Other economically advanced democracies, particularly in Western Europe, structure legal and regulatory institutions and processes in ways, discussed in this book, that suggest plausible alternatives to American adversarial legalism. But the practice that works well in Amsterdam or London might not work as well in Seattle or Miami. And those Dutch or British practices may also entail a downside not revealed by current comparative studies. Moreover, adversarial legalism is deeply rooted in the political institutions and values of the United States. American legal elites and political leaders are not likely to accept wholesale replacement of familiar legal practices with those drawn from rather different political traditions. Some Western European legal and regulatory practices may achieve higher levels of legal certainty than American adversarial legalism, without nearly so much expenditure on lawyers and legal conflict, but those practices are nested in political systems that impose high taxes and expect deference to governmental bureaucracies—neither of which has much political appeal in the United States. For good and for ill, adversarial legalism is at the heart of the American way of legal governance, and it is likely to remain so.

The purpose of this book, therefore, is not to provide a definitive overall assessment of adversarial legalism, nor is it to propose specific improvements. Rather, my principal intent is descriptive and explanatory—to enhance understanding of American adversarial legalism's characteristic features; to show how and why it has come to differ from the legal and regulatory styles of other economically advanced democracies; and to highlight its salient consequences, negative as well as positive. Secondarily, by devoting attention to adversarial legalism's negative consequences, I hope to stimulate constructive thought about possible reform pathways. Yet that focus, I hope, will not obscure the vitally important virtues of adversarial legalism listed above—virtues that are threatened by heavy-handed measures to cripple adversarial legalism without providing effective alternatives.

Offering generalizations about the American legal system as a whole, I should note, is a bit quixotic. The United States has fifty separate state legal systems, sets of administrative agencies, and judiciaries, crosscut by federal law, agencies, and courts. Within states, there are scores of city and county law-making and law enforcement bodies. Just as importantly, the United States is a huge, continent-wide country—a nation that has never been fully united but rather has been riven by differing political and social subcultures (Woodard, 2011). Those subcultures tend to favor conflicting views about how law should deal with economic liberty, religion, individual responsibility, crime, race, environmental protection versus economic growth, how much money should be devoted to tax revenues and aid to the poor, and other important but divisive issues. Those conflicting attitudes are reflected in substantial regional and local differences in the law on the books and the law in action. Thus any generalization I make in this book about American laws and legal practices, even if based (as I try to do) on empirical studies, can probably be contradicted by those familiar with actual practices in particular states, counties, or cities.

On the other hand, respect for the rule of law is one idea that unites these barely united states. The scores of law schools in the United States assign the same books, instill in their students the same common law mode of legal reasoning, and teach the same basic elements of due process of law. State supreme courts cite cases from other states and the U.S. Supreme Court. The U.S. Constitution, federal regulatory and civil rights law, and many other areas of federal law have been powerful unifying forces and have strongly influenced the evolution of state law. Overall, therefore, I believe that there is as much or more that characterizes the American legal system as a whole than divides it, and that those commonalities are worth highlighting and examining. And I think the intra-U.S. differences fade in significance when trying, as this book does, to discuss how and why the American way of law differs from that of other economically advanced democracies.

The picture of the American legal system painted in this book reflects sociolegal, comparative, and political perspectives. The sociolegal strand draws on empirical studies of the system as it actually operates—studies that focus not merely on the law on the books or famous court opinions but on the law in action, including the day-to-day outcomes of its processes. The comparative strand draws on studies that contrast legal and regulatory processes in the United States with similar processes in other economically advanced democracies. The political strand traces the links among the distinctive characteristics of the American legal system and fundamental features of American political culture, political structure, and political processes.

The discussion bridges categories of American law and policy that typically are treated as separate and distinct—criminal justice, liability law, environmental regulation, social welfare law, and so on. By viewing these different legal spheres holistically, it becomes clear that the different streams of the American legal process share a common set of characteristics. That is what undergirds the claim that adversarial legalism is the American way of law. The very pervasiveness of American adversarial legalism, moreover, suggests that it is best viewed not merely as a method of solving legal disputes but as a mode of governance, embedded in the political culture and political structure of the United States. In an important sense, therefore, this book can be viewed as a study of the relationship between law and politics in America, examined in comparative perspective.

The goal of the comparative analysis, let me re-emphasize, is not to recommend specific transplants from other political and legal systems. The appropriate analogy is not transplant surgery but psychotherapy. Like that practice, comparative analysis in this book attempts to reveal roads not taken, unconsciously maintained patterns, and sources of resistance to change. At the same time, by emphasizing the deeply entrenched political roots of adversarial legalism in the United States, this book will repeatedly remind us that legal and political traditions, like individuals, are not easily changed. And that also suggests caution about attempting to uproot parts of adversarial legalism without providing reliable functional alternatives.

American Legal Exceptionalism

Everywhere in the modern world, legal control of social, political, and economic life is intensifying (Galanter, 1992; Dewees, Trebilcock, and Coyte, 1991). Law grows from the relentless pressures of technological change, geographic mobility, global economic competition, and environmental pollution–all of which generate social and economic disruption, new risks to health and security, new forms of injustice, and new cultural challenges to traditional norms. Some citizens, riding the waves of change, demand new rights of inclusion, political access, and economic opportunity. Others, threatened by change, demand legal protection from harm and loss of control. Democratic governments pass laws and issue judicial rulings responsive to both sets of demands (Schuck, 2000: 42; Kagan, 1995).

In some spheres of activity, such as land use regulation and worker protection, Western European polities typically have more restrictive laws than does the United States. Compared to the United States, Japan has a more detailed and extensive set of legally mandated product standards and premarketing testing requirements (Edelman, 1988: 292; Vogel, 1990). Germany has stricter recycling regulations and much tighter legal restrictions on the opening and operating of new retail enterprises (Davis and Gumbel, 1995). Compared to most American states, Sweden has tougher laws, and tougher law enforcement, concerning fathers' obligations to provide child support. The Netherlands regulates how much manure a farmer can spread on his fields (Huppes and Kagan, 1989: 215) and, like Germany, has more stringent emission standards than the United States for some major air pollutants (Rose-Ackerman, 1995: 27–28). An increasing number of nations, as well as the European Union, now have active constitutional courts (Kapiszewski, Silverstein, and Kagan, 2013), supporting Torbjorn Vallinder's (1995: 13) claim of a worldwide trend toward the "judicialization of politics," defined as "(1) the expansion of the province of courts or the judges at the expense of politicians and/or the administrators . . . or . . . (2) the spread of judicial decision making methods outside the judicial province proper." As the European Union has extended its regulatory reach, rights-oriented judicial rulings and litigation have become increasingly salient aspects of governance in European member states (Kelemen, 2011; Stone Sweet, 2000; Lasser, 2013).

But the United States, as mentioned earlier, has a unique legal style. That is the message of an accumulating body of careful cross-national studies, such as those listed in Table 1. Each study examines a specific area of public policy, law, or social problem-solving in the United States and at least one other economically advanced democracy. The studies focus not merely on the formal law but on how the law is implemented in practice. Cumulatively, the studies compare national systems for compensating injured people; regulating pollution; punishing criminals; equalizing educational opportunity; promoting worker safety; discouraging narcotics use; deterring malpractice by police officers, physicians, and product manufacturers; and so on. The studies do not, of course, cover all of the many fields and subfields of law. But the comparative empirical studies mentioned are sufficient to show that for one social problem after another, the American system for making and implementing public policy and resolving disputes is distinctive. It generally entails (1) more complex bodies of legal rules; (2) more formal, adversarial procedures for resolving political and scientific disputes; (3) a much larger role for private lawsuits in enforcing antidiscrimination, consumer protection, and regulatory law; (4) more adversarial and costly forms of legal contestation; (5) stronger, more punitive legal sanctions;[1] (6) more frequent judicial review of and intervention into administrative decisions and processes;[2] (7) more political controversy about legal rules and institutions; (8) more politically fragmented, less closely coordinated legal decision-making systems; and (9) more legal uncertainty and instability. More recently published comparative studies suggest that these differences have persisted into the twenty-first century.[3]

Comparative studies are hardly necessary, moreover, to show that in no other economically advanced democracy are judges elected, or appointed, through such an openly partisan political process. In no other democracy do judges so readily make new law rather than simply apply it. The legal system of no other democracy so fully empowers and encourages lawyers and non-governmental advocacy organizations to act as private attorneys general, bringing lawsuits against government bodies and business corporations for violating statutory or Constitutional rights. Thus in no other economically advanced political system do public policy entrepreneurs and advocacy groups so readily turn to the courts to achieve policy goals that have been ignored or blocked by legislatures. And nowhere have judges so often made crucial decisions in political struggles over the delineation of electoral district boundaries, the management of forests, the breakup of business monopolies, the appropriate funding level for inner-city versus suburban public schools, or the effort to discourage cigarette smoking.

Consequently, the United States has by far the world's largest cadre of politically-oriented cause lawyers who seek to influence public policy by means of innovative litigation—and who use the threat of litigation in order to promote institutional change (Epp, 2009, 1998a; Kawar, 2015; Hensler, 2016). In no other country are lawyers so entrepreneurial in seeking out new kinds of business, so eager to challenge authority, or so quick to propose new liability-expanding legal theories. In no other countries are the money damages assessed in environmental and tort suits nearly so high, or have major manufacturers been driven into bankruptcy by liability claims, or have disagreements over tort law generated such intense interest group clashes in the legislatures. Notwithstanding the aggressive prosecution of governmental corruption by Italian and French magistrates, the United States leads the league of nations in the extent to which political parties' struggles for political advantage regularly include investigations and prosecutions arising from charges that the chief executive, his aides, cabinet members, or legislators have committed criminal violations (Ginsburg and

TABLE 1 Cross-national studies

Author	Policy area	Countries compared with U.S.
Badaracco (1985)	Exposure to polyvinyl chloride	France, Germany, Japan, U.K.
Bayley (1976)	Police behavior	Japan
Bok (1971)	Selection of labor represen-tatives	Several West European
Boyle (1998)	Litigation in the licensing of nuclear power plants	France, Germany, Sweden
Braithwaite (1985)	Coal mine safety	Australia, Japan, Germany, France
Braithwaite (1993)	Nursing home care	Australia, U.K.
Brickman et al. (1985)	Hazardous chemicals regulation	Several West European
Charkham (1994)	Corporate governance	France, Germany, Japan, U.K.
Church & Nakamura (1993)	Hazardous waste cleanup	Denmark, Germany, Nether-lands
Day & Klein (1987)	Nursing homes	U.K.
Feldman (2000)	Blood safety	France, Japan
Glendon (1987)	Regulation of abortion and child support	Several West European
Greve (1989b)	Public interest litigation in environmental regulation	Germany
Hoberg (1993)	Environmental regulation	Canada
Jacob et al. (1996)	Role of courts	France, Germany, Japan, U.K.
Jasanoff (1986)	Carcinogens regulation	Several West European
Johnson (1998)	Criminal prosecution	Japan
Kagan & Axelrad (2000)	Environmental and product safety regulation; patents; labor; debt collection	Germany, Japan, U.K., EU, Canada, Netherlands
Kelman (1981)	Workplace safety	Sweden
Kirp (1979)	Racial discrimination in schools	U.K.
Kirp (1982)	Special education	U.K.
Langbein (1979b)	Criminal adjudication	Germany
Langbein (1985)	Civil litigation methods	Germany
Litt et al. (1990)	Banking regulation	Japan
Lundqvist (1980)	Air pollution regulation	Sweden
Pizzi (1999)	Criminal adjudication	Germany, Netherlands, Norway, U.K.
Quam et al. (1987)	Medical malpractice com-pensation	U.K.
Schwartz (1991)	Products liability lawsuits	Several West European
Sellers (1995)	Land use decision making	France, Germany
Tanase (1990)	Compensation for vehicle accidents	Japan
Teff (1985)	Pharmaceutical products regulation	U.K.
Vogel (1986)	Environmental regulation	U.K.
Wallace (1995)	Environmental regulation	Japan, several West European
Wokutch (1992)	Workplace safety regulation	Japan

Shefter, 1990). The United States is remarkable in its propensity to stage highly publicized, protracted legal donnybrooks such as the multicourt battle over Florida's votes in the 2000 presidential election, and the waves of litigation by political conservatives opposed to the 2010 Affordable Care Act—struggles that inject huge televised doses of politicized legal argument into the nation's everyday experience.

What *Is* Adversarial Legalism?

All these legal propensities are manifestations of what I call "adversarial legalism"—a method of policymaking, policy-implementation, and dispute resolution with two salient characteristics. The first is *formal legal contestation*—competing interests and disputants readily invoke legal rights, duties, and procedural requirements, backed by recourse to formal law enforcement, litigation, and/or judicial review. The second is *litigant activism*—a style of legal contestation in which the assertion of claims, the search for controlling legal arguments, and the gathering and submission of evidence are dominated not by judges or government officials but by disputing parties or organizations, acting primarily through lawyers. Organizationally, adversarial legalism typically is associated with and is embedded in decision-making institutions in which *authority is fragmented* and in which *hierarchical control is relatively weak*.

Table 2 presents a typology designed to contrast adversarial legalism with other modes of policymaking: policy-implementation and dispute resolution.[4] The table outlines a two-dimensional space based on two variables: (1) the relative density of controlling legal rules and (2) the degree to which legal authority is organized and exercised in a hierarchical as opposed to a participatory fashion (that is, influenced by the affected parties). Along the horizontal, "density of legal control" dimension of Table 2, legal processes vary in the extent to which substantive decisions and procedures are structured by, and expected to conform to, specific legal rules, rights, and duties. The more detailed and prescriptive those pre-existing legal rules—that is, the further along the continuum toward the right side of the table, the more formal or legalistic the system can be said to be.[5] Conversely, decision-making systems can be placed toward the left side, and characterized as informal, to the extent that guiding legal rules are more general, less constraining, both substantively and procedurally.

In the second dimension, displayed vertically on the table, the higher up toward the top that a policy-implementation or dispute-resolution process is located, the more hierarchical it is—that is, dominated or controlled by an official who is relatively insulated from pressures from disputing parties or affected individuals and organizations. Toward the bottom end of that

TABLE 2 Modes of policy implementation and dispute resolution

Organization of decision-making authority	Decision-making style		
	Informal	⟵⟶	Formal
Hierarchical	Expert or political judgment		Bureaucratic legalism
↑ ⏐ ↓			
Participatory	Negotiation/mediation		Adversarial legalism

continuum, authority is exercised in a more participatory manner, so that affected parties have considerable opportunity to make arguments and actually influence legal outcomes.

Taking each of these dimensions to their extreme form produces four ideal types—conceptual constructs which real world decision processes may approximate to various degrees. In fact, legal systems often employ hybrids—policy-implementation and dispute resolution systems in which one ideal type predominates but which combine elements of two or more others. Such real-world hybrids thus occupy various intermediate points on either the informal–formal dimension, or the hierarchical–participatory dimension, or on both, edging closer to the center of the two-dimensional space. The ideal types, however, give us images or conceptual starting points for comparing and contrasting real-world systems.

Negotiation / Mediation

A process in the lower left quadrant of Table 2 is participatory in the sense that it is dominated by the contending parties, not by an authoritative governmental decision maker. But it is informal or nonlegalistic, since neither procedures nor normative standards are dictated by formal law. One example would be dispute resolution via negotiation, with or without lawyers. For example, the congressional statute mandating special education programs requires local school districts to negotiate an individualized education plan with the parents or guardians of each special needs student.[6] The quadrant would also include mediation, whereby an official third party attempts to induce contending parties to agree on a policy or settlement but refrains from imposing a settlement based on law or official policy. Often, for example, regulatory officials charged with implementing antidiscrimination or consumer protection law mediate disputes between a complainant and an employer or a merchant, fostering a negotiated settlement (Silbey, 1984).

Expert / Political Judgment

In modern administrative states, many administrative decision processes would fall in the upper left quadrant of Table 2. They are *hierarchical* in the sense that an official decision maker (as opposed to the individual or organization subject to agency action) controls the process and the standards for decision; yet they are *informal* in the sense that decisions are entrusted to the professional or political judgment of individual officials rather than requiring them to conform to detailed legal rules. For example, in many Western European countries decisions concerning eligibility for disability benefits and the extent of workers' compensation benefits are made by a panel of government-appointed physicians (or a mixed panel of physicians and social workers) without significant probability of intensive judicial review. In Japan disputes over fault in motor vehicle accidents regularly are resolved by special traffic police who rush to the scene, question the parties, "hammer out a consensual story as to what happened," and file a detailed report on their findings (Tanase, 1990: 651, 673–674). In the United States, government programs to protect human subjects and laboratory animals in biomedical research are characterized by broadly worded legal standards, implemented by university review boards consisting of scientific professionals.

Bureaucratic Legalism

A policy-implementing or decision-making process characterized by a high degree of hierarchical authority and legal formality (the upper right quadrant of Table 2) resembles the ideal-typical bureaucratic process as analyzed by Max Weber. Governance by means of bureaucratic legalism emphasizes uniform implementation of centrally devised rules, vertical accountability, and official responsibility for fact-finding. The more hierarchical the system, the more restricted the role for legal representation and influence by affected citizens or contending interests. In contemporary democracies the pure case of bureaucratic legalism usually is softened in some respects, but it is an ideal systematically pursued, for example, by tax collection agencies. Also tending toward this ideal are German and French courts, where judges are bureaucratically recruited and supervised—as contrasted with America's emphasis on election or political appointment. In court, these bureaucratically recruited and embedded judges—not the parties' lawyers and not lay juries—dominate both the evidence-gathering and the decision-making processes (Langbein, 1994). Another illustration: in contrast to American criminal prosecutors' offices, in which individual assistant district attorneys usually make their own judgments about which charges to make and bargain with defense counsel about how much to reduce them in return for guilty pleas, prosecutors in Japan are subject to detailed rules and close hierarchical supervision concerning the investigation of facts, determination of the proper charge, and the recommendation of penalties (Johnson, 1998).

Adversarial Legalism

The lower right quadrant of Table 2 includes policymaking, policy-implementing, and decision processes that are procedurally formalistic but in which hierarchy is relatively weak and party influence on the process is strong. Regulatory and antidiscrimination laws in the United States, for example, frequently are implemented and enforced not merely by government bureaucracies but also, and sometimes primarily, by means of lawsuits that are initiated by a decentralized array of private individuals, entrepreneurial lawyers, and advocacy organizations. American methods for compensating victims of highway and medical accidents prominently include a decentralized and adversarial tort law system driven by claimants and their lawyers, as contrasted with Western European compensation systems, which operate primarily through social insurance or benefit-payment bureaucracies. In American civil and criminal adjudication, the introduction of evidence and invocation of legal rules are dominated not by the judge (as in continental Europe) but by contending parties' lawyers. Even in comparison with the British adversarial system, hierarchical, authoritative imposition of legal rules is relatively weak in the United States (Atiyah and Summers, 1987). Trial court judges share decision-making power with lay jurors, whose decisions are not explained and largely shielded from hierarchical review, which reduces legal certainty and magnifies the influence of skillful legal advocacy. Hierarchical control of judges in the United States also is weakened by jurisdictional fragmentation between the federal and the fifty separate state judiciaries. Due to the large role of political parties and interest groups in the selection of judges, American judges, compared to more professionally selected and supervised judiciaries, more often are influenced by their political commitments, so that decisions are more often influenced by which judges decide the case or by which city or county court deals with the case (Levin, 1972: 193–221; Rowland and Carp, 1983: 109–134).

Similarly, compared to European democracies, in which regulatory policymaking tends to prioritize a combination of expert judgment and officials' negotiations with affected interests, regulatory policymaking in the United States is more legalistic and adversarial. Complex legal rules concerning public notice and comment, restrictions on ex parte and other informal contacts with decision makers, legalistically specified evidentiary and scientific standards, mandatory official findings and responses to interest group arguments all are intended to facilitate interest group participation and judicial review of administrative decisions. But hierarchical authority is correspondingly weak. Policymaking and implementing authority are often shared by different agencies, at the same or at different levels of government, with different interests and perspectives. Agency decisions are frequently challenged in court by dissatisfied parties and not infrequently reversed by judges, whose rulings can precipitate further changes in administrative policymaking routines. Lawyers, scientists, and economists hired by contending industry and advocacy groups play a large role in presenting evidence and arguments. Overall, the clash of adversarial legal argument has a larger influence on decisions than in other countries' regulatory systems, where policy decisions more often are characterized by a combination of political and expert judgment and consultation with affected interests (Badaracco, 1985; Brickman, Jasanoff, and Ilgen, 1985; Strauss, 2006).

Sequential Decision Systems

As the example of judicial review of regulatory agency decisions shows, governments often establish a sequence of modes of policymaking and policy-implementation. Often legal decisions made the first instance via bureaucratic legalism can then be appealed to court or an administrative body that more closely resembles adversarial legalism. For example, in the massive U.S. Social Security Disability program, where front-line decisions are structured via bureaucratic legalism, an individual whose application has been denied can obtain a de novo rehearing that has some features of adversarial legalism. The appeal is heard by an intra-agency (but quasi-independent) administrative law judge. The applicant appears and speaks in person, often with the assistance of legal counsel—although the Social Security Administration itself is not represented by counsel defending the initial decision. Ultimately, however, applicants who are turned down by repeated intra-agency appeals can (and often do) appeal to a U.S. Circuit Court of Appeals, in which both sides are represented by lawyers (Mashaw, 1983: 139–140; Kagan, 2017). More generally, a very wide array of legal decisions made in the first instance in the United States by administrative bodies—from local police departments and land use permitting agencies to state regulatory enforcement offices and federal immigration authorities—can be appealed to courts, where the processes of adversarial legalism kick in. Conversely, the vast majority of processes *initiated* via adversarial legalism—everyday criminal prosecutions and civil lawsuits—end up being resolved via negotiation, primarily to avoid the costs, delays, and uncertainties of full-scale adversarial legalism. In automobile accident cases in the United States, most legal claims for damages against the allegedly negligent other driver, based on tort law, are resolved via bureaucratic processes in the potential defendants' liability insurance company.

No modern democratic legal system is characterized entirely by any of the quadrants in Table 2. National legal styles are not monolithic; their ways of making, invoking, and enforcing law vary internally. Litigation resembling adversarial legalism can and does occur in more cooperation-oriented nations, such as the Netherlands and Japan (Niemeijer, 1989: 121–152; Upham, 1987). Privatization, deregulation, intensified economic competition, and the advent of transnational regulation by the European Union and the European Court of Justice all have increased the role of courts and litigation in the governance of European countries (Kelemen, 2011; Kagan, 1997a). Meanwhile, in the United States, bureaucratic legalism is common. Most bureaucratic decisions are not appealed to courts. Most accident victims, outraged customers, and others with legal grievances do *not* resort to lawsuits as their first recourse (Hensler et al., 1991; Miller and Sarat, 1981). Politicians and legal elites have often created less adversarial, less costly alternatives to adversarial litigation—juvenile courts, family courts, small claims courts, workers' compensation tribunals, court-annexed mediation processes, negotiated regulatory compliance plans, and so on. American judges and legislatures periodically issue rulings and enact statutes that are designed to *discourage* lawsuits and appeals. A wave of such reforms affected the tort systems in many states in the 1980s and 1990s. The early twenty-first century has seen an even stronger wave of anti-adversarial legalism, as discussed in the Afterword.

Most importantly, to reemphasize a point made earlier, in social arenas in which the processes of adversarial legalism often *are* invoked, full-scale legal contestation usually does not occur. The overwhelming majority of criminal and civil cases are resolved short of a jury trial. This is largely because the extraordinary costs, delays, and uncertainties associated with formal adversarial litigation impel most disputants to negotiate an informal plea bargain or settlement—even if it means abandoning valid claims or defenses (Feeley, 1979; Macaulay, 1979). Thus it is helpful to think of adversarial legalism as referring both to (1) *a method of policy implementation and dispute resolution* (characterized by a set of legal institutions, rights, and rules that facilitate or encourage adversarial, party-dominated legal contestation) and (2) *the day-to-day practice of adversarial legal contestation*—adversarial legalism in action. In principle and in practice, institutionalizing the methods or structures of adversarial legalism—that is, establishing the kinds of judiciaries, legal rules, and law firms that facilitate adversarial litigation—does not completely determine how often conflicting parties actually *use* those institutions. The incidence and intensity of adversarial legalism in action varies over time and across settings, depending on the motivations and resources of potential disputants.

Yet viewed in comparative perspective, the United States is distinctive in both dimensions. At the level of legal structures and rules, it is much more inclined to authorize and encourage the use of adversarial litigation to implement public policies, to challenge existing laws and policies, and to hold law enforcement officials, administrative agencies, school systems and business corporations legally accountable. And according to the comparative studies of particular policy fields listed in Table 1, adversarial legalism as a matter of day-to-day practice is far more common in the United States than in other democracies.[7]

The dual aspect of adversarial legalism—as decision-making structure or method and as day-to-day practice—is crucial to understanding its social consequences. It means that adversarial legalism's importance cannot be measured by litigation or adjudication rates alone, any more than the significance of nuclear weapons rests on the frequency of nuclear war. Even if only a small minority of aggrieved persons or organizations actually file lawsuits, and even if most lawsuits are settled before trial, the mere threat of costly, embarrassing, and potentially punitive adversarial litigation can deter malpractice by hospitals, business organizations, and governmental bodies. Even if only a small percentage of those who object to plans for new waste disposal facilities challenge the proponents' permits in court, and even if only a handful of businesses mount legal appeals against new regulations, the legal rules and practices that facilitate such adversarial legal actions matter a great deal because the governmental officials who formulate solid-waste permits and new regulations cannot predict either the incidence or the outcomes of such actions. Because its structures always stand ready to be mobilized, adversarial legalism—litigant-driven, potentially costly legal contestation—is a barely latent, easily triggered potentiality in virtually all contemporary American political, economic, and administrative processes. It creates a set of incentives and expectations that have come to loom very large in American governmental, commercial, and social life. For these reasons, adversarial legalism can meaningfully be called the American way of law.

The Roots of Adversarial Legalism

By drawing many conflicts over law and public policy into the courts, adversarial legalism enhances the role of judges in legal change, and in that sense blurs the line between law and politics. And so, especially since the 1980s, it has stimulated partisan political battles concerning judicial selection. Those features of adversarial legalism are jarring to the professional legal elites of European democracies who have long regarded legal change as the province of representative legislatures alone. Judges in those countries are selected, trained, and supervised in nonpolitical ways that emphasize careful legal craftsmanship, consistency, and predictability. Thus their adjudicatory processes lean more toward the ideals of bureaucratic legalism than toward adversarial legalism.

Adversarial legalism *is* consonant, however, with the legal culture of American judges, lawyers, legal scholars, and teachers, who tend to view law as a "pragmatic instrument of social improvement" (Atiyah and Summers, 1987: 404), and view courts as essential checks on the elected branches of government. Consequently judicial creativity and problem-solving is valued, as is creative legal advocacy. Adversarial legalism is used and defended by politically conservative lawyers for advancing conservative values and by politically liberal ones for advancing liberal values. But the roots of adversarial legalism go deeper than American professional legal culture alone. Adversarial legalism in the United States stems primarily from distinctive American political traditions, attitudes, structures, and interest group pressures.

Most of the men who founded the United States had rebelled and fought against a powerful, distant monarchy. Great Britain, they believed, had violated their fundamental political and legal rights and had squelched their desires for local self-government. They believed in individual liberty, at least for white males, and they understandably were wary of concentrated government authority. Most "federalists" (who wanted a stronger national government) and "antifederalists" (who did not) believed that government should be mostly decentralized, subject to accountability by state and local electorates, and constrained by law. In his comparative analysis of political cultures, Seymour Martin Lipset (1996: 21) wrote that with its emphasis on individualism and its mistrust of government, "America began and continues as the most antistatist, legalistic, and rights-oriented nation."

Those attitudes were embedded in the political structures of the young nation. Through written constitutions, both federal and state, government was to be decentralized and divided into cross-checking branches, and limited by law. The constitutions also contained bills of rights, enforceable in independent courts at the behest of ordinary people. The states also adopted the British common law tradition, which vested considerable law-making power in judges. That pattern of fragmenting authority was repeated in the states' separate court systems: the adjudicatory power of judges was shared with locally selected juries and, via the adversary system, was checked by contending lawyers. By the mid-nineteenth century, a majority of states had instituted democratic election of judges to ensure accountability and political responsiveness.

Adversarial legalism, therefore, soon was woven into the fabric of American life and politics. In the early nineteenth century, the county courthouse, for most people, was the most salient institution of government. Courts and juries were widely used, widely valued. Lawyers, as Alexis de Tocqueville observed in the late 1820s, were prominent at every level of government. Because state legislatures met only for short periods each year, state court judges, deciding case-by-case under the common law, became the primary policymakers for broad swaths of property, contract, and tort law. Thus four basic engines of American adversarial legalism were already chugging away: (1) a politically selected judiciary that not only applied but also *made* law, via common law adjudication and via constitutional review of legislative and other governmental decisions; (2) litigant-and-lawyer-dominated modes of dispute-resolution and adjudication, structured around the right to trial by jury; (3) a large, entrepreneurial, and politically-active legal profession; and (4) a legal culture that reflected a view of law, litigation, and courts as important instruments for protecting individual rights, improving governance, and checking the exercise of political power. In the economic sphere, American businesses, compared to their counterparts in Europe, relied more on lawyers, litigation, and judges to resolve conflicts, to adapt the law to a nascent capitalist economy, and later in the century, to limit governmental regulation of markets.

Fast forward to the second half of the twentieth century. In that period, adversarial legalism's role in American governance expanded and intensified. Starting in the late nineteenth and early twentieth centuries, a more pro-government strand had developed in American political culture. Prairie populists and urban Progressives, responding to the social disruptions and harms generated by industrialization, urbanization, and larger-scale market dynamics, demanded government regulation of public utilities and railroads, food and workplace safety, and agricultural price supports. That strand of political culture flourished again during the Great Depression. The Roosevelt Administration's New Deal instituted nationwide stabilization measures for price and labor and financial markets, regulation of antilabor union practices, and social insurance programs for the retired workers, the unemployed, and single-mother families. During the New Deal and World War II, the national government's taxing powers and administrative capacities grew enormously. Washington had become expected to play an active role in stabilizing the economy and promoting economic growth. In the postwar decades, most of the population enjoyed markedly higher standards of living, was better educated, and was linked by modern communications technologies.

In that context, the pro-government strand in American political culture intensified, generating demands for higher nationwide standards concerning criminal and social justice, health and safety, and environmental protection. It was manifested in the powerful political movements that swept the United States beginning in the 1960s—the civil rights movement, environmentalism, and feminism—as well as in the efflorescence of public-interest groups that demonstrated, petitioned the courts, and lobbied legislatures on behalf of Latinos, consumer interests, the aged, tenants, children, disabled persons, impoverished families, and more.

Cumulatively, these movements were demanding a major expansion of governmental authority, particularly on the part of the federal government. That demand, however, ran up against an inherited political tradition and political structures grounded in distrust of centralized political authority and big government. From that tension sprang increases in adversarial legalism's role in governance. Following are two illustrations of that dynamic, summarized quickly here but explicated more fully in Chapter 3.

Between 1965 and 1977, responding to the new political movements, Congress passed twenty-five major environmental and civil rights acts, plus far-reaching statutes regulating workplace safety, consumer lending, product safety, private pension funds, and local public education. It created federal regulatory agencies or bureaus to issue implementing regulations, binding on millions of business firms. But to enforce those laws and regulations, Congress was compelled to bow to the inherited demands for decentralization of government. Rather than creating and funding large new national regulatory inspectorates with offices in every locality, Congress often delegated implementing authority to state and local governments. Yet the politically liberal reformers and their congressional allies had little trust that many of these politically varied governments would be enthusiastic or competent enforcers of the transformative new federal statutes and regulations. To meet those concerns, Congress turned to adversarial legalism. It empowered individual citizens and public interest organizations to haul state and local governments into court for noncompliance or to sue non-complying regulated businesses directly. Lawyers and judges, it was hoped, would ensure the faithful implementation of law. Similarly, responding to partisan distrust, by both liberals and conservatives, of how *federal* regulatory agencies would employ their broad new law-making powers, Congress—and the federal courts themselves—expanded interest groups' rights to demand searching judicial review of new administrative regulations. Judges thus became deeply involved in enforcing and definitively interpreting federal regulatory law.

Second, as suggested above, the judiciary itself expanded the realm of adversarial legalism. To mention just one example, in the realm of criminal justice, politically liberal reformers were increasingly critical of unfair—and often brutal and racist—practices by local police departments and courts, not only in Southern states but also in the big cities and racial ghettos of the North. But the national government had no European-style ministry of justice that could discipline and impose national norms on the hundreds of local police departments, prosecutors' offices, and courthouses. The federal courts, however, had a point of leverage. In the 1960s during Chief Justice Earl Warren's tenure, the U.S. Supreme Court reinterpreted the Constitution, elaborating new, nationally binding constitutional rules regulating pretrial detention, interrogation of suspects, police searches for evidence, and jury selection. And to help ensure local police, prosecutors, and judges would enforce the norms, often described as the "due process revolution," the Court also ruled that state and local judges were constitutionally obliged to block the use of unconstitutionally obtained evidence. And to prod them to do so, the Court ruled that state governments were constitutionally obliged to provide free defense counsel for indigent defendants. Over time, responding to defense lawyers' arguments, *judges*, not state or federal legislatures, worked out the principles for when police can arrest and use lethal force, when they can search a suspect's car, and much more.

In those and myriad other ways, in state law as well as federal law, adversarial legalism became a crucial component of the American version of the contemporary activist state. It is only a slight oversimplification to say that in the United States, lawyers, legal rights, judges, and lawsuits became functional equivalents for the large central bureaucracies that dominate governance in the activist states of Western Europe.

Adversarial legalism has given the United States the most politically and socially responsive court system in the world. Compared to most national judiciaries, American judges are less constrained by legal formalisms; they are more policy-oriented, more attentive to the equities (and inequities) of the particular situation. In the decentralized American legal system, if one judge closes the door on a novel legal argument, claimants not infrequently can find a more receptive judge in another court. By threatening government officials, business corporations, and other organizations with litigation and its accompanying harmful publicity, adversarial legalism helps institutionalize measures to ensure compliance with legal norms (Epp, 2009; Lytton, 2008). Adversarial legalism makes the judiciary and lawyers more fully a part of the governing process. It thus makes America's pluralistic form of democracy even more pluralistic (Peretti, 1999), and as the Constitutional framers might have appreciated, operates as an essential check on governmental malpractice.

But this kind of "responsive law," to use Philippe Nonet's and Philip Selznick's (1978) term for this approach to legal governance, is also, as they warned, a "high-risk strategy" of legal ordering. When judges take on contentious policy issues, political factions battle to place their adherents in the judiciary, and judicial decisions often appear driven primarily by judges' political values. Adversarial legalism is used by political conservatives to advance conservative interests and values as well as political liberals to advance theirs. In its willingness to sidestep legal formalism in order to seek substantively desirable outcomes, responsive law generates legal unpredictability and political criticism. The cumbersomeness and costliness of adversarial litigation compel many victims of legal wrongs to shy away from asserting legal claims or defenses, leaving patterns of wrongdoing unremedied. Overall, adversarial legalism is a promising way of meeting the public's demand for justice and protection but also an inefficient, uncertain, and sometimes divisive way of doing so. The world's most responsive legal system does not necessarily give Americans the world's most reliable legal system or the world's most responsive system of governance.

Contours, Consequences, Causes

The tension between adversarial legalism's desirable and undesirable consequences is discussed more fully in Chapter 2, "The Two Faces of Adversarial Legalism." Chapter 3, "The Political Construction of Adversarial Legalism," explains in greater detail why adversarial legalism is more common in the United States than in other democracies, and why, despite a great deal of criticism, it has persisted and even increased in recent decades.

Parts II, III, and IV circle back and elaborate those themes, demonstrating that the same general contours, causes, and consequences of adversarial legalism recur in four broad spheres of policy—criminal justice, civil justice, social justice, and governmental regulation of economic activity. The Afterword focuses on the conservative legal movement and its attack on adversarial legalism in the early twenty-first century, as it was strengthened by the Republican Party gains in political power. That movement, the discussion shows, has limited adversarial legalism as used to advance politically liberal values, yet has mobilized adversarial legalism to advance conservative values. At the same time, political liberals *have* mobilized adversarial legalism to combat a conservative president's efforts to dismantle the regulatory state and to override legal and constitutional rights. Deeply rooted in American political structure and culture, and useful to both major political parties, adversarial legalism, the chapter concludes, will remain the American way of law.

CHAPTER TWO

The Two Faces of Adversarial Legalism

L ike the blind men of legend who felt different parts of an elephant and described it variously as resembling a tree, a snake, and a wall, critics and defenders of the American legal system often seem to be referring to entirely different phenomena. In 1996 plaintiffs' lawyers in California supported a ballot measure that would facilitate securities class actions. Their television ads portrayed elderly investors who claimed that only by virtue of such lawsuits had their life savings been recouped from fraudulent companies. Electronics companies opposed to the measure put forth ads about greedy lawyers who brought frivolous lawsuits that extorted settlements from honest companies. Both sides, like the blind men, did have a piece of the truth—but only a piece.

Adversarial legalism encompasses many kinds of legal actions, some socially beneficent, some socially problematic, many a bit of both. In the aggregate, it generates both social benefits and social costs. Analysis must begin by recognizing both faces of adversarial legalism, as exemplified by the following case studies, one involving southern prison reform and one concerning a legal deadlock over dredging a major commercial harbor in Oakland, California. The story of Southern prisons' litigation illustrates adversarial legalism's capacity for making law and governance more responsive to claims for decency and justice. The Port of Oakland story shows how adversarial legal structures designed to increase governmental responsiveness can also lead to governmental paralysis and to injustice. Together, they prompt the question: Is it possible to shed adversarial legalism's justice-defeating costs and adverse side effects without undermining its capacity to enhance justice and good governance? This chapter provides no answer to that difficult, perhaps overly broad question, but it does take some steps along that path by looking directly at both the attractive and the troublesome faces of adversarial legalism and by analyzing the anatomy of each.

Adversarial Legalism in Action: Alabama Prison Reform

In the early 1970s, Alabama prisons, in the impassioned words of a public health officer, were "unfit for human habitation." Inmates were packed in crowded, unsupervised dormitories. Fights, stabbings, and brutal sexual assaults were common. Inspecting a punitive isolation unit, an investigator found five black inmates packed into a tiny cell with no mattresses, no running water, and a hole in the floor for a toilet. "It was completely dark. The odor would make one's eyes water and throat burn from BO, feces, urine, and general filth" (Bass 1993: 335). One of the inmates had been there for fourteen days, two for twenty-one days. Throughout the prison system medical care was intermittent and abysmal: unsupervised prisoners, without formal training, regularly pulled teeth, dispensed medication, and gave injections. Severely disturbed and violent psychotics were placed in the general inmate population.

State correctional officials, despite some prodding, did little to remedy these atrocious conditions. Nor did the state legislature, despite committee reports raising the issue; nor did the opposition political party or the judges of Alabama's courts; nor did Alabama's governor, George Wallace (famous for defying laws, courts, and a presidential order demanding an end to racial segregation in public schools, colleges, and universities). In the decentralized American political system, moreover, there was no congressional law governing state correctional systems, no national official charged with supervising state prisons. Adversarial legalism, however, provided a possible way to bypass an unresponsive political system and force some improvements on the Alabama prison system.

Earlier, in 1963, the U.S. Supreme Court held that prisoners in state penal institutions could petition federal courts for writs of habeas corpus in order to challenge the constitutionality of their conviction in state courts or confinement by state and local governments.[1] Before then, federal judges had not been responsive to prisoner petitions about unbearable prison conditions (Friedman, 1993: 309–313). As long as the legal process that had led to the prisoner's incarceration had been formally proper, the judges had seen no *constitutional* defect in harshly run prisons. In 1965, however, U.S. District Court Judge J. Smith Henley, having heard testimony about Arkansas prisoners who were savagely whipped for "infractions of discipline" and for not working hard enough in the fields, adopted a novel theory: inhumane prison conditions could be considered violations of the prohibition of "cruel and unusual punishment" in the Eighth Amendment of the U.S. Constitution. On those grounds, in 1970 Judge Henley ruled the whole Arkansas prison system unconstitutional (Feeley and Rubin, 1998). That decision spurred a broader prisoners' rights movement. It attracted idealistic lawyers from the civil rights movement. In 1972 the American Civil

Liberties Union established the National Prison Project. The Southern Poverty Law Center provided financial help and legal advice to dedicated lawyer-reformers.

In October 1971 Frank Johnson, U.S. District Court judge for the Middle District of Alabama, received a handwritten petition signed by N. H. Newman, a prison inmate; it described in shocking detail the inadequacy of medical care in the state prison system. Newman had reached the right judge. Frank Johnson exemplified the political independence, diversity, and individualism of the American judiciary. He was a Republican in Democratic Alabama, a former small-town lawyer and U.S. District Attorney, appointed a U.S. District Court judge by President Eisenhower. Soon after his appointment in 1956, during the Montgomery bus boycott that launched the civil rights movement, Johnson had struck down the city of Montgomery's law that required segregated seating on buses; he ruled that the condemnation of official segregation in *Brown v. Board of Education* (1954) applied not only to schools but also to other public services. Earlier in 1971, before receiving prisoner Newman's petition, Judge Johnson had ruled that Alabama's horrible state-run mental institutions were unconstitutional; because they did not provide meaningful treatment, he reasoned, they deprived involuntarily committed patients of liberty without due process of law. The mental institutions case provided Johnson, once he encountered inmate Newman's petition, a model for prison reform.

Judge Johnson appointed a local lawyer to represent Newman, urging him to bring a civil lawsuit against the state. The judge also urged the U.S. Attorney for Alabama to intervene in the case; the petition, Johnson told him, "raises extremely serious . . . 8th Amendment questions" (Bass, 1993: 325). Previously, some federal judges had dismissed such prisoner petitions, arguing that the cruel and unusual punishment clause of the Constitution had not been intended to guarantee convicted criminals any particular level of medical care. Judge Johnson disagreed, and the case went to trial. Newman's court-appointed lawyer and a U.S. Justice Department attorney presented hours of deeply disturbing testimony from experts who (pursuant to court order) had toured the prisons' medical facilities. Judge Johnson held that the prison system's woeful neglect amounted to unconstitutionally cruel and inhuman punishment. He ordered the state to take twenty-four specific corrective steps, including arrangements that would guarantee prompt medical treatment and would bring the infirmary into compliance with federal standards for Medicare-accredited facilities (Bass, 1993: 326–327).

In response to additional prisoner petitions in 1974 about other oppressive penal conditions and practices, Judge Johnson appointed two other Alabama lawyers to represent the inmates. After consulting with experienced prisoners' rights lawyers from other states, the lawyers filed class action lawsuits claiming that the whole Alabama prison system was so thoroughly pervaded by violence, overcrowding, inedible food, and brutal methods of punishment that it was unconstitutionally cruel and inhumane.

Again, the mechanisms of adversarial legalism opened up the prisons to outside scrutiny. A weeklong trial featured detailed testimony by an inmate who had been repeatedly raped and also by professional prison officials from other states. The state attorney general conceded that the system was legally indefensible. Judge Johnson issued detailed orders closing the current disciplinary cells and demanding reduction of overcrowding, controls on violence, improved sanitation and food, and increases in professional staff (Bass, 1993: 335–339).

Governor Wallace appealed to the U.S. Court of Appeals, stating that his attorney general had been wrong in admitting the Eighth Amendment violations. The appellate court, however, upheld Johnson's constitutional ruling and most of his specific orders. As had become customary in institutional reform cases (such as those demanding school desegregation), the trial judge kept the case alive pending full compliance with the injunction; the state officials charged with compliance thus remained subject to punishment for contempt of court should they engage in overt resistance. Judge Johnson also appointed the newly elected governor, Forest James, receiver for the state prison system; the governor thus was obligated to oversee compliance and report back to the judge. By keeping the case open, the judge enabled the prison reform lawyers to keep adversarial pressure alive–by monitoring prison conditions, meeting with the receiver, and complaining to the judge when they detected noncompliance.

In 1990 the case was closed. Observers still criticized Alabama's correctional system, but they also noted far-reaching, positive changes. Correctional officials and guards "professed astonishment, and no small pleasure, that the prisons had changed so drastically" (Bass, 1993: 343). The minimum standards specified in Judge Johnson's order had precipitated the development of nationwide professional standards and an accreditation system run by the American Correctional Association. Moreover, the widespread publicity generated by Judge Johnson's order helped bring about the enactment of a 1980 congressional law that authorized the U.S. Attorney General to bring lawsuits to correct constitutional deprivations in state or local jails, prisons, mental health facilities, and nursing homes (Bass, 1993: 345–346; Feeley and Rubin, 1998).

By 1990 state prisons in forty-one states were operating under court orders that demanded that they remedy unconstitutional conditions of confinement, as were nearly one-third of large county jails.[2] In the course of the prison reform litigation, Malcolm Feeley and Edward Rubin (1998) observed, federal court judges forged a comprehensive regulatory code for prison management, covering residence facilities, sanitation, food, clothing, medical care, discipline, staff hiring, libraries, work, and education. Throughout the country, prison officials began to consult attorneys to ensure that they were in compliance with the law.[3]

In the 1990s, however, a conservative political backlash developed. In 1996, Congress enacted restrictions on prison reform litigation and on the duration of judicial oversight. Many consent decrees were terminated (Sullivan, 2000). In many states, legislation that increased the length of prison sentences and urban crime control efforts stressed incarceration for nonviolent as well as violent offenses. In the face of mass incarceration, state and county budgets were strained, prison and jail overcrowding increased, and with more older inmates held for longer times, prison medical care systems also were stressed. A 2019 U.S. Department of Justice investigation of Alabama prisons found high levels of violence and a "flagrant disregard" for an inmate's right to be free from excessive and cruel punishment (Benner and Dewan, 2019). Nevertheless, the basic legal structures of adversarial legalism remained in place. In the early twentieth century, in lawsuits against California's massive prison system, federal courts found the facilities unconstitutionally overcrowded; judges ordered not only major improvements in medical care but also sharp reductions in prison populations. The Supreme Court upheld those orders, perhaps helping penal policy turn a corner (Simon, 2014; Aviram, 2015).

The Virtues of Adversarial Legalism

The reforms that dragged Alabama's correctional system into the twentieth century were not instituted by a national ministry of justice or corrections, as they might have been in a European country, or implemented through a hierarchically organized bureaucracy. The reforms were thrust on Alabama laterally by the mechanisms of adversarial legalism. They were made possible by the fragmented, decentralized structure of the American legal system, its openness to individual legal complaints, its tradition of entrepreneurial legal advocacy, and the creativity and boldness of its politically selected, diverse judiciary.

The Southern prison reform cases highlight the fact that in the American legal order, even the most marginalized citizens, convicted felons, feel entitled to petition a court for relief and that courts at times can provide it. Adversarial legalism, in Samuel Johnson's phrase, gives the ordinary individual "adventitious strength" (Muir, 1973: 112). It encourages Americans, more than the residents of other democracies, to regard themselves as legal rights-bearing citizens. They might be less inclined do so, however, if American judges were not so open to creative advocacy, so powerful, so often willing to reshape prior law in order to achieve substantively just results. In the Arkansas and Alabama cases, prisoners' lawyers advanced a novel interpretation of constitutional law, undeterred by the fact that it had been rejected by other judges in the past. Armed with tools provided by the adversarial American pretrial and trial processes, the prisoners' rights lawyers could investigate and bring to light the hidden malpractices of closed institutions. As a result of recurrent successes of that kind in a wide variety of cases, adversarial legalism energizes the American legal profession as a whole; hence American lawyers, overall, are far more entrepreneurial and proactive than their counterparts in other democracies (Osiel, 1990).

Similarly, because hierarchical constraints on American lower court judges are looser than those that prevail in other judiciaries, individual judges, such as J. Smith Henley in Arkansas and Frank Johnson in Alabama, often enjoy enough legal discretion to reinterpret the law and act on the basis of their moral convictions. Even more startling from the standpoint of legal scholars and judges from hierarchical legal systems, the lower court judges in Arkansas and Alabama had the power to issue structural injunctions—judicial orders to elected state governors that included detailed legal instructions, along with procedures that enabled plaintiffs' lawyers to monitor and ensure compliance. Similarly, lower federal courts used structural injunctions to prod recalcitrant local school boards, particularly in Southern states, to comply with the Supreme Court's 1954 *Brown v. Board of Education* ruling, which required an end to decades of legally mandated discrimination against black schoolchildren (Melnick, 2016; Peltason, 1961).

The Southern prison reform and the desegregation litigation exemplify American adversarial legalism's capacity to push government and society a bit further along the arc of justice, to expose and challenge governmental neglect and rigidity. Repeatedly, adversarial legalism has enabled political activists to break or circumvent political deadlocks on controversial issues. It has enabled the politically weak, neglected by legislative politics, to demand and obtain better treatment from the government, first and foremost in the cause of racial equality but also in the quest for honest and effective government, more compassionate welfare administration, and more civilized law enforcement practices. Richard Emery, a public interest lawyer in New York City, brought a class action lawsuit that ended a common police practice in that city of conducting humiliating strip searches of persons arrested for minor offenses (Herbert, 1998). In more than half the states, courts have compelled legislatures to restructure public school funding to increase spending on children in tax-poor municipalities (Reed, 1998; Howard and Steigerwalt: 2012: 123–128). In 2017, the first year of the Trump administration, adversarial legalism was an important mechanism for blocking or requiring amendments of hastily drafted administrative orders that violated constitutional rights—and also for invalidating regulatory initiatives that violated federal administrative law's insistence on rational, evidence-based policymaking.

By creating incentives for private litigation, adversarial legalism also amplifies the law's capacity to *publicize* legal wrongs committed by corporations and other large organizations—and thereby to promote reforms in their practices. Through the pretrial discovery powers it grants private litigants, adversarial litigation exposed the tragedy of widespread asbestos poisoning (Barnes, 2011) and scared many corporations into strengthening internal systems for product design, quality control, and fair personnel management. Litigation against the Catholic Church on behalf of victims of clergy sexual abuse generated widespread publicity about the Church's repeated failures to acknowledge and deter such behavior, punished it with huge money damages, helped compel it to make epochal policy reforms, and made it more acceptable for law enforcement officials to prosecute clergy abuse cases criminally (Lytton, 2008). In a cross-national analysis of laws forbidding racial discrimination in employment, Robert Lieberman (2005) observes that compared to the United Kingdom and France, enforcement in the United States has been significantly more energetic and effective (even if shortfalls remain) because its legal system provides much greater scope for enforcement via private litigation, pretrial discovery, and costly judicial remedies. At a more mundane level, adversarial legalism, even if more often merely threatened rather than actually employed, makes insurance adjusters, public prosecutors, and administrative agencies attend more carefully to the evidence and the equities of individual cases.

As in the Southern prisons' litigation, adversarial legalism also facilitates (and hence encourages) new *kinds* of justice claims. Imaginative lawyering and receptive judges, not legislatures, first established the right to win money damages for sexual harassment, to recover damages for negligent infliction of emotional injury, and same sex couples' rights to adopt children and to get married. Japanese and European environmentalists look across the ocean somewhat jealously, for they see in the United States a legal system that more readily enables community groups and advocacy organizations to haul government planners and private developers into court—and hence to compel redesign of housing projects, highways, waste dumps, and factories. Midwestern city administrators interviewed by political scientist Charles Epp complained about the time and money their municipal governments had to devote to defense of civil lawsuits. They acknowledged, however, that to ward off liability their cities had instituted more systematic checks of road conditions and playground equipment, intensified training for police and other employees who deal with the public, and acted more rapidly to weed out problem officers. Here are some of the things that three senior city administrators told Epp (1998b: 12):

We're much more responsive to complaints and concerns raised by citizens, apart from the election process, because we know in the back of our minds that the complaint might conceivably become a lawsuit.

The biggest changes for the better in this city have come as a result of lawsuits or threatened lawsuits, not as a result of political changes in the council or anything else. The courts have done a far better job than politics of improving our policies.

The rights of citizens and employees are far better protected as a result—and only as a result of litigation, not other changes. And the safety of our citizens is better protected. Remember all that training and inspection I mentioned? It makes a difference. Our roads and streets are safer, our playgrounds are safer, our whole operation is safer.

In a later publication, Epp (2009) describes how police reformers used the threat posed by aggressive plaintiffs' lawyers to prod urban police departments to adopt stricter standards concerning use of firearms, backed by a proactive mode of training, data-gathering, and supervision. When the Kentucky courts held that the state's entire public school system was so badly underfunded that it was unconstitutional, the governor and state legislature, previously reluctant to raise taxes, quickly moved to enact a school finance reform project. "It's the law," said the governor (Paris, 1998). Adversarial legalism, therefore, can sometimes inject principle into the political process, providing legal and hence political legitimacy for politicians and agency leaders to act as statesmen.

When one focuses on such achievements, American adversarial legalism is a bright sun indeed. It is this heroic side of adversarial legalism that Owen Fiss (1984: 1086–1087) contrasts with paler methods of dispute resolution such as negotiated settlement or mediation:

There is, of course, sometimes a value to avoidance, not just to the judge, who is thereby relieved of the need to make or enforce a hard decision, but also to society, which sometimes thrives by masking its basic contradictions. . . . But when one sees injustices that cry out for correction—as Congress did when it endorsed the concept of the private attorney general and as the Court of another era did when it sought to enhance access to the courts—the value of avoidance diminishes and the agony of judgment becomes a necessity. Someone has to confront the betrayal of our deepest ideals and be prepared to turn the world upside down to bring those ideals to fruition.

The confronters in Fiss's vision, of course, are activist judges, such as J. Smith Henley and Frank Johnson, and the lawyers who argue such cases to

court, and perhaps even the law professors who spell out the legal theories
that judges can cite when turning the world upside down.

Adversarial Legalism's Other Face: Disorder in the Port

Ice-cream cones are no good if you eat too many of them. Even one is bad
if you eat it at the wrong time or place. In some times and places, judges
shouldn't turn the world upside down. And if too many judges are striving
to turn the world upside down, the world may not work so well. Adversarial
legalism's sword, honed by distrust of authority, can be used against the
trustworthy, too. Adversarial legalism can be invoked by the misguided,
the mendacious, and the malevolent as well as by the mistreated. Its complexity, costliness, and malleability can produce injustice as well as justice.
The Port of Oakland's frustrating struggle to dredge its harbor at the edge
of San Francisco Bay illustrates the other face of adversarial legalism.

In 1988 international shipping lines launched a new generation of
containerships—huge, efficient, and costly ($40 million each). The new
vessels furthered a technological revolution that in the 1970s and 1980s
transformed international trade, as it moved cargo across oceans, through
ports, and across continents with dramatically greater speed, reliability,
and economy. Shoppers in Dutch food stores now could buy green beans
and oranges shipped in refrigerated containers from Senegal and Florida.
A moving inventory of shirts, jeans, and dresses, packed in containers in
a Hong Kong warehouse, whisked from ship to train in Los Angeles, now
flowed to the loading docks of shops in Cincinnati and Atlanta at transportation costs of pennies per garment. Technological change brought order
to the port: today's electronically coordinated, mechanized container ports
bear little resemblance to the seaports of the past, notorious for costly delays, labor exploitation, pilferage, drunkenness, and crime. On both sides
of the Atlantic and Pacific, local monopolies and stodgy oligopolies are
threatened by distant competitors, spurring productivity and innovation
(Kagan, 1990b).

In the 1970s the Port of Oakland in San Francisco Bay initiated plans to
deepen its harbor to forty-two feet in order to accommodate the larger ships
of the future. In 1986 the U.S. Congress, which finances improvements in
the national navigation system, authorized funding for the project. For the
next eight years, however, a seemingly endless series of regulatory actions
and lawsuits blocked the dredging of the harbor.

Before the early 1970s seas and harbors were used as free disposal
sites for sewage sludge, garbage, and chemical wastes. Regulatory officials and environmentalists had little input into port expansion decisions.
Dredging and disposal operations destroyed marshlands, disrupted fish-

eries, and dislodged chemical wastes buried in urban rivers and bays, (National Research Council, 1985). Today, however, dredging projects require a permit from the U.S. Army Corps of Engineers; pursuant to the National Environmental Policy Act, the Corps must first prepare and circulate a comprehensive analysis of all potential environmental impacts and methods of mitigating unavoidable adverse consequences. The Corps of Engineers' decisions, in turn, are checked by other governmental bodies—the U.S. Fish and Wildlife Service, the National Marine Fisheries Service, the relevant state department of fish and game, the U.S. Environmental Protection Agency, the state agency charged with protecting water quality, and the relevant state coastal zone management agency. Each of these agencies, responsible for enforcing a specific relevant statute, is legally instructed to object to or block dredging projects that fail to meet those statutory standards. There is a third level of legal control: citizens, local politicians, and environmental advocacy groups who think that the Corps or the other agencies have not fulfilled their statutory responsibilities are legally empowered to file a lawsuit and seek judicial review of their decisions.

In the Port of Oakland case, the Army Corps of Engineers issued an environmental impact statement (EIS) in 1986. It approved disposal of the dredged harbor floor sands at an established dumping site in San Francisco Bay, near Alcatraz Island. But environmentalists, fishing interests, and state regulatory officials raised concerns about damage to water quality and fisheries. The Corps, in response, conducted further sediment tests and in September 1987 released a supplementary EIS. It called for special care disposal and capping methods for about 21,000 cubic yards of sediment (less than 1 percent of the total project) that was to be dredged from certain contaminated areas, but it concluded that for the bulk of noncontaminated sediments, in-Bay disposal would have no adverse environmental effects. State and local regulatory agencies, however, had legal power to block in-Bay disposal under state environmental law. And they preferred disposal in the deeper waters of the Pacific Ocean to the Alcatraz site.

Confronted with this regulatory deadlock, in January 1988, Port of Oakland officials proposed disposal at an ocean site designated 1M, although that would double the cost of dredging. New regulatory hurdles then arose. Fishermen claimed that disposal at 1M would harm ocean fisheries. The Corps prepared another supplementary EIS. Its analysis disputed the fishermen's claims. Nevertheless, the U.S. Environmental Protection Agency (EPA), statutory guardian of ocean waters, refused to issue a permit for 1M. An environmental advocacy group prepared to bring a lawsuit challenging the Corps' supplementary EIS and argued that the sediments should be dumped beyond the continental shelf, fifty miles out to sea. The Corps responded that it was legally precluded from authorizing disposal beyond the continental shelf because that would cost at least twice as much as 1M without being demonstrably better in environmental terms.

Prodded by increasingly anxious Port of Oakland officials, in March 1988 the Corps and the EPA negotiated a compromise, also agreed to by environmental groups and a federation of Pacific fishing associations. Ocean site B1B, ten miles off the coast, would be used for the first 500,000 cubic yards of the dredged material (except for sediments from the clearly contaminated area); further testing and study would precede any decision concerning disposal of the remaining 6.5 million cubic yards. The dredging machinery and barges moved into place. When access to court is easy, however, compromise is unstable. In mid-April of 1988, just before the dredging commenced, the Half Moon Bay Fishermen's Marketing Association brought suit in federal court, alleging that the B1B disposal decision violated a number of federal regulatory provisions and would disrupt fisheries. The U.S. District Court judge, and then the federal court of appeals, rejected the fishermen's legal claims. The dredging machinery completed one day of digging before, on May 16, 1988, a state court judge, responding to a new lawsuit based on another legal argument, held that the dredging permit had been issued without a requisite certification from the California Coastal Commission. The dredging stopped.

By that time, shipping lines using the Port of Oakland, it was said, were screaming for deeper water. Desperate port officials announced an alternative plan: to dispose of the first 500,000 cubic yards of dredged material in the Sacramento River Delta, where it would be used to reinforce levees. Local regulatory processes then creaked into action. The Port of Oakland prepared a new EIS. After a year or so, a California regional water quality agency approved the plan, but the local Contra Costa Water District challenged the Port's EIS in state court. Yet another year later, in July 1990, the court *upheld* the delta plan. But by then, the Port of Oakland had decided not to go forward, since regulatory conditions designed to safeguard delta water quality had pushed estimated disposal costs to $21 per cubic yard, ten times the cost of disposal at Alcatraz.

As Oakland officials searched for other disposal alternatives, new legal obstacles arose. The Water Quality Control Board for San Francisco Bay explicitly banned deposit of *all* new dredge project spoils in the Bay, as did the National Marine Fisheries Service, which cited dangers to already diminished salmon populations. Officials from the National Marine Sanctuaries program and other environmental groups objected to ocean disposal off the Continental Shelf. The EPA, having been burned by litigation, retreated into legalistic defensiveness, refusing to approve any new ocean disposal site. It noted that federal law required agency officials to make scientifically grounded findings about the environmental impact of ocean disposal, and yet the requisite mapping of the ocean bottom and currents had not even been initiated until 1990. No decision that would hold up in court, EPA indicated, could be made before 1994.

All this time, while possible environmental harms were debated and investigated, very tangible economic and social harms mounted. The costly hydraulic dredging equipment stood idle. Big ships that sought to call at Oakland, nearly scraping bottom (and thereby risking truly significant environmental harm), had to carry reduced loads and wait for high tides. Schedules of container trains and waiting warehouses and factories were disrupted. Shipping companies, facing higher costs and customer complaints, scrapped plans to expand operations at the Port of Oakland. The previously successful port *lost* money, and hence the municipal government lost substantial revenues from the port–funds needed to help maintain municipal social services. Port-related employment, too, was adversely affected.

Finally, political pressure mounted, new studies were funded, new impact statements were prepared, and more regulatory hearings were held. In late 1992 partial phase I dredging, encompassing 500,000 cubic yards of sediment, was at last permitted. The contaminated sediment (21,000 cubic yards) was deposited in a lined upland site. Regulation officials allowed the port to dump the remaining half-million cubic yards near Alcatraz in San Francisco Bay–just where the port and the Corps of Engineers had first proposed in 1986 (U.S. Army Corps of Engineers, 1992a). In the interim, additional *sampling and testing* costs incurred by the Port of Oakland and the Corps of Engineers had reached almost $4 million, or $8 a cubic yard for phase I–more than double the cost of the actual barging and disposal operation. For the next six million cubic yards, a final decision did not come until late 1994, after a multimillion-dollar research and analysis program. The relevant agencies endorsed a much more expensive disposal plan: some dredged sediments would be barged by sea to the edge of the Continental Shelf, and some (in order to win the support of environmental groups) would be used to create new wetlands far up the Sacramento River Delta. Funding the wetlands disposal project required a $15 million appropriation from Congress and an additional $5 million from the California legislature–at an estimated cost of about $20 per cubic yard. In 1995 the port finally was dredged to the planned forty-two-foot depth (Busch, Kirp, and Schoenholz, 1999: 193–194; Kagan, 1999b).

Some Adverse Propensities of Adversarial Legalism

The laws and legal procedures that for eight years blocked dredging in Oakland Harbor reflect fundamental ideals of pluralistic democracy–that public policy should be formulated and implemented only after full and fair deliberation; that meaningful attention should be given to the claims of the individuals and groups who are not politically powerful (such as the Half Moon Bay fishermen); that environmental protection should be given special weight in planning urgent development projects that might deprive future generations of irreplaceable ecological amenities; and that to vindicate those values, a variety of interest groups and agencies should be able to challenge official assumptions and judgments in court, where they can be tested by smart lawyers, competing experts, and independent judges. In New York City, as shown by William Buzbee's (2014) detailed play-by-play account, adversarial legalism did just that. In the course of a legally protracted process, citizen groups, their attorneys, and federal judges exposed flawed scientific and regulatory judgments by the Corps of Engineers and thereby halted development of the Westway, a massive landfill-and-highway plan that would have had significant adverse effects on aquatic life in the Hudson River. That legal decision ultimately stimulated the formulation and implementation of a reasonable compromise plan.

In the Port of Oakland story, however, the procedures designed to protect those environmental, analytic, and participatory values seemed to fall into the hands of the sorcerer's apprentice, multiplying themselves beyond control. Month after month, regulatory officials, scientists, and lawyers, arguing first in one legal forum, then in another, debated the propriety of decision-making procedures, the adequacy of sediment samples and tests for chemical contamination, and the reliability of environmental impact models. No proceeding produced any definitive finding that the proposed disposal plans were environmentally dangerous (which in that regard makes the Port of Oakland story an extreme case). For years, no court or agency was able to authoritatively designate an environmentally acceptable, economically sensible alternative. The governing body of law, detailed and complex, generated only uncertainty, inconsistency, and legalistic defensiveness. When one agency found a plan legally acceptable, another would disagree. When one court upheld a regulatory decision, another overturned it. No agency could ever be sure that its legal rulings would hold up in court. The mere threat of adversarial litigation, with its capacity to impose further crippling delays, induced both the port and the Corps of Engineers to accept successively more remote (and far more costly) disposal sites and methods, regardless of the merits of the objections. In the tangled web of adversarial legalism, port officials argued, mollusks received far more protection than the human communities that depended on the jobs and revenues generated by the seaport's operations.[4]

Rotterdam, at the mouth of the Rhine in the Netherlands, is Europe's largest seaport. It must deal with far larger volumes of far more seriously contaminated dredged material. The Netherlands, like the United States, adheres to the London Dumping Convention preventing ocean disposal of toxins. There is a strong Dutch green movement that pushes officials to comply with national environmental laws, which, like those in the United States, call for detailed impact analyses and detailed mitigation plans. Thus the Port of Rotterdam has had to deal with its massive dredging and disposal problems in an environmentally responsible manner. It has done so, however, far more expeditiously than the Port of Oakland, without resource-draining and dispiriting adversarial litigation (Hanf and Smits, 1991). The deadlock in Oakland, the Rotterdam experience suggests, is not inherent in the task. It stemmed from a particular institutional structure, characterized by fragmented authority, complex and constrictive legal rules, wide access to litigation, and unpredictable risks of judicial reversal.

Because it derives from basic structures of American government, the Oakland story is far from unique. The same kind of expensive, time-consuming, legally unpredictable, extortive, and economically destructive legal wrangling is a common occurrence in the United States. Virtually every major port-dredging plan, on the East Coast as well as the West, must slog through the quicksand of litigation or invest huge sums in mitigation projects extorted by the threat of litigation.[5] Adversarial legalism often slows and greatly increases costs for many other kinds of large-scale development or construction plans—from siting garbage dumps (Welles and Engel, 2000) and rebuilding bridges (Howard, 2014) to building highways (Detlefsen, 1995), factories (Harris, 1995), and housing projects (Frieden, 1979). Further examples are provided in Chapter 10, which explores more fully the role of adversarial legalism in dealing with tensions between economic development and environmental protection.

Perhaps most importantly, the complexities and costly delays of adversarial legalism also affect vast numbers of everyday legal processes, from commercial dispute resolution to criminal prosecutions. In comparison with parallel legal structures in other rich democracies, adversarial legalism, even as it seeks to (and often does) do good, imposes higher expenses on American processes for compensating injured people, collecting debts, choosing labor union representatives, preserving wildlife habitats, running hospitals and schools, and cleaning up chemical waste sites. In lawsuits seeking damages for personal injuries, lawyers for both sides absorb an astonishing 40 or 50 percent of the sums that liability insurers expend on claims (Kakalik and Pace, 1986; Abraham and Liebman, 1993: 108)—far more than is absorbed by the transaction costs of injury compensation systems in Western Europe or Japan.

The U.S. Superfund program for cleanup of hazardous waste disposal sites, one study noted, generated so much time-consuming litigation among former chemical waste disposers that "by mid-1990 . . . after 10 years of program operation, only sixty-three of the more than twelve hundred National Priorities List sites had been cleaned up" (Church and Nakamura, 1993: 129). As several studies of regulatory rulemaking have shown, new federal rules concerning workplace health risks (Mendeloff, 1987), hazardous air pollutants (Dwyer, 1990), and motor vehicle safety features (Mashaw and Harfst, 1987) often are bogged down in the federal bureaucracy for years, as administrators call for additional scientific research, economic analyses, and legal opinions, hoping to ward off judicial reversal–a threat that their counterparts in other economically advanced democracies do not experience (Badaracco, 1985; Brickman, Jasanoff, and Ilgen, 1985). European and Japanese multinational corporations generally maintain larger staffs of in-house attorneys in their U.S. subsidiaries than in their corporate headquarters and other subsidiaries combined, and they spend more in the United States for reporting, testing, and certifying to regulators that their companies are complying with the law (Kagan, 2000; Kagan and Axelrad, 1997).

Finally, as in the Port of Oakland story, adversarial legalism tends to turn the legal process, designed to settle conflict, into a divisive political struggle, which makes the leaders of major institutions, both public and private, more critical of the courts. Rival political parties and private interest groups openly strive to elevate judges who will be more sympathetic to their particular values and to block the appointment of judges whose political attitudes they fear. Not infrequently, business interests who have lost in court persuade legislators to enact laws designed to counteract a court decision (Barnes, 2004) or to squelch entire categories of litigation. Comparing different public policies for compensating injury victims, Jeb Barnes and Tom Burke (2015) found that policies implemented via adversarial legalism generated more ongoing political conflict than those implemented via bureaucratic legalism, compensated victims more erratically, and spread the costs of compensation more unequally.

When Leila Kawar (2015) compared immigrant rights litigation in the United States and France, she found striking differences in the role of courts and in the political conflicts that ensued. In the United States in the 1980s and 1990s, a sequence of class actions challenged the policies and practices of the U.S. Immigration and Naturalization Service (INS) concerning the deportation of illegal immigrants. The litigation entailed extended pretrial discovery processes, scores of depositions of agency officials, and intrusive consent decrees. It also stimulated "highly adversarial relations between advocacy groups and agencies" (110–111). In 1996, a Republican Congress passed a statute that limited courts' ability to grant class-wide injunctive remedies that would limit agency practices related to removals (119). But immigrant rights lawyers did not give up. They continued to sue the agency for serious rights violations in *individual* removal cases and to demand continued compliance with existing broad consent decrees (122). In France, Kawar found, immigrant rights litigation, conducted in a very different kind of legal system, was not so politically divisive. Yet it is important to remember that American adversarial legalism's political divisiveness in this realm coexists with, and does not nullify, its compensating virtues. In 2018, adversarial legalism, mobilized by the American Civil Liberties Union lawyers, prompted and enabled federal judges to compel revision of a Trump Administration policy that was imposing harsh treatment on asylum-seeking refugees—a policy that was also traumatizing hundreds of children separated from their parents at the border and sent to detainment centers around the country.

The Janus-Faced Nature of Adversarial Legalism

In the Port of Oakland saga, the American legal and regulatory system was not malfunctioning. It was being used as directed, or at least as officially permitted and encouraged. Each regulatory agency and interest group whose legal actions postponed harbor dredging was invoking regulatory standards, procedures, and analytical requirements that are written into law. The redundant reviews by a multiplicity of specialized agencies, along with the laws that enabled fishermen and county water districts to haul government officials into court, were consciously designed bulwarks against environmental heedlessness. Each of those laws, viewed on its own, seems rational and balanced, attentive to economic as well as to environmental values, well grounded in democratic opinion. Nevertheless, the cumulative outcome was irrational, unjust, divisive, and lamentably inefficient. And that is because the mechanisms of American adversarial legalism—the very kinds of mechanisms that sometimes block environmentally obtuse development projects, that produced a judicially-mandated cleanup of Boston's polluted harbor (as described in Chapter 10), that yielded *Brown v. Board of Education* and the Southern prison reform decisions, and that sometimes free the unjustly accused—produce irrational, unjust, and inefficient outcomes as well. Once again, adversarial legalism is Janus-faced.

That the same thing can produce both good and bad results should not be regarded as a paradox. Bureaucracies repeatedly are created because they provide higher levels of honesty and consistency than other modes of administration, but bureaucracies are perpetually reviled for their frustrating caution and red tape. The welfare system that generously assists the needy also generates a certain amount of fraud, dependency, and irresponsibility. "For every jury that departs from the law in order to acquit Vietnam War resisters," George Fletcher (1994: 14–15) observed, "another convicts the Scottsboro boys." In the same way, the heroic image of adversarial legalism is not false. It is only incomplete. As a system for administering criminal justice and resolving civil disputes, the engines of American adversarial legalism can and often do advance the cause of justice in uniquely progressive ways. But the engines don't always work well or work the same for everyone, particularly for those who can't afford them. To offer one more metaphor, American adversarial legalism is like a professional baseball slugger who leads the league in magnificent home runs—but who also misses routine plays in the outfield, often arrives late to the game, and commands such a large salary that many fans can't afford to come to the ballpark.

In most cases, of course, adversarial legalism produces neither home runs nor terrible errors. Often the outcome is mixed: adversarial legalism produces generally desirable outcomes but at a disturbingly high price in time and money, or has radiating consequences that some think good, on balance, but others do not. Quite often, because full-scale adversarial legalism is so cumbersome, time-consuming, and costly, disputants seek informal compromise rather than all-out adversarial litigation and adjudication. Or they shy away from legal conflict altogether—which also has varied effects. Sometimes, like the city governments and police departments described in Charles Epp's research (1998b; 2009) mentioned above, organizations make salutary efforts to comply with the law rather than risking the costs, delays, uncertainties, and negative publicity of adversarial litigation and adjudication. But those anticipated costs also deter many individuals with valid and painful legal grievances from asserting them at all. In yet other cases, the potential costs and delays of adversarial legalism inspire conflicting parties to negotiate creative, mutually acceptable settlements. An example is provided by round two of the Port of Oakland story:

Not long after the Port of Oakland finally emerged from the swamp of adversarial legalism and received approval to dredge its harbor to a depth of forty-two feet, it began planning to deepen the ship channels in San Francisco Bay to fifty feet in order to accommodate a new generation of still larger transpacific containerships. Where would the millions of cubic yards of dredged sediments be deposited? This time, the port, after consulting with a multiagency, broadly consultative committee organized by the Corps of Engineers, proposed dumping some of the mud in a shallow area near the edge of San Francisco Bay. There it would be planted with marsh grasses, restoring the shoreline wildlife habitat. Environmental groups, instead of threatening to litigate, embraced the plan. The Bay Conservation and Development Commission, usually opposed to any plans to fill the bay, gave its approval. A new federal law, passed in the wake of the first deadlock over dredging the harbor, authorized the Corps of Engineers to accept (and fund) environmentally constructive dredging disposal plans even if they are not the least expensive alternative. In other port areas as well, interagency teams and inclusive local planning groups now work at formulating dredging plans consensually (Busch, Kirp, and Schoenholz, 1999: 247). As David Kirp and his colleagues suggested, this chapter of the Port of Oakland story shows that politicians, agencies, and interest groups can learn from past fiascoes, adopting decision processes that tame adversarial legalism and produce creative compromises (247). That happens virtually every day in many parts of the United States. Finding ways to avoid litigation is the stock in trade of most practicing lawyers.

Yet adversarial legalism is rarely fully tamed. It may be pushed out of the clearing on particular issues, but it always lurks in the bushes, ready to be goaded into action, since the legal structures of adversarial legalism are always in place, ready for use. In October 1997 a West Oakland citizens' organization brought a suit against the consensually negotiated harbor dredging plan, demanding that federal funds be withheld until planners examine measures to reduce air pollution from the increase in traffic that will flow from larger containerships (DelVecchio, 1997). The plaintiffs also threatened a suit arguing that the port expansion would violate environmental justice regulations by disproportionately polluting the minority neighborhood adjacent to the port. To avoid further delay, the port settled the cases by agreeing to spend considerable sums on refitting port equipment to reduce air pollution, although its analyses indicated that the resulting contribution to cleaner air in the vicinity would be minimal. On the other hand, research has now demonstrated that very serious adverse health effects stem from exposure to fine particulate emissions from diesel engines like those that operate intensively in seaport areas (Thornton, Kagan, and Gunningham, 2009: 410–411). That suggests that the West Oakland neighbors' complaints were entirely justified. It also emphasizes the complexity of assessing and weighing the radiating costs and benefits of adversarial legalism.

Let us stipulate, then, that adversarial legalism sometimes works well, yielding social benefits that far outweigh its costs; that it sometimes works badly, generating costs that outweigh its intended benefits; and that often it produces a difficult-to-evaluate-or-agree-upon mix of costs and benefits. In principle, a comprehensive evaluation of adversarial legalism would attempt to work out an overall ledger. But gathering the data, coding the outcomes, and comparing incommensurable consequences (better environmental protections versus the costs they impose on economic efficiency and employment) all present unfathomable problems. In the alternative, one might focus only on the system's successes as an inspiration or model for future cases. Those successes, and adversarial legalism's vital role in combatting and deterring governmental oppression and disregard of human rights, are of incalculable worth. This book, I trust, will not be thought to disregard those virtues. Yet the book does concentrate to a considerable extent, perhaps disproportionately, on the social *costs* of adversarial legalism.

Why focus on adversarial legalism's dark shadow as opposed to its luminous successes, or its many modest, everyday successes? First, as an academic colleague suggested, "self-congratulation is not as valuable as self-reflection."[6] In institutional analysis, as in medicine, pathological cases have diagnostic value, revealing fundamental systemic mechanisms. Thus one goal is to better understand the *reasons* for the adverse effects of adversarial legalism. Second, those effects are socially important. They include costly "defensive medicine" in many spheres of business and government. They deter the assertion of just claims and defenses. They distort and delay the implementation of government programs. They weaken faith in the justice system. As Peter Schuck (2000: 421) has observed, "Law that arouses and then dashes peoples' hopes discredits [law's] melioristic impulses, leaving corrosive cynicism and mistrust in its wake." And that mistrust can trigger political overreactions that disable law's best capabilities—as illustrated by the conservative attacks on adversarial legalism discussed in Chapter 11.

Such overreactions remind us that even as this book discusses adversarial legalism's vices, it would be a serious error to forget, devalue, or discard its virtues. In that connection, it may be helpful to develop a deeper understanding of *why* adversarial legalism has come to loom so large in the American legal system. To that exploration, we turn next.

CHAPTER THREE

The Political Construction of Adversarial Legalism

The Netherlands is a pluralistic, intensively regulated nation. Nevertheless, Dutch civil litigation rates are much lower than those in neighboring Germany and Belgium. The reason is that "Dutch jurists have found many ways to avoid handling conflicts in a legalistic way. A rich supply of institutions offers legal aid, legal protection, and conflict resolution alternatives" (Blankenburg and Bruinsma, 1991: 51). In this lies an important lesson: institutional alternatives to courts, more than cultural dispositions toward litigiousness, shape the propensity to rely on litigation to resolve disputes.

Similarly, adversarial legalism in the United States does not arise from an inherent American propensity to bring lawsuits. Many, perhaps most, Americans are reluctant to sue, even when they have grounds to do so, and they often disparage those who do.[1] Rather, American adversarial legalism arises from political traditions and legal arrangements that provide *incentives* to resort to adversarial legal weapons. Put another way, American adversarial legalism arises from the relative absence of institutions that effectively channel contending parties and groups into other ways of resolving disputes, ensuring accountability, regulating business, and compensating victims of injury or economic misfortune (Wilensky, 1983).

Glance again at the list of comparative studies in Table 1 in Chapter 1. In virtually every policy area studied, the other democracies, rather than relying on adversarial legalism, tend to implement public policy and resolve disputes by other means. These include powerful national bureaucracies or corporatist bodies in which internal administrative or political mechanisms, not lawsuits and judicial review, provide the primary mode of accountability for regulatory and other policy decisions.[2] The other countries generally have more comprehensive social insurance programs, which serve as the primary recourse for injured persons and victims of misfortune;

accordingly, liability law recoveries in court are limited. Those kinds of institutional arrangements, however, do not grow easily in the shifting sands of American politics.

Adversarial legalism does. Its growth has been nurtured, particularly in the post-World War II era, by a political culture with two conflicting strands. One major strand demands comprehensive governmental protections from harm, injustice, and environmental dangers—and hence a more powerful, activist government. The other strand, rooted deep in American history, mistrusts governmental power; thus it values the fragmentation of political authority and seeks to keep government (as well as large, powerful businesses) accountable through lawsuits and judicial review. This chapter shows how America's political culture and governmental structure first shaped adversarial legalism in the late eighteenth and nineteenth centuries, expanded its range and intensity in the years since 1960, and assures its persistence despite much criticism and efforts to curtail it.

The phenomenon to be explained—increases in adversarial legalism in the United States as a whole—is dauntingly complex. "Adversarial legalism," as noted earlier, refers both to the everyday incidence of adversarial legal contestation and to the legal structures and laws that foster such contestation. Much of American law is made by the fifty state governments, which vary significantly politically and hence legally. There are many steadily evolving fields of law. The explanatory variables discussed—political structure, political culture, economic structure, and legal culture—are all expansive terms, encompassing multiple strands. Quantitative, longitudinal measures of most these variables are not readily available. What follows, therefore, does not rise to the level of a parsimonious causal model, backed by quantitative proof of each variable's weight. Rather, it is a mostly qualitative account, highlighting the legal changes and causal factors that appear to matter most.

Something Old, Something New

We nod with familiarity when modern authors cite Alexis de Tocqueville's observation that in the United States of the 1820s and 1830s, most major political issues became judicial issues. Later, the Supreme Court's *Dred Scott* decision helped precipitate the Civil War. Afterwards, litigation by Southern white supremacists led to Supreme Court decisions that undercut the thrust of postwar federal civil rights laws and constitutional provisions, opening the door to decades of racial apartheid and subordination. In 1884, a federal court judge ordered California's gold mine companies to stop dumping toxic mining effluent and debris into rivers and streams; the order simultaneously shut down the state's most profitable industry and halted a process that imposed extensive damage on the Central Valley's agriculture and environment (Vogel, 2017). An 1895 editorial in the *Street Railway Journal,* Lawrence Friedman (1978) reports, referred to accident liability lawsuits as a "nightmare" and a "sword of Damocles," and railroad executives complained about ambulance-chasing lawyers. In the late nineteenth century and the first third of the twentieth, business interests often resorted to adversarial legalism, persuading the courts to strike down prolabor statutes and to issue injunctions against striking workers.

Adversarial legalism, in sum, has always been woven into the fabric of American life and politics. Early in the nation's history, four basic engines of adversarial legalism were put in place: litigant-and-lawyer-dominated modes of adjudication, oriented toward trial by jury; a large, entrepreneurial, politically active legal profession; a politically selected judiciary that could *make* law, both through common law adjudication and through constitutional review of legislative and administrative decisions; and a legal culture that valued law, litigation, and courts as essential parts of governance as well as of dispute resolution.[3] John Coffee, Jr. (2015: 10–11) points out:

> In Europe, judges were the appointees of the central government and were often charged with enforcing its policies against recalcitrant regions or provinces. In the United States, by the early to middle nineteenth century, the majority of state judges were popularly elected. . . . This combination of politically responsive state judiciaries and juries representing and reflecting the local community led to the perception of litigation as "democracy in action."

Thus compared to their counterparts in England and Western Europe, nineteenth-century Americans probably were more likely to use law and litigation to maintain a sense of moral order. They lived in a more pluralistic, more transient, society with weaker institutions of social control. Free from traditions of deference to kings and priests and guilds, Americans were not reluctant to mount adversarial legal challenges to authority (and to each other) (Kessler, 2017).[4]

Yet the adversarial legalism that came to pervade the United States in the last third of the twentieth century is both more extensive and more intense than that of the nineteenth century and the first half of the twentieth. Before the 1960s, there were few legal struggles akin to the Alabama prison reform case and the long legal battle over dredging Oakland Harbor. In 1960, public interest advocacy organizations, acting as private attorneys general, appeared in court less often than in later decades.[5] Class actions against business corporations, government agencies, and prison systems were rare, as were successful damage suits against police departments, hospitals, and physicians. The average civil and criminal trial was far shorter than today's. Before the late 1960s, American administrative agencies, school boards, highway planners, and zoning boards were much less likely than their contemporary counterparts to see their policy decisions successfully challenged in court. In 1960 the threat of litigation was not an omnipresent consideration, as it is today, in corporate finance, electoral redistricting, land use planning, enforcement of immigration law, and the practice of medicine. Nominations to the Supreme Court and to U.S. Courts of Appeals did not unleash intensely partisan, interest group conflicts of the magnitude that began in the 1980s—partly because the Supreme Court had not yet issued rulings establishing, and then threatening to restrict, women's constitutional right to abortion.

In 1960 there was one lawyer for every 627 people in the United States. By 1995 the ratio had doubled to 1:307 (Curran and Carson, 1994). Between 1960 and 1987, expenditures on lawyers in the United States grew sixfold, from $9 billion annually to $54 billion (in constant 1983 dollars), almost tripling the share of GNP consumed by legal services (Sander and Williams, 1989: 434–435). Between 1960 and 1980, federal court appellate cases involving constitutional issues increased sevenfold (Kagan, 1987). Between 1970 and the late 1980s, federal indictments of public officials swelled from fewer than 100 per year to almost 1,000 per year, which, as Ginsberg and Shefter (1990: 5–7) point out, "suggests growing use of criminal investigation of public officials as a mode of partisan struggle for political advantage." Medical malpractice suits, rare in 1960, reached 4.3 per 100 insured physicians in 1970 and 18.3 per 100 in 1986 (Quam et al., 1987: 1529–1531, 1597–1600; Dewees, Trebilcock, and Coyte, 1991). The volume and rate of state appellate and federal court cases involving public schools, roughly stable from 1920 through 1960, doubled in the 1967–1981 period (Tyack and Benavot, 1985).[6] In the decades following the California Supreme Court's 1971 decision in *Serrano v. Priest,* litigants filed more than sixty cases in forty-one states challenging the constitutionality of school finance methods, and in many states litigants and judges assumed a significant ongoing role in reshaping school-funding policy (Heise, 1995). In 1990 a former CEO of a major American bank told me, "I sit on a lot of corporate boards of directors. I started using my stopwatch to see how much of each board meeting is taken up by lawyers. Years ago it was about 5 percent. Recently it has gone up to 40 or even 50 percent."

The period before 1960 was not a golden age. It was harder to challenge governmental and economic power, and power was not always benign. Racial, ethnic, and gender discrimination usually went unchallenged. Government controls on pollution were weak or nonexistent. Many regulatory agencies were soft on the industries they were supposed to control. Citizens, especially poorer citizens, often had little recourse when highways were thrust through their neighborhoods, when chemical waste sites were located near their homes, or when policemen, school principals, or bureau-crats treated them arbitrarily. The point is that the 1960s initiated a period of striking change in the intensity and reach of adversarial legalism. Some-thing new had been added to the stew of American law. It became spicier. It was served up more often and in larger portions. It nourished more people—while giving indigestion to others. To understand these changes, we must attend to the complex interaction of political structure, political and legal culture, and shifting political pressures and opportunities.

The Demand for "Total Justice"

Most obviously, the increases in adversarial legalism reflected an out-pouring of new legal rules, rights, and obligations. State courts made sweeping changes in tort law, which made it easier for injured people to sue and obtain substantial damage awards from doctors and landlords, manu-facturers and municipal governments. The Supreme Court's "due process revolution" enlarged the legal rights of criminal defendants, prisoners, and welfare recipients. Judicial decisions and congressional statutes prompted the growth of government-funded public defenders' offices for criminal cases and of legal services offices for the poor. Between the mid-1960s and mid-1970s, federal and state governments enacted an unprecedented wave of regulatory statutes and administrative regulations concerning pollution control, land use, consumer protection, worker safety, and nondiscrimina-tion in employment and education. They also mandated a more legalistic and punitive approach to regulatory enforcement, not only by regulatory officials (Bardach and Kagan, 1982) but by private lawyers and advocacy groups (Farhang, 2010; Burbank and Farhang, 2017).

But why was there such an outpouring of new law? The proximate causes were the politically liberal social movements that swept through the United States in the 1960s. Beginning midway through that decade, the United States experienced what political scientist Samuel Huntington (1981) labeled a period of "creedal passion." During such recurrent episodes in American history, he argued, many citizens become outraged by the gap between America's liberal, egalitarian political creed and the inequali-ties that stem from contemporary institutional practices. Caught up in the politics of creedal passion, citizens leap the channels of electoral politics and turn to demonstration and protest, as in the case of the populist agrarian rallies of the 1880s or, during the Great Depression, the sit-down strikes and marches by the labor movement and the unemployed. Similarly, in the 1960s the moral passion, street demonstrations, and civil disobedience of the civil rights movement—and then of the anti–Vietnam War movement—overwhelmed the incremental processes and compromises of "normal politics." These movements energized and provided a model for others, such as environmentalism and feminism. Specialized public interest groups were organized to demonstrate and lobby on behalf of ethnic minorities, consumer safety, the aged, poor tenants, children, the handicapped, welfare recipients, and so on. Cumulatively, they demanded major transformations in established social and economic patterns and a major expansion of the role of the federal government.

Political leaders in Congress and many judges were extremely responsive (Jenkins and Milkis, 2014: 5; Wilson, 1994: 669; Wilson, 1980). The federal government's Voting Rights Act of 1965, enacted by a Democratic Congress and presidency, commanded Southern states to register black voters en masse. Technology-forcing statutes instructed industry to control pollution and prevent accidents. The Supreme Court banned prayer in public schools, ordered reapportionment of state legislatures, and gave women the legal right to obtain abortions. Judges ordered cities to bus clumps of white children and black children across towns to achieve racial balance in the schools. Other judges, horrified by conditions in state mental institutions, ordered the deinstitutionalization of mental patients. State court judges reshaped tort law in order to compel businesses, professionals, and local governments to develop better safety precautions.

To some observers, moreover, the legal revolution of the 1960s and 1970s reflected not merely a periodic burst of idealism and political activism but a more enduring social and intellectual change. Surveying the evolution of American legal culture since the late nineteenth century, Lawrence Friedman (1985) discerns a striking increase in popular expectations of "total justice"–the notion that because rich, technologically advanced societies now *have* insurance systems, large well-funded governments, and greater administrative capacities, those capacities *ought to be* employed to remedy serious social problems and sources of harm. To be sure, political conservatives and political liberals may have different priorities in that regard. Conservatives, upset about increases in street crime and drug additions, might demand more law and order, while liberals might demand laws and government programs that would provide financial aid to families devastated by physical injury or poverty. The key notion is that fatalism has declined; solutions are possible. Hence government and law ought to be responsive to pressing social problems.

For example, Friedman notes, late-twentieth-century Americans, in contrast to their more fatalistic forebears, readily observe that modern societies have the capacity to devise means of *preventing* misfortune and mistreatment–regulatory inspections, double hulls for oil tankers, tests to detect carcinogens, better education and nutrition for poor children. If those techniques exist, the logic goes, it is unjust not to use them. The law, therefore, should require them. Such ideas, Friedman suggests, had penetrated the thinking of much of the law-shaping governmental elite—law professors, appellate court lawyers, judges, legislative staffers, advocacy organizations, and journalists. Hence the judges' expansion of liability in tort law. Hence the endorsement by political and legal elites of politically liberal social activists' demands for stringent environmental and safety regulation, broader antidiscrimination laws, and more potent judicial remedies against legally recalcitrant organizations, public and private.

On the other hand, popular demands for governmental social engineering and for total justice are not unique to the United States. In the 1960s Western European democracies extended preexisting governmental protections against misfortune and added new ones to limit environmental degradation and unfair treatment. Like the United States, they liberalized divorce laws, created women's rights to obtain legal abortions (Glendon, 1987), banned discrimination in employment, and expanded long-standing national social insurance and health care schemes (Wilensky, 1975; Kamerman and Kahn, 1988). European Green parties battled successfully for pollution controls, restrictions on nuclear power, and limits on hazardous chemicals—regulations that compare in stringency with those of the United States (Vogel, 1986; Brickman, Jasanoff, and Ilgen, 1985; Lundqvuist, 1980). Western European laws protecting employees from arbitrary termination, restricting urban sprawl, and guarding tenants' interests generally are much stricter than those in the United States.

But as shown by the comparative studies in Table 1, Chapter 1, the expansion of entitlements and regulation in Western Europe did not produce American-style adversarial legalism. There, national governmental bureaucracies and corporatist bodies implemented ambitious regulations and welfare state entitlements without much reliance on—and hence without much interference from—courts and lawyers. That has changed a bit in recent decades: the European Union and the European Court of Justice have relied more on litigation and member state courts to implement their regulations and rulings (Kelemen, 2011) and overall, courts play a larger role in governance (Kapiszewski, Silverstein, and Kagan, 2013). Still, even in contemporary Western Europe, American-style class actions, waves of toxic tort cases, and court-ordered institutional reform plans are far less frequent and potent than their American counterparts. In European courts, money damages awarded to injured plaintiffs in tort cases are substantially lower (Sugarman, 2006). Fierce legal and regulatory controversies sometimes erupt in Europe, as in the case of siting decisions for development projects, but they usually are resolved in political and administrative forums, not in the general court system. Outcomes much less often are shaped, as in the Port of Oakland dredging story, by the sheer costs and delays of legal procedures.

In sum, similar winds of change blew through both Western Europe and the United States, but the winds were filtered through sharply contrasting political structures and traditions. Somewhat similar basic *policy norms* emerged on both sides of the Atlantic, but the national *methods* of establishing and implementing those norms were markedly different. To understand why, we must examine more fully the interaction between (a) the inherited American political structure and (b) increasing political demands for justice and governmental regulation.

Fragmented Governmental Authority and Adversarial Legalism

To condense this section's argument, the intensification and expansion of adversarial legalism in the United States since 1960 has been stimulated by a fundamental mismatch between a changing legal culture and an inherited set of political attitudes and structures. Americans have attempted to articulate and implement the socially transformative policies of an activist regulatory-and-welfare state through the political and legal institutions of a decentralized, nonhierarchical governmental system. In the absence of cohesive political parties, a dominant national bureaucracy, and a widely trusted social insurance system, the proponents of increased protection of individual rights, stronger regulatory measures, and expanded social welfare programs sought laws and judicial decisions that would authorize litigation to implement legal change. Legislatures and judiciaries responded accordingly.

Damaska's Typology

In *The Faces of Justice and State Authority* (1986), Mirjan Damaska formulates a typology of legal processes built on two dimensions. The first dimension contrasts hierarchical with coordinate modes of organizing administrative and legal processes. The hierarchical model, toward which continental European states incline, emphasizes strong, highly professional national bureaucracies, directly responsible to a parliamentary cabinet. The reigning ideals of hierarchical law and administration are fidelity to official policies and uniformity of case-by-case decision-making. Legal and administrative officials, therefore, are to be professionally trained and organizationally insulated from the potentially corrupting influence of local politicians, wealthy citizens and businesses, and public opinion. In contrast, American legal and administrative processes lean toward what Damaska labels a coordinate model of authority, designed to counteract the potential for tyranny or political bias inherent in centralized, hierarchically-organized political and legal authority. The power to make and apply policy and law, therefore, is fragmented, delegated to many governmental bodies and courts, staffed by officials and judges chosen to be responsive to local political communities. Coordination is exercised horizontally rather than hierarchically by empowering one governmental body to check another and by granting citizens' rights to challenge governmental decisions in court.

The second dimension of Damaska's typology contrasts two polar visions of the proper role of government. At one extreme is the activist state, dedicated to the aggressive management, mobilization, or transformation of the national economy and society. At the other pole is the reactive state, expected only to provide an orderly framework for private economic and social interaction. The reactive state formulates and implements policy primarily by resolving conflicts generated by competing interests.

There are obvious affinities between an activist state and a hierarchical organization of authority, with its centrally managed bureaucracy and judiciary, willing and able to implement official policy. Similarly, a reactive state fits nicely with a coordinate organization of authority, with its wide openings for civilian influence, its skepticism about state-enforced norms, and its reliance on adversarial argument. In the reactive, conflict-resolving state, when government is involved in a dispute with citizens, the government official stands on the same plane, in theory, as the individual; he or she represents just another competing interest. A judge attentive to individual rights must have the last word, not (as in the activist state) the government official focused on systematic policy implementation.

Coordinate Authority and Reactive Government

Through the nineteenth century and well into the twentieth, the United States blended a reactive state and coordinate authority. Both flowed in large part from the political liberalism and suspicion of centralized governmental power that animated the American Revolution, the constitutional founding, and the developing nation (Hartz, 1955).[7] In the liberal vision, governmental power must be limited and restrained by law, invoked and applied by rights-bearing citizens.

American political culture has also harbored a turbulent populist strain, mistrustful of concentrated economic as well as governmental power, quick to believe that government officials will engage in self-dealing or will be corrupted by business interests (Lipset, 1996; Goodwyn, 1978). If powerful men cannot be trusted, power should be fragmented, held accountable not only to watchful local electorates but also to the law, and applied in courts that are staffed by ordinary people serving as judges and jurors. Since American bankers and merchants, too, tended to mistrust politicians and their appointees, business interests joined grassroots populists in advocating constitutional and other legal controls on government, enforceable in the courts. So did one further source of distrust of government: Southern political leaders, who feared that a strong central government could be influenced by Northern states to forbid or restrict slavery—a stance Southern states maintained even after the Civil War and the abolition of slavery.

These basic political attitudes were embodied in constitutions, state as well as federal, that splintered governmental authority among separate branches, establishing legal constraints on each. The federal Constitution also compelled the new national government to leave much governing power to the states, while state constitutions guaranteed generous measures of home rule to local governments (Briffault, 1990). Both federal and state constitutions included a government-limiting bill of rights, enforceable in local courts at the behest of ordinary citizens. And in courts, the adjudicatory power of judges was checked by assertive lawyers (Kessler, 2017) and shared with locally-selected juries (Hale, 2016).[8]

American government in the nineteenth century was far from absent (Novak, 2008). The common law shaped and regulated markets. Local governments regulated dangerous and obnoxious land uses. State governments built canals (Scheiber, 1969). The federal government established agencies to distribute public lands, deliver the mail, and regulate the safety of steamship boilers (Mashaw, 2012). But with a tradition of decentralized government, the United States developed what some students of comparative politics have called a "weak state"—not "weak" in the sense of wholly inactive or ineffective but in the sense that such a state is highly responsive to political factions, popular opinion, and organized private interests—as opposed to a "strong state," one that is capable of dominating civil society through unified governmental will and powerful bureaucratic structures (Krasner, 1978: 55–70). In contrast to Western European nations, where strong, politically autonomous central governmental bureaucracies *preceded* the development of democracy, nineteenth-century American government was dominated through much of the nineteenth century not by bureaucrats in Washington or state agencies but by decentralized political parties and by locally selected judges (Skowronek, 1982; Shefter, 1994; Fukuyama, 2014). State legislatures met for limited terms and for limited pay. That further enabled and encouraged judges to become active policymakers by reinterpreting and readjusting the common law (Hurst, 1956, 1964; Horwitz, 1977)—a mode of policymaking that was decentralized, incremental, and consistent with Damaska's conception of a reactive, conflict-resolving state. It was that political system that prompted de Tocqueville's (1835) observations that in America important political issues repeatedly were transmuted into judicial questions and that politics and social life were pervaded by lawyers and the vocabulary of the law.

Decentralized, coordinate governmental structures reinforced a reactive approach to governance. Decentralized government favored political parties built by the dispensation of patronage to local supporters—rather than by tight adherence to a particular political philosophy and policy agenda.[9] Federalism, separation of powers, bicameral legislatures, and locally oriented political parties resulted in legislative processes that were full of veto points at which particular interests could block governmental action that displeased them; that too, meant that courts were often a more *responsive* government institution. Economic competition among states generated pressures against raising taxes, making regulation too strict, and expanding state bureaucracies. Professional governmental bureaucracies were thus slower to develop in the United States than in Europe.[10] In the late nineteenth century, American state and city governments—as well as Congress (White, 2011)—were often corrupt and distrusted.

Moreover, in the late nineteenth century and early in the twentieth, politically conservative interests often turned to adversarial legalism to ward off the expansion of governmental controls. In legal appeals from Southern states, the U.S. Supreme Court limited the reach of the post-Civil War Fourteenth Amendment[11] and of congressional statutes designed to combat white vigilantism and protect the civil rights of former slaves.[12] Business interests persuaded Congress to expand the lower federal courts (Gillman, 2002) and used them to retard the growth of labor unions, to issue injunctions against striking workers, and to declare unconstitutional both state and federal laws designed to foster unionization or to directly protect employees (including child workers) from onerous working conditions. Court rulings on these and other forms of regulation further retarded expansion of national regulatory bureaucracies. So did a 1895 Supreme Court decision invalidating a federal income tax[13]—a ruling that took almost twenty years and a constitutional amendment to overturn.

The courts did not strike down *most* regulatory statutes. The federal government established the Interstate Commerce Commission to regulate the rapidly growing railroad industry, and also built bureaucracies to administer the Homestead Act for settling the Western plains and for doling out pensions for the families of Civil War veterans. As knowledge of causes of communicable disease spread, cities and counties established departments of public health, sewage, and garbage disposal. State governments established public utility commissions to regulate insurance companies, electricity companies, water supply companies, and other businesses "affected with a public interest" (Novak, 2017). During the Progressive Era, city, state, and even federal bureaucracies grew rapidly (Friedman, 1973: 396–405). The 1883 federal Civil Service Act represented a significant (although still only partial) step away from staffing federal agencies anew after each election (the "spoils system") and toward building professional, merit-based national bureaucracies (Mashaw, 2012).[14]

Nevertheless, even as American government became more robust, it remained much smaller, less centralized, and less dominant in society than the governments of such countries as France, the unified Germany, and Japan. Compared to Western Europe, economic life in the United States—not only in the nineteenth century but in the twentieth as well—was more fully the province of private business firms, which were less subject to governmental financing, control, and guidance. Business relationships, labor relations, and business–government interactions were policed to a large extent by litigation and by judge-made rules that favored entrepreneurial energy, freedom of contract, and private property (Hurst, 1956; Horwitz, 1977). This too reinforced a reactive, conflict-resolving approach to governance.

Activist Government and the New Deal

In all industrialized democracies, twentieth-century political demands pushed governments to become more activist—to steer and stabilize the economy and to provide a measure of economic security to injured workers, the unemployed, and the aged. In the United States, however, those political demands were channeled through entrenched political structures that had fragmented and decentralized power. And as Damaska (1986: 13) pointed out, "A state with many independent power centers *and* a powerful desire to transform society can be likened to a man with ardent appetites and poor instruments for their satisfaction." When that hungry man was an American political activist in the 1960s, he grabbed an instrument that best seemed to address his dilemma—adversarial legalism. In the 1930s even hungrier men reached for more radical governmental changes.

Confronted with the crisis of the Great Depression, Franklin Roosevelt's New Deal directly addressed the tension between fragmented government and demands for transformative governmental action. To the New Dealers, "a system of centralized and unified powers, bypassing the states and the judiciary, seemed indispensable to allow for dramatic and frequent governmental regulation" (Sunstein, 1990: 23). The Roosevelt administration strengthened the central government and extended its administrative reach, substituting national, bureaucratically administered programs for markets and state law. The president and Congress established public works programs, agricultural stabilization programs, national bank insurance, and the social security retirement program, all administered by federal agencies. The 1933 National Industrial Recovery Act (NIRA), in a move evocative of European corporatist arrangements, mandated nationwide price-and-wage stabilization agencies for each industrial sector, to be staffed by representatives of business, labor, and consumers (Hawley, 1966). But the Supreme Court, dominated by defenders of the inherited reactive regime, held that the NIRA and several other major New Deal statutes were unconstitutional.

In response, Congress reenacted those statutes in different form. More generally, in a backlash against the politically conservative uses of adversarial legalism, it tried to push the courts out of the ring. Congress forbade judicial injunctions against strikes by labor unions and it shifted legal disputes about antiunion practices (as prohibited by the National Labor Relations Act) from the courts into an administrative tribunal, the National Labor Relations Board. President Roosevelt sought to expand the Supreme Court and pack it with supportive Democrats. But before that plan came to a vote in Congress, the Court backed down and upheld two major New Deal laws—and subsequently upheld others. Roosevelt and his successor President Truman reshaped the judiciary; they appointed federal judges who generally believed in judicial deference to federal legislation and to the decisions of federal administrative agencies. Through the 1950s, the new constitutional and administrative law doctrines forged by the New Deal judges limited litigation by business interests who opposed the expansion of federal regulation and taxation.

The huge increases in federal taxation, spending, and military procurement that occurred during World War II, together with the federal bureaucracies they spawned, persisted into the Cold War. The postwar federal government continued to assume responsibility for national economic policy. It invested heavily in infrastructure development, higher education, scientific training, and research. Thus from the New Deal on, the American state no longer could be characterized as mostly reactive. It fostered a "mixed economy" characterized by a large measure of business-government cooperation, and, compared to the pre-New Deal period, an even higher degree of activism and governance by the federal government (Hacker and Pierson, 2016).

Total Justice + Fragmented Government = Adversarial Legalism

Notwithstanding the centralizing impact of the New Deal, World War II, and the Cold War, in the 1950s and early 1960s government in the United States, viewed in cross-national comparative terms, remained structurally and politically fragmented (Wilensky, 1965: xvi–xix). Many salient realms of law, policy, and administration—policing and criminal law; education; land use control; family, tort, and commercial law; welfare administration; and antidiscrimination policy—were still the province of state and local governments and courts. Due in large part to Southern Democrats' race-based resistance to administration by federal government bureaucracies, a number of important federal programs, such as unemployment insurance, disability insurance, and Aid for Families with Dependent Children, were actually administered by state and county agencies whose procedures and standards in social benefit programs often differed from state to state and county to county (Mashaw, 1971, 1983). But as the postwar economy flourished and governmental capacity grew, so did the political demands on the federal government for total justice and more unified national legal remedies. The congressional response, however, was hampered by the many veto points in the complex legislative process, by regional political divisions, and by Constitutional restrictions on the federal government's powers. It was that collision—between politically fragmented government and strong political demands for governmental action—that ignited increases in adversarial legalism.

To note one prominent example, in the 1950s, partly because of their Cold War claims about America's democratic virtue, national political elites had become sensitive to the contradiction between the egalitarian "American creed" and the ugly reality of Southern apartheid (Dudziak, 1988; Rosenberg, 1991). Due to the constitutional limits of federalism, however, the national government could not displace local democratic control of public school policy and law enforcement in southern states. There was no national minister of education or minister of justice who could give direct orders to segregationist local school officials or racist sheriffs or replace them if they were recalcitrant. Because American political parties were not hierarchically controlled, Southern Democrats in the Senate repeatedly blocked congressional civil rights legislation that was proposed by the national Democratic Party and by Democratic presidents.

The coordinate structure of American government, on the other hand, enabled both presidents and civil rights leaders to circumvent the legislative deadlock by turning to the courts. In the late 1930s, President Roosevelt had created what became the Office of Civil Rights in the Department of Justice, dedicated to using the courts to attack Southern racism (McMahon, 2000). The National Association for the Protection of Colored People (NAACP) filed lawsuits in various school districts arguing that because legislatures, federal and state, had persistently failed to act against a nationally recognized injustice, it was incumbent on the courts to step into the breach. President Truman's and then (in the 1950s) President Eisenhower's attorney general filed supportive legal briefs in the Supreme Court (Pacelle, 2003: 70, 72). The American judiciary was staffed with ex-politicians (Goldman, 1967),[15] including many political liberals appointed by Democratic presidents and steeped in the pragmatic, social-problem-solving ethos of "legal realism" (Teles, 2008: 22–25) and "responsive law" (Nonet and Selznick, 1978). The Supreme Court, led by Chief Justice Earl Warren, a moderate

Republican ex-prosecutor, ex-governor, and ex-candidate for vice president, was open to arguments based on substantive justice—arguments that emphasized the social consequences of Constitutional interpretations, not merely the text. Thus in 1954, in *Brown v. Board of Education,* the Court ruled that racially separate schools mandated by law were inherently and fundamentally unfair, contrary to the Constitution's equal protection clause.

The NAACP had cast its argument and requested remedy in the form of a constitutionally grounded legal right. This meant, in the American legal tradition, that the Court's ruling could be invoked by ordinary citizens and by citizens' groups like the NAACP. It could be enforced against a segregated school district by any local trial court judge, state or federal—although in the South, the *federal* district courts, though staffed by Southerners, were most open to doing so (Peltason, 1961). Consequently, private enforcement of constitutional law by means of adversarial litigation became a primary method of implementing national antisegregation policy—albeit a minimally effective method, especially in the Deep South, until the 1964 U.S. Civil Rights Act led to federal *bureaucratic* regulation and more far-reaching judicial reform orders (Melnick, 2016).[16] The main point for this chapter, however, is that as part of the shift from Damaska's reactive state to an activist one, the Supreme Court and lower federal courts were transforming constitutional law—which earlier had been a mechanism primarily for telling the government what it could *not* do—into a mechanism for telling government what it *must* do (Silverstein, 2009), demanding that it take affirmative action to help solve pressing but inadequately addressed social problems.

The 1960s due process revolution in criminal procedure repeated this pattern. The national legal elite, prodded by the civil rights movement, had become increasingly dismayed by abusive police practices in segregated Southern states and in crime-ridden black neighborhoods in Northern cities. Yet Congress and the Department of Justice did not have clear hierarchical authority to impose reforms on hundreds of local police departments and courthouses. The only viable strategy for change seemed to be a further elaboration of *coordinate* controls, using the tools of adversarial legalism—lawyering, litigation, and judicial policymaking. Responding to a series of individual petitions for review, the Supreme Court during Chief Justice Earl Warren's tenure reinterpreted the Constitution, applying most provisions of the Bill of Rights to state and local government. In doing so, the Court elaborated new nationwide rules to regulate pretrial detention, interrogation of suspects, searches for evidence, station-house lineups, and jury selection. In addition, the Court mandated adversarial enforcement mechanisms for those new legal standards—free counsel for indigent defendants and an exclusionary rule that required rejection of evidence obtained in violation of the Supreme Court's rules. Again, because these new policies and procedures were cast as constitutional rules, they were largely insulated from reversal or amendment by legislatures or police administrators, state or federal. This ensured that policy development and implementation would remain in the province of adversarial legalism. Defense lawyers' motions to suppress illegally obtained evidence and confessions became a routine practice in local criminal prosecutions,[17] and the appellate courts, not state legislatures, laid down the principles for determining when police need a warrant, when they can search a suspect's car trunk, and so on. Later, private lawsuits against police departments, seeking money damages for violations of individuals' constitutional rights, became an additional mode of enforcement (Epp, 2009). The result has been an adversarial (and politically controversial) way of regulating local criminal justice officers (Walker, 1993; Bradley, 1993).

The tension between impulses toward total justice and fragmented government also stimulated changes in the civil justice system. In Damaska's model of the reactive state, the dominant purpose of civil law is conflict resolution. In the spirit of the activist state, however, lawyers, judges, and legal scholars increasingly focused on the achievement of substantively just legal outcomes and the effective implementation of public policies and legal norms (Marcus, 2014: v127). They pushed for changes in civil procedure that would reduce the advantages that legally experienced "haves" traditionally enjoyed vis-à-vis inexperienced "have not" parties (Galanter, 1974). More and more states, following the lead of the federal court system, jettisoned legalistic pleading standards in favor of simplified notice pleading and expanded plaintiffs' rights to searching pretrial discovery—both of which facilitated enforcement of legal norms by private litigants (Marcus, 2014: 134). To increase the deterrent or regulatory effect of the law, judges and legislatures authorized class actions, which enabled lawyers to aggregate an alleged legal wrong affecting many victims into one potentially lucrative—and very threatening—lawsuit. Reinterpreting tort law to enhance its regulatory goals, judges reduced legal barriers to successful, remunerative lawsuits by injured individuals against businesses, hospitals, and local government bodies. Adversarial legalism thus became a more salient form of policy implementation and influence in the myriad social, economic, and political relationships mediated by civil law.

Fragmented Government and the Private Enforcement of Public Law

In the 1960s and 1970s, Democratic majorities faced the same structural problem that confronted New Deal reformers: how to implement socially transformative legislation in a coordinately organized, decentralized political system. The New Deal tried to consolidate and extend the powers of the central government and its new bureaucracies, displacing state governments and the courts. In the 1960s and 1970s, in contrast, Congress embraced adversarial legalism.

Between 1964 and 1977, in a truly extraordinary surge of activity, Congress, controlled by the Democratic Party and prodded by social movements and liberal advocacy groups, passed twenty-five major environmental and civil rights acts, plus far-reaching statutes regulating workplace safety, consumer lending, product safety, private pension funds, and local public education.[18] At the same time, Congress was reluctant or unable—for political, fiscal, and constitutional reasons—to create huge federal bureaucracies, with offices in every metropolitan area, to enforce all these demanding regulatory programs. In many cases, therefore, Congress assigned primary enforcement responsibility to state and local governmental officials. But then how could reformers and their congressional allies be sure that the new federal norms would be faithfully implemented? Or ensure that the vast numbers of business firms brought into the ambit of federal regulation would *comply* with the growing array of new legal obligations?

Adversarial legalism provided one answer.[19] Regulatory reformers couched their goals in the form of sweeping legal rights—to equal treatment, a safe workplace, clean water, clean air (Melnick, 1995; Landy and Levin, 1995). Congress embedded those rights in statutes. In many cases, Congress specifically authorized private individuals and energetic reform lawyers to enforce those rights by acting as private attorneys general; that is, to bring lawsuits against state and local governments for half-hearted implementation of federal laws, or directly against regulated businesses, unions, and local government bodies. To further mobilize private lawyers as enforcement agents, Congress enacted scores of one-way fee-shifting statutes, which enabled successful plaintiffs to recover lawyers' fees from governmental and corporate defendants—but did not require plaintiffs, if they lost, to pay the defendants' lawyers' bills (Farhang, 2010; Greve, 1989a; O'Connor and Epstein, 1985). These fees, together with direct aid from large, politically liberal private foundations, provided funding for a rapidly growing number of politically liberal public interest law firms (Burbank and Farhang, 2017).[20] "During the 1970s," observed David Vogel (1989: 293), "the public interest movement replaced organized labor as the central countervailing force to the power and values of American business."

In interpreting the new statutes, the courts themselves often did so in ways that expanded opportunities for litigation. Even when congressional statutes were silent on the subject, federal judges sometimes held that those laws contained *implied* private rights to sue businesses and government entities that arguably had not complied (Melnick, 2016).[21] In addition, judges often interpreted the statutes broadly. Referring to a provision of the 1964

Civil Rights Act barring racial, ethnic, and gender discrimination by private businesses, Melnick (2018a: 33) writes:

> It is more accurate to say that the federal courts *rewrote* Title VII, turning a weak law focusing primarily on *intentional* discrimination into a bold mandate to compensate for past discrimination, to prohibit employment practices that have a "disparate impact" on racial minorities (and later women), and above all to substantially increase the job opportunities available to African-Americans.

Increases in adversarial legalism in practice quickly followed. Private litigation to enforce federal statutes grew from a rate of 3 per 100,000 population in 1967 to 13 by 1976, to 21 by 1986, to 29 in 1996 (Farhang, 2014). In the early 1990s, the municipal government of Washington, D.C., was operating under at least seven separate judicially supervised decrees, requiring city officials to meet higher standards in food subsidy programs, jails, public mental health services, public housing, institutions for the mentally ill, juvenile detention facilities, and public schools (Plotz 1994). In 2000, more than thirty state welfare agencies were operating under court orders demanding improvements (Sandler and Schoenbrod 2003: 122). After a 1991 statute authorized judges to award compensatory and punitive damages for civil rights law violations, there followed a surge in sexual harassment complaints and other civil rights suits in federal courts (Melnick 2018a: 39). Similarly, after the Supreme Court interpreted an 1871 law to authorize monetary damages from state and local government agencies for violations of a citizen's civil rights, networks of reform lawyers brought scores of lawsuits against city police departments for racial discrimination or excessive use of force by individual officers (Epp, 2009: 64–72). All in all, the federal judiciary, noted Paul Frymer (2008: 16), "became one of the leading engines of the regulation state."

In sum, whereas European polities generally rely on hierarchically organized national bureaucracies to hold local officials and business firms accountable to national policies, the U.S. federal government, politically impeded from exerting such direct hierarchical controls, mobilized a distinctly American army of enforcers—a decentralized array of private advocacy groups and lawyers and federal district court judges. To offer one example, the landmark federal Education for All Handicapped Children Act (EAHCA), enacted in 1975, required local public schools to provide all children, regardless of handicap, an "appropriate public education." Rather than creating a federal enforcement bureaucracy, Congress imposed detailed due process procedures on local educators and gave parents of handicapped children legal rights to challenge educational plans with which they disagreed, first administratively, then to court. Predictably, adversarial, legalistic hearings became common (Neal and Kirp, 1986), and federal courts became the principal forums for defining "appropriate public education" (Melnick, 1995).[22]

Fragmented Government and Adversarial Administrative Law

Congress also invited private attorneys general to police policy implementation by *federal* agencies. The public interest movement of the 1960s and 1970s wanted to expand the regulatory power of the federal government—but it was deeply suspicious of centralized power (McCann, 1986). Books published by consumer advocate Ralph Nader had argued that regulatory agencies were all too easily captured by powerful regulated businesses and their allies in government. The reformers' solution was to subject the more powerful federal regulatory state to the checks of adversarial legalism. In Michael McCann's phrase, they sought to institutionalize a "judicial model of the state," in which public interest advocacy groups, by invoking administrative legal procedures—in court if necessary—could counterbalance business litigation against and influence on federal administrative agencies (McCann, 1986:114; Stewart, 1975; Burbank and Farhang, 2017).

The national legislature and the courts were sympathetic. Especially after 1968, when the executive branch was controlled by Republicans, a Democratic Congress willingly gave citizen watchdog groups and courts more leverage over administrative policymaking and enforcement. Reinforcing the spare 1946 Administrative Procedure Act, new statutes expanded advocacy groups' ability to participate in policymaking and to challenge regulations and permitting decisions in court for being insufficiently stringent. At the same time, judges' reviews of new regulations became more searching and demanding. Agency regulations could be rejected, the courts held, for failure to provide adequate rationales, or a sufficiently detailed supporting factual record, or meaningful responses to objections by advocacy groups or by regulated businesses (Shapiro, 1988; Mashaw, 2006; Croley, 2008). New presidential administrations could not repeal regulations issued by their political predecessors, the Supreme Court held, without meeting the demanding notice and comment, data analysis, and reason-giving standards required for new regulations.[23] The goal was to substitute judicially enforced legal rationality for one-sided, politically engineered backroom deals.

In addition, to try to ensure faithful implementation of new regulatory statutes by Republican agency leaders, Democratic Congresses adopted a more legally constraining *statutory* style. In contrast to New Deal regulatory statutes, which granted administrative policymakers a great deal of discretion, the regulatory statutes of the late 1960s and 1970s set forth more detailed rules and strict deadlines. Business lobbyists and Republican legislators, in turn, fought for specific statutory provisions that would protect *their* interests and values. The increased legislative specificity enabled liberal advocacy groups to challenge administrative leniency or inaction in court more effectively (Melnick, 1992), while also helping businesses argue that agency decisions were legally unauthorized or insufficiently grounded in reliable data.

Lawsuits against the federal government and appeals of governmental decisions, not surprisingly, increased, at least vis- à-vis some agencies. More than 50 percent of the Environmental Protection Agency's major regulations issued in the early 1980s were blocked, at least temporarily, by court challenges (Coglianese, 1997). Lawsuits and appeals in that decade also blocked or delayed virtually every U.S. Forest Service management plan, (*Economist,* 1990: 28), new motor vehicle safety regulation (Mashaw and Harfst, 1991), federal lease for offshore petroleum exploration (Lester, 1992), and, as exemplified by the Port of Oakland story in Chapter 2, almost every seaport dredging plan (Kagan, 1991). Beginning in the 1970s, the Office for Civil Rights in the U.S. Department of Health, Education, and Welfare was subjected to a decade-long lawsuit and series of court orders demanding more rapid agency investigation of complaints of civil rights violations (Rabkin, 1980).

Political Distrust, Statutory Complexity, and Adversarial Legalism

During the late 1960s and early 1970s, even as the federal government was responding to demands for racial justice, environmental protection, control of dangerous technologies, and worker safety, the American electorate, including liberal Democrats, became far more mistrustful of government (Griffin, 1991: 701–709; Jenkins and Milkis, 2014: 6–7).[24] Political leaders seemingly became more mistrustful of each other. Voters more often elected legislatures and chief executives of different parties (Fiorina, 1991: 646–650; Thurber, 1991: 653–657)—a pattern that became prevalent over the next forty years (Burbank and Farhang, 2017: 6). The civil rights and anti–Vietnam War movements splintered the authority of political party leaders, instigating a more decentralized political primary and fund-raising system (Polsby, 1983). The power of congressional committee chairmen was redistributed among a multiplicity of subcommittees (Davidson, 1981). Campaign finance reforms intensified each legislator's search for independent sources of funding and support. Taking all these changes together, political party leaders were stripped of a considerable measure of control over policy formulation (Huntington, 1981; Polsby, 1983; Ranney, 1983). The resulting hyperpluralism further promoted adversarial legalism. Here is why.

In political systems without consistently dominant, highly disciplined political parties, scholars have argued it makes sense for interest groups and momentarily strong political coalitions to demand enactment of highly detailed laws, enforceable in court, for that will help insulate today's policy victories from reversal following tomorrow's electoral loss (Cooter and Ginsburg, 1996: 305; Moe, 1989; Landes and Posner, 1975). Thus in the United States, beginning in the late 1960s, politically divided government and less-disciplined political parties enabled organized interest groups—groups representing particular localities, industries, or ideologies—to demand statutory amendments that would help them exert influence on policy implementation and challenge unsympathetic administrative officials in court (Moe, 1989). American statutes have always been less carefully drafted, and hence less coherent, than those of, say, the British Parliament, in which cohesive majority governments need not compromise with the current minority (Atiyah and Summers, 1987). But especially in an era of divided government and weak political party unity, congressional statutes had to be painfully stitched together by shifting, issue-specific coalitions. Often, legislative leaders and presidents could gather support for their bills only by adding a variety of loopholes and amendments demanded by various stakeholders. Individual senators and House subcommittee chairs often added hastily drafted last-minute amendments (Smith, 1989). Increasingly, responsibility for statutory implementation was divided among two or more federal government agencies,[25] so that each might check the others' expected political biases (Moe, 1989). Similarly, implementation of congressional programs was often devolved on state and local governments, so statutes contained detailed accountability and federal oversight provisions (Melnick, 2018a: 22). That added much more procedural complexity (Schuck, 2014: chapter 9) and more potential for delay and for litigation—again as exemplified by the Port of Oakland saga.

In consequence, American statutes (and implementing administrative regulations) became—and have continued to be—much more complex, longer, and more densely worded than statutes on similar subjects enacted by legislatures in other rich democracies (Kagan, 2010). Multisubject omnibus acts—as well as the impenetrable Employee Retirement Income Security Act (ERISA), the 400-page 1990 Clean Air Act, and the 900 page Affordable Health Care Act of 2010—resemble enormous patchwork quilts, often laden with legally contradictory or incomprehensible provisions. This style of legislation magnifies legal uncertainty, virtually demanding subsequent litigation and judicial interpretation (or reinterpretation) of congressional policy. Tax legislation provides a striking example. Comparing American, British, and Swedish taxation systems, political scientist Sven Steinmo (1993: 38) observed:

The American tax system is by far the most complex system in the world. There are myriad special exemptions, deductions, credits, adjustments, allowances, rate schedules, special tariffs, minimum and maximum taxes designed to affect certain classes, groups, regions, industries, professions, states, cities, companies, families, and individuals. No other tax system in the industrialized world comes anywhere close to the degree of specificity found in the U.S. Federal Revenue Code.

Steinmo (1993, 141) notes that British and Swedish politicians, like their American counterparts, are under constant pressure to make tax adjustments in the name of equity or efficiency or special need. But Great Britain and Sweden, with their unified political parties and strong parliamentary governments, are better at containing interest group pressures. The mind-boggling complexity of American tax law, says Steinmo, directly reflects the fragmentation of power in Congress and in American political parties, which "made an already overly open process even more open and made an already porous system even more loophole-ridden (141)." In the preceding thirty years, the *Economist* (2017c) wrote, the federal tax code tripled in length, as lobbyists and receptive Congress members inserted carefully-drafted tax breaks for particular constituents, making an ostensibly progressive tax law system into one that magnifies economic inequality. Compared to other democracies, not surprisingly, the implementation of tax law in the United States is far more burdened by expenditures on tax lawyers and consultants and far more prone to adversarial legal contestation.

Beginning in the 1960s, as courts were drawn further into the policy-making process, *judge-made law* also became more complex, uncertain, and malleable—thereby inducing more litigation. As some—but not all—judges responded to popular demands for total justice, political divisions within the American judiciary became sharper. Supreme courts, both state and federal, were riven by higher dissent rates (Friedman et al., 1981). Political struggles over judicial selection intensified. The resulting changes in judicial personnel often led to rapid changes in legal doctrine. A politically-divided Supreme Court's shifting rulings on search and seizure law left police officers and lower court judges confused (Bradley, 1993). Judges' conflicting political ideologies affected their rulings on tax law, which in turn produced different enforcement policies by the tax agencies whose decisions the judges reviewed.[26] Political differences among federal judges not infrequently led to conflicting rulings and to pressures on Congress to override one of the conflicting judicial precedents; but even such override statutes, one study found, put an end to partisan judicial dissensus only about half the time (Barnes, 2004). Again, the consequence has been more adversarial legalism: when legislation is unclear and court decisions unpredictable, then disputants have more incentive to hire lawyers and try to reshape the law to their own ends.

Political Conservatives and Adversarial Legalism

For all their criticism of "excessive litigation" in recent decades, Republican presidents and legislators often have been active supporters of measures that promote adversarial legalism, which helps explain its persistence even in the more conservative 1980s, 1990s, and 2000s. Just as the politically liberal public interest movement mistrusted the federal agencies created in the 1960s and 1970s, fearing they might betray reformist goals, political conservatives worried that agency bureaucrats might be too zealous, hostile to business and economic growth. Hence, as noted earlier, Republicans too fought for legislative provisions that would restrict administrative discretion and subject it to legal challenge. Unable to block regulatory legislation, they tried to ensure that regulatory statutes would insist on high standards of economic and technological rationality. This gave business firms leverage for attacking regulatory decisions in court, which they did with considerable regularity—just as they did in the late nineteenth and early twentieth centuries.

Similarly, conservatives exploited the populist strain in American political culture that, while eager for the benefits of total justice, mistrusts "big government" and is hostile to tax increases. Republican legislators, when unable to fully block the enactment of regulatory statutes, often supported the idea of shifting enforcement responsibility to private litigants. For example, conservative senators' reluctance to fund a federal enforcement bureaucracy led liberal sponsors of the 1968 Truth-in-Lending Act to accept an enforcement system that relied primarily on private lawsuits against lenders (Rubin, 1991). Similarly, in 1991, as the understaffed Equal Employment Opportunity Commission struggled with huge backlogs of discrimination claims, the response of Republican president George H. W. Bush (and the Democratic Congress) was not to bolster the EEOC but to strengthen private lawsuits to enforce antidiscrimination laws. The 1991 Civil Rights Restoration Act empowered employees hurt by discrimination to sue employers for higher money penalties, including punitive damages— an enforcement strategy that required no new federal bureaucrats and no new taxes (Potter and Reesman, 1992; Farhang, 2010). Even after Republicans gained control of Congress in the early twenty-first century, they continued, albeit at a slower pace, to add to the stock of statutes that relied on adversarial legalism for implementation (Burbank and Farhang, 2017).

In addition, public interest law firms financed by political conservatives developed a conservative brand of judicial activism. As Thomas Keck

(2014: 14) put it, "In a world of constant litigation by friend and foe, any decision not to litigate would amount to an act of unilateral disarmament, leaving the field to [one's] ideological opponents." So litigate conservative legal activists did. In the 1980s, conservative lawyers persuaded the Supreme Court to expand constitutional rights against regulatory restrictions on private property and to strike down some race-based preferences in affirmative action programs. Supreme Court rulings on both topics propelled judges throughout the country into the business of adjudicating the validity of university admissions policies, governmental set-asides for minority-owned (or ostensibly minority-owned) contractors, and the decisions of local and regional zoning boards. In 2008, after a long campaign in law reviews as well as in the courts by National Rifle Association lawyers, a 5:4 conservative Supreme Court majority reversed prior understandings of the Second Amendment of the U.S. Constitution, holding that it protected an individual right to bear arms[27]—a ruling which encouraged further litigation to overturn state and local gun control laws.

Fragmented Economic Power and Adversarial Legalism

While fragmentation of *governmental* authority is a principal causal factor, adversarial legalism also has been encouraged by the fragmented *economic structure* of the United States. From the start, American capitalism, resistant to control by guilds and governments, has been more decentralized and open than European market-oriented economies. In the nineteenth century, competition was promoted by constitutional restrictions on local governments' protectionist measures and by pro-business judges' interpretation of the common law (Horwitz, 1977). Compared to Europe and Japan, American markets have less often been dominated by cartels, centralized banks, governmental ministries, or nationalized companies (Levy, 1997; Roe, 1991; Katzenstein, 1978). In the American tradition of limited government, private enterprise has performed many social functions—the financing and operation of railroads and public utilities, the provision of health insurance and pensions, and more—that long were dominated by government or corporatist bodies in Europe.

In the competitive American economy, business factions often have used law and litigation to advance their interests and disadvantage competitors. In the late nineteenth century small American merchants, farmers, and shippers, pressed hard by railroads and other large corporations, pushed Congress to enact antitrust laws and make them enforceable in the courts by private lawsuit. Local American bankers, allying with populist politicians, lobbied for laws that forbade interstate expansion by Wall Street banks and blocked them from owning controlling shares in corporations

(Roe, 1991). One consequence is that corporations in the United States historically have been controlled not by a handful of central bankers or by a governmental finance ministry but by the shifting pressures of competitive financial markets and aggressive investors. And American businesses, compared to their counterparts in other rich democracies, historically have relied more on lawyers and litigation to resolve conflicts.

Relatedly, David Vogel (1986) points out, American businessmen, compared to British business leaders, have tended to be more suspicious of government and antagonistic toward governmental controls.[28] Nor have American businesses found it necessary or desirable to submit to governance by strong national private industrial associations and the corporatist business-government relationships of the kind that thrive in the Netherlands, Germany, and Japan. Consequently, in the United States, unfair competitive practices, financial problems, and other sources of conflict among business firms cannot be resolved informally by powerful bankers, dominant industrial groups, or business-government control systems. Instead, regulation of commercial conflicts is left more fully to the realm of defensively worded contracts and the threat of litigation.

The fragmented, competitive American business structure also has made government regulation more adversarial and legalistic. In the 1960s and 1970s, when the federal government enacted demanding environmental and safety laws, there were few powerful trade associations with whom regulators could negotiate and implement specific regulations and compliance plans. Consequently, in comparison with comparable bodies of law in Japan and in Europe, American corporation law, securities regulations, and safety and environmental regulations are formulated in an arm's-length, legally formalistic, and adversarial manner (Badaracco, 1985; Brickman, Jasanoff, and Ilgen, 1985). Laws and regulations in the United States are more detailed (Kagan, 2010; Braithwaite, 1985) and are enforced more legalistically. All this breeds more legalistic resistance from business and more appeals to the courts (Bardach and Kagan, 1982; Kelman, 1981).

Business-labor relations in the United States also occur in an organizational context that is particularly fragmented. In many Western European countries, such as the Netherlands and Germany, collective bargaining occurs at the national level, among peak associations of labor and industry. Such labor agreements in the Netherlands cover most workers and employers, whether they are signed-up union members or not (Kagan, 1990a). In the United States, in contrast, the National Labor Relations Act (1935) encouraged *plant-level* union-organizing and bargaining. The Taft-Hartley Act (1946) enabled politically-conservative states, especially in the South, to discourage unionization, which led to large-disparities in worker wages and benefits across regions, and encouraged employers in higher-wage areas to fight unionization (Flanagan, 1987). In this exceptionally fragmented system,[29] industry-wide bargains became the exception rather than the rule (Rogers, 1990; Kagan, 1990a).

Lacking hierarchical systems of governance, American labor-management relations, viewed in comparison to those of European countries and Japan, are more pervaded by adversarial legalism. Lawyers guide employers' antiunion campaigns. Union elections are routinely appealed to the National Labor Relations Board (NLRB) (Flanagan, 1987). In Japan during the 1990s, labor commissions, established to hear claims of unfair labor practices, heard between 500 and 1,500 cases a year, most of which were settled by conciliation. In the United States during the 1990s, between 30,000 and 45,000 unfair labor practice cases were filed with the NLRB each year (Sanders, 1996: 379; Gould, 1984: 48). Both organized labor and business interests battle to control presidential appointments to the NLRB, whose regulations, not surprisingly, end up shifting in the wake of presidential elections (Moe, 1989).

Compared to Western European countries, American pension, workplace-injury insurance, and health care systems are left far more fully to the private sector. As profit-seeking firms, those benefit-providing companies have stronger incentives to maintain a hard line on claims and to qualify their obligations in contractual fine print. In consequence, although hard evidence is lacking, litigation in court over benefits and coverage almost certainly is far more common in the United States. Similarly, governmental regulation of the privatized, employer-dominated American system for employee pension funding and pension rights is legalistic, complex, and frequently litigated.

Put the more fragmented, more competitive American economic system under greater financial stress and adversarial legalism increases. In recent decades, a more competitive world economy has generated rapid shifts in corporate management, corporate downsizing, and contracting-out, and more risky, high-stakes relationships among strangers. In response, American legislatures and courts formulated new regulations and rights of action aimed at financial deception, insider trading, and unjust employee dismissals. Thus the United States experienced sharp increases in class-action stockholder lawsuits against corporate managers (Romano, 1991: 65), more lawsuits between business debtors and creditors (Nelson, 1990), more suits between insurance companies and their insureds (Dunworth and Rogers, 1996), and more lawsuits by dismissed employees (Dertouzos, Holland, and Ebener, 1988). During the wave of hostile corporate takeovers that swept the restructuring U.S. economy in the late 1970s and 1980s, law firm partners deployed teams of young lawyers like squadrons of fighter planes, bombarding their corporate adversaries with preemptive lawsuits, demands for truckloads of documents, and pretrial motions, trying to spend and to stall their adversaries into submission (Stewart, 1983: 146). In Europe and

Japan there have also been sharp increases in competitive pressures, but adversarial legal conflict among businesses, and between business and government, is much less frequent than in the United States (Kagan, 1997a).

Lawyers, Legal Culture, and Adversarial Legalism

One further contributing cause of American adversarial legalism must be mentioned—the legal profession and the legal culture it generates. Beginning in the 1960s, the advent of a distinctively American brand of activist government—one that seeks total justice through decentralized governmental and economic institutions, legalistic regulation, adversarial legal challenge, and citizen-initiated lawsuits—vastly increased the demand for lawyers. Within a few decades there were far more of them, housed in larger organizations. There were many more economically and politically important cases of the kind that warrant big investments in creative, aggressive lawyering. In no other country have lawyers been so entrepreneurial in seeking out new kinds of business, so eager to challenge authority, and so quick to propose new liability-expanding legal theories.

Lawyers themselves have not been the primary cause of the expanding domain of adversarial legalism. Broader political currents and interest groups, as suggested earlier, were the sorcerers that called forth adversarial legalism—thereby generating demands for more legally trained apprentices. These sorcerers' apprentices, however, soon became richer, better organized, more energetic. While many judges and lawyers strive to dampen adversarial legalism (Kagan, 1994; Suchman and Cahill, 1996), thousands of lawyers who believe in or profit from litigation exploit every opportunity to extend it further and to thwart the sorcerers' occasional efforts to rein it in. Organized networks of activist lawyers—ranging from the National Prison Project in the Alabama prison reform case, to plaintiffs' lawyers who focus on particular hazardous products (e.g., asbestos, tobacco, breast implants), and to conservative organizations like the U.S. Chamber of Commerce—systematically push courts to extend the law in the directions each values. The American Trial Lawyers Association lobbies legislatures and mobilizes large campaign contributions to block reforms that would reduce adversarial legalism (Kagan, 1994; Heymann and Liebman, 1988: 309).

Moreover, American lawyers and law professors, in sharp contrast to their counterparts in other democratic nations, have created and defended a body of legal ethics that exalts adversarial legalism. In the United States (far more than elsewhere) lawyers' codes of ethics endorse zealous advocacy of clients' causes—short of dishonesty—but without regard to the interests of justice in the particular case or broader societal concerns (Osiel, 1990: 2019). American lawyers' professional culture is unique in permitting and implicitly encouraging them to advance unprecedented legal claims, coach witnesses, and attempt to wear down their opponents through burdensome pretrial discovery. In the hands of some practitioners—not all, but not merely a few—manipulative and aggressive modes of getting clients and litigating push the limits of adversarial legalism even further (Kagan, 1994: 1, 53–58).

Perhaps most important, American law professors, judges, and lawyers have elaborated legal theories that actively promote adversarial legalism not as a necessary evil but as a desirable mode of governance. In doing so, they reflect an important strand of American political culture that, as mentioned earlier, became entrenched in the early nineteenth century: a view of lawyer-driven litigation and judges as guardians of liberty and democracy. The heroic view of the judiciary's role in government—exemplified by Professor Owen Fiss's statement quoted in Chapter 2—has not been uncontested in the law schools or in the judiciary. But on balance, by the 1960s and thereafter, many prominent American legal scholars and judges have supported a social engineering vision of law and the judicial role—and hence have supported legal rules that facilitate adversarial legalism. Michael Greve (1989b: 231) observed: "In the United States, there has been a broad consensus for public interest litigation among legal scholars, judges, and the legal establishment in general. In the Federal Republic [of Germany], there is a similarly broad consensus against it. Judges on the Federal Constitutional Court and the Federal Administrative Court voiced their opposition to association lawsuits not only on the bench but in legal periodicals and in public."

Whereas European legal scholars speak of law as a logically coherent set of authoritative principles and rules, American legal scholars often speak of law as a manifestation of the ongoing struggle among groups and classes for political and economic advantage, or as a manipulatable set of tools for achieving better government (Kagan, 1988: 728–730; 1994: 24–27). In contrast to Great Britain, Atiyah and Summers (1987: 404) observe, "American law schools have been the source of the dominant general theory of law in America . . . 'instrumentalism' . . . [which] conceives of law essentially as a pragmatic instrument of social improvement."[30] Thus the language of the American law school classroom is the language of policy analysis. Law reviews bristle with arguments for new legal rights, not for legal stability. American legal scholars tend to celebrate those American judges who, like the Supreme Court justices in *Brown v. Board of Education* or Frank Johnson in the Alabama prisons case, feel authorized or even obligated to "do justice" when the other bodies of government have failed to take action against social problems. A cross-national comparison of styles of statutory interpretation classified the American judiciary as the most freewheeling and creative (Summers and Taruffo, 1991). The dominant strain in the legal culture of American law teachers supports easy access to courts, along with policy solutions that take the form of judicially enforceable individual rights, government liability for violations of legal rights, and judicially-enforceable legal controls on official power.

———

American legal culture is far from monolithic in its endorsement of adversarial legalism. Beginning in the 1980s and accelerating in the 1990s, conservative politicians, foundations, lawyers, and business organizations launched a political movement that attacked and sought to erode the legal attitudes, legal structures, and legal practices that had fostered the expansion of adversarial legalism in the 1960s and 1970s. Republican electoral victories led to the appointment of more conservative judges, motivated to chip away at liberal, litigation-encouraging doctrines forged by the Warren Court. Beginning in the mid-1990s, as discussed more fully in the Afterword, a narrow conservative majority on the U.S. Supreme Court has issued numerous rulings on procedural issues that have made it more difficult for individuals to successfully sue governmental bodies and corporations for violations of civil rights law (Burbank and Farhang, 2017; Wasserman, 2012; Siegel, 2006). Legislatures in many states have enacted restrictions on tort litigation. Congress enacted restrictions on class-action securities, prison reform, and immigration policy litigation. The Supreme Court also strengthened corporations' ability to impose form contracts on their employees and customers that substitute industry-run arbitration plans for rights to seek redress in court (Staszak, 2015). Republican legislators and business lobbyists espousing an intense antigovernment ideology blocked the enactment of regulatory legislation and watered down regulations that did pass, diluting what had been an important stimulant for adversarial legalism in preceding decades.

In sum, adversarial legalism has become more politically contested. On the other hand, the *basic* structures of adversarial legalism in the United States have not been and are not likely to be dismantled. The basic forces that foster adversarial legalism—popular demands for fair treatment, recompense, and protection, combined with mistrust of government and fragmentation of political and economic power—remain unchanged and perhaps are unchangeable. Three decades of expanded adversarial legalism imprinted the ideas of American *legal* culture on the country's *political* culture. As political scientist Michael McCann (1999: 87) has pointed out, such salient political issues as "discrimination against women, ethnic minorities, gays and lesbians; the incendiary abortion issue; pornography and hate speech; campaign finance regulation; the relationship between religion and public education; gun control; restrictions on police abuse; [and] death penalty policy . . . have been understood and contested in distinctly legal terms delineated by the federal courts over time." In consequence, he adds, "Even those citizens who oppose prevailing court constrictions and legal frames typically [must] pose their own counter-claims in terms of legal traditions authorized by the courts" (87).

Indeed, as discussed in the Afterword, conservative politicians and business interests, while denouncing adversarial legalism when deployed to advance or vindicate the values of political liberals, not infrequently expanded the use of adversarial legalism to advance or vindicate conservative values—just as they did in the late nineteenth and early twentieth centuries. Moreover, in the first decades of the twenty-first century, as political party polarization has often led to gridlock in Congress, activists in *all* political factions, conservative as well as liberal, have even more eagerly turned to the courts to seek legal remedies and legal changes that they have been unable to wrest from legislatures or government agencies. Adversarial legalism thus remains the American way of law.

PART II

CRIMINAL JUSTICE

CHAPTER FOUR

Adversarial Legalism and American Criminal Justice

In the United States, the index of reported crime per 100,000 population tripled between 1960 and 1980. Fear of violence drove much of the middle class to the suburbs, robbing many cities of their economic and cultural vitality. In England, too, the index of indictable crimes increased tenfold between 1955 and 1991. While homicide rates in the United States remain much higher than in other economically advanced democracies, by the end of the 1980s or the early 1990s reported burglary rates in Australia, Great Britain, Denmark, Sweden, and the Netherlands exceeded the rate in the United States, and car theft was more common in France than in America (Marshall, 1996; *Economist*, 1996a: 23–25; Wilson, 1994: 25).

Perhaps people in fatalistic societies bear the risk of criminal victimization silently. But in rich, democratic societies, citizens expect government to protect them. The American response to public demands for security and justice, however, has differed from those of other economically advanced democracies. Substantively, the criminal law of the United States is distinctive in its greater punitiveness, its political volatility, and its inconsistency across regions of the country. Procedurally, American criminal justice is more pervaded by adversarial legalism—lawyer-driven legal contestation in a relatively nonhierarchical, organizationally decentralized system. Adversarial legalism provides powerful tools for challenging bias, abuse of power, and error by law enforcement authorities. But those tools do not significantly temper the substantive harshness of the American system of criminal justice, and they exacerbate its potential for inconsistency and unequal treatment. This chapter provides an overview of how and why the American criminal justice system differs from those of other democracies and with what consequences.

Adversarial Legalism in Action: The McCleskey Cases

In 1978 Warren McCleskey, an African American, entered a store in Marietta, Georgia, together with three armed accomplices. Brandishing a gun, McCleskey commanded all the customers to lie face down on the floor while his accomplices robbed the store manager at gunpoint. Responding to a silent alarm, Frank Schlatt, a white police officer, entered the store. Two shots rang out. Officer Schlatt was killed. The county prosecutor charged McCleskey with murder and armed robbery. McCleskey denied having fired the shots, but at trial the prosecutor introduced evidence indicating that at least one of the fatal bullets was fired from a gun of the type that McCleskey had carried during the robbery. In addition, two witnesses (one a codefendant, one an inmate in the county jail in which McCleskey was held) testified that they heard McCleskey admit to the shooting. The jury found McCleskey guilty. A Georgia statute provides that homicide in the course of an armed robbery and the killing of a police officer are aggravating circumstances that warrant capital punishment. Based on that law, McCleskey was sentenced to be executed.

McCleskey appealed. His lawyers alleged that he had been denied due process of law in various ways.[1] But on January 24, 1980, the Georgia Supreme Court affirmed the conviction and the sentence. McCleskey's lawyers then asked the U.S. Supreme Court to review the case, but the petition was denied (like all but a tiny percentage of the several thousand that reach the Court each term). McCleskey's lawyers then petitioned another Georgia court, asserting over twenty legal arguments, but in April 1981 that court too denied relief. McCleskey appealed that decision. In June 1981 the Georgia Supreme Court turned down McCleskey's request for review. McCleskey's lawyers again sought review by the U.S. Supreme Court; that petition was denied in November 1981.

On December 30, 1981, McCleskey, still incarcerated, filed a petition for habeas corpus in federal court. His lawyers made eighteen separate arguments concerning the unconstitutionality of his conviction and sentence. The claim that the lawyers pushed hardest was that the Georgia capital sentencing process was administered in a racially discriminatory manner. McCleskey's lawyers relied on a statistical study of Georgia murder cases in the 1970s. The study, funded by the National Association for the Advancement of Colored People (NAACP) and conducted by Professor David Baldus and others, indicated above all the fateful importance of prosecutorial discretion in homicide cases. In more than 2,000 murder cases, only about 5 percent of defendants were sentenced to capital punishment. Even in the 463 cases in which the defendant was "death eligible" due to the presence of statutorily specified aggravating factors, only 100 defendants

(22 percent) had received a death sentence, mostly because prosecutors often did not seek to impose the death penalty.

If county prosecutors in Georgia sought capital punishment in only a minority of death eligible cases, what guided their decisions to do so? Those decisions, the Baldus study suggested, were influenced, consciously or unconsciously, by race. Surprisingly to many, a *smaller* percentage of black defendants (4 percent) than white defendants (7 percent) were sentenced to die. Rather, the race of the *victim* seemed to matter. In death eligible cases, the prosecution sought the death penalty in 70 percent of cases in which black defendants had killed white victims, but did so only in 32 percent of cases in which white defendants had killed whites, in 15 percent where black defendants had killed blacks, and in 19 percent where white defendants had killed blacks (*McCleskey v. Kemp,* 1987). The racial disparities persisted when the researchers controlled for the number of aggravating factors. In sum, Georgia defendants charged with killing white victims, and especially blacks who killed white victims, were much more likely to receive a death sentence, while black killers of blacks (one of the largest categories of cases) were least likely to receive a death sentence (Baldus et al., 1983).[2] In Georgia's criminal justice system, black lives did not seem to matter as much as white lives.

Nevertheless, in 1984 the U.S. District Court ruled that the Baldus study did not support McCleskey's claim that the entire system was so tainted by racial discrimination that his conviction was unconstitutional. McCleskey's lawyers appealed that decision. On January 29, 1985, the U.S. Court of Appeals affirmed the district court decision. McCleskey again petitioned the U.S. Supreme Court for review, and this time the Court accepted the case. Yet in 1987 the Court, by a bare 5–4 majority, affirmed the district court ruling. The majority opinion argued that "discretion is essential to the criminal justice process" and that the statistical evidence fell short of proving that "the decision makers in McCleskey's case acted with discriminatory purpose" (*McCleskey v. Kemp,* 1987). The Constitution, in this interpretation, condemned only proven discriminatory purpose, not unconscious racism or racially disparate outcomes.

In July 1987, five days before his scheduled execution, McCleskey's lawyers, perusing records obtained as a result of a change in Georgia's open-records law, discovered that the jail inmate who had originally testified against McCleskey had in fact been a government informant, planted in an adjoining cell by law enforcement officials. The defense lawyers filed another petition for habeas corpus in the U.S. District Court in Georgia, arguing that the use of an informant constituted a violation of McCleskey's Sixth Amendment right to have an attorney present during pretrial interrogation. The district court agreed and scolded the prosecution for misconduct (Kaplan, 1991: 68). The state of Georgia then appealed. In December 1989, the federal court of appeals reversed the district court, holding that McCleskey had abandoned his Sixth Amendment claim in his December 1981 petition for habeas corpus, and hence could not now argue it again (notwithstanding his claim that his lawyers then had no knowledge of the government's deliberate use of an informant).

McCleskey appealed that decision to the U.S. Supreme Court, which again accepted his case, now labeled *McCleskey v. Zant*. In 1991 the Court held, by a 6–3 vote, that second and subsequent habeas corpus petitions could properly be dismissed as abusive unless the defendant could show that his counsel had been impeded from raising the same claim earlier and that the claimed constitutional error probably affected the outcome of his trial and sentencing (*McCleskey v. Zant*, 1991). By these standards, the Court held, McCleskey's Sixth Amendment claim, even if legally supportable, had been properly dismissed.

The Georgia authorities prepared to carry out McCleskey's death sentence. His lawyers petitioned the Georgia Board of Pardons and Paroles for clemency. On September 24, 1991, the board turned down this appeal. McCleskey's execution was scheduled for 7 p.m. that day. McCleskey's attorneys immediately filed nearly identical appeals in Georgia and in the federal district court. The state court just as immediately rejected the Georgia appeal; McCleskey's attorneys quickly appealed that decision to the U.S. Supreme Court. At 10 p.m. the Supreme Court, by a 6–3 vote, denied the appeal from the Georgia court.

Meanwhile, in the federal appeal, U.S. District Court Judge Owen Forrester summoned attorneys and witnesses to an emergency hearing. He issued an order staying the execution until 7:30 p.m., then until 10 p.m., and then until midnight in order to hear further evidence (Montgomery and Curriden, 1991; Applebome, 1991: A18; Harris and Curriden, 1991). At 11:20 p.m. Judge Forrester denied McCleskey's petition but stayed the execution until 2 a.m. to permit McCleskey's lawyer to file an appeal. At 1:50 a.m. the federal court of appeals affirmed Judge Forrester's denial of McCleskey's claim and lifted the stay of execution. At 2:17 a.m. McCleskey was placed in the electric chair. Three minutes into his final statement, the warden informed him that the U.S. Supreme Court was considering his case. McCleskey was removed from the chair. At 2:42 a.m. the Supreme Court issued a ten-minute stay of execution. At 2:52 a.m., it denied the last of McCleskey's twenty appeals. At 3:06 a.m. on September 25, 1991, Warren McCleskey was electrocuted, thirteen years after the killing of Officer Schlatt.

In Georgia in 1910 a Warren McCleskey might well have been lynched.[3] In 1950 he might have been physically coerced into confessing before trial. In that year, if there had been a trial, it would have been conducted before an all-white jury and a judge who had been put in office by white local politicians. Upon conviction, McCleskey would have been executed promptly. By 1978, however, adversarial legalism had helped change the criminal justice system of Georgia and the nation, providing poor defendants with lawyers and providing defense lawyers with new opportunities to challenge criminal charges and law enforcement methods in court. That in turn forced prosecutors, police, and judges to attend more closely to the law. Supreme Court constitutional rulings had narrowed the range of persons subject to capital punishment and had reduced (but clearly not eliminated) the risk of discrimination based on the race. By 1978, police chiefs, judges, and prosecutors in many counties throughout the country had become more attentive to the risk of racially unequal treatment, although racially biased law enforcement—often based on charging decisions by prosecutors—remained painfully persistent (Spohn, Gruhl and Welsh, 1987: 183–84) and still does to this day (Caravelis, Chricos, and Bales, 2013; Crawford, Chiricos, and Kleck, 1998).

The McCleskey case also brings into sharp relief some equally salient and troublesome features of the American criminal justice system: its tendencies toward punitiveness, cumbersomeness, inconsistency, inequality, and political volatility—tendencies that pervade the handling of crimes other than homicide as well.

Punitiveness. Ultimately, Warren McCleskey was electrocuted. As of 2016, twenty of the fifty American states did not authorize the death penalty. In the thirty states that do, only a small, steadily shrinking minority of death eligible murderers actually are sentenced to die,[4] and in only a handful of states are the condemned actually executed. Nevertheless, the United States stands alone among economically advanced democracies in employing capital punishment at all (Zimring and Hawkins, 1997: 33–39). Putting aside the death penalty, penal policy in the United States is distinctively harsh (Whitman, 2003). In 1995 its incarceration rate—565 per 100,000 people—was more than five times as high as the rate in other rich democracies (*Economist,* 1997: 46, 1995: 25), and those disparities have continued (*Economist,* 2017d). The incarceration rate for black Americans, moreover, is five times the rate for whites,[5] and for black males higher still.

The cross-national disparity in incarceration rates is not explainable by differences in crime rates. It is due in large measure to the much longer prison terms prescribed by American legislatures for repeat offenses and for drug-related activity (Frase, 1990: 658; Selke, 1991), and partly to America's higher rates of *violent* crime (Zimring and Hawkins, 1997: 33–39). In addition, American courts are much more likely to impose jail sentences for "victimless" infractions such as disorderly conduct, prostitution, and public drunkenness (Frase and Weigend, 1995: 320–321).[6] American police are more likely than their French or German counterparts to arrest and lock up crime suspects rather than simply issuing a summons, and American defendants are more likely to be held in jail until both their first court appearance and the final decision (Frase and Weigend, 1995: 329; Frase, 1990: 599–601).

In some European countries, such as Finland, France, Germany, and Sweden, traffic violations and other minor offenses are punished according to statutorily-prescribed "day fines that are scaled to the offender's average daily income" (Tonry and Frase, 2001: 306–11). Here too, punishment in the United States tends to be harsher. In many cities and counties, fines and court costs imposed for nonaccident traffic offenses, for failures to appear in court, and even for using a public defense attorney often exceed poor peoples' ability to pay. The penalty for nonpayment of fines and fees not infrequently is jail time or suspension of a driver's license (both of which can precipitate job loss) (Harris, 2016; Bannon, Nagrecha, and Diller, 2010). These penal practices have a disproportionately adverse effect on poor black people (Dewan, 2015). In many localities, moreover, black people are substantially more likely to be stopped by police for nonaccident traffic offenses (Baumgartner, Epp, and Shaub, 2018; LaFraniere and Lehren, 2015) and more likely to be subjected to a search in that connection (Epp, Maynard-Moody, and Haider-Markel, 2014; Epp and Maynard-Moody, 2014). In many states, divorced fathers who fail to make child support payments they cannot afford are jailed, and that too often leads to job loss and continued failure to pay (Robles and Dewan, 2015). The severity and disparate racial impact of American penal law is extended by the tendency of rental housing managers (Desmond, 2016) and employers (Pager, 2007) to reject applicants with a record of criminal incarceration. The harshness of American criminal law is also extended by sweeping residential and employment restrictions imposed on sex offenders (including nonpredatory ones) for years *after* they have been released from prison terms (Elman and Elman, 2015). In many states, people who have served their prison terms for a felony conviction are barred from voting; in ten states they are barred for life.

In one respect, American criminal law is less harsh and restrictive. Warren McCleskey and his companions in crime carried guns. If law in the United States made guns as hard to get as laws in other countries do, Officer Schlatt almost surely would not have been shot and the law enforcement establishment would not have been so vengeful. The liberality (or laxness) of United States gun control laws, viewed in comparative perspective, goes a long way towards explaining why the United States suffers much higher levels of *lethal* crime (and hence harsher penal sentences) than other economically advanced democracies with comparable overall crime rates (Zimring and Hawkins, 1997: 33–39). The U.S. Constitution is almost unique in entrenching a "right to bear arms." (Law and Versteeg, 2012: 805).

Due to weak legal restrictions on gun sales and possession,[7] rates of firearm homicide in the United States in 2010 were more than twenty-five times greater than in other high-income countries (Grinshteyn and Hemenway, 2016).[8] American robbers are much more likely to use guns,[9] as are people involved in fights and acts of revenge.

American police officers, therefore, face armed citizens, or potentially armed citizens, much more often than their counterparts abroad, and police officers in the United States are vastly more likely to be physically assaulted, shot, and killed (Zimring, 2017). Fear of armed citizens gives American police greater incentives to treat suspects warily, to search them aggressively, and to shoot defiant suspects who are armed or perhaps armed. The rate at which suspects are shot and killed by police is much higher in the United States than in other economically developed countries (Zimring, 2017),[10] and the rate of for black suspects is especially high.[11] Citizens' fear of police, in turn, results in defensiveness, hostility, and criminogenic "legal cynicism"[12]—especially (and tragically) in urban neighborhoods that suffer from disinvestment, multigenerational deep poverty, chronic joblessness, competing street gangs, high violent crime rates, and high rates of arrest and incarceration for black men and youths. The distinctive harshness of American criminal penalties may also help explain the multiplication of formal procedural rules designed to prevent conviction of innocent suspects. These complex procedures are responsible for another distinctive feature of American criminal justice systems: adversarial legalism's cost and cumbersomeness.

Cumbersomeness. With its unusually extended, agonizing legal jousting, the McCleskey case dramatically illustrates adversarial legalism's capacity to drag the legal process into a costly, protracted procedural morass. The prosecution and trial of a typical capital case has become so legally complex that appellate courts have found defense lawyers, prosecutors, or judges guilty of reversible legal error in two out of three death penalty appeals (Butterfield, 2000b). As a result of sequential appeals stretching over years, each execution in the United States has been estimated to cost at least $2 million in public and private legal expenses—three or four times the cost of life imprisonment (Chiang, 1996a: A1).[13] One consequence, as indicated earlier, has been a major decline in actual executions in all but a few Southern states (Smith, 2012: 227).

Adversarial legalism makes other aspects of the criminal justice system extremely cumbersome as well. Even in ordinary, noncapital cases, the routine criminal jury trial is so complex, slow, and costly that it can only be used sparingly: well over 90 percent of felony prosecutions are either dismissed or resolved through guilty pleas (Langan and Grazadei, 1995: 9). To refer back to the typology in Table 2, Chapter 1, the legal structures and cumbersome procedures of adversarial legalism divert the disposition of most serious criminal charges into the informal negotiation quadrant. This dynamic is discussed more fully in Chapter 5.

Inconsistency. If Warren McCleskey had *not* committed his offense in a Southern state where the death penalty is employed far more frequently than elsewhere in the United States, his execution would not have occurred or would have been far less likely.[14] Had he been tried in Alabama rather than in Georgia, the trial judge could have imposed a death sentence even if the jury had decided to show mercy.[15] Within the handful of states that most often resort to capital punishment, the propensity of locally elected prosecutors to seek the death penalty—and hence the risk that an accused murderer will get a death sentence—varies markedly from county to county (Paternoster, 1991: 176–180).[16] In Bronx County Courthouse in New York City, dealing with criminal cases of all kinds, predominantly minority juries have at times acquitted black felony defendants at almost three times the national acquittal rate (Holden, Cohen, and de Lisser, 1995). In sum, legal inconsistency—dissimilar outcomes for similar cases—is built into the politically decentralized, locally responsive American criminal justice system (Levin, 1972; Eisenstein, Flemming, and Nardulli, 1988).

Inequality. Warren McCleskey's legal fate was shaped in large part by the state-appointed defense counsel assigned to his case. In the procedurally complex, adversarial American justice system, defense lawyers in trial courts bear primary responsibility for contesting the prosecution's evidence, arguments, and any violations of the defendant's legal rights. In the postconviction stage, McCleskey's lawyers were extraordinarily persistent. So are the experienced private defense attorneys hired by wealthier individuals charged with white collar crimes, such as financial fraud, and by members of organized crime families. But the great majority of criminal defendants are represented by state-employed public defenders or by private attorneys appointed by local criminal justice system officials. At the crucial initial stages of many cases, and at trial, overworked public defenders or poorly compensated private defense counsel often fail to mount an aggressive investigation and defense, even in capital cases.[17] Prosecutors too are often inexperienced or overloaded. Therefore, to a far greater degree than in most democratic nations' criminal justice systems, outcomes in the United States are shaped by the shifting and often unequal balance of competence, commitment, and resources between prosecuting attorneys on one side and defense lawyers on the other. Adversarial legalism is good for establishing rights to challenge police and prosecutorial procedures, but it does not ensure that governmentally supported defense and prosecutorial offices will be supported at levels that guarantee energetic and competent assertion and protection of those rights (Stuntz, 1997).

Political and Legal Volatility. McCleskey v. Zant, the second Supreme Court opinion in McCleskey's case, was a judicial boy-who-cried-wolf response to adversarial legalism in capital cases. Reacting against sequential appeals and midnight requests for stays of execution, a politically conservative Supreme Court majority began in the 1990s to impose limits on appeals and habeas corpus petitions, reversing liberal precedents established not many years earlier. Congress imposed limits via new statutes.[18] The U.S. Supreme Court (*Herrera v. Collins*, 1993) and other courts (Redelet, Bedau, and Putnam, 1992) have rejected appeals by defendants who belatedly turn up evidence pointing toward their innocence. This politically conservative movement to restrict judicial review has continued into the twenty-first century, even as violent crime rates have declined and even as scores of individuals convicted of homicide have been officially exonerated (Garrett, 2011)—revelations which suggest that significant numbers of wrongful conviction needles exist in the haystack of all criminal convictions.[19] At the same time, the legal finality that the conservative backlash hoped to create remains elusive. In states that retain capital punishment, defense lawyers continue to devise new legal arguments for postconviction judicial hearings and restrictions on executions. And politicians' restrictions on funding for postconviction legal aid have *increased* legal delay, leaving convicted capital case inmates to languish on death row waiting for a governmentally-funded lawyer (LaChance, 2014).

The contentious legal struggles concerning in capital cases reflect the uniquely politicized American system for making and remaking criminal law and procedure for all kinds of offenses. In most other economically advanced democracies, penal policymaking is dominated by a professionalized national ministry of justice, and judges are appointed and promoted almost exclusively on the basis of professional qualifications and performance. In the United States, in contrast, individual politicians often compete by proposing ad hoc legislative measures that purport to be "tough on crime." Hoping to soften the law's harshness, defense lawyers, as in McCleskey's case, take the political struggle to the courts. Often they lose—but sometimes they win, since the American judiciary is politically diverse, independent, and creative. And because judges play a significant role in reshaping criminal law and its administration, their decisions often generate further political controversy. The United States, in consequence, is distinctive in the extent to which judges are nominated, elected, or voted out of office on the basis of their attitudes toward crime control and defendants' rights. This makes the criminal law politically malleable. A legal expert on death penalty jurisprudence noted that due to retirements by one judge and replacement by another, Supreme Court "decisions decided no more than a year apart often seem to manifest totally different priorities" (White, 1987: 21). Thus in cross-national perspective, American criminal law is perpetually enmeshed in political and legal challenge.

Why is American criminal law distinctively punitive and politicized? Why are its procedures, shaped and pervaded by adversarial legalism, so cumbersome and susceptible to inconsistent and unequal implementation? To address these questions, we must begin by considering the basic political structures of the United States, first as they affect the making of the criminal law, then as they affect the law's implementation.

Making Criminal Law: Political Permeability and Penal Policy

In the 1980s convicted burglars and thieves in the United States spent three or four times as many months in prison than did their counterparts in Denmark (Selke, 1991) and other Western European countries. Since then the gap undoubtedly has been expanded by the mandatory sentence enhancements (greatly extended prison sentences for third felony convictions, use of firearms in a crime, and narcotics dealing) that were enacted by Congress and by many American state legislatures in the 1990s (Lowenthal, 1993).

American penal laws may be harsher, one might speculate, because crime rates are higher in the United States and the voting public therefore demands tougher penalties. This is not quite right. Crime rates in Copenhagen, a comparative study found, are comparable to those in Indiana (Selke, 1991: 232–233). In the 1990s, burglary rates in London exceeded those in New York (Zimring and Hawkins, 1997). Crucially, however, street crime in gun-ridden American cities is much more *deadly*; armed robbery is much more common, as is murder (Zimring and Hawkins, 1997). This probably explains why Americans, bombarded with news of violent crime on competing commercial television stations, are significantly more likely than Western Europeans to endorse imprisonment and favor longer prison terms (Savelsberg, 1994: 929–930).[20]

Popular sentiment, however, does not automatically produce tougher penalties. "In many countries besides America," The *Economist* (1995: 25) observed, "public opinion strongly supports capital punishment. . . . The difference is that, in America, politicians are more likely to follow public opinion . . . not try to change it." Leading politicians in Great Britain and New Zealand sometimes have emphasized the crime problem during election campaigns. But the much-publicized tough-on-crime measures enacted by Tory governments in Great Britain during the 1980s and 1990s did not come close to matching the large increases in punitiveness and incarceration rates in the United States during those years. The "central difference," writes James Q. Wilson (1997: 81), "is that the gap between public opinion and official governance is wider in England than in America."

In most other rich parliamentary democracies, policymaking on crime-related issues is generally dominated by professionals in the Ministry of Justice and by respected academic experts. The United States does not lack for experts, both in and out of government. But in the United States, far more than in other rich democracies, the making of criminal law often proceeds along a different, more populist, political track, spurred by interest groups and ambitious politicians reacting to highly publicized crimes. The populist track is kept busy by fragmentation of political authority. Criminal law is forged by fifty state legislatures as well as by Congress. In contrast to parliamentary systems, in which individual representatives defer to their party's leadership, American legislators, largely on their own in raising campaign funds and building constituent support, face stronger incentives to introduce or support legislation that will demonstrate they are not soft on crime. In a number of American states law-and-order advocacy groups can put initiatives and referenda concerning crime policy directly to the electorate. In California, for example, following a highly publicized kidnap-murder, voters (ignoring the objections of many law enforcement professionals) passed a sweeping "three strikes and you're out" ballot initiative in 1994, mandating life imprisonment for a third felony conviction (even if the third felony is not a violent crime).

In this political environment American politicians often are unwilling to defer to criminologists, bar associations, law professors, police chiefs, or judges who argue that harsher methods will be ineffective, impossible to implement, or unjust.[21] Fearing electoral retaliation from the politically powerful National Rifle Association (Sykes, 2017) and other advocacy groups hostile to gun control laws, politicians in many states fall over each other in the scramble to deal with the crime problem by enacting laws that enhance rather than restrict gun-owners' rights, even in the wake of mass-killings. A study of nine states, conducted in the 1960s and 1970s, indicated that legislatures passed several new criminal statutes virtually every year, almost always pushing penal policy in a more legalistic and punitive direction (Jacob, 1984: 143–147; Berk, Brackman, and Lesser, 1977: 182). This pattern continued into the 1990s, even as violent crime rates began a steady decline. In 1984 Congress sought to rationalize sentencing by federal judges according to guidelines written by a professional sentencing commission. But in 1986 a panicky Congress responded to mass media accounts of a crack cocaine epidemic by hastily enacting the Anti-Drug Abuse Act, which mandated sentences for selling crack that were vastly harsher than those for selling powder cocaine.[22] At the time and in the years that followed, Congress ignored the U.S. Sentencing Commission's argument that the disparity between crack and powder penalties was unjustified and ignored also the enormous sentence disparities between whites and blacks convicted of cocaine trafficking (since blacks constituted the overwhelming majority of those convicted of crack sales).[23] A surge of adversarial legalism resulted, as hundreds of defense lawyers (and some lower court judges) challenged the constitutionality and enforcement of the federal crack cocaine law (Provine, 1998).

The 2008 collapse of the subprime-mortgage-fueled housing bubble and the subsequent deep recession resulted in overwhelming fiscal pressures on both the federal and state governments. In response, political leaders finally began to focus on the extraordinary costs generated by giant state and federal incarceration systems. Some states sought to shrink prison populations by reducing the lengths of sentences for nonviolent offenders. Judges found the crowded conditions and overstretched health services in California's prisons unconstitutionally inhumane, forcing the state to spend much more money on health care for inmates and to substantially downsize the prison population (Simon, 2014; Aviram, 2015). Some state legislatures legalized marijuana and many local police departments adopted nonenforcement policies for marijuana users and medical marijuana purveyors (*Economist*, 2014b). These more liberal developments in some states, however, confirm the point that compared to other democracies, the permeable American political structure generates more frequent, more uncoordinated, and regionally inconsistent changes in the criminal and penal law.

Implementing Criminal Law: Two Models of Authority

Criminal justice systems empower police officers to capture and subdue those who resist their commands, to search for evidence, and to lock suspects in jail. For democratic nations a perennial and pressing problem is guarding people from the guardians; that is, preventing abuse and error by those who exercise officially granted coercive powers. One fundamental mechanism of control is the rule of law; another is democratic accountability. Most democracies seek a measure of both, but the two principles coexist in uneasy tension.

Recall Mirjan Damaska's (1975) distinction between hierarchical and coordinate models for organizing governmental authority, discussed in Chapter 3. The hierarchical model, which Damaska abstracts from the systems of Western Europe, centralizes political control of law enforcement and adjudicative processes. It is designed first and foremost to minimize the inconsistency, bias, and injustice that can stem from local, parochial influences on criminal justice system officials. If the hierarchical model could dream, its nightmares would be haunted by the corrupt, incompetent local police chief, the ideological judge who disregards national policies she dislikes, and the jury that acquits or convicts because of the defendant's race, religion, or ethnicity. Hence the hierarchical model strives to substitute the rule of law for the rule of men. It emphasizes apolitical professionalism in the recruitment and training of police, prosecutors, and judges. It organizes them in carefully structured bureaucracies and subjects their performance to close hierarchical supervision and review. To the same end, hierarchical systems grant a national minister of justice far-reaching powers to guide and discipline local officials and supervisors. Democratic responsiveness is focused at the top of the hierarchy of offices—not at the level of frontline, local officialdom—by making the minister of justice directly accountable to the national government and to the parliamentary opposition.

Damaska's coordinate model erects a different set of defenses against a different set of injustices. Its nightmares would feature an overly powerful central government that uses the criminal code as an instrument of political repression or makes laws that, even if not meant to be repressive, are too harsh and unbending, too unresponsive to the values of minority subcultures or to the equities of particular cases. The coordinate ideal, accordingly, emphasizes the fragmentation of power and grassroots democratic responsiveness. Police, prosecutors, and judges are selected and held accountable by local political processes. Politically independent defense lawyers are empowered to dispute the state's evidence, to expose misbehavior by enforcement officials, and to question the fairness of the law itself. Hence the coordinate model exalts the techniques of adversarial legalism—party-influenced (as opposed to hierarchically controlled) legal contestation—to provide legal coordination and ensure accountability.

No nation's criminal justice system conforms entirely to either the hierarchical or coordinate model. Germany, for example, employs nonprofessional lay judges who sit alongside professionals (although the latter are clearly dominant) (Machura, 2000; Casper and Zeisel, 1972). Conversely, there are some hierarchical elements in the United States: trial court decisions can be appealed up the ladder of courts, as in the McCleskey case; the U.S. Supreme Court's constitutional rulings are binding on state and local officials; large urban police departments and prosecutors' offices employ bureaucratic modes of supervision and coordination. Still, the Japanese and most European criminal justice systems lean much more strongly toward the hierarchical ideal (Damaska, 1975: 487, 488; Bayley, 1979),[24] while the criminal justice systems of the United States approximate the coordinate model—and do so far more than their British parent or their Canadian and Australian cousins.

In the United States authority over the making, enforcement, and adjudication of criminal law is scattered over the fifty states and their many counties and municipalities. There is no comprehensive nationwide criminal code and no truly national police force (Bayley, 1979).[25] The authority of the U.S. Attorney General in Washington extends only (and rather weakly) to the ninety-four locally based U.S. attorneys who prosecute federal crimes, and hardly at all to the hundreds of locally elected district attorneys who prosecute state crimes or to the thousands of municipal police chiefs and county sheriffs. In contrast to their counterparts in Japan, France, Germany, or the Netherlands, American trial court judges, police chiefs, sheriffs, and district attorneys have not been selected, socialized, and supervised by an overarching state bureaucracy that administers entrance exams, provides systematic training, coordinates policy, rewards the diligent, and weeds out the incompetent. Rather, American law enforcement officials and judges are elected by local constituencies or appointed by local political leaders—a practice that reflects the coordinate model's concern for independence and political responsiveness rather than for carefully honed legal craftsmanship or fidelity to legal rules.

"Becoming a prosecutor in France," writes Richard Frase, "is a long-term career choice," whereas the average tenure of prosecutors in the United States is relatively short. And compared to the French system, "procedures for training American prosecutors are rudimentary at best" (Frase, 1990: 562–563). In the Netherlands five senior prosecutors meet twice monthly to discuss and revise nationwide guidelines governing the waiver of prosecution for different kinds of offenses and offenders (Downes, 1988: 15). Conversely, "in most American states, prosecutors are locally elected officials with surprisingly great and virtually uncontrolled authority" (Damaska 1975: 502, 512). Hierarchical supervision of individual prosecutors' case-by-case discretionary decision-making is weak. Compared to their Japanese counterparts, David Johnson found, assistant prosecutors in the United States have much more leeway to act on the basis of their own individual judgment—and their judgments are more subject to the influence of complaining victims, grand juries, defense lawyers, and criminal defendants themselves (Johnson, 1998: 247).

Similarly, compared to European (or British or Japanese) judiciaries, American judges have remarkably diverse social, educational, and career backgrounds. Since many are selected for political reasons rather than on the basis of prior experience, a tort lawyer can end up on the bench for criminal cases, and a prosecutor or politician who has never been a trial judge can be catapulted onto the state supreme court or even the U.S. Supreme Court (Kagan, Detlefsen, and Infelise, 1984). Newly appointed American judges do not receive the intensive, specialized training required of new European judges. One consequence is the variability that is the hallmark of the American judiciary. Some American judges are gifted, some well prepared, some neither (Atiyah and Summers, 1987: 345, 357). Some judges are tough sentencers, while others are much more lenient. Judges differ in individual personality, political philosophy, and local political culture, and those differences have been shown to affect their decisions (Levin, 1972; Gaylin, 1974; Gibson, 1980). Notwithstanding a New Mexico statute that mandated imprisonment for drunk-driver recidivists, a study found that at least half of New Mexico judges did not incarcerate repeat offenders—sometimes because they disagreed with the legislative mandate or resented the legislature's attempt to limit their discretion—while other judges faithfully followed the statute (Ross and Foley, 1987).

In the adjudicative process, a still more diverse and localistic institution, the jury, tugs against rule-of-law ideals. Guilt or innocence is determined by a small group of legally untrained citizens drawn from the local community; they hear a single case and then disperse. In German criminal adjudication lay citizens serve on panels with professional judges, but the lay people serve for a period of time, thereby gaining some experience. Moreover, in every case in Germany a professional judge writes an opinion explaining and justifying the panel's decision (including the sentence); that opinion makes decisions reviewable by an appellate court and ultimately makes them more uniform and predictable.[26] American juries, in contrast, decide in secret. If jurors acquit, they do not have to explain in an intellectually defensible way that their doubts about the prosecution's case were reasonable. If they convict, they need not explain why they found the defense unpersuasive. Juries' decisions are essentially impervious to post hoc rational analysis or hierarchical legal review. The American jury's unreviewable powers mirror the powers of American police, prosecutors, and judges to make discretionary decisions—particularly decisions to drop or reduce criminal charges—without meaningful possibility of legal review.

From the perspective of a Japanese or a European criminal lawyer steeped in the values of the hierarchical model, the American criminal justice system is an uncoordinated, weakly supervised, potentially inconsistent mess. The coordinate model, however, deliberately sacrifices some legal regularity in order to make the criminal process more responsive to popular notions of justice. Thus Michigan jurors could decline to convict a physician who, contrary to law, helped terminally ill patients commit suicide. Ordinary American trial court judges can declare statutes unconstitutional and impose novel conditions of probation on convicted persons. Juries have declined to convict women who attacked or even killed husbands who previously had physically abused them. As political opposition to the Vietnam War increased in the late 1960s and early 1970s, juries often acquitted young men charged with draft evasion (Levine, 1992: 114–115).

But the coordinate model also means that a criminal defendant's fate may rest on contingencies such as where and by whom he is tried. Some judges are known to be biased in favor of the prosecution (Brill, 1989).

Conviction rates are higher in politically conservative than in politically liberal counties (Levine, 1983). The white Los Angeles police officers who were captured on videotape brutally beating Rodney King (an African American) after a high-speed car chase were acquitted by a jury in a white suburban community (triggering a violent riot by African Americans), but were convicted by a predominantly minority jury when reprosecuted in federal court in downtown Los Angeles (Holden, Cohen, and de Lisser, 1995: A1, A5). Jurors can (and sometimes do) vote for conviction and even the death penalty based on misunderstandings of the evidence, of the judges' instructions, or of the operations of the legal and penal system (Paduano and Stafford-Smith, 1987: 211; Garvey, Johnson, and Marcus, 2000).[27]

Regulating the Coordinate Model: Adversarial Legalism

Americans may value the democratic responsiveness inherent in the coordinate model, but they also believe that similar cases should be treated similarly and that official power should be constrained by law. The decentralized coordinate model, accordingly, seeks to promote legal regularity via a sequence of lateral legal checks. American prosecutors can reject charges pushed forward by the police if the prosecutor thinks the evidence is inadequate. Judges have the authority and obligation to reject charges made by prosecutors when a preliminary hearing indicates insufficient evidence or legal grounds to proceed against the suspect. There are some hierarchical checks as well, triggered by defendants' appeals to higher courts. In principle, and to a considerable degree in practice, each decision-maker anticipates the possibility of rejection by the next one in the sequence and thus will avoid legal errors or factually weak cases that may result in dismissal at the next stage.

Defense lawyers are the enzymes that catalyze the coordinate model's sequential checking system. Their job is to slow the rush to judgment, directing judges' or prosecutors' attention to police malpractice or to weaknesses in the prosecutor's case. At trial, defense lawyers cross-examine police and other witnesses (a job that falls primarily to the judge in continental European systems).[28] American defense lawyers remind the judge about legal precedents, build a record that can sustain an appeal, and summarize the evidence for the jury, a job done by the judge in British jury trials.

Suppose, however, that a criminal suspect does not have a defense attorney or that his lawyer is inept, lazy, or overburdened. In such cases the coordinate system's checking mechanisms can easily lie dormant. In Philadelphia on a February morning in 1954, soon after the police (responding to political pressures) had opened a drive against "vagrants and habitual drunkards" in the central city, officers herded fifty-five defendants before a magistrate. As Caleb Foote described the court, there were no prosecuting attorneys and no defense lawyers. Within fifteen minutes, the magistrate discharged forty defendants and found fifteen guilty, sentencing each of the latter to three-month terms in the House of Correction. Foote (1956: 603) wrote: "Four of these committed defendants were tried, found guilty and sentenced in the elapsed time of seventeen seconds. . . . The magistrate merely read off the name of [each] defendant, took one look at him, and said, 'Three months in the House of Correction.' As the third man was being led out he objected, stating, 'But I'm working . . . ,' to which the magistrate replied, 'Aw, go on.'" In the Philadelphia magistrate's court and thousands like it, in 1954 and in previous decades, whenever defendants were not represented by counsel—as was common for working class and poor defendants—little adversarial legalism prevailed in practice (Friedman and Percival, 1981). The method of adjudication in actuality was judge-dominated, yet without the same level of commitment to norms of legality that are inculcated in highly professional, hierarchically organized European judicial systems.

Professor Foote's account, published in a law review, sought to induce legal elites to recognize the huge gap between the ideals of the judicial system and its tawdry reality, especially as it applied to poor Americans. But how could that gap be closed? In theory, after reading about the Philadelphia magistrate's disregard of legal norms, reformers might have called for nationwide or at least statewide professional standards for recruiting, training, and supervising judges, along the lines employed in Great Britain and continental European democracies. No more political cronies of the mayor on the bench. Alternatively, reformers might have urged welfare bureaucracies to provide noncriminal alternatives for dealing with panhandling vagrants and alcoholics—such as government-provided shelter, aid, and treatment—rather than arrest and jail.

In the politically decentralized United States, however, neither Congress, the president, nor the U.S. Attorney General had the political authority to change judicial recruitment and training systems in fifty states. Nor was there a national social welfare department with funding or authority to induce scores of municipalities to provide shelters and treatment facilities. The predominant strategy of American legal reformers, therefore, was to sharpen the weapons of adversarial legalism, that is, to arm "vagrants" and other victims of unprofessional local judiciaries with stronger legal rights and with free legal advocates, capable of challenging and resisting governmental control. To achieve these goals, the reformers turned to the sole national institution with a modicum of hierarchical control over local courthouses—the U.S. Supreme Court, interpreter of the U.S. Constitution, which proclaims itself the "supreme law of the land." In a series of cases in the 1960s and 1970s the Supreme Court held that individual rights to liberty were violated by laws that made it a crime to be drunk in a public place, absent proof that the defendant actually was disturbing the peace.[29] In *Argersinger v. Hamlin* (1972), the Supreme Court announced a constitutional right to free counsel for indigent defendants in any prosecution that might result in substantial imprisonment, even for misdemeanors such as disturbing the peace. *Argersinger,* along with the Supreme Court's 1963 *Gideon v. Wainwright* decision, transformed the institutional landscape of American criminal justice, inducing cities and urban counties to establish offices of full-time public defenders or to fund court-appointed lawyers for indigent criminal defendants (Spangenberg and Beeman, 1995: 31; Hall, 2011: 78–80).[30]

In the early 1970s Malcolm Feeley studied a lower criminal court in New Haven, Connecticut. In contrast to Philadelphia in 1954, public defenders were consistently present in the court. So were prosecuting attorneys, for Connecticut felt compelled to provide prosecuting lawyers to match its state-funded defense lawyers. The prosecutors in turn demanded more systematic, documented evidence of guilt from the police; there was a written file and police report for each case. Feeley (1979: 184) observed that while approximately 40 percent of New Haven misdemeanor defendants were not represented by counsel (usually because they said they didn't want one), they benefited because others did have lawyers: "By pressing their clients' interests, occasionally raising legal defenses, and pressing for openness and trust between themselves and the Prosecutor's Office, defense attorneys have helped carve out the factors which enter into the assessment of the case. . . . Once they are established, these norms . . . are applied more or less equally to all."

In the 1960s legal reformers also pressed for nationwide legal controls over repressive and often racist local police practices. Again, in a politically decentralized, coordinate system, neither the president nor his attorney general had constitutional authority to fire a racist chief of police in Birmingham, Alabama or any other city. Moreover, Congress, hamstrung by federalism and by Democratic Party division, was of little help. But confronted with television pictures of Southern sheriffs beating civil rights marchers, national political, journalistic, and legal elites came to believe that something had to be done. Adversarial legalism again was the answer. It provided the tools for circumventing the power vacuum on Capitol Hill, using litigation and federal courts to impose federal legal standards on politically autonomous local police departments and courts.

In a series of appeals from state court decisions, the Supreme Court, as noted in Chapter 3, reinterpreted the Constitution, applying to the states the criminal procedure provisions of the Bill of Rights, which traditionally had been understood to operate as a check only on the *federal* government. Case by case, the Court elaborated detailed nationwide rules concerning pretrial detention, interrogation of suspects, and police searches for evidence. The Court required local judges to exclude evidence obtained by means of illegal searches or interrogations (as defined by the federal courts). The Court expanded opportunities for locally convicted defendants to seek collateral review in lower federal courts (as exemplified by Warren McCleskey's habeas corpus petitions) and opened the door for federal reprosecution of racist law enforcement officers who had been acquitted by local juries in state courts. More recently, even after the Court became more conservative in the 1990s, it interpreted the "cruel and unusual punishment" clause of the Constitution to ban the death penalty and life imprisonment without parole for juveniles under eighteen convicted of murder.

In addition, the Supreme Court, reinterpreting a post-Civil War congressional statute, expanded opportunities for victims of police misconduct to bring lawsuits for money damages against local police departments for violation of citizens' constitutional rights.[31] Consequently, between 1961 and 1977 constitutional tort suits against government officials in federal courts increased from 296 to over 13,000 annually (Skolnick and Fyfe, 1993: 300–305; Schuck, 1983: 41–51, 200–201). In 1990 lawsuits against the Los Angeles Police Department cost the city about $11.3 million in settlements and verdicts (Skolnick and Fyfe, 1993: 202). In the wake of a $25 million verdict against the Torrington, Connecticut, police department for failing to arrest a repeatedly violent and abusive husband, 84 percent of urban police departments adopted policies calling for mandatory or preferred arrest policies in cases of domestic violence (Sherman, 1992).[32] Police reformers used the *threat* of expensive and embarrassing constitutional tort lawsuits to convince many departments to adopt regulations, plus monitoring systems, to control excessive use of force by officers (Epp, 2009).[33] (More recently, however, as discussed in the Afterword, the U.S. Supreme Court's rulings have made it more difficult to win constitutional tort cases against police departments and prosecutors' offices).

What Adversarial Legalism Cannot Do

Adversarial legalism is not the only set of tools that the United States employs to foster the rule of law. In larger American law enforcement organizations, legal professionals, fighting the centrifugal tendencies of the coordinate model, develop regulations and guidelines designed to enhance legal uniformity. For example, the district attorney's office in Los Angeles convenes a weekly Special Circumstances Committee that reviews homicide cases and strives to impose normative coherence on the decision of whether or not to seek the death penalty. New Jersey created a statewide office to train, assign, and oversee defense lawyers who handle capital cases for indigent defendants (Lewin, 1995).

To some extent, moreover, adversarial legalism has accelerated the development of such internal bureaucratic controls. As a result of the Supreme Court's exclusionary rule and the adversarial challenges to illegally seized evidence that it makes possible, most municipal police and federal law enforcement officers now receive extensive (and by most accounts reasonably effective) training in the law of search and seizure (Bradley, 1993: 37; Walker, 1993: 46–53; Orfield, Jr., 1987). Similarly, as noted above, judicial decisions making it easier to sue police departments for damages have encouraged many police departments in many cities to codify and implement policies on use of force and to work harder at training police officers and weeding out bad ones (Skolnick and Fyfe, 1993: 203; Epp, 2009). But clearly, not all municipal police departments do so. In 2014–2016, mass protests erupted in Baltimore, Maryland; Cleveland, Ohio; Ferguson, Missouri; and elsewhere after police killings of unarmed black men. U.S. Department of Justice investigations of police departments in those and other cities resulted in scathing reports of racial bias, unwarranted use of lethal force, and a tradition of impunity for the officers responsible (Smith and Apuzzo, 2015).[34] Those federal investigations, while in some sense introducing a new hierarchical-supervision element into the decentralized American law enforcement system, nevertheless are ad hoc responses to headline events. And the U.S. Department of Justice obtains its leverage from the threat of a federal lawsuit against the municipality in question; the U.S. Attorney General can sue the local police chief, but has no hierarachical authority to fire him or her. Moreover, politics can intrude: the Trump Administration, as it came to office in early 2017, claimed that the U.S. Department of Justice investigations of local police departments had resulted in less effective law enforcement and announced that such investigations would no longer be launched.

Thus adversarial legalism can at best temper, not control, the centrifugal tendencies of the United States' coordinate model of organizing law enforcement, prosecution, adjudication, and punishment. In comparative perspective, American police officers, prosecutors, and trial judges are remarkably independent-minded and often resistant to hierarchically imposed administrative controls (Heilbroner, 1990). With disturbing frequency, newspaper reports of an exonerated prisoner are traced back to a local prosecutor's or police officer's failure to comply with their legal duty to disclose exculpatory evidence. Moreover, political fragmentation means that a suspect's or defendant's fate often depends significantly on *where* he or she is, for different states continue to enact different penalties for similar offenses. Within a single state, prosecutors in different counties, locally elected or appointed, often "will treat the possession of a small amount of cocaine, a first time property offense, or drunk driving differently" (Pizzi, 1993: 1344; Ross and Foley, 1987).[35] The incidence of police shootings of suspects varies significantly among regions of the nation, and even among cities in the same region, primarily because of variation among municipal police departments in their protocols, training, and supervision (Zimring, 2017).

In addition to political fragmentation, the weaknesses of adversarial legalism as a regulatory mechanism are products of its limited reach, its inefficiency, and its counterproductive effects, which include the politicization of the criminal justice system. A few words on each topic will illustrate the point.

The Limited Reach of Adversarial Legalism. Adversarial legalism exerts little control over the *discretionary* decisions that constitute the most frequent, crucial, and potentially discriminatory actions by law enforcement officials. These include district attorneys' determinations concerning when to decline to prosecute, or for whom to demand high bail, or in which cases to file multiple as opposed to single charges. Thus the United States still contrasts sharply with hierarchical prosecutorial systems, which have well-developed mechanisms for selecting and training prosecutors and subjecting their decisions to the rule of law (Johnson, 1998: 255–257; Pizzi, 1993: 1337). Similarly, in the absence of statewide, hierarchical influence on the training and supervision of city and county police forces, adversarial legalism has not been able to impose legal uniformity (or racial neutrality) on police officers' decisions about whom to stop and question (Epp, Maynard-Moody, and Haider-Markel, 2014),[36] whom to arrest (Stuntz, 1997: 5, 50), whether to resort to coercion in making arrests, or whether to disclose exculpatory evidence to suspects being interrogated.[37] And because the juvenile justice system, designed as an alternative to adversarial legalism, operates in a more informal, discretionary manner, adversarial legalism has not been capable of eliminating the substantial differences in outcomes for African American youth, who, according to a Department of Justice report, are significantly more likely than young white offenders to be arrested, held in jail, sent to either juvenile or adult court for trial, convicted, and sentenced to long periods of incarceration (Butterfield, 2000a).

Adversarial legalism's protections, for the most part, involve rights that *may* be invoked by the defendant rather than restrictions on police imposed automatically as a matter of hierarchical legal command. Hence adversarial legalism's protections crumble when a naïve or scared criminal suspect does not invoke them. Police investigators often persuade suspects in custody to waive the right to silence and to legal counsel guaranteed by the Supreme Court's *Miranda* decision. A study in one city found that police obtained such waivers and confessions in some two-thirds of all interrogations (Leo,

1996, 2008). Nationwide, this common practice has been a primary source of false confessions, as shown by Richard Leo's analysis of tens of cases in which homicide or rape suspects were convicted after a jailhouse interrogation but subsequently were exonerated, often after having spent many years on prison (Leo, 2008).

Constitutional law, and hence adversarial legalism, also has little influence on the fifty state legislatures' decisions concerning how much funding to provide to public defenders' offices, which in turn strongly influences how often the protections against police and prosecutorial misconduct established by the courts actually are invoked (Stuntz, 1997). In many states and counties, funding of public defenders is abysmal.[38] The general point is that regulating criminal law enforcement via the legal rules and structures of adversarial legalism—whose efficacy depends on persistent invocation by defendants and their lawyers—is only inconsistently successful.

And of course, adversarial legalism could not stem the politically-driven increase in mass incarceration in the United States. Similarly, adversarial legalism could not stanch the steady increase of private gun ownership, including sale of semiautomatic military assault rifles, as the Republican Party, cowed by the grass-roots political power of National Rifle Association and its committed members, has blocked serious regulation of firearms in most places. This has left the United States government unique among economically advanced democracies in failing to maintain anything close to a monopoly over the means of violence—a fundamental condition of political and legal order. In 2015, a thorough compilation of local news reports indicated that in the United States, a mass shooting—defined as one that left four or more people dead—occurred, on average, more than once a day (LaFraniere, Cohen, and Oppel, Jr., 2015).

Adversarial Legalism and Inefficiency. First, as a mechanism of legal accountability, litigation is far more costly than bureaucratic supervision. Secondly, as will be elaborated in Chapter 5, adversarial legalism has made the American criminal trial a distinctively inefficient method of deciding disputes—a method so complex and costly that it has become a relatively uncommon event. Third, by making courts the primary lawmakers for much of criminal procedure, adversarial legalism has produced a confusing and erratic body of procedural rules, especially when compared to the professionally drafted codes and guidelines implemented by ministries of justice in Western European countries. As lawmakers, American courts proceed reactively, case by case, making rules in the form of highly contextualized judgments about which appellate judges themselves often disagree (Bradley, 1993). Hence Supreme Court rulings concerning car searches or the waiver of *Miranda* rights are commonly misunderstood and misapplied by police officers and lower court judges alike (47–49).[39]

Of course, legal confusion and malleability breed more costly litigation as well as inconsistent treatment.

The Politicization of Criminal Procedure. Viewed in comparative perspective, adversarial legalism's techniques of legal challenge seem to turn the processing of criminal cases into a legal slalom course in which a rule violation by the police or an arguably prejudicial statement by the prosecutor, the trial judge, or a juror results in the exclusion of incriminating evidence, a mistrial, or an appellate court reversal. When such legal errors seem disproportionate to the seriousness of the criminal offense, the public, like Charles Dickens's Mr. Bumble in *Oliver Twist,* is prone to view the law as an ass, focused on legal technicalities rather than on the truth or falsity of the criminal charge. For that reason, adversarial legalism has been a politically controversial mechanism for increasing accountability in the criminal justice system.

Once liberal reformers made constitutional litigation a primary strategy for imposing nationwide standards on local police, courts, and prosecutors, then conservative interest groups and politicians turned their attention to the judiciary, trying to stack the courts with judges inclined to reverse or restrict liberal judicial precedents. On the U.S. Courts of Appeals, where judges sit in panels of three, judges appointed by Republican president Ronald Reagan disagreed with colleagues appointed by Democratic president Jimmy Carter in almost one of four criminal appeals during the 1980s (Gottschall, 1986: 52). In 1986 political conservatives, complaining that the California Supreme Court had reversed the trial court in sixty-four of sixty-eight appeals in capital punishment cases, mounted a successful electoral campaign to oust the chief justice, Rose Bird, and two liberal colleagues (Wold and Culver, 1987). In the next decade, with a new cast of Republican judges, the California court *upheld* most of the death sentences it reviewed—much more often, in fact, than almost every other state supreme court (Kamin, 1999). In Congress and in some states liberals have fought back, battling to block conservative judicial appointments and working to put politically liberal judges on the bench. In many states "judicial election campaigns have come to resemble other [electoral] races, complete with attack advertising and multimillion-dollar war chests" (Glaberson, 2000, A8). America's uniquely partisan political struggle to control the courts thus exacerbates the malleability, inconsistency, and indeterminacy of criminal procedure in the United States.

———

Adversarial legalism does fill an organizational void, at least partially. It has prodded a highly decentralized, politically responsive criminal justice system toward the uniform application of legal rights and penalties.

It enables dedicated lawyers and judges to expose malpractice or legalistic inflexibility on the part of police and prosecutors. It enables them to employ imaginative constitutional interpretation to make improvements in the justice system. But adversarial legalism is an indirect, incomplete, and inefficient mechanism of control and legal coordination—especially when compared to the professionalized, bureaucratically-supervised police, prosecutorial, and judicial systems of some parliamentary democracies. Adversarial legalism also has made American criminal procedures distinctively cumbersome, inconsistent, and confusing. And those characteristics, as we will see in Chapter 5, increase the risk of injustice in the disposition of individual cases.

CHAPTER FIVE

Deciding Criminal Cases

In the eighteenth century, English juries sitting in the Old Bailey tried between twelve and twenty felony cases a day (Langbein, 1979a: 262). In the late nineteenth century, jury trials in Oakland, California, probably averaged half an hour at most (Friedman, 1979). But during the twentieth century, wrote Albert Alschuler (1986: 1825), "the American jury trial . . . has become one of the most cumbersome and expensive fact-finding mechanisms that humankind has devised."

In 1968 felony trials in Los Angeles averaged 7.2 days. A detailed study of nine county courts in the mid-1980s found that the median jury trial in felony cases (excluding trials in which the death penalty is at issue) took more than fourteen hours (National Center for State Courts, 1988: 19).[1] Since actual trial days averaged less than 3.5 hours (9), the median trial probably lasted over four days. In Oakland, California, the study also revealed, homicide trials, which accounted for a third of all criminal trials in the county, averaged forty-four hours (before jury deliberations)—probably at least two weeks (30).[2] In North Carolina the average trial in a capital murder case in 1991 cost the state about $80,000, and some cost more than $150,000; by 2000–2010, such cases cost more than ten times those amounts.[3] "England may be the cradle of the adversary system," Graham Hughes (1984: 568) observed, "but the child it reared never grew to the giant proportions of the sibling who crossed the Atlantic."[4]

The expansion of the American criminal trial springs from the intensification of adversarial legalism. Litigation and court rulings have generated a set of constitutional rights and legal practices that encourage criminal defendants to remain silent and that empower criminal defense lawyers to challenge the prosecution's evidence, the composition of the jury, and the conduct of the adjudicatory process. Each right was elaborated in hopes of reducing the risk of unjust conviction. And Americans have long prized the jury as democratic institution, giving ordinary citizens the opportunity to make critical normative decisions and even to serve as a check on unpopular laws and incipient governmental tyranny (Hale, 2016). But the pumped-up adversarial jury trial has become so complex, legalistic, and costly that, in the words of comparative legal scholar John Langbein (1979a: 265), it is "unworkable as an ordinary or routine dispositive procedure." Average citizens sense this too: in many cities a large proportion of people summoned for jury duty fail to show up.[5] After comparing criminal trials in the United States to those in the Netherlands, Germany, Norway, and England, William Pizzi (1999: 74, 184) concluded that American trials are much more susceptible to variability in the intensity of adversarial advocacy and are a more uncertain mechanism for determining the truth, which exacerbates the risk of both unjust conviction and unjust acquittal. Indeed, Pizzi notes, defense lawyers and judges in the United States commonly refer to trials as crapshoots and go to great lengths to avoid them.

Instead of trial, therefore, the overwhelming bulk of criminal charges are dismissed or are decided by defendants' guilty pleas. In Phoenix, Arizona there were approximately 20,000 felony convictions in the 1983–1986 period. Only 4.27 percent were tried; the rest were disposed of by guilty plea (Lowenthal, 1993: 80). Trial rates of less than 5 percent also have been found in Los Angeles, Denver, and Manhattan (Boland et al., 1990: 91–97). Nationwide, it is estimated that more than 90 percent of all criminal convictions are obtained via guilty pleas (Stuntz, 1997: 24; Alschuler, 1983: 935). According to Thomas Weigend (1980: 411), a German comparative legal scholar, "The admirable American preoccupation with safeguarding the individual's procedural rights has backfired. By affording the whole collection of procedural rights to a small minority of defendants, the system deprives the great majority of rights [particularly the right to a meaningful day in court] available to the accused in most civilized countries."

Adversarial Legalism's Ugly Child: Plea Bargaining

Plea bargaining isn't a new practice (Friedman, 1979), and most other nations too, Weigend (1980) observes, have established a simplified, speedy, and inexpensive dispositional system for the majority of criminal cases— those in which the evidence is strong and defendants do not have any plausible defense. In most countries, full-scale, labor-intensive adjudication, replete with opportunities for the defendants and their lawyers to challenge the prosecution's case, tends to be reserved for more serious crime charges and those in which defendants strongly claim to be innocent.

The key normative issues revolve around the character of the simple model and how much pressure is exerted on defendants to be cooperative—to confess. In Germany and France, Weigend (1980: 420) notes, the simple model involves either a less complicated, quicker trial in a lower court or a payment of a fine in return for dismissal of criminal charges (as in American traffic courts). But, and this is Weigend's critical point, in Germany and in France "the cost of choosing the more complicated model is not prohibitive." In the United States, Weigend says, the "situation is dramatically different." Compared to a rapid plea negotiation (the simple model in the United States), the American jury trial is vastly more complex, labor-intensive, expensive, and anxiety-provoking. Unlike a plea negotiation, Weigend notes (1980: 420–421), an American jury trial not only requires the lawyers to spend many days in court but imposes the following responsibilities on them:

> finding, interviewing, and coaching witnesses; submitting briefs on, and arguing, pretrial motions to suppress evidence; fighting over discovery and inspection rights; devising tactics for questioning witnesses and generally for the conduct of the trial; analyzing and challenging the composition of the jury; preparing lengthy opening and closing arguments; presenting the evidence in a fashion understandable to uneducated and ignorant laypersons; arguing, again and again, about objections to particular lines of questioning and to the introduction of evidence; attacking the credibility of the opponent's witnesses and preparing drafts of jury instructions.

"It is the disproportion in America between the simple and the complicated models of adjudication," Weigend concludes (1980: 421), "which induces the American system to use coercion and deceit in order to reach the quick dispositions it has come to depend on for survival."

Weigend overstates the point a little. In the United States many guilty pleas are not the product of coercion, and many do not stem from the disparity he refers to. Rather, guilty pleas often reflect straightforward confessions by defendants with no plausible defense and the ensuing sentence reflects a "going rate" well understood by the courthouse community.[6] Many other guilty pleas reflect negotiations between prosecutors and defense counsel that probe the evidence, assess the defendant's record and degree of culpability, and tend to arrive at sensible and fair dispositions (Utz, 1978). On the other hand, many guilty pleas *do* reflect the extraordinary legal complexity and stressfulness of adversarial jury trials, which cast fear into the heart of the unpracticed defense lawyer and vastly increase the difficulty of a prosecutor's and a trial judge's job. In the criminal process, as in other spheres of American law, adversarial legalism enables disputing parties to threaten their adversaries with very large costs and delays, which encourages case disposition by means of informal (and often extortionate) bargaining.

Defense lawyers in the United States are keenly aware that prosecutors and judges, obligated by law to dispose of criminal cases within a few months, cannot afford to mount many seven-day trials. Hence, whereas Japanese defendants are encouraged to confess and apologize (Foote, 1992),[7] American defense lawyers routinely encourage even clearly guilty defendants to maintain a stony silence and to plead not guilty,[8] for the lawyer can then threaten, implicitly or explicitly, to insist on trial unless the prosecutor offers concessions. Prosecutors, in turn, often feel compelled to reduce charges (and hence penalties) in order to elicit guilty pleas, thereby avoiding a laborious, schedule-wrecking trial. Judges also encourage the aversion to adjudication. In many jurisdictions, researchers have shown, judges give defendants who insist on trial stiffer sentences than those imposed on comparable defendants who plead guilty (Lynch 1994, 120; Brereton and Casper, 1981: Uhlman and Walker, 1979). By emphasizing the "trial penalty" (or, from the prosecutor's standpoint, the guilty-plea discount), defense lawyers pressure at least some defendants who might prefer a trial to plead guilty to a lesser offense (Lynch, 1994: 127).

The risk that innocent (or legally "acquitable") defendants will be coerced into pleading guilty has been intensified, many observers assert, by the enactment of sentence enhancement statutes that mandate extremely long prison terms for offenses involving certain circumstances, such as use of a firearm or conviction for a third felony. These statutes raise the stakes for defendants. Consequently, they are more inclined to insist on trial, which threatens to overwhelm both the courts and the prosecutors' offices.[9] But prosecutors are tempted to avoid trial by offering not to charge the aggravating circumstance (thereby offering an enormous reduction in the prison term) if the defendant will plead guilty to a lesser offense (Lowenthal, 1993: 80).[10] For an alleged burglar with a long prior record, faced with twenty-five or thirty years in prison if convicted, the prosecutor's offer can be almost impossible to refuse—even if the defendant is inclined to contest the charge.

Plea bargaining is troubling on other grounds as well: for the guilty, it transforms the act of confession from a ritual of moral and social healing into a cynical game, reinforcing many criminal defendants' alienated view of society (Casper 1972: 80–81). American prosecutors, unlike their European counterparts, can freely reduce charges at any time; hence in a regime of plea bargaining, prosecutors have a strong incentive to inflate and multiply the initial charges to fortify their bargaining position (Frase, 1990: 621; Alschuler, 1983: 939). Even if many ethically committed prosecutors resist this temptation, not all of them do.

Overall, actual control over sentencing shifts from judges to prosecutors because they control the ultimate *charge*. Yet in the United States, in contrast to Western Europe and Japan, prosecutors receive little formal training in sentencing theory; often, especially when burdened by very high caseloads in in high crime-rate counties, they decide the fates of defendants rapidly and intuitively, without obligatory coordinating guidelines and without any institutionalized requirement to explain and compare their decisions in a reviewable manner (Lynch, 1994: 125–126).[11] American prosecutors also spend less time and effort than Japanese prosecutors, for example, probing the facts of each case and assessing the proper legal disposition. Consequently, David Johnson (1998) concluded, outcomes for similar offenses and offenders in the United States are likely to be far less uniform—and in that sense, less just—than in Japan. In a regime of plea bargaining, moreover, defendants' fates are deeply affected by differences in bargaining skills among attorneys (Lynch, 1994: 130–131). That imbalance is worse in many counties and states that seriously underfund the provision of defense counsel for poor defendants (*Economist*, 2017b), and in others where misdemeanor defendants often do not have lawyers at all (Van Cleve, 2016; Williams, 2017)

Ironically, then, the rules and structures of adversarial legalism, because they generate such a cumbersome and costly mode of dispute resolution, produce *too little* adversarial legalism in practice—a pattern that recurs in many areas of American law.

Criminal Case Disposition in Comparative Perspective

Most European democracies forbid large sentencing differentials between defendants who confess and those who insist on trial, or at least carefully limit such disparities (Myhre, 1968: 650; Alschuler, 1983). Most strictly forbid prosecutors to bargain over reductions in charges; with some sub rosa slippage, that seems to be the practice as well.[12] Many legal systems insist, in fact, that a confession should not preclude a trial, both as a safeguard against coerced confessions and for reasons suggested by Alschuler's assertion that plea bargaining "is inconsistent with the presumption that a decent society should want to hear what an accused person might say in his defense" (Alschuler, 1983: 933–934).

Many European legal systems can attain or at least approximate those goals because in contrast with the radically decentralized and adversarial American system, their prosecutorial and judicial systems and processes are hierarchically organized, and their adjudicatory processes are vastly more efficient. Germany, John Langbein (1979b: 204–225) asserted in an illuminating article, is a "land without plea bargaining." This is no longer entirely true, particularly in complex cases involving economic, environmental, and narcotics charges (Pizzi, 1993: 1325) but also in routine cases, in which prosecutors offer to file only a "penal order" (which entails a fine, not incarceration) in return for defendants' acquiescence to the charge (Dubber, 1997: 559).[13] Nevertheless, knowledgeable comparativists insist that plea bargaining in Germany, compared to the more prevalent American version, is "less likely to cause major sentencing disparities, to encourage initial overcharging, or to create undue risks of convicting the innocent" (Frase and Weigend, 1995: 354). Charging decisions by German prosecutors are constrained by written guidelines, and prosecutors are part of a carefully trained and hierarchically supervised career bureaucracy.

But most importantly, Langbein pointed out, German prosecutors have less *need* to bargain than do their American counterparts because German criminal trials are short. According to a 1970 study, they averaged a day in length for major trials, about two hours for average cases (Casper and Zeisel, 1972: 149–150).[14] In the 1990s Germany experienced a fair number of strongly contested "monster trials," in which a sequence of hearings spread out over months or even well over a year. Still, a systematic 1989–1990 study found that trials for more serious crimes averaged 2.8 days; in somewhat less serious cases, 2.4 days (Dubber, 1997: 569). Why are German trials substantially shorter than American trials?

No Juries

In Germany adjudication is entrusted to a panel of judges and lay persons.[15] As we have noted, the court's decision (including the sentence) must be explained in writing and is subject to searching appellate review. Since there are no juries, with their unexplained and unreviewable verdicts, German criminal trials have no need for the time-consuming prophylactic procedures the United States employs to prevent juror bias or error. These American procedures include lengthy interrogation of prospective jurors and adversarial procedures concerning selection,[16] disputes concerning "the vast exclusionary apparatus of the law of evidence" (Langbein, 1979b, 207; Damaska, 1997b), and adversarial debates over the proper wording of jury instructions.

Less Adversarial, More Focused Trials

In Germany (as in France and several other continental European democracies), defendants have a right to remain silent, and the judge reminds them of it, but defense lawyers rarely advise their client not to answer the judge's questions. In contrast with the United States, where defense lawyers often preclude a defendant from testifying at trial, the defendant in Germany generally tells his or her version of the story and is then questioned by the judge (Van Kessel, 1992: 421; Frase and Weigend, 1995: 343; Langbein, 1979b: 208).[17] As in England and other European countries, the defendant typically is the *first* witness, which immediately focuses the trial on the most important points at issue (Langbein, 1979b: 208–209). The U.S. Supreme Court actually held unconstitutional a state law requiring the defendant to testify first (Pizzi, 1999: 165–168). Because the defendant testifies last, or not at all, in the United States, the prosecution must painstakingly prove every potentially contestable point since it doesn't know which will be contested. In Germany the defendant and other witnesses are questioned by the presiding judge, who then "invites his fellow judges (professional and lay), the prosecutor, the defense counsel, and the accused to supplement his questioning" (Langbein, 1979b: 207).[18]

The Pretrial Investigation

At trials in Germany (and in the Netherlands and Norway) (Pizzi, 1999: 112–113), the questioning of the defendant and other witnesses is based on a detailed file of pretrial statements and other evidence gathered by police, prosecutors, or investigating magistrates. Well before trial, the file is made available to the defense—which then can suggest further, potentially exculpating lines of inquiry by prosecutors, who are obligated to investigate such leads. According to Langbein (1979b: 208), "This thorough, open, and impartial pretrial preparation effectively eliminates surprise and forensic strategy from the trial," while enabling the judge to zero in on the real issues, avoiding the repetitive and often trivial testimony that characterizes American trials.[19]

Because of the thorough pretrial investigation, in fact, many German trials are uncontested. One study found that German defendants made a full confession during their testimony in 41 percent of trials, and another 26 percent offered partial confessions (Casper and Zeisel, 1972: 142–147). In the Netherlands, a British scholar observed, the facts are "mainly established at the investigating stage, so that . . . the Dutch public trial is mainly a check on whether the investigations have been properly carried out" (Downes, 1988: 94–97). The primary focus of the trial judge (as opposed to the investigating magistrate) is developing an understanding of the defendant's motivations and degree of culpability.[20]

Americans may be inclined to characterize such trials as little more than a slow plea—the equivalents of the many cases resolved in the United States by guilty plea because the defendants do not contest the charges. But the short European trials are vastly different from American plea bargaining. The short European trials take place in open court, the defendant speaks for him- or herself, and most important, their fate is decided by a judge (or panel of judges), who must explain and justify the decision orally and in writing. The decision in one case can be compared to the decision in others, and it can be appealed. American plea bargaining, in contrast, is a low-visibility process; the decisions it reaches are unexplained and essentially unreviewable, which means that there is no official mechanism for imposing uniformity on the system.

The dominance of the investigatory phase in criminal justice processes in Europe does not mean that there is no scope for adversarial argument. In the Dutch process, for example, where all evidence collected by prosecutors or investigating magistrates must be shared with defense counsel, "the investigation *by* the examining magistrate" can be "turned into a procedure *before* the examining magistrate," introducing a *trial* element into the pretrial phase (Peters, 1992: 285. The defense lawyer often takes a role in the building of the file, which ultimately contains testimony from witnesses suggested by the defense and reports by forensic social workers and psychiatrists (288). Within a judge-dominated structure, however, adversarial interaction by attorneys rarely devolves into the contentious brand of adversariness often employed by American defense counsel and by prosecuting attorneys, in which each often strives to prevent the other from introducing evidence that would detract from the goal of winning (Pizzi, 1999).[21]

Of course, it is not easy to imagine transplanting European methods of criminal adjudication to the United States. Nor is that the point of this comparison, which is only to highlight the structural causes and the consequences of American adversarial legalism. A hierarchically supervised investigatory system and a short, less adversarial criminal trial seem to avoid, or to at least mute, the more coercive and inconsistent effects of unrecorded and unreviewable plea bargaining—the unattractive but affordable offspring of the costly and inefficient American jury trial.

London and New York

Criminal case disposition shaped by the structures of American adversarial legalism remains distinctive even when compared with England, the birthplace of trial by jury and the adversarial system. British prosecutors and courts, like their American counterparts, have had to cope with rising urban criminal caseloads. A form of implicit plea bargaining is not uncommon; defendants' lawyers let them know that a substantial penalty reduction is available if they plead guilty (Hughes, 1984). But British criminal defendants have another option. For a large range of serious crimes, British defendants can decline to plead guilty and can demand a prompt, non-jury trial in a magistrate's court rather than a jury trial in Crown Court. The magistrate's court also deals with misdemeanor cases; hence "roughly 98 percent of all criminal matters are handled in magistrate's courts" (Pizzi, 1999: 105), which cannot impose prison sentences exceeding six months.

In the 1980s Graham Hughes (1984: 606) compared lower criminal courts in New York City with London's magistrate's courts. In the New York courthouse, he wrote:

> The physical plant is run down . . . , with sickening rancid bathrooms. . . . A general air of seething disorder, verging on chaos prevails. Officials appear harried and angry and information is almost impossible to obtain. Clerks are bored and patronizing, police are cynical and indifferent. In the court-rooms . . . a hum of noise prevails. . . . Events taking place before the bench are meaningless to all except a few insiders. A series of rapid and muttered colloquies take place . . . between lawyers [for defense and prosecution] and judges with a mute defendant physically present but rarely involved. . . . When judges can be heard at all they often appear angry and at times abusive.

In the London magistrate's court, Hughes observed that the proceedings are dominated not by the prosecutor and the defense lawyer but by a professional magistrate. In American lower courts, the opposite is true because only a tiny proportion of misdemeanor prosecutions result in trials; as Malcolm Feeley (1979) explained in *The Process Is the Punishment*, almost all defendants plead guilty because the delays and other costs of insisting on a jury trial make it an unattractive option.[22] Not so in the London magistrate's court. The trials often last only an hour and "rarely last more than a day" (Hughes, 1984: 600). As Hughes saw it:

> London's magistrate's courts also have an air of . . . considerable bustle. But the business and bustle usually appear to be under firm control by the magistrates and the police who are in charge of the courts. . . . The proceedings are conducted smoothly with some formality, a great deal of decorum, general civility, and an air of considerable authority. The prevailing tone is one of benevolent paternalism coupled with recognition of defendants' procedural rights. Magistrates are almost unfailingly polite to defendants, and this appears . . . to express itself in an institutional concern that the defendant is aware of the nature of his situation and can appreciate his choices and exercise his rights. The police behave in court . . . in a strongly authoritative but not unkind way to defendants. The proceedings are easily audible and make sense to even the casual, untrained observer. . . .
>
> Defendants participate in the process more than in a New York court. They are spoken to directly by the clerk and the magistrates in clear and simple language which is repeated until there is confidence that the defendant has understood. The defendant is listened to carefully and any ambiguities . . . in his responses are usually examined. . . . At the end of the proceeding, most

defendants appear to be satisfied that they have taken part in a reasonably fair process in which they were treated in a dignified fashion and given an opportunity to express choices on significant questions.

Hughes was by no means an unqualified admirer of the English system, and his comparison, focusing on two courts at a particular moment in time, may not be fully representative. Outside British urban centers, for example, magistrates are lay persons, advised by a lawyer-clerk (Pizzi, 1999: 105).[23] For our purposes, the primary value of Hughes's account is to highlight the difference between two ways of enhancing protection for defendants in routine criminal cases. The American approach, imposed via the Supreme Court's constitutional decisions, is to emphasize adversarial legalism, guaranteeing defendants the right to a jury trial and to representation by defense counsel. In principle, therefore, fairness increases, but so do the costs and delays of trial, so that, as noted earlier, most cases are resolved by informal, lawyer-dominated bargaining. The British, in contrast, seek to enhance both efficiency and fairness by muting adversarial legalism and by concentrating more power in a reasonably well-staffed, apolitical judiciary.[24] As Hughes (1984: 608–609) puts it:

> The virtues of these English magistrate's courts are, in the end, those of benevolent authority and paternalistic order. The strong control of the court by the magistrate, the firm control of the defendants and the public by the police, the relative dearth of lawyers and their deference and brevity of speech when they appear at all, converge to produce this picture. Questions of defendants' rights are certainly not absent, but raising them will often depend on the magistrate himself, and, if defendants are treated fairly and all the norms of procedure and substantive criminal law are followed with decent fidelity, it is often not because of the vigilance of any representative of the defendant, but because of the traditional behavior of the courts.

The contrast between the American emphasis on lawyer-driven adversariness and British judicial paternalism is also reflected in comparisons of felony cases that go to full-scale jury trial. For example, in the United States adversarial rights to purge racial and other forms of bias from jury selection have become routinized into what Alschuler (1986: 1824) justifiably labels a "prolonged, insulting, privacy-invading jury selection process,"[25] as prosecutors and defense lawyers both try "to kick people they don't like off the jury" (Pizzi, 1999: 18; Hale, 2016: 324–26).[26] In Los Angeles criminal trials in 1984, jury selection averaged five hours (Kakalik et al., 1990). In England criminal juries usually are impaneled in a matter of minutes (Alschuler, 1983: 971; Hughes, 1984: 590). Similarly, in the United States adversarially invoked rights to prevent unfair trial practices generate lengthy in-court wrangles over evidentiary issues. When that happens, jurors often are marched out of the courtroom like children kept from hearing their parents' arguments. In English criminal trials lawyers rarely tie up proceedings with objections and disputes about the admission of evidence,[27] partly, William Pizzi (1999: 176, 180) argues, because British appellate courts are less likely than American appeals courts to reverse a trial court's decision for procedural error, unless it appears to have resulted in a "miscarriage of justice."[28]

Hughes (1984: 589–599) remarks on the muted adversariness of the average British barrister, as compared to the typical American criminal lawyer.[29] American lawyers feel no compunction about coaching friendly witnesses before trial (which British barristers would not do) or about using facial expressions to signal to the jury that a hostile witness's testimony should not be believed. Too often, the American adversary system's competitive ethos leads prosecutors to engage in heavy-handed or even illegal tactics, such as withholding exculpatory evidence.[30] Encouraged by the adversarial ethic, American prosecutors and defense lawyers engage in "frequently repetitive (as well as pointless and degrading) cross-examination" (Alschuler, 1986: 1824) punctuated with objections and arguments from opposing counsel about the cross-examiner's questioning style. This rarely occurs in English criminal trials, where, Hughes (1984: 589) observed, "judges are forthright and dominating" and opposing counsel are "correspondingly restrained"—again, this is partly because British judges are considerably less likely to be reversed on appeal for a remark or ruling that an appellate court regards as prejudicial to the defendant's interests (109). In contrast to American judges (Friedman, 1993: 387–388), British judges in jury trials summarize and comment on the evidence (Wolchover, 1989). In American trials that task is left entirely to the competing lawyers, who have leeway to resort to obfuscation and appeals to general values rather than to close analysis of the evidence—which may be responsible for the substantial (and frustrating) incidence of mistrials due to hung juries (between 10 and 15 percent, according to existing studies) (Hale, 2016: 312–313).

One other difference: in the U.K., a 1994 parliamentary statute authorized British judges and juries to draw inculpatory inferences from a defendant's refusal to answer questions or explain his or her actions, either to the police or in court (Schmidt, 1994: A17).[31] The United States, in contrast, bans such inferences and prevents prosecutors from calling the jury's attention to the defendant's refusal to offer a defense in his or her own words. By thus making proof of guilt more difficult, the American interpretation of the privilege against self-incrimination encourages a more adversarial posture by both sides. Defense lawyers in the United States prod most defendants not to testify at trial and also to be silent when arrested and interrogated in the police station. Prosecutors, in turn, often adopt a reciprocally adversarial posture. And police interrogators regularly resort to psychological trickery to induce criminal suspects to waive their right to silence and answer police questions (Leo, 2008, 1996; Parloff, 1993: 58–62). One result, as Leo (2008) has convincingly shown, is a disturbing number of manipulated, false confessions.

In sum, British trials, while adversarial, entail a much larger dose of hierarchical control, hence more constraints on party-driven adversariness, than criminal adjudication in the United States. That does not mean that English tribunals are kangaroo courts; acquittal rates in British Crown Courts are considerably higher than in American jury trials. It does mean that British trials are shorter and less costly. And that moderates incentives to resolve cases via the kind of low-visibility, sometimes extortive, sometimes coercive plea negotiation that occurs in American criminal courthouses.

Unequal Justice

No criminal justice system can always provide equal justice. Compared to the typical defendant, wealthier, better-educated, better-connected defendants enjoy many advantages. Typically, they have a shorter criminal record, and better lawyers, and a larger number of respectable friends who might be able to provide favorable evidence (Cooney, 1994: 833–858). But *costly* systems of justice exacerbate these inequalities.

In regimes that lie closer to the ideal type of bureaucratic legalism, the prosecutor and judge are the dominant figures; they can be trained and reviewed in ways that tend to offset social inequalities in the defendant population. But in a regime of adversarial legalism, the parties' *lawyers* are the crucial actors. Hence, compared to European criminal justice systems, outcomes in the United States are far more sensitive to variations in the energy and skill of particular defense counsel and prosecutors, and especially to any *imbalance* of effort and competence between the two sides. Moreover, those imbalances are common, partly because full-scale adversarial legalism is so slow, complex, and costly that advantages flow to those who can best afford the battle.

When asked in opinion surveys if there is a different system of justice in court for the rich and the poor, Americans tend to say, "Yes, indeed" (McClosky and Brill, 1983: 150–151).[32] They are right. The overwhelming majority of criminal defendants, black and white, are poor.[33] Their legal representation is provided by public defenders, who often are overburdened, or in some counties by court-appointed (often poorly compensated) private lawyers, or in misdemeanor courts in many smaller counties, by no lawyer at all.[34] The inequality arises from the capacity of well-financed defendants, or of defendants represented by especially dedicated defense lawyers, to create an entirely different kind of legal proceeding, mobilizing all the weapons afforded by adversarial legalism.

In white-collar crime cases, for example, well-paid defense lawyers often get involved early, maneuvering to restrict the prosecution's access to information and negotiating with prosecutors even before the indictment is handed down (Mann, 1985; Penner, 1992: 3; Eisinger, 2017). Well-financed defense counsel hire consultants to help them select sympathetic juries or try out arguments before mock juries (Adler, 1994). To enhance defense witnesses' ability to withstand adversarial cross-examination, well-financed defense counsel spend hours coaching them (although, as suggested above, most other legal systems forbid witness coaching and encourage witnesses to tell their stories in their own words) (Pizzi, 1999: 197–198). At complex trials, American jurors are sometimes befuddled by the complexity of evidence and by the tactics of skilled defense lawyers, whose reputations rest on winning, not merely ensuring that defendants reliably get a fair trial.[35] But most public defenders' offices cannot come close to consistently mounting full-scale aggressive defenses even in capital cases,[36] and certainly not in the great mass of lower-visibility noncapital cases (Stuntz, 1997). Even the most competent public defender lacks the time and resources for requisite factual investigation, research, and legal argument for every plausible claim in each defendant's case (Stuntz, 1997). The poor defendant thus gets fewer legal arguments made on his behalf than the rich defendant, and some poor defendants get less than others.

Although most (not all) state legislatures have steadily increased appropriations for public defenders' offices and assigned criminal defense counsel, these expenditures have not kept pace with the volume of criminal cases. Reviewing the available data, William Stuntz estimates that *in constant dollars* public expenditures *per case* on defense lawyers for indigent defendants "declined significantly" between the late 1970s and the early 1990s–"a period in which the law of criminal procedure mushroomed" and hence in which litigation costs ought to have *risen* (Stuntz, 1997: 9–10). Numerous studies have concluded that public defenders, while hardworking and generally competent, are terribly overburdened (Stuntz, 1997; Hanson et al., 1992; McIntyre, 1987). Stuntz cites a New York City study that found that court-appointed defense lawyers filed written pretrial motions on procedural issues in only 11 percent of nonhomicide felony cases, but even this exceeded the proportion of cases in which appointed defense lawyers visited the crime site (4 percent), interviewed witnesses (4 percent), and used experts to challenge the prosecution's evidence (2 percent) (McConville and Mirsky, 1986–1987: 762–767).

Resource inadequacy affects prosecutors' offices as well. When caseloads are high, prosecutors, who operate under legal mandates to try or dispose of criminal cases within a few months, tend to treat defendants more leniently. Law professor Randy Barnett (1994: 2595–2596) writes:

> In 1976, when I was a law clerk for the State's Attorney's Office of Cook County [Chicago], the average caseload per judge was well over 400. In those days, plea bargaining was notorious. . . . Rapes routinely were reduced to aggravated battery. Car thieves and burglars had to be convicted dozens of times before being imprisoned. It simply was not possible to bring even a small fraction of cases to trial, and defense lawyers knew it. So most cases ended with extremely lenient deals. . . .
>
> By the time I returned to the felony trial courts as an Assistant State's Attorney in 1979, the caseload in each courtroom was down to between 125 and 135 [due to federal funding assistance]. This meant that I could credibly threaten to try any case . . . and could offer plea bargains that were in my judgment correct sentences. . . . By the 1990s, [due largely to the war on drugs] the caseload had once again climbed to over 400, even though the number of courts had greatly increased. Give-away plea bargaining was once again rampant, especially for those accused of property crimes.[37]

Even aside from heavy caseloads, incentives to resolve cases by plea bargaining stem from the nature of jury trials, which for both prosecutors and defense counsel are highly labor-intensive, complex, and stressful. Recalling his first few jury trials, an American public defender (Bellows, 1988: 78) wrote:

> During the government's direct exam you must listen to what the witness is saying; take copious notes; make objections before—not after—the answers are given; refine and replan your cross-examination; and watch the jury's reaction. I repeatedly found my mind wandering and had no idea what the witness had said. When I did focus carefully on what the witness was saying, I forgot to make objections. When I managed to listen and make objections, I found that I had taken no notes (and thus had only the vaguest recollection of the testimony).

Considering those formidable demands, we can be sure that not all lawyers rise fully to the occasion. Yet others do. That is crucial, because in a regime of adversarial legalism, the quality of justice is *especially* dependent on the relative commitment and ability of the dueling lawyers. In a study of death penalty litigation, Samuel Kamin (1999: 124) writes:

> Experts with whom I've spoken have generally agreed that the most important variable in determining whether a capital defendant will be sentenced

to death is not the details of the crime, the locale in which the case will be tried or the race of the defendant but rather the competence of the defendant's attorney in trying death cases. This opinion is shared by death penalty scholars as well.

Some of the unequal outcomes generated by the American criminal justice system stem from its greater emphasis on *political responsiveness* than on legal uniformity. Thus legal penalties for similar crimes differ from state to state, or from time to time within the same state, as legislatures respond to public opinion or organized interest groups. But those inequalities in outcome are not regarded as wholly improper, for they are legitimated, at least in part, by democratic processes. Similarly, American reliance on locally selected police chiefs and prosecutors, who make discretionary decisions about enforcement priorities and charging policies, means that similar offenders in different communities will often be treated differently. Reliance on trial by panels of randomly selected citizen jurors, whose decisions are unexplained and unreviewable, virtually guarantees unequal outcomes. Such county-to-county, jury-to-jury inequalities, justifiable or not (and they're surely troublesome in terms of the ideal of equal treatment under the law), were deliberately built into the system long ago. They are the inherited legacy of a polity that feared a government strong enough to impose legal uniformity across a whole continent or even a whole state.

Inequalities that stem wholly from the expense and complexity of highly adversarial criminal trials, however, are of a different order. Those inequalities arise from the relegation of most criminal case dispositions to informal, legally unreviewed negotiations between weakly supervised individual prosecutors and poor defendants' lawyers, who vary in quality and resources.

Legal Culture and Adversarial Legalism

In 1995 Eric Leonard, a twenty-two-year-old man accused of serial murders, was sitting in a Sacramento, California, courtroom. His lawyers were arguing for a change of venue for his trial. According to a reporter (Coronado, 1995) attending the hearing:

> The defendant raised his hand, waving it ever so slightly. "I am guilty," Leonard said. Immediately, . . . the courtroom fell silent. . . . When it appeared that Leonard was about to repeat his statement, . . . Assistant Public Defender Caroline Lange swung her arm around Leonard and whispered frantically in his right ear. His other attorney . . . spoke into the left ear. Before anything else could happen, Judge Thomas M. Cecil—noticeably jarred—said

"Let's take a break and go off the record." He quickly left the bench, and proceedings were adjourned for the day. Neither Cecil, Deputy District Attorney John O'Mara nor the defense attorneys would comment on Leonard's unsolicited remark.

In this remarkable scenario, lawyers and a judge did not treat a serial killer's voluntary courtroom confession as a welcome discovery of the truth or of the defendant's capacity for remorse. They treated it as a disturbing interruption. Their response shows how deeply the American legal profession is wedded to the ideology of adversarial legalism.

From one perspective, the Sacramento defense attorneys were simply responding rationally to the incentives created by the institutions of American adversarial legalism. This was, after all, a prosecution for several murders. In California, as in many other American states, the defendant's life was at stake. If a defendant is going to confess, the lawyers take it as their obligation to see that the confession is withheld until it can be traded for a plea bargain ensuring that the penalty will be imprisonment, not execution. Until then, their job, as they see it, is to use adversarial techniques—such as ensuring the defendant's silence, making motions to exclude evidence, trying to obtain the most favorable jury they can, arguing that the trial should be moved to a distant county—in order to increase the prosecution's costs and increase its willingness to agree to a plea bargain.

I suspect, however, that the defense lawyers' desperate efforts to stop their murderous but perhaps now contrite client from saying more was dictated not so much by instrumental calculations but by a professionally inculcated adversarial instinct. Put another way, the defense lawyers' adversarial stance was rooted in the ethos of American legal culture. American lawyers—unlike British barristers and European lawyers—are trained to believe that their primary responsibility is not to uncover the truth and produce the correct legal disposition but to get the best possible result for their clients.

Consider too the *judge*'s behavior in the Sacramento hearing. Why did he not immediately follow up on the defendant's statement? Was he not interested in determining the truth? Underlying his passivity too, I suspect, is a set of beliefs shaped by adversarial legalism: the lawyers for both sides, not the judges, are responsible for bringing out the relevant evidence. It also is risky for a judge to depart from the adversarial script, for an appellate court might find that he has transgressed the defendant's constitutional rights. Finally, in the system's list of goals, following the adversarial procedures properly ranks somewhat higher, it seems, than determining the truth. The power of this ethic is underscored by the *prosecutor*'s failure to follow up on the defendant's confession.[38]

Significantly curtailing adversarial legalism in the criminal justice systems of the United States, therefore, would conflict with the ethos of the legal profession and the American judiciary. Both could be counted on to fight like wildcats against significant changes in basic legal rules and the structure of legal institutions. And given the structure of American government, that makes sense. Adversarial legalism has been the American substitute for hierarchical methods of guaranteeing the rule of law. In a politically fragmented system, lacking systematic ways of funding and imposing uniformly high levels of professionalism on local police and prosecutors and judiciaries, adversarial legalism has indeed provided valuable legal weapons for combating blatantly unjust laws and law enforcement processes.

But adversarial legalism is far less effective for achieving equal justice in everyday criminal legal processes. It is too costly, cumbersome, and complicated for everyone to wield it equally. It undermines, rather than promotes, the assumption (or ideal) that decisions in criminal cases should be based on law, accurately applied to the facts of each case by prosecutors, judges, and juries (Johnson, 1998). In that sense, adversarial legalism tends to erode the legitimacy of the criminal justice system.

PART III

CIVIL JUSTICE

CHAPTER SIX

Adversarial Legalism and Civil Justice

A nthropologists tell us that before systems of criminal justice, before police departments and jails, human societies established systems of *civil* justice. Victims of theft, violence, and betrayal could assert their claims before headmen, chiefs, or elders; persons charged with those acts could offer denials, excuses, and counterclaims; the authorities adjudicated and imposed penalties, typically involving restitution or other compensatory payments (Schwartz and Miller, 1964; Hoebel, 1964). Contemporary governments too, as part of the implicit bargain on which their claim to legitimacy rests, establish courts to decide disputes over property, allocate responsibility for injuries, and compel the payment of debts. Criminal law, by and large, is used only for offenders who cannot afford to pay restitution (hence most often against poor offenders), for certain offenses that are deemed politically dangerous, and for those serious offenses for which compensation is deemed morally inadequate.

In modern pluralistic societies, however, the civil law is complex. Jurisdictional rules and formal requirements are daunting and confusing. Litigants need lawyers, and lawyers are expensive. Courts often are underfunded and overburdened; justice is delayed and hence denied. The true facts of a dispute often are hard to determine. Established legal rules may not quite fit the protean variety of particular situations. Dealing with these problems—accessibility, affordability, delay, effective fact-finding, adaptability—is the day-to-day challenge faced by every contemporary civil justice system. The United States, however, struggles with those challenges in distinctive ways.

Compared to other economically advanced democracies, the American system of civil justice, like its system of criminal justice, adheres more closely to an organizationally fragmented coordinate model (Damaska, 1975) than to a governmentally guided hierarchical model. The American system is shaped not by a national ministry of justice but by state legislatures; by politically selected federal and state judiciaries; and by an exceptionally large, entrepreneurial, and politically assertive legal profession. The United States more often relies on privately initiated civil litigation and judges to resolve commercial disputes, implement public policy, and enforce regulatory statutes and civil rights laws. Hence an unusually large range of problems can be taken to court in the United States. Finally, civil litigation and adjudication systems in the United States are structured not via a hierarchical, judge-dominated process but by adversarial legalism—lawyer-and-party-dominated litigation, with the added complication of trial by jury.

A civil justice structured by adversarial legalism, however, is characterized by costliness, cumbersomeness, and legal uncertainty. As a result, ordinary citizens with legal grievances often are deterred from hiring attorneys and venturing into court at all. If they do, full-scale adversarial trials are statistically rare. Plaintiffs usually feel compelled to settle before trial, and often to abandon or severely compromise just legal claims. For the same reason, defendants—even prosperous individuals and business corporations—often feel compelled to surrender or severely compromise legally meritorious defenses.

Overall, however, a civil justice system structured by adversarial legalism increases the advantages that "repeat-player" business litigants have over "one-shotter" individual plaintiffs, both in litigation and in prelitigation and pretrial negotiations (Galanter, 1974). Most individual claimants' hopes for civil justice hinge on the variable responsiveness of private mediation and arbitration forums or on the informal complaint systems operated by large business enterprises. This chapter discusses American civil litigation in general. Chapter 7 explores in more detail the realm of tort law, the most politically controversial form of civil justice in the United States.

The Two Faces of Adversarial Legalism in Action

This distinctively American system of civil justice, John C. Coffee Jr. (2015, 9) points out, has roots "that are closely entangled with core American political ideals." In the early nineteenth century, civil litigation, as implemented through lawyers, juries, and popularly elected judges, "represented democracy in action" (11) and was seen as a bulwark of "the rights of the common man"(11).[1] By the end of the nineteenth century, Coffee continues, the American civil justice system had acquired two additional distinctive features: (a) the contingent fee (whereby plaintiffs' lawyers often can be paid via a share of any monetary legal recovery) "as a necessary means by which the common citizen could finance and afford litigation"(13); and (b) the "American rule" whereby each party pays his own lawyer (13–14)—as contrasted with the loser pays rule that prevailed in England and Europe. The American rule removed the plaintiff's concern that an unsuccessful suit against a large company would saddle him or her with the defendant's lawyers' fees. In the second half of the twentieth century another distinctive feature was added: entrepreneurial plaintiffs' lawyers were authorized to pursue class actions on behalf a large numbers of individuals, greatly multiplying the potential monetary recovery, their own contingent fees, and the monetary threat that civil litigation poses to potential defendants. In addition, by placing pretrial discovery powers in the hands of competing parties' lawyers, adversarial legalism provides more probing forms of fact-finding than do other civil justice systems.

This potent and positive face of adversarial legalism is illustrated by a lower court case named *Gilmore v. Columbia Falls Aluminum Company*. In 1985, according to a lengthy *New York Times* article by Jim Robbins (1998), Columbia Falls Aluminum Company, located in northwestern Montana, had become a perennial money loser. Its corporate owner, Atlantic Richfield Company (ARCO), sold the company to Brack Duker and Jerome Broussard for $1, plus $3 million for unsold inventory. As part of the deal, the parties agreed that Columbia Falls workers would be entitled to at least 50 percent of any future annual profit, an agreement referred to in a letter from ARCO to Duker. After taking over Columbia Falls Aluminum, Duker and Broussard embarked on a major cost-cutting program, persuading hundreds of workers to accept a 15 percent pay cut in return for the promise of a 50 percent share of future profits. Faced with the alternative—shutting down the plant—the workers consented. Beginning in 1986, Columbia Falls Aluminum started making money. The new owners split the $2.6 million in profits for that year with Columbia Falls employees. Robbins goes on (1, 11):

> But over the next five years, rather than splitting the take, [Duker and Broussard] funneled much of the money into offshore bank accounts. Before they cut off their union and salaried employees altogether, the two men had awarded $84 million to them and $231 million to themselves. . . .
>
> In 1989, Mr. Duker and Mr. Broussard dismissed their chief financial officer after he raised concerns about their financial practices. . . . [Later] a 39-year-old accountant at the plant named Roberta Gilmore challenged the company's bookkeeping practices and was promptly told, she says, to keep her mouth shut.
>
> Instead, after fuming for a couple of years, she filed a [class action] lawsuit. . . . At one point, the two small-town lawyers she hired showed up in Federal Court in Missoula, Mont., wearing polar fleece jackets and Sorel boots. They were greeted by Mr. Duker—flanked by three bodyguards and 13 lawyers in finely tailored suits.

Clearly, Mr. Duker had the upper hand in any [legal] war of attrition. And yet, five years and 10 months after the suit was filed [after pretrial discovery and other investigation by the plaintiff's lawyers unearthed the diversion of funds noted above and a letter from ARCO memorializing the profit-sharing requirement] he threw in the towel. Just two weeks before Ms. Gilmore's lawsuit was scheduled for trial, he agreed to pay the [approximately 1,000] workers $97 million. . . . When she heard the news, Ms. Gilmore broke into sobs.

Gilmore's lawyers—who at one point had to take out an $800,000 bank loan to pay their expenses—were to receive $6 million of the $32 million settlement for salaried employees. Labor union lawyers were to receive 10 percent of the $65 million settlement for hourly employees. Later, Duker's lawyer sued him, claiming that Duker had refused to pay a promised bonus of $3 million for holding the final settlement to $100 million or less (Robbins, 1998: 11).[2]

Gilmore v. Columbia Falls Aluminum Company exemplifies the strengths of American adversarial legalism. By validating class actions, which offer plaintiffs' attorneys the prospect of very large fees, the American civil justice system taps the energy of entrepreneurial lawyers like Ms. Gilmore's. And that enables legally inexperienced citizens such as the Columbia Falls employees to pursue legal claims against economically powerful repeat players. By authorizing wide-ranging, lawyer-guided pretrial discovery, adversarial legalism enabled plaintiffs' lawyers to uncover even carefully concealed evidence of malfeasance. Gilmore and her lawyers also gained courage from the American rule concerning attorneys' fees and court costs; even if they had lost, they would not be responsible for Mr. Duker's massive lawyers' bills. In giving ordinary people these extraordinary legal weapons, American adversarial legalism contrasts with civil justice systems that are cheaper and more expeditious but less creative and less threatening to potential and actual defendants. Doris Marie Provine (1996: 239) writes:

France has taken considerable pains to keep the fees for civil litigation at a reasonable level. A 1991 law, for example, makes civil litigation free to those who cannot afford it. The system encourages laypersons to represent themselves and a significant minority do, especially before administrative tribunals. Even when people do hire lawyers, self-imposed and court-imposed restrictions on the scope of their activities tend to keep the fees much lower than in the United States. What the system does *not* provide, however, is a check on the excesses of powerful institutions. The problem, as Cappelletti and Garth observe, is that "a right of individual access, however liberally granted, does not necessarily lead to the vindication of new rights on a very large scale."

In the United States, conversely, the combination of contingency fees, class actions, and probing pretrial discovery *has* made civil litigation a potent mechanism for individuals and for social activists to seek in court the vindication of new rights on a large scale. Concomitantly, the politically selected American judiciary, schooled in flexible common law reasoning, often has responded by articulating new, politically liberal interpretations of contract law, civil rights laws, consumer protection law, securities law, and personal injury law. That judicial creativity encourages both social activists and entrepreneurial lawyers to file civil lawsuits proposing extensions of existing legal rights. Thus more than in other countries, the American civil litigation system has become a prominent component of the modern activist state (Marcus, 2014), a mechanism for implementing the ideals of what Nonet and Selznick (1978) labeled policy-oriented "responsive law."

Consider, however, a less attractive face of adversarial legalism, exemplified by a lower court case called *Johnson v. Johnson*. In 1983 Seward Johnson, heir to the Johnson & Johnson health care products fortune, died at the age of eighty-seven. Johnson's will, drafted in the last months of his life, left the bulk of his $400 million estate to his third wife, Basia. In 1968 Basia, a recent immigrant from Poland, had come to the Johnson home as a kitchen employee; three years later she married Johnson, forty years her senior. Johnson's will left nothing to his six children, from whom he had long been estranged (apparently for good reason); years earlier, however, he had given each child a trust containing tens of millions of dollars' worth of Johnson & Johnson stock (Margolick, 1993).

Seward Johnson's children challenged the validity of his will in the New York Surrogate's Court. They claimed that Basia—who had become increasingly imperious as Seward declined—used undue influence in getting Johnson to change the will in her favor. Their case, according to David Margolick's detailed account, was legally (as well as morally) weak: in a sequence of earlier wills, Johnson had consistently left nothing to his dissolute children on grounds that their trust funds were enough, and he had made successively more generous bequests to Basia (Margolick, 1993: 198, 268). But Johnson's children employed smart, aggressive lawyers from a big New York City firm. They conducted marathon pretrial depositions of Basia, the Johnson children, and Seward Johnson's lawyer (Goldsmith, 1987). They concocted enough of an argument, in the judge's view, to get a jury trial. Before and during the over-three-month trial, the presiding judge displayed "astonishing partiality" toward the claimants, according to law professor John Langbein (1994: 2041). Before the trial ended, Basia agreed to a settlement that gave about $40 million of the estate to the Johnson children and paid their legal fees. The legal fees for both sides amounted, amazingly, to $25 million (Goldsmith, 1987)—enough to pay a year's salary for at least 300 police officers, nurses, or schoolteachers.

Reviewing Margolick's account of the Johnson litigation, Langbein (1994: 2043) points out that litigation based on claims of undue influence or unsound mind, "which occupy so prominent a place in American probate law, are virtually unknown both on the Continent and in English and Commonwealth legal systems."[3] "Anywhere else in the Western world," Langbein continues (2045), "the Johnson children's lawsuit would have been suppressed in short order. In the United States, it became a license to exploit the shortcomings of the procedural system. Skilled plaintiffs' lawyers extorted a multimillion-dollar payoff for themselves and their unworthy clients." The Johnson will litigation, with its huge stakes, is far from a typical case. But its costliness, legal unpredictability, and arbitrary outcome, Langbein suggests, are the legacies of two distinctive features of the American system of civil justice—features that structure ordinary cases as well: (1) a lawyer-dominated, adversarial, and potentially manipulative system of evidence-gathering and presentation; and (2) trial by jury and by politically selected, highly autonomous judges.

Johnson v. Johnson does hint at some positive features of American adversarial legalism as well. In some European civil law systems courts are reluctant to look behind the words of a formal legal document (Hazard and Taruffo, 1993). Adversarial legalism, with its potent weapons of pretrial discovery wielded by private attorneys, gives litigants more opportunity to uncover the human truths that lie behind the documentary curtain. It is not difficult to find cases in American law reports in which courts thwarted a fortune hunter who really did subvert an ailing testator's mind, hoping to cheat deserving children of their birthright.[4] American judges, less carefully socialized to the bench and less closely supervised than their counterparts in many other countries, may be less predictable, but they also tend to be more flexible and more oriented to practical problem-solving.

Johnson v. Johnson reminds us, however, that adversarial legalism can be used by the unscrupulous, as well as against them, and that a politically selected judiciary, trial by jury, entrepreneurial lawyering, and aggressive pretrial discovery also have some disturbing side-effects. Viewed in comparative terms, seriously-contested civil litigation in the United States is extraordinarily costly to the parties, and it entails more legal unpredictability. Costliness and legal uncertainty often result in injustice, as parties (like Basia Johnson) feel compelled to abandon legally justified positions in order to avoid the costs and risks of adjudication. Another result is inequality: in the United States, parties who can better withstand the costs and risks of litigation and can obtain better lawyering enjoy a greater advantage over parties who cannot.

Adversarial legalism's costliness, unpredictability, and risks of injustice and inequality disturb even those who are sometimes in a position to benefit from them. In 1994 John Lande surveyed 143 American business executives, corporate inside counsel, and outside counsel. Asked to assess how the court system has been working on a five-point scale, half the executives and one-third of outside counsel said "poorly." A majority expressed severe doubts about its capacity to determine the truth correctly (Lande, 1998). Not surprisingly, therefore, business firms (*and* individuals) usually negotiate settlements before trial—typically as strongly advised by their lawyers and by judges.

Consequently, putting aside small claims courts (which are limited to very small amounts in dispute), in most populous jurisdictions the percentage of civil cases resolved by trial (as opposed to settlement, withdrawal, or early judicial dismissal) has fallen well below 5 percent (Galanter and Frozena, 2014).[5] Put otherwise, only a very small percentage of American litigants actually get their day in court and have their cases decided by the application of law to the facts as found by a judge or jury. As powerfully summarized by Marc Galanter and Angela Frozena:

> With ever more elaborate rules and procedures, [judges] preside over a movement toward trial that provides the frame for bargaining or summary disposition. Even if it doesn't occur frequently, the trial is a ghostly presence. It is present not as the culmination of the proceedings but as a doomsday machine—a demanding and risky thing, unwelcome to all the players (including the judge), that will occur if the matter is not resolved by settlement or dismissal. (Galanter and Frozena 2014: 126)

What makes American trial such a frightening "doomsday machine?" How does its "ghostly presence" influence the fate of litigants in the *pretrial* process, during which most cases are settled or abandoned, and the nature of civil justice as a whole? Comparisons with civil case adjudication in some other countries will help explain the distinctive qualities and consequences of the American civil justice litigation system mentioned above: costliness, unpredictability, injustice, and inequality.

Adversarial Legalism and the Cost of Civil Litigation

If one were starting from scratch, it would be difficult to imagine, much less design, a mode of adjudication that, as in *Johnson v. Johnson,* would spend $25 million on lawyers to resolve a single dispute. The absolute size of the legal fees in the Johnson conflict was very unusual, to be sure, but the fact that the legal transaction costs incurred by the parties were more than half of the amount actually paid to the claimant was not. In the average American product liability lawsuit, lawyers' fees for both sides, added together, are larger than the amount received by the plaintiff. Even in routine auto accident lawsuits, payments to lawyers account for more than 40 percent of total liability insurance payouts (Hensler et al., 1987: 27–28). In the 1970s, the Wisconsin Civil Litigation Project constructed a systematic sample of 1,649 lawsuits that had been filed in federal and state courts. The researchers found that in cases in which the plaintiffs' recoveries were less than $10,000, the median plaintiff's legal costs amounted to about 35 percent of the recovery when the lawyer took the case on a contingent fee basis—and 46 percent when the lawyer was paid on an hourly basis (Trubek et al., 1983: 111). Defendants' legal fees generally were almost as large. Hence total transaction costs for both sides amounted to well over 50 percent of the total settlement.

One 1988 study indicated that when employers were sued in wrongful discharge cases, their legal defense costs alone averaged over $80,000 (Dertouzos, Holland, and Ebener, 1988); in a later study, those costs averaged $124,000 (Maltby, 1994: 107). The American Intellectual Property Law Association estimated in 1994 that in patent infringement cases the median litigation cost for each side was $280,000 through pretrial discovery and $518,000 through trial (Gerlin, 1994a: B1). According to a 1993 survey, in defending stockholders' fraud claims against their officers and directors, corporations paid law firms an average of $967,000 per case; this average included the less expensive cases that the responding companies won without paying a settlement (Lambert, 1995: B6). Why does American adversarial legalism generate such enormous legal bills? Some cross-national comparisons will provide a large part of the answer.

Lawyer-Dominated versus Judge-Dominated Litigation. In 1987, as part of a research project, I interviewed Dutch representatives of cross-Atlantic shipping lines and marine insurance companies. I asked them if the legal resolution of disputed cargo damage claims differs when the cargo damage is discovered in Rotterdam, and hence is subject to Dutch courts rather than in New York. "Oh yes," I was invariably told. "You have to pay a great deal more in lawyers' bills if the cargo is in the United States." This was not merely because American lawyers charged higher hourly rates. It was primarily because they put in far more time—and hence more billable hours—on each case.

American lawyers do more because American judges do less. In civil cases filed in Rotterdam or in other continental European cities, the *judge* is primarily responsible for interrogating parties and witnesses, selecting expert witnesses, demanding production of relevant documents, identifying the relevant law, and summarizing the evidence. In American litigation those burdens are shouldered by opposing counsel. In continental Europe, legal advocates for the contending parties play only a supporting role, identifying witnesses to be interrogated by the judge and suggesting avenues of inquiry or legal analysis the judge may have omitted (Langbein, 1985). Thus in comparative perspective continental European legal systems are "judge-heavy," while the American system is "lawyer-heavy" (846). A 1973 study indicated that California had about 18 practicing lawyers for each judge, compared to 8 in Italy, 3 in France, 2.5 in Germany, and 2 in Sweden (Council on California Competitiveness, 1992: 88).[6] The Swedish and West German governments spent more on courts, prosecutors, and legal-aid lawyers than their citizens spent on private legal services. In contrast, "public sector expenditures in the United States were about one-fourth to one-fifth of private expenditures" (Johnson and Drew, 1978: 10, 55).

Although there are no systematic comparative data, the European practice of allocating many costs of litigation to judges almost certainly results in a much less costly civil adjudication system not only for disputing parties but for society at large (Brookings Institution, 1989: 6). Richard Hulbert (1997: 747), who has practiced law both in the United States and in Paris, writes that when viewed from an American perspective, the French system of civil justice "is cheap. It is quick. It produces judgments that overall seem to be satisfying." In a widely cited article, John Langbein (1985) argued that compared to civil justice in the United States, Germany's adjudicatory system is both cheaper and quicker, mainly because its fact-gathering process is far more efficient. "Probably no unbiased observer would disagree," says Herbert Bernstein (1988: 594), holder of law degrees from both countries. That conclusion is bolstered by considering some additional differences between European and American methods of civil litigation.

Redundancy. In strongly contested, higher-stakes cases in the United States, separate lawyers for all parties participate in lengthy pretrial depositions during which parties and witnesses are first questioned by one lawyer, then often cross-examined by another. If the case goes to trial, the lawyers, parties, and witnesses repeat virtually the same interrogation in open court. In high-stakes cases, lawyers often meet with their parties and witnesses both before depositions and before trial for another run-through—a rehearsal of the anticipated interrogation (Reitz, 1990: 989). German civil litigation is remarkably different. Langbein (1985: 826) notes that "there is no distinction between pretrial and trial. . . . Trial is not a single continuous event. Rather, the court gathers and evaluates evidence over a series of hearings, as many as the circumstances require." The lawyers for each side nominate the witnesses they wish the judge to question (Bernstein, 1988: 592–593). Hence in contrast to American litigation, German parties and witnesses testify just once, when interrogated by a judge (Reitz, 1990: 989). Because witnesses are not coached in advance by lawyers and it is the judge's responsibility to assess the evidence, there is far less emphasis than in the United States on adversarial challenge—and hence less necessity to have lawyers for both sides present (and paid for) each time a piece of evidence is examined by or presented to the judge (Damaska, 1997a: 846).

All-at-Once versus Episodic Trials. American pretrial discovery is complex and costly, Langbein observes (1985: 831), partly because the sharp division between pretrial and trial encourages American lawyers to "investigate everything that could possibly come up at trial." That is because once trial begins—with the parties, their lawyers, and witnesses all assembled in the court house at a long-scheduled date—the trial cannot be suspended for more than a day, so lawyers "can seldom go back and search for further evidence" (831). In contrast, the episodic character of German fact-gathering, unfettered by the need to accommodate the jury, means that "if the case takes an unexpected turn, the disadvantaged litigant can count on developing his response in another hearing at a later time" (831).

Dueling Expert Witnesses. In complex cases in which expert technical assessments are required, contending American litigants each hire and carefully coach their own expert witness. In a more hierarchical system such as Germany's, the court appoints a single neutral expert witness, who is not coached in advance by anyone (Langbein, 1985: 835–840).[7] A corporate counsel experienced in intellectual property disputes writes that "European litigation . . . also involves the use of experts. But in the United States there are experts, and . . . experts, and still more experts" (Pantuliano, 1993, 308; see also Somaya, 2000). Thus, according to patent attorney James Maxeiner (1991: 601, 604), "expert testimony in U.S. patent litigation is much more costly than in Germany." In French courts, practicing attorney Richard Hulbert (1997: 749) tells us, the judge appoints an expert for "controverted issues of fact, particularly facts of a technical nature." Then:

> The appointee will conduct an investigation outside the courtroom, under no formal rules of evidence or relevance, at sessions to which the parties are convoked with full freedom to present their views and those of their experts or other representatives, orally or in writing. The results of the *expertise* is a report that in principle the judge need not accept, but in the absence of other evidence, it is difficult to see how it could be rejected, provided that the judge is satisfied that the *expert* [whose investigative and reporting procedures are regulated by law] has done what he was commissioned to do and that no material procedural irregularities have been committed.

Trial by Jury. European courts (including in the United Kingdom, which has abandoned the jury in most civil cases) avoid the extraordinary inefficiencies of the American civil jury trial, which include lengthy, adversarial jury selection (National Center for State Courts, 1988: 110; Kakalik et al.,

1990) and legalistic wrangling over what evidence and arguments must be suppressed because they might mislead amateur decision makers. Civil trials in the United States that are conducted by a judge alone tend to be at least 50 percent shorter than jury trials.[8] And because American jurors, in contrast to judges in Europe, are not given written summaries of the issues and evidence in advance, the whole story of the dispute must be presented to them orally. Each witness is questioned first by one set of lawyers, then cross-examined by another. Unlike a European judge, American jurors cannot comment during trial or indicate that they are satisfied on a certain point. Hence lawyers, uncertain which issues will be regarded as crucial, must cover all issues and, playing it safe, often call extra witnesses to testify (Reitz, 1990: 989; Langbein, 1985: 830). Consequently, according to studies in the 1980s, the average urban jury trial in the United States—in all likelihood a fairly routine motor vehicle accident or other personal injury case—took about 13.5 hours, spread over several days (National Center for State Courts, 1988). (The median for contract and nontort cases was about 14.5 hours.) In 1984 half of all jury trials in Los Angeles and Oakland, California, lasted more than thirty hours, spread over seven days (Kakalik et al., 1990: 110).[9] That is one reason that in many large cities a quarter or even half the citizens summoned for jury duty fail to appear.[10]

Pretrial Discovery. As the *Columbia Falls Aluminum* case teaches, adversarial pretrial discovery is a powerful tool for unmasking phony defenses and for undermining spurious claims. Information gathered in pretrial discovery very often becomes the basis for a settlement. Nevertheless, even when it works well, the adversarial American pretrial discovery and negotiation process is costly and slow. In lower-stakes cases, therefore, lawyers make minimal use of pretrial discovery. With respect to more intensely-contested cases, Second Circuit Court of Appeals judge Ralph K. Winter (1992: 264), a member of the federal courts' Advisory Committee on Civil Rules, lamented: "In private conversations with lawyers and judges, I find precious few ready to argue that pretrial discovery involves less than considerable to enormous waste. . . . [The Advisory Committee found] a no-stone-left-unturned . . . philosophy of discovery governs much litigation and imposes costs, usually without corresponding benefits. . . . Second, discovery is sometimes used as a club against the other party . . . solely to increase the adversary's expenses." This can compel a less-wealthy plaintiff to surrender, settling on disadvantageous terms.

Delay. Besides adversarial legalism's direct costs, American litigants inclined to insist on a jury trial must endure extraordinary delays. According to Albert Alschuler (1990: 6), "the average civil case tried during 1988 in the Circuit Court of Cook County [Chicago] had been filed more than six years before." In Los Angeles the median time between filing and trial of a civil action, only 4.2 months in 1942, grew to 19 months in 1962, and 41.5 months (almost three and a half years) in 1982 (Selvin and Ebener, 1984: 27). More typically, in a 1987 study of thirty-seven urban jurisdictions, the median time from filing to jury trial was slightly more than two years, although in Detroit, it was more than three years, and in Providence, Rhode Island, almost five (Goerdt, 1991: 296; Ostrom et al., 1996: 24).[11] In a *well-funded* civil law court system, exemplified by Germany's, half of civil court plaintiffs have a decision within six months, three-quarters within nine months, and summary proceedings are even faster (Blankenburg, 1994: 806).

The much longer waits for adjudication in the American civil justice system stem partly from the complexities of merely scheduling a jury trial—an all-at-once performance at which all parties, lawyers, witnesses, and the judge, with all their varied schedules, must be on hand at the opening curtain, on a day when an empty courtroom is available. Multiple postponements are not uncommon. Lengthy pretrial discovery processes, with their own scheduling issues, also contribute. So do lengthy jury selection processes, complicated by legal requirements designed to produce juries that satisfy conflicting ideals: the jurors must be competent, *and* representative of all segments of the community, *and* unbiased (Hale, 2016: 193). Delay is also closely associated with Gillian Hadfield's conclusion, based on a variety of measures, that "American courts are woefully underfunded and understaffed" (Hadfield, 2014: 84) For example, Hadfield found that "whereas the United Kingdom has 126 judges per 100,000 cases; France, 205; and Germany, 283, the U.S. system struggles through with just 65" (84).

Legal Complexity. The decline of adjudication in the United States, Sam Gross and Kent Syverud (1996: 62) argue, also has been propelled by the interaction between judicial underfunding and legal complexity. The American political and legal system, they note, has been more intent on elaborating the tools of adversarial legalism than on investing in the courts (or in inexpensive, more expeditious methods of civil dispute resolution):

> The essence of adversarial litigation is procedure. . . . When we want to improve our judicial system we pass a procedural reform, which invariably means elaborating old procedural rules or adding new ones—rules that govern the presentation of evidence and arguments, rules that create opportunities to investigate and prepare evidence and argument. . . . The upshot is a masterpiece of detail, with rules on everything from special appearances to contest the jurisdiction of the court, to the use of exhibits during jury deliberation. But we cannot afford it. As litigants, few of us can pay the costs of a trial; as a society, we are unwilling to pay even a fraction of the cost of

the judicial apparatus that we would need to try most civil cases. We have designed a spectacular system for adjudicating disputes, but it is too expensive to use.

Adversarial Legalism and Legal Unpredictability

In all modern legal systems, most civil cases are settled before trial, as the litigants, advised by their lawyers, come to recognize what their chances would be in court. The cases that go to adjudication usually are those in which the basic facts are strongly contested and litigants can't agree on the likely outcome. Hence in all countries the cases that reach adjudication involve a substantial dose of uncertainty. Yet it appears that in the civil justice systems of the United States, legal unpredictability is greater than in many other economically advanced democracies. Here is a dramatic example:

On January 4, 1984, Getty Oil and Pennzoil Corporation, a Houston-based company, announced Pennzoil's purchase of three-sevenths of Getty's stock for $112.50 per share. The press release described the proposed sale as an "agreement in principle" that was "subject to [the] execution of a definitive merger agreement" (Petzinger, 1987: 198; Mnookin and Wilson, 1989: 301). Pennzoil, however, apparently refused to withdraw its *original* tender offer of $100 per share until a final agreement was signed, sealed, and delivered (Baron and Baron, 1986: 256). Meanwhile, Getty Oil's bitterly divided board of directors continued to seek out a "white knight" who would not only increase the purchase price but would also support current management in its battle with minority shareholders. Then Texaco, after being assured by leading corporate takeover professionals that Getty Oil remained "free to deal," offered to buy all of Getty Oil's outstanding stock for $125 per share. Texaco's offer was formally accepted by the relevant parties on January 7, 1984.

Pennzoil sued Getty Oil for breach of contract in Delaware, but the judge declined to block the sale to Texaco. Pennzoil then filed a new lawsuit against New York-based Texaco in Houston, seeking a staggering $14 billion in compensation. Legal analysts agreed, based on an independent analysis of the court file, that (1) no contract existed between Pennzoil and Getty under the law of New York, where the Texaco-Getty deal was negotiated; (2) even if Texaco were liable, under either New York or Texas law, Pennzoil's damages should not have exceeded $422 million (Baron and Baron, 1986: 269, 279). Nevertheless, a Houston jury awarded Pennzoil $7.5 billion in actual damages and $3 billion in punitive damages. A Texas appeals court reduced the punitive damages to $1 billion. Even Texaco, however, couldn't write an $8.5 billion check. It filed for bankruptcy—which was temporary but resulted in a fire sale of $5.1 billion in assets, deeply strained business relationships, and the near collapse of a company that employed thousands of workers (Brown, 1988: H1, H7).

How could a sophisticated company such as Texaco, with its cadre of experienced attorneys and investment bankers, fail by such a wide margin to discern the legal risks to which it was exposed? The answer is that in the decentralized American legal system, constantly being shaped and re-shaped by adversarial argument, the ostensibly solid legal path mapped by one's sophisticated lawyer can suddenly turn to quicksand. This is not an endemic feature of all legal regimes. When asked about transatlantic cargo damage disputes that *reach adjudication*, the shipping line and insurance firm representatives whom I interviewed all asserted that results in the courts in Rotterdam are far more *predictable* than in similar cases litigated in the United States. Patent attorney Michael Pantuliano (1993, 307) writes, "I believe most U.S. house counsel . . . would approach the prospect of European patent litigation with less trepidation than they would approach U.S. patent litigation," largely because European adjudication entails lower "downside risk."

After analyzing the record in the Johnson estate case, Professor Lang-bein, along with David Margolick, the experienced legal correspondent who chronicled the litigation, felt certain that the Johnson children's case lacked legal merit (Margolick, 1993: 198, 268). But the lawyers representing the Johnson estate apparently were not sure that the court would recognize the legal merits of their defense, so Johnson's widow Basia acceded to the children's legal gamble, buying them off with a $40 million settlement. Langbein traces the source of this legal uncertainty (and the defendant's consequent vulnerability to extortionate demands) to two factors: (1) the less-thoroughly professional, more political character of the American judiciary, and (2) the almost unique American insistence on using untrained citizen-jurors to resolve civil cases.

Professional versus Political Judiciaries. German courts have a specialized chamber that deals with commercial disputes and another that deals with patent disputes, along with specialized labor courts and specialized tribunals that deal with disputes concerning social benefits.[12] In the Netherlands cargo damage disputes are channeled into a chamber of the court system staffed by judges who specialize in maritime cases. The United States has specialized federal courts for bankruptcy and for patent appeals, but most litigation comes before generalist judges. The U.S. District Court judge who hears a cargo damage dispute or a patent infringement case may not have dealt with such cases recently—and perhaps never.[13] She relies on the litigants' attorneys to point out the relevant statutes, precedents, facts, and arguments. Supported by a pragmatic, results-oriented legal culture, the generalist American judge is more likely to rely on her own judgment to reach a result that she thinks is just (Atiyah and Summers, 1987). The corollary of that responsiveness to individual contexts, however, is a higher probability that different judges will make different assessments of what is substantively just, which reduces legal predictability.

In the Netherlands (and in other hierarchically organized European legal systems) judges are recruited, socialized, and supervised in a manner explicitly designed to maximize adjudicative predictability. After a closely supervised apprenticeship, open only to law graduates who have done very well on a nationwide exam,[14] a young judge's progress to more responsible and prestigious posts depends on merit ratings she receives from senior judges in the chambers through which she rotates, as well as on periodic evaluations by the ministry of justice (Meador, 1983: 22–23).[15] The goal of this bureaucratically organized career-management system is to homogenize the judiciary, to make its decisions legally competent, uniform, and predictable.

The American judiciary is professional too, in its own way. All judges have had legal training. They often reaffirm that their obligation as judges is to apply the law uniformly to all, regardless of their own beliefs. They are legally constrained by the possibility of appeal and reversal by higher court judges and also by the risk of open criticism by lawyers and judicial colleagues for unjustifiably violating the conventions of legal reasoning (Cross and Tiller, 1998). Millions of potential disputes are resolved, therefore, when American lawyers tell their clients, with a high degree of conviction, that they will lose if they go to court. Thus the American legal system is far from wholly unpredictable. But its residual level of unpredictability–which is of course difficult to measure–is probably greater than in economically advanced democracies whose judiciaries are selected in a professionally controlled, nonpolitical manner. American judges, unlike their counterparts in Western Europe or Japan, come to the bench after prior careers as practicing lawyers, prosecutors, or political activists.[16] Some have had little courtroom experience. In most American states, new judges get little formal training, and there is no systematic merit-oriented promotion system (Meador, 1983: 26). Compared to their European counterparts, American judges enjoy far more autonomy vis-à-vis their judicial superiors, both with respect to their career prospects and to their day-to-day legal decision-making; most of the countless procedural decisions that American judges make in the course of pretrial hearings and trials are de facto unreviewable.

There is a method to this ostensible madness. Free from the homogenizing influence of European-style legal bureaucracies, the American judiciary, precisely because it is politically responsive and less formalistic, is more pragmatic, more willing to adapt the law to changing circumstances and new justice claims. But there is a touch of madness to the method as well; its symptom is vulnerability to comparatively higher levels of legal unpredictability. Comparing trial judges in England with their politically selected counterparts in the United States, Atiyah and Summers (1987: 164) observe: "It cannot be doubted that in England the judge brings on average a higher level of competence to the entire trial process. The judge is invariably a former barrister of many years' experience and high standing at the bar. . . . In America . . . the situation is much more variable" (see also Hazard and Taruffo, 1993: 68). An observational study of small claims courts found that some American judges are narrowly legalistic, while others tend to act as mediators, and still others tend to decide cases according to their own notions of fairness and desert (Conley and O'Barr, 1987). Decisions by U.S. District Court judges appointed by Democratic presidents are demonstrably more liberal than those appointed by Republican presidents (Rowland and Carp, 1983), and similar findings recur for studies of other courts, both state and federal (Pinello, 1999; Cross and Tiller, 1998). American lawyers, as documented by Sarat and Felstiner's (1986) study of divorce lawyers, often tell their clients that the legal outcome will depend on which judge ends up hearing the case. Dutch divorce lawyers, according to a study by John Griffiths (1986), simply tell their clients what the law prescribes and hence what they can expect in court.

What's more, stories of seriously biased and incompetent American judges are far from rare (Brill, 1989). The Texas trial judge who instructed the jury in the Pennzoil-Texaco case acknowledged afterward that "there is a good chance that perhaps I read the cases wrong and not have applied [the law] correctly." In fact, he had adopted nearly verbatim the jury instructions proffered by Pennzoil's lawyers while ignoring Texaco's submissions (Petzinger, 1987: 463, 453). Similarly, day by day, the Johnson estate's lawyers saw what seemed to be an airtight case crumble as the trial judge, a politically active former personal injury lawyer, repeatedly acted in a biased and improper manner (Margolick, 1993: 301–313). "Americans can only look with envy," Langbein (1985: 2044) asserts, "to the esteemed and meritocratic chancery bench that conducts probate adjudication in English and Commonwealth jurisdictions." The American judiciary, far from homogenized, is not even reliably pasteurized, and it is not always the cream that rises to the top. In many states, lawyers with no prior experience as trial judges have been catapulted directly onto state supreme courts (Kagan, Detlefsen, and Infelise, 1984).

Juries. "American law is unique," says Langbein (1985: 2043), "in undertaking to resolve will contests by means of civil jury trial" in which skillful lawyers strive "to evoke the jurors' sympathy for disinherited offspring and to excite their likely hostility towards a devisee such as Basia, who can so easily be painted as a homewrecking adventurer." Ironically, some scholars suggest, Americans have preserved trial by jury because they fear the biases of a politically appointed judiciary (Schuck, 1993: 310). But juries bring to the courthouse their own form of legal unpredictability. The jury system entrusts judgment to an ever-changing cluster of individuals who are not told about the applicable rules of law until the trial is over, nor instructed how similar cases have been decided by other juries. Jurors are not expected to explain and justify their decisions. And because a jury's decision is not explained in writing (like that of a European trial court), it cannot be systematically compared with, and hence harmonized with, others.

That is not to say that juries usually or even frequently ignore the judge's legal instructions or often reach decisions on the basis of emotion rather than evidence. On average, research has found, jurors regard plaintiffs' claims for money damages with some skepticism (Hans and Lofquist, 1992). Marc Galanter (1993: 70) concludes: "The literature, on the whole, converges on the judgment that juries are fine decision makers. They are conscientious, collectively they understand and recall the evidence as well as judges, and they decide on the basis of the evidence presented."[17] When researchers presented similar tort cases to over 500 mock juries, they found that *individual jurors* drawn from different states, ethnic groups, income levels, and age groups tended to make remarkably similar average judgments about the defendant's moral culpability and about the severity of the harm (Schkade, Sunstein, and Kahneman, 2000: 1156). But that does not mean that the jury system yields a high level of legal predictability.

In the University of Chicago Jury Project in the 1950s, researchers asked judges who had presided over jury trials how they would have decided the case had it been a bench trial. The judge agreed with the jury's decision on liability in 79 percent of the cases (Kalven, 1964; Kalven and Zeisel, 1966: 56; Galanter, 1993).[18] That is only moderately encouraging. Legal uncertainty stems from two problems: first, one cannot tell in advance whether any particular jury (or judge) will be the one in five or so that decides idiosyncratically; and second, the idiosyncratic judgment is likely to go uncorrected. A Philadelphia judge, referring to two asbestos disease cases he had presided over, commented: "Two men had similar physical problems. They each had pleural thickening and some shortness of breath. In the case involving the man who counsel believed to be the sicker of the two, the jury awarded $15,000. For the other plaintiff, the jury awarded $1,200,000" (Hensler, 1985: 65).[19] To a legal scholar from another country, the striking point would be not only that the juries decided inconsistently, but that there was no systematic, reliable mechanism for reconciling their judgments.[20]

Peter Huber (1990) compared verdicts by different juries in a sequence of cases concerning claims of harm from Bendectin (a morning sickness drug), and in another sequence of cases involving an alleged defect in Audi motor cars, and sequences of cases involving several other allegedly dangerous products. Most juries, in accordance with the weight of the scientific evidence presented, found that the product in question was not defective or not responsible for the plaintiffs' injuries. But, as Huber noted, "Every new case has a new jury, and one jury's finding is not binding on the next's" (290). In each sequence of trials concerning a particular product, one or a few juries, hearing the same evidence as those that found no liability, decided otherwise and awarded the plaintiff massive compensatory and punitive damages. The modal jury award was nothing at all, but the average award was in the millions of dollars. For each manufacturer in question, the result was inescapable legal uncertainty and enormous litigation expenses (278; Sugarman, 1985b: 599–602; Bork, 1996: A15).

Examining the inconsistent outcomes in the Bendectin trials, Joseph Sanders (1993) locates the problem not in the jury per se but in the organization of adversarial, jury-focused trial system. Information on causation was provided by conflicting, lawyer-coached expert witnesses, presenting different kinds of scientific evidence, not back-to-back but at widely separated points in the trial. The lawyers' cross-examinations of the witnesses was designed more to generate contradictions and to obfuscate than to inform. The result, Sanders concludes, was a body of testimony that failed to enable the lay fact-finders to weigh properly the quality of experts or the scientific findings on Bendectin's effects.

Importantly, guessing what a jury will do is made even more difficult by the infrequency of jury decisions. Since only a tiny percentage of civil cases go to verdict, the jury system sends only weak and static-filled signals to the trial bar.[21] News media coverage of trial verdicts is selective, oversampling very large jury verdicts or cases in which juries find liability in unlikely situations (MacCoun, 1993; Aks et al., 2000). The result, as indicated by a number of studies summarized by Galanter (1993: 81–86), is that lawyers come up with widely divergent pretrial estimates of a case's likely outcome at trial. When Douglas Rosenthal (1974) asked five experienced New York trial lawyers to read the files and estimate the recovery value of fifty-nine recently settled cases, their predictions were far from accurate or consistent. The median recovery was about 75 percent of the experts' estimates, and 40 percent of recoveries were less than two-thirds of the experts' estimates. And in a study of 443 back and neck injury cases, Philip Hermann (1962) found that only one-sixth of the final demands and offers by plaintiffs and defendants came within 25 percent of the jury's actual verdict.

One might wonder if these and similar studies (Danzon, 1985: 50; Kritzer, 1990: 31; Clermont and Eisenberg, 1992: 1170–1172; Priest, 1993: 129) reflect the incompetence of the average lawyer rather than any defect in the jury system. But a legal system in which the average lawyer is very poor at predicting outcomes, for whatever reason, is by definition rather unpredictable. One might object too that these studies focus on personal injury cases, in which both the substantive law and the law of damages are unusually vague, and in which clever appeals to jury sympathy might (but might not) sway the verdict. But legal uncertainty, as indicated by *Johnson v. Johnson,* reigns in nonjury civil cases as well. An analysis of sample of a broad range of cases found substantial variation between attorneys' expectations and actual awards after trial by judges and juries (Osborne, 1999: 193).[22] Kent Syverud (1997: 1943) points to "the almost universal election of businesses and governments to opt out of fact finding by a civil jury when they are civil plaintiffs," because they perceive "that there is less predictability ... in fact finding by a civil jury than in dispute resolution by other methods."

Legal unpredictability also pervades American family law (Ellman, 1999), in which judges, not juries, decide alimony, child custody, and marital property distribution disputes. The authors of a study of divorce and custody litigation in Wisconsin note: "Several of the lawyers we interviewed report that they have difficulty in discerning court standards and that they cannot predict the outcomes of court processes. . . . Even the lawyers . . . who do think there are set standards and who do say they can predict outcomes differ in their opinion of the content of those court standards" (Erlanger, Chambliss, and Melli, 1987: 599).[23] In a survey of attorneys (Lande, 1998: 32), one respondent said:

> I started out as a plaintiffs' trial attorney with a strong belief in the jury system. . . . I don't believe that anymore. I think . . . it behooves you to do anything possible to avoid it. . . . You can go through all of the different systems, whether it be family law through divorce, products claims, malpractice claims, securities litigation, you know, virtually every category of major litigation. . . . Is it predictable, reliable in terms of a rule? Are the transaction costs reasonable in terms of a result? Does it provide guidance for the future? Not a single one of these systems would even get a passing grade.

Because of the costs and delays of trials, many busy court systems have encouraged "managerial judging," whereby judges pressure the parties' lawyers to settle cases before trial. But this adds another source of legal uncertainty, for judges differ in the intensity with which they apply pressures to settle and in their knowledge of the facts of the case (Frankel, 1975: 1042; Resnick, 1982; Yeazell, 1994; Molot, 1998: 992). In European civil justice systems, where judges dominate the fact-gathering processes, settlement negotiations occur under the nose of a third party who is deeply familiar with the case. In both kinds of legal systems, pretrial settlements occur in the shadow of the law. But the greater predictability of European adjudication means that the boundary of the shadow there is far clearer.

Injustice

By making litigation and adjudication slower, more costly, and less predictable than a civil justice system that more closely resembles bureaucratic legalism, adversarial legalism often transforms the American civil justice system into an engine of injustice in the sense that it induces litigants, both plaintiffs and defendants, to abandon just claims and defenses. Dixie Flag Manufacturing Company, a firm in San Antonio, Texas, with sixty-three employees, makes and sells American flags. In 1991 Dixie Flag was sued by a person who had seen some men lowering a large flag in a parking lot and then volunteered to help so that the flag would not touch the ground. As the volunteer grasped the flag, according to his subsequent legal complaint, a gust of wind billowed the massive banner high into the air. The plaintiff, apparently more patriotic than he was quick-witted, failed to let go, and the flag pulled him high off the ground. *Then* he let go. He crashed to the ground and was injured. Later, his patriotism now brushed aside, he sued Dixie Flag for compensatory damages. The company's president spent considerable time combing old company records but could find no evidence that his company had even made that particular flag. Nevertheless, Dixie Flag's liability insurance carrier paid the plaintiff $6,000 to settle the suit, much to its client's outrage. The insurers explained that it would have cost $10,000 in attorneys' fees to prevail in court (Van de Putte, 1995: A14).[24] The Dixie Flag settlement is not at all unique. In a 1992 survey of 234 municipal government attorneys, "over 80 percent acknowledge that on occasion they settle cases that would be winnable . . . just to save money in the short term" (McManus, 1993: 835).

At the same time, the costs and unpredictability of adversarial legalism often induce potential *plaintiffs* to back away from asking the courts to vindicate entirely just legal claims, especially when they are met with questionable but costly-to-rebut legal defenses. California debt collection agencies, the president of their trade association estimated, take no more than 20 percent of their debt default cases to court, largely because of litigation expenses, complexities, and delays (Kagan, 1984: 338). Charles Ruhlin (2000) found that a major multinational bank with credit card operations in the United States and Germany is more reluctant to sue delinquent debtors in the United States because German courts deal with collection cases far more efficiently and reliably; the bank ends up writing off a significantly larger proportion of unpaid debt in the United States than it does in Germany. Berrey, Nelson, and Nielsen (2017) analyzed a 1,788 case random sample drawn from all employment discrimination cases filed in seven regional federal courts, 1988 to 2003, and also conducted 100 in-depth interviews with civil rights case parties and legal counsel. They found that only a tiny percentage of claimed discrimination victims persist to the point of filing a case in court. Those who do sue "are likely to settle or lose. Only . . . 6 percent reach trial." Nevertheless "adversarialism casts a shadow over all aspects of the cases, shaping the behavior and experiences of parties on both sides" (177). That adversarialism weighs more heavily on plaintiffs, who "as 'one-shotters,' challenge defendant employers, 'repeat players.' This disparity in legal experience puts plaintiffs at a distinct disadvantage at virtually every stage of the dispute" (13).[25] Yet the researchers' interviews also revealed that along with plaintiffs, "those representing defendant employers have a shared feeling of being unfairly treated in the litigation process. Both parties believe that the litigation process disfavors them" (177).

Manipulative Lawyering. As the Dixie Flag and the Johnson estate cases suggest, adversarial legalism's expense and unpredictability tend to encourage and reward manipulative lawyering and extortive demands. An experienced corporate lawyer, comparing patent litigation in the United States and in Europe, observed that one is much more likely to encounter hyperaggressive lawyering and obstructionist defenses in the United States (Pantuliano, 1983). Dutch and American shipping company and insurance officials told me that when settlement negotiations in cargo damage claims take place in the shadow of Dutch courts, they are "more logical" than negotiations that occur in New York, where the lawyers are more likely "to see what they can get away with" or to take an uncompromising stand based on a legalistic reading of the bill of lading. The American lawyers' goal, in the claims agents' view, was not to work out a reasonable agreement based on the facts and the law but to manipulate the law and its cumbersome processes so as to extort concessions from the other side.

In terms of personal character, Rotterdam lawyers may be no less Machiavellian, on average, than are New York lawyers. But compared with the United States, professional codes of ethics in the Netherlands, as in England and other countries in Western Europe, more strongly enjoin lawyers to temper one-sided advocacy in the search for objective legal truth (Osiel, 1990: 2019; Atiyah and Summers, 1987: 163). Moreover, in the decentralized, adversarial American court system—with its long delays before adjudication, its weak hierarchical controls over lawyer-controlled pretrial discovery, its legal uncertainty, and its opportunities for forum shopping— lawyers have much stronger *incentives* to "see what they can get away with" than they do in Holland. Because litigation in Holland is less costly and more legally predictable, Dutch litigants have less reason to succumb to a settlement that departs from the law solely in order to avoid the costs of further pretrial discovery and the risks of going to trial.

To be sure, manipulative American lawyers run some risk that their adversaries will haul them before a judge, where they can be sanctioned for pretrial discovery abuse or for making factually unfounded legal claims. Within some tight-knit communities of lawyers, reputational networks discourage excessively adversarial litigation activity (Gilson and Mnookin, 1994). In cases in which the monetary stakes are small, neither side, typically, invests much in legal maneuvering (Trubek et al., 1983). Many, perhaps most, American lawyers prefer an ideal of gentlemanly (or ladylike) interaction to that of the warrior litigator (Kagan and Rosen, 1985). Nevertheless, studies suggest that superaggressive, manipulative lawyering— explicitly designed to increase the other side's litigation bills and thereby to induce them to compromise their claims or defenses—is sufficiently common that any potential litigant would rationally be afraid of encountering it (Garth, 1993: 939–945, 949). In the late 1970s, Chicago lawyers who frequently were involved in large-stakes litigation admitted to a researcher that they had used discovery tools in 40 percent or more of their cases simply to impose work burdens or economic pressure on their adversaries. More than 80 percent said they had sometimes done so, employing discovery tactics in order to slow down the progress of the suit, shipping huge numbers of documents to opponents in hopes of obscuring crucial information, or tutoring witnesses to give evasive answers in depositions (Brazil, 1980: 857).

It is all quite logical. In a regime of adversarial legalism, disputing parties' litigation costs are higher than in more hierarchically organized, less adversarial legal systems; hence the incentives to compromise just claims and defenses are greater. In the United States, moreover, because even a party who wins at trial generally must pay his or her own legal fees, lawyers and disputing parties have greater incentives to inflict litigation costs or delays on their adversaries in order to induce them to make greater concessions. As in the Dixie Flag case, even weak legal arguments force one's adversary to expend resources to rebut them, and hence may have some "settlement value" (Molot, 1998: 992).[26] One consequence is that in the United States, as discussed further below, parties' and their lawyers' relative capacities to bear the costs and delays of litigation play a much larger role in case disposition than in judge-dominated adjudicatory systems.

Large Stakes and Extortive Settlements. The extortive settlement in *Johnson v. Johnson* stemmed from the combination of very large financial stakes ($400 million) and adversarial legalism's legal unpredictability (as embodied in a biased, amateurish judge and a potentially swayable jury). This potential arises in other high-stakes lawsuits as well, particularly in class actions by very large groups of consumers, investors, and employees. The class action is a distinctively American legal invention, generally eschewed by other political systems but quite congruent with American political propensities.[27] During the 1970s civil rights and environmental advocates, judges, and politicians saw in the class action a mechanism that, by cumulating small money claims into one gigantic one, would help impose higher normative standards on business corporations and local governments—and would do so without having to rely on government bureaucracies (Farhang, 2010). The class action also offered entrepreneurial American lawyers potentially very large fees for successfully suing offending business corporations on behalf of all the company's consumers, stockholders, female employees, neighbors, or so on. The *Columbia Falls Aluminum* case, discussed at the outset of this chapter, illustrates the virtues of the class action device, as do many class actions based on claims of racial or gender discrimination in employment (Gaiter, 1996: A1, A11). In addition, class actions on behalf of corporate stockholders have been a very important mechanism for enforcing laws against security fraud and corporate managers' self-dealing.

On the other hand, the powerful class-action weapon can be misused so as to extract a large settlement even if the legal case for imposing liability on the defendant is very weak. After learning of a government investigation of alleged price fixing by major airlines, attorneys filed twenty-one cases on behalf of 12 million passengers. Although each passenger's losses would be small, aggregating 12 million small claims created potentially massive liabilities for each airline. Three years later the consolidated cases were settled for $458 million in cash and discount coupons, plus $14.4 million in fees for the plaintiffs' lawyers—even though the presiding judge said he "would assess the chances of the plaintiffs recovering as not good" and that he believed "the case would have a hard time surviving a motion for summary judgment" (*Wall Street Journal,* 1993: A14). But it made sense for the defendants to settle, especially once they hit on the idea of paying the individual plaintiffs in the class via coupons worth a 10 percent discount off purchased tickets for off-peak travel. The plaintiffs' attorneys got a big payoff while providing only minimal benefits to each individual client—that is, to the minority of class members who were very determined, able to prove they fell within the affected class, and persistent enough to collect and use the coupons. To a number of legal scholars, that was not an isolated case but rather fit a pattern.

John C. Coffee Jr. (1995: 1347–1348), having reviewed a large number of cases, wrote that "the modern class action . . . has long been a context in which opportunistic behavior has been common and high agency costs have prevailed. Settlements have all too frequently advanced only the interests of plaintiffs' attorneys, not those of class members." Other researchers have come to similar conclusions.[28] During the 1980s, according to studies by law professors Janet Alexander (1991) and Roberta Romano (1991), certain lawyers routinely filed class actions, alleging fraud, against virtually any high-tech company whose stock values had recently fallen; defendants routinely settled quickly in order to avoid the risks and adverse publicity of a public trial (which the plaintiffs' lawyers were also eager to avoid). At a 1996 meeting of dozens of corporate attorneys who specialize in defending product liability class actions, a law school professor asked how many had "bought off" plaintiffs' counsel by offering to boost their fees in return for a settlement. "Roughly half the audience members raised their hands," a journalist reported (Boot, 1996: A18). Since in some cases the aggregate claimed damages could be large enough to propel a defendant corporation into bankruptcy—which did happen in litigation concerning alleged risks from silicone breast implants[29]—one can see why the defendants were willing to strike such deals.

The misuse of class actions does not nullify the very considerable compensatory and deterrent value of class actions when the plaintiffs have legally valid claims. But the revelations or charges of misuse have had political ramifications. As noted in the Afterword, a conservative political backlash in the 1990s and early twenty-first century led to congressional statutes and court decisions that sought to limit class actions. It is still unclear to what extent those legal changes have in fact discouraged such suits. But those changes probably have overreached, discouraging legally justifiable class actions based on serious corporate and governmental violations of civil rights, consumer protection standards, and other legal protections for ordinary individuals.

Inequality

Adversary theory suggests that the detrimental effects of manipulative lawyering will even out as each side's lawyers fight fire with fire. But that faith seems justified, at best, only when both sides can afford and are willing to engage in an intensive firefight. That type of strict equality of wealth and motivation often is absent. In a regime of adversarial legalism, where privately hired lawyers perform the demanding tasks of interviewing and cross-examining witnesses, devising litigation tactics, and conducting trials, it is quite likely that these tasks will not be performed adequately and equally for all parties (Johnson and Drew, 1978). In their study of employee civil rights litigation, Berrey, Nelson, and Nielsen (2017:199–200) interviewed an experienced defense lawyer who told them:

> All defense lawyers, especially . . . large companies . . . represented by [large law firms] filed [motions for] summary judgments whether they had merit or not . . . because many plaintiffs [lawyers] . . . don't put a lot of investment in their cases. They take the case and then they sit on them. The filing of the summary judgment motion tells them that they've got basically forty-five days to take whatever depositions and other things they want to take.

If they're like most plaintiffs' lawyers in the region, they're inundated with other cases. So they'll push for an early mediation, because there is a summary judgment hanging over their heads. . . . They're inclined to just get rid of the case. . . . I have been doing this work exclusively now for several years, and I can't think of a single case where I haven't filed a summary judgment motion.

That account highlights the significance of a point made by Amalia Kessler (2017: 340), referring to Western European legal systems: "In systems that empower judges to play a greater role in the fact-finding process . . . disparities in the quality of legal representation are less likely to affect the outcome of the adjudication." Great Britain, while retaining the adversary system, strives to even out the quality of advocacy by limiting trial practice to a specialized corps of barristers whose links to particular clients are attenuated and who are constrained by strong legal constraints on overzealous action. Atiyah and Summers (1987: 162–163) observe, "There are . . . cases in the American courts in which the opposing lawyers are strikingly mismatched. . . . Such gross mismatches rarely occur in England."

In a lawyer-dominated litigation system even small differences in opposing counsel can make a big difference. Gerald Williams (1983: 7) divided forty Iowa lawyers into pairs, gave them identical case files (plus photocopies of comparable case jury awards from the Des Moines area), and asked them to negotiate a settlement. Among the fourteen pairs who completed the exercise and were willing to submit a signed statement of results, settlements ranged from $15,000 to $95,000; none were within 20 percent, plus or minus, of the average settlement. And when Robert Condlin (1985: 66) examined transcripts of arguments by 100 teams of law students in a simulated lawsuit negotiation, he concluded that negotiators' experience, preparation, and intellectual abilities, "along with tolerance for conflict, stamina, ruthlessness, oratorical skill and emotional force, play as large a role in determining the extent to which norms are invoked and elaborated as do qualities inherent in the norms themselves."[30]

Unequal legal representation in the United States does not occur randomly, of course. Rich litigants generally can hire better lawyers than opponents who are not rich, and in high-stakes cases they also can buy the services of consultants to help them choose a favorable jury and test out arguments before mock juries (Alschuler, 1998: 410–411; Adler, 1994). In Marc Galanter's (1974) well-known formulation, repeat players, on average, get better lawyering than inexperienced one-shotters. The repeat players do better at the difficult job of shopping for lawyers, marshaling evidence, producing supportive witnesses, and preparing beforehand the contracts and record-keeping systems that will strengthen their legal position in disputes that may arise in the future (Galanter, 1974; Cooney, 1994). Even if parties can afford equal lawyering, their capacity to endure the lengthy, frustrating process of litigation often varies. In a study of divorce cases in Wisconsin the authors concluded that "instead of reflecting the parties' interests, settlements most typically reflect the parties' relative stamina and vulnerability to the pressures of a prolonged dispute" (Erlanger, Chambliss, and Melli, 1987: 592). In a more hierarchical, judge-dominated civil litigation system, these differences in the capacity of parties probably matter but almost certainly not as much as they do in the United States.

Adversarial legalism also compels many victims of injustice to acquiesce in violations of their legal rights because the cost of civil litigation exceeds the monetary value of their losses. For losses under $1,500 or so (depending on state law), American claimants can pursue their legal rights in small claims courts, where the trappings of adversarial legalism (juries, lawyers, pretrial discovery) are banned—and hence adjudication is affordable. For tort cases, a lawyer might be found to take a relatively small-stakes case on a contingency fee basis, that is, in return for a third of the winnings. But for countless moderate-stakes commercial, contract, or property disputes, the court system is simply out of reach—not only because adversarial legalism is expensive but because under the American rule, even if a court upholds your claim, you, and not the guy whose legally unfounded defense forced you to trial, must pay your lawyer's fees. The best that can be done is to find a lawyer who will see what can be accomplished by means of a threatening demand letter or telephone call (Macaulay, 1979). And as shown by detailed sociolegal studies (Desmond, 2016) and journalistic investigations (MacGillis, 2017), low income *defendants* usually can't find a lawyer at all to present their defenses in eviction procedures or debt collection cases. They stand little chance against determined landlords' attorneys or collection agencies—and the resulting court-orders often plunge them deeper into debt, marginalization, and despair.

Other economically advanced democracies, such as the Netherlands and Great Britain, attempt to minimize the legal effect of economic inequality by ensuring that not only the poor but a substantial proportion of the working and middle classes are eligible for government-provided-or-reimbursed legal services.[31] The United States, despite its commitment to lawyer-dominated methods of litigation, provides governmental support for civil legal services only to the poor—and gradually has been shrinking the level of support.[32] Most importantly, Japan, the Netherlands, and the United Kingdom also deal with the problem of inequality by providing a richer array of free or inexpensive precourt dispute resolution institutions for personal plight cases; these include legal advice clinics as well as specialized administrative tribunals for landlord-tenant conflicts, employee dismissal issues, and consumer complaints—tribunals in which lawyers are not needed (Kritzer, 1996; Blankenburg, 1994; Tanase, 1990; Rosch, 1987).

Moreover, in contrast to the Netherlands, Great Britain, Japan, and some Scandinavian countries, American state legislatures, prodded by state bar associations, generally have prohibited the provision of lower-cost legal services by trained nonlawyers housed in legal advice bureaus, community organizations, banks, large retail stores, and other businesses (Hadfield and Heine, 2016). Professor Hadfield suggests that such restrictions on the market for legal services helps explain why, according to national household surveys of legal problems, Americans who experience legal problems more often "lump it"—that is, fail to seek legal advice or other remedy—than citizens in the Netherlands or the U.K. And for those reasons, a World Justice report ranks the United States below the U.K., Netherlands, Germany, Sweden, Australia, Canada, and France in individual access to civil justice (Hadfield and Heine, 2016).

In their dealings with each other, many business firms and other legally experienced repeat players in the United States avoid the expense and unpredictability of adversarial legalism by contracting in advance to deal with serious disputes only via "alternative dispute resolution" (ADR) by private third parties—mediators, arbitrators, or retired judges whom the parties pay to adjudicate their dispute according to law. Arbitrators decide without juries; some American arbitration proceedings look a bit like European civil adjudication. Arbitration clauses have become standard in architectural and construction contracts, industrial supply contracts, and real estate transactions. Experienced companies in those fields—although not in quite a few others[33]—apparently have come to believe, as Hazard and Taruffo's (1993: 171) comparatively oriented study of American civil procedure asserts, that "arbitration required by contract . . . usually affords better justice than a prohibitively expensive right to litigate."

Ordinary citizens are far less likely than sophisticated business firms to plan their way into ADR systems. Increasingly, however, legislatures and courts are compelling litigants in some kinds of cases to submit to arbitration or mediation before granting them a trial (Alschuler, 1990: 17). Plaintiffs, defendants, and their attorneys, whether winners or losers, tend to be quite satisfied with such *court-annexed* ADR (Hensler, 1990: 417; Brazil, 1990). One reason may be that in ADR, in contrast to lawsuits settled before trial via bargaining through lawyers, the parties often participate themselves and get a respectful hearing (Alschuler, 1990: 24).

Less happy, however, are many ordinary American citizens who are virtually forced into *industry-dominated* ADR programs. Understandably seeking to avoid the costs and unpredictability of litigation and the huge risks of class actions, stock brokerage firms, hospitals, health maintenance organizations, banks, telecommunications companies, insurance firms, and many corporate employers require new customers and employees to sign form contracts (or click "accept" online) by which they (unwittingly or reluctantly) sign away their rights to a jury trial and to file or join a class action. Instead, as prescribed by the form contracts, customers and employees must pursue their legal claims through mandatory arbitration, often without the right to legal representation.[34] The managers of the arbitration system chosen by the corporation set the basic arbitration rules and choose the pool of arbitrators. The arbitration decisions are final, ordinarily nonappealable to courts for judicial review.

Data on outcomes in these privately operated mandatory arbitration systems are rarely available. But journalistic investigations repeatedly report disturbing individual stories of bias and denials of remedies for apparent serious injustices, including civil rights violations by employers, medical malpractice, and fraud by for-profit technical schools (Silver-Greenberg and Corkery, 2016a, 2016b; Jacobs and Siconolfi, 1995). Female employees regularly complain that sexual harassment complaints do not get a fair hearing from business-oriented arbitration panels (Jacobs, 1994: B2; Meier, 1997: A1). A systematic study by Shauheen Talesh (2012) has shown that in implementing a California "lemon law" designed to protect new motor vehicle buyers, the state's *industry-influenced* mandatory arbitration system vindicates buyers' claims significantly less often than does a similar *government*-staffed and operated arbitration system in Vermont. Another study showed that in mandatory arbitration systems for employment-related disputes, the employee win rate was 21.4 percent, which is lower than employee win rates in court trials, and median awards for cases employees won were much lower than court awards (Colvin, 2015). The author of that study also pointed out that the lower win and recovery rate in mandatory arbitration sharply reduced employee bargaining power in claims of unfair treatment or dismissal. Most significantly, evidence has surfaced suggesting that a great many customers or employees with grievances simply "lump it" rather than pursuing their claim in an industry-run mandatory arbitration system (Resnick, 2015).

In the early twenty-first century, corporate mandatory arbitration causes became a focus of intense political and legal conflict. As noted in the Afterword, U.S. Supreme Court rulings by the Court's conservative majority upheld corporate arbitration clauses that ban customer or employee participation in class actions notwithstanding state laws to the contrary. The Consumer Financial Protection Bureau (an Obama administration creation) issued a regulation that would have *outlawed* mandatory arbitration clauses in the financial services industry, but in 2017 a Republican Congress and President Trump repealed that rule. The same kind of partisan back and forth first banned and then sustained such clauses in nursing home contracts.[35]

A civil justice system bloated by adversarial legalism thus is a twofold source of inequality: sophisticated litigants gain an advantage because they are better at withstanding the costs and uncertainties of adversarial litigation and also because they are better able to devise ways of circumventing it. Knowledge that the court system is too costly, complicated, slow, and uncertain to vindicate many legal rights and defenses, and in many cases is simply inaccessible, must surely have a deeply corrosive effect on American citizens' faith in the justice system. The average citizen thinks it favors the rich. The average businessperson, like the owner of the Dixie Flag Company, sees the feckless and the unscrupulous aided by the cost and uncertainty of adversarial litigation and feels that the system is unfair to the honest. Both are right–certainly not all the time, but all too often. Amalia Kessler (2017: 340) writes "in countries less wedded to adversarialism, it has been easier to engage in rational reform aimed at developing alternative, non-litigation-based (and nonlawyer-based) approaches to dispute resolution of benefit to the public as a whole." Americans sometimes try. In the 1970s, an extensive academic study and a congressionally established reform commission recommended that routine bankruptcy cases be diverted from federal courts into an administrative agency. An agency, it was argued, could process routine cases nonadversarially, more efficiently, and more cheaply than the courts–bureaucratic legalism instead of adversarial legalism. Federal bankruptcy judges and bankruptcy lawyers reacted by lobbying hard against the proposed reform bill. They succeeded. Congress enacted instead the Judges' Bill, which kept bankruptcy cases in the courts. The reform bill died, Jeb Barnes (1997) explained, partly because American lawyers, as such, are politically influential and many key members of Congress (and of leading consumer advocacy groups) are lawyers. But the reform bill was also opposed by the American Bankers Association, the National Consumer Finance Association, the Department of Justice, organized labor, and congressional leaders of both parties. These politically diverse opponents all expressed misgivings about creating a new federal bureaucracy, which they feared would be less politically insulated than bankruptcy courts, might be underfunded and incompetent, or might end up being biased against their constituencies' interests.

For all its cost and inefficiency, therefore, a system structured by adversarial legalism persisted. It persisted because of a political tradition that is mistrustful of the competence and political neutrality of bureaucratic authority. That political tradition, therefore, prefers to fragment authority and to hold it legally accountable through individually activated rights and adversarial litigation. American politicians, interest groups, many lawyers, and broad swaths of the American public may complain bitterly about adversarial legalism, but they have trouble accepting any alternative that smacks of hierarchically organized bureaucratic legalism or expert judgment.

They are left, therefore, with more reliance either on (a) litigation and higher lawyers' bills than those who seek civil justice in other economically advanced democracies or on (b) opaque private dispute resolution systems established by business corporations and other large organizations.

Yet it is worth keeping in mind that a civil justice system pervaded by adversarial legalism has virtues as well as vices. Americans have a civil justice system that, for all the faults discussed above, can produce the Columbia Falls Aluminum case and many like it—cases in which determined individuals manage to get committed legal representation, mobilize the weapons of adversarial legalism, prove that a powerful business firm or government body has violated their legal rights, and thereby obtain some measure of justice. The challenge for justice-minded reformers, in seeking to limit adversarial legalism, or fix its shortcomings, or institute nonlitigious substitutes for routine cases, is to preserve adversarial legalism's capacity to expose and remedy serious wrongdoing.

CHAPTER SEVEN

The Tort Law System

Tort law enables people to bring lawsuits for the recovery of monetary damages from individuals or organizations who wrongfully harm them, intentionally or negligently. In principle, therefore, one of tort law's social functions is compensation of individuals and their families for significant expenditures, financial losses, and emotional harms caused by the malfeasance of others. Simultaneously, tort law functions, at least in theory, as a regulatory system: through adjudication, it establishes legal norms, defining what behavior is wrongful; and by imposing monetary penalties it deters wrongful behavior and stimulates precautionary measures by those whose activities might endanger others. This chapter examines how the American tort law system seeks to fulfill those functions, the ways in which it is distinctive, and how those distinctive features matter.

In most other economically advanced democracies, those who sustain serious injuries seek monetary compensation primarily from governmentally mandated, bureaucratically administered social insurance programs, without having to prove who was at fault in causing the injury. For that reason, the tort law system in those countries is less prominent than in the United States and less potent. The American tort law system authorizes plaintiffs' lawyers to conduct more probing pretrial discovery into defendants' activities, records, and behavior. It imposes larger monetary damage awards. Those features reflect the efforts of (and finance) America's much larger, more entrepreneurial, and more legally creative population of plaintiffs' attorneys. American tort law, consequently, is a prominent mechanism for developing new, more demanding legal norms of precautionary behavior—and often for punishing business companies, professionals, government bodies, and other organizations that fail to comply with those norms. On the other hand, the American tort law system's distinctively adversarial quality makes it a costly, erratic, inefficient, and often inequitable way of adjudicating normative disputes and compensating injured people. Yet it remains threatening and costly for business firms, medical providers, and other potential defendants, who are compelled to pay for expensive liability insurance and precautionary measures. For that reason, the American tort law system, viewed in comparative perspective, is much more politically controversial, as competing pro-and-anti-tort reform lobbyists besiege legislatures for changes in the law and mount electoral campaigns to oust state court judges whose tort rulings they dislike.

Adversarial Legalism in Action: Asbestos Litigation

In the 1970s and 1980s the incidence of asbestos-related diseases among workers in Holland was five to ten times as high as in the United States. As of 1991 almost 200,000 asbestos-based tort cases had been filed in the United States. Fewer than *ten* had been filed in the Netherlands, although Dutch law authorizes tort claims against employers. The primary reason for the huge discrepancy in tort claims, according to Harriet Vinke and Ton Wilthagen (1992: 12, 17), is that "in the Netherlands employees get reasonable benefits in a non-confrontational way"–that is, through the collectively funded social security system. Disabled Dutch workers are entitled to all needed medical care and lifelong benefits equal to 70 or 80 percent of their lost earnings, without having to prove that an employer or product manufacturer did anything wrong. In the Dutch nonfault system, compensation is modest in amount but far more certain and consistent than in the adversarial American tort system (21).[1]

Asbestos was once hailed as an extremely beneficial magic mineral, used in thousands of products. But it turned out to be deadly, the source of lethal lung diseases and a gigantic, long-lasting public health crisis. Years after exposure, tens of thousands of workers who inhaled asbestos fibers while working in mining, manufacturing, shipbuilding, construction, and demolition projects became disabled and died. According to Andrea Boggio (2013: 3), past exposure to asbestos "kills nearly one person every two hours in the United States, one every four hours in the United Kingdom, three every day in Italy and Germany, two every day in France, Japan, and Australia, and one every day in the Netherlands." But as late as the mid-1960s, the causal link, while it had become known to leading asbestos manufacturers (Barnes, 2011: 25–26), was not entirely clear to most workers, physicians, and workers' compensation judges–even as the number of deadly asbestos-caused diseases started to mount and epidemiological studies began to demonstrate the causal pathway.

In the United States, disabled asbestos workers first began to seek compensation for medical bills and lost earnings by filing claims in state-level workers' compensation programs. But as recounted by Jeb Barnes (2011), workers compensation tribunals either rejected the claims or granted very modest benefits. Most state legislatures, pressured by business interests, failed to amend workers' compensation laws to cover work-caused injuries that were not immediately manifest—such as asbestosis and cancer that stemmed from exposure to asbestos dust, chemical fumes, and the like. But adversarial legalism provided an alternative route to policy change: it enabled creative trial lawyers and politically responsive judges to expand the regulatory and compensatory power of tort law.

In 1969, armed with newly published scientific research on the health effects of asbestos exposure, a tort lawyer in Texas successfully sued eleven asbestos manufacturers in a U.S. District Court. The court concluded that the manufacturers had breached an emerging strict liability tort doctrine that required manufacturers to warn users about dangerous properties of its products (Barnes, 2011). The defendants appealed, but the 5th Circuit U.S. Court of Appeals affirmed the lower court judgment, stating "Here there was a duty to speak, but the defendants remained silent" (*Borel v. Fibreboard Products Corporation,* 1973: 1103). That duty, the court added, extended to "all users and customers, including the common worker in the shop." The court's ruling also enabled claimants to circumvent state workers' compensation systems, file tort suits in court against asbestos manufacturers, and demand a jury trial. There they could demand money damages not only for medical expenses and lost wages but also, as required by tort law in most states, for "pain and suffering" as defined in each case by a jury.[2]

Other federal courts of appeals adopted the same liability doctrine, creating an opening for a stream of lawsuits. The stream became a river after 1977, when pretrial discovery by a plaintiff's lawyer revealed correspondence showing that years before, leading asbestos manufacturers had commissioned studies of asbestos's health effects and had concealed the disturbing results (Barnes, 2011: 26). Swamped with cases, federal court judges authorized entrepreneurial lawyers to aggregate thousands of cases into class actions. The class actions threatened such massive liability obligations that within a few years all major asbestos manufacturers, hoping to salvage their companies' future, filed for Chapter 11 bankruptcy—a judicially supervised process that typically trims and restructures a company's debts while attempting to sustain core production operations and employment (Coffee, 1995: 1386). The tort system thereby sent a loud normative and regulatory message to all American business executives: take affirmative steps to identify deadly hazards associated with your products and, at a minimum, warn all users about them.

Yet as a mechanism for *compensation*, adversarial legalism proved to be costly, inconsistent, and inequitable. Studies indicated that close to two-thirds of expenditures by defendant firms' liability insurance companies ended up in the pockets of lawyers and experts for both sides as opposed to going to asbestos victims and their families (Kakalik et al., 1984: vviii).[3] Judicial decisions and jury awards in asbestos cases varied from state to state and case to case; hence some victims obtained far less compensation than others with similar illnesses and losses. Many victims whose claims were harder to prove got nothing (Sugarman, 1989: 46). In a multi-plaintiff asbestos case in Texas, five different juries, after hearing exactly the same evidence and asked to rule on a series of specific issues relating to causation and liability, reached substantially different decisions (Bell and O'Connell, 1997: 22; Green, 1989: 221–223, 228–235). Claimants in class action settlements reached later in time received substantially lower recoveries than those who sued on their own or were in earlier class settlements (Coffee, 1995: 1384–1396).[4] Appellate courts invalidated some huge class action settlements as procedurally unsound (Schuck, 1992: 553–568; Brickman, 1992; Kakalik et al., 1983). The Supreme Court concurred, arguing that some massive class actions included too many diverse types of plaintiffs to be fairly represented by one attorney and be treated in common (Coffee, 2015: 108–116)

In the 1980s, Congress was repeatedly petitioned to create a more fair and efficient way of compensating the huge numbers of asbestos victims—a way that would reduce the claimant's burden of proof, much as Congress had done in 1969 for thousands of coal miners afflicted with black lung disease, caused by inhaling coal dust. That law, besides simplifying the claimants' burden of proof, guaranteed payment by creating a government-run fund, financed by a tax on coal producers. Disputes would be resolved by an administrative agency. In the 1980s, Congress came close to creating such an administrative system for asbestos victims, but amidst pressures from conflicting interests, no law was passed (Anderson, Warshauer, and Coffin, 1983). The flood of claims and lawsuits continued. In 1999, the Supreme Court urged Congress to act, stating "the elephantine mass of asbestos cases . . . defies customary judicial administration and calls for national legislation" (*Ortiz v. Fibreboard Corp,* 1999; Barnes, 2011: 29). A bipartisan group of senators and representatives proposed an administrative compensation program, but again it bogged down due to conflict among insurance companies, plaintiffs' lawyers, and asbestos-related companies. A similar stalemate blocked a 2004 effort, even though it was endorsed by President George W. Bush and the leaders of the Republican-controlled House and Senate (Barnes, 2011, chapter 4).[5] Consequently, individual and class action lawsuits remained the primary recourse for asbestos victims and their families. But by then most cases were actually resolved by more efficient bureaucratic processes developed in bankruptcy courts, thus avoiding the costs and delays of adversarial tort litigation.

In 1982 Johns-Manville, the largest asbestos manufacturer, had filed for Chapter 11 bankruptcy, pleading that the corporation's enormous financial obligations under existing and anticipated tort suits threatened its solvency. The bankruptcy filing transferred all litigation against the company to a single federal bankruptcy court, where there is no right to trial by jury. Under supervision of a bankruptcy court judge, Johns-Manville created a trust fund and an administrative system to compensate claimants according to a fixed schedule (based on type of medical problem). Plaintiffs' lawyers' fees were capped at 25 percent of the amount paid to claimants. As of December 31, 2004, the Manville trust (and its successor, after the first ran out of money) had settled almost 640,000 claims and distributed more than $3.4 billion (Barnes, 2011: 36–38). Johns-Manville was compelled to jettison entire divisions, slashing its workforce by one-third, or about 9,000 employees. Ultimately, more than seventy other companies that had mined, manufactured, or used asbestos initiated bankruptcy proceedings; they too established compensation trusts, which collectively distributed billions of dollars, doing so more efficiently than tort litigation in the court system.

As a compensation method, however, the bankruptcy trust system has been far from ideal. In contrast with the never-enacted legislative plans for a comprehensive, tax-funded, administrative compensation system, the company-by-company bankruptcy trusts varied in how well they were funded. Over time, as the trust funds declined, many paid out less per claim. Thus a victim's compensation has depended on how soon his or her disease manifested itself and into which company's trust the claim was routed.[6] Meanwhile, the shrinking of the earlier-created bankruptcy trusts led plaintiffs' lawyers to sue ever more companies that had used asbestos in some form, although many of them had nothing to do with the original concealment of asbestos risks (Barnes, 2011: 42). Some lawyers started inventing claims. In December 2012, A West Virginia jury found two Pittsburgh lawyers guilty of civil racketeering for conspiring with a radiologist to fabricate evidence in asbestos lawsuits (Fisher, 2012). This is one of scores of accounts of fraudulent claims, generated by unscrupulous attorneys, that have appeared in the press and the courts.

Overall, the asbestos saga illustrates both the virtues and the limitations of the American tort system. When state governments and Congress remained paralyzed, failing to punish corporate heedlessness and ignoring the harm suffered by tens of thousands of disabled and dying workers, adversarial legalism provided an alternative, more responsive mechanism for public policymaking and implementation. Plaintiffs' lawyers, motivated by American tort law's contingent fee and class action mechanisms, and empowered by litigants' rights to pretrial discovery, brought asbestos-makers' wrongdoing to light. The lawyers' legal arguments, reflecting the work of creative legal scholars, were adopted by judges who had been steeped in a judicial culture open to legal innovation. The judges thereby created new legal norms—business firms' obligation attend to nonobvious hazards created by their processes and products, to abate or mitigate them, and to warn employees and customers about them. The court-made law motivated plaintiffs' lawyers to alert more than half a million asbestos disease sufferers or their survivors that compensation was available.[7] As emphasized by Jeb Barnes (2011) the financial risks and delays of a litigation process structured by adversarial legalism triggered a search for a quicker (although also far less than ideal) way to settle the former asbestos workers' claims—in this case, quasi-administrative proceedings crafted by defendant companies, plaintiffs' lawyers, and bankruptcy judges. Absent adversarial legalism, the financial burdens of tens of thousands of disabled and dying workers and their families almost certainly would have been worse.

Another dramatic example of the American tort system's capacity to generate new regulatory norms, mentioned in Chapter 2, is provided by the litigation against the Catholic Church on behalf of victims of clergy sexual abuse. As analyzed by Timothy Lytton (2008), that litigation occurred in three waves, beginning in 1984 and continuing into the first decade of the twenty-first century. Tort law enabled plaintiffs' lawyers to use pretrial discovery to expose the systematic nature of the problem and then attack not merely the wrongful misbehavior by individual priests but wrongful behavior by the Catholic hierarchy—for failing to report the offenses to the police, or even to bar deviant priests from the church, and for failing to institute systems for preventing recurrences. The lawsuits compelled many dioceses to pay large amounts in money damages. But perhaps most importantly, the lawsuits generated widespread publicity about the church's failures, compelling it, at least in the United States, to make very significant—even if not fully adequate—policy reforms.

Alongside the American tort system's capacity for such heroic action, however, it is important to bear in mind its weaknesses. As a compensation system for victims of wrongful behavior, such as asbestos-poisoned workers and their families, it is more inefficient, unequal, and unreliable than a bureaucratically administered, tax-funded (but never-enacted) system could have been. The reasons for those shortcomings are the focus of the next sections of this chapter.

Tort Law or Social Insurance, Courts or Bureaucracies?

Throughout most of the nineteenth century, sunken ferries and exploding boilers evoked little legal response. Accidents "just happened" (Friedman, 1978: 374). By the end of the century, however, legal culture was changing. Fatalism declined. Reformers asserted that if engineers could make locomotives that roared along at fifty miles an hour, they also could make better braking and signaling and coupling systems; if they didn't, the railroad corporation, not God, was responsible for train wrecks and their human carnage (376). The rise of mass markets for casualty insurance meant that courts could compel business firms to compensate the victims of their technologies without bankrupting useful companies (Friedman, 1986). At a sharply increasing rate, therefore, accident victims brought tort suits against factory owners, railroads, and streetcar companies.[8]

But tort law called for detailed factual and moral inquiries, tailored to the particular case. Didn't the plaintiff know some danger would be involved? Was his or her own negligence a contributing cause? How fast was the train really moving? What could the defendant company reasonably have done to reduce the risk? Did the plaintiff have back pain *before* the accident? Confronting these kinds of issues, the legal rules and adjudicatory processes of tort law grew ever more complicated. Legal complexity made the relative economic capacity and legal sophistication of the contending parties just as important as the law itself in determining which accident victims would be compensated and in what amounts. Examining California trial court records from the late nineteenth century, Lawrence Friedman (1978: 367) found that although some accident victims obtained substantial recoveries, "it is likely that nothing was paid—not a penny—to most victims and their families." Railroads systematically coerced workers into relinquishing injury claims (370–371). Nonetheless, railroad executives complained about ambulance-chasing lawyers and the fraudulent claims they arranged through "rascally confederates in the medical profession" (373).

In the decade after 1910 American state legislatures began to carve one major type of legal claims out of the tort law/jury system—work-related injuries. For these, they made employers absolutely liable for medical expenses and for about two-thirds of lost earnings. The injured worker no longer had to prove the employer was at fault. The employer no longer could escape liability by blaming the employee's contributory negligence or claiming that the worker had voluntarily assumed the risk. Employers were required by law to carry workers' compensation insurance. In that regard, the workers' compensation systems reflected the ideal of "enterprise liability," whereby businesses would be held responsible, regardless of fault, for compensating, and hence for failing to reduce, harms that flow from their enterprises, services, and products—while presumably passing on most of the cost of prevention and compensation to the customers who want those services and products.[9] Procedurally, to resolve arguments about the extent of accident-related disabilities, the workers' compensation systems substituted bureaucratic legalism for adversarial legalism: the disputes were diverted from costly jury trials to less formal, state-run administrative tribunals that were to apply statutorily-specified monetary compensation rules and in which lawyers' fees would be limited.

Western European democracies also adopted collective approaches to compensating workplace accident victims. To fund compensation systems, however, they were more inclined to rely on payroll taxes on both employers and employees rather than on employer-provided private insurance (Williams, 1991: 117–197). Since World War II many European democracies have expanded coverage beyond the workplace, further restricting the role of tort law. In Germany, for example, mandatory industrial accident insurance has been extended to cover injuries to students at school as well as accidents in the course of travel to and from work and school; it thus covers at least one-third, possibly half, of all traffic accident injuries—including the many injuries to negligent drivers who have no one to blame but themselves (for whom tort law is useless) (Nutter and Bateman, 1989). Switzerland extended workers' compensation insurance coverage to injuries at home and at play (Duffy and Landis, 1988). Disputes are resolved not in court but in specialized administrative tribunals. Sweden and Denmark have adopted administrative systems requiring all health care providers to carry liability insurance that will pay compensation for "avoidable" injuries incurred through medical treatment (Mello, Kachalia, and Studdert, 2011).[10]

Further, in most post–World War II Western European welfare states, medical care for victims of any kind of accident or chemical exposure has been provided through tax-supported universal public health care programs. Lost wages are replaced in large part by tax-funded disability plans. Tort law damages are limited to economic losses that are not covered by such medical and social insurance programs; noneconomic damages are legally specified and moderate in amount. Consequently, most disputes concerning compensation for injury are decided not by courts but by bureaucratic agencies and panels of medical and occupation experts.[11]

New Zealand represents the purest version of the collective responsibility/social insurance approach. A governmentally operated social insurance scheme, funded by levies on employers, motor vehicle owners, and general taxes, provides moderate but certain compensation—the cost of medical attention and rehabilitation, plus 80 percent of lost earnings—for all personal injuries arising out of accidents, including "medical errors and medical mishaps,"[12] regardless of fault (Gellhorn, 1988: 188–212).[13] For unintentional injuries the tort law system is marginalized. In contrast to the enormous litigation costs of adversarial legalism in the United States, in New Zealand "about 90 percent of expenditures go to or on behalf of injured people; administration and other transaction costs claim only 10 percent" (Sugarman, 1989: 40).[14] Moreover, surveys indicate that New Zealanders are overwhelmingly supportive of their current tort-free regime (Gellhorn, 1988: 194).

The American Pattern: Social Insurance *and* Adversarial Legalism

The United States, too, has gradually implemented a collective responsibility/social insurance model for compensating victims of harm, although its moves in that direction have been more tentative and limited, and it has been less willing to restrict the role of tort law and adversarial legalism. Workers' compensation coverage has not been extended beyond the workplace. Moreover, the workers' compensation process, originally designed to provide insured benefits to injured workers without costly legal conflict, has become adversarial and legalistic (Nonet, 1969; Schroeder, 1986: 151).[15] A study of workers' compensation claims for permanent partial disability indicated that in Maryland, New Jersey, and some categories of cases in Wisconsin, dueling adversary experts were employed in 63 percent, 79 percent, and 63 percent of cases, respectively, and that legal friction costs added up to 38 percent, 46 percent, and 42 percent of the total disability payments awarded (Workers Compensation Research Institute, 1988). In workers' compensation tribunals in Great Britain and Western Europe, in contrast, governmentally appointed physicians and other experts (not American-style dueling doctors) make disability analyses (Kritzer, 1993: 16).

Nevertheless, the collective responsibility/social insurance model of injury compensation has steadily expanded its importance in the United States. Most importantly, the Social Security Disability (SSDI) system, created in 1956, provides substantial benefits for workers who become permanently disabled and unable to work, whether through accident or illness. Funded by payroll taxes and administered by state and federal bureaucracies, SSDI's internal appeals system has become the largest adjudication system in the nation. An extensive 1988–1989 survey found that the overwhelming majority of Americans who experience personal injuries do not file tort suits.[16] They seek payment for their medical bills and lost wages from employer-provided health and disability insurance, workers' compensation insurance, casualty insurance (most often for motor vehicle accidents), government-provided Medicaid, and if permanently disabled, from SSDI (Hensler et al., 1991). Only about 10 percent of injured people each year—mostly motor vehicle accident victims—obtain compensation via the fault-based tort liability system. The tort system, that survey indicated, ends up compensating only 7 percent of total *economic* loss resulting from injuries, and 11 percent of loss if one includes payments for pain and suffering, but 33 percent of all compensation received for motor vehicle accident injuries (18).

Although the American fault-based tort system occupies only a secondary place as a monetary source of compensation for injuries, it remains legally and conceptually primary. For example, except in the states that have recently modified the "collateral source rule," tort case juries are not supposed to be told if the plaintiff's medical expenses or earnings losses are covered by health or disability insurance. Revealing that information to the jury, the argument goes, would erode the moral and deterrence rationales for tort damages, which require negligent defendants to pay for the full measure of the harm they cause. Thus, Stephen Sugarman (1989: 40) points out, "When payments for losses already covered by collateral sources and for pain and suffering are subtracted, one finds that only about 10–15 percent of the costs of the tort system go to compensating victims for out-of-pocket medical expenses, lost income and the like."[17]

Intensifying Tort Law

During the 1960–1980 period, as Western European democracies were bolstering their social insurance programs and marginalizing fault-based tort law, the United States, always ambivalent about big government, drew on the political demand for "total justice" (Friedman, 1985) for a dramatic expansion of tort law's coverage and potency. Beginning in the 1960s, increasingly sophisticated plaintiffs' lawyers (Witt, 2007) and responsive reform-minded judges reshaped American tort law and practice, case by case. State court rulings greatly modified the common law rule that tort claimants are barred from recovery by their own contributory negligence, adopting instead a more claimant-friendly comparative negligence doctrine (Ursin, 1981: 243–244). They abolished governmental and charitable institutions' legal immunity from tort liability. They changed evidentiary rules for medical malpractice cases, and (as in the asbestos cases) imposed strict liability for product defects. They expanded the right to recover compensation for accident-related emotional distress (244). They made it easier to sue out-of-state businesses in the injured party's county courthouse. And perhaps most significantly, judges enabled entrepreneurial lawyers to aggregate the claims of large numbers of accident or defective product victims into massive class action suits (Coffee, 1995: 1356–1358; Priest, 1985: 461). All of this made it far easier for plaintiffs to win lawsuits and enhanced the regulatory reach of tort law.

The doctrinal changes did not induce a universal litigation explosion; for many categories of accidents and in some regions, the rate of tort litigation grew only modestly.[18] Most of the many tort claims arising from motor vehicle accidents, for example, continued to be resolved bureaucratically; for example, by preemptive monetary settlements offered by potential defendants' liability insurance companies. Nevertheless, tort litigation gradually became an enormous presence in American life. In 1989, 447,374 tort cases were filed in state courts (National Center for State Courts, 1991: 3). Medical malpractice tort claims increased from 1 per 100 American physicians in

1960 (when malpractice suits, however justifiable, were very difficult to win)
to 10.6 per 100 in 1980 and then to 17 per 100 in 1986 (by way of comparison, there were only 1.8 malpractice claims for every 100 Canadian physicians in 1986, and the average American physician's medical malpractice
insurance bill was eleven times that of his or her Canadian counterpart)
(Dewees, Trebilcock, and Coyte, 1991: 219, 221; Danzon, 1990: 56; Nutter
and Bateman, 1989). Tort claims against officials of municipal and county
governments in the United States grew dramatically (Tort Policy Working
Group, 1986).

European and Japanese tort law governing liability for physicians and
product manufacturers also changed in the 1980s and 1990s, coming "reasonably close to American doctrine" (Schwartz, 1991: 28; Gifford, 1991:
10). Nevertheless, "the rates of litigation and the costs of liability in those
countries," according to Gary Schwartz (1991: 28, 47–51), "are only a small
fraction of what they are here." Dow Chemical reported that in 1986 it
incurred $100 million in legal and insurance expenses for product liability
in the United States, compared to $20 million for such expenses on a com-
parable volume of manufacturing and sales elsewhere, and it was engaged
in defending 456 lawsuits in the United States, compared to only four elsewhere (Chinloy, 1989: 57; Nutter and Bateman, 1989). The asbestos class
actions provided a precedent for other "mass tort" cases in which tens of
thousands of claims were aggregated into a single lawsuit calling for millions or even billions of dollars in damages on behalf of individuals who
claimed that their maladies stemmed from pharmaceutical and chemical
products (such as Bendectin and Agent Orange), silicone breast implants,
and intrauterine birth control devices (Coffee, 1995).

American courts also expanded the moral boundaries of responsibility
in tort law, paralleling the expansion of regulatory law in the same era.
Motorists and pedestrians injured in auto or sidewalk accidents, judges
in many states ruled, could hold municipal governments responsible for
not making traffic signs more visible or fixing uneven sidewalks. Occasionally, shoppers who had been mugged in shopping center parking lots
lodged tort claims against the center, arguing that management should
have posted security guards there (Lee, 1997). Some tenants victimized
by crime sued landlords for repeatedly failing to make the building more
secure (Woo, 1993).

But despite cases of this nature, the new American tort law did not really
achieve the ideal of enterprise liability, under which—as Swedish pharmaceutical accident insurance—any injury arising out of an enterprise's activity is compensable without proof of the enterprise's fault. American tort
plaintiffs still must present evidence indicating that the defendant company
or governmental body was primarily at fault (Bell and O'Connell, 1997: 32).
That has a chain of consequences. Defendants resist blame; hence tort

lawsuits often are contentious, costly, and risky to pursue. Consequently, most victims of medical malpractice or product injuries or parking lot muggings do *not* file claims and do not recover anything (Saks, 1992: 1147; Abel, 1987: 448–451). And thus the tort system does not compel negligent injurers as a class to bear anywhere near the full economic cost of the harms they inflict on their victims.

The Tort Industry

For all its weaknesses as a compensation system, American tort law became enormously threatening to actual and potential defendants. Juries are granted wide discretion to assign monetary values to the plaintiff's pain and suffering and in some cases to impose very large punitive damages without explaining why (Blumstein, Bovbjerg, and Sloan, 1990). Between 1960 and 1980 a substantial majority of jury verdicts in product liability and medical malpractice cases in Chicago went against the plaintiff; but in cases that plaintiffs *won*, average awards increased more than tenfold— more rapidly than the consumer price index and the price of medical care. Verdicts in which damages exceeded $1 million grew from 0.1 percent of all trials in 1960–1964 to 3.5 percent in 1980–1984, and those million-dollar verdicts accounted for 85 percent of the money awarded in all 1980–1984 trials (Peterson, 1987: 22, 33, 35, 51). An insurance industry study of large product liability claims revealed an increase in payments of $1 million or more from none in 1975 to 13 percent of all claims closed in 1985 (Soular, 1986: 3).

Like government lotteries with growing jackpots, the large-recovery cases, even if statistically infrequent, acted like magnets, drawing new cases into the liability system. With the prospect of collecting one-third of the awarded damages through contingency fees—a practice prohibited in most other countries—American plaintiffs' lawyers geared up to seek out accident victims and to aggregate cases. An intensely competitive litigation industry developed. The Supreme Court held that laws and regulations that barred advertising by lawyers amounted to unconstitutional restrictions on freedom of speech (*Bates v. State Bar*, 1977). Ads for tort lawyers blossomed on bus-stop benches and late-night television.[19]

Entrepreneurial plaintiffs' lawyers developed sophisticated methods of what critics called ambulance chasing (or more benignly stated, of alerting suffering victims about their rights), such as holding press conferences near the sites of dramatic plane crashes and chemical spills and deploying representatives to advertise for and sign up potential claimants. The American Trial Lawyers Association (ATLA), the Public Citizen Health Research Group, and the Center for Automotive Safety created databases, lists of expert witnesses, and litigation kits for plaintiffs' lawyers, helping (and encouraging) them to bring lawsuits concerning harms caused by particular defective automobile models, medical products, lead paint, and other chemicals (Rabin, 1993: 128; Stipp, 1993; Kolata, 1995). Conversely, liability insurance companies and other defendants learned to contest large tort claims all the more fiercely, throwing costly legal obstacles into the paths of serious claims (Lohr, 1995: 19; Opatrny, 1995: C1). Overall, as the financial stakes rose in tort litigation, so did the level of adversarial legalism, the transaction costs, and the unpredictability of outcomes.

The American tort industry reached one of its twentieth-century peaks in litigation against major tobacco companies. For years, American juries, in scores of lawsuits, declined to find the tobacco companies liable; jurors apparently were unsympathetic to cigarette-addicted smokers who did not quit after tobacco's hazards became widely known.[20] By the 1980s some 50 million smokers in the United States *had* quit. Polls indicated that 90 percent of respondents knew that cigarette smoking can cause lung cancer (Viscusi, 1990; 1992), and a majority of respondents polled said that smokers, not tobacco companies, are primarily responsible for the adverse health consequences of smoking cigarettes (Kagan and Nelson, 2000). Nevertheless, each year, millions of young people were becoming addicted to cigarettes. Smoking remained a major cause of death, and the cause most preventable. And plaintiffs' lawyers who had made millions of dollars in mass tort actions against asbestos companies had the skills, the resources, and the incentives to keep trying.

In the mid-1990s plaintiffs' lawyers persuaded several state attorneys general to hire them, on a contingency fee basis, to file lawsuits against the tobacco industry on behalf of the state governments (Mather, 1998). Each lawsuit. emphasizing the tobacco companies' years of cynical denial that cigarette smoking is addictive and carcinogenic, demanded compensation for billions of dollars that the states had paid (via Medicaid health benefit program) for the care of tobacco-related illnesses. As the publicity mounted, virtually every state attorney general filed a parallel suit. The tobacco companies, however, mounted a determined legal defense.[21] But they also faced trillions of dollars of total claims and an unpredictable court system. So in 1997, before any judge had yet accepted either side's legal arguments (Mather, 1998: 920), the tobacco companies agreed to a massive $368 billion settlement of the states' lawsuits in exchange for relief from further liability.

A congressional statute, however, was required to satisfy the tobacco companies' demand for legal immunity in future. But inflamed by mounting evidence of the tobacco companies' duplicity, key congressional leaders proposed an increase in the settlement amount to $516 billion and declined to provide legal immunity. The tobacco companies cried foul, as did their allies in Congress, and the congressional bill died. The lawsuits, however, did not. In 1998 the tobacco companies settled the state lawsuits for $246 billion–still a massive amount–*without* a promise of exemption from liability in other cases. Tobacco companies also agreed to significant restrictions on marketing and advertising. To varying degrees, state governments used the settlement moneys paid to fund smoking cessation programs. The settlements encouraged the filing of still more individual and class action suits against the major tobacco companies, including one by the U.S. Department of Justice. And by contributing greatly to the political demonization of tobacco companies, the tobacco litigation helped pave the way for the enactment of federal legislation in 2009 that gave the Food and Drug Administration authority to regulate tobacco products (McCann and Haltom, 2018; McCann, Haltom, and Fisher, 2013). So overall, the tobacco litigation story highlights adversarial legalism's regulatory potential. In no other country has tort litigation played such a large role in countering the political influence of huge tobacco companies and forging tobacco control policy.

The Critique of American Tort Law

By the 1980s adversarial legalism had made American tort law the world's most politically controversial liability law system, generating heated legislative battles, ballot propositions, and controversies about judicial appointments. The political attack was initiated by organizations that directly face the costs and uncertainties generated by adversarial litigation–insurance companies, physicians' associations and hospitals, product manufacturers, municipalities, and school districts. They funded the American Tort Reform Association (ATRA), which mounted a costly mass media advertising campaign, focused on the theme of "lawsuit abuse" (Bell and O'Connell, 1997: 188–189). The arguments that ATRA and other tort critics made in the political arena have tended to be one-sided, based on unsupported statistical claims and on unrepresentative, often distorted stories of excessive or undeserved overcompensation. Those stories, however, often circulate like viruses in the business press and in the mass media (Daniels and Martin, 1995; Galanter, 1998; Haltom and McCann, 2004). Putting aside these exaggerations, however, there are other reasons why American tort law became politically controversial. As we shall see, a body of academic analysis and cross-national comparisons suggest that a tort law system shaped by adversarial legalism is a very inefficient and inconsistent means of compensating accident victims and that its regulatory contribution to deterrence and safety, while sometimes quite significant, is erratic.

Inefficiency

The inefficiency of the American tort system is revealed most strikingly by comparing it to a more efficient one. In Japan, as noted by Takao Tanase (1990), fewer than 1 percent of automobile accidents involving death or an injury result in tort litigation. In the United States the comparable figure is 21.5 percent. The disparity does not stem from passivity on the part of Japanese accident victims. They commonly make claims based on tort law and they receive compensation from negligent drivers and their insurance companies.[22] The litigation rate is low because Japan provides nonlitigious methods of assessing fault, advising victims of their legal rights, and determining the appropriate level of compensation. It is instructive to examine how this is accomplished.

First, Japan invests heavily in *official investigation of traffic accidents* to determine the facts and the relative responsibility of the parties. Accidents must be reported to the police immediately; this obligation is widely obeyed, Tanase reports, partly because insurance companies may refuse to pay compensation to motorists who fail to report. Members of a large cadre of police officers who specialize in traffic accidents come to the site rapidly, question parties and witnesses, "and hammer out a consensual story as to what happened to which the parties agree and formally endorse by signing." These police reports are given great weight and rarely are challenged in court (Ramseyer and Nakazato, 1989: 673–674). In addition, in assessing an accident victim's medical bills and permanent injuries, insurance companies and courts rely heavily on the victim's own treating physician, who is trusted because Japan's "Compulsory Insurance Investigative Bureau" employs medical consultants to reexamine dubious reports and crack down on hospitals or physicians who seem out of line. Overall, in terms of the typology outlined in Chapter 1, Japan's method of investigating the facts is both more hierarchical and more reliant on expert judgment than the American system. In the United States, a great many accident injury claims are resolved bureaucratically, that is, through insurance company claims processes. But in contested cases, a large number of claims shift into a litigation process characterized by lawyer-driven adversarial fact-gathering, costly pretrial discovery (in large stakes cases), and negotiation between plaintiffs' lawyers and insurance companies' lawyers.

Second, before a court case is filed in Japan, contested claims generally are resolved by *nonlitigious dispute resolution mechanisms*. These include Traffic Accident Dispute Resolution Centers, which along with courts, provide mediation services, as do a network of consultation centers operated by provincial and municipal governments, the bar association, and insurance companies. In the consultation centers, claimants get free advice on legal rights from specialized counselors (nonlawyers, who mostly are retired government officials) (Ramseyer and Nakazato, 1989: 675–677). The mediation services and advice centers work effectively because the Japanese legal system works hard at developing clear rules that guarantee virtually automatic, predictable, and moderate compensation for most accident victims. In the 1960s Japanese judges took the lead in developing fixed formulae for determining damages and assessing liability.[23] Special traffic sections in the Japanese judiciary continue to produce, update, and disseminate legal standards for compensation. Moreover, Ministry of Finance regulations, compulsory loss-sharing arrangements among insurance companies, and other governmental controls strive to standardize the damages offered by insurance companies. In court, decisions are made by judges, not juries, and these decisions are subject to review for conformity to the traffic and compensation law (Tanase, 1990: 667–673). To return to the typology in Chapter 1, the establishment of standards for compensation approaches the ideal of bureaucratic legalism, as contrasted with the more flexible and powerful but less predictable adversarial legalism of the American system.

In Japan probably fewer than 2 percent of accident victims hire lawyers (Tanase, 1990: 660). Japanese auto accident victims need not hire a lawyer and go to court because they and the defendants' insurance companies can agree what the court decision will be.[24] In contrast, in civil cases tried in Chicago between 1960 and 1980, George Priest (1990: 196) found that the majority of jury time was spent on routine, small-stakes auto accident or slip-and-fall cases "because the difficulty of predicting how Chicago juries will decide makes it impossible for the parties to agree on a settlement amount to save litigation costs." Tanase estimates that in Japan legal fees comprise only 2 percent of the total compensation paid to injured persons and that mediating and claims process costs amount to about 0.2 percent of the total amount paid to injured persons. In the United States, according to an in-depth survey in the late 1980s, 24 percent of individuals hurt in motor vehicle accidents involving potential defendants hire a lawyer, which generally compels the defendant to employ a lawyer too; the figure goes up to 57 percent of claimants with serious injuries (defined as fractures, burns, or worse) (Hensler et al., 1991: 124). When persons with serious motor vehicle injuries hire lawyers, more than half file lawsuits (116, 122). The resulting transaction costs are shocking. According to a 1968 Department of Transportation nationwide study of motor vehicle accident tort claims (not just lawsuits), lawyers for both sides were paid almost $1 billion, which equaled 47 *percent* of the total personal injury benefits ($2,059,100,000) paid by liability insurers to third party accident victims (Bombaugh, 1971: 229–230). Similar results emerged from a RAND Civil Justice Institute study in the mid-1980s (Kakalik and Pace, 1986: 70–72). In the words of Peter Bell and Jeffrey O'Connell (1997: 67), "No one wants to compensate injured people with a bucket brigade of money that wastes every second bucket."

As in other areas of law, the economic costs of adversarial legalism in tort law have ramifying economic and social consequences. The average driver's automobile liability insurance policy costed her 250 percent more in 1990 (in constant dollars) than the same coverage cost in 1980 (RAND Institute for Civil Justice, 1995; Carroll, Abrahamse, and Vaiana, 1995). In consequence, huge numbers of poorer motorists—up to a quarter of all drivers in California, for example—have been tempted into outlawry, driving illegally without insurance.[25] Others can afford only minimal coverage; hence many victims of negligent driving by underinsured motorists have little hope of obtaining meaningful compensation through the tort system (Sugarman, 1993a).

Injustice

All of that expense might be tolerable if it produced just decisions and reliable, meaningful levels of compensation for the injured. But here too study after study seem to support the conclusion that the American tort system does not attain those goals (Abraham and Liebman, 1993; O'Connell, 1979). One survey revealed that almost two-thirds of those who had filed a personal injury lawsuit considered the legal process they experienced unfair (Hensler et al., 1991: 139–140). Summarizing several studies concerning motor vehicle cases, Robert Rabin (1988: 34) wrote: "Research has shown that the tort system only erratically compensates the victims of traffic accidents, often undercompensating the most seriously injured, overcompensating others, and spending more money on litigation costs than on payments that end up in injured plaintiffs' pockets."[26]

Both the American adjudicative system and the law of damages encourage that kind of inconsistency. Whereas the Japanese make clear, specific laws and organize the judiciary to maximize uniformity and reliability of compensation, the American tort law system seems designed to encourage the opposite. Decisions are entrusted to amateur juries, who are uninformed about decisions in comparable cases, are not compelled to explain their decisions or coordinate them with those of other juries, and are subject to the competitive tactics of truth-manipulating lawyers, who all too often are unequally matched. The law of damages, particularly with respect to the crucial category of compensation for pain and suffering (which accounts for 30 to 40 percent of all compensation awarded), is completely vague (Blumstein, Bovbjerg, and Sloan, 1990: 174–176; Geistfeld, 1995). In a typical jury instruction, the judge tells the jury that it may award the plaintiff compensation for past and future physical pain stemming from the defendant's wrongdoing, but "there are no objective guidelines by which you can measure the money equivalent of this element of injury;

the only real measuring stick, if it can so be described, is your collective enlightened conscience" (Douthwaite, 1988: 274). Jurors, not surprisingly, interpret that standard quite differently (Vidmar, 1993: 253–54; Greene and Bornstein, 2000).

Studies show that injury severity explains only about 40 percent of the variation in pain-and-suffering awards (Bovbjerg, Sloan, and Blumstein, 1989: 923–924; Sloan and Hsieh, 1990: 1025), and that plaintiffs with similar painful and debilitating injuries are often awarded significantly different amounts of damages (Geistfeld, 1995: 784; Leebron, 1989: 310). A study of California malpractice case verdicts found wide variation between physicians' ratings of injury severity and jury awards for noneconomic damages (Studdert, Yang, and Mello, 2004). Experienced medical malpractice insurance companies, one careful study of their files showed, were "seriously off the mark" in estimating the amount of damages a jury would award and "failed to establish anything like a going rate" (Metzloff, 1991, 46). In a study of more than 500 mock juries, researchers found that in deliberating over the appropriate *monetary damage* award, juries were more unpredictable than they were with respect to liability questions, producing a wide range of results (Schkade, Sunstein, and Kahneman, 2000: 1139). Comparative analyses indicate that in the United States, verdicts in personal injury cases provide both much larger and much less predictable awards for pain and suffering than similar tort cases in Western Europe, where they are decided by *judges* in accordance with fixed guidelines (Sebok 2006: 392; Sugarman 2006: 418).

The law of punitive damages, authorized for egregious behavior by the defendant, also vests much discretion with individual juries (or in the trial judge, when neither party demands a jury trial), which widens the door for inconsistency. Punitive damage amounts—awarded in far fewer than 10 percent of all tort cases (Eisenberg et al., 1997; Polinsky, 1997: 666; Ostrom et al., 1996: 237–238)—have a positive correlation, at the aggregate level, with the amount of compensatory damages awarded (Eisenberg et al., 2006).[27] But it remains difficult for lawyers in an individual case to predict how high punitive damage awards will be or whether judges will subsequently reduce them. In 20 to 25 percent of cases in which juries grant very large awards for punitive damages—or for pain and suffering alone—trial court judges reduce the award as legally unjustified, more often for extraordinarily large verdicts (Shanley and Peterson, 1983: ix–x; Broder, 1986; Ostrom et al., 1993; Adler, 1994: 244; Vidmar, Gross, and Rose 1998). But that judicial check does not produce legal predictability and consistency, since the judges' decisions in that regard are not subject to definitive legal rules. Appellate courts sometimes reduce very high jury verdicts, but those decisions too are not closely guided by law. The one predictable element is that judges almost never reverse a jury decision for awarding *insufficient* damages.

In the American tort system, compensation payments to injured claimants also are strongly affected by factors that have nothing to do with the legal validity of a claim or a defense. For example, jury awards tend to be substantially smaller if the case is tried in a small county rather than a big city (Danzon, 1984: 143). Moreover, as Stephen Sugarman (1989: 38) has pointed out, answers to the following questions make a significant difference: "Was your injurer insured? Do you happen to have (or did the other side make or destroy) the right evidence? Do you have the right lawyer, the right expert, and the ability to endure the settlement process? Do you look like you will make a good witness? Who happens to be the insurance adjuster or lawyer with whom the settlement is being negotiated?" The result, Sugarman says, is a system in which "lawyers' talents, plaintiffs' demeanor, defendants' grit, and the idiosyncrasies of jury composition hand similar victims altogether dissimilar results" (38).

That the American tort system fails to compensate or undercompensates many legally deserving accident victims is best revealed by the extensive research on malpractice litigation. Partly because of the costliness and uncertainty of the tort system, the great majority of patients injured by medical malpractice do not even file claims (Danzon, 1985: 42; Bell and O'Connell, 1997: 105).[28] Among those who *do* file claims or bring suit, many victims give up and recover nothing once they confront the problems of obtaining expert witnesses and overcoming legalistic resistance (Munch, 1977: 76).[29] At trial, liability verdicts are difficult to predict. When a panel of eleven expert anesthesiologists was asked to evaluate malpractice case files, the physicians' judgments on liability coincided with the actual jury verdicts in only 57 percent of the cases (Liang, 1997: 125–126; Sanders, 1998: 360). Even in a sample of cases in which a physician evaluator employed by the defendant's own insurance company had rated the defendant's behavior indefensible, juries decided against plaintiffs in 42 percent of subsequent malpractice trials (Taragin et al., 1992: Sanders, 1998: 360).

At the same time, the American tort system often results in *overcompensation*. One reason is that defendants often pay damages to tort victims for losses that had been covered by other sources (Sugarman, 1989: 40). Another reason is that the tort system not infrequently rewards legally doubtful claims. In the study mentioned above, medical malpractice plaintiffs won at trial in 21 percent of cases that had been rated defensible by physicians whom the defendant's insurer had retained to evaluate malpractice claims (Taragin et al., 1992; Sanders, 1998: 360). The Harvard Medical Malpractice Study found that while most patients hurt by substandard care did not file legal actions, more than 80 percent of patients who *did* bring suit had *not* received substandard care (Huber, 1997). Those patients brought suit, notwithstanding the questionable validity of their legal claim, because they stood to gain by doing so. As indicated by a number of careful studies, insurance companies, faced with an expensive and legally uncertain adjudicative system, seem willing to buy off many tenuous medical malpractice claims with small settlements—as in the analogous Dixie Flag product liability case discussed in Chapter 6.[30]

The insurers (like other repeat-player defendants such as municipalities and mass transit systems) prefer to devote their legal firepower to fighting claims by victims with the most serious injuries, for those could result in million-dollar jury awards. But that fierce resistance tends to result in *undercompensation of the most seriously injured*. To be sure, some victims of very serious and disabling medical accidents succeed in obtaining very large jury awards. That happens often enough to frighten doctors (because of the tort system's unpredictability) (Weiler, 1991: 6; Songer, 1988; Kennedy, 1985) and to drive up the level of malpractice insurance premiums (for the large-award cases account for almost half the total compensation paid) (Sugarman, 1989: 39). The fact is that more than two of every three jury decisions go *against* the plaintiff (Eisenberg et al., 1995; Moller, 1996). Moreover, victims of serious injuries often are desperate for money and cannot afford the delay of waiting for a trial (which always entails a risk of losing). Thus research shows that most malpractice claimants with legally strong claims receive much less than full compensation for even their economic losses (Sloan and Van Wert, 1991: 158; Weiler, 1991; Munch, 1977: 80). In other spheres of tort law too, Bell and O'Connell (1997: 63–64) summarize the research as indicating that "persons with minor injuries on average receive a much higher percentage of their economic loss from a tort claim than do persons with serious injuries."

The measure of justice also depends on whom one gets to sue. Controlling for severity of injury, jury awards in medical malpractice cases are several times higher than awards in auto accident cases, according to a study based on jury verdict reporters in five states in the 1980s.[31] And in the 1960–1980 period, Chicago juries awarded plaintiffs who had fallen in a building owned by a corporation significantly higher damages than plaintiffs who had fallen on government-owned property and three times as much as those who fell in a private dwelling (Chin and Peterson, 1985).[32] Had those injured claimants received similar injuries in falls at their own workplaces, they would have been barred from the tort system and relegated to filing workers' compensation claims, which would yield much smaller awards (although with more certainty).

Uncertain Deterrence

With its energetic plaintiffs' lawyers—fueled by contingency fees, far-reaching powers of pretrial discovery, and the prospect of large money damages—American tort law is uniquely capable of exposing and penalizing those responsible for unsafe products and negligent practices (Speiser, 1980). It stands to reason, defenders of the system argue, that reforms that would diminish tort law's fierceness or replace it with a more efficient, nonfault-based compensation system would deprive us of tort law's regulatory and condemnatory function. Life in the United States, it is argued, would be more dangerous. Perhaps so, but accurately assessing the regulatory effects of American tort law is not easy. As Stephen Sugarman (1989) reminds us, besides the threat of tort liability, individuals and organizations are simultaneously subject to other, often more salient, inducements for safe and responsible behavior. Pilots and motor vehicle drivers are motivated by the instincts of *self-preservation*. The precautions taken by physicians and product engineers are motivated primarily by *professional ethics*. For airlines and product manufacturers, *market forces* provide strong inducements to construct multiple layers of precautions because serious fatal accidents, dramatized on television news programs, can destroy a company's reputation and market share. Finally, *direct governmental regulation*, with its roadway speed limits, factory inspections, and permit systems (plus the threat of criminal penalties for willful violations that result in accidents), provide more immediate and more specific instructions on how to prevent harm than tort law does. It is not clear how much tort law adds to those regulatory factors.

In that regard, Sugarman points out, the liability system's deterrent threat is muted by liability insurance. In addition, it is diminished by the uncertainty as to whether tort liability will actually be imposed. Then there is the stubborn persistence of human incompetence, inattentiveness, and calculated corner-cutting, which lead truck drivers, emergency room doctors, and the crew of the Exxon *Valdez* to make mistakes, no matter how large the potential tort liability. After surveying American corporate product design staffs, George Eads and Peter Reuter (1984: 263, 291) wrote, "Although product liability exerts a powerful influence on product design decisions, it sends an extremely vague signal. Because the linkage between good design and a firm's liability exposure remains tenuous, the signal says only, 'Be careful, or you will be sued.' Unfortunately, it does not say how to be careful, or, more important, how careful to be" (292).[33] Moreover, the tort law system does not aim its deterrent threat accurately. A study of 1,465 nursing homes, 1998–2006, found that those with the *best* records on three national data bases on quality of care had a 40 percent annual risk of being sued for negligence, scarcely different from a risk of 47 percent for those with the very worst deficiency records (Studdert et al, 2011).

Consequently, efforts to sort out how much tort law really adds to the regulatory equation generally have been mixed and rather inconclusive (Schwartz, 1994: 379; Deweese and Trebilcock, 1992: 59–60; American Law Institute, 1991: 32). Research on medical malpractice litigation illustrates that point. A comprehensive study concluded that American tort law had stimulated "broad-based improvements in the institutional environment and procedures through which medical care is delivered" (Weiler, 1991: 91). Physicians report having adopted new standard procedures following well-publicized court cases (Weiler, 1991: 127; Givelber et al., 1984; Wiley, 1981). Liability risks stimulated anesthesiologists to study risk factors, publicize best practices, and spur the development of new oxygen-measuring technologies, all of which significantly reduced dangerous and sometimes fatal adverse events in operating rooms. Indeed, some studies indicate that American malpractice law not only deters but sometimes "overdeters," leading not only to sensible extra precautions but also to unnecessary hospitalizations, lab tests, and other defensive procedures.[34] On the other hand, a multistate quantitative study of millions of births, 1991–2002, found that the odds of adverse birth outcomes was not associated with medical malpractice risk (measured by malpractice insurance premiums) (Yang et al., 2012).

Dewees and Trebilcock (1992: 83) observed that while the level of medical malpractice claims in Canada was only 20 percent that of the United States, "there appears to be no evidence that Canadian physicians are more careless than their U.S. counterparts"–although they did not cite any comprehensive medical-record study, analogous to several conducted in the United States, that carefully examined the incidence of medical malpractice. For the same reason, disagreement arises about whether the substitution of social insurance for medical malpractice law in New Zealand adversely affected the quality of care.[35] Nevertheless, a more recent study of the administratively implemented no-fault systems for medical injury compensation in Sweden, Denmark, and New Zealand concluded, "There has been no discussion of returning to a fault-based system of tort liability for medical injuries. Strong, separate systems of complaints investigation and physician discipline appear to have allayed any concern that injury deterrence may be undermined by a move to a compensation system that does not involve judgments of fault or economic penalties for clinicians "(Mello, Kachalia, and Studdert, 2011). The Danish and Swedish systems disseminate analyses of claims data to hospitals, systematically using them to improve patient safety practices–which the fragmented American tort system does *not* do systematically.

Overall, it is by no means clear that life is more dangerous in economically developed countries where tort suits are far less common and less fearsome than in the United States. Nor do other democratic countries, comparing their accident and injury rates with those in the United States, seem inclined to emulate American adversarial legalism. Yet it is hard to believe that the deterrence argument is wholly wrong. In addition to new medical risk-reduction practices, many safety-enhancing measures in the

United States—such as warning beepers on trucks and construction machines that are put in reverse gear, improved helmets for football players, and softer surfaces under climbing structures in children's playgrounds (Epp, 2009)—were stimulated by tort cases that imposed liability on companies or municipalities that had failed to institute those improvements. Recall the midwestern city administrators quoted in Chapter 2 who recounted improvements in municipal safety inspections, personnel training, and supervision that had been stimulated by lawsuits (Epp, 1998b). In a 1987 study by an international consulting firm, more than half of the 101 top corporate executives surveyed said that their companies had added safety features to their products as a result of the threat of lawsuits (Zehnder, 1987; Schwartz, 1994: 480).

On the other hand, systematic studies of some particular industries have found little evidence that American tort law consistently or significantly affects product design or safety. Multinational motor vehicle manufacturers claim that no other country comes close to the United States in terms of the incidence and cost of product liability litigation (Kagan, 2000a). A major Japanese auto manufacturer asserted that with twice as many of its cars on the road in Japan than in the United States, "its American operations lead to about 250 product liability claims against the company each year. By contrast, in Japan the number of annual product liability filings averages about two" (Schwartz, 1991: 51). But two careful analyses of the development of particular safety improvements in motor vehicles (ergonomics, braking, lights, crashworthiness) contend that American product liability law—in contrast with direct government safety regulation—has made only negligible or, at best, secondary contributions to better design (Graham, 1991; Mackay, 1991). One reason, the analysts noted, is that by the time a company's engineers hear that an American jury has found defects in their design for a model currently on the road, they usually have completed work on new designs and safety features for subsequent model years.[36]

Similarly, in the 1970s and 1980s crashes of small airplanes often led to lawsuits against the aircraft manufacturers, alleging that the crash stemmed from product defects. Two analyses of safety improvements in small aircraft, however, concluded that litigation and escalating liability insurance costs did not lead to improved aircraft design or lower accident rates (Martin, 1991; Craig, 1991).[37] Meanwhile, sales plummeted, and by the late 1980s domestic production of light aircraft had virtually ceased. Thousands of workers were laid off. Flying probably became riskier, not safer, since users kept flying (rather than retiring) older used planes. In 1994 Congress enacted the General Aviation Revitalization Act, which limited lawsuits involving planes more than eighteen years old.[38]

There are other contexts in which American tort law appears to over-deter, inducing precautions that make products and services much more (and arguably unreasonably) expensive or that suppress the provision of products and services that would actually reduce the risk of harm. According to a 1992 survey of 500 public accountancy partnerships in the United States, more than half had limited their audit services or had shunned certain clients engaged in higher risk markets in order to protect themselves from lawsuits by disappointed investors (Berton and Lublin, 1992; Berton, 1995); both of those defensive tactics may well have increased the risk of financial deception.[39] A 1995 survey by the Society for Resource Management found that 63 percent of personnel managers declined to make negative evaluative comments when asked for an assessment of a former employee for fear of landing in court (Louis, 1987: C1).[40] That, of course, is a recipe for enabling incompetent or abusive executives (such as someone dismissed for sexual harassment) to do the same in the future.

In the mid-1980s lawsuits led manufacturers of the DPT vaccine to exit the business, which threatened the supply of a product that has all but wiped out childhood diphtheria, whooping cough, and tetanus—diseases that killed thousands of children in previous generations (Burke, 2002).[41] In response, Congress in 1988 enacted a vaccine injury compensation program. It removed vaccine cases from the tort-jury trial system, routing adverse-reaction claims to an enterprise liability/limited compensation scheme, administered through the Federal Claims Court and funded mostly through a tax on vaccines (Burke: 2002, Barnes and Burke, 2015). Manufacturers again started making and marketing new vaccines. In its first six years of operation, the new vaccine injury compensation program resolved 3,451 claims and paid a total of nearly $600 million to 827 successful claimants (Barnes and Burke, 2015: 169).

Overall, the spotty existing evidence suggests (but only speculatively) that American tort law probably has a net positive regulatory effect, but an erratic one. Potential targets of tort liability vary in their attentiveness. Many manufacturers, physicians, and corporate personnel officers *overestimate* the actual risk of being sued, perhaps because of the publicity accorded unrepresentative jury verdicts (Bailis and MacCoun, 1996: 419–429; Edelman et al., 1992: 47–83; Songer, 1988: 585–605. Hence tort law sometimes deters, inspires new or better precautionary measures, and improves safety. Sometimes tort law overdeters, compelling adoption of precautions that reduce overall social welfare. But for still other potentially hazard-creating entities and individuals, tort law is too uncertain and unpredictable to affect behavior very much at all, or it is far less salient than other inducements to responsible behavior, or it sends deterrent signals that are simply not strong enough to get through the mix of other signals and daily pressures. Critics of the system therefore have argued that American tort law's regulatory effects are too mixed, uncertain, and scattered to justify an adversarial system that generates large economic costs, pours a great deal of money into lawyers' bills, and fails to provide just and reliable compensation.

Supporters of the system, in contrast, argue that tort law's positive regulatory effects, even if not always effective, are far too valuable to dispense with, particularly in a political system in which direct governmental regulation of health, safety, and professional standards is politically contested, often underfunded, or too accommodative vis-à-vis regulated entities. Supporters would also call attention to the assertive tort law campaigns of the kind mentioned earlier in this chapter—the litigation against asbestos makers and against tobacco companies—campaigns in which plaintiffs' lawyers, wielding the tools of pretrial discovery, brought to light unconscionable corporate cover-ups and stimulated new legal or regulatory reforms. One might add the tort litigation campaign, mentioned earlier in this chapter, against the Catholic Church concerning sexual abuse by priests (Lytton, 2008). Through tort law, therefore, adversarial legalism can mobilize a decentralized battalion of law enforcers, enabling them to publicize and punish wrongdoing in a wide range of contexts—wrongdoing that lies outside the range of government's existing regulatory safety net or which slips through its holes. That capacity also is too vital, it often is argued, to be legally or politically weakened.

The Tort System and Popular Morality

Tort litigation provides Americans with a steady stream of morality tales—challenging, dramatizing, reaffirming, and extending the society's moral judgments about wrongdoing and responsibility. For many citizens, however, tort law seems to have lost its moral groundings, conflicting with traditional notions of individual responsibility (Polisar and Wildavsky, 1989; Sanders, 1987; Engel, 1984). Those citizens shook their heads when they read about Sheila Leibeck, an automobile passenger who was badly burned while leaving a McDonald's takeout window because she had put a cup of hot coffee between her legs and it spilled—but then won a $2.9 million verdict (including $2.7 in punitive damages) against McDonald's. Her lawyer's argument was that the fast food chain knowingly served unusually hot coffee and failed to warn customers about it adequately (Gerlin, 1994b; Rhode, 1999: 143–144).

To those Americans who are inclined toward what political scientist Aaron Wildavsky (1990) called an "egalitarian" political culture—rather than toward a political culture that emphasizes individual responsibility—the McDonald's case verdict was entirely defensible; in their view, businesses ought to be held accountable for preventable harms that flow from their profit-making activity. Scholars pointed out that McDonald's had decided not to reduce the temperature of its coffee even after other previous patrons had been scalded and that the plaintiff had initially requested payment only for her medical and attendant expenses (about $11,000)—a request McDonald's had refused, although it *had* compensated other coffee burn victims (Haltom and McCann, 2004; Galanter, 1998: 732).[42] Moreover, the tort system's defenders point out, the public has been getting distorted messages from the media, leading them to a false impression that the system is morally out of control. Most newspaper accounts of the McDonald's hot coffee verdict failed to mention that the trial court judge subsequently reduced the award to $500,000, or McDonald's inconsistent treatment of Leibeck's (as compared to other burn victims') claim (Galanter, 1998). Nor did news media give much prominence to a later U.S. Court of Appeals decision that *rejected* the claim of a plaintiff who had sued a manufacturer of coffee-making machines after spilling hot coffee on herself in a moving car (*McMahon v. Bunn-O-Matic Corp.,* 1998). In general, the news media are far more likely to report jury verdicts *favoring* tort plaintiffs—especially those involving quirky claims or huge punitive damage awards—than verdicts for defendants (Bailis and MacCoun, 1996; Chase, 1995).

Moreover, the public at large, in contemplating the McDonald's coffee case, probably did not consider the fact most tort claims are morally uncontroversial, or researchers' findings that juries tend to regard plaintiffs' claims with skepticism (Hans and Lofquist, 1992; MacCoun, 1996). To many legal scholars, therefore, the common view that the tort system is morally out of control stems from distorted reporting and from propaganda spread by a business community seeking to avoid its social responsibilities (Haltom and McCann, 2004; Rhode, 1999; Daniels and Martin, 1995).

There is much more than a grain of truth in that diagnosis. But the adverse political reaction to tort law also reflects the fact that notions of individual responsibility are as widely ingrained in Americans' beliefs as are politically liberal notions of total justice. As noted earlier, in the late 1990s a majority of survey respondents asserted that cigarette smokers, not tobacco companies, should be responsible for the health care costs stemming from smoking-related diseases (Kagan and Nelson, 2000). To believers in individual responsibility, no amount of explanation or the subsequent reduction of the verdict can obliterate their sense that the woman who foolishly put a cup of hot coffee between her legs was primarily to blame, so that imposing legal responsibility on McDonald's, however rational from a regulatory standpoint, violates a basic moral principle.

The tort system also seems morally unhinged to many Americans because of the common knowledge that it unintentionally rewards and encourages corruption. In 1991 the vice president of State Farm Insurance noted that "the ratio of bodily injury claims to property damage claims [in auto accident cases] has increased about 50 percent over the last 10 years . . .

at a time when automobiles have become safer and there should be fewer bodily injury accidents" (Sloane, 1991: 15). The rise of such claims is concentrated in major urban centers: in 1991 the ratio of bodily injury claims to accidents was less than 13 percent in Harrisburg, Pennsylvania, but 75 percent in Philadelphia (Brickman, Horowitz, and O'Connell, 1994: 33). A report by the RAND Institute for Civil Justice (1995: 32–33) observed that "the availability of general damages ('pain and suffering') and the fact that they are usually calculated as some multiple of economic losses provide the incentive to submit claims for nonexistent injuries and to build medical costs." The RAND researchers found that motor vehicle accident claimants represented by attorneys accumulate significantly more visits to doctors and chiropractors than similarly injured claimants who do not retain attorneys; and other studies also provide strong suggestive evidence of lawyer-driven medical bill padding (32–33). The RAND scholars' analysis led them to the astonishing estimate that "about one-third of the automobile industry accident costs submitted to insurers appear to be excess" (1; Carroll, Abrahamse, and Vaiana, 1995; Grady, 1996).[43] In 2012, as noted earlier, a jury found two Pittsburgh lawyers liable for civil racketeering and $429,000 in damages for conspiring with a radiologist to fabricate evidence in hundreds of asbestos lawsuits against railroad operator CSX (Fisher, 2012). Sociolegal scholars correctly point out that there is a great deal of underclaiming as well as overclaiming by accident victims (Saks, 1992). But the tort system's overclaiming, claim-padding, shadow has been more politically explosive—perhaps because it has been illuminated more brightly by media-savvy conservative interests (Haltom and McCann, 2004).

Many Americans also accuse the tort system of undermining traditional notions of individual responsibility by encouraging legal blaming. According to an extensive survey, more than 90 percent of American drivers injured in two-car accidents blamed someone else for the crash, but so did 37 percent of drivers involved in *one-car* accidents (Hensler et al., 1991: 159). Comparing these results to a similar survey of British accident victims, Herbert Kritzer (1991: 400–427) noted that Americans were considerably more likely than the British to blame someone else for an auto accident; and among motorists who blamed the other driver, Americans were considerably more likely to demand compensation. Kritzer speculates that the difference is at least partly attributable to the incentives provided by the American tort system.

Similarly, a tort system shaped by adversarial legalism seems to encourage legal defensiveness. American drivers repeatedly are instructed not to apologize when they get into a collision so as not to compromise their bargaining position in a subsequent lawsuit.[44] Americans are accustomed to encountering business enterprises that decline reasonable requests by saying, "Sorry, our insurance company won't let us."[45] The citizens who are disturbed by this law-induced defensiveness are easily recruited to the political constituency for tort reform.

Tort Politics: The Conservative Reform Movement

In the 1980s and early 1990s critiques of American tort law spilled out of the law reviews, appellate courts, and the business press into the broader political arena. Business groups urged state and federal legislatures to curtail judge-made liability rules. Republican candidates for office courted votes by calling for limits on tort litigation. Ballot initiatives in California twice asked the electorate to approve plans substituting no-fault self-insurance for tort suits arising from motor vehicle accidents; each time, opponents and proponents spent tens of millions of dollars on television commercials designed to sway the voters, who ended up rejecting both initiatives. Subsequent decades have seen intense, increasingly expensive judicial election campaigns in a number of states; anti-tort business interests poured money into efforts to replace state supreme court judges they saw as biased toward tort plaintiffs, and trial lawyers' associations responded by financing those targeted judges' retention campaigns.

This kind of battle over tort law is unique to the United States. In no other economically advanced democracy do plaintiffs' tort lawyers, or organized business advocacy groups, or partisan clashes between political parties, play such a prominent political role in shaping the civil justice system. In most rich democracies, changes in the codes of civil justice are enacted only after long deliberation and consultation among legal experts, jurists, relevant central government bureaucrats, and cabinet ministers. But in the United States, where political power is fragmented among the branches of government, across states, within legislatures, and within the political parties, no single national or state bureaucracy, no party leader, no business or labor confederation, no high legal or judicial commission, and no court controls policy development in civil justice. The ebbs and flows of partisan elections often are decisive.

In recent decades, those ebbs and flows have enabled the conservative critics of the American tort system to make significant headway, as a more ideologically conservative Republican Party gained control of more state legislatures. Between 1985 and 1991 forty-one state legislatures enacted changes in tort law (Lipsen, 1991: 248–249). More states followed suit in the mid-1990s; several more did so in the first decade of the twenty-first century. Except for a handful of narrowly targeted measures,[46] there was little movement toward what Thomas Burke (2002: 18) labels *replacement* reforms—legislative enactments that, like workers' compensation programs, replace adversarial tort claims and jury trials with a system that provides injured people with moderate benefits without any need to prove fault and that relies on administrative dispute resolution. Models for such reforms do exist. The authors of the previously mentioned study of administratively implemented no fault medical injury compensation systems in New Zealand, Sweden, and Denmark (Mello, Kachalia, and Studdert, 2011: 5–9) concluded that:

> In addition to easing injured patients' access to compensation for preventable injuries,[47] [each of those systems] preserves physician-patient relationships, encourages transparency about adverse events, and fosters physician participation in the claims process. In this way, an administrative compensation system can help move American health care toward the culture of safety necessary to prevent medical injuries.

Nevertheless, American legislatures, even in less conservative states, have shown little inclination to extend the existing workers' compensation or the black lung program replacement model to other kinds of frequently recurring injuries, such as motor vehicle accidents, medical accidents, asbestos disease, adverse reactions to pharmaceuticals, or tobacco-related illnesses—all of which remain the province of contingency-fee tort litigation and erratic compensation.

Instead, most state tort reform laws have been what Burke (2002: 18) labels *discouragement* measures—enactments designed simply to inhibit lawsuits by making it more difficult for plaintiffs to sue, to win, and/or to win a lot, but which keep the basic adversarial, court-based tort law system intact. For example, many such laws modified joint and several liability rules so that "deep pockets" government and business organizations that are only partly responsible for injuries will not be stuck with the whole cost of compensation. Other laws shortened statutes of limitations, placed caps on pain and suffering and punitive damage awards, and changed the collateral source rule under which tort victims can claim damages even for losses covered by their own insurance. Still other reform laws called for penalties on refusals to accept early settlement offers, imposed limits on contingency fees, or mandated arbitration or mediation as a prerequisite to a jury trial.[48]

In at least seventeen states plaintiffs' lawyers associations successfully took the battle to the courts, persuading judges to hold that tort reform statutes, particularly those imposing caps on damages, are unconstitutional under state law (Nutter and Bateman, 1989: 16–18). On the other hand, conservative tort reformers often secured the appointment or election of conservative state supreme court judges who issued court decisions that limited damages, pulled back from notions of strict liability, and required stronger evidence that defendants had actually caused the harms in question

(Schwartz, 1992; Eisenberg and Henderson, 1992; Sanders and Joyce, 1990). In California, business interests made sizable contributions supporting a successful 1986 ballot measure that compelled the ouster of liberal California Supreme Court justice Rose Bird (Wold and Culver, 1987). In 1996 a member of the plaintiffs' bar commented that Bird's conservative replacement, Chief Justice Malcolm Lucas, had been "more effective than any Republican legislator in the past 10 or 15 years" in curbing civil litigation.[49]

At the federal level, the increasingly conservative U.S. Supreme Court held in 1996 that huge punitive damage awards that are unrelated to the seriousness of the harm violate the Due Process Clause of the U.S. Constitution. That principle ordinarily would apply, the Court subsequently ruled, if the ratio of punitive to compensatory damages decided on by the jury is greater than 9:1.[50] The Court also urged federal trial court judges to exclude the testimony of expert witnesses who relied on uncorroborated "junk science" to draw causal connections between defendants' products and claimants' maladies (*Daubert v. Merrill Dow Pharmaceuticals*, 1993; Sanders, 1998); issued a number of rulings that pre-empted state tort laws that imposed or threatened liability for products subject to federal product safety regulation; and most significantly, restricted the bundling of large numbers of separate individual injury claims in a class action settlement (Coffee, 2015: 110–116).

Overall, the conservative push for tort reform may well have diminished the rate and intensity of American tort litigation—although there is only scattered evidence on how much of a diminution. A 1995 study showed that from 1986 to 1993 the number of tort cases filed in twenty-two selected states stopped rising, but the number remained steady at about 390,000 per year (Bureau of Justice Statistics, 1995). There is some evidence that conservative discouragement measures, such as statutory caps on pain and suffering damages, deter some lawsuits—although they also diminish access to justice for persons with less lucrative damage claims and curtail the size of damage settlements for the most severely injured plaintiffs.

For example, a 2003 Texas law imposed a $250,000 cap on noneconomic damages in medical malpractice cases. Absent the cap, noneconomic damages typically amounted to three times plaintiff's economic damages (lost earnings, medical care costs). Stephen Daniels and Joanne Martin (2015: 212) found that as a result of the cap, plaintiffs' lawyers have become less willing to take on factually complex, intensely contested malpractice claims unless the potential money damage recoveries are very large. (A plaintiff's lawyer's pretrial disbursements, the authors state, can easily approach $100,000 if the case is especially complex.) Over the first five years after the cap was put in place, the average annual number of medical malpractice case filings in Harris County, Texas, which includes the huge city of Houston, declined 46 percent from the 1997–2002 average (Daniels and

Martin, 2015: 206). Moreover, a Texas lawyer noted, the reform law, "essentially closed the courthouse door to the [medical] negligence that could kill a child, a housewife, or an elderly person"–all categories of victims who would have no lost earnings and hence very limited economic, and hence noneconomic, damages (Daniels and Martin, 2015: 206).[51] A Texas lawyer wrote Daniels and Martin: "I found jury verdicts decreased due to the propaganda disseminated by insurance companies and big business and this resulted in insurance adjusters offering less money to settle cases. I began to decline representation in cases I used to accept" (11). In contrast with the Texas study, on the other hand, a statistically sophisticated study, focusing on tort damages caps adopted in eight states, 1993–2004 (and on eleven states that had not done so), found that "medical malpractice caps have not altered the number of medical malpractice awards or settlements" (Donohue and Ho, 2007: 96).

Moreover, as the following examples indicate, the American tort system still can be prodded into potent action when widespread serious harms flow from heedless business practices. Starting in the mid-1990s, litigation against nursing homes (generally in the wake of patient deaths or of serious injuries stemming from neglect) grew rapidly, particularly in Florida and Texas, resulting in average recoveries of over $400,000 (Stevenson and Studdert, 2003; Studdert and Stevenson, 2004). And echoing the earlier litigation against tobacco companies, in the first decades of the twenty-first century hundreds of lawsuits have been filed across the United States against manufacturers and distributors of massive quantities of opioid painkillers–drugs that have been widely blamed for triggering and feeding a devastating epidemic of addiction. The suits, brought by several state attorneys general and by private tort lawyers representing scores of cities, argue that starting in the 1990s leading opioid makers unleashed false and misleading marketing campaigns that knowingly underplayed the risks of addiction and exaggerated the benefits of their products (Lopez, 2018).

The Persistence of Adversarial Legalism

As the opioid litigation suggests, despite the legal changes they have wrought, the political conservatives' discouragement-oriented reforms have not changed the basic shape of the adversarial tort law system. In contrast to other democracies, the United States still has few constraints on contingency fees. It has not moved to a "loser pays" system with respect to attorneys' fees. Viewed in cross-national comparison, the American reforms (aside from caps on punitive damages and pain and suffering damages in some states) have not prescribed systematic, detailed money damages schedules (as in Japan and Western European tort law), and hence have not significantly constrained jury discretion in that regard. The conservative reforms have not significantly reduced the cost of litigation or displaced the cumbersome jury system—which, as we have seen, resolves only a small percentage of personal injury cases by trial but which shapes the adversarial settlement process. Nor have the conservative reforms replaced an inefficient and inequitable adversarial tort system with broadly funded, administratively implemented, injury-compensation systems for recurrent kinds of cases administered via bureaucratic legalism.

Instead, an important legacy of the political struggle over tort law has been greater *instability* in the law of personal injury and greater *inconsistency* in compensating similarly injured accident victims. Consequently, an accident victim's chances of obtaining compensation and the level of compensation he or she will get (as well as a defendant's insurance company's liability) may vary not only from state to state and case to case but from year to year, depending on shifts in political party control of the legislature and the state supreme court.

One abiding source of adversarial legalism's persistence is its general consonance with some significant strands in America's increasingly polarized political and legal culture. In 1996, California voters were presented with three ballot initiatives designed to curtail adversarial legalism. One would have instituted no-fault compensation for motor vehicle accidents, displacing tort law. Another sought to discourage extortive stockholder class actions. A third called for limits on contingency fees in quickly settled cases. Opponents of the measures, led by the California trial lawyers' association, bombarded the electorate with television commercials that showed ravenous-looking wolves on the hunt, while a voice-over warned voters not to vote for ballot propositions that would benefit "corporate wolves." Another commercial, portraying a female motorist whose car suddenly was hit by a reckless driver, proclaimed: "Under no-fault, it's always your fault"—a trope that underscored the normative core of tort law. All three ballot measures were defeated at the polls.

The trial lawyers' commercials skillfully tapped two enduring strains in American political culture—populism and individualism (Lipset, 1996: 20). Populism is ever suspicious of the corporate wolves, from Wall Street to the insurance company boardroom, and of the politicians and bureaucrats who are thought to be under the baleful influence of the wolves. American individualism has long emphasized the right of the individual to pursue his or her own interests and seek justice in the courts (which are distrusted less than other governmental institutions) against those who wrongfully impinge on one's liberty or property. Both strains are suspicious of collectivist methods of compensating accident victims, especially if they totally displace individual rights to sue and strong legal sanctions against corporate and other wrongdoers.

Of course, in the broad bay of American politics there are yet other currents that are supportive of collectively funded income security policies, such as the Social Security Disability program. Adherents of this tradition endorse the basic propositions of total justice—the idea that government bears responsibility for ensuring that the innocent victims of misfortunes and injustices (and especially their families) should not be plunged into destitution. But many Americans do not trust the government to implement that responsibility properly. Democrats, who generally support active government, worry that government-funded injury compensation programs will be subjected to Republican budget-cutting pressures and be besieged by business lobbyists, so that eventually they will shortchange powerless injured individuals and their families. The history of state workers' compensation programs—in some states, during some eras—provides some support for this concern. Republicans, on the other hand, worry that Democratic administrations will turn collectivist accident-compensation programs into undisciplined, fraud-ridden boondoggles, engines for increasing benefit payments and higher tax or insurance charges.

Thus political mistrust of government and politics leaves adversarial legalism, for all its flaws, not as the only game in town but as a very important one for developing and implementing regulatory norms concerning proper business behavior, for compensating the victims of heedless behavior, for seeking vindication in particular cases. But adversarial legalism is a game that remains erratic, very expensive, and economically inefficient, leaving many players and attentive bystanders concerned that justice often is not done nor safety guaranteed. For that reason, too, the conservative effort to roll back tort law is not likely to fade away.

PART IV

PUBLIC LAW

Social Justice and Regulation

CHAPTER EIGHT

Adversarial Legalism and the Welfare State

In France governmental efforts to trim costly welfare state benefits are regularly met by mass demonstrations in the streets. In the United States a different mode of protest prevails. In August 1999, a group of welfare recipients filed suit against the State of Florida, contending that the state had illegally cut off their Medicaid benefits when it ended their cash assistance (Families, USA, 2000, 16). In January of that year, a federal district judge ruled that New York City had improperly denied Medicaid to poor people who failed to comply with work requirements of the city's welfare program (Pear, 1999). Two decades later, in January, 2018, the same partisan political struggle over welfare state benefits again was thrust into the courts, as three public interest law firms sued the U.S. Department of Health and Human Services, arguing it had violated federal law when it authorized Kentucky to impose work requirements on Medicaid recipients (Goldstein, 2018a).

The Florida, New York City, and Kentucky lawsuits were far from unique. The American welfare state differs from those of most economically advanced democracies. Substantively, social provision in the United States is less comprehensive and less generous. Structurally, the American welfare state is marked by the fragmentation of authority among federal, state, and local government in the formulation and administration of social policy, and the United States relies more on *private* provision of social insurance, post-secondary education, health care, social services, and housing for low-income people. To coordinate and control this fragmented system, American social programs tend to rely on detailed legal rules and rights, enforceable in court. The judiciary is often is asked to block legislative or administrative restrictions on social benefits for failing to comply with federal statutes or the Constitution. On similar legal grounds, judges not infrequently order state or local governmental agencies to reform and improve social service delivery. Thus litigation, courts, and adversarial legalism play a much more significant role in shaping and administering social policy in the United States than in other countries. This chapter describes and explains the distinctive prominence of adversarial legalism in the American welfare state and examines some of its consequences.

The American Welfare State in Comparative Perspective

The welfare state is one of the most striking public policy developments of the twentieth century. Its rise reflected both a political and a humanitarian desire to soften the harsh edges of dynamic capitalist systems. In country after country, governments have imposed taxes and created programs to buffer families from the devastating effects of illness, sudden economic loss, and poverty. Germany's 1920 Weimar Constitution declared a right to social insurance. Chile's 1925 constitution "guarantees to all the inhabitants of the country . . . social security, especially regarding healthy housing and economic conditions of life such that each inhabitant . . . would have a minimum of welfare for his needs and that of his family."[1]

Neither Weimar Germany nor early twentieth-century Chile truly fulfilled their constitutional promises, of course, but the aspirations expressed in such documents have been of great political and practical importance. By the last third of the twentieth century, most economically advanced democracies had guaranteed their citizens free public education and medical care. They had enacted laws assuring families a meaningful level of income in the event of a breadwinner's injury, unemployment, disability, or retirement, and had created programs to alleviate destitution regardless of cause. Many nations provide or subsidize daycare for preschool children of working mothers, mandate paid vacations and maternity leaves for workers, provide job training for the unemployed, and construct low-cost housing for poor families.

In the United States governments have been subject to similar political pressures to improve economic opportunity, reduce economic inequality, alleviate misfortune, and provide a social minimum to all residents. American governments, therefore, have participated in the construction of the welfare state. Early on, American state and local governments provided universal public education and subsidized mass college-level education. In the depths of the Great Depression, newly elected president Franklin Roosevelt declared that ensuring the economic security of all Americans should be the highest priority of government. In his 1944 "Four Freedoms" speech Roosevelt declared that "individual freedom cannot exist without economic security and independence" (Goldman, 1977: 287, 386).

Yet in the United States the welfare state idea has always been contro-versial. Neither the federal nor state constitutions establish sweeping rights to social welfare. Compared to their counterparts in Western Europe and Canada, politically conservative American political elites and much of the public at large have been quicker to express concern about fraudulent claims generated by governmental benefit programs, particularly those designed to serve poor families and individuals. These concerns have been intensi-fied, it has been argued, by persistent beliefs among substantial numbers of white voters that such policies disproportionately benefit black Americans (Alesina and Glaeser, 2004) or are unfair to hard-working, taxpaying fami-lies (Haidt, 2012). Americans also have been more reluctant to accept the high tax burdens required by generous cradle-to-grave benefits.

In the political arena, American business interests have been more effec-tive than their counterparts abroad in warning against the labor market ri-gidities and inefficiencies associated with mandatory job-related protections and benefits—and labor interests have been less effective in countering those concerns. More fundamentally, it has been argued that the U.S. Constitu-tion, by fragmenting political power, inhibited the formation of a strong socialist or labor party akin to those that propelled the expansion of worker rights and the welfare state in other economically developed democracies (Alesina and Glaser, 2004). The Democratic Party did not fulfill that role because throughout the first two-thirds of the twentieth century, it was split between liberal Northern Democrats and conservative Southern Demo-crats. American labor law, consequently, is not as strongly pro-union as Eu-ropean labor law.[2] That weakness contributed to the steady and ultimately drastic shrinkage of the unionized private sector in the nation as a whole, and hence to drastic shrinkage of organized labor's political influence on social policy (Hacker and Pierson, 2010: 56–61). Just as significantly, begin-ning in the 1970s, powerful segments of the business community and the Republican Party moved toward a fervently antitax, antistatist ideology (Hacker and Pierson, 2010)—a political posture that hardened in the early twenty-first century as the Republicans gained political power, both in state governments and in Washington. One consequence has been the further weakening of organized labor's political influence[3] and a decline in funding and staffing of government agencies charged with delivering social services and administering social programs.

For all these reasons, legally guaranteed welfare rights and benefits in the United States are markedly less comprehensive and less generous than in post–World War II Western Europe (Alesina and Glaeser, 2004; Wilensky, 2002; Esping-Anderson, 1990; McFate, Lawson, and Wilson, 1995). Most prominently, although a majority of Americans obtain health care coverage through a complex array of government programs and employer provision, the United States stands out among economically advanced democracies in failing to guarantee universal health care benefits as a basic right of citizenship, and millions of Americans—a higher percent than in most economical advanced democracies—remain uninsured.[4] In ten Southern states, it was reported in 2015, a single, childless person is not eligible for Medicaid, the federal-state program for health care coverage for the poor. In Alabama, an adult in a four-person household with an annual income of $4,400, well below the official United States poverty line, earns too much to qualify for Medicaid (Robertson and Fausset, 2015). The infant mortality rate in the United States is higher than in other rich democracies (Porter, 2018; Central Intelligence Agency, 2017).

In the sphere of labor rights and benefits, as noted above, a much smaller proportion of American workers, especially in the private sector, enjoy the bargaining power, benefits, and protections provided by labor unions. In the United States, compared to other Organization for Economic Cooperation and Development (OECD) countries, a markedly greater share of corporate earnings goes to top corporate officers and to capital rather than to labor. And American laws, viewed in comparative perspective, provide American workers far weaker governmentally-guaranteed rights and benefits. In many Western European countries, such as the Netherlands (Kagan, 1990a), laws ensure that the wages and benefits agreed upon in industry-specific collective bargaining agreements are extended to all workers in those industries, whether the workers are labor union members or not; not so for workers in nonunion firms in the United States. American minimum wage laws are set significantly lower (vis-à-vis median income) than those of other rich democracies (Alesina and Glaeser, 2004: 38–39). Unskilled male workers in the United States earn less, and they enjoy fewer legally mandated benefits (Freeman, 1994),[5] such as paid holidays and sick days. Compared to their counterparts in France and Germany, a detailed study shows (Carre and Tilly, 2017), American retail workers are paid far less than their counterparts in France and Germany, who also benefit from more government regulation of life-disrupting irregular schedules and from stronger collective bargaining protections against sudden, at-will dismissal.

Governmentally supplied unemployment benefits in the United States are available for a much shorter period and replace a smaller percentage of the laid-off employee's wages than unemployed workers in other rich democracies receive (McFate, 1995: 636).[6] Labor law in Western European countries and Canada provides workers with rights to severance payments in the event of layoffs or dismissals; American labor law does not (Freeman and Katz, 1994; Abraham and Houseman, 1993). Except for Italy, the United States spends far less than other rich countries, as a percentage of GDP, on public employment services and job training for unemployed workers, leaving them much more vulnerable to the negative effects of globalization and automation (McFate, 1995: 641, 644). The U.S. income security program for retirees and their families (Social Security) is less generous, especially for the relatively poor retiree, than are publicly-provided pension systems in other OECD countries (Alesina and Glaeser, 2004:2 6).

In a study of fourteen economically advanced democracies, the United States ranked a distant last in terms of legislation mandating maternity leave benefits and job protection for employed mothers-to-be (Gornick, Meyers, and Ross, 1997: 138; *The Economist,* 1998: 110). In comparison with virtually all Western European countries, American public policies have done less to prevent or ameliorate poverty among single mothers and their children, either by direct income transfer programs or by programs encouraging employment, such as subsidized child care (Gornick, Meyers, and Ross, 1997).[7] Overall, the United States taxes its citizens less[8] and spends less on social benefits, as a percentage of GDP, than comparably rich countries (Wilensky, 2002; Alesina and Glaeser, 2004), although that gap is partially reduced by a complex array of tax credits and loan subsidies (Howard, 2007; Hacker, 2002; Tach and Edin, 2017).[9]

The American economy, less burdened by taxes and restrictive labor laws, has generally been more successful than most European welfare states in fostering entrepreneurship, generating jobs, and reducing unemployment. At the same time, as Hacker (2005: 157) notes, "U.S. social programs and tax policies reduce inequality less than do similar programs and policies abroad, and they have done less to blunt the post-1970s increase in inequality." Based on 2015 data, the U.S. poverty rate, measured by living on less than half the nationwide median income, was higher than that in all other economically advanced nations (OECD Data, 2018), and benefits and subsidies for families below that line are much lower (*Economist,* 2017a). And strikingly, in recent years, according to OECD analyses, the U.S. rates of upward socio-economic mobility have declined significantly (Chetty et al., 2017); indeed, the United States has fallen behind many rich democracies in that regard as well as in access to easily affordable higher education (Hacker and Pierson, 2010: 29, Porter, 2014).[10]

The American welfare state, as noted earlier, also has a distinctive political and organizational structure. Viewed comparatively, social benefits and services in the United States tend to be administered or delivered in a more politically decentralized—and therefore uneven—fashion. Historically, public education has been governed and largely funded (via local property taxes) by *municipal* governments, which vary widely in taxable wealth—although in recent decades those local revenues have been matched by state governments. Since the 1930s the federal government has instituted a number of nationwide social programs, but many—Social Security Disability Insurance, Medicaid, unemployment insurance, and direct financial aid for poor families ("welfare" and food subsidies)—are administered not by federal bureaucracies but by state and local governments. Moreover, the central government often provides only partial funding; state and local governments retain considerable discretion in setting spending and eligibility levels. Compared to Europeans, moreover, American citizens rely much more heavily on *private* insurance companies, hospitals, employers, and nonprofit organizations (rather than on government agencies) for health care provision, for compensation for workplace injuries, for treatment of the mentally ill and the elderly, and for retirement pensions.[11] In the United States provision of low-income housing has relied much more on governmental subsidies to private developers and nonprofit organizations. Indeed, in recent years, as private sector rents have climbed steeply in many cities, those subsidies have become woefully inadequate,[12] deepening the poverty of many poor families (Desmond, 2016).

These structural arrangements affect the legal character of social welfare program administration in the United States. Because benefit provision is entrusted to far-flung (and sometimes financially hard-pressed) county governments, private insurance companies, banks, school districts, private nursing homes, private employers, and private colleges and universities, the United States, in contrast with more statist European welfare systems, often employs detailed, judicially enforceable statutes, regulations and procedures to ensure that those benefits are made available responsibly, uniformly, and fairly. The House of Representatives report on the 1977 amendments to the federal Food Stamp Act filled 869 pages and "contained advice on such matters as how late intake offices should be open and which court decisions had identified the proper method for counting the income of migrant workers" (Melnick, 1993: 34; Katzmann, 1995). The Affordable Health Care Act of 2010, which relied on private insurance companies and state governments for implementation, was a staggering 910 pages long (Giffey, 2012), and by 2013 it had been elaborated by almost 11,000 pages of regulations (O'Donnell and Akinnibi, 2013).[13]

To ensure compliance with those and many other legal standards and procedures, Congress has often encouraged adversarial legalism. In the 1975 Education for All Handicapped Children Act, for example, Congress provided sweeping rights to an "appropriate education" in public schools throughout the country–but provided only limited funding to the local schools, which had to absorb the high costs of implementing those rights. To promote compliance, Congress armed parents of handicapped children with legal rights to contest school administrators' decisions about their child's placement and services. In contrast to Great Britain, which in that era also adopted ambitious special education policies, litigation by dissatisfied parents became a common feature of the special ed programs in the United States (Kirp, 1982). American (but not British) judges regularly ended up deciding what an appropriate education entails for particular children or categories of children (Melnick, 1995)–and hence how local school funds should be divided between special needs and other students (Sandler and Schoenbrod, 2003).[14]

More broadly, the United States is unique in the extent to which individuals and advocacy groups appeal to courts to challenge administrative decisions and social policies. In 2000, according to Sandler and Schoenbrod (2003: 122), more than thirty state or local welfare agencies were operating under court orders demanding improvements. Similarly, in 2016, a study reported, "almost 20 states are currently working to implement consent decrees or other court orders related to the reform of their child welfare systems" (Meltzer, Joseph, and Shookhoff, 2012). Even more common are appeals to the courts by individual applicants whose petitions for benefits have been turned down by agencies or by administrative law judges who hear intra-agency appeals. For example, more than 10,000 such appeals to the regular court system are filed each year by applicants for federal disability benefits (Barnes and Burke, 2015: 91).

In other economically advanced democracies, litigation and courts play some role, perhaps an increasing one, in policing the fairness of decisions by welfare state bureaucracies, but the litigation has a different character. Germany diverts complaints by patients who are denied special medical services into free social courts, where they are decided by panels staffed by a professional judge who specializes in such cases, a lay judge who represents the patient, and another lay judge who represents the employer or doctor (Jost, 1998).[15] Great Britain provides a system of relatively informal administrative tribunals in which citizens can dispute bureaucrats' decisions concerning entitlements. But neither these tribunals nor regular courts, Herbert Kritzer (1996: 135, 147, 174) observes, "exercise the kind of direct control over other governmental institutions that courts in the U.S. have done repeatedly over the past several decades." The same is true in France, which operates an extensive administrative court system for processing individual complaints against government agencies but which excludes the judiciary from significant influence on governmental policy (Provine, 1996). This has implications for everyday administration. In response to American judges' assertive decision-making concerning social provision, agencies are compelled to adopt internal administrative rules and procedures that seem designed more to prevent legal error than to make the agency more responsive to persons the agencies are supposed to serve. Based on his observational research in Germany, Sweden, and the United States, Christopher Jewell (2007) found that in making eligibility and benefit determinations, officials in American welfare agencies are more tightly restrained than their German and Swedish counterparts by detailed legal rules and procedures—and hence are more legalistic and inflexible in their interactions with needy clients.

The patchiness of the American welfare state indirectly encourages adversarial legalism in other fields of law. As illustrated by Chapter 7's discussion of the asbestos problem (and tort litigation in general), the American legal system's failure to provide guaranteed universal health care coverage is reflected in the country's vastly higher rates of tort litigation, as accident victims seek monetary damages to cover their past and future medical needs. Litigation also is stimulated by American workers' greater vulnerability to arbitrary dismissal (due to relatively weak statutory and labor-union protections and to America's less-generous unemployment benefits). Thus employers in the United States more often experience lawsuits by dismissed employees, such as unjust dismissal suits based on state common law, or racial or gender discrimination claims based on civil rights laws. Laura Beth Nielsen (2000) studied the consequences of "forced separations" of mostly white-collar employees by a multinational corporation. The company's U.S. branch experienced lawsuits by almost 23 percent of the dismissed employees during the year studied, compared to 7 percent in its Canadian branch—even though the corporation prescribed uniform company-wide personnel management and employee termination policies, and even though Canadian law provides more comprehensive protections against arbitrary dismissal than does American law.

In sum, adversarial legalism plays a prominent role in the American version of the welfare state, and that role has been extremely important. Adversarial legalism has lent strength to segregated black schoolchildren, to welfare mothers, to handicapped children and workers, to pregnant teenagers who desperately want abortions, to the children of illegal immigrants, to seniors in nursing homes, and to arbitrarily treated nonunionized workers. Advocates for members of these and other groups have used the courts to challenge and sometimes to reverse public policies and administrative practices that reflect racist attitudes, repressive moralism, or bureaucratic callousness. In many states, adversarial legalism has resulted in meaningful improvements in child welfare programs (Meltzer, Joseph, and Shookhoff, 2012). But as stressed in earlier chapters, adversarial legalism is Janus-faced. It does make American government and business firms more responsive to individualized claims of justice and to the policy arguments of the politically less powerful. But as the following case study suggests, adversarial legalism also is an inherently uncertain and politically contested method of policy implementation and dispute resolution.

Adversarial Legalism in Action: Naming Deadbeat Dads

American states, like governments in most economically advanced democracies, legally require divorced or absent men to provide financial support for children they have fathered. While state family law traditionally defers to the custodial mother if she declines to enforce her children's rights to paternal support,[16] the policy considerations are somewhat different when the mother is receiving welfare benefits. In those circumstances, if the father can be compelled to pay child support, the state's obligation is reduced or disappears entirely. That was the focus of a detailed case study by Stephen Sugarman (1985a) concerning litigation that affected the implementation of the AFDC (Aid for Families with Dependent Children), a program embedded in the 1935 U.S. Social Security Act. In 1996, AFDC was superseded by the TANF (Temporary Assistance for Needy Families) welfare reform program, which triggered a major decline in the importance of direct welfare grants—a decline counterbalanced to some degree by increases in food aid programs and the federally-administered Earned Income Tax Credit program, which provides cash subsidies to employed workers. But despite these program changes, the Sugarman case study of the earlier AFDC litigation illustrates some recurrent consequences—some positive, some negative—of efforts to change social programs via adversarial legalism.

In the late 1960s, the number of unmarried mothers receiving AFDC expanded dramatically. Some states decided to compel mothers, as a condition of receiving AFDC benefits, to disclose the father's identity to welfare administrators. Forcing absent fathers to recognize their illegitimate children, it was argued, would deter both men and women from having babies they were not prepared to support on their own and might deter welfare fraud, since in some cases the father actually may be providing child support and the mother wishes to cover up that source of income in order to qualify for AFDC.

Without disparaging those concerns, welfare rights activists argued that in some cases a mother on welfare might have good reasons for not seeking support payments from the father or for not divulging his name to state authorities. She might be afraid that the father will be abusive toward her or the child. She might believe that the father might decide to marry her and help support the child, but that governmental demands will drive him away. She might have other, more personal reasons to conceal the father's identity or fear that disclosure would be psychologically harmful for the child. In any event, welfare rights advocates argued, an innocent child should not be denied assistance because his or her mother refuses to accede to the local welfare officials' demand for information about the father. In 1968 an unmarried "welfare mother" in Connecticut, defying state regulations, refused to name the father of her illegitimate child, "Scott Doe." Connecticut, as its regulations prescribed, terminated both Scott's and his mother's AFDC benefits. Scott's mother sued the state. Welfare rights lawyers championed her case, seeing it as a vehicle for advancing their legal reform agenda. Understanding her legal argument requires some further background.

The AFDC program, initiated in the depths of the Great Depression, arose from a plan to revive insolvent state pension funds for widows or children with absent or disabled fathers. Bowing to pressure from state governments (which wanted both federal money and continued political autonomy), New Deal reformers crafted a joint federal-state AFDC program. The federal government provided matching funds for state-administered programs that aided single-parent families; state governments were allowed to set both benefit levels and eligibility requirements "under the circumstances of each State." Within states, welfare administration typically was further decentralized to city and county governments. Intercounty differences in attitudes toward welfare and welfare recipients compounded interstate differences, leading to wide variations in the application of eligibility rules and in levels of aid to needy families (Mashaw, 1971: 818–839).

By 1967 state and local government control over AFDC rules and welfare administration had become enmeshed in controversy and in adversarial legalism. In the 1960s, as welfare rolls swelled, political conservatives complained that the AFDC system was riddled with fraud, that it encouraged sexual and financial irresponsibility, and that it led to ongoing dependency. In some cities, welfare authorities conducted so-called midnight raids to find out if there was a "man in the house" (who was presumed to be an undeclared source of support). Some states, particularly in the South, required the agencies that administered AFDC to deny benefits to applicants who failed to provide a "suitable home" for the aided children. Welfare rights lawyers—led by attorneys in the federally funded Legal Services Program—claimed that many such state and city rules were motivated by racism; they systematically challenged those rules in federal courts (Davis, 1993; Lawrence, 1990).

The federal judiciary was remarkably responsive. In a flurry of decisions beginning in the late 1960s, judges transformed AFDC from a program grounded in state and local discretion in setting eligibility and benefit policies into a system of entitlements subject to federal legal supervision (Melnick, 1993: chapters 4, 5). For example, some states, such as California and New York, which provided comparatively generous AFDC payments, had enacted regulations imposing one-year residency requirements before immigrants from other states (such as Southern states that provided much lower AFDC benefits) could qualify for aid. In *Shapiro v. Thompson* (1969), however, the Supreme Court held that the Constitution contained a fundamental (albeit nontextual) right to travel, which it interpreted as overriding California's one-year residency requirement. In *Goldberg v. Kelly* (1970), the Court, asserting that welfare was not a privilege but a right, held that before a state or local government could terminate aid on grounds of a recipient's ineligibility, the government is constitutionally obliged to provide the AFDC recipient a right to a hearing before a neutral administrative adjudicator.

In the 1968 case of *King v. Smith,* the Court dealt with an Alabama regulation providing that if a single mother had a "regular boyfriend" she was ineligible for AFDC assistance; the Court held that certain congressional amendments to the AFDC law had restricted states' rights to establish eligibility requirements and that the Alabama rule illegally conflicted with federal law. "Immorality and illegitimacy," the Court pronounced, "should be dealt with through rehabilitative measures rather than measures which punish dependent children" (Davis, 1993: 68). In *Townsend v. Swank* (1971) and *Carleson v. Remillard* (1972), the Court, rejecting eligibility rules promulgated by Illinois and California, asserted that states could not exclude AFDC applicants who were eligible according to federal administrative guidelines and that in enacting the AFDC program, Congress, far from allowing states discretion (as had been generally assumed), "intended to provide a program for the economic security and protection of *all* children" (*Carleson*, 604). Thus federal court administrative officials and judges were able to impose national rules (and reject more conservative local governments' policies) on a wide range of issues—such as what resources should be counted in determining an AFDC applicant's eligibility, AFDC recipients' obligations to seek employment, and whether children in college or still in the womb should receive benefits (Melnick, 1993: 97).

Now we can return to the Connecticut case of young Scott Doe. In August 1969 in *Doe v. Shapiro*, a U.S. District Court judge in Connecticut, citing *King v. Smith* (1968), ruled that Connecticut's law, by cutting off benefits to AFDC children if mothers declined to name the father, was unlawful. Connecticut appealed, but the court of appeals refused to hear the case because state lawyers had filed the appeal a day after the prescribed deadline. Connecticut policymakers were unwilling to abandon the basic principle of parental responsibility, however. They amended their regulations, declaring that an AFDC *mother's* (rather than her children's) benefits would be cut off for failure to cooperate with welfare officials in seeking paternal support payments. Welfare rights lawyers brought suit again. In this case, *Doe v. Harder* (1970), the U.S. District Court held in March 1970 that Connecticut's partial cutoff too violated federal law (Sugarman, 1985a: 377). The state's welfare commissioner was held guilty of contempt of court. Connecticut appealed directly to the U.S. Supreme Court. Once again its appeal was rejected on technical grounds; Connecticut's lawyers, the Court ruled, should first have sought review in the court of appeals. Connecticut responded not by re-appealing but by enacting a new law in 1971. This one stipulated that if an AFDC mother refused to identify her child's father, welfare officials could take her to court, and if she still refused, the judge could jail her for contempt. While in jail, the mother and her child would continue to receive AFDC benefits. Not surprisingly, reform lawyers attacked this law in court, in a case designated *Roe v. Norton* (1973).

Roe v. Norton took more than ten years to resolve. The case was first heard in early 1973 by a three-judge U.S. District Court panel which unanimously *upheld* Connecticut's law. Doe's lawyers took the case to the U.S. Supreme Court, which quickly granted review. The Children's Defense Fund filed an extensive amicus curiae brief challenging Connecticut's contempt rule and helped persuade twenty-six other organizations, ranging from the American Academy of Child Psychiatry to the Salvation Army, to join as fellow amicus curiae.

But meanwhile, the lower court's *Doe v. Shapiro* (1969) decisions (along with similar court decisions invalidating coerced maternal cooperation rules in other states' AFDC programs)[17] had aroused congressional interest in the policy issue. Senator Russell Long of Louisiana, the influential chairman of the Senate Finance Committee, had long been opposed to liberalizing AFDC requirements with respect to absent fathers' obligations. In 1974, before the Supreme Court decided *Roe v. Norton*, Long pushed through a congressional law requiring *all states* to terminate AFDC benefits for mothers who refused to name the fathers of their illegitimate children. In response, the Supreme Court remanded *Roe v. Norton* to the lower courts for evaluation in light of the new congressional act.

In 1975, however, Congress amended the 1974 law. Prodded by lawyers for the Children's Defense Fund and the Welfare Rights Center, legislators prescribed a "good cause" exception to the cutoff rule. The exception was not to come into effect, however, until its details were specified in regulations to be drafted by the Department of Health, Education, and Welfare (HEW). And HEW, then led by Republicans in the last years of President Gerald Ford's administration, moved slowly in drafting those regulations, while also declaring that in the interim states should follow the 1974 rules that authorized coerced maternal cooperation in virtually all cases. Nevertheless, in the remanded *Roe v. Norton* case, U.S. District Court judge Joseph Blumenfeld, interpreting the more liberal 1975 law, held that Connecticut must withhold all sanctions from noncooperating mothers until HEW defined "good cause." Connecticut appealed that decision, once again putting *Roe v. Norton* on the U.S. Supreme Court's docket.

There's more: welfare rights lawyers sued HEW, demanding that it revise its interim regulations to extend Judge Blumenfeld's ruling nationwide. When a U.S. District Court ruled against the plaintiffs in that case, they too appealed to the Supreme Court. However, before the Court heard the case, Democrats won an electoral victory and a reconstituted HEW urged states to issue their own good faith exception regulations, pending final HEW rules.

In June 1977 the Supreme Court, still confronted with Connecticut's appeal from Judge Blumenthal's ruling, remanded *Roe v. Norton* back to the lower court, noting that Connecticut had by then adopted its own good cause provision. The plaintiffs agreed to abandon *Roe v. Norton* in 1981, after the HEW good cause exception rules became final. The regulations provided that an AFDC mother could be excused from identifying her child's absent father if she could show at a hearing that disclosure would create a risk of serious physical or emotional harm.

The net result of thirteen years of litigation, Stephen Sugarman (1985a: 380) observed, is that "the law on maternal cooperation is not very different from Connecticut's policy in 1968 before the lawyers ever got involved." True, he noted, there is now a narrow set of formal excuses for noncooperation, and only the mother's share of AFDC is at risk. But those excuses are not easy for her to establish (430). In 1979, among some 50,000 cases in which Connecticut mothers were asked to name the father, 236 mothers refused to cooperate and only 21 established good cause. At the same time, it is equally far from clear that the struggle was worth it for Connecticut. In 1978 and 1980, Sugarman noted, the support payments that Connecticut managed to get "deadbeat dads" to pay amounted to 6 and 7 percent, respectively, of all AFDC payments—about 4 or 5 percent after subtracting the state's collection costs—and it is not clear how much of that came from coerced identification as opposed to identification that would have been made voluntarily, absent the legal requirement (430). In the 1990s, notwithstanding the issues raised by the *Roe v. Norton* litigation, a new federal welfare law ordered states, on pain of losing substantial amounts of federal welfare money, to produce annual increases in the percentage of unwed fathers acknowledging paternity (Jacobs, 1997). And the 1996 welfare reform litigation, which imposed time limits and demanding work requirements in its new TANF program, resulted in drastic reductions in the number of women and children on welfare. (As noted above, the major federal sources of financial aid for the poor or low income people then became a food purchase subsidy program and a tax credit/cash-subsidy program).

The Positive Effects of Adversarial Legalism

From one perspective, the "naming deadbeat dads" story illustrates how adversarial legalism sometimes has enabled idealistic American lawyers and judges to help shape the welfare state. It highlights how adversarial legalism enables legal advocates for the poor to challenge alleged legislative and bureaucratic malpractice, to expose the prejudices or lack of imagination that may be embodied in statutes and regulations, and to argue that considerations of social justice sometimes should outweigh fiscal concerns and considerations of bureaucratic efficiency. Whereas legislation states general rules, litigation forces judges to focus on the plight of particular individuals whose situations may differ from the typical problem situation envisaged by legislators. Thus in *Roe v. Norton* the lawyers pointed out that in some cases it is *not* in the best interests of a child for the state to require AFDC mothers to identify the child's father and to compel him to meet his support obligations. In such cases the legislature's assumption–in this case, that the welfare mother who declines to identify the father is socially and morally irresponsible–is incorrect. Ultimately, the *Roe v. Norton* litigation and the debate it generated led to a nationwide HEW regulation authorizing an AFDC-supported mother who can show good cause to decline to identify the father.

Similarly, in some other welfare rights cases mentioned–*King v. Smith* (1968), *Goldberg v. Kelly* (1970), *Shapiro v. Thompson* (1969)–adversarial legalism operated as a check on stringent administrative rules and practices that reflected politically-conservative, probably overbroad assumptions about the prevalence of welfare cheating. The Supreme Court's decision in *Goldberg v. Kelly* compelled thousands of counties and municipalities to institute "fair hearings" by neutral officials when claimants argued that the agency had erred in terminating their badly-needed benefits–thereby requiring agencies to substitute legal proof for potentially arbitrary administrative judgments.

Adversarial legalism sometimes serves not only as a procedural check on the administration of public policies but as a political catalyst for legislative reforms that *expand* social provision. For example, in the early 1980s, the politically-conservative Reagan administration embarked on a rushed effort to purge ineligible recipients from the Federal Social Security Disability Program; benefits were terminated for at least 500,000 individuals. The structures of adversarial legalism, however, enabled many to appeal their terminations to the federal courts. There, as recounted by Jeb Barnes and Tom Burke (2015: 75), judges "abandoned their traditional deference to the SSA, reversing terminations in 41 percent of the cases [they heard] and a whopping 91 percent in cases involving mental impairments." The courts' opinions contained ideas that liberal reformers then drew upon in lobbying Congress, which in 1984 enacted legislation updating the legal standards and methods for assessing disability (76).

Similarly, in the early 1970s, public interest litigation on behalf of handicapped children enabled educational reformers to expose the fallacy (and the heartlessness) of state policies that assumed it was too difficult or too costly to provide a public education for handicapped children or to integrate them into the regular schools; these lawsuits, which included some striking victories for rights advocates, precipitated enactment of federal legislation that mandated an appropriate public education for handicapped children (Melnick, 1995). Many state governments, fearful of the costs of such litigation and the enormous additional costs of educating physically and mentally disabled children, supported enactment of the Congressional law because it also promised federal financial aid to state and local schools when they instituted special education programs.

As in the field of education for children with disabilities, when an injustice or hardship can be framed as invidious discrimination or as a violation of a constitutional right, adversarial legalism has provided a vital mechanism for addressing issues of social justice that had simply been ignored by the elected branches. In 1950s and early 1960s, when African Americans were still disenfranchised in Southern states, litigation in the federal courts, based on federal statutes or the U.S. Constitution's Equal Protection clause, was the only effective means of challenging and dismantling governmental laws and practices that entrenched racial inequality. Subsequently, after the enactment of the federal Civil Rights Law in 1964, Shep Melnick (2014: 97–98) writes, adversarial legalism was crucial in building "the civil rights state" via a "symbiotic relationship between federal courts and federal agencies." In implementing Title VI (which prohibited discrimination in federally funded programs and contracts) and Title VII (forbidding discrimination in employment), administrators promulgated politically liberal regulations and guidelines. Then judges, prodded by civil rights lawyers, legally endorsed the agencies' interpretive guidelines and enforced them. Melnick (97–98) adds:

> Courts' ability to issue injunctions, award monetary damages, and provide attorney's fees not only put real teeth into the enforcement process, but provided strong incentives for private litigants to monitor the behavior of employers and recipients of federal funding. The growth of the civil rights bar, in turn, provided crucial political support for these institutional arrangements when they were threatened by adverse Supreme Court decisions.[18]

Of course, banning discrimination and mandating procedurally fair hearings do not guarantee more adequate social provision or better employment benefits. But a legal right to fair treatment is a helpful step in that direction.[19] In a political system that has been reluctant to establish comprehensive, well-funded social welfare programs and employee protections comparable to those provided by other economically advanced democracies, adversarial legalism has often been the only game in town as far as reformers were concerned, or at least the game that could best put relative socioeconomic deprivation on the political agenda.

The Downsides of Adversarial Legalism

Consider the "naming deadbeat dads" story again, but this time from the perspective of one of its less auspicious consequences—perpetuating costly litigation, political conflict, and legal uncertainty. For more than ten years, adversarial legalism struggled to impose a definitive legal solution on the coerced maternal cooperation controversy. Judicial decisions, far from providing authoritative legal guidance, succeeded primarily in stimulating legal and political counterattacks. When a U.S. District Court judge rejected Connecticut's cutoff of AFDC funds to children of uncooperative mothers, Connecticut responded by recasting its rules to cut off only the mother's benefits. When a court said that too was unlawful, Connecticut passed a law calling for the jailing of noncooperative mothers, stimulating multiple appeals to the courts. Similarly, when other district courts held that state rules requiring coerced maternal cooperation rulings were illegal, the U.S. Department of Health, Education, and Welfare declined to acquiesce in the judges' interpretation of federal law, stimulating more appeals. In these and other instances, litigation bred more litigation, conflicting decisions, legal complexity, and legal uncertainty.

More generally, by opening the courts to challenges to governmental authority and lawyers' creative arguments, adversarial legalism turns the judiciary into an arena of continuing political struggle over social policy and its implementation. Because judges can and do make policy decisions, the competing political parties each strive to appoint judges who will be ideologically sympathetic. In consequence, while approximately 80 percent of cases decided by the U.S. Courts of Appeals are decided unanimously, about 20 percent generate split decisions, and in these more politically controversial cases, judges appointed by Republican presidents tend to vote differently from judges appointed by Democrats (Gottschall, 1986: 49–54; Cross and Tiller, 1998). That affects the implementation of social programs: in appeals of U.S. Social Security Administration decisions concerning an employee's eligibility for a pension based on permanent disability, three-judge panels of the courts of appeals dominated by Republican judges differ significantly from predominantly Democratic panels (Haire and Lindquist, 1997: 230–236).

The politicization of the judiciary tends to vitiate legal authority. As in the coerced maternal cooperation story, administrative agencies and state governments often are inclined to treat judicial decisions that reject their policies as just one more political obstacle to be overcome by tactical means—including the possibility of drawing a more sympathetic judge in the next round of litigation or of persuading Congress to pass legislation overriding the judge's decision. Opponents of the previously-mentioned liberal judicial rulings on AFDC administration repeatedly sought congressional legislation that would overturn them—but in vain. Yet later, after President Reagan was elected in 1980, Congress enacted laws that reversed many of the earlier court rulings (Melnick, 1993: 120–130). Overall, on a wide range of legal policy areas, Congress reversed or modified at least 300 lower court and 100 Supreme Court decisions between 1975 and 1990 (Eskridge, 1991). On the other hand, Jeb Barnes (2004) found that such congressional override statutes, ostensibly aimed at resolving politically partisan division among federal judges, succeed in doing so only about half the time. In sum, by channeling policy disputes to a decentralized, politically-selected judiciary system, adversarial legalism engenders a balkanized, uncertain, and continually contestable body of public law. In continental European countries, where legal review of administrative decisions is entrusted to specialized administrative courts, judicial decisions are more predictable and stable (Garoupa and Matthews, 2014).

American benefit-granting agencies, acting in the shadow of frequent appeals of their decisions to the courts,[20] often include intra-agency appeal systems that partially mimic the adversarial formats of American courts (Kagan, 2017). But here too, adversarial legalism is not a recipe for greater legal order. In his classic study of decision-making in the U.S. Social Security Administration's disability benefits (SSDI) program, Jerry Mashaw (1983) found that in a typical year in the 1970s, more than half of the 250,000 SSDI benefit denials, even after administrative reconsideration, were appealed to intra-agency administrative law judges (ALJs). While ALJs technically are agency employees, they are substantially independent; in 1983 they brought a class action against the Social Security Administration (SSA) in federal court, arguing that in attempting to monitor and sanction ALJs who deviate from agency policy, the SSA was improperly constraining their independent legal judgment. In 1979, in over half of the appeals, the ALJ reversed the administrative denial. Reversal rates by different ALJs ranged from 70 percent to 20 percent (Mashaw, 1983: 42; Kagan, 1984: 823). Similar disparities have been found among the intra-agency adjudicators who hear appeals from front line agency decisions in immigration and asylum cases (Ramji-Nogales, Schoenholtz, and Schrag, 2007).

High reversal rates by administrative law judges, and wide inter-ALJ disparities in reversal rates, does not mean that such appeal systems should be discarded. Nor does the protracted litigation, political conflict, and legal uncertainty that often accompanies reform litigation efforts like *Roe v. Norton* provide grounds, in my view, for disallowing that kind of adversarial legalism. But these are troublesome aspects of adversarial legalism, since they stimulate political backlashes against social welfare programs or government in general, and may compel less well-funded reform advocates to simply give up.

Social Justice and Civil Justice

In the early, idealistic days of the national Legal Services Program, Geoffrey Hazard (1969) argued that while courts at their best can provide civil justice—remedying particular illegal actions by individuals or organizations—they have only limited powers to provide social justice. After all, whom can judges hold legally responsible for the systemic inequalities in income and wealth that are inherent in dynamic capitalist economies? How can a court remedy those inequalities, short of massive redistributions of money and power that are well beyond the authority and competence of judges to order? Hazard may have overstated his point. As noted earlier, in the late 1960s and early 1970s, welfare rights lawyers successfully used litigation to drive state and local governments toward higher standards of *procedural* justice. That kind of litigation and judicial decision-making has continued to strengthen the just implementation of laws, state and federal, designed to provide social benefits, rights, and protections of various kinds. Moreover, some procedural court rulings have broad substantive consequences. *King v. Smith* (1968), the previously-mentioned case in which the Supreme Court struck down Alabama's presumption that a "man in the house" demonstrated ineligibility for welfare benefits, made an estimated 500,000 children eligible for public assistance (Davis, 1993: 68).

Yet for the most part, Hazard's dictum was correct. One reason is that victories in court—especially when they have significant budgetary consequences for governments—often trigger political or administrative reactions that reverse or erode the apparent gains. For example, the Supreme Court's previously mentioned decision in *Goldberg v. Kelly* (1970) sought to prevent the mistaken termination of welfare benefits to families who were actually eligible. Before terminating benefits, the Court held, the Constitution's due process clause required local welfare agencies throughout the country to provide for a pretermination hearing. But those hearings slowed the process of terminating truly ineligible recipients, thereby raising local governments' welfare costs. In response, politicians required welfare administrators to adopt tougher evidentiary standards for *new* applicants, which delayed payments to eligible needy families (Brodkin and Lipsky, 1983). Caught between the threat of lawsuits by rights advocates and intensified accountability demands from conservative politicians, welfare officials often sought refuge by mechanically following rules. Welfare offices came to be staffed with checklist-oriented clerks, displacing social workers and their discretionary assessments of clients' particular needs

(Simon, 1983). As the administrative system was reshaped by adversarial legalism and political counterreaction, welfare clients increasingly felt lost in impenetrable legal mazes (Sarat, 1990; Jewell, 2007)

Another reason Hazard was correct: in the United States, courts' authority over substantive rights is limited. Even in its most liberal era, the Supreme Court declined to read a right to subsistence or a socially guaranteed minimum standard of living into the U.S. Constitution, a document that was drafted before the modern welfare state had been dreamed of.[21] Lacking the power to tax, judges have only limited authority to promulgate redistributive policies or compel legislatures to do so.[22] Nor can the *courts* do much to remedy the major differences between politically liberal and politically conservative states in the social and health care benefits they provide for low income households (see Robertson and Fausset, 2015).

Adversarial legalism has proved to be a limited weapon in other areas of social policy as well. The United States is close to unique in the extent to which liberalization of abortion laws came about through litigation and judicial decisions, rather than legislation, and unique in establishing an untrammeled, judicially-established constitutional right to first-trimester abortion (*Roe v. Wade*, 1973). But in contrast to most European governments, which include abortion services in their universal health care programs, adversarial legalism has not provided American women with a constitutional right to a *government-funded* abortion, and in a great many locations political resistance has made actual access to abortion services either impossible or very difficult (Glendon, 1987). Similarly, during the 1960s and 1970s crusading lawyers used the federal courts to expose the abominable conditions in underfunded state mental hospitals (Rothman and Rothman, 1984), which led to reductions in commitments to those institutions. Yet adversarial legalism was a thoroughly ineffective mechanism for providing alternatives, such as adequate halfway houses for the mentally ill, or for ensuring that persons who formerly would have been involuntarily committed could be induced to move to shelters to take helpful medicines (Curtis, 1986). Nor has American adversarial legalism been capable of expanding governmental guarantees for child care, subsidized housing, or effective job training and placement of the unemployed.

In sum, returning to Hazard's distinction between civil justice and social justice, adversarial legalism has had some impact on social justice. It has helped and continues to help reduce the most blatant forms of discrimination and insensitivity in the *administration* of existing law. Nevertheless, the American system of social provision for the unemployed and the needy (especially and ironically in poorer, more politically conservative states), remains significantly less comprehensive and generous than the welfare states of northwestern Europe, more suspicious of fraud and abuse, and for recipients, more demeaning, legalistic, and difficult to deal with.[23]

Moreover, as a mechanism of *civil justice*, adversarial legalism, as discussed in Chapter 6, has serious limitations. For example, in the United States, the effective implementation of civil rights laws forbidding racial discrimination by employers or landlords relies heavily on aggrieved individuals' readiness and capacity to document evidence to prove their case, obtain a competent lawyer, and if necessary, pursue their claims in court. But the difficulties, costliness, and stress for claimants of taking that route means that those laws are bound to fall short. To be sure, more than 10,000 job discrimination and other kinds of wrongful termination cases are filed in the courts each year, and employers find such suits threatening and costly to defend (Dertouzos, Holland, and Ebener, 1992).[24] But nationwide, only a tiny fraction of employees with claims of workplace discrimination actually file lawsuits. That is the finding of a detailed study of civil rights court filings and of in-depth interviews with parties and their legal counsel by Ellen Berrey, Robert Nelson, and Laura Beth Nielsen (2017: 21).[25] They add that, "When targets do sue, they are likely to settle or lose" due to the typical disparity in resources between inexperienced plaintiffs and better-represented defendant business firms. Moreover, "Plaintiffs often are treated by the EEOC [Equal Employment Opportunity Commission] and court bureaucrats, defendant organizations, defense lawyers, judges, and even their own lawyers as unworthy claimants" (201).

In fact, as part of the conservative attack on adversarial legalism, as discussed in the Afterword, the U.S. Supreme Court has gradually made it even more difficult for employees to win civil rights cases. Lauren Edelman (2016) documents part of that legal evolution with respect to workplace discrimination claims. In *Meritor Savings Bank v. Vinson* (1986) the U.S. Supreme Court held that workplace sexual harassment violates the 1964 Civil Rights Act's prohibition of discrimination based on sex, and held that right enforceable via lawsuits for money damages against the victim's employer. The Court suggested, however, that an employer might be protected from liability if it had instituted an effective antiharassment policy and complaint procedure. Large corporate employers rushed to adopt programs that could sail them into that possible safe harbor. In a 1998 Court opinion,[26] the "might protect" idea in the *Meritor* opinion became "would protect" as long as the employer had a written antiharassment policy and an effective complaint procedure. That sounds like a sensible and constructive way to change sexually abusive workplace cultures without costly and cumbersome adversarial legalism. But Edelman (2016, chapter 8) shows that in sexual harassment suits that are brought to court, the judges often dismiss the suit based only on the defendant corporation's assertion that it has such a policy and procedure; the judges don't consider whether the procedure it is actually effective. Edelman (2017) adds: "Judges frequently discount evidence plaintiffs present that, despite having such policies, employers condone or fail to correct a culture in which harassment and degradation of women are common. And even where employees . . . [avoid] complaint procedures [due to] fear of retaliation, courts generally see an employee's failure to complain as a bar to winning a sexual harassment case."

A Partial Exception: Adversarial Legalism and Educational Inequality

Among economically advanced democracies, wrote historian Kenneth Jackson (1996: E15): "Only in America are schools, police and fire protection and other services financed largely by local taxes. . . . In Europe, Australia, and Japan, such [funding] functions are essentially the responsibility of national or at least regional governments."[27] Compared to the United States, European central governments raise proportionally far more money through national (rather than provincial or municipal) taxation. They also exert stronger controls on urban sprawl and provide far more public housing, dispersed more widely (Weir, 1995). In the United States, local governments operate more on their own, desperately searching for sources of revenue to meet political demands for education, transportation, and public safety. County governments, which control land use outside city limits, often are inclined to let developers supplant farms and open spaces with revenue-generating housing developments, golf courses, shopping centers, and industrial parks. And in the United States (unlike Western Europe), newly settled areas have been able to incorporate as new suburban municipalities with relative ease (Briffault, 1990); henceforth they operate as semiautonomous principalities, mostly free to zone out low-income housing and reject public housing for the poor.

This is the political structure that drove suburbanization in the second half of the twentieth century, especially after urban crime grew in the 1960s. In many counties, middle-class and successful working-class families—mostly whites but successful black families as well—increasingly moved to the suburbs, seeking better public schools and safer neighborhoods. Businesses followed, along with the jobs they support. Racial discrimination in the housing market made it harder for black families to escape inner city neighborhoods. In 1969, Congress enacted a law banning racial discrimination in housing, but proponents could enact it only by jettisoning strong legal enforcement provisions (both public and private). Consequently, until amended in 1988, the 1968 law proved wholly ineffective in pushing federally-subsidized affordable housing into the suburbs and in fighting private racial discrimination (Massey and Denton, 1993: 191–200). Even since then, residential racial (as well as socioeconomic) separation has increased. Many American cities contain large areas characterized by levels of poverty, ethnic and racial isolation, physical deterioration, drug addiction, and violence that, according to French sociologist Loic Wacquant (1995), are quantitatively and qualitatively very different from the immigrant neighborhoods of Western European cities.

The tradition of local educational governance and finance meant that schools (and students) in property-tax-rich suburbs generally enjoyed more resources per student than those in declining older cities (as opposed to thriving ones), in less wealthy suburbs and in rural school districts. In many urban schools, moreover, vandalism and violence were far more common than in the suburbs; so was the proportion of students with behavioral or developmental problems. Teacher turnover generally was higher. Student achievement and aspiration levels generally were far lower. The realities of public education massively contradicted America's stated, and widely held, ideals of the ideal of equal educational opportunity. But state and federal politicians, confronting electorates dominated by families who had bought a hard-to-afford suburban house in order to find better schools, generally declined to establish *metropolitan* school systems, blending the resources and students of city and suburb (Peterson, 1996; Weir, 1995: 226–229). Adversarial legalism, as in other policy areas, sprang from this tension between American ideals of equal opportunity and a fragmented, veto-prone political system that is ill-prepared to respond to those ideals.

Beginning in the 1970s, for example, reformers brought lawsuits challenging suburban zoning laws that banned construction of multiple-unit apartment houses, trailer parks, and small-lot single-family homes. They argued that such laws were unconstitutional because they excluded low-income African Americans from affordable housing in suburban towns and their schools. The U.S. Supreme Court held, however, that the Constitution is not offended absent explicit proof that a suburban municipality's single-family zoning rules had been adopted *in order to* exclude African Americans rather than simply to maintain amenities and control growth (*Village of Arlington Heights v. Metropolitan Housing Development Corp.*, 1977). The Court also rejected constitutional challenges to state laws stipulating that community residents must be allowed to vote on (and reject) plans to build low-income housing projects in their towns or neighborhoods (*James v. Valtierra*, 1971).

The New Jersey Supreme Court acted more boldly to integrate the suburbs, as recounted by David Kirp, John Dwyer and Larry Rosenthal (1995). In a ruling known as *Mt. Laurel I* (1975), it held that suburbs were obligated by the state constitution to provide their fair share of low-income housing, and in 1983 the court authorized builders to file lawsuits to compel suburbs to adjust their zoning regulations accordingly (*Mt. Laurel II*, 1983). But in 1985 the state legislature, besieged by the suburbs, enacted a compromise law that blunted the impact of the *Mt. Laurel* cases.[28] The New Jersey Supreme Court, with its chief justice up for renomination and under political attack, upheld the compromise law (*Mt. Laurel III,* 1986), which watered down suburbs' obligations to provide affordable housing. By the mid-1990s very little low-income housing had been built in New Jersey's wealthier suburbs (Kirp, Dwyer, and Rosenthal, 1995).

Reformers' assault on exclusionary zoning via adversarial legalism was not meaningless, however. It helped stimulate legislatures in several states to enact laws that required suburbs, when approving new housing developments, to make provision for low-income units. But for most families in declining cities, a path to a better, suburban education for their children would require saving enough money to afford a single-family house in the suburbs—a motive that unscrupulous salesmen of high-risk, low down-payment mortgages exploited during the housing bubble of the first decade of the twenty-first century, with disastrous financial results for such families after the bubble burst.

Another equalizing strategy, at least for African Americans, was to file lawsuits charging that the racial imbalance between city and suburban schools amounted to unconstitutional racial discrimination. In *Milliken v. Bradley,* first filed in 1970, NAACP lawyers asked a U.S. District Court to order that black students from Detroit, where about 70 percent of public school students were black, should be bused to predominantly white suburban schools. Judge Stephen Roth held the Detroit school board and the state government guilty of de jure discrimination—for example, by maintaining optional attendance zones within Detroit that enabled white families to avoid sending their children to largely black schools and by other measures apparently intended to *retard* "white flight" from the city schools. The judge then ordered that some 310,000 of the region's 780,000 pupils be bused from city to suburb or vice versa (Wilkerson, 1979).

The U.S. Supreme Court reversed that decision (*Milliken v. Bradley* (1974). In a five-four decision, the Court held that judges could not order metropolitan busing absent a finding of deliberate discrimination by the suburban school districts in question. Chief Justice Burger's opinion asserted that a ruling that allowed a judge to become a "de facto legislative authority" and "school superintendent" for the whole area would be beyond the qualifications of judges and antithetical to democratic governance. In Los Angeles, Wilmington, and Louisville, courts nevertheless did order metropolitan busing; the results were mixed, the downside being considerable additional white flight and a great deal of political opposition, even from some black parents and educational leaders.[29] But by and large, *Milliken* stanched the effort to bridge the city-suburb structural divide by means of court-ordered busing of students.

One other litigation strategy, however, has been somewhat more successful, perhaps because it involves redistributing money rather than housing or school children. In 1971 the California Supreme Court had held in *Serrano v. Priest* that California's local property tax system for funding public schools, as then operated, violated the California Constitution because it resulted in sharp disparities in educational expenditures. In 1973, the U.S. Supreme Court held in a five-four decision that even substantially different per-pupil spending in property-tax-rich and property-tax-poor municipalities did *not* violate the *U.S.* Constitution. But reformers continued to initiate legal attacks against state property tax systems as violative of *state* constitutions. In twenty-five of the forty-two states in which a state supreme court decided the issue, the court held the school-funding system unconstitutional (Howard and Steigerwalt, 2011: 127–30; Paris, 2010; Reed, 2001: 176; Heise, 1995: 1743). Often, the reformers returned to court repeatedly, arguing that a state had failed to comply adequately with the court order. Judges often ended up micromanaging the school funding formulae adopted by state legislatures.[30] But progress was made. Comparing five states in which reformers won in court with three in which they lost, Douglas Reed (1998: 182–201) found that court orders generally resulted in increased funding for the most poorly resourced school districts; they also led to increased state funding for education overall.

Just as importantly, the litigation publicly dramatized the problem of unequal educational funding. Many state legislatures increased the share of local public school spending provided by state revenues (sales and income taxes) as compared to local property tax revenues—reaching parity by the 1980s (Chingos and Blagg, 2017). And they distributed that money more progressively, increasing funding for the bottom fifth of school districts, on average, by 50 percent between 1990 and 2012, bringing them roughly in line with high income districts (*Economist*, 2017f). By the late 1990s and continuing into the twenty-first century, as researchers put it, in virtually every state "the average low-income student attends districts that are as well funded as districts the average nonpoor student attends" (Chingos and Blagg, 2017: 2).

Yet it has become apparent that equal funding, while helpful, does not lead to equal educational outcomes[31]—or even in adequate ones for children in schools whose social and familial environment deprives large proportions of students of the kinds of socialization, stability, and encouragement enjoyed by children in higher socioeconomic school districts. "Of young Americans whose parents did not finish high school," The *Economist* (2017f) reported, "only 5 get a degree, compared with nearly 20% in the OECD as a whole." Thus adversarial legalism has not been able to overcome the disparities in educational equality that stem from a political structure that facilitates the socioeconomic stratification of public education.

———

In the United States privately initiated litigation over public provision arises and persists because it seemingly promises to narrow the gap between legal ideals and a fragmented, fiscally pinched governmental system. In the 1980s and 1990s, as mentioned in Chapter 3, public interest law firms filed lawsuit after lawsuit against the city of Washington, D.C.—one class action on behalf of poorly served children in foster care, others on behalf of food stamp recipients, prisoners in overcrowded city jails, recipients of governmental mental health services, households awaiting public housing, detainees in appallingly bad mental institutions, and youths in juvenile detention facilities. In each case the judge, appalled by the gap between the promises of the welfare state and the performance of a poorly administered, poorly funded municipal government, imposed a reform program on the relevant department (Plotz, 1994).

Yet litigation, as stressed above, cannot bridge the gap. Courts can and do issue orders against maladministration and penalize overt discrimination, but they cannot increase the tax base of cities, eliminate socioeconomic disparities between the poor and the suburban middle classes, create governmental programs, guarantee jobs, build subsidized housing, or operate halfway houses for the mentally ill. The same fragmentation and weakness of governmental authority that create the opening and the justification for adversarial legalism tend to impede the realization of egalitarian social goals, even in the face of litigation and court orders.

That is not to say that litigation on behalf of the poor has done no good. When governments are unresponsive to social needs, adversarial legalism, even if not a panacea, often is far better than doing nothing. Litigation sometimes helps mobilize groups for direct political action and helps change public perceptions of the issues (McCann, 1994). As in the case of education for educationally handicapped children, court rulings and the threat of further costly litigation sometimes impel local governments to join egalitarian reformers in pushing for new statutory laws that expand rights and benefits for the needy or marginalized. Moreover, one should not underestimate the value of the *procedural* reforms—the protections against official arbitrariness, discrimination, and invasion of privacy—that have flowed from litigation by American civil rights groups, poverty lawyers, and advocates for particular disadvantaged groups.

Nevertheless, the fact remains that adversarial legalism has not significantly narrowed the differences between the American welfare state and those of other rich democracies, or turned the early legal victories of the civil rights movement into victories over urban poverty and racial isolation. To make changes of that order would require not litigation but a sustained intellectual and political movement yielding sweeping legislative changes in American tax, labor, and educational policy and in traditions of local home rule. That does not seem likely in view of the current political structure and political culture of the United States.

CHAPTER NINE

Adversarial Legalism and the Regulatory State

Protect us, O Government, from harm! Protect us, surrounded as we are by the side effects of dynamic capitalist economies and modern technologies. For we dwell in fear that we and our children will ingest or inhale invisible toxins. Agricultural chemicals, mechanized logging, industrial pollutants, and massive construction projects threaten our remaining forests, marshes, and streams. We are vulnerable to dangerous machines and products, deceitful promoters, discriminatory treatment, and all kinds of human error. In the name of human decency, O Government, protect us from harm!

Versions of this fervent prayer are voiced every month in legislative hearing rooms, on television programs, and in the newsletters of public interest advocacy organizations. In democracies governments take those prayers seriously. They don't answer every prayer, of course, but every year they commission studies to analyze risks and they enact additional regulatory obligations into law. Governmental inspectors fan out across the community, a white-collar police force enforcing regulations designed to prevent a wide range of harms, ranging from workplace injuries, environmental pollution, and food-borne disease to substandard care in nursing homes and inadequate maintenance of airliners, train tracks, and school buses. Inside office buildings, regulatory experts evaluate permit applications for factory expansions, new construction projects, new pharmaceutical products, and new stock issues. All in all, the cumulative growth of the regulatory state has transformed the legal systems of economically advanced countries. It has proactively inserted law into every corner of society, compelled transformations in business practices, and significantly reduced many risks and forms of injustice.

Despite much political rhetoric about overregulation, few politicians push hard to eliminate (as opposed to fine-tune) protective regulation programs of the kind mentioned in the preceding paragraph. Most regulatory programs are widely regarded, by political conservatives as well as liberals, as essential correctives for serious market failures—that is, for hazards and injustices that are inadequately controlled by market incentives and liability law (Singer, 2015). Yet for several reasons, regulation remains a focus of political conflict. One reason is that regulation never fully answers the prayer for protection. Underregulation is inevitable. An ever-changing economy constantly generates new, unanticipated, not-yet-legally-designated hazards, new openings for heedless, greedy, or incompetent behavior. New intensifying economic pressures invariably tempt some businesses to take risky short-cuts. Regulatory officials are not omnipresent; they cannot detect, correct, or punish all violations. So serious harms slip through the gaps in or around the edges of existing regulatory programs. Charges and investigations occur. And the regulatory system is decried as corrupt or tragically inadequate.

Second, regulation stimulates political conflict because the mandated regulatory requirements often impose significant costs on regulated entities. Some regulatory restrictions threaten the market share and earnings of particular regulated firms—and sometimes of whole segments of an industry. That can stimulate organized political efforts to roll back certain regulations and to block the promulgation of new ones.

A third reason for conflict is that regulations have an inherent tendency to be overinclusive. Regulations that mandate precautionary measures often are stimulated by, and designed to prevent, specific harmful practices—usually those that have characterized a handful of unscrupulous or negligent business firms. But typically the new regulations, designed to be even-handed, apply not only to those "bad apples" but to all firms in an industry, including the "good apples," the generally responsible firms. For those good apples, the across-the-board regulatory requirements often seem unnecessary, costly to comply with, and hence unreasonable (Bardach and Kagan, 1982: chapter 3). To use a familiar analogy: millions of law abiding, well-intentioned people endure inconvenient security screenings designed to catch or deter a tiny number of terrorists or madmen. The constant chafing of perceived regulatory unreasonableness, stemming from having to comply with a multitude of such prophylactic regulations on different subjects, makes many businesspeople critical of the bureaucratic regulatory state, resistant to its expansion, and eager to see it cut back. That dynamic, moreover, is exacerbated by America's distinctive regulatory style.

American bodies of regulatory law do not differ greatly from those of other economically advanced democracies. They address the same kinds of social problems. The substantive thrust of different nations' regulatory standards also tends to be similar. On some subjects, American regulations are more demanding, on others less stringent (most prominently, concerning reduction of carbon emissions) (Swedlow et al., 2009; Wiener, 2007).[1] But in terms of *regulatory style*, the United States is clearly different. American forms of regulatory law, its processes for making regulatory policy, and its methods of enforcing regulatory rules tend to be more legalistic and more reliant on adversarial legalism. This sometimes makes American regulation more effective than regulation in other economically advanced democracies. Sometimes it does not. But it almost always makes American regulation, viewed in comparative perspective, more costly, more inefficient, and more inflexible. One consequence is that regulation in the United States, viewed in cross-national comparison, more often evokes hostility—and that hostility undermines the support from and cooperation by regulated entities that are essential if the public's regulatory prayers are to be answered.

Adversarial Legalism in Action: PREMCO's Regulatory Experience

Between 1995 and 1998 I directed a research program that conducted ten detailed case studies of multinational corporations that have similar business operations in the United States and in Europe, Canada, or Japan. Each company studied interacts repeatedly with different national regulatory regimes concerning the same production technologies and regulatory issues. By holding the regulated entity constant (or as close as one might expect to come to that condition), the research highlighted the differences in national legal regimes as they actually operate. For example, Kazumasu Aoki and John Cioffi, authors of one of the case studies (2000), compared the Japanese and American regulatory regimes for industrial wastes by studying the regulatory experience of PREMCO (a pseudonym), a Japanese multinational corporation that manufactures precision metal parts, with facilities in many countries. PREMCO operates similar factories in the United States and Japan, generating similar manufacturing wastes—solvents, oily water, and contaminated metal particles. Some of those wastes are classified as hazardous; if disposed of improperly they can badly contaminate soil, waterways, or underground aquifers, endangering ecosystems and human health. After years of uncontrolled industrial waste disposal, sloppy management of hazardous waste storage sites, midnight dumping by unscrupulous waste disposal services, and revelations of serious harm to many people, both the United States and Japan enacted legislation that mandates rigorous waste storage and disposal methods.

It appears that PREMCO strives to be an environmentally responsible corporation. The company won recognition from the United States Environmental Protection Agency (EPA) for developing a method to phase out the use of chlorofluorocarbons and trichloroethylene two years before the deadline established by the Montreal Protocol (designed to protect the earth's ozone layer). PREMCO also instituted an aggressive corporation-wide environmental auditing and waste reduction program, certified under the International Standards Organization's important ISO 14000 series. Aoki and Cioffi found that in its U.S. and Japanese factories, PREMCO had instituted similar shop floor controls on the collection and storage of wastes, as well as controls on their shipment and disposal. The two governmental regimes' regulatory styles differed sharply, however. According to Aoki and Cioffi (2000: 34):

> Viewed through the lenses of PREMCO's comparative experience, American environmental regulations are more detailed and prescriptive, and American enforcement processes, in contrast with Japan's, emphasize the legalistic interpretation of formal regulations and the imposition of sanctions to modify economic behavior. In contrast to Japanese waste management regulation, the complex American regulatory scheme poses more difficulties in compliance, imposes substantial additional economic costs on regulated entities, and engenders antagonism and defensiveness on the part of firm personnel.

The Japanese mode of environmental regulation is far more cooperative and nonadversarial. Use of nonlegally binding administrative guidance (gyōsei shidō) reduces the Japanese regulatory system's reliance on formal legal rules, sanction-based enforcement, and litigious relations.[2] In addition, the Japanese regulatory framework tends to emphasize (1) performance standards rather than specific, mandatory methods of waste control and (2) informal regulatory initiatives formulated and implemented jointly by industry associations and government ministries and agencies. In comparison with the United States, corporate antagonism towards regulators in Japan is extremely low, as the system appears to facilitate corporate acceptance of regulatory norms. Shop floor environmental practices as implemented in PREMCO's Japanese plant are equal or superior to those imposed on the U.S. factories by prescriptive American regulations.

To illustrate this contrast Aoki and Cioffi (2000) recount the experience of AMERCO–PREMCO's U.S. subsidiary–as it interacted with the state environmental regulatory agency in an eastern American state in which three AMERCO factories are located. The federal Resource Conservation and Recovery Act (RCRA), enacted in 1976, authorized the U.S. Environmental Protection Agency (EPA) to turn over the administration of the mandated waste control program to state governments, so long as the state adopts each provision of RCRA, plus implementing regulations and procedures that are at least as stringent as the federal program. The federal statute and rules, moreover, are extraordinarily detailed and prescriptive. The regional EPA office monitors state RCRA enforcement regarding the number of violations found and penalties imposed.

Comprehension as well as compliance is a primary challenge under RCRA. A U.S. Court of Appeals opinion described the effort to comprehend RCRA a "mind-numbing journey" (*American Mining Congress v. EPA*, 1987).The facilities managers at two AMERCO plants estimated that they spend approximately 15 to 20 percent of their time on RCRA issues (Aoki and Cioffi, 2000). One prescriptive provision, for example, is "the twelve-hour rule," which provides that hazardous wastes must be moved from shop floor collection containers to a satellite or a main storage area once every shift or every twelve hours. The state agency classified waste oil as a hazardous waste under RCRA, which brings most of AMERCO's production processes within the ambit of RCRA regulations, including the twelve-hour rule.

In October 1992 state RCRA inspectors visited AMERCO Plant A, a facility that was scheduled to close two weeks later. The inspectors issued a citation to the plant manager for a number of violations, including failures to properly collect, label, and store waste oil under the twelve-hour rule and other state RCRA provisions. AMERCO's current management officials insisted to Aoki and Cioffi that these violations did not result in any environmental contamination, or even in any significant environmental risks, and none was alleged by the regulators. Plant A's manager promised the inspector, "We'll go ahead and fix these problems, but we're not going to send you documentation that we have fixed the problem . . . since in two weeks this plant is not going to even exist" (40–41). The regulators, write Aoki and Cioffi, "perceived this response as evidence that AMERCO was indifferent or resistant to environmental regulation." That perception was colored by an earlier conflict involving AMERCO's Plant B. PREMCO had bought Plant B in 1985, soon after it had been placed on the EPA's Superfund list of badly contaminated chemical disposal sites. Years before, between 1960 and 1967, sloppy disposal or leakage from Plant B had caused extensive contamination of soil and a municipal water supply well. By the mid-1990s, AMERCO had been obligated to spend $14 million on cleanup and related fees, with more to come. But adversarial negotiations over the details of the cleanup plan, during which PREMCO's Washington lawyers had employed "aggressive negotiation and litigating tactics," had been interpreted by state regulators as evidence of "corporate hostility to environmental obligations" (36–37).

In April 1993 state regulatory officials launched simultaneous RCRA inspections of AMERCO Plants B and C (located in different cities) and cited them for numerous violations similar to those found in the 1992 inspection at Plant A. Once again, according to company officials and AMERCO's outside counsel (a former state environmental agency attorney), the vast majority of these violations posed no significant risk to the environment and none had caused any environmental contamination.

At that time, each of the three AMERCO factories regarded itself as autonomous in production, management, and regulatory affairs. But to the regulators, the failure of Plants B and C to respond to the warning provided by the Plant A inspection was symptomatic either of persistently haphazard waste management practices or of outright defiance. Consequently, for each violation of the twelve-hour rule, regulators cited the company not merely for violating the rule but for violating labeling, sealing, and storage requirements for hazardous wastes. Thus a single violation immediately mushroomed into four or five violations; two-thirds of the approximately 150 citations issued following the April 1993 inspections were derived from violations of the twelve-hour rule. Subsequently, AMERCO submitted two status reports and additional correspondence confirming rectification of all violations, and in March 1994 the agency issued a notice of compliance to both plants. Nevertheless, two months later the agency sent AMERCO a legal notice demanding $495,000 in fines for violations found during the inspections at *all three* plants.

The company and its attorneys, outraged by the punitive response to its efforts to remedy the violations, argued that the regulators had grossly inflated the environmental risk factor and thus the size of the fine. Aoki and Cioffi's review of the litigation file convinced them that the company managers' position was justified.[3] Negotiations between AMERCO and the government took six months and cost the company over $50,000 in attorneys' fees—far more than the cost of remedying the original violations themselves. The government ultimately settled for approximately $200,000— $100,000 in fines, a $10,000 donation to a local environmental group, and a credit of $92,500 in return for $185,000 in capital expenditures for new pollution controls that addressed issues that had not constituted violations and required the company to undertake waste reduction measures not mandated by RCRA.

AMERCO also hired a new environmental manager with responsibility for coordinating environmental compliance across all plants. But the bitterness between AMERCO and the agency reportedly persisted into the late 1990s when Aoki and Cioffi interviewed company officials, and shop floor supervisors still regarded any possible governmental RCRA inspection with trepidation. In the late 1990s a statewide political backlash led to the total repeal of the regulation that classified machine-lubricating waste oil as a hazardous waste under RCRA—a change that reduced the risk of overregulation but increased the risk of underregulation.

PREMCO-Japan's regulatory experience could hardly be more different. Rather than employing detailed, prescriptive legal rules, Japanese environmental statutes articulate broad regulatory goals. They are implemented through informal administrative guidance and custom-tailored agreements between individual firms and the prefects or municipal governments that enforce the national laws, a pattern also noted by Wallace (1995) and Young (1984). Japanese regulators view extensive consultation with regulated industry trade associations and with individual facilities as the most important means of formulating and achieving policy goals. Japanese law and administrative guidance, rather than prescribing the *means* of achieving regulatory goals—such as the U.S. twelve-hour rule—simply require industries, in Aoki and Cioffi's paraphrased translation, "to employ any necessary measures to prevent [hazardous wastes and ordinary wastes] from scattering, flowing away, seeping into the ground, or emitting an offensive odor." The sole prescriptive rule requires factories to enclose waste storage areas, post signs identifying them as such, and store wastes in sealed containers to prevent evaporation or exposure to high temperatures.

When violations of these waste storage provisions are found, Japanese law requires regulators to issue an improvement order containing no financial penalties. Only if an improvement order is ignored or if harm to human health occurs are officials authorized to seek legal sanctions—criminal penalties, for instance. But resort to formal enforcement mechanisms is discouraged and extremely rare. Thus, in the municipality in which PREMCO's Japanese plant is located, regulators told Aoki and Cioffi that formal sanctions have never been imposed for violation of storage standards and, in contrast with AMERCO's experience, regulators inspecting the Japanese plant have never formally found a violation of waste management regulations—although that might reflect the pervasive reluctance of Japanese environmental regulators to resort to formal legal sanctions (Kitamura, 2000).[4] Japanese regulators instead focus on monitoring the firm's waste manifests and on waste reduction as their primary regulatory goal.

Japanese environmental law requires companies and individual facilities to appoint a senior plant official as the factory's pollution control supervisor and in addition to appoint a pollution control manager. These officials are then legally responsible for compliance with, and violations of, environmental regulations and orders. Here too the emphasis is on institutionalizing responsibility for overall environmental outcomes rather than for complying with specific legal rules. According to Aoki and Cioffi (2000: 46):

> In contrast with AMERCO, PREMCO has taken advantage of the opportunities afforded by the performance-based character of the Japanese waste storage standards to diffuse environmental knowledge, training, and respon-

sibility throughout the firm, including to shopfloor workers and supervisors. Performance-based regulation also allows greater flexibility in compliance efforts. Perhaps as a consequence, PREMCO's Japanese managers display none of the negative attitudes towards environmental regulation and regulators detected among AMERCO's managers.

The American Regulatory Style

The PREMCO case, like the other case studies in the research project from which it emerged, replicates the findings of a substantial body of comparative sociolegal studies, covering different regulatory programs that highlight the distinctiveness of the American style of social regulation. Of course, there are a great number of regulatory programs in the United States at all levels of government, and they vary in regulatory style. While some regulatory statutes and implementing rule books, like RCRA's, are highly prescriptive, setting out regulatory obligations in excruciating detail, others grant implementing agencies considerable discretion to balance regulatory goals and economic considerations, depending on the particular circumstances. Some American regulatory agencies, like ticket-issuing highway patrolmen, have a legalistic enforcement style, automatically imposing fines on detected rule violations, even those that pose no immediate risk of harm, but many other agencies employ a more flexible enforcement style (Kagan, 1993). Many state environmental agencies are much less likely than the U.S. EPA to resort to formal legal penalties against or to sue serious violators (Institute for Policy Integrity, 2017)—although that sometimes is because the agency is understaffed or less than fully politically independent. Different regional and different state offices charged with implementing the same law have been found to employ different enforcement styles (Shover et al., 1984; Scholz and Wei, 1986). Repeatedly, politicians and agency chiefs announce plans for making regulation more cooperative (Fiorino, 1996: Michael, 1996; Freeman, 1997).

Nevertheless, as in the Aoki and Cioffi study, whenever researchers have carefully compared specific regulatory regimes in the United States with their counterparts in other economically advanced democracies, the American regulatory regime has been found to entail a number of distinctive features. First, American regulatory statutes and regulations generally are more legalistic—that is, more detailed, prescriptive, and complex (yet confusing and difficult to comply with). Second, American regulatory regimes *more often* (even if not always) enforce the law legalistically: they are more likely to issue formal legal sanctions when they encounter rule violations, and their legal penalties tend to be much more severe. Third, relationships between regulators and regulated entities in the United States are much more often *adversarial*; legal contestation of regulatory rules and decisions, in administrative appeal boards or in courts, is far more common, both by regulated entities and by citizen advocates of stricter regulation. American regulatory statutes, including but not limited to civil rights laws and antitrust laws, are far more likely than similar laws in other countries to authorize and provide incentives for private lawsuits against violators. Fourth, regulatory rules and methods in the United States more often are enmeshed in political controversy and conflict, as rival interests and politicians battle over regulatory appointments, funding, and efforts to lock their policy preferences into statutory amendments or revised regulatory rules.

The European Union, in order to implement its growing body of business regulations, has had to rely on member state governments. Thus like the U.S. federal government, the EU in recent decades has tended to promulgate more detailed rules, to demand more formal procedures, and to encourage tougher sanctions for violators. Daniel Kelemen (2011) has labeled this regulatory style "Eurolegalism," a cousin of American adversarial legalism. Empirical studies in several regulatory policy areas indicate that the EU has thereby injected a dose of legalism into previously cooperation-oriented national enforcement styles (National Academies of Sciences, 2017, chapter 3; Bastings, Mastenbroek, and Versluis, 2017; Bignami, 2011). Nevertheless, those studies reaffirm the proposition that Europe remains a goodly distance from the American regulatory style, which remains distinctive—more adversarial, less collaborative, and more reliant on litigation.

The Form of the Laws

Law professor Edward Rubin, aware that the U.S. Federal Reserve Board's authorizing statutes and regulations governing bank safety and soundness fill numerous three-inch-thick binders, was astonished to learn that Germany's comparable statute and the Bundesbank's implementing regulations are bound in a pamphlet that is less than 100 pages in length. Part of the explanation, Rubin learned, is that German bank regulatory officials are career employees, subjected to much more extensive training than their American counterparts, and they are trusted to make programmatically sensible judgments without constraint by immensely detailed legal rules (Rubin, 1997).

German *environmental* regulations are implemented by state (*lander*) and municipal officials, and are perhaps the most detailed of any nation's save the United States. Still, they are much less prescriptive than American rules.[5] Moreover, the purpose of detail in German regulations is different, according to Daniel Kelemen (1998). The prescriptiveness of American statutes and regulations reflects politicians' and interest groups' desire to control regulatory agencies that they do not fully trust; the rules are designed to prevent the agency's capture by regulated entities or, on the other hand, by regulatory zealots, and to facilitate judicial review that will check unwarranted administrative decisions. In Germany, in contrast, the detail of federal environmental regulations is designed to provide guidance to the state and local officials who are responsible for implementing federal law, and to *shield* regulatory administrators from judicial interference. Moreover, the detailed German air pollution regulations have the legal character of administrative guidance, not binding law; hence administrators can (and often do) lawfully depart from them in individual permitting decisions based on their duty to adjust regulatory requirements to particular circumstances and economic conditions.[6]

Comparisons of U.S. environmental statutes and regulations with those of Sweden (Lundqvist, 1980), Great Britain (Vogel, 1986; Cooter and Ginsburg, 1996), and Canada (Graben and Biber, 2017) have also noted the far greater legal formality, complexity, and prescriptiveness of the American laws. Unique to the United States, for example, is Congress's tendency to stipulate firm deadlines by which a regulatory agency must promulgate implementing regulations and achieve specific regulatory goals; because agencies often cannot meet those deadlines and goals, they are sued by environmental groups demanding compliance (Melnick, 1992a). Prescriptive, deadline-laden statutes, moreover, lead to prescriptive, deadline-laden regulations,[7] and at the level of individual regulated enterprises, to permits, remediation plans, checklists for inspectors, and reporting requirements that far exceed in specificity those imposed by other countries (Axelrad, 2000; Dwyer, Brooks, and Marco, 2000).

The complexity of American statutes also is exacerbated, Peter Schuck (2014: 281–294) has noted, by Congress's tendency to enact statutes that assign implementation responsibilities to multiple, crosschecking federal agencies, or to divide it between federal and state agencies—which greatly complicates compliance for regulated entities. In the realm of civil rights law, Shep Melnick (2018b: 34–35) writes:

> In its investigations of complaints [to the U.S. Department of Education's Office for Civil Rights (OCR)] under the federal Individuals with Disabilities Education Act, OCR expects schools to follow the 320 pages of regulations promulgated by its Department's Office of Special Education and Rehabilitative Services. Federal contractors must follow the guidelines established by the Office for Contract Compliance (OFCC) in the Department of Labor. OFCC's *Federal Contract Compliance Manual* runs over 700 pages. The [Equal Employment Opportunity Commission's] rules run to almost 270 pages [of fine print] in the *Code of Federal Regulations* (CFR). . . . The rules established

by Department of Justice's Civil Rights Division are even longer–slightly more than 360 pages in the *CFR*. [The Department of Housing and Urban Development's] fair housing rules are a bit shorter, just over 200 pages. These figures do not include those agency guidelines, interpretations, compliance manuals, technical assistance documents, memoranda of understanding, and resolution agreements that are the daily fare of regulation. The bottom line is that modern civil rights state has produced an intricate web of rules that apply to almost all businesses, educational institutions, government units, and nonprofits in the country.

The Regulatory Policymaking Process

Many governments seek to manage the political struggle over regulatory standards by entrusting regulatory decisions to technocratic bureaucracies, largely shielded from political and legal interference. Other governments create corporatist forums in which representatives of the regulated industry and of pro-regulation advocacy groups, along with relevant scientific and regulatory experts, bargain toward consensus in formulating regulatory standards. In the United States, in contrast, there is much less trust in agency expertise and political neutrality, and understandably so: the leaders and top echelon of regulatory agencies are politically appointed. Often, they are not specialists drawn from the regulatory bureaucracy. In Republican administrations, they often are former executives, lawyers, or lobbyists for regulated entities. In Democratic administrations, they often are drawn from pro-regulation advocacy organizations. And hence regulatory agencies are the foci of partisan political struggles over regulatory policy. At the same time, reformers have sought to subject those political struggles to the constraints of *legal rationality*, and with some success. The American administrative process for making regulatory policy thus is distinctive in its legal formality, its openness to formal participation by interest groups, its adversarial quality, and its subjection to judicial review.

Specifically, American statutes and court decisions insist that in elaborating regulatory policy, administrative agencies must publish draft regulations, invite comments by affected parties, and conduct hearings in which advocacy groups, business organizations, and other interests may present their critiques and demands. Private consultation between regulators and regulated firms is legally proscribed in many circumstances and politically dangerous in many more. Administrative law compels policymakers to spell out the scientific, technological, and economic evidence they think will justify the regulatory standard chosen. Major regulations often are challenged in court; there judges scrutinize the fairness of the agency's rulemaking procedures, its interpretation of the relevant statutory language, and the quality of its response to arguments submitted by industry and advocacy organizations. The complex requirements of administrative law, however, slow down the regulatory policymaking process, often delaying the issuance of badly needed new rules (Mendeloff, 1987; Mashaw and Harfst, 1987). The fate of new rules is often determined by whether the court that reviews them has a majority of Republican or Democratic judicial appointees (Cross and Tiller, 1998). Nevertheless, the complex requirements of administrative law, as shown by Steven Croley's (2008) detailed case studies, have a valuable function. They push agencies to conduct reasoned, evidence-backed policy analyses. In that and other ways, they reduce the capacity of members of Congress, lobbyists, and lawyers representing regulated business interests to pressure regulatory agency policymakers to water down demonstrably valuable proposed regulations, and make it more difficult for incoming presidential administrations to simply repeal regulations they don't like.

In Great Britain, in contrast, the regulatory policymaking process is far less formal and less open to legal contestation. As indicated by David Vogel's (1986) comparative study of environmental policy, regulatory officials in the U.K. issue nonbinding administrative guidelines stating presumptive emission limits and control technologies. They do so after *private* discussions among staff members, selected technical representatives of affected companies and trade associations, and "responsible" environmental groups. Judicial review of agency decisions is infrequent. Lawyers, therefore, do not play a significant role in the rulemaking process. The same contrasts emerge from Rose-Ackerman's (1995) comparison of German and American environmental policymaking; from Badaracco's (1985) detailed comparative account of occupational health regulation in the United States, France, Germany, England, and Japan; and from Brickman, Jasanoff, and Ilgen's (1985) analysis of how Germany, France, the United Kingdom, and the United States regulate potential chemical carcinogens in pesticides, food additives, and workplaces.

In the European nations Brickman, Jasanoff, and Ilgen (1985: 305) studied, "the absence of legislative-executive competition," together with the traditions of governance by professional, apolitical public agencies and by corporatist bodies, have reduced "pressure for rigorous procedural and judicial controls on the bureaucracy." In consequence, "A confidential process of consultation and accommodation permits government officials to mediate among conflicting private interests. As a result, regulators are able to make the necessary trade-offs and compromises without presenting reasoned public justifications or drawing open political fire." In contrast, the authors found (304) that American regulatory agency policymakers implement statutes under the critical eye of other governmental institutions and . . . warring private interests, each advancing interpretations of law, science, and economics consistent with its narrower objectives. Unable to strike bargains in private, American regulatory agencies are forced to seek refuge in "objectivity," adopting formal methodologies for rationalizing every action. . . . [The courts'] searching review . . . has forced administrators toward greater formality and rigor in building the evidence to support their decisions.

Precisely the same contrast is illustrated in the above-mentioned comparative analysis by Joseph Badaracco (1985: 120–21) and in a comparison of rulemaking by the United States and the EU by Peter Strauss (2006).

Implementation and Enforcement

The punitive fine imposed on PREMCO for only moderately serious, quickly remedied regulatory violations is not entirely representative of American regulatory enforcement. During the administration of President Ronald Reagan, the Occupational Safety and Health Administration's (OSHA) propensity to impose fines declined significantly (Scholz and Wei, 1986), as did the proportion of OSHA fines contested by employers (Kniesner and Leeth, 1991). Some American agencies, as noted earlier, consistently pursue a flexible or even an accommodative enforcement style, emphasizing remedial orders more than punishment (Kagan, 1993). Some American regulatory regimes employ a "soft touch" strategy; rather than prescribing and policing governmentally formulated regulations, they require individual regulated entities to make and enforce their own intrafirm standards and procedures for reducing hazards in ways tailored to their particular operations. Some American agencies shy away from punitive action; reports regularly surface of cases in which regulatory officials declined or failed to punish obvious and significant regulatory violations (Barstow, 2003; Lifsher, 1998).

Nevertheless, in many American agencies, regulatory officials are at risk of criticism from elected politicians or their own superiors for not citing or punishing regulatory violations. Agencies often seek to demonstrate their diligence by highlighting the number of prosecutions initiated and fines imposed. As noted in the PREMCO case, the federal EPA systematically audits state environmental agencies' records with respect to failure to seek legal sanctions against violators; EPA reports that criticize failures to prosecute often make newspaper headlines (Fialka, 1998: 40; Adler, 1998: 40). Therefore, notwithstanding variation among American agencies, numerous cross-national studies of particular regulatory programs have found regulatory implementation in the United States to be more legalistic and deterrence-oriented than in other economically advanced democracies, where enforcement officials who encounter shortcomings among regulated entities more consistently employ a problem-solving, cooperation-seeking style (Boden and Wegman, 1978: 43, 45; Kelman, 1981; Wilson, 1985; Kagan, 2000b).

When John Braithwaite, John Walker, and Peter Grabosky (1993) compared nursing home regulation in the United States, England, Japan, and Australia, they found that enforcement in the United States was more legalistic and punishment-oriented. For most violations, American state nursing home regulators accept the filing of a satisfactory plan of correction, but formal legal enforcement—administrative fines, suspensions of new admissions, and license revocations—is far from infrequent and far more common than in the other countries.[8] Each journalistic report of substandard care, the researchers found, triggers demands for harsher penalties. Thus nursing home regulation in the United States, Braithwaite concluded, is "tougher than nursing home regulation in the rest of the world" (25–27). Braithwaite also was struck by the culture of distrust generated by the legalistic approach to regulation. Writing in 1993, Braithwaite observed that federal training of state inspectors "emphasized the need for inspectors to be in control during [end-of-inspection] exit conferences, not to be distracted by questions raised by nursing home staff, [and] to stick to the facts of the deficiencies that require a written plan of correction"—a posture that would be shocking to nursing home regulators in Australia or England (36). In consequence, Braithwaite pointed out (48):

> Inspectors in the United States spend most of their time alone in a room poring over resident charts, whereas English and Australian inspectors spend most of their time out in the nursing home observing care and talking to staff, residents, and visitors about care. The theory of the recent [1990 federal statutory] reforms was that the inspection process would become more resident-centered and less document-centered. But our research team's observation is of no significant change because the new element of resident interviews has been balanced by extra documents for inspectors to check and extra pieces of paper for them to fill out.

This kind of impersonal, by-the-book regulatory style has been noted in other sociolegal studies (Bardach and Kagan, 1982; Axelrad, 2000).

Another striking feature of American regulatory style is the relative severity of the legal sanctions it imposes for serious violations.[9] No other nation authorizes and imposes such weighty *criminal* penalties for violations of regulatory laws. In 1988 Congress increased criminal fines for insider trading to $1 million for individuals and $2.5 million for entities, and doubled the maximum prison term for violations of any securities law provision from five to ten years (Pitt and Shapiro, 1990: 238). In the late 1980s and early 1990s Congress upgraded criminal offenses in most environmental laws from misdemeanors to felonies, thereby increasing the maximum potential prison sentences. Under both federal and California law, courts can impose a criminal fine of up to $1 million on a corporation for violations of water pollution law that knowingly endanger another person; for such violations individual corporate officers found responsible can be fined up to $250,000 and sentenced to prison for up to fifteen years.[10]

Of course, the vast majority of regulatory violations—including those detected and cited by enforcement officials—do not lead to criminal prosecutions and penalties. The major reason is that most regulatory rules require precautionary preventive measures, so most violations (like AMERCO's violation of the twelve-hour rule), while they may increase the *risk* of harm, do not result in *actual harm*; the usual regulatory response, therefore, is an administrative citation and order requiring remedial action. Secondly, even when serious harm does occur, it often is difficult for prosecutors to pin down individual responsibility and prove *criminal intent* (see the "knowingly endanger" standard in the preceding paragraph), especially with respect to officials in large corporations with complex decision processes and sophisticated legal defense teams. Thus despite intense political pressures to punish individuals responsible for the disastrous 2008 Wall Street meltdown and the ensuing deep recession, restrictive court rulings discouraged even able and dedicated prosecutors from convicting and imprisoning top executives of the financial institutions that fraudulently sold, bundled, and mislabeled risky home loans, bonds, and derivatives (Eisinger, 2017: xviii). For serious violations, therefore, prosecutors and regulatory agencies are more inclined to file criminal charges or civil lawsuits against the corporation as a whole and then to settle for large money penalties (Eisinger, 2017; Garrett, 2014; Firestone, 2003; Uhlmann, 2014).[11]

Nevertheless, the risk of criminal prosecution for regulatory violations is very salient for regulated entities in the United States. In the 1995–1997 period, after Congress increased the EPA's funding for criminal investigators (Blabolil et al., 1997), prosecutions for environmental violations more often targeted individual corporate officers, rather than corporate entities, and more than a third of those convicted were sentenced to prison (1997; Kagan and Lochner, 1998). A study of 700 prosecutions for violations of federal environmental laws between 2005 and 2010 found that virtually all stemmed from repeat violations, deceptive conduct, outright defiance, or significant harm to the environment or public health (Uhlmann, 2014). A survey of American corporate environmental managers in 2004 found that on average they estimated a 70 percent probability that a serious environmental law violation by their company would be prosecuted and punished, and most *overestimated* the severity of such punishments (Thornton, Kagan, and Gunningham, 2005).

American law also provides for much heavier *civil* penalties for regulatory offenses than does the law of other countries. The federal Clean Air Act and the Toxic Substances Control Act authorize civil penalties of up to $25,000 per day for ongoing violations. The EPA can also impose administrative penalties equal to the financial benefit the violator gained by not making the required abatement. Several federal environmental statutes require violators to pay for the damages to natural resources caused by unauthorized pollution (Privatera, 1992: 3–6). In 1989 the Exxon *Valdez* (with a third mate named Robert Kagan at the wheel) went aground in Prince William Sound, Alaska, spilling 11 million gallons of oil in the wildlife-rich waters (Davidson, 1990). Exxon Corporation, after spending $2 billion on cleanup efforts, pled guilty to criminal charges and was fined $125 million, based on damages to the environment. In addition, the state of Alaska and the federal government each brought civil actions against Exxon for natural resource damages, and Exxon settled those suits for almost $1 billion (*Washington Post,* 1991: A14; Verhovek, 1999). Exxon also was sued for damages by scores of plaintiffs' lawyers who signed up thousands of fishermen, Indian tribes, and other private parties allegedly injured by the spill, and a federal court jury handed down a $5 billion punitive damages award. These figures seem almost quaintly small when compared to the over $20 billion in combined criminal fines, civil damage claims, and natural resource damages assessed two decades later against British Petroleum in the wake of the giant oil spill from its Deepwater Horizon well in the Gulf of Mexico in 2010.[12] Volkswagen's combined criminal and civil penalties for intentionally rigging their diesel cars to pass government emission tests (while in practice emitting illegal levels of harmful particulate matter) resulted in over $4.3 billion in criminal and civil penalties, plus more money in civil case settlements with cheated customers (Vlasic, 2017).

Exxon's, BP's and Volkswagen's simultaneous exposure to criminal prosecution, governmental civil penalties, and private lawsuits for damages for the same violations highlights another distinctive feature of American regulatory law: its encouragement of *private* enforcement of regulatory law. In the 1890 Sherman Antitrust Act, Congress enabled plaintiffs to file civil lawsuits against and collect treble damages from companies that had engaged in prohibited anticompetitive practices. The treble damage provision encouraged lawyers to represent such claimants on a contingency fee basis; that is, in return for a substantial percentage of the damages obtained. Since then, in over 250 statutes, Congress has provided incentives for entrepreneurial lawyers to act as private attorneys general (Farhang, 2014, 2010). The incentives also include one-way fee shifting provisions whereby successful plaintiffs' lawyers' fees must be paid by the defendant—but if plaintiffs lose, they do not have to reimburse the prevailing defendant's lawyers' fees. In addition, some statutes, beginning with the 1964 Civil Rights Act, provide that many individual claims can be aggregated into class actions—remember the Columbia Falls Aluminum case; that too multiplies incentives for entrepreneurial plaintiffs' lawyers and enhances the deterrent threat to regulated companies. Some statutes combine multiple legal incentives for private enforcement suits. The federal Truth-in-Lending Act (1968), for example, (1) gave debtors a cause of action against lenders who violate the statute's complex disclosure rules; (2) provided that prevailing plaintiffs would receive a $100 minimum award, regardless of actual losses, (3) plus their attorneys' fees; and (4) provided that attorneys could bundle thousands of bank customers together in a class action, "raising the specter of enormous damages suits [even] for minor violations of the statute" (Rubin, 1991: 237).

These kinds of statutory incentives—together with plaintiffs' rights of pretrial discovery and the remarkable volume of reports that American corporations must file (disclosing financial data, industrial emissions, product complaints, chemical inventories, bank lending patterns, and more)—have made litigation by entrepreneurial lawyers a prominent and often potent means of enforcing American regulatory law in many spheres, from securities laws and civil rights laws to the Clean Water Act. Neither the private class action, the contingency fee, nor other special incentives for private enforcement actions are prominent features of regulatory law in other countries (Greve, 1989b; Coffee, 2015). What Sean Farhang (2010) has labeled "the litigation state"—in which a decentralized, legally incentivized army of private attorneys is a vital aspect of the regulatory system—is a uniquely American phenomenon.

All in all, the combination of criminal, civil, and private enforcement results in regulatory penalties in the United States that dwarf those in other countries. Karpoff, Lott, and Rankine (1998: 4), after studying legal responses to 283 environmental violations by publicly traded companies in the 1980–1991 period, wrote, "The mean fine or damage award in our sample is $9.43 million (the median is $600,000), and the average forced compliance or remediation cost is $59.97 million (the median is $8 million)." In recent years, the European Union has imposed extremely large monetary penalties on giant high-tech companies for violating EU fair competition law and privacy protection regulations. But overall, multinational corporations view American regulatory regimes as more threatening than those of any other economically advanced democracy (Kagan, 2000a).

Is Adversarial Legalism Necessary?

If adversarial legalism makes American regulation particularly threatening, does it also make American regulation more *effective* than regulation in other rich democracies? For several reasons, that question, posed in such general terms, is not easy to answer. First, the term "regulation" encompasses scores of different kinds of regulatory programs and rules, some very ambitious and demanding, some less so. Second, there are no settled metrics for measuring "effectiveness," and whatever metric one chooses, there rarely is inadequate comparative data enabling one to apply it across different countries. Third, both across and within countries, specific regulatory programs' priorities and levels of ambition shift over time, often rather rapidly (Vogel, 2012). Fourth, regulatory agencies both within and across countries face different task environments. Some police industries with a relatively high prevalence of recalcitrant bad apple enterprises, while others face a higher percentage of cooperative firms (Shover et al., 1984). Different agencies cope with different levels of political resistance versus support, and differentially severe funding shortfalls. Fifth, when American regulation succeeds, as it very often does, in reducing risks and harms, it often is not clear whether or to what extent those successes are due to the extra deterrent punch provided by adversarial legalism. In a study of fifteen pulp and paper mills in the United States and Canada, Neil Gunningham, Dorothy Thornton, and I found that all had reduced the harmful chemicals in their effluent to levels below the requirements in their regulatory permits. But in explaining *variation* in environmental performance across those firms, nonlegal factors—such as local social pressures, adverse publicity, and managers' normative beliefs—were more important than variation in regulatory agency enforcement style. (Kagan, Gunningham, and Thornton, 2011; Gunningham, Thornton, and Kagan, 2003).

Yet although social pressures, reputational concerns, and cultural norms of good corporate citizenship play a large role in supporting regulatory compliance, regulation's deterrent threat clearly does matter. Studies showed that firms in highly competitive markets (such as pulp and paper manufacturing or trucking) are unlikely to invest in *very* costly preventive measures absent legally binding, regularly enforced rules that compel those firms' competitors to make comparable investments (Thornton, Kagan, and Gunningham, 2009; Gunningham, Thornton, and Kagan, 2003; Vogel, 2005). Lewis-Beck and Alford (1980) found that, after controlling for other factors, increases in regulatory penalties played a major role in sharply reducing the high death rate of underground coal miners in the United States. The American propensity to supplement government enforcement with incentives for enforcement via private lawsuits also has mattered in some regulatory spheres. For example, some comparative studies indicate that American laws forbidding racial discrimination in employment and workplace sexual harassment, while far from fully rooting out those offenses, have been far more potent than comparable laws in nations that do not foster the private enforcement of public law (Lieberman, 2005; Saguy, 2000; Gelb, 1989: 206). Conversely, private enforcement (as well as government enforcement) has been relatively weak in implementing the 1968 U.S. Fair Housing Act, which helps explain the tragically slow progress in reducing racial discrimination in housing markets (Massey and Denton, 1993).[13]

On the other hand, some research, such as the above-discussed study of PREMCO by Aoki and Cioffi (2000) and the study of nursing home regulation by John Braithwaite (1993), indicate that the legalistic American regulatory style, by discouraging cooperative relationships between regulators and regulated entities, sometimes makes regulation in the United States less effective than other nations' regulatory style, at least in some spheres of regulation. Lyle Scruggs (1998; 1999) used national reports to the Organization for Economic Cooperation and Development (OECD) to analyze *rates of progress* by seventeen economically advanced democracies in reducing pollution during the 1970s and 1980s. Notwithstanding the greater prescriptiveness and deterrent threat of American environmental regulation, Scruggs found that the United States ranked thirteenth of the seventeen nations in reducing air pollution (sulphur dioxide, nitrous oxide), solid wastes (measured by reductions in municipal wastes and proportion of paper and glass recycled), and water pollution (measured by percent of population served by waste water treatment plants and by reduction in pesticide use per acre of arable land). In terms of rates of progress, the United States trailed Germany (which ranked first) and several countries with decidedly nonlegalistic enforcement styles—the Netherlands (second), Sweden (third), Japan (fourth), and the United Kingdom (eleventh) (Scruggs, 1998, 70). The most important correlate of rapid environmental improvement, Scruggs found, was whether the nation had neo-corporatist institutions that fostered a more consensual mode of regulation—that is, whether well-organized, comprehensive industry associations were incorporated into the regulatory policymaking and enforcement process. Pluralist systems, in which political and economic power is more fragmented, ranked lower—and the United States is surely the most hyperpluralistic of all the OECD countries.

Relatedly, according to Allen (1989: 72), from the mid-1970s to the mid-1980s German chemical companies invested twice as much money as their American counterparts in complying with environmental protection measures. Verweij (2001) found that Swiss, German, and French regulatory regimes reduced toxic effluents in the Rhine River more completely than did the comparable American regime for the Great Lakes. Like the PREMCO study, several previously mentioned case studies of multinational corporations (Kagan and Axelrad, 2000) showed that while the corporations experienced more adversarial and legalistic regulation in the United States, the levels of protection that the companies provided in their parallel operations in Germany, Japan, the Netherlands, and the United Kingdom were substantially similar to those achieved in the United States.

Still, one might argue, even if some other countries achieve comparable regulatory outcomes with less legalistic, more cooperative regulatory methods, such methods would not work in the United States. American businesses are not enmeshed in strong industry associations of the kind that Scruggs found so significant in promoting regulatory effectiveness. American businesspeople, some observers have contended, are less deferential to governmental authority than are Japanese and European firms.[14] Indeed, American business interests work hard and make very large campaign contributions to elect political leaders whose regulatory appointees will relax enforcement of existing regulations and block promulgation of new ones. That is what indeed occurred during the administration of George W. Bush (2001–2008) and is currently occurring, even more consistently, during Donald Trump's presidency.

Moreover, corporatist political systems that engage in cooperative regulatory policymaking are vulnerable to slipping into overly cooperative patterns. Japan's collaborative regulatory policymaking, which Aoki and Cioffi (2000) describe positively in their PREMCO account, has been marked by significant failures. It received some of the blame for the terrifying and immensely costly 2011 Fukashima nuclear power plant disaster. The cooperation-seeking Japanese enforcement style, while generally effective vis-à-vis large regulated entities, has been shown by some studies to be far less so vis-à-vis smaller firms, with adverse consequences for worker safety (Wokutch and Vansandt, 2000) and environmental protection (Aoki and Cioffi, 2000: 53). Milhaupt and Miller (2000) describe how the Japan's collaborative financial regulatory system failed to attend to the growth of nonbank financial institutions whose high-risk lending practices stimulated a real-estate bubble, the collapse of which in 1990 had devastating economic effects—much like the way American financial regulators' hands-off approach to new forms of mortgage lending and finance led to the equally devastating Wall Street financial meltdown in 2008.

Perhaps, then, American regulatory policymaking, so open to partisan political influence *must* be more constrained by administrative law, adversarial legalism, and judicial review. Those processes make the rule-making process more transparent, open to a wide range of information and opinion, and more reliably evidence-based. They make agencies less vulnerable (although not invulnerable) to capture, corruption, or crippling by regulated business interests and their political allies. Similarly, perhaps American regulatory *enforcement* sometimes must be rather adversarial, legalistic, and deterrence-oriented. Legalistic agency enforcement, some studies indicate, often is necessary in the initial phase of a new regulatory program or regulation; and in regulatory task environments characterized by many small competing firms and high compliance costs (Thornton, Kagan, and Gunningham, 2009; Kagan et al., 2013); and for regulated firms in market niches characterized by significant levels of antiregulation recalcitrance (Shover et al., 1984). Enforcement via private litigation provides also vital added punch for regulatory programs when the relevant government agency's monitoring capacity is limited—as is often the case due to inadequate budgets. Consequently, to sharply curtail adversarial legalism in the American regulatory state without somehow replacing it with a more effective and reliable way of assuring cooperation from regulated enterprises almost surely would pave the way to much larger numbers of harmful violations of important, public-protecting regulatory norms.

Nevertheless, it is important to recognize that the benefits provided by adversarial, legalistic regulation in some situations come at a price in others. American adversarial legalism imposes higher costs on regulated businesses, and hence on the economy as a whole, than comparable regulatory approaches in other economically advanced democracies. The next section explores further the nature of those costs.

The Social and Economic Costs of Legalistic Regulation

It is fairly clear that American adversarial legalism, when contrasted with cooperative modes of regulation, generates more legal uncertainty, much higher litigation and lawyering expenses, higher compliance and opportunity costs, and more defensiveness and alienation among regulated enterprises. These costs, by incrementally reducing aggregate economic efficiency, are borne by society at large as well as by regulated firms.

Unpredictability

In theory, a regulatory regime that emphasizes detailed, strictly enforced legal rules should be more stable and predictable than regimes that emphasize discretionary adjustment of policies to particular circumstances. Paradoxically, however, regulatory compliance officials in multinational enterprises characterize American regulation as more legally uncertain than regulation in Western Europe or Japan. The uncertainty stems from several features of American regulatory systems. Institutional fragmentation results in overlapping, imperfectly coordinated regulation by numerous local, state, and federal agencies, which may be dominated by different political parties with different regulatory policy preferences. Business groups and advocacy organizations battle for regulatory changes in agencies, courts, and legislatures, rendering American regulatory law particularly malleable. The ever-present prospect of legal and political challenge means that regulatory officials in the United States, compared to their counterparts in other countries, typically demand more scientific evidence to support permit applications, requests for variances, and new regulations. Consequently it is often unclear to regulated enterprises when a regulatory decision on a permit application, for example, will be made and whether the evidence and certifications provided will be regarded as legally sufficient.

Consider, for example, the experience of "Q Corp.," a multinational electronic-parts maker with similar factories in California and Japan, subject to parallel water pollution regulations. Aoki, Kagan, and Axelrad (2000: 82) found that:

> Q USA environmental managers spend much more time than their Q Japan counterparts striving to assimilate and reconcile regulatory requirements that are promulgated—separately and not always consistently—by federal agencies, state agencies, municipal agencies, and courts. Q USA officials spend much more time attending meetings, communicating with regulatory enforcement officials, and going to private workshops aimed at clarifying the law and ascertaining how it applies to particular industrial operations. Q USA officials spend more time communicating with environmental lawyers retained by the company, from whom they seek a second opinion in an effort to reduce the legal uncertainty that they regularly experience.

Even so, legal uncertainty remains, because U.S. regulatory law is often in flux. To mention one example that affected Q USA, in 1987 Congress directed the states to adopt by 1990 numerical ambient water quality objectives for certain toxic pollutants. States were slow to do so, however, partly because of concern that their decisions would be challenged in the courts, either by industry or by environmentalists, for lack of an adequate scientific basis. In 1991 California promulgated the Inland Surface Water Plan (ISWP), but it omitted objectives for some bodies of water and some pollutants. The EPA then disapproved California's regulations as incomplete. Meanwhile, local California governments sued the state on the ground that the ISWP rules were too stringent and would compel them to renovate water treatment plants or build new ones, either way at great expense. A California court invalidated the ISWP rules for violating certain procedural requirements in the promulgation process. Back at the federal level, an environmental organization sued the EPA for failing to meet the 1987 law's deadline, and a federal court ordered EPA itself to issue regulations setting standards for the pollutants, which the agency did in 1992. The impact of the ongoing federal-state jousting on the local water treatment plant to which Q USA's effluents flow, and hence on Q USA's in-house treatment obligations, thus took years for the company to figure out (Aoki, Kagan, and Axelrad, 2000: 94, note 51).

More generally, a survey of American environmental lawyers (Ruhl et al., 2002) uncovered strong agreement that the sheer number, complexity, and changeability of regulations is the chief cause of noncompliance (far outranking costs of compliance) and indeed made it virtually impossible to achieve full compliance 100 percent of the time, even for committed firms.

Lawyering Costs

Officials of PREMCO, the Japan-based metals manufacturing company mentioned earlier, assert that the corporation has spent more money on legal services for its U.S. subsidiary than for its corporate headquarters plus all its other manufacturing plants in Asia and Europe. Officials of several other multinational enterprises in the same research project said that their U.S. subsidiaries consult lawyers more often and longer on a wider range of matters because American law is generally more complex, changeable, and difficult to master; because the legal sanctions for being wrong are generally much higher; because litigation is more common; and because litigation in the United States is vastly more expensive than in other economically advanced democracies (Nielsen, 1999; Ruhlin, 2000; Kagan, 2000a).

Welles and Engel (2000) found that "Waste Corp.," a multinational builder and operator of waste disposal facilities (which nobody wants near their backyard), spent a staggering $15 million on legal services in the course of its efforts to obtain approval for a single municipal solid waste landfill in California; for over ten years the company had approximately seven lawyers on retainer, busy addressing numerous regulatory agencies, two major administrative appeals, and three extended lawsuits. In Pennsylvania the same company retained seven lawyers (but only part-time) for the five years it took to get a landfill permit there, a process that entailed two administrative appeals but no lawsuits and "only" $1.45 million in lawyering costs. When Waste Corp. sought to develop a similar landfill in England, by contrast, the company retained two lawyers, part-time, for an eight-year process that also included at least one administrative appeal; its legal costs there were about $137,000. And in the Netherlands, despite having undergone two administrative appeals, the company did not have to retain lawyers at all (since lawyers are not required in administrative appeals) and it spent less than $50,000 on legal services.

Accountability Costs

Viewed in cross-national perspective, American regulatory regimes generally impose more extensive and specific requirements concerning reporting, record-keeping, testing, employee education, certifications, and so on. Besides the costs of complying with substantive regulatory standards, therefore, regulated firms spend more in the United States than they do overseas to *prove* that they are complying (Dwyer, Brooks, and Marco, 2000; Kagan, 2000a). For example, in the early 1990s "B Corp." notified regulatory authorities in the United States, England, and the Netherlands that it had discovered that solvents had leaked from deteriorating underground tanks and pipes in its factories in those countries. The American regulators, Lee Axelrad (2000) found, demanded far more comprehensive analysis, more voluminous documentation, and more costly reports than did the European authorities. The documents submitted to American regulators for contaminated sites, said B Corp. regulatory compliance officials, would fill a four-drawer filing cabinet, compared to the less than half of a single file drawer of documentation submitted to regulators in the other countries. And behind each additional ten pages of documentation lay scores of hours that company officers devoted to research, testing, measurement, analysis, and preparation and checking of draft reports.

All in all, B Corp. officials estimated that "extra" studies, submissions, and negotiations with U.S. regulators added $8 to $10 million to the costs of designing the cleanup plan for the two sites in the United States (out of total costs per site of an estimated $22 million), whereas the "extra" regulatory accountability costs for comparable site investigations and cleanup planning in the United Kingdom and the Netherlands were negligible (Axelrad, 2000). Moreover, as of the time Axelrad interviewed B Corp. officials, actual remediation efforts in England and the Netherlands were well under way, but at the American sites action remained on hold while the firm still waited to learn if officials considered the company's analysis sufficient. In this case, therefore, the additional demands of the U.S. regulatory regime confirmed the maxim that when pushed too far, *accountability* (proving one has done the right thing) can displace *responsibility* (doing the right thing) (Bardach and Kagan, 1982).

Opportunity Costs

Regulatory permitting systems are designed to slow the headlong rush of development and technological change, forcing business firms to look more carefully at potential adverse side effects before they leap. But prior regulatory review may also impose opportunity costs on society. Each month's further scrutiny of a new, perhaps more benign, pesticide means another month's delay in supplanting a more harmful pesticide. For most products and processes, however, American regulatory regimes impose longer delays and larger opportunity costs than comparable national regimes in Western Europe.[15] American opponents of new projects generally have more opportunities to challenge regulatory approvals in court than their counterparts in other countries, and litigation, crawling at a deliberate pace, typically results in substantial opportunity costs. The greater prospect of judicial review, moreover, often seems to make American regulatory officials more cautious and legalistic in reviewing proposals than their counterparts abroad. When Ford applied for air pollution permits for new painting processes in its two German plants, the time from application to approval in Germany took five months and seventeen months, respectively; the parallel permit applications for Ford's plants in Minnesota and New Jersey took over four years (Dwyer, Brooks, and Marco, 2000).

Divisiveness and Defensiveness

One of adversarial legalism's chief *intangible* costs is its corrosive effect on business-government relationships and ultimately on regulatory politics. When a regulatory inspector and a regulated enterprise become locked in an adversarial posture, exchange of information and cooperation, so essential to effective regulation, are often reduced (Bardach and Kagan, 1982). Comparing U.S., British, and Australian nursing home regulation, Braithwaite (1993: 17) observed, "American nursing homes have higher fire safety standards than Australian nursing homes, better food and nutrition standards than English nursing homes . . . better care planning, and more varied activities." But overall, Braithwaite (15–16) concluded, quality of care in the United States is worse, primarily because the highly prescriptive and legalistic American enforcement system drives nursing homes toward a defensive, legalistic approach to compliance–rather than motivating them to do their demanding work more carefully and compassionately. After sitting in on meetings that included a facility director of nursing, a dietician, and a quality assurance coordinator (a position required by law), Braithwaite (41) observed, "The question that holds center stage during quality assurance meetings is not, 'What is the best way to design this program to deliver maximum improvement in quality of care?' It is, 'What is it that they [the regulators] want of us here? What is the minimum we have to do to satisfy the requirement of having a quality assurance program?'" Defensiveness is also manifested in a disturbingly high incidence of falsification of medical and other records in order to avoid violations (41).

Similar observations pervade comparative studies of other regulatory programs. Comparing Q Corp.'s environmental compliance programs at its factories in the United States and Japan, Aoki, Kagan, and Axelrad (2000, 83) say, "One can think of [environmental managers in the U.S. plant] as playing legal defense instead of playing environmental offense. Q Japan officials have more time to do the latter." They go on (83):

> Whereas Q Japan environmental officials express dismay that Q USA has actually violated the law on occasion, Q USA officials, while clearly committed to the goals of environmental protection, seem to regard occasional violations of particular regulatory rules as something close to inevitable and as something less than shameful. In the U.S., where legal penalties often are imposed for unintentional violations that do not entail serious harm, the social stigma attached to a regulatory "violation" seems less severe than in Japan, where sanctions are reserved for serious violations.

> In Japan, we conclude, the regulatory regime appears to have gathered greater "normative gravity," partly because Q Japan officials view it as comprehensible, reasonable and predictable. This appears to facilitate the internalization of regulatory norms by operating managers and workers. The fluctuating, polycentric character of the American regime, in contrast, seems to *impair* the law's normative gravity (although not its threat) and to make it more difficult for regulatory norms and the idea of perfect compliance to permeate the corporate culture and the planning process.

To be sure, many efforts to institute more cooperative modes of regulation in the United States occur, and many succeed (Rees, 1988; Weber, 1998). But a regulatory system structured by adversarial legalism makes it *more difficult* to successfully institutionalize informal cooperative methods. And as a number of scholars have found (Brickman, Jasanoff, and Ilgen, 1985: 27; Wallace, 1995: 111), the defensiveness that legalistic enforcement engenders often keeps American regulation from achieving the gains that would flow from cooperation.

———

Compared to other economically advanced democracies, the United States has been remarkably successful in fostering vibrant financial markets, promoting innovation and entrepreneurial activity, facilitating industrial restructuring, and creating new jobs. However costly American social regulation may be, and however annoying the extra costs generated by adversarial legalism may be, its overall social benefits, as many analyses have shown, massively outweigh those costs. Notwithstanding those costs and annoyances, most American firms willingly comply with most regulations. They are motivated to do so by social pressures, by business managers' belief in the rule of law, and by their normative agreement with the basic norms of most regulatory programs (Kagan et al., 2011 Gunningham, Thornton, and Kagan, 2003; Vandenberg, 2003). The costs and annoyances of adversarial legalism have not been a major source of relocation of manufacturing or other business operations to other countries (Anderson and Kagan, 2000), a process driven much more by differential labor costs. Indeed, in contrast to the closed-door decision-making methods of many other nations, American adversarial legalism provides both domestic and foreign companies greater assurance that they are competing on a relatively level regulatory playing field and that they have legal recourse against official arbitrariness or favoritism. Adversarial legalism, ironically, helps legitimate the American regulatory process because it emphasizes legal accountability, transparency, and rights of public participation.

Nor should we overglamorize the regulatory systems of other economically advanced democracies. It would not be difficult for those knowledgeable about particular regulatory problems to point to instances or entire regulatory arenas in which American regulation is considerably more effective and efficient or in which other countries' regulatory regimes are poorly enforced. That said, it does not follow that adversarial and legalistic regulation is optimal for the United States. The United States benefits from the enormous market it offers both American and foreign businesses; they cannot afford to abandon the United States even if its regulatory system is especially litigation prone and legalistic. But those extra costs, even if they do not sink a dynamic economy, are often very significant for particular firms and in principle wealth-depleting for the society as a whole.

Even more significant, perhaps, are the social and political costs of adversarial regulation. Through its prescriptiveness, punitiveness, and contribution to formalization of business-government relationships, American adversarial legalism often induces mutual resentment, defensiveness, and mistrust. It thereby discourages the kind of cooperation that is essential to the full achievement of regulatory goals. Most importantly, it gives regulation a bad name, obliterating attention to its positive achievements, ubiquity, and essentiality in competitive, rapidly changing modern societies. That negative view of regulation has contributed to—and has been amplified by—the upsurge of ideological hostility to government regulation led by conservative business activists and Republican politicians during the early twenty-first century. As discussed below, their antiregulation agenda has aimed, for the most part, not at reforming or improving regulation but at repealing or impeding implementation of morally-essential, economically desirable (even if imperfect) regulatory statutes and rules, brushing aside the prayers for regulatory protection that had led to those laws' enactments.

That is deeply troublesome. The existing American regulatory state, even if partly burdened by (and partly enhanced by) adversarial legalism, is preferable to a crippled, dismantled regulatory state.

The Regulatory State in the Early Twenty-First Century

Beginning in the 1970s, conservative activists and business organizations created and funded think tanks that published critical analyses of federal regulation. Those analyses sought to be constructive. They often highlighted the extent to which particular regulations imposed costs that arguably exceeded their intended benefits or in which the regulations, as formulated, were not the most cost-effective way to achieve the regulatory objectives. By the 1980s and 1990s, however, both the Republican Party and some major business organizations had moved sharply away from their earlier stance of regulatory cooperation. They adopted a more intense, ideologically driven opposition to government regulation (Hacker and Pierson 2016; Mayer, 2016). The goal, it seemed, was not to reform regulation but to simply to repeal it or cripple the regulatory state. Comparing the politics of regulation in the United States and in Europe, David Vogel (2012) observed that by the early twenty-first century, "Each claim about a new risk is likely to be challenged by a counter-narrative contending that it was misinformed" (264). Prominent conservative politicians and television commentators referred to government regulation as "job-killing" and denounced global warming, or the human contribution to it, as a hoax. And as the Republican Party enjoyed increasing electoral success, conservative opponents of the regulatory state gained opportunities to turn their ideas into law.

From 2001 through 2008, during George W. Bush's presidency, a Republican Congress slowed the growth of the regulatory state, even as new risks became evident. Political conservatives allied with regulated businesses were appointed to head federal departments and regulatory agencies. During President Barack Obama's tenure, 2009–2016, congressional Republicans often used legislative tactics to block new regulatory legislation, to weaken laws they could not block, and to cut funding for regulatory agencies' policy research, risk assessment, and compliance-monitoring programs. When regulatory laws, administrative regulations, and executive orders *were* promulgated, Republican state attorneys general and the U.S. Chamber of Commerce often challenged their legality in court, delaying their implementation. Republican electoral victories also gave conservatives control of a majority of state governments and hence over state regulatory agencies and their budgets.[16] Since the mid-1990s, according David Vogel's (2012) analysis, European countries, prodded by the EU government, have replaced the United States as the world's leader in enacting stringent risk-control regulations. The federal government in the United States failed to adopt more stringent new EU regulatory standards concerning, among other things, food safety, chemical safety, control of genetically modified agricultural products, and most significantly, regulations designed to counteract global warming.[17]

Moreover, after the 2016 election, Republicans again won the presidency and retained control of both the House and the Senate. President Donald J. Trump promised to implement a more radical antiregulation agenda. His strongly antiregulation appointees to federal government departments, agencies, and commissions moved quickly to repeal existing regulations and policies, to abandon existing prosecutions of regulatory violations, and to purge their organizations of regulatory experts and scientists (Davenport, 2018; Protess and Silver-Greenberg, 2017; Cowley and Silver-Greenberg, 2017; Goodnough and Zarntke, 2017). In many agencies, in Republican states as well as in Washington, there were signs that an energetic, sometimes legalistic enforcement style was being replaced not merely by a less legalistic one but by an undemanding, very accommodative enforcement style (Lipton and Ivory, 2017).

The saying "It is difficult to make predictions, especially about the future," has been attributed to Niels Bor, Mark Twain, Yogi Berra, and many others. Probably, I have read, it is an old Danish adage. In any case, it suggests why it is difficult to predict to what extent conservative assault on regulation, during the Trump administration and thereafter, will shred the portrait of the American regulatory state painted in this chapter. Nevertheless, a number of factors point to the long-run resilience and continuity of the American regulatory state and of the distinctive American regulatory style, rather than to their disintegration.

First, by 2000, the major laws, institutions, and legal practices that constitute the federal regulatory state had been entrenched for several decades, creating change-resistant "path dependencies." That is, many businesses, activist organizations, and members of the public who had adapted to, relied on, and benefitted from those laws and practices could be expected to—and did—fight hard against efforts to change them. Moreover, as Joseph Singer (2015) wrote, while many Americans in opinion polls affirm the generalization that there is too much regulation, they also express strong approval for most specific regulatory policies and wish they were stronger or better enforced. So by the end of the 1990s, conservative opponents of the regulatory state had already learned a hard political lesson: because of the many veto points in the American policymaking and legislative process, *and* because of the depth of public support for most major environmental, health and safety, and civil rights policies, it is rarely possible to repeal or substantially weaken important regulatory statutes (Burbank and Farhang,

2017). During the 2000–2018 period, Republican congressional leaders did not even try to repeal any major regulatory statute, other than the 2009 Obama-era Affordable Health Care Act, or even to amend any, save for the 2010 Dodd-Frank Act, which sought to stabilize the financial services industry.

Scores of regulatory statutes and rules, therefore, remain on the books. Most do not evoke partisan political conflict or opposition from regulated entities, who generally have accepted and adapted to them. Drawing on those statutes and the rich body of administrative law, attorneys general from politically liberal states, as well as a large array of proregulation advocacy organizations, regularly and immediately file lawsuits that challenge the legality of Trump administration antiregulatory initiatives. Thus far, the lower courts have ruled in the challengers' favor almost every time, holding that the Trump administration initiatives were inconsistent with the underlying regulatory statutes, or had been issued in violation of the tenets of administrative law, or had blatantly lacked scientific or other evidentiary support.(Sanger-Katz, 2019; Institute for Policy Integrity, 2019). And each day, existing regulatory law triggers complaints of violations and propels the actions of thousands of regulatory inspectors and bureaucrats, state as well as federal. In that important sense, the American regulatory state and the adversarial legal contestation that it generates have remained intact.

The lawsuits by attorneys general from liberal states remind us, too, that in America's politically fragmented and divided political system, there are many sources of political and legal resistance to the Republicans' anti-regulation movement. In a 2011 survey, while 84 percent of Republicans asserted there is too much government regulation, only 22 percent of Democrats thought so (Carrigan and Coglianese, 2012: 3). In politically liberal American states, from California, Oregon, and Washington to Maryland, New York, and Massachusetts, legislatures and courts continue to make and enforce new law aimed at regulating environmental degradation and greenhouse gas emissions, dangerous technologies and products, workplace discrimination, unfair labor and commercial practices, and other harms. Historically, an American political party that moves toward an ideological extreme, rather than toward the position of the median voters, risks being defeated at the polls sooner or later. The Republicans have managed, for periods of time, to govern as desired by their more ideologically extreme voter and donor base (Hacker and Pierson, 2005). But that strategy could also lead in the future, as it did in the 2008 election, to a Democratic counterreaction, in which some or many of the conservative changes in regulation may be reversed.

More fundamentally, a basic support for and propellant of the American regulatory state and regulatory style—the political and legal culture of "total justice"—while more politically contested, still seems far from dead.

That political culture, as noted in Chapter 3, has two elements. The first is the political idea, stemming from the eighteenth-century Enlightenment and the nation's founding, that the role of government, as the U.S. Constitution's preamble promises, is to promote the general welfare. The second element, as Lawrence Friedman (1985) argues in *Total Justice*, stems from the technologically and organizationally sophisticated nature of economically advanced modern societies, which makes evident to the public that government has the *capacity* to devise and implement laws that will prevent serious harm. Together, those elements are widely interpreted as imposing on government the *obligation* to devise and implement regulatory laws to deal with serious, evident problems, and to hold those who cause serious harms legally accountable. Thus in the aftermath of highly publicized disasters like fatal coal mine explosions, petroleum spills, food poisonings, the September 2001 terrorist attack, and the 2008 financial collapse, politically overwhelming demands arise from civil society, demanding government action to prevent a recurrence. Almost uniformly, elected political leaders scramble to respond, proposing new laws, tougher regulations, and more aggressive enforcement.[18]

The idea of total justice, as noted in Chapter 3, stimulated and became embedded in the wave of civil rights, environmental, health and safety, and consumer protection laws enacted in the 1960s and 1970s. Support of that idea is why, as noted above, Republicans have not attempted to repeal or significantly weaken most of those laws, realizing that to do so would be politically difficult or even disastrous. Polls suggesting that Republican respondents agree that there is "too much" regulation does not mean they think there should be no regulation. Moreover, the total justice idea impels a free press to document and publicize obvious regulatory failures and to analyze their apparent causes. The total justice idea gives Democrats principles to invoke in criticizing Republican governments and electoral opponents who appear unresponsive to such regulatory failures. And failures, as suggested at the outset of this chapter, are close to inevitable.

In our technologically dynamic, interdependent, highly competitive economic world, opportunistic or heedless behavior by some business firms will occur and recur. Tragedies, unfortunately, will ensue. Some will be attributed to regulatory cutbacks by the Trump administration (or subsequent administrations), some to scandal-triggering revelations about government favoritism to the responsible regulated enterprise. Public demands for better protections also will ensue. Over time, therefore, it is likely that government regulation will grow, regardless of the partisan tides of politics. And in the United States, both the shortcomings and the excesses of regulation will continue, as in the past, to spur adversarial legalism, both as a mode of making government more responsive and as a mode of policing regulated enterprises.

CHAPTER TEN

Economic Development, Environmental Protection, and Adversarial Legalism

D uring the eighteenth century, agricultural production in England and
France lagged behind growing populations. Concerned about maintaining political stability, the central governments in both countries strove
to increase food supplies. One obvious strategy was to increase agricultural
efficiency by privatizing communally held lands. Another was to extend
the amount of land under cultivation by draining and reclaiming low-lying
areas (and in France by building irrigation projects as well). In England, as
described in Jean-Laurent Rosenthal's *The Fruits of Revolution* (1992), these
programs moved ahead rapidly. The plans of the French monarchy, however, were almost completely stymied by an eighteenth-century version of
adversarial legalism.[1] By the end of the century, France experienced a violent revolution. England did not.

In France local opponents of irrigation and reclamation projects repeatedly brought lawsuits against the developers who had been chartered by
the royal government. Litigation over each project typically lasted for
years. Judges had to slog through a confusing legal tangle of ill-defined
feudal property rights, local privileges, and easements. Project opponents
who lost in one court often appealed to another, extending the litigation
until the developer simply gave up (Rosenthal, 1992: 44–47, 86–87, 132).
When the royal government in Paris sought to replace the lengthy judicial proceedings with a streamlined administrative process, a fragmented
welter of politically entrenched local courts, church authorities, nobles, and
local governments managed to block the reforms (138, 167, 177).

In England, conversely, the agricultural improvement plans moved ahead
because property rights were relatively clear, as were legal rules for compensating dispossessed property holders (at least to some extent). The Kings'
Bench–judges trained in the Inns of Court in London and paid by the Crown–
applied the law relatively consistently. Agricultural development projects

moved ahead in France only after the French Revolution established the legal and political primacy of the National Assembly and of a strong, hierarchically organized, central bureaucracy. Sweeping aside feudal rules, the revolutionary government systematized the law of property. Proposals for draining communally held lands were subjected to an up-or-down vote by village councils (Rosenthal, 1992: 32). Disputes were channeled into administrative offices. The central government took over the finance and supervision of the judiciary, which henceforth emphasized legal predictability and tended to defer to the national legislature and the central bureaucracy on matters of policy.[2]

While the French Revolution was centralizing political authority and diminishing the centrifugal influence of locally responsive courts, the American Revolution was expressing an entirely different spirit. The American revolutionaries wanted to *limit* the power of a distant central government. As discussed earlier, the federal and the state constitutions established a large measure of autonomy for democratically elected local governments. They guaranteed individual and property rights against governmental abridgment, and to enforce those rights the Americans *fortified* judicial power. By insisting on trial by jury and on local selection of judges, they also made the courts responsive to community values and interests.

The centrifugal impulses of the American Revolution help account for some surprising analogies between eighteenth-century France and the contemporary United States. Here too, local and philosophical opponents of change often institute sequential lawsuits against ostensibly valuable development projects—efforts to build highways, expand manufacturing plants, implement forestry plans, open waste disposal facilities, and construct new housing clusters. As in eighteenth-century France, litigation drags on—and projects are delayed, abandoned, or made more costly—because adjudicatory processes are both slow and legally unpredictable. Like the French judiciary of the eighteenth century, American judges enjoy a large measure of independence from the central government, as well as from state government, and are willing to challenge decisions of governmental planners. In the contemporary United States, too, adversarial legalism arises from the fragmentation of governmental authority.

New construction projects, of course, are not always unmitigated boons. Infrastructural improvements, however beneficial for the collectivity, can disrupt neighborhoods, harm local ecosystems, and desecrate places of beauty. Not infrequently, infrastructural development projects benefit politically influential business interests and self-interested politicians far more than they benefit the collectivity. Ideas of what is a "good" development conflict and evolve: by the end of the twentieth century, swamp drainage and reclamation, even for agricultural uses, had come to be viewed by many as heedless destruction of rapidly vanishing, environmentally essential wetlands. As in eighteenth-century France, local communities often oppose development projects, crying NIMBY—not in my back yard. In many contemporary democracies, government officials structure decision-making to accommodate those concerns. In the early 1990s, according to a comparative study by Jeffery Sellers (1995), local opponents of development projects filed legal appeals in Germany and in France (albeit in specialized administrative courts) about as often as they did in the United States.

The United States, however, remains unique in the *extent* to which adversarial legalism shapes the struggle between continuity and change, between environmental protection and economic growth, between private interests and the public interest. American developers, Sellers noted, are far more likely than their French or German counterparts to be accompanied by lawyers at every step of the planning process. One reason is that in the United States, broad standing-to-sue rules enable local and national environmental advocacy groups to challenge in court the decisions of land use planning boards, private developers, highway departments, and other governmental bodies responsible for infrastructure projects. In their lawsuits, the challengers cite detailed statutory rules and judicial precedents that require developers to provide fact-based analyses of the social costs and as well as of the presumed benefits of proposed highways, dams, mining operations, resorts, and shopping centers.

Adversarial legalism has a bright side: because it can subject new projects and policies to sober second thought, they often are changed for the better. But adversarial legalism in this realm also has a darker side: it can make planning *less* rational. Faced with complex laws and the possibility of litigation, governmental planners often get mired in legal defensiveness, which can greatly postpone desirable public initiatives (Howard, 2014). And as in the Port of Oakland dredging saga described in Chapter 2, adversarial legalism sometimes turns planning processes into a panicky scramble to avoid the risks, delays, and costs of extended, legally unpredictable litigation. When threatened with litigation, project developers often feel compelled to make expensive side-payments demanded by local or ideological opponents. Some of these side-payments are justifiable mitigations of environmental or social harms caused by the project, but some simply dip into the perceived deep pockets of the developer to provide public goods that the community has not been willing to pay for itself. In sum, trying to ensure governmental accountability through adversarial legalism is an inherently erratic method of striking a sensible balance between environmental and economic development concerns. This chapter explores that phenomenon and discusses why it is so deeply entrenched in the American way of governance.

The Bright Side of Adversarial Legalism:
The Boston Harbor Cleanup

In the 1980s, a decade after the enactment of the demanding Federal Clean Water Act of 1972, Boston, Massachusetts still had what was widely considered the most polluted harbor in the United States. The Metropolitan Sewerage System (MSS) still did not have the required secondary treatment plants. Concentrated sewage sludge, created by its outdated primary sewage treatment facilities, regularly was dumped in the harbor. The sewage treatment facilities, moreover, frequently broke down and overflowed, gushing raw sewage into the waters.[3] Beaches often had to be closed, fishing restricted, and acres of shellfish beds placed off limits (Savage, 1995; Dolin, 2005). The responsible agency, the Metropolitan District Commission (MDC), was dependent on the state legislature, which repeatedly underfunded the MDC's sewerage division. The political system was so paralyzed that the generous federal funding assistance provided by the 1972 law was no longer available. Politicians in Boston and the forty-three surrounding communities served by the MSS were reluctant to impose on households and businesses the large increases in water charges needed to finance the renovation of miles of old, leaky, municipal sewerage pipes and to build the massive secondary treatment facilities needed for processing and recycling sewage sludge—projects estimated to cost as much as $2 billion (Dolin, 2005: 118). And instead of appropriating money to aid in building those required facilities, the state government had petitioned the U.S. Environmental Protection Agency (EPA) for a waiver, leading to extended negotiations. President Reagan's first head of EPA, appointed in 1981, applied little pressure on Boston or the Massachusetts government to come into compliance with the law (Dolin, 2005: 129–130).

In December 1982, in Quincy, a municipality adjacent to Boston, a city solicitor was so appalled by the human waste he encountered while jogging on the beach that he pushed the city to file a lawsuit in state court against the MDC and various state officials. Citing violations of the Massachusetts Clean Water Act, Quincy requested a preliminary injunction against any additional sewer hookups to the MSS so as to keep the pollution problem from worsening pending resolution of the case. Judge Paul Garrity responded by appointing a special master (Charles Haar, a Harvard Law School professor) to investigate and resolve any disputed factual issues. Haar's August 1983 report stressed the need for a better funding mechanism for the MDC and MSS. Judge Garrity then approved an agreement with state and MDC officials aimed at rectifying the pollution problem. Meanwhile, the Boston Conservation Law Foundation (CLF) filed a parallel suit against MDC in federal court, citing violations of *federal* law and demanding a court-mandated cleanup; that suit was suspended, however, awaiting developments in Quincy's state court litigation (Savage, 1995: 370).

Thirteen months later, on November 29, 1984, having seen no significant alleviation of the ongoing pollution or of the deadlock in the state legislature concerning reform proposals, Judge Garrity issued an injunction imposing a moratorium on most new sewer hookups to the MSS. That order, by threatening to bring construction projects to a virtual halt in Boston and throughout the MSS region, drew swarms of business lobbyists to the state capitol, all demanding action on the sewage problem (Savage, 1995: 371; Dolin, 2005: 120–21). The Massachusetts attorney general, however, quickly appealed Judge Garrity's injunction and a Massachusetts Supreme Court judge overturned it. But in the United States, when one court shuts the door, another might open it. A new head of enforcement at the EPA regional office announced that his agency would sue the MDC in U.S. District Court and petition a federal judge to impose a moratorium on sewer hookups. Meanwhile Judge Garrity too increased the pressure for a political solution. He granted news media interviews about the harbor case. The *Boston Globe* and *Washington Post* displayed front-page photos of Garrity, dressed in his judicial robe, standing at the edge of Boston Harbor. The adverse publicity helped push the Massachusetts legislature into action.[4] It enacted a law that replaced the MDC with a new Massachusetts Water Resources Agency (MWRA), vested with powers to issue bonds to finance the harbor and sewer system cleanup measures and to set water rates that would be sufficient to finance the bonds as well as ongoing operating and maintenance costs (Dolin, 2005: 121–124).

A month later, January 31, 1985, the EPA, as promised, sued the MDC, the MWRA, and the state of Massachusetts in federal court, seeking a judicial order compelling them to submit plans and schedules for remedying the ongoing violations of the Clean Water Act and to ensure the implementation of those plans. EPA officials argued that federal law provided stronger legal sanctions and remedial powers than the state court could muster. They also argued that since Judge Garrity had retired at the end of 1984, the federal court could better counteract the anticipated political pressures on the MWRA. In May 1985, U.S. District Court Judge A. David Mazzone consolidated EPA's lawsuit with the dormant case filed in 1983 by the Boston Conservation Law Foundation, thus adding another urgent voice to the court's deliberations. Subsequently, in September 1985 Judge Mazzone found that the defendants were clearly in serious violation of the federal Clean Water Act. Governor Dukakis of Massachusetts (who would be the Democratic Party's candidate in the 1988 presidential election) chose not to appeal but to cooperate. Judge Mazzone ordered the parties to agree on a plan and schedule for curing the violations.

The negotiations were complex. It was far from easy to agree on very costly remedial measures. Judge Mazzone's intervention frequently was needed to conduct hearings, resolve differences, and establish new deadlines for next steps. Ultimately, he ordered that a proposed new primary treatment facility, sited on Deer Island in Boston Harbor, must be finished and operational by 1995 and that a state-of-the-art secondary treatment facility must be ready by 1999—demanding deadlines in view of the scale, cost, and technical complexity of these installations. Despite setbacks during construction, the project—celebrated in 1999 by *Engineering News Record* as one of the greatest projects of the last 125 years—was completed in twelve years. Miles of huge tunnels had to be designed and dug deep under Boston Harbor. The projects ended up costing $3.8 billion. Even with federal and state subsidies to the MWRA, water and sewer service charges to an average family in the communities affected grew from an average of $113 annually to $477 in 2000; those charges, it was estimated, would grow to $792 in 2010 (Dolin, 2005:155).

But by 1991, direct sludge discharges into the harbor had ceased. Huge digesters on Deer Island were turning the sludge into disinfected pellets that could be distributed or sold for fertilizer. By 2005, the vast majority of the harbor met federal water quality standards (157). Boating, fishing, and beach-going had returned. EPA officials and environmental activists proclaimed the Boston Harbor project "one of America's greatest environmental success stories" (162). In 2015, my wife and I walked a nicely landscaped trail around the circumference of Deer Island, admiring spectacular views of Boston and the harbor, and marveling at the massive sewage treatment and reprocessing facilities that fill most of the island's interior. At the start of the trail is a bronze statue of Judge Mazzone.

The Darker Side of Adversarial Legalism: The Los Angeles Century Freeway

The Century Freeway was designed to link Los Angeles Airport in west Los Angeles with communities and freeways to the east. After receiving federal funding for the Century Freeway in 1968, the state highway department (Caltrans) moved rapidly to acquire property along the seventeen-mile right-of-way, relocate displaced families, seek construction bids, and negotiate agreements with the several municipalities through which the roadway would pass. (Each municipality's consent is legally necessary when highways, as is often the case, require local street closures.) In early

1972, however, the Center for Law in the Public Interest filed a federal class action against state and federal transportation agencies—Caltrans and the U.S. Department of Transportation (DOT)—on behalf of people who lived along the freeway path. The center's legal complaint was joined by other parties: the city of Hawthorne, which had a politically active neighborhood group that was upset about the thought of a highway carving up its area; the Sierra Club and the Environmental Defense Fund, which argued that the highway was environmentally unwise; and the NAACP, which argued that the choice of route denied minority communities and families the equal protection of the law (Hebert, 1972; Detlefsen, 1995: 20; 1994).

In terms of prior precedent, none of the plaintiffs' legal arguments appeared to be very strong. The Center for Law in the Public Interest argued that Caltrans and the DOT had not circulated an environmental impact statement (EIS) evaluating the project, as required by the National Environmental Policy Act (NEPA). Caltrans and DOT responded that NEPA had been enacted in 1969, *after* the Century Freeway project had been approved, and their lawyers had determined that its requirements were not applicable to the Century Freeway project. In any case, Caltrans and DOT argued, their environmental analysis had in fact been adequate.[5] Because the equal protection and other constitutional claims seemed rather far-fetched, Caltrans lawyers felt sure they would prevail on the merits. Nevertheless, U.S. District Court Judge Harry Pregerson issued a preliminary injunction against further property acquisition pending the court's decision, and he ordered Caltrans to prepare an EIS.

The preparation and circulation of the EIS took from 1972 to 1978. During that time, work on the Century Freeway remained on hold. By the time of the 1972 injunction, 60 percent of the parcels had been acquired, and relocation funds had been paid to displaced residents. One-third of the right-of-way had been cleared, leaving large deserted areas that during the pendency of the litigation became sites for crime and illegal trash disposal. Local, state, and federal officials urged Caltrans to get the project completed. However, California's liberal governor Jerry Brown, elected in 1974, appointed a Caltrans director who was generally opposed to any further highway construction in Los Angeles (Detlefsen, 1994). Hence in 1979 Caltrans (over the objections of its senior engineers and planners) settled the litigation via a consent decree that made major concessions to the plaintiffs.

Two lanes of the planned highway were to be reserved for buses and multipassenger vans. Caltrans and the federal government would finance construction of 4,200 new housing units in the communities through which the freeway would pass, at an estimated additional cost of $300 million— even though most displaced residents presumably had already found new housing.[6] (The originally budgeted cost of the freeway had been $500 million.) In addition, the consent decree, as formulated under Judge Pregerson's

auspices, provided for an elaborate affirmative action plan and an employment center, supervised by a plaintiff-dominated committee and paid for
by Caltrans, using state and federal highway funds. The decree splintered
the highway construction project into eighty-four contracts and subcon-
tracts, which presumably would make it more feasible to hire companies
owned by women and minorities (Hebert, 1986: 4). Minority hiring goals,
based on the proportion of minorities in the freeway corridor, were fixed
for each construction trade on all freeway and housing construction projects, bolstered by an apprenticeship program to be funded by Caltrans.
Detailed rules were established to help plaintiffs' counsel hold Caltrans to
the agreed-upon goals.

A decade of often acrimonious judicial hearings ensued, revolving
around the implementation, interpretation, and amendment of the consent
decree. Despite the judicial mandate commanding cooperation among the
parties, an adversarial spirit prevailed. Although hardly anyone, including
the communities along the route, thought that the Century Freeway should
not be built, the freeway was not completed until 1993, more than twenty
years after Judge Pregerson's injunction. One can scarcely imagine the in-
tervening financial, environmental, and emotional harm engendered by
thousands of pollution-spewing traffic jams.[7] Pursuant to demands made by
plaintiffs during implementation of the consent decree, one of the planned
high occupancy vehicle lanes was converted to provide for a light rail
system, although transportation planners doubted it would prove to be cost-
effective.

For years, the policy preferences of elected governors and mayors
were subordinated to the preferences of the judge and the various plaintiffs' lawyers. The overall cost of the project ballooned to approximately
$2.2 billion (Reinhold, 1993). Construction and administrative costs for
the housing program were grossly inflated (Trombley and Hebert, 1987a,
1987b). Caltrans funds ultimately provided not only job training programs
for minorities but tutoring and scholarships for poor children and housing
for AIDS patients in West Hollywood, ten miles from the freeway (Reinhold, 1993). Those certainly were meaningful benefits, but all in all, actual
highway construction ended up accounting for only 54 percent of the
project's total cost. Even without those extras, construction costs for the
highway itself, burdened by the scores of separate contracts and subcon-
tracts demanded by the affirmative action portions of the consent decree,
reached over $100 million a mile, "more per mile than any other road
in American history" (Reinhold, 1993, 1).[8] The Century Freeway consent
decree drained Caltrans's budget, curtailing projects elsewhere in the
state. California sank to last place among the fifty states in new highway
construction.

The Prevalence of Troublesome Adversarial Legalism

The Century Freeway is not the only highway to be reshaped by litigation. Even the threat of a lawsuit sometimes suffices. After years of planning, for example, transportation officials in Boston, striving to ameliorate an infamously congested traffic pattern, obtained federal and state funding to build a third tunnel across Boston Harbor and a new, underground highway through the city, replacing unsightly, outmoded elevated roadways. The officials' environmental analysis showed that the new tunnel/artery, by reducing congestion, would significantly improve air quality. But the Conservation Law Foundation (CLF) opposed the project, contending that the new roadway ultimately would worsen pollution by drawing more cars onto the roads (Stipp, 1991). Backed by a number of transportation and environmental groups, CLF threatened to sue unless the Federal Highway Administration compelled Massachusetts project planners to institute a costly set of traffic-cutting measures. To ward off such litigation, which threatened to unravel the delicately balanced web of political and financing commitments supporting the plan, the Massachusetts environmental affairs secretary conditioned his 1990 certificate of approval on a series of environmental mitigation projects demanded by CLF, including improvements to Boston's rapid transit rail system. Research showed that these measures not only would add some $3.6 billion to the project's original $5 billion cost but would be extremely inefficient ways to reduce pollution (Palmer, 1994). Other municipalities, environmental agencies, and neighborhood groups followed CLF's example, using the threat of litigation to extract an additional $2.8 billion for mitigation projects, many of them rather far removed from any direct impacts of the tunnel/artery project.[9] As in the Century Freeway saga, adversarial legalism served in part as a mechanism through which particular interests could extort public funds for their desired projects while delaying widely demanded public works and injecting less, not more, rationality into the search for a sensible balance between economic development and environmental protection.

A list of similar stories is not difficult to assemble. To give just a few examples, plans to establish badly needed, more secure disposal sites for both low-level (Gunnison, 1993) and high-level nuclear wastes (Topol, 1991; Deese, 1982) were blocked or delayed for years and were subjected to large side-payments as a result of lawsuits filed by neighborhood groups and advocacy organizations. Welles and Engel (2000) studied the experience of a multinational corporation that specializes in designing and constructing waste disposal sites. They found that the firm took much longer and paid vastly more money on lawyers and litigation to obtain permits for municipal landfill sites in California and Pennsylvania than in England and in the Netherlands. Conversely, business firms have often turned to adversarial legalism to obstruct government projects designed to enhance environmental conditions—as when corporate sugar growers used litigation to block a federal government plan to restore the Florida Everglades by flooding huge sugar plantations built on former wetlands (McKinley, 1999). In the 1970s and 1980s the construction of nuclear power plants in the United States was slowed to a crawl, then virtually abandoned, but not because elected governments or even the public decided to reject nuclear power; American voters generally *rejected* ballot measures designed to block nuclear power plants (Boyle, 1998: 153). Like eighteenth-century France's marsh drainage program, American efforts to license nuclear plants were so often tied up in lengthy litigation by opponents that project sponsors, burdened by endless legal and financial uncertainty, often simply gave up.[10]

Not every American development project or plan, of course, is held up and distorted by litigation. Other scenarios often unfold. First, politically skillful governmental officials often invoke the specter of costly adversarial legalism to bring project proponents and opponents together and forge an acceptable compromise (Busch, Kirp, and Schoenholz, 1999; Kagan, 1997b: 872). Second, as in the Boston Harbor case, adversarial legalism, by circumventing or breaking *political* deadlocks, sometimes actually promotes infrastructural development *and* environmental protection. And third, all too often there is not enough adversarial legalism: it remains dormant because potential project opponents lack the knowledge, organization, or resources to find willing lawyers and bring lawsuits to block environmentally harmful projects (Foster, 1998). For the balance of this chapter, however, it may be useful, as in this book as a whole, to focus on the more troublesome manifestations of adversarial legalism. For as in engineering failure analysis, thinking about why things go wrong may illuminate pathways to getting things to come out right.

Why Troublesome Adversarial Legalism Recurs

Adversarial legalism of the kind exemplified by the Century Freeway recurs, despite outraged protests by elected officials, because it reflects three distinctive features of American law and governance: (a) reliance on (or at least provision for) litigation to ensure governmental accountability; (b) court-enforceable statutory demands for comprehensive environmental analysis as a precondition to developmental action; and (c) high levels of legal uncertainty. Those three features, in turn, arise from the confluence of the two basic factors referred to repeatedly in this book: (1) the distrust and consequent fragmentation of governmental authority in the United States, combined with (2) powerful political demands for governmental action to solve social problems.

Accountability through Lawsuits

In all economically advanced democracies, highway planning officials are expected to consider the interests of affected local communities, to analyze the impacts of various alternatives, to mitigate environmental disruption, to pay compensation and provide relocation assistance to displaced property owners along the right-of-way, and to act honestly and fairly in awarding construction contracts. In most democratic countries officials are held accountable to those standards primarily by administrative supervision and political oversight. Opposition political parties and the news media play an additional watchdog role. Thus in the Century Freeway and the Boston tunnel cases, highway planners had to prepare detailed cost-benefit and environmental analyses. They had to defend their choices to superiors in the state capital and to the DOT in Washington, to legislative appropriations committees, and, in mandatory public meetings, to the community and the press. But far more than other democracies, the United States employs an additional accountability mechanism: litigation (and the threat of litigation).

Because of the unusually broad American rules concerning standing to sue, virtually any interested party—including members of the world's widest array of public interest lawyers, acting as self-appointed private attorneys general—can bring lawsuits against alleged violations of public law. Thus in the Century Freeway case, the motive force was the Center for Law in the Public Interest, not particular clients. In the Boston tunnel project story, the Conservation Law Foundation, with hardly a mention of who its client might be, threatened to sue the agencies that financed the project. As described in Chapter 2, the Port of Oakland sued a local water district for raising what a court ultimately ruled were legally unfounded—but project-delaying—objections to the Port's badly needed disposal plan for dredged material.

Accountability through litigation both reflects and reinforces the extraordinary power of American courts. The United States is distinctive, Mirjan Damaska (1990: 424–425) emphasizes, in granting politically selected lower court judges the power to overturn decisions made by high officials of the central government, and in perpetuating a legal culture in which even lower court judges do not "shy away from deciding matters of great political importance . . . ; being people in their second career, relatively unconcerned about promotions, they make use of these powers in a comparatively bold manner." In the Port of Oakland story told in Chapter 2, a state court judge halted dredging disposal operations that had been authorized by the U.S. Army Corps of Engineers, the EPA, various state agencies, and a federal court. In sum, when decentralized litigation becomes a primary method of ensuring governmental accountability, individual judges, applying the law, can trump the plans of democratically elected governments—*or*, as in in the Boston Harbor case, order unresponsive governments to remedy serious neglect of their legal duties and environmental responsibilities.

The Slow-Motion Search for Comprehensive Rationality

Under the Marine Protection, Research, and Sanctuaries Act the EPA has authority to designate an ocean disposal site for dredged material—as it did on the Port of Oakland story—but the agency must first make official findings concerning:

> (A) The need for the proposed dumping; (B) The effect of such dumping on human health and welfare, including economic, esthetic and recreational values; (C) The effect of such dumping on fisheries resources, plankton, fish, shellfish, wildlife, shore lines and beaches; (D) The effect of such dumping on marine ecosystems, particularly with respect to (i) the transfer, concentration and dispersion of such material and its byproducts through biological, physical and chemical processes, (ii) potential changes in marine ecosystem diversity, productivity, and stability, and (iii) species and community population dynamics; (E) The persistence and permanence of the effects of the dumping; (F) The effect of dumping particular volumes and concentrations of such materials; (G) Appropriate locations and methods of disposal or recycling . . . ; (H) The effect on alternate uses of oceans, such as scientific study, fishing, and other living resource exploitation, and nonliving resource exploitation.

The U.S. Army Corps of Engineers may issue a dredging permit when it would meet "the public interest," but federal regulations say the Corps must first consider and weigh

> all factors which may be relevant . . . including the cumulative effects thereof: among these are conservation, economics, aesthetics, general environmental concerns, wetlands, historic properties, fish and wildlife values, food hazards, land use, navigation, shore erosion and accretion, recreation, water supply and conservation, water quality, energy needs, safety, food and fiber production, mineral needs, considerations of property ownership and, in general, the needs and welfare of the people.[11]

These legal demands for careful study and evaluation before public action reflect the ideal of *comprehensive rationality*. Who would not want government to look before it leaps? Shouldn't we expect project planners to attend to all the values and interests at stake and gather all the relevant facts? Well, perhaps not *all* the facts. As decision theorists such as Herbert Simon and Charles Lindblom have explained, *fully* complying with the demands of comprehensive rationality often entails intolerable costs, both in money and delay (Simon, 1957; Braybrooke and Lindblom, 1963). In the Port of Oakland case, for example, the EPA could not make the findings required by the statute quoted above until Congress appropriated the millions of dollars needed to do the requisite research—funds for which other socially useful programs also were clamoring. Even after the funds are authorized, research is usually painstakingly slow and costly. By 1991, after four years of environmental impact analysis, expenditures by the Port of Oakland and the Corps of Engineers on sediment sampling and testing had reached almost $4 million, the equivalent of $8 a cubic yard for phase I of the dredging project—more than the physical act of phase I dredging ultimately cost. And since relevant research methodologies are adversarially scrutinized, scientific controversy erupted at every step, further delaying the regulatory and legal decision processes.[12]

American laws demand comprehensive analysis but they also often display an abiding distrust of the analysts. Thus the Corps of Engineers, before granting a harbor dredging permit, must submit its analyses to and consult with a variety of other agencies—the U.S. Fish and Wildlife Service (statutory guardian for migratory birds, fisheries, and threatened and endangered species), the National Marine Fisheries Service, the relevant *state* Department of Fish and Game, both federal and state environmental protection and water pollution control agencies, and the state Coastal Zone Management Agency. Each of those agencies, in turn, is legally bound to file evaluations of the project in terms of the agency's own particular governing statute and to object to the Corps of Engineers' analysis if they find it wanting. In addition, relevant studies and plans often must be made available for public review and public hearings. Objections from other agencies and advocacy groups must be recorded and given a formal, reasoned response.[13]

In practice, the ideal of comprehensively rational analysis rarely can be fully achieved. Perfect research is too expensive. There is no methodology by which agencies can rationally find the "correct" balance among the multiplicity of factors they are legally supposed to take into account. Administrative decisionmakers, therefore, often just muddle through. They make a rough "guestimate" based on the information obtainable within a reasonable period of time (Braybrooke and Lindblom, 1963; March and Simon, 1958). They try to strike reasonable compromises among conflicting values. But when the law demands comprehensive rationality, including the filing of specific scientific findings, guestimates and compromises may not be good enough. Any relevant private advocacy organization, any affected local government, any competing agency that objects to a particular compromise decision can challenge it in court. Adversarial legal procedures ensure embarrassing exposure of the inevitable gaps in the project planners' analysis or of their incompletely rationalized "satisficing" judgments.

Judicially enforceable statutory demands for analytic perfection thus provide sturdy footholds for project opponents and delaying lawsuits. The Conservation Law Foundation's threatened lawsuit against the Boston artery and tunnel project was based on a challenge to the highway department's analysis, which concluded–plausibly, but surely not conclusively–that large reductions in congestion would reduce harmful air pollution (Stipp, 1991). Aware of such stories, agency officials and project planners view litigation as an ever-present threat. Perhaps it won't materialize, but if it does, it could delay the start of the project by at least another year, perhaps more. In consequence, agencies expend a great deal of time and resources on "defensive science," striving to make their decisions judicially bulletproof. In that regard, transportation agencies trying to build a toll road near San Diego (the first new highway to be constructed in the increasingly traffic-jammed county in decades) produced more than 100 volumes of environmental impact reports, hoping to repel legal challenges. But environmental groups eventually sued the agencies in both state and federal courts–and petitioned the U.S. Fish and Wildlife Service to block the road-building by declaring the California gnatcatcher an endangered species. Outside the courthouse, opponents of the San Diego toll road announced to supporters and the press that their goal was to stop the planned freeway (as well as any alternative routes) entirely. Inside the courthouse, however, their lawyers' arguments focused not on the basic policy debates concerning transportation or enhancement of air quality but on claimed defects in the environmental analyses (Fulton, 1992).

Legal Unpredictability

The threat of litigation is not terribly problematic when the law is clear and the adjudicative process is expeditious and predictable. Under those circumstances, a rational defendant, if confronted with a legally meritorious claim, would leap to comply. If the defendant asserts a legally sustainable defense, the rational plaintiff would retreat, saving time and money. But in the American legal system, as we have seen, legal certainty is elusive. In the Century Freeway case, Caltrans officials and their lawyers felt sure that they had complied with the applicable laws and that the constitutional claims advanced by the NAACP and women's advocacy groups, viewed in light of existing legal precedents, were weak. But Judge Pregerson issued a preliminary injunction, pending trial. Caltrans officials still felt they would prevail after a full trial. The trial never occurred, for Caltrans came under intense political pressure to settle and the Caltrans officials could not be totally sure that they would have won in court.

The legal disagreement and uncertainty arose partly because American law governing land use and environmental protection, viewed in cross-national comparison, is both extraordinarily complex and extraordinarily vague (or as legal scholars often put it, "indeterminate"). The *complexity* of American law reflects the characteristic fragmentation of governmental authority in the United States: to secure permission to transport petroleum by pipeline from a giant offshore oil well and recovery station on the California coast, Chevron had to obtain approvals from no fewer than forty-four federal, state, regional, and local governmental bodies—each applying its own statutes, regulations, and ordinances (Lee, 1990: D1; Lucas, 1990; Benedict, 1993). The *indeterminacy* of U.S. environmental law arises in large measure from the method of lawmaking in American legislative bodies, which tend to be more politically permeable than legislatures in parliamentary systems and to operate on a more ad hoc basis. American environmental laws are drafted by fractious legislative committees, responding to particular crises and to crosscutting political pressures. Lobbyists corner committee members to push for last-minute amendments. A motor vehicle manufacturing company official, reflecting on his experience with Congress when it was enacting standards for hydrocarbon emissions, complained: "You'll never tell me . . . this process of running around the hall in and out of a conference committee at 11 o'clock at night . . . is a rational process. The people bartering on what the emission levels should be on automobiles wouldn't know a hydrocarbon if they tripped over it. . . . But there they are, [saying] 'I'll give you this, if you give me that.' It's almost like you're out in [Las Vegas] Nevada." (Dimento, 1986: 118–119).

Legal unpredictability is exacerbated by the politically selected nature of the American judiciary. In most other democracies, as noted in earlier chapters, the professionally selected and evaluated judiciary treats legal consistency as a preeminent ideal (Garoupa and Matthews, 2014). In the United States many judges do value consistency, but to many others, achieving justice in the particular case (or acquiring a reputation for being a compassionate judge—or, for a Republican judge, a defender of conservative values)—is even more important. Individual judges who feel strongly about a policy issue, such as Judge Pregerson in the Century Freeway case, do not hesitate to turn their feelings into law. Legal variability and malleability encourage continued adversarial struggle. As in the Port of Oakland and the Boston Harbor cases, interests that lose a policy battle in one agency or court may try another, or run to the legislature to seek ad hoc corrective legislation, for there is almost always a chance that a different decision-maker will be more responsive. Thus to the participants in these controversies, the law often appears to be simply an arena for ongoing political struggle, not the authoritative normative anchor that it represents in some other democratic nations.

Fragmented Government and Adversarial Legalism

Many American politicians and scholars have been troubled by the role of adversarial legalism in American economic and environmental governance. The U.S. Advisory Commission on Intergovernmental Relations (1992, 1) reported that badly needed "new highways, airports, . . . wastewater treatment plants, and solid waste facilities" have frequently been subjected to immensely costly delays because "federal rules and procedures governing decisionmaking for protecting the environment often are complex, conflicting, difficult to apply, adversarial, costly, inflexible, and uncertain." Yet the same politicians who are disturbed when *their* favorite programs are bogged down by litigation rarely take a public stand against legal rights to challenge national bureaucracies in court. The rights to litigate that frustrate a political office-holder today may come in handy when his or her partisan opponents are in power tomorrow.

More fundamentally, the whole pattern of governance via adversarial legalism, as emphasized throughout this book, is sustained by the tensions generated by a political culture that demands "total justice"–active governmental protection from harm, injustice, and environmental degradation–but remains highly mistrustful of governmental authority. Responding to electoral pressures, politicians of both parties repeatedly endorse ambitious regulatory goals, but they also insist, again in response to political traditions and pressures, that governmental regulatory authority be structurally fragmented, procedurally checked, scientifically grounded, and legally constrained. Policies intended to control hazardous technologies and other sources of harm are therefore forced through the complex gates of detailed legal prescriptions, demanding scientific and economic analyses, and judicial oversight.

The reasons for the persistence of American adversarial legalism are highlighted by comparing the United States with its neighbor to the north. Like the United States, Canada is geographically huge, environmentally diverse, and politically decentralized, with strong provincial governments. Canada has active environmental advocacy groups, and its environmental policies address the same issues as those covered by U.S. law (Hoberg, 1991: 107–131; Harrison and Hoberg, 1991: 3–28).[14] As in the United States, Canadian communities have often resisted plans for expanding ports and constructing waste disposal facilities. Yet Canada has not experienced high levels of adversarial legalism (Hoberg, 1993; Nemetz, Stanbury, and Thompson, 1986). Canadian law does not favor class actions by private attorneys general. In 1972 and 1973 the Canadian national government established an environmental impact analysis requirement akin to that established by the 1969 U.S. National Environmental Protection Act (NEPA), but Canadian courts usually have not been inclined to halt ongoing projects pending the completion of an environmental analysis. Canadian judges do not emulate American judges' willingness to reexamine the adequacy of administrative bodies' policy responses to arguments against their proposed plans or regulations (Lucas, 1993: 170; Howlett, 1994). Thus Canadian environmental activist organizations generally refrain from litigating; instead, they concentrate on lobbying and public education (Roman and Pikkov, 1990). In contrast to the adversarial legalism that has accompanied the U.S. Endangered Species Act, Canadian species protection policies are governed by legal provisions that grant broad discretion to environmental agencies and their wildlife experts. The implementation process is based on cooperative decision making by committees, which include provincial governmental officials and the leaders of major environmental organizations.

How can we account for these differences? *Political culture* undoubtedly plays a significant role. Unlike their American cousins, Canadians didn't revolt against the British crown. In comparative opinion polls Canadians tend to be more respectful of authority and more communal in their attitudes, while Americans are more individualistic, antistatist, and rights-oriented (Lipset, 1991). James Q. Wilson (1989: 304) points out, "Americans always entertain the suspicion that the government is doing something mischievous behind their backs."

In addition to political culture, however, differences in *political structure* help explain the American emphasis on adversarial legalism. In a study of environmental regulation in federal governments, Daniel Kelemen (1998) observed that compared to the central governments of *parliamentary* federal systems such as Canada, Australia, and Germany, political authority in the United States is more fragmented. Not only is power divided between Congress and the presidency, which often have been dominated by competing political parties, but American political parties generally exert less control over individual legislators than do parties in parliamentary regimes. Frequent elections mean frequent shifts in power and influence. The president, various congressional committees, and competing interest groups all engage in a nonstop battle for control of regulatory personnel and policies whose funding and enforcement priorities shift from administration to administration, congressional session to congressional session (Wood and Waterman, 1991). Worried that their political adversaries will gain control in the future, contending interests fight for detailed statutory provisions, mandated analytic requirements, formal participatory procedures, or bureaucratic arrangements that will enable them to reshape unfavorable administrative decisions, by appeals to court if necessary (Moe, 1989). Richard Lazarus

(1991: 311) writes: "Amendments to the Clean Air Act and Clean Water Act in 1977, to the Clean Water Act, CERCLA, FIFRA, RCRA, the Safe Drinking Water Act, and TSCA during the 1980s, and to the Clean Air Act in 1990, all exhibit the same trend. Each eliminated substantial EPA discretion, imposed more deadlines, and included more prescription."[15]

Accountability by detailed law and litigation provides a means of continuing the struggle to constrain power and influence policy. Administrators find themselves without the capacity to set priorities and implement them flexibly. With reference to the EPA, Lazarus (id.) continues:

> Congress has repeatedly demanded that the agency perform impossible tasks under unrealistic deadlines. Courts have rejected many of the agency's efforts to provide itself with more leeway in their implementation, while the White House, OMB [the Office of Management and Budget], and congressional appropriation committees have simultaneously resisted subsequent agency efforts to comply with judicial mandates. The agency spends much of its limited resources defending its decisions in court, negotiating with OMB and the White House, and justifying its decisions to Congressional committees. A virtual state of siege and a crisis mentality have persisted at the agency for much of its existence as Congress has responded to each EPA failure by passing even more restrictive deadline legislation that the agency again fails to meet.

In Canada's parliamentary central government (and in its parliamentary provincial governments as well), bureaucracies are less politicized, and they are subject to unified political control by governments that are dominated by a single, cohesive political party for four or five years on end. The dominant party does not need courts to control administrative decisions. As a senior Canadian official put it: "Canadian regulatory officials are directly subject to the authority of Parliament's leadership in Cabinet. Thus it is unnecessary for Parliament to spell out legislative intent in great detail . . . this is in contrast to the American context where social regulation was written with the explicit objective of denying discretion and flexibility to the regulators."[16] In parliamentary systems, such as Canada's, the government in power can quickly amend the law to reverse administrative or judicial decisions that displease it. Hence it does not feel the need to write such detailed rules or encourage citizen suits to monitor the bureaucracy. Tight legal controls are not necessary because political controls suffice. Relations among regulators and the regulated are therefore less likely to be abraded by legal conflicts about the applicability of highly prescriptive regulations.

Another structural feature of American government—the strength of its political traditions of local government—is also of great importance. With respect to environmental protection, for example, the regulation of land use, waste disposal, and drinking water supply have remained primarily the province of locally elected, locally financed, municipal or (for unincorporated areas) county governments. For the most part, local officials, not state and federal governments, control the location of new housing developments, shopping centers, and industrial parks. To a larger degree than most economically advanced democracies, local governments in the United States rely heavily on local taxes, particularly property taxes, to finance basic governmental services, including education, public safety, infrastructure maintenance, and so on. The national government in the United States, therefore, has fewer *financial* controls over state and local governments. Policy clashes between separately elected city and state governments, and between state and federal regulatory officials, are common. For environmental advocacy groups—such as the Center for Law in the Public Interest and the NAACP in the Los Angeles Century Freeway case—adversarial legalism provides a vital mechanism for pushing state and local governments to adhere to national policy norms.

In contrast, in Great Britain, the Netherlands, Germany, and Japan, much land use planning authority is vested in provincial governments. Cities are confined to tight borders. Suburbs are not created at will. Municipalities and provincial governments get large proportions of their budgets from the national government, and hence tend to be responsive to their political paymaster's concerns. Since towns are less dependent on local revenues than in the United States, business firms are less inclined to base location decisions on variations in local property tax rates. In America, conversely, revenue-hungry (or job-hungry) local governments face stronger incentives to favor economic development over environmental protection (Peterson, 1995; Kagan, 1999a). In short, decentralized governance makes environmental protection more difficult in the United States than in more hierarchically ordered polities.

From the perspective of American environmentalists, the logical remedy would be to mimic European land use regulation, shifting authority over local land use decisions to a higher level of government at which environmental values might weigh more heavily than local concerns about maximizing property tax revenues or speeding the flow of traffic. But in the United States the powerful political forces maintaining local control generally have blocked that route. The next best strategy, from the environmental standpoint, has been to construct a more complex set of institutional and legal checks on local decisions that threaten environmental values. That strategy has led to national or state laws that require local project proponents—those who wish to build paper factories, dredge ports, or drill for oil—to obtain permits not only from local governments but also from a network of federal, state, or regional agencies responsible for protecting specific environmental values—for example, water, air, endangered species, wetlands, beaches, and so on. Secondly, the environmental regulatory strategy has been to empower neighborhood groups and environmental advocacy groups to file lawsuits that challenge local land use decisions or development projects pushed by the state or federal government (such as new highways), alleging that they fail to meet legally mandated environmental assessment criteria embodied in law. Thus the patterns of costly litigation evidenced in the Century Freeway story, the Port of Oakland dredging project, and so on arise from laws and procedures that were designed to implement national environmental policies in a highly decentralized governmental structure. Sometimes adversarial legalism has positive effects in that regard. But often, what Richard Stewart, a former assistant attorney general for environment and natural resources (1990: 346), has called a "self-contradictory attempt at central planning through litigation" tends to misfire.

Skewed Consequences

It should be restated that adversarial legalism often results in *improvements* in public policy. As in the Boston Harbor case (and the New York Westway case, mentioned in Chapter 2), lawsuits have often exposed governmental failures to deal with environmental impacts adequately. But the Century Freeway and Oakland Harbor cases illustrate how accountability through litigation can readily generate two unfortunate outcomes: the use of the legal process to extort particularistic benefits and skew political responsiveness.

Litigation-Based Delay and Extortion. When public law is constantly subject to judicial reinterpretation and legislative intervention, those who oppose governmental programs and projects are encouraged to try their hand at litigation, or at least the threat of it. The National Research Council panel (1986: 89–90) that studied the port expansion decision process observed: "Objectors do not necessarily have to win in the courts to win their point. If the courts provide a vehicle for substantial delay and that delay is costly to the proposers of the project, the threat of going to court becomes a powerful negotiating tool in the hands of objectors. . . . It is an essential reality for all of the participants in regulatory decision-making." When Caltrans, hoping to avoid further litigation in the Century Freeway case, agreed to construct costly mass transit facilities and to build a large housing project, that decision was not backed by a careful cost-benefit analysis. Nor did that decision flow from a legislative debate or a carefully prepared state or national transportation plan. It was an ad hoc decision, made in private, often hectic negotiations in the shadow of the courthouse. The decision was shaped primarily by the wish list of a particular public interest law firm and the other plaintiffs—whose desires evidently had not managed to gain approval through democratic and administrative political processes.

The Asymmetrical Responsiveness of Governance via Litigation. Adversarial legalism was injected into the planning and implementation of American development projects because governmental and corporate project planners are not infrequently insensitive to local and environmental concerns. Once built, superhighways cannot be dismantled or moved; the communities and neighborhoods they disrupt cannot be reassembled. Tree farms do not recreate the ecosystems or the beauty of mature forests mauled by clear-cutting. Lawyers and courts, the advocates for adversarial legalism hoped, would make public policy responsive to *all* relevant voices in the affected community, not just the powerful proponents of development. Sometimes that hope is realized. But often it is not.

One reason is that many communities adversely affected by development projects lack the knowledge, contacts, or resources to use adversarial legalism effectively. In the declining industrial town of Chester, Pennsylvania, 65 percent African American and very poor, the mechanisms of adversarial legalism lay dormant in the 1980s and 1990s as government officials, local and state, issued permit after permit to waste processing companies of various kinds. According to a *New York Times* reporter who visited Chester in 1996, the air was "thick with acrid smells and, often, smoke. Dump trucks rumble through throughout the day" and "the first thing you notice is the smell" (Janovsky, 1996: 15). Property values in Chester plummeted. There is significant evidence that cancer rates were much higher than might be expected (Foster, 1998). In the mid-1990s, when a Philadelphia public interest lawyer contested a permit for yet another waste processing facility in Chester, and then appealed it to the courts, a victory in one court was overturned by another. Only direct political action, both in the streets and the election of a new city government, belatedly started to turn the tide. Across the nation, minority neighborhood victories in such "environmental justice" lawsuits have been few and far between.

Conversely, the powerful weapons of adversarial legalism can make the government *disproportionately* responsive to those who *do* wield them. Consider, for example, the Century Freeway case. Once the Center for Law in the Public Interest, the Sierra Club, and the NAACP obtained a preliminary injunction, they were guaranteed not only a voice throughout the subsequent negotiations and the administration of the consent decree, but the dominant voice; they could demand particular benefits for particular groups in return for agreeing to let the project proceed. Once Judge

Pregerson incorporated the settlement in a judicial decree, the Center for Law in the Public Interest and the other advocacy groups retained a virtual veto over any subsequent proposals to change the plan. The judge and a committee dominated by the plaintiffs' lawyers became a special, undemocratic government for the highway project—impervious to the views of the elected government of Los Angeles or of two subsequently elected Republican governors (who did not share the antihighway attitudes of the Democratic administration that embraced the settlement years earlier).

A similar skewing of political responsiveness characterized the Port of Oakland story. For years, as a sequence of regulatory bodies and courts slowly processed repeated challenges to proposed disposal sites for dredged sediment, local elected political leaders—the mayor of Oakland, state and federal legislative representatives—were powerless to respond to the resulting loss of port business, municipal revenues, and jobs. As in eighteenth-century France, adversarial legalism paralyzed political leadership, enabling particularized interests to trump the general interest.

———

In eighteenth-century France, it took a violent revolution to reverse the fragmentation of governing authority. The fragmentation of power created by the American Revolution, however, persists in large measure, even as the central government has grown stronger. Municipal governments insist on retaining control of local land use permitting, so state and federal governments enact environmental laws that seek to regulate local land use officials. Environmentalists, wary about the Army Corps of Engineers' control over landfill permits for wetlands, battle for laws that grant the EPA oversight or veto authority in that regard; business interests, wary of the EPA, battle to preserve the Army Corps' authority. In consequence, control over wetlands is divided between both agencies, plus state and local agencies, all of whom must interact in accordance with detailed legal rules. Both pro-regulation advocacy groups and regulated businesses jealously guard their rights to challenge either agency's decisions or procedural omissions in court. And so adversarial legalism persists as a prominent way of mediating the tensions between economic development and environmental protection.

Adversarial Legalism in the Twenty-First Century

In the nineteenth and first third of the twentieth century, politically conservative interests were the primary drivers of adversarial legalism—to enforce contracts, protect property rights, and to block or reshape government efforts to regulate private market activity. During the second half of the twentieth century, however, adversarial legalism was developed and used more widely. Its role in American governance expanded. As living standards and access to higher education increased, American voters, advocacy groups, and political leaders wanted governments to do more: to control hazards, protect the environment, combat crime, eradicate discrimination, provide some measure of economic security, and remedy injustice. But even as governments responded, enacting new laws and programs, popular mistrust of government increased. Political interest groups and politicians, both liberal and conservative, insisted that enhanced governmental authority should also be fragmented and constrained by court-enforceable legal prescriptions, procedures, and citizens' rights. Legislatures and courts empowered individuals, businesses, and advocacy groups to pursue their legal claims, financial interests, moral passions, and political goals through litigation and adjudication. To negotiate the ensuing set of legal opportunities and legal risks, individuals, business firms, universities, local school systems, and government agencies armed themselves with lawyers.

The expansion of adversarial legalism was propelled—not entirely, but primarily—by politically liberal lawyers, legal academics, judges, and politicians. Pushing aside traditional conservative political values, they brought about politically liberal changes in constitutional law, civil rights law, regulatory law, and tort law. Liberal statutes and judicial precedents bred additional regulations and judicial rulings, each designed to specify or advance the normative goals underlying their legal forebears. Illustrating this logic of legal expansion, Shep Melnick (2018b, 19) writes:

> The American civil rights state was originally constructed to destroy the racial caste system in the south. Attacking state-sponsored segregation, discrimination, and disenfranchisement required an unprecedented assertion of federal authority. Before long these same powers were being used to address sex discrimination, the barriers faced by English language learners and students with disability, age-based rules on hiring and retirement, and social norms regarding sexual orientation and gender identity. Regulation slowly moved from the most public—state laws mandating segregation—to the most private—sexual relations among adults.

This kind of expansion of the regulatory state, together with the adversarial legalism that both propelled and flowed from it, grated on conservatives. Conservative Christian leaders in Southern and border states denounced "the secular, sexually liberated, science based, 'big government' ethos" that they felt liberal elites had imposed upon their way of life (Woodard, 2011: 278). Business firms, health care providers, and local governments complained about ever tighter legal constrictions, higher compliance costs, the threat of disruptive litigation, growing legal bills, and the injustices that (as this book has shown) can flow from adversarial legalism. Beginning in the late 1970s, politically conservative business interests, legal academics, judges, lawyers, and political leaders initiated what Steven Teles (2008) has called "the conservative legal movement." They challenged many legal ideas, rules, and practices that in the 1960s and 1970s had propelled and legitimated the use of adversarial legalism to advance politically liberal values (Staszak, 2015).

By the 1980s, diminishing adversarial legalism—or more assertively employing it to advance politically conservative values—had become part of the Republican Party's political agenda. That agenda intensified in the 1990s, as important elements of both the business community and the Republican Party veered toward a more fervent antitax, antistatist stance (Hacker and Pierson, 2010; Fiorina and Abrams, 2009). Urged on by conservative funding sources and news media outlets, Republican politicians and lawyers openly expressed ideological hostility toward the regulatory state, plaintiffs' lawyers, and "judicial activism." In the first two decades of the twenty-first century, as political polarization increased, a more uncompromisingly conservative Republican Party gained political power at both the state and federal levels of government. It then was able to advance the conservative legal agenda by enacting tort reform laws, by impeding the enactment and implementation of regulatory law, and by appointing or achieving the election of ideologically conservative judges who adopt the legal arguments of conservative legal activists.

To what extent has the conservative legal movement actually diminished adversarial legalism? Can one still regard adversarial legalism as the American way of law? Should we expect it to persist in the future? This Afterword addresses those questions—while acknowledging that they sweep too broadly to be answered definitively. The battle between activists demanding politically conservative legal change and those who resist them is fought in many fields of law, in fifty politically diverse state governments and judiciaries, and in the federal government and judiciary. The resulting forest of legal developments and judicial decisions is immense and politically varied. Systematic empirical research on the law in action illuminates only some patches of that forest. So this chapter will focus only on some of the prominent clumps of trees, drawing on a necessarily selective sample of scholarly books, articles, and journalistic reports. The account is tilted toward especially salient areas of federal (rather than state) law and politics, up until late 2018. Based on that imperfect sample, here are the tentatively offered conclusions.

First, the conservative legal movement has successfully chipped away at some of the legal rules and legal structures that had stimulated the growth of adversarial legalism in the 1960–1990 period, particularly those that had been used to advance politically liberal values. Despite its electoral successes, the Republican Party has not repealed or amended the major pieces of regulatory or civil rights legislation that propelled the earlier growth of adversarial legalism, but as noted in Chapter 9, it has significantly slowed the pace of enactment of such laws and the litigation they would have spawned. Most importantly, a conservative U.S. Supreme Court majority has overturned many judicial precedents that previously have been used to attack violations of individual constitutional rights, civil rights statutes, and other federal laws. Many state governments that came under Republican control have constricted legal doctrines that foster tort litigation.

Second, in its zeal to reduce the costly and threatening aspects of adversarial legalism, the conservative legal movement has not tried to provide reliable *alternative* ways of remedying injustice and ensuring governmental and corporate accountability. Its dominant goal, it appears, has been to squelch adversarial legalism, not to reform it. Thus the legal changes the movement has wrought, focused on the reduction of type II errors (ill-founded legal claims) almost certainly have generated many more type I errors (injustices unremedied, harmful business and governmental practices undeterred, and rights violated with impunity).

Third, chipping away at adversarial legalism, however significant, is far from dismantling it. Still intact are its basic legal foundations: an adversarial, lawyer-driven system of litigation shaped by the right to trial by jury; politically-selected, policy-minded judiciaries; a large, entrepreneurial and creative legal profession, armed with powerful tools of pretrial discovery; and a legal culture still pervaded by the idea that law and courts are or should be instruments for effectively protecting individual rights, improving governance, and controlling the exercise of political and economic power.

Fourth, while conservative antilitigation reforms have in fact diminished litigation rates in a number of policy areas, particularly torts and civil rights, they have not done so in other legal spheres, and some *new* genres of adversarial legalism have flourished. Increased political polarization and legislative deadlock have driven conservatives as well as liberals to turn to adversarial legalism to advance their policy objectives and to block their ideological opponents' legal actions. Litigation campaigns and Supreme Court rulings have continued to generate important policy changes—some politically liberal, some conservative—ranging from the right to same-sex marriage to the right to bear arms and the right of wealthy individuals, business organizations, and other associations to expend unlimited funds, free of regulation, on political speech.

Fifth, this overall persistence of adversarial legalism reflects the continuity and embeddedness of the political attitudes and structures that *undergird* it: (a) a stream of American political culture that harbors a deep-seated mistrust of concentrated power; (b) a high level of fragmentation of political authority; and (c) a still vibrant (although more often contested) strain in political and legal culture that reflects the idea of "total justice," that is, that modern economically and technologically advanced societies and their governments have the capacity and obligation to enact and enforce laws designed to prevent serious harm and to provide effective remedies for serious injustices. As argued throughout this book, the interaction of factor (c)—which demands the exercise of governmental authority—with factors (a) and (b)—which inhibit the exercise of centralized power—perpetuates recourse to litigation and courts in order to change and implement public policies and to hold governments at all levels legally accountable. Political polarization has intensified that conflict in political attitudes, stimulating and perpetuating adversarial legalism.

Sixth, by further politicizing regulation, judicial selection, and adversarial legalism itself, the conservative legal movement has magnified a distinctive feature of the American way of law: the extent to which law and legal institutions in the United States are politically controversial, perpetual targets of conflicting political efforts to bend the law toward particular moral, economic, or political ends.

The Conservative Counterattack

The "conservative legal movement," Teles (2008) observed, has entailed the deliberate infusion of conservative political activism into the legal profession and the judiciary. Most prominently, in the early 1980s, conservative activists sponsored the growth of the Federalist Society, a network of lawyers and legal academics who favored a less powerful federal government and hence rejected the policy-oriented "judicial activism" and the liberal constitutional doctrines epitomized by the Warren Court's rights revolution. Leading members of the Federalist Society network identified smart, ideologically conservative lawyers and worked to appoint them to influential positions in the Reagan administration, to federal judgeships and clerkships, and to legal professorships (Teles, 2008, Hollis-Brusky, 2015). Conservative interests also funded ideologically focused public interest law firms, modeled on the many liberal ones that had been major players in the expansion of adversarial legalism (Decker, 2016). The U.S. Chamber of Commerce, under new, more antigovernment leadership, threw energy and vast amounts of money into litigation, lobbying, and electoral campaigns, all designed to advance the conservative legal and political agenda in appellate courts, Congress, and state legislatures (Hacker and Pierson, 2010). Christian conservatives, dedicated to a different set of issues, launched their own legal movement, creating Christian law schools, funding legal advocacy organizations, and launching litigation campaigns (Bennett, 2017; Hollis-Brusky & Wilson, 2017).

Other conservative activists concentrated on changing public perceptions of adversarial legalism. Some sought to replace the image of the plaintiffs' class action lawyer as a private attorney general with a vision of him or her as "a predatory, self-seeking opportunist" (Coffee, 2015: 16). The Manhattan Institute for Policy Research, financed by business interests, funded the dissemination of polemical books and newspaper articles that derided the American tort system and plaintiffs' lawyers (Haltom and McCann, 2004). The American Tort Reform Association (ATRA), whose members are predominantly defense lawyers, prodded editorial writers and Republican politicians to take public stands criticizing the tort system. The conservative tort-reformers' most politically potent tool, William Haltom and Michael McCann argue, was the deliberate dissemination of "tort tales" about ostensibly outrageous jury verdicts. Many tort tales were apocryphal, while others (like the distorted version of the McDonald's hot coffee case) omitted crucial details that would have made the legal outcome sound much more reasonable. These tort tales, however, were repeated by editorial writers, politicians, comedians, talk show hosts, and workplace conversations until they came to be taken as emblematic of an out-of-control tort system (Burke, 2002: 30).[1] In a recent survey, even *plaintiffs* in civil rights cases agreed with the statement "There are far too many frivolous lawsuits today"—as did 80 percent of defendants' representatives (Berrey, Nelson, and Nielsen, 2017: 178).

To translate these ideas and sentiments into law, however, conservative Republicans had to gain political power. And indeed, after decades as a minority party in Congress, Republicans gained majority control of the House of Representatives in the 1994 election and (except for 2009–2010, the first two years of Barack Obama's presidency) maintained that control until the Democratic victory in November 2018. Republicans also enjoyed majorities in the Senate, and hence in both houses of Congress, from 1995 through 2008, and again since the 2014 elections. Republicans controlled the presidency and the executive branch of the federal government during George W. Bush's administration (2001 through 2008) and regained it in 2017, following Donald Trump's election in 2016. Just as importantly, Republican electoral victories also gave conservatives control of a healthy majority of state governments.[2]

With these Republican electoral successes, political activists imbued with a conservative, antistatist philosophy moved into leadership positions in Congress, in regulatory agencies, on the airwaves, and in the federal and state judiciaries.[3] Scherer and Miller (2009) found that Federalist Society members appointed to the U.S. Supreme Court and the U.S. Courts of Appeals in the 1989–2005 period made more conservative rulings than Republican judges who were not Federalist Society members. In a number of states, conservative activists mounted well-financed electoral campaigns that often ousted liberal (or moderate) state supreme court judges and replaced them with hardline conservatives. In West Virginia, Republican legislators exploited complaints of excessive spending by some state supreme court judges to impeach the entire court and replace the ousted judges with party loyalists (Krugman, 2018).

The more judiciaries tilted toward conservative judges, the more conservative activists, lawyers, and politicians turned to litigation to attack government policies they disliked and to advance their own ideas for legal change. The U.S. Chamber of Commerce and other conservative law reform organizations regularly have filed briefs in the U.S. Supreme Court arguing for rule-changes that would impede litigation against business corporations by consumers, employees, and other civil rights plaintiffs (Burbank and Farhang, 2017: 177). Lawyers affiliated with the Federalist Society filed briefs in politically controversial high court cases, providing ideas which conservative Republican judges and Supreme Court justices frequently embraced (Hollis-Brusky, 2015, 2011). In the first year of the Trump administration, the White House counsel was quoted as saying that nearly all the lawyers in his office are Federalist Society participants—a political takeover that has strongly influenced the president's markedly conservative nominees for the many open positions in the federal courts. These appointments are likely to have a significant influence on federal law for years to come.

Curtailing Adversarial Legalism:
Conservative Legal Movement Successes

As noted in Chapter 9, even before the George W. Bush and Barack Obama administrations, conservative activists realized that it was politically difficult or even hazardous to try to shrink the regulatory and civil rights state by repealing major federal statutes. A lower-visibility strategy was to restrict adversarial legalism as a mode of enforcing those laws effectively (Burbank and Farhang, 2017) and as the engine of state level tort law. Beginning the late 1990s, John Cioffi (2010: 104–105) observes, "Political conflict over the scope, role, and litigious means of enforcing regulatory norms grew increasingly intense."[4] Conservatives attacked adversarial legalism on three fronts: in state legislatures and courts (with respect to tort law), in Congress, and in the federal courts. Their successes with respect to tort law were discussed in Chapter 7. Here we will focus on how they have fared so far in Congress and the federal courts.

In Congress. As discussed in Chapter 6, civil case defendants often face incentives to settle cases even if they have valid legal defenses, simply to avoid adversarial legalism's costliness, disruptions, and capacity to generate adverse publicity. Those risks are heightened in class actions involving hundreds or thousands of plaintiffs. Thus after the Republican Party gained control of Congress in the 1994 election, one legislative priority was to restrict class actions that claim mass violations of statutory and constitutional rights. In 1996, Congress severely limited class action lawsuits that challenged the Immigration and Naturalization Service's policies and practices in deporting aliens (Kawar, 2015: 103). That same year, Republican legislators inserted in an omnibus appropriations act a provision that restricted government-funded legal services lawyers' ability to pursue damages stemming from an unlawful government policy (Albiston and Nielsen, 2007:1105).[5] Congress also enacted the Prison Litigation Reform Act of 1996, which weakened "prisoners' ability to bring, settle, and win lawsuits" for claimed violations of constitutional rights (Schlanger, 2015, 153).[6] In 2005, Congress passed a law granting the gun industry immunity from civil suits involving the criminal misuse of firearms and ammunition (Lytton, 2005b).[7]

Congress devoted even more attention to private *securities* class actions. Overriding President Clinton's veto, a new Republican majority passed the Private Securities Litigation Reform Act of 1995, requiring plaintiffs in securities class actions to provide more specific facts in their initial pleadings; that, reformers hoped, would weed out speculative (but nevertheless threatening) class actions before they entered the expensive pretrial discovery phase (Cioffi, 2010: 106).[8] After the 2001 dot-com stock collapse, Congress imposed new fraud-prevention obligations on accounting firms that audit corporate financial reports, but it pointedly declined to give investors (and hence private law firms) authority to enforce those regulations, entrusting that responsibility solely to the Securities and Exchange Commission (which business interests perceived as less threatening) (Cioffi, 2010: 107). Similarly, due to opposition by Republicans in Congress, the 2010 Dodd-Frank Act regulating financial services companies did not authorize private litigation to enforce major rules.

During the George W. Bush administration, the Republican Congress enacted the Class Action Fairness Act (CAFA), which diverted large consumer and personal injury class actions from state courts to federal courts—thus responding to business interests' desire to escape class actions under state law, particularly those often filed in counties notorious for a proplaintiff, anti-big-business bias (Coffee, 2015: 126–127). Moreover, as pointed out by Burbank and Farhang (2017: 140), CAFA meant that class action litigation, since confined to federal courts, could be curtailed by conservative amendments to the Federal Rules of Civil Procedure and by the ever-more-conservative class action jurisprudence of the Supreme Court.[9]

From a broader standpoint, however, conservative reformers' successes in getting Congress to roll back adversarial legalism have been limited. Stephen Burbank and Sean Farhang (2017) assembled a database of all bills—some 500 of them—that were introduced into Congress in the 1973–2014 period and were aimed at *reducing* incentives for private actions to enforce public law.[10] In fact, Burbank and Farhang found that only a handful of those bills were enacted, mostly narrow in scope. Tellingly, Burbank and Farhang note that in the 1980s the conservative Reagan administration abandoned its effort to pass a statute designed to deter private enforcement—"having concluded that it was broadly perceived as 'anti-rights,' threatening unacceptably high political and electoral costs to the administration" (18). Indeed, even when the Republicans controlled one or both houses of Congress, they enacted some new laws that explicitly *authorized* private enforcement and included special incentives to sue, such as enhanced money damages and attorneys' fee reimbursement for successful plaintiffs (Farhang, 2014; Burbank and Farhang, 2017). After all, as might appeal to conservatives, adversarial legalism outsources the costs of implementing federal law from government-funded bureaucrats to private citizens and lawyers.

In the U.S Supreme Court. Conservatives found a more receptive venue for restricting adversarial legalism in the Supreme Court, which is more shielded from public opinion than is Congress. During the Chief Justiceships of William Rehnquist (1986–2005) and John Roberts (2005–), a conservative majority on the Supreme Court, ruling on low-visibility cases that seemingly involved only legal technicalities,[11] and lobbied by briefs from conservative legal advocacy organizations,[12] made considerable strides in undercutting the legal supports for adversarial legalism as a mechanism of enforcing public law (Staszak, 2015; Burbank and Farhang, 2017; Wasserman, 2012; Siegel, 2006). The list of rulings that propelled those strides is a long one.

Reversing previously entrenched interpretations of the Federal Rules of Civil Procedure, the Court made it easier for defendants to win dismissal of plaintiffs' claims via pretrial summary judgment,[13] and for failing to state their initial claims with sufficient specificity or legal plausibility.[14] By adopting new interpretations of federal statutes, conservative majorities on the Court limited the ability of plaintiffs who win settlements in civil rights cases to obtain reimbursement of attorneys' fees from government or corporate defendants.[15] They expanded government immunity-from-lawsuit doctrines and interpreted civil rights statutes narrowly,[16] which helped shield state and local governments from liability for rights violations, including those involving police and prosecutorial misconduct (Dodd, 2015). The conservative justices held unconstitutional the 1994 federal Violence Against Women Act, which had authorized victims of sexual violence to file civil actions against their attackers in federal courts.[17] They overturned earlier Court precedents holding that certain federal civil rights and regulatory statutes authorized private lawsuits against governments or corporations for noncompliance.[18] The Court made it considerably more difficult for plaintiffs' lawyers to consolidate huge numbers of tort or employment discrimination claims into class actions demanding multimillion dollar (hence potentially extortive) damage awards.[19] Perhaps most importantly, the Court's conservative majority, through expansive interpretations of the 1925 Federal Arbitration Act, made it easy for business corporations to avoid consumer and employee class actions altogether by inserting mandatory arbitration provisions into the form contracts commonly required of corporate customers and employees (Staszak, 2015: chapter 3; Resnik, 2015). "The domain of the class action," writes John Coffee Jr. (2015: 132) "has substantially shrunk."

Assessing these and many other Supreme Court decisions in the 1994–2005 period, law professor Andrew Siegel (2006: 1097) argued that "hostility to litigation" was an "organizing theme in the Rehnquist Court's jurisprudence." Howard Wasserman (2012) offers the same conclusion about the Court during the chief justiceship of John Roberts, beginning in 2005. In Burbank and Farhang's (2017: 3) summary, "The Supreme Court has transformed federal law from friendly to unfriendly, if not hostile, toward enforcement of rights through private lawsuits." To other scholars too, most of these rulings have not been straightforwardly-desirable "efficiency reforms" but in effect operate as "discouragement reforms"–that is, rulings that protect corporate and government defendants not only from frivolous litigation but also, and more importantly, from liability for some serious violations of individual rights.[20] Five or six years after the Court's *Buckhannon* decision,[21] which limited plaintiffs' rights to obtain reimbursement of attorneys' fees, a survey of public interest law firms indicated that *Buckhannon*, along with subsequent decisions applying it, had in fact inhibited the filing of class actions to enforce rights (Albiston and Nielsen, 2007: 1121). Albiston and Nielsen, drawing on their survey results, add that the symbiosis between *Buckannon* and the Court's expansion of the sovereign immunity doctrine (shielding state governments from some lawsuits alleging violation of federal constitutional and statutory rights) leaves public interest lawyers "little incentive to bring equitable claims against states: 'Why engage in protracted litigation with scant prospect for recovering the cost of that litigation?'" (1121).

These "hostility to litigation" arguments gain support from the increasing frequency with which the Court has divided along ideological lines in these procedure cases, with forceful dissents by Democratic justices. Stephen Burbank and Sean Farhang built a database of 365 Supreme Court cases, from 1961 to 2014, that involved disputes about private enforcement of public laws or interpretations of the rules of civil procedure. Their analysis of these cases reveals both (a) an increasing decline, since the Warren Court era, in the probability of a plaintiff victory in such cases; and (b) a steadily growing partisan division between conservative and liberal judges—a divide driven, especially since 2000, by conservative justices' ever-more-consistently antiplaintiff decisions (Burbank and Farhang, 2017: 153–155). And finally, to taste the flavor of the kinds of decisions that have provoked the hostility to litigation claims, consider the following case.

In 1984, John Thompson, a twenty-two-year-old African American, was tried and convicted of armed robbery in New Orleans, Louisiana. Then, in a separate case, he was tried and convicted of murder and sentenced to death. But years later, in 1999, a private investigator hired by Thompson's lawyer discovered that the county prosecutor Harry Connick (and several assistant prosecutors) had failed—contrary to a long-established constitutional obligation—to inform Thompson's defense lawyer of blood samples and other evidence indicating that Thompson was not guilty. In 2003, after eighteen years in prison, including fourteen years in isolation on death row and several close calls with the executioner, Thompson was retried. His lawyers presented evidence that another man had committed the murder. A jury quickly found Thompson not guilty.

Subsequently, Thompson sued the county government for violation of his constitutional rights. His lawyers showed that the exculpatory evidence had been concealed in the county district attorney's office for fifteen years.[22] A jury awarded Thompson $14 million in damages—$1 million for each year he spent in prison. The 5th Circuit Court of Appeals affirmed, emphasizing that the trial evidence showed that Prosecutor Connick *knew* his staff was seriously undertrained on their duty to turn over exculpatory evidence to the defense, and that he had failed to fix it. But in 2011, by a 5–4 vote with five conservative justices in the majority, the U.S. Supreme Court reversed the award, deciding that the county attorney's office was not liable (*Connick v. Thompson*, 2011). Misconduct in one case, Justice Thomas's majority opinion argued, does not meet the legal standard for liability—a *pattern* of inadequate training and supervision of individual prosecutors. Thomas implied that an opposite decision might have led to more legally unsustainable lawsuits, which would force prosecutors' offices and police departments to spend precious time and resources defending legally unfounded claims. The majority justices appeared to regard that risk as more serious and frequent than the risk of rights violations by poorly trained, poorly supervised law enforcement personnel.

Justice Thomas's opinion acknowledged that in the ten years preceding Thompson's trial, "Louisiana courts had overturned four convictions because of . . . violations by prosecutors in Connick's office." Nevertheless, the Court's majority brushed aside the lower courts' findings as well as defense lawyers' arguments that liability in such cases is important for prodding district attorneys' offices to adequately train and supervise their prosecutors. That such incentives might be helpful also is suggested by a March 2012 study by the respected Innocence Project (2012). It showed that in ninety-one criminal cases since 2004 in the adjacent state of Texas, courts had ruled that prosecutors had committed misconduct, ranging from hiding evidence to making improper arguments to the jury.[23] As noted earlier in this book, Charles Epp's *Making Rights Real* (2009) makes a strong empirical case that private lawsuits for damages against police departments (which the *Connick* and other Court rulings make much more difficult to win) have in fact spurred the institutionalization of better, rights-respecting standards in local law enforcement bodies.

In 2017, John Thompson, who never got a penny of the $14 million jury award, died of a heart attack at age fifty-four, after having worked for a decade at Resurrection After Exoneration, a residential and education program he and friends had started in New Orleans to aid people leaving prison without money, family, or friends to help them (*New York Times*, 2017). In a *New York Times* op-ed piece, Thompson had written: "I don't care about the money. I just want to know why the prosecutors—who hid evidence, sent me to prison for something I didn't do and nearly had me killed—are not in jail themselves. There were no ethics charges against them, no criminal charges, no one was fired and now, according to the Supreme Court, no one can be sued" (Dodd, 2015: 664).

The Persistence of Adversarial Legalism

Politically conservative activists, abetted by the U.S. Supreme Court, have in fact provided corporations and government bodies some measure of insulation against some genres of adversarial legalism. On the other hand, the basic *institutional structures* of adversarial legalism are still intact: (a) an independent, politically-selected judiciary; (b) a rich array of constitutional precedents and administrative law rules that facilitate claims against and resistance to governmental actions; (c) a large legal infrastructure of politically and morally engaged activist lawyers, conservatives as well as liberals, eager to pursue their causes in court; (d) trial by jury (actually conducted in only a small percentage of criminal and civil cases, but still a potent influence on dispositions); (f) contingency fees and statutory fee-shifting rules that attract entrepreneurial lawyers; and (g) lawyers' powers to engage in extensive, probing, and costly pretrial discovery.[24]

Consequently, although conservative legal changes have made it *more difficult* to successfully initiate and win class actions, civil liberties lawsuits, and tort suits that yield giant damages for pain and suffering, it is by no means impossible to do so successfully. Moreover, the legal culture of total justice, although perhaps more contested, is still alive. Serious legally-culpable injuries clearly caused by large corporations—such as British Petroleum's 2010 Gulf of Mexico oil spill or the mortgage security fraud by large financial institutions during the housing bubble that burst in 2008—still trigger extensive litigation by public prosecutors and by hordes of private lawyers, resulting in massive money damage awards or settlements.[25] As mentioned in Chapter 7, hundreds of such lawsuits recently have been filed against manufacturers and distributors of opioid painkillers for fraudulent and unconscionable marketing of huge quantities of these drugs, which fed an epidemic of addiction. Moreover, political polarization has increased the incentives for both liberals and conservatives to turn to the courts to obtain legal changes they cannot obtain in deadlocked legislatures or to block legal changes they dislike. Overall, therefore, the available evidence suggests that the conservative legal and political movement has had mixed consequences for adversarial legalism in practice. Litigation of some kinds has declined. But its persistence, and in some domains its growth, are more salient than its diminution.

Domains of Decline. The National Center for State Courts conducts periodic studies of civil litigation rates in state courts of general jurisdiction. Those rates, according to the most recent studies, were basically flat from the mid-1990s to 2009, rising slightly after 2000 (National Center for State Courts, 2017).[26] Then, coinciding with the economic recession that began in 2008, litigation rates began to decline—as of 2015 by about 11 percent (National

Center for State Courts, 2017). Those figures, however, are dominated by smaller-stakes civil cases,[27] which usually do not involve extensive pretrial discovery and jury trials—the features of adversarial legalism that have pre-occupied the conservative legal movement.

Those aggregate numbers, moreover, do not show the growing extent to which lawsuits, once filed, shift from full-scale adversarial legalism into other modes of dispute-resolution—negotiation, mediation, and arbitration. Many state court systems have instituted efficiency-oriented reforms such as court-sponsored mediation (as a first step before resuming the path to litigation), limits on pretrial discovery, and assertive case management and settlement procedures implemented by "managerial judges" (Resnik, 2015, 1982). Many states, as well as the U.S. Supreme Court's rulings, have made it easier for parties to obtain summary judgments before trial. Thus in both state and federal courts, the rate at which civil lawsuits are decided via ad-versarial jury trials has continued to shrink, almost to the vanishing point (Galanter and Frozena, 2014)—although that trend, spurred by the costli-ness and cumbersomeness of jury trials, has proceeded largely indepen-dently of the conservative legal movement.

With respect to higher-stakes civil cases, which have been the primary targets of the conservative legal and political movement, the trends are mixed. Notwithstanding the Supreme Court decisions discussed above, Burbank and Farhang (2017: 1) report that, "In the past decade, more than 1.25 million federal lawsuits were filed to enforce federal statutes, spanning the waterfront of federal regulation." But *civil rights* enforcement cases have declined. Although complaints of discriminatory mistreatment filed with the Equal Employment Opportunity Commission increased between 2000 and 2014 (Berrey, Nelson, and Nielsen, 2017: 42), the rate of civil rights cases filed in federal *courts* went down from 16.1 per 100,000 population in 1997 to 10.9 in 2014 (Burbank and Farhang, 2017: 230). In another realm, the securities class action reform acts, as intended, made such suits "less easy to file and more costly to prosecute" (Coffee, 2015: 78). But the number of such suits did *not* significantly decline (NERA, 2012; Bratton and Wachter (2012: 215) and average settlement amounts increased (Coffee, 2015: 78). Civil enforcement actions by the Securities and Exchange Commission, which long had outnumbered private enforcement suits by two or three to one, increased significantly in the first decade of the twenty-first century (Bratton and Wachter (2012: 215).

The 2011 America Invents Act, enacted during the Obama administra-tion, was a bipartisan effort to reduce a steadily growing scourge of abusive litigation by patent trolls—companies that systematically file legally doubtful patent infringement claims against successful pharmaceutical or high-tech companies, extorting monetary settlements from defendants reluctant to endure the costs and delays of adversarial legalism (Porter, 2017a). This statute was a rare example of a "replacement reform," as it substituted an expert administrative dispute resolution body for decision-making via adversarial litigation.[28] Thus far, however, it seems to have been only slightly successful in reducing patent-trolling litigation, which continued to rise, at least through 2015 (PWC, 2017; Cohen, Gurun, and Kaminers, 2016).[29]

The tort law field has seen discouragement-oriented reforms rather than replacement reforms. And in fact, some kinds of claims clearly have been discouraged. Beginning in the 1990s, in Franklin County, Ohio, (which includes Ohio's capital city, Columbus), product liability and medical malpractice cases declined significantly; in the cases that went to trial, defendants won most jury verdicts, and when plaintiffs won, the amounts awarded declined (Merritt and Barry, 1999). As noted in Chapter 7, state laws that have imposed strict caps on money damages for pain and suffering in medical malpractice cases appear to have discouraged plaintiffs' lawyers from taking on some kinds of cases—particularly those of seriously-injured children or nonemployed mothers, for whom lost earnings (the base for calculating pain and suffering damages) are small or nonexistent (Daniels and Martin, 2015, 2010). But overall, a multistate comparative study found that "medical malpractice caps [enacted in the 1994–2004 period] did not alter the number of medical malpractice awards and settlements" (Donohue and Ho, 2007).

The 1996 Prison Litigation Reform Act, as intended, resulted in a decline in prison reform litigation and in the number of prisons and jails operating under judicially mandated reform orders (Schlanger, 2015). But that doesn't mean adversarial legalism has faded away. In a momentous 2009 decision, for example, a federal court ruled that California's chronic prison overcrowding not only exacerbated an unconstitutional insufficiency of adequate health care but made any adequate remedy impossible. Consequently, the court ordered the state to reduce prison populations by approximately 40,000 prisoners within two years (Simon, 2014: 7). In *Brown v Plata* (2010), the U.S. Supreme Court upheld that order. By highlighting the enormous fiscal as well as the human costs of America's extraordinarily high levels of mass incarceration and crowding, the *Plata* case helped stimulate a nationwide political movement by state legislatures to rescue state budgets by reducing prison populations, particularly with respect to nonviolent and older offenders (Aviram, 2015; Simon, 2014).

Similarly, a 1996 congressional statute, mentioned earlier, barred judicial review of many Immigration & Naturalization Service (INS) expulsion and treatment decisions, and it also limited judicial injunctions against the agency's immigrant removal-related operations (Kawar, 2015: 119). But here, too, adversarial legalism persisted at significant level, as immigrants' rights lawyers worked pathways around the edges of the statute, seeking judicial relief for governmental violations of existing permanent judicial reform orders and settlement agreements. Moreover, pursuant to a 2001 Supreme Court decision, rights lawyers continued to file numerous lawsuits and appeals against individual case decisions by the Board of Immigration Appeals and against the INS with respect to *non-removal* cases (122). Then in the 2017–2019 period, state attorneys general and the American Civil Liberties Union repeatedly challenged the Trump administration's immigration orders in court, usually successfully. Separate U.S. District Court rulings compelled the administration to reverse or suspend numerous policies, among them, refusing to process asylum claims by illegal border-crossers; refusing to consider credible fear of gang violence grounds for asylum; ending an Obama administration program protecting immigrants brought to the country illegally as minors (Weiss, 2018); separating migrant children from parents arrested at the border and detaining them (Shear et al., 2018); and forcing refugees seeking asylum to wait in Mexico to be processed in the United States (Shear, Kanno-Youngs, and Haberman (2019).

In terms of squelching adversarial legalism, perhaps the most significant conservative legal victories have been the Supreme Court decisions that encouraged large corporations to tuck binding private arbitration provisions into long, rarely read, form contracts, such as those required by large employers, financial services companies, cell phone providers, cable television companies, hospitals, and online retailers and service providers.[30] Under the Court's interpretation of the Federal Arbitration Act, such contractual provisions can prevent customers and employees from filing lawsuits alleging violations of antidiscrimination laws and from filing or participating in class actions, even when applicable state laws seek to preserve consumers' and employees' rights to pursue claims in court.[31] There is little systematic evidence about what actually occurs in most private (and hence opaque) mandatory arbitration systems. But there is some evidence that individuals, left with that alternative alone, rarely turn to it for smaller-stakes grievances of the kind they often have against cable companies, large retailers, telephone and credit card companies, and the like.[32] And it is quite clear that the many companies that employ such form contracts have sharply reduced the risk of being sued by lawyers, undergoing pretrial discovery, and dealing with threatening class actions (and resulting adverse publicity)—a reduction that also blunts the deterrent effects of civil rights and consumer protection laws and regulations. As the impact of the Supreme Court's endorsement of these contractual arrangements became clear, they evoked political protest. Two Obama-era regulatory agencies banned them, one in the nursing home industry, the other when required by banks, credit-card issuers, and other financial companies. In 2017, however, the Trump administration, lobbied by the relevant industries, moved quickly to repeal those bans.[33]

Domains of Persistence and Growth. For some kinds of cases adversarial legalism remains salient and even on the rise. Systematic research by Burbank and Farhang (2017: 2, 14) reveals that although private *civil rights* cases tailed off, in 2014 the rate of private litigation in federal courts enforcing federal statutes in general was over 40 per 100,000 population—up from 29 per 100,000 in 1996 (and from 21 per 100,000 in 1986 and 13 per 100,000 in 1976). Undergirding this steady growth has been Congress's previously mentioned propensity to foster adversarial legalism by enacting statutes that include not only private rights of action but also special incentives to sue, such as enhanced money damages and attorneys' fee reimbursement for successful plaintiffs (Burbank & Farhang, 2014). For example, in several cases decided in 1999, the U.S. Supreme Court majority endorsed a restrictive interpretation of "disability" in the Americans with Disabilities Act (ADA), which until then had been a fertile source of private litigation. In 2008, however, Congress enacted the ADA Amendments Act, which not only overrode the Court's interpretation but actually broadened the definition of "disability," *enhancing* claimants' legal rights and incentives to sue (Barnes and Burke, 2015: 103–105). Also, the 1990s saw a rapid increase in "qui tam" lawsuits brought under the Federal False Claims Act—cases in which a private party sues another individual or corporation for fraud against the government and is awarded a percentage of moneys ultimately returned to the federal treasury. Even *more* qui tam cases were filed in the 2000–2009 period (Engstrom, 2013).

The river of product liability suits based on exposure to asbestos also continued to flow. As of 2002, an estimated 730,000 individual claims had been filed in total, and more were projected for the future. By 2013, the *rate* of new claims was only 20 percent the rate in 2003, but the average paid to resolve claims was three times the average 2001 payment (Barnes and Burke, 2015: 125). Moreover, asbestos claims were being filed against an ever-wider range of companies (over 8,400 in all), including many that had nothing to do with covering up the dangers of asbestos (the original basis for manufacturers' liability) but merely used asbestos products, such as insulation (125). And as noted earlier, as in the tobacco litigation of the 1990s (discussed in Chapter 7), entrepreneurial tort lawyers have teamed up with state attorneys general and impacted city governments to sue pharmaceutical companies and wholesalers for irresponsible or fraudulent marketing of the opioid drugs that have fueled a devastating, often lethal, epidemic of addiction cases (Whelan and Randazzo, 2018).

In addition, adversarial legalism has remained an undiminished, and perhaps growing, feature of administrative policy-implementation in the United States. Studies of particular programs indicate that it has intensified, not diminished. With respect to the massive Social Security Disability Insurance (SSDI) program, Barnes and Burke (2015: 90) observe:

In the initial years of the program only about 2% of denied claims were appealed [to administrative law judges]; today about one in three are, about 800,000 per year. Second . . . nearly 80% have representatives . . . at the appeals stage, and most of those representatives are lawyers; an entire industry of Social Security claims advocates has been created.

Barnes and Burke (2015: 91) also note an increase in appeals of such cases to the federal *courts*, reaching more than 10,000 SSDI cases a year—partly because federal judges "have remanded to SSA for reconsideration about half of the appeals brought and in most of those the appellant [whose claim thus far had been denied] eventually receives benefits."

Rebecca Hamlin (2014) compared the processing of refugees' applications for asylum in the United States, Canada, and Australia. In the twenty-first century, she observed (78–82), there has been a "litigation explosion" in the United States, which further complicates a multistage administrative decision-making system that was already, in comparative perspective, "highly adversarial, legalistic, and contentious." Refugee appeals to the courts from administrative asylum denials, already 40 percent of *all* administrative appeals in the U.S. Courts of Appeals in 1996, leapt to over 80 percent in the 2003–2012 period. Why so many appeals? First, Hamlin learned, because immigration judges and the Board of Immigration Appeals have to cope with a "chronic underfunding" of the frontline agencies, that curtails careful, professional determination of the facts of asylum claims. Second, the federal courts of appeals, regularly confronted with gross inconsistencies and procedural flaws in Board of Immigration Appeals' decisions, often overturn them, which stimulates more appeals in other cases. "The Supreme Court has tried to limit this trend, and Congress has responded by creating legislation that strips court jurisdiction and limits administrative discretion, but these steps do not seem to have reduced the likelihood of Courts of Appeals [decisions] to overturn asylum denials" (82).

Litigation challenging *state* governments' administrative agency performance also continued to thrive. In 2016, nineteen states were facing system-wide lawsuits claiming that the state's agency for protection of neglected or abused children had consistently failed to deal effectively with high rates of abuse or neglect and had serious shortages of decent foster homes (Palmer and Robertson, 2016). The lesson is that the characteristic American distrust of bureaucracy—reflected in politicians' reluctance to increase administrative budgets and invest in improving their staffs' professional abilities—remains a reliable source of more adversarial legalism.

New Frontiers for Adversarial Legalism. In the structurally fragmented American political system, when political leaders and policy advocates are stymied in one set of institutions, they often use adversarial legalism to advance their agenda in the courts. Their incentives to do so have increased in the early twenty-first century, as the Republican Party's move to the political right has intensified political polarization and legislative deadlock. In consequence, the American legal system has seen the development of new genres of adversarial legalism.

One new genre has been policy-oriented litigation by government agencies and public prosecutors. According to David Engstrom (2013 :616): "judicial constriction of class actions and punitive damages helps explain the rising use of so-called agency restitution actions, in which [politically liberal government] agencies litigate and secure large monetary judgments against regulatory targets and then distribute the proceeds to private individuals or entities who have suffered harm"–an observation made also by Zimmerman (2011: 542–43). In addition, U.S. attorneys, frustrated by Supreme Court decisions that made it more difficult to successfully win criminal convictions against prosecute top corporate officials (Eisinger, 2017), more often have used criminal prosecutions against corporate *firms* to achieve *regulatory* goals. (Barkow and Barkow, 2011). The corporate defendants, fearing the negative publicity associated with criminal prosecution, face strong incentives to settle the cases and agree to make substantial ongoing changes in industry practices (and sometimes to hire independent monitors to police their compliance). Federal prosecutors negotiated eleven such agreements between 1993 and 2001, but that number rose to twenty-three in the 2002–2005 period, and sixty-six in the 2006–2008 years (Spivak and Raman, 2008). Settlements in those cases imposed regulatory changes on large firms in telecommunications, banking, medical device manufacturing, student loans, fashion, and more (Barkow and Barkow, 2011: 4).

Even more prominent has been the upsurge of litigation by state attorneys' general (AGs). These independently elected, politically partisan state government officials traditionally have concentrated on enforcing state law in state courts and on serving as defense counsel in lawsuits against state agencies. But beginning in the 1990s, as shown by Paul Nolette (2015), politically ambitious state AGs repeatedly used adversarial legalism to influence *national* policy. The AGs' technique was to coordinate their lawsuits–to file, in their respective state courts, separate but legally similar prosecutions or civil lawsuits, all with common regulatory objectives. Nolette assembled a database of 686 such cases of coordinated litigation; two-thirds were filed after 2000. In some of these collaborations, state AGs sought court orders against national government agencies, demanding that they take new regulatory actions. Most prominent in that regard were the multiple cases they filed against the U.S. Environmental Protection Agency (EPA), arguing that the 1970 Clean Air Act obligated the EPA to issue regulations requiring diminished emissions of greenhouse gases. The U.S. Supreme Court sustained that legal claim. In collaborative multistate lawsuits against *corporate* defendants, the state AGs sometimes have demanded such massive combined monetary penalties that the defendants succumbed to pretrial settlements requiring nationwide behavioral change. Such settlements, according to Nolette, have significantly reshaped regulatory norms and corporate practices concerning tobacco control, mortgage foreclosure and lending, and the pricing and marketing of pharmaceutical products.[34]

During the Obama administration, 2009–2016, coalitions of politically *conservative* Republican AGs, closely allied with regulated industries, brought coordinated lawsuits with an *anti-regulatory* valence—suits that challenged the legality or constitutionality of various federal, state, and local environmental regulations, presidential executive orders, and various aspects of the Affordable Care Act. Not infrequently (though not always) the AGs steered their cases to conservative judges who blocked or substantially delayed the laws and regulations in question. Then, in the wake of the 2016 election, in which Donald Trump's victory gave Republicans control of the executive branch as well as Congress, attorney generals from Democratic states geared up for collaborative multistate litigation to block Republican statutes, regulations, and executive orders meant to roll back rights and regulations created by Democratic administrations, federal and state. In the first seven months of the Trump administration, the Associated Press found, more than forty such legal actions were filed (Peoples, 2017). By the end of 2017, the attorney general of New York alone had launched 100 such legal or administrative actions (Hakim and Rashbaum, 2017). These kinds of lawsuits, like those brought by the Republican AGs during the Obama administration, promise to keep dragging the courts into the political maelstrom.

Similarly, the American "culture wars" concerning moral and religious issues, further intensified by political polarization, have been fertile source of adversarial legalism. A recurring scenario is that conservative state governments enact laws that restrict access to abortion; or chip away at the separation of church and state; or push back against demands for equality for gays, lesbians, and transgender people. Then liberal activist groups and local governments contest those restrictions in court, ensuring that judges remain key decision makers in these fields and that judicial selection processes will elicit conflicting pressures from each side in the culture wars. In a detailed analysis of the politics of the culture wars in the United States, 1992–2014, political scientist Thomas Keck (2014: 11) found that "advocates on the left and the right are more or less equally likely to frame their demands in the form of rights [and] to appeal to courts to vindicate those demands." Moreover, on most of the issues he studied [abortion, affirmative action, LGBT rights] "the policy landscape today would be substantially different in the absence of independent judges and rights advocates determined to appeal to those judges" (244). Keck adds, "Every state legislator . . . who cast a vote on any of these policy questions was aware that his or her state's existing discriminatory policies were a magnet for litigation (244)."

New subgenres of adversarial legalism also have welled up in the field of criminal justice. Increased *national* attention to shootings and rights violations by local police (Zimring, 2017: 9–16) prompted citizen groups and reform lawyers to seek novel judicial remedies against municipal police departments and county sheriffs' offices whose shortcomings have not been addressed adequately by state political leaders. In 1994, Congress authorized the U.S. Attorney General to bring civil actions and obtain reform-oriented court injunctions against local police departments shown to have engaged in a pattern or practice of institutional misconduct. During the 1994–2013 period (but most intensely during President Obama's administration, beginning in 2009), the U.S. Department of Justice, drawing on that statutory authority, conducted investigations of fifty-seven police departments to determine if grounds for a lawsuit and reform-oriented injunction existed. Most of those threatened lawsuits resulted in negotiated reform agreements. Because many of these agreements involved major cities,[35] they covered departments responsible for policing approximately one-fifth of the nation's population and a much larger proportion of the demographic groups most at risk of serious police misconduct (Rushin, 2015).[36]

Another example: beginning in the late 1990s, determined defense lawyers, aided by an "innocence network" of clinics in dozens of law schools, mounted scores of legal challenges to the convictions of hundreds of prison inmates incarcerated for rape, murder, or both. A great many of these challenges were based on DNA evidence (Garrett, 2011: 5–6). As of 2017, the Innocence Project reports, more than 350 such inmates had been exonerated. These cases have been consequential politically as well as legally, weakening support for capital punishment and contributing to the steady decline in its actual use. And by showing conclusively how wrongful convictions were obtained, the "actual innocence" movement has stimulated a number of state and urban police departments to institutionalize the use of DNA, the videotaping of interrogations, and better modes of preventing erroneous eyewitness identification of suspects (Garrett, 2011: chapter 11).

Perhaps the most remarkable new genre of adversarial legalism—and one that highlights its irrepressibility in contemporary American governance—was stimulated by the "war on terror" that followed the September 11, 2001 al-Qaeda terrorist attack on the World Trade Center and the Pentagon. A series of petitions to the courts, aided by lawyers who volunteered to represent detainees at the Guantanamo Bay military prison, drew the judiciary into reshaping the military commissions established by the George W. Bush administration. The Supreme Court twice held that detainees indeed had the right to petition federal courts for writs of habeas corpus to review the legality of their detention and the commissions' procedures.[37] The Court also held that preliminary review tribunals created by the administration violated detainees' rights under the Geneva Convention and the U.S. Constitution's Fifth Amendment.[38] As described by political scientist Gregory Burnep (2017), the litigation (and the threat of more) repeatedly convinced the Bush administration and Congress to ward off further litigation by making additional procedural changes in the commission system, such as barring the use of evidence obtained through torture or other coercive methods; expanding detainees' rights to counsel and participation in their defense; rights to learn about classified evidence against them in the military's possession; and rights to more meaningful appeals within the commission system. One consequence, as noted by Burnep (2017: 273)—adding to an analysis by law professor Jack Goldsmith (2012)—is that "the realm of war and national security has become deeply legalized," expanding the role and authority of national security lawyers in the executive branch and of lawyers embedded, even at field level, in the military.

Using Adversarial Legalism for Conservative Political Purposes. One of the most significant effects of the conservative legal movement has been to forge new legal rights or doctrines designed to advance conservative values. Conservative majorities on the U.S. Supreme Court have been important allies in that regard, as illustrated by the following rulings.

  The Right to Bear Arms. In 2008, culminating a sophisticated legal campaign led by the National Rifle Association, a conservative majority of the Supreme Court abandoned long established legal assumptions and held that the Second Amendment to the U.S. Constitution establishes an *individual right* to acquire and possess firearms. Its ruling struck down Washington, D.C.'s gun control law for violating that right.[39] That decision, together with a subsequent one holding that the right is "fundamental" and binding on state and local governments,[40] invited the National Rifle Association, gun manufacturers, and other pro-gun advocacy organizations to challenge in court existing and future state and local laws regulating the sale and possession of guns—a litigation process likely to continue for years to come.[41]

  Affirmative Action. In order to maintain racial diversity and minimize racial isolation in its public schools, Seattle, Washington instituted a program that limited interschool transfers so as to maintain racial balance and that used race as a tiebreaker for admission to particular schools. Similar affirmative action plans had been in place in hundreds of school districts around the country. For years, they had been upheld by lower federal courts on the grounds that maintaining racial diversity was a

particularly compelling governmental interest in the education and socialization of children. But in 2007, the Court's conservative majority,
by a 5 to 4 vote, invalidated Seattle's program and a similar one in Louisville, Kentucky. Such programs, wrote Chief Justice Roberts, were
"directed only to racial balance, pure and simple," a goal he said was
forbidden by the Constitution's guarantee of equal protection.[42] A dissenting opinion by Justice Breyer claimed the Court's decision was a
radical step away from settled law and practice and predicted that the
ruling would "substitute for present calm a disruptive round of race-
related litigation"–presumably by opponents of affirmative action plans.

Federal Regulatory Authority. One controversial provision of the 2010 Affordable Care Act (ACA) required individuals who remain uncovered
by expanded public and private health insurance plans to purchase
their own health insurance policies, mostly at heavily subsidized
rates. Twenty-six Republican state governors, a small business association, and conservative legal advocacy groups filed separate lawsuits in many states arguing that the so-called "individual mandate,"
exceeded Congress's constitutional powers under the Interstate Commerce Clause. Republican U.S. District Court judges tended to strike
down the individual mandate or all of the law, Democratic judges
all upheld it. In 2012, a closely divided U.S. Supreme Court *upheld*
the individual mandate.[43] Chief Justice Roberts voted with the four
Democratic justices in that regard–but without endorsing their view
that the individual mandate was well within Congress's established
Commerce Clause power. Indeed, Roberts joined the other four
Republicans in an opinion that limited the reach of the Commerce
Clause–an opinion that implicitly invites business firms and conservative lawyers in the future to challenge laws and regulations enacted
under the Commerce Clause, and invites judges to employ more demanding standards in scrutinizing those provisions.

Conservatives also frequently challenged government regulation by arguing for more expansive interpretations of the First Amendment.
The Affordable Care Act required employers to provide health insurance to employees, including coverage for birth control pills for female
employees. In *Burwell v. Hobby Lobby* (2014) the conservative Supreme
Court majority, citing the First Amendment's "free exercise of religion"
clause, invalidated those provisions of the act insofar as they applied
to privately held businesses whose owners objected to providing birth
control pills on religious grounds. This decision widened the door for
litigation by religious groups eager to expand the realm of religious
liberty, overriding antidiscrimination law.[44] Similarly, the Supreme

Court's conservative majority, broadly interpreting the First Amendment's freedom of speech clause, issued fateful antiregulatory decisions by striking down provisions of a clause in a political campaign finance statute that had limited spending on campaign advertising and advocacy by business corporations and other associations;[45] by invalidating a California law that required all crisis pregnancy centers (including religiously oriented ones) to provide clients information about abortion options;[46] and, in a major blow to public employee unions (long an electoral opponent of the Republican Party), by holding, contrary to a forty-year-old precedent, that the unions could no longer automatically collect dues from employees who had not voluntarily become union members (*Janus v. AFSCME*, 2018).

Voting Rights. In *Shelby County v. Holder* (2013), a lawsuit instigated and supported by conservative activists and funding sources (Hartocollis, 2017) a 5–4 conservative majority on the U.S. Supreme Court struck down a major provision of the federal Voting Rights Law that required certain Southern states, counties, and cities with a history of racial discrimination in voting to submit voting rule changes to the U.S. Justice Department for preclearance—a measure designed to ensure that the planned changes do not discriminate against racial and ethnic minorities. The Court's ruling eliminated the preclearance regulatory process. It led to numerous state voting rule changes intended to or likely to suppress voting by black citizens, which politically liberal activists sought to block after the fact by filing Voting Rights Act lawsuits.

In sum, the conservative Supreme Court justices—along with their ideological mates in the conservative legal movement at large—have been skeptical about, even hostile to, adversarial legalism when it facilitates individual claims against law enforcement bodies, business corporations, and local governments based on constitutional due process norms, civil rights laws, product liability law, and environmental law. But the conservative judges have had no compunctions about making rulings that *expand* adversarial legalism by facilitating lawsuits by businesses or individuals who challenge government regulation or who challenge affirmative action programs designed to promote racial equality. The weaponry of adversarial legalism, it seems clear, will be kept in working order by conservatives as well as liberals when it is likely to advance their values and interests.

———

In the early twenty-first century, the United States, viewed in cross-national perspective, still remains distinctive in the degree to which its modes of governance and dispute resolution are pervaded or influenced by adversarial legalism. Because of the fragmented political structures and political culture of the United States, American laws and regulations remain much more detailed and complex than similar laws and regulations in other rich democracies (Kagan, 2010). American regulations, even taking into account various reform efforts, still are implemented in a relatively more legalistic manner and engender more adversarial legal contestation (Bignami and Kelemen, 2018). Despite some limits on tort law, class actions, and civil rights litigation brought about by the conservative legal movement, there is little doubt that businesses, universities, hospitals, and government bodies in the United States still feel compelled, as they did two decades ago (Kagan and Axelrad, 2000) to retain the services of far larger cadres of lawyers than do their counterparts abroad. The risk of lawsuits for police misconduct, workplace sexual harassment, and playground accidents has had significant regulatory effects on many police departments, corporate employers, and municipal government departments (Epp, 2009). American presidents and their appointees to head regulatory agencies—again, unlike their counterparts in other rich democracies—still often find their policy initiatives delayed and sometimes blocked by judges.

The judiciary's role in governance has increased markedly in the European Union and some member states (Kelemen, 2011), as well as in a number of other countries (Kapiszewski, Silverstein, and Kagan, 2013). But the American judiciary remains unique in the extent to which it responds to partisan political efforts to shape the law. In contrast to their counterparts in Western Europe, American judges are selected or elected through partisan—indeed increasingly partisan—political processes. In controversial cases, judges' partisan backgrounds continue to influence their rulings and the ideological direction of the law (Howard and Steigerwalt, 2012), which encourages political activists and their lawyers to steer their legal claims to judges whom they believe are ideologically sympathetic. By way of contrast, Germany's specialized Federal Constitutional Court is regarded as one of the world's most powerful and interventionist high courts. Its members—in contrast with the professionally selected judges in the ordinary German courts—are selected by the two chambers of the federal legislature, which might be regarded as a recipe for intense political party struggles over judicial selection. But as described by comparativist Kim Lane Scheppele, "For years there has been a convention that the two senates of the Court, with eight judges each, should not have a majority from either side of the political spectrum. Any majority decision of at least five judges must therefore of necessity have convinced someone from the 'other side' to join the decision. That is why the Courts decisions don't sound like they are party programs by another name. . . . The contrast with the US could hardly be more striking."[47]

In sum, notwithstanding the efforts and successes of the conservative legal movement, adversarial legalism continues to play a major role in shaping public policy in many areas of American governance. Lawyers and judges (including bankruptcy judges), not Congress or any government agency, have been the key actors in shaping a protean, decentralized regime for compensating tens of thousands of victims of asbestos poisoning (Barnes, 2011). In systematic studies, political scientists have found that courts became and have remained key decision makers in affirmative action in admission to higher education, equity and adequacy in public school financing,[48] the right to same-sex marriage and adoption (Gash, 2015), and the legitimacy of state government restrictions on abortion services (Howard and Steigerwalt, 2012; Hall, 2011). More than once, adversarial litigation placed in the hands of the Supreme Court the fate of the 2009 Affordable Care Act—and hence the fates of millions of uninsured families. Perhaps most dramatically, adversarial litigation has continued to be critically important in shaping and reshaping the rules that seek to channel the struggle over political power and fair electoral practices. Thus American judges repeatedly determine the constitutionality of electoral district lines,[49] of campaign finance laws,[50] of Republican state legislatures' efforts to restrict access to the polls, and—as in the fateful 2000 case of *Bush v. Gore*—the outcome of elections. Consequently, partisan political battles over the staffing of the federal judiciary and many state courts have become *more* intense, more overtly ideological. American law thus remains distinctively malleable, politically controversial, and a focus of political and legal action.

The persistence of adversarial legalism reflects the ongoing mistrust and fragmentation of political authority in the United States—factors which, as this book has stressed, make the law more complex and stimulate judicial challenges to government decisions. Indeed, in the last two decades, the Republican Party's ideological shift to the political right has made the American political and legal system more fragmented and polarized. Law and legal practice varies more sharply between politically liberal states and states dominated by antitax, antigovernment Republican politicians. Whereas the government in Louisiana, as allowed by the U.S. Supreme Court's 2011 *Connick* decision, may ignore the failure of locally selected prosecutors to ensure compliance with constitutional norms, New York's high court has reinforced those norms, ordering lower court judges in that state (a) to require prosecutors to search their files and disclose all evidence favorable to the defense at least thirty days before trials in major cases; and (b) to hold in contempt prosecutors who fail to do so (Feuer & McKinley, 2017). As the law on politically salient issues *diverges* in politically conservative and politically liberal states, activists on both sides of the partisan divide have incentives to turn to the federal courts, where they invoke congressional laws and the Constitution to challenge state laws they oppose and to demand judicial rulings that will impose *their* legal values on *all* states. Similarly, as noted above, the Republicans' and President Trump's further lurches to the political right on regulatory policy and individual rights issues have propelled liberal activist groups and state attorneys general into the courts at a startling rate.

More fundamentally, adversarial legalism's persistence in the United States reflects a self-perpetuating, path-dependent dynamic. In a model developed by Alec Stone Sweet (1999), the more often courts in any social or political context appear to be reasonably effective for resolving (or dampening) potentially destructive conflicts and for generating legal norms, the more legitimacy courts are accorded, and the more often they tend to be used. So too in the United States. For decades, the mechanisms of adversarial legalism have been used for a wide array of grievances and conflicts. Those mechanisms, notwithstanding complaints about particular decisions or legal doctrines, have come to be widely regarded as valuable and essential, legitimately available to those whose justice-claims or policy demands have been rejected or ignored. The web of legal precedents thus continues to expand, influencing the way grievances and desires for justice are perceived and framed by individuals, business organizations, lawyers, journalists, and political activists of all stripes (Silverstein, 2009). Those who have profited from, adapted to, and relied on the mechanisms of adversarial legalism strive to preserve them. Legal academics, judges, journalists, activist groups, and at least some prominent political leaders often rearticulate the legal values that the mechanisms of adversarial legalism reflect. Litigation stories appear daily in the news media and in popular entertainment, weaving the prominence and legitimacy of adversarial legalism ever more densely into American culture.

The ideological tunes played by adversarial legalism, we have seen, are subject to shift over time, as partisan politics and cultural tides bring about change in particular legal rules, doctrines, and procedures. But the musical instruments of adversarial legalism—its basic legal rules and remedies, and the entrenched institutions and norms that sustain them—remain in place, ready to be played by determined individuals and organizations with justice-claims that other institutions are failing to remedy. Thus the musical genre of adversarial legalism, sometimes sweet, sometimes discordant, will continue to pervade American law, politics, and society, perpetuating its legal exceptionalism.

NOTES

REFERENCES

INDEX

Notes

***

1. The Concept of Adversarial Legalism

1. Feldman (2000) describes an exception. He shows that in the United States, Japan, and France alike, contaminated blood products infected thousands of hemophiliacs with HIV. Litigation ensued in all three countries, but the legal sanctions levied against respondent companies and government officials in Japan and France were harsher than in the United States, and the litigation in those countries became more of a political cause célèbre. It does appear, however, that the behavior by Japanese and French government officials and companies was more clearly egregious, since "both Japan and France delayed the licensing of a U.S. blood test and continued using unheated blood products months after they had been abandoned in the United States" (694).

2. Sellers (1995) is a partial exception, since he found that appeals to courts of local land use decisions in the 1980s and 1990s were as common and just as likely to be successful in France and Germany as in the United States. The French and German appeals were to special administrative courts rather than to courts of general jurisdiction, as in the United States.

3. See Hamlin (2014; determination of refugee asylum cases, the United States, Australia, Canada); Kelemen (2011; securities regulation, competition policy, and disability rights, the United States and European Union); Lieberman (2005; antidiscrimination law in the United States, Great Britain, France); Kawar (2015; immigrant rights litigation in the United States and France); Cioffi (2010; corporate governance law in the United States and Germany); Jewell (2007; welfare administration in the United States, Germany, and Sweden); Bignami (2011; data privacy regulation in Europe and the United States); Saguy (2000; sexual harassment regulation in France and the United States); Hensler (2016; class action litigation in the United States and numerous countries, especially Australia and Israel).

4. The typology in Table 2 reflects the distinction between hierarchical and party-influenced modes of legal decision making and adjudication developed by Thibaut and Walker (1978) and Damaska (1986), as well as the typology of

bureaucratic decision modes in Mashaw (1983), from which I derive the additional category "expert judgment."

5. The term "legalistic" is used here to refer to a rule-oriented style of governance or decision making. See also Shklar (1964); Wilson (1968); Levin (1972: 193). In this context, I do not use the term "legalistic" in the more pejorative sense of the rigid adherence to rules without regard to their purpose or to the fairness of the outcome. In that regard, see Nonet and Selznick (1978); Kagan (1978: 6, 92–93).

6. U.S.C. sec 1414 (d). When parents are passive, the plan may be hierarchically imposed by the school's special education staff, making the process de facto an expert judgment one.

7. Cross-national and historical data on national litigation rates—for example, focusing on civil litigation per 100,000 population—are very spotty and probably misleading. Litigation rates are very sensitive to differences in the various kinds of civil courts: those dealing with smaller versus larger claims, courts of general jurisdiction versus those that specialize in certain types of cases. Those jurisdictional boundaries are not the same across nations and change over time, making it difficult for researchers to be sure they are comparing like with like. Review articles dealing with such studies indicate that the American litigation rate, while higher than that of most countries, is not extraordinarily higher. Galanter (1983); Clark (1990); Markesinis (1990); and Kritzer (1991).

2. The Two Faces of Adversarial Legalism

1. *Fay v. Noia* (1963).

2. National Prison Project (1990); Bureau of Justice Statistics (1991). In California during the 1980s, thirty-five of the state's fifty-eight county jail systems had been sued and were operating under court orders (Welsh, 1992: 601).

3. For a more critical view of judicial reform orders in prisons, arguing that they may have adverse consequences for internal authority and inmate security, see DiIulio (1990).

4. There was little doubt that deepening Oakland's harbor would be economically desirable, both for the region, where port activity is a vital source of economic sustenance, and for the national economy as a whole. If, moreover, Oakland should become incapable of handling the most modern vessels, the only major ports on the entire West Coast would be in Los Angeles and in Puget Sound, hundreds of miles away from Oakland's valuable rail and highway links to California's Central Valley and to the East.

5. A search in 1989 revealed 123 reported court cases, in federal courts alone, concerning dredging and disposal plans (McCreary, 1989: 43). See also National Research Council (1985: 89–90); Wessel and Hershman (1988: 253–286); Kagan (1991: 327); Strum (1993a, 1993b, 1993c).

6. Comment by law professor Edward Rubin in a workshop on the manuscript for this book, Georgia State Law School, Atlanta, April 24, 2018.

3. The Political Construction of Adversarial Legalism

1. On the incidence of lawsuits by injured people, see Hensler et al. (1991); Sloan and Hsieh (1995). On disparaging those who do litigate, see Engel (1984: 551); Greenhouse (1986); and Sanders (1987: 601–616).

2. In a corporatist political economy, private actors are represented by a limited number of large, relatively stable, interest associations. Business firms are represented by federations of sectorial employers' organizations, employees by federations of labor unions. Their negotiations over policy take place under the watchful eye of a government ministry (Schmitter, 1979:13).

3. Amalia Kessler (2017) has shown that in the early nineteenth century, courts of equity were important competitors to the adversarial legalism of the common law courts. Equity courts operated without juries. Chancellors (as equity judges were called), assisted by masters whom chancellors appointed in complex cases, used an inquisitorial method of fact-gathering, and, rather than being bound by detailed legal rules, enjoyed broad discretion in fashioning decisions and remedies. However, with the rise of Jacksonian democracy in the 1830s, the equity courts faded in prominence or were pushed to adopt lawyer-dominated, adversarial procedures.

4. Kessler (2017: 327–28) refers to the widespread view, among lawyers and non-lawyers in nineteenth-century America, "that American (political and economic) liberty hinged on the availability of adversarial dispute-resolution mechanisms that encouraged . . . the aggressive, competitive assertion of rights." See also Dennis Hale (2016).

5. In the 1940–1960 period, Elizabeth Magill (2009) notes, the Supreme Court held that Congress could authorize lawsuits by parties aggrieved by an administrative agency decision, even if the decision had not violated such parties' specific legal rights. Those kinds of suits, however, were brought mostly by business firms complaining of administrative decisions that they claimed were legal errors that disadvantaged them vis-à-vis competitors. It was in the 1960s that Congress started authorizing and encouraging lawsuits and appeals by liberal public advocacy organizations and lawyers.

6. R. Shep Melnick (2016: 17) notes that federal court rulings on elementary and secondary education, "rare events" in the 1950s, had by 2016 become so "commonplace" that "a 2004 survey of public school law devotes over 500 pages to such diverse topics as 'church-state relations,' 'school attendance and instruction issues,' 'student classifications,' 'rights of students with disabilities,' 'student discipline,' 'teachers' substantive constitutional rights,' 'discrimination in employment,' and 'tort liability.'"

7. Some scholars have argued that Hartz and others have neglected the extent to which profoundly illiberal political ideas, such as nativism, sexism, and racism, have contended with liberalism in American political culture and law. See, for example, Smith (1993). Regional subcultures, particularly in the slave-holding South and Appalachian regions, pulled in other directions (Woodard, 2011). Still, viewed comparatively, liberalism is what best distinguished American political culture in the late eighteenth and early nineteenth centuries from that of most other relatively economically advanced countries.

8. In the immediate post-Revolutionary period, Dennis Hale (2016: 164) notes, juries in many state courts were legally empowered not only to decide factual disputes but to "judge the law" as applied to a particular case, "even if this meant contradicting the judge's instructions." This view emerged from Americans' distrust of unchecked judicial power stemming from pre-Revolution conflicts with local British-appointed judges over libel law and the enforcement of the British Navigation and Revenue Acts. In that context, Hale tells us, John Adams asserted that if a judge's view of the law violates a fundamental political principle, "it is not only . . . [the juror's] right but his duty, in that case, to find the verdict according to his own best understanding, judgment and conscience" (61).

9. Francis Fukuyama (2014) classifies nineteenth-century American government as a clientelistic state, in which political parties accumulated support and power by offering voters patronage—government jobs, permissions, and other particularized benefits. The result was often incompetent and hence distrusted government bureaucracies, which fed voters' antipathy to big government.

10. This is not to say that the federal government was absent or passive. For example, it spurred national economic growth by fostering private enterprise. It distributed or sold (cheaply) huge swaths of public lands in frontier territories or states to thousands of small farmers (Hacker and Pierson, 2016: 108). It helped privately financed railroads cross the country via land grants and loan guarantees (White, 2011). The U.S. Bureau of Lands grew to become a substantial, relatively professionalized federal government bureaucracy (Mashaw, 2012). Thus the government was active and effective in some areas, but it relied heavily on private initiative and implementation.

11. *The Slaughter-House Cases* (1873).

12. *U.S. v. Cruikshank* (1876); *U.S. v. Harris* (1882); *Civil Rights Cases* (1883).

13. *Pollock v. Farmers' Loan and Trust Co.* (1895).

14. The Civil Service Act called for competitive examinations for hiring and promotion, and it provided security of tenure, during good behavior. Within five years, over 50 percent of the federal public service, outside of the post office, was covered by the new civil service regime. But the reforms were also partial in the sense that the top levels of federal administrative bodies continued to be staffed primarily via patronage appointments, used by political leaders to reward political party loyalty and ensure that their ideological allies, or allies of their primary supporters, were in administrative leadership positions (Mashaw, 2012). Even today, Francis Fukuyama observes, "each incoming [federal] administration makes more than four thousand political appointments . . . far more than in any other advanced democracy" (Fukuyama, 2014: 477).

15. Sheldon Goldman (1967) found that four-fifths of federal appellate court judges had been political activists at some point in their careers. See also Kagan, Detlefsen, and Infelise (1984).

16. For years, political and legal authorities in Southern states and cities blunted the thrust of the Supreme Court's decision by intimidating potential litigants (Peltason, 1961: 58; Rosenberg, 1991). Significant progress toward desegregation occurred only in the latter half of the 1960s, after black activism in the streets and violent resistance by Southern white supremacists combined to compel Congress

to enact the Civil Rights Act in 1964. The Act enabled federal bureaucrats to employ hierarchical levers, such as the threat to withdraw federal funds from the recalcitrant school districts, as well as providing incentives for private enforcement litigation and enabling federal judges to craft powerful injunctive legal remedies (Melnick, 2014: 91–93). Neither Congress nor the courts, however, were able to stanch white flight from judicially integrated public schools to suburban school districts and to private schools, thus "legally" resegregating a large percentage of black schoolchildren.

17. According to some studies in the 1970s, pretrial hearings on motions to suppress evidence occurred in almost one in ten criminal prosecutions and in almost 40 percent of prosecutions relying on evidence obtained by search warrant (Nardulli, 1983: 585; Davies, 1983: 611).

18. Among these major enactments were the Civil Rights Act (1964), the National Traffic and Motor Safety Act (1966), the National Environmental Protection Act (1969), the Clean Air Act (1970), the Occupational Safety and Health Act (1970), the Clean Water Act (1972), the Equal Employment Opportunity Act (1972), the Employee Retirement Income Security Act (1974), and the Surface Mining and Reclamation Act (1977). See Vogel (1989: chapters 3–4); Sunstein (1990). In addition, congressional regulation of state and local government bodies reached new heights, sometimes through direct regulations, such as the Voting Rights Act; sometimes by means of conditions attached to federal laws providing funding for housing and welfare programs, mass transit, and so on (Mayhew, 1991; Conlan, 1985).

19. As Daniel Kelemen (2011: 25) puts it in his analysis of the rise of a variant of adversarial legalism–"Eurolegalism"–in the European Union, "as political authority becomes more fragmented, adversarial legalism becomes a more attractive mode of governance for lawmakers. Political fragmentation creates agency problems and simultaneously offers a tempting solution to them."

20. For a superb political account of how Congressional Democrats developed these private enforcement regimes and a quantitative analysis of their growing prevalence, see Burbank and Farhang (2017). For an excellent, detailed account of evolution of adversarial legalism in the civil rights state, see Melnick (2016).

21. See also Schuck (1983); Taylor (1984; implied rights to sue to ensure compliance with the National Environmental Protection Act); Rabkin (1989; implied private rights to sue the Office of Civil Rights concerning enforcement priorities); Chen (2014; implied private rights to sue public school districts for violations of federal guidelines that interpreted the Civil Rights Act to require bilingual education under some circumstances).

22. Moreover, in 1986, after the Supreme Court had recently ruled that plaintiffs who prevailed in court in EAHCA cases could not collect attorneys' fees from the school district, Congress unanimously passed legislation providing for such fee payments in administrative as well as judicial proceedings (Melnick, 1995: 44; Kirp, 1982).

23. *Motor Vehicles Manufacturers Association v. State Farm* (1983).

24. In 1960, write Hacker and Pierson (2016: 197) "over 70 percent of Americans said they trusted the federal government to 'do what is right' most of the

time." But in 1980, after the deep civil conflicts unleashed by the civil rights movement and the Vietnam War, the Nixon Administration's Watergate scandals, and
the stagflation of the late 1970s, "only 25 percent of Americans expressed that level
of trust" (197).

25. Enforcement of the various provisions of the federal civil rights laws, Shep
Melnick (2018b: 34–35) points out, is delegated not only to the Department of Education's Office for Civil Rights but also to the Civil Rights Division of the Department of Justice, the Equal Employment Opportunity Commission, the Department
of Labor's Office for Federal Contract Compliance Programs, and several units in
the Department of Housing and Urban Development.

26. On the basis of their empirical research, Howard and Steigerwalt (2012:
36–39) show that (a) the complexity of the federal tax laws generates a high rate
of litigation, giving courts a large role in interpreting tax law; (b) those judicial
tax law decisions are significantly influenced by the judges' partisan ideology; and
(c) variation in partisan judicial ideology across U.S. District and Appeals courts
affects the ideological valence of audit policy and enforcement decisions by the
regional offices of the Internal Revenue Service.

27. *District of Columbia v. Heller* (2008).

28. Elsewhere Vogel (1996: 3) writes, "The most characteristic, distinctive, and
persistent belief of American corporate executives is an underlying suspicion and
mistrust of government. It distinguishes the American business community . . .
from every other bourgeoisie." Vogel (1978) traces this distrust partly to the fact
that, in contrast to Western European nations and Japan, corporate business became a formidable national presence well before the growth of large national bureaucracies that sought to manage the economy.

29. Scholars measure labor union centralization in terms of the level at which
bargaining is conducted (national, regional, the local plant), the degree of control
central federations exert over local union strike activities and finances, and the absolute number of union organizations. Merging various studies, Joel Rogers (1990)
found that, on a scale of 0 (least centralized) to 7 (most centralized), Austria in the
1980s scored 7, the Netherlands 5.7, Germany 1.3, and the United States 0. See also
Wilensky (1976: 21–25, 48–50; 1983: 53–54, 71–72).

30. Legal historian Amalia Kessler (2017: 336) notes that American law schools,
since the founding of Harvard Law School in the 1870s, have insisted that civil
procedure be taught as a required first year course, and adds that "it is deemed essential to conveying the view that law is not a neutral science composed of abstract
principles . . . but instead a form of difficult, contested policymaking, implicating
the heartfelt interests of real flesh-and-blood people."

4. Adversarial Legalism and American Criminal Justice

1. McCleskey's lawyers argued that the conviction was flawed, inter alia, because
(1) Georgia's death penalty was applied in a discriminatory manner; (2) the lineup
at which McCleskey was identified was improperly conducted; (3) McCleskey's
inculpatory pretrial statements were improperly admitted into evidence because

they had not been given voluntarily; and (4) McCleskey's prior criminal record had been improperly admitted into evidence (*McCleskey v. State*, 1980).

2. For the prosecution's counter-argument, see Rothman and Powers, 1984, 10–11. Subsequent studies in Florida, North Carolina, Mississippi, and Illinois found similar race-of-victim effects in capital cases (Butterfield, 1998; Weisburd, 1999).

3. In the decade 1900–1909 there were at least 885 lynchings in Southern states, and 621 between 1910 and 1919 (Paternoster, 1991).

4. Juries impose death sentences on convicted murderers in about 20 percent of the cases presented to them (Paternoster, 1991: 168–69; Baldus, Woodworth, and Pulaski, 1990: 88–89).

5. In analyses that include inmates in local jails and other facilities as well as in state and federal prisons, the U.S. incarceration rate in 2014 was 691 per 100,000 (Wagner and Walsh, 2017). Those analyses indicate an incarceration rate for whites of 450 per 100,000 and blacks of 2,306 per 100,000 (Sakala, 2014). That disparity reflects the higher recorded crime rates for black citizens, who are arrested approximately eight times the white rates for homicide (Cooper and Smith, 2011) and for robbery (Bureau of Justice Statistics, 2002). But bias plays a role too. Arrest records have been shown to reflect racially targeted policing, especially for drug offenses and minor crimes (Rothwell, 2015; Mauer, 2009). The huge incarceration disparity also has been shown to reflect somewhat longer sentences for black than for white defendants with respect to the same crimes (especially for minor offenses), even after controlling prior criminal record and other legally relevant factors (Nellis, 2016; Spohn, 2000; 481). Half of the racial disparity in *sentencing*, researchers have estimated, is explained by prosecutors' tendency to demand longer sentences for black defendants than for similarly situated whites (Nellis, 2016:10; Rehavi and Starr, 2012).

6. In 1980, 6 percent of all criminal charges in France involved victimless or consensual crimes; in the United States, "comparable offenses accounted for over 30% of all arrests, notifications, or citations for nontraffic violations" (Frase, 1990: 569–570).

7. For a brief survey of U.S. gun control laws in comparative perspective, see Masters (2012).

8. In 2010, there were over 16,000 homicide deaths in the United States, a rate of 5.3 per 100,000 population. In twenty-one other high-income countries, that rate was 0.8. About two thirds of the U.S. homicide deaths were firearm homicides, which occurred at a rate of 3.6 per 100,000. In the other high-income countries, the firearm homicide rate was 0.1 per 100,000 (Grinshteyn and Hemenway, 2016).

9. A comparative study in the 1980s found that approximately 40 percent of robberies reported to the police in the United States involve firearms, compared to 12 percent in Germany and 9 percent in England (Lynch, 1988: 196–197; Zimring and Hawkins, 1997: 115).

10. The *Economist* (2014c: 27) reported that "in recent years, the New York Police Department was called to an annual average of almost 200,000 incidents involving weapons, shot 28 people and saw six of its officers shot (mostly non-fatally)." In contrast, "in the year to March 2013 police in England and Wales fired weapons three times and killed no one." Nationwide, Franklin Zimring (2017) has estimated,

based on a variety of sources, that there are more than 1,000 deadly shootings by police each year in the United States.

11. According to systematically collected newspaper accounts of police shootings in the United States in 2014–2015, police killed a higher number of white than black suspects overall, but on a population-adjusted analysis, a black suspect was more than twice as likely to be killed by police than a white suspect (Zimring, 2017: 45–46). Some large police departments, like New York City and Houston, Texas, collect more detailed data on use of force by officers. Using that data, economist Roland Freyer (2016) found that in those cities black suspects were *not* more likely than whites to be killed by police, but *were* significantly more likely to be subjected to lesser uses of force, such as searches, being pushed to the ground, and handcuffed.

12. Sociologists David Kirk and Andrew Papachristos (2011, 1191) define legal cynicism as "a cultural frame in which people perceive the law as illegitimate, unresponsive, and ill equipped to ensure public safety." Controlling for other factors, they found that "legal cynicism explains why [high rates of] homicide persisted in certain Chicago neighborhoods during the 1990s despite declines in poverty and declines in violence citywide."

13. Moreover, the cost of legal defense in capital cases adds to delay, as states postpone adequate appropriations for death penalty appeals (Verhovek, 1995).

14. Between 1977 and March 1990, only thirteen states actually executed anyone, and only six (Alabama, Florida, Georgia, Louisiana, Texas, and Virginia) executed more than five persons (*Economist*, 1990: 26). Between 1977 and 2013, Texas, Virginia, Oklahoma, and Florida accounted for 60 percent of all executions (*Economist*, 2014a: 27). Nationally, total annual executions declined from ninety-eight in 1999 to twenty in 2016 (*Economist*, 2017e). That decline may have stemmed partly from a 50 percent drop in the national homicide rate between 1980 and 2012. Another factor was the fact that more states authorized juries to impose a sentence of life without parole for first-degree murder.

15. See *Harris v. Alabama* (1995). The U.S. Supreme Court upheld an Alabama law granting judges broad discretion to disregard jury decisions on sentencing. Justice Stevens, in dissent, noted that Alabama judges had overridden five jury recommendations of death sentences under that statute, while sentencing to death forty-seven defendants for whom the jury had recommended life sentences.

16. Within capital punishment states, most county criminal justice systems never or rarely impose the death penalty; in 2010, just twenty-nine mostly rural counties (fewer than 1 percent of all counties) were responsible for approximately half of all death sentences imposed nationwide (Smith, 2012: 227; Berger, 2011, 2).

17. On inadequate funding of defense counsel in capital cases, see Coyle et al. (1990: 30–44); Redick, Jr. (1993: 22); Margolick (1994); Bright (1994). On funding of defense counsel and the low level of adversarial activity in general, see McConville and Mirsky (1986–1987); Stuntz (1997).

18. The Anti-Terrorism and Effective Death Penalty Act of 1996, enacted April 1996, limited the ability of state prisoners to file more than one habeas corpus petition in federal courts. The Supreme Court quickly upheld its constitutionality (*Felker v. Turpin*, 1996). Two years later, Congress restricted funding for defense lawyers to help defendants in capital cases pursue federal appeals.

19. The National Registry of Exonerations, maintained by the University of California and the University of Michigan, declared that as of October 2016, the Innocence Project, begun in 1989, had thus far led to a total of 1,896 official exonerations. A 2012 report by the registry stated that between 1989 and 2012, 416 homicide convicts had been exonerated, plus 306 persons convicted of rape or other sexual assault, 94 for other crimes of violence, and 58 for drug or property crimes. See http://www.law.umich.edu/special/exoneration.

20. In a 1994 poll 85 percent of American surveyed said that courts in their area did not deal with criminals harshly enough (Bureau of Justice Statistics, 2000: 130–131). Although burglary rates, according to 1999 victimization studies, were higher in several Western European countries (England, Denmark, and Belgium) than in the United States (with the Netherlands about the same), American survey respondents were most likely to recommend imprisonment (rather than community service) for a hypothetical twenty-one-year-old recidivist burglar, and they recommended significantly longer prison terms than respondents from other Western European countries (OECD, 2005).

21. Between 1955 and 1971 the number of groups that lobbied the California legislature on crime policy issues expanded, and the "elite or professional model of legislation faded" (Berk, Brackman, and Lesser, 1977: 86). In Great Britain, in contrast, a later study showed that civil servants, after initially having been ignored by the Thatcher administration, reasserted influence on British crime policy (Reiner and Cross, 1991: 4–7).

22. According to a former counsel to the House Judiciary Subcommittee on Crime, no separate hearings were held on the crack penalty provision. It was written into the comprehensive bill with only about three and a half hours of discussion. "The 100-to-1 ratio [between penalties for crack and powder cocaine] was originally a 50-to-1 ratio in the subcommittee's bill, and was arbitrarily doubled to symbolize redoubled congressional seriousness." (Manley, 1994, 14).

23. In 1995, 88.4 percent of those convicted in federal courts for selling crack cocaine were black; 4.5 percent were white. In large part due to the preponderance of black crack dealers, the average sentence served by black inmates in federal prisons (seventy-one months) far exceeded the average served by white inmates (fifty months). In the early 1980s, before the crack law, the average time in federal prisons served by blacks was comparable to that of whites (Skolnick, 1998: 90, 94; Tonry, 1995).

24. In Germany, a federal polity, police and prosecutorial offices are organized at the level of the states (lander). But the German Penal Code and Code of Criminal Procedure are federal laws, operating nationwide. And, as Damaska (1975: 488) observes, "a striving for [national] uniformity is nevertheless obvious."

25. The federal government in the United States does operate many specialized police forces with narrow mandates, such as the FBI, the Drug Enforcement Administration, the Border Patrol, and the Immigration and Nationalization Service, together with the small criminal branches of regulatory agencies such as the Environmental Protection Agency, the Food and Drug Administration, and the Securities and Exchange Commission.

26. As David Johnson (1998: 295) points out in a comparison of prosecutorial decision making in the United States and Japan, "when judges write detailed opinions

justifying verdicts and sentences, and when those decisions are themselves standardized by the judicial bureaucracy—as in Japan—prosecutors enjoy higher levels of . . . [predictability]."

27. Researchers in the Capital Jury Project also found that jurors who voted for the death penalty frequently did not follow or understand their instructions (Mansnerus, 1995).

28. In Germany lawyers have the right to cross-examine witnesses but generally prefer to ask the judge to pursue any additional line of questioning that the lawyer thinks would be helpful (Frase and Weigend, 1995: 367).

29. In its 1972 decision in *Papachristou v. City of Jacksonville*, the Supreme Court invalidated laws that criminalized vagrancy, reasoning that their inherent vagueness violated the right to due process of law and invited discriminatory application. Many cities responded by establishing noncriminal detoxification centers to which the police could commit (for a short time) incapacitated chronic public inebriates (Aarmson, Dienes, and Musheno, 1978).

30. State and local expenditures on defense lawyering in criminal cases increased from $46 million nationally in 1970 to $315 million in 1978 (Stuntz, 1997: 5, 50).

31. The key decisions were *Monroe v. Pape* (1961) and *Monell v. Department of Social Services* (1978).

32. Mandatory arrest policies were also spurred by a Minneapolis study indicating that arresting abusive men reduced recidivism in domestic violence cases, although subsequent research has questioned the benefits of mandatory (as opposed to discretionary) arrest in such cases (Sherman, 1992).

33. In *Tennessee v. Garner* (1985), the Supreme Court held it unconstitutional for police to use deadly force unless their lives or the lives of others were directly threatened by an offender (half of the states had by then already adopted that standard by statute) (McCoy, 2010: 121).

34. Lizette Alvarez (2014, A12), summarizing her lengthy article, reported:

> For decades Florida has had a history of deadly, racially tinged police confrontations, many of them involving unarmed men, which have led to riots, protests and a steady undercurrent of rancor between minorities and the police. But in the past 20 years, not a single officer in Florida has been charged with using deadly force.

35. In recent years, it still appears that police, prosecutors, and judges in rural counties tend to impose significantly harsher legal penalties than their counterparts in big cities (Keller and Pearce, 2016).

36. State highway patrol officers, researchers have found, stop and question African American drivers much more often than white motorists. In addition, studies of several California cities revealed that the rate of arrests subsequently determined to be unfounded for African Americans is at least four times as high as for whites, and in some places seven or twelve times as high (Bass, 1997: 8-10). For a systematic account and analysis of reasons this occurs, see Epp, Maynard-Moody, and Haider-Markel (2014). It should be noted that very similar findings have been found in studies of police stops of black persons in Canada and the United Kingdom, notwithstanding national efforts, at least in the United Kingdom, to outlaw and prevent racial profiling (Smith, 2006).

37. Fisher (2000) points out that England enforces the obligation to disclose exculpatory evidence in criminal cases quite effectively by means of a hierarchical system that prescribes and regulates police recording and communication of all evidence. In the decentralized American system, in contrast, each police department is essentially self-regulating in this regard. The failure of police and prosecutors to disclose evidence has been a primary factor in cases in which defendants convicted of serious crime have subsequently been completely exonerated (Leo, 2008). For a comparison of efforts to control racial profiling by police in the United States and the U.K., see Smith (2006).

38. In Louisiana, two-thirds of funding of public defenders comes from local courts' fees and fines, principally traffic violations—an erratic source of revenue. A study by the American Bar Association found that Louisiana has only one-fifth of the defense lawyers needed to provide adequate representation (*Economist*, 2017b).

39. Craig Bradley found that in 1980–1984, the U.S. Supreme Court decided thirty-five cases involving the interpretation of the Fourth Amendment's restrictions on searches and seizures. Few were decided unanimously. Seven had no majority opinion at all, as the justices disagreed about what restrictions the Constitution should be read to require (Bradley, 1993: 49). After examining 223 state appellate decisions on search and seizure issues, Bradley concluded that in at least a third of the cases, either the trial court judge or the state appellate judges had misunderstood Supreme Court precedents (47–48). Between 1985 and 1990 an increasingly conservative Supreme Court decided forty-three Fourth Amendment cases, reversing the court below in 85 percent of the cases that had been decided in the defendant's favor (Bookspan, 1991). Two legal scholars asked 547 police officers about the legal propriety of searches undertaken in six fact situations described in cases that had been decided by the Supreme Court. Taking the Court decision as the correct answer, the police officers' mean score was 3.4 out of 6—only slightly better than the 3.0 one would expect from random guessing. A group of lawyers scored 4.4 on the same test (Heffernan and Lovely, 1991: 537).

5. Deciding Criminal Cases

1. Excluding jury deliberation time, which averaged about three hours (National Center for State Courts, 1988: 19), the median trial took slightly more than eleven hours.

2. A study of nine urban trial courts in 1986–1987 indicated that trial days averaged less than three and a half hours (National Center for State Courts, 1988: 79).

3. In a 1995 California trial of a man charged with murdering two police officers, the defense alone cost the state nearly $1,000,000, including $255,000 on forensic and legal experts; $100,000 for private investigators; $50,000 for paralegals; and the rest for attorneys' fees (Verhovek, 1995: A1, A13). In a 2003 case, New York spent more than $1,000,000 in defense of a man charged with a capital crime, and a 2008 study showed that it cost Maryland $1.9 million more to prosecute a death penalty case than to prosecute a noncapital murder case (Berger, 2011, 4).

4. On the other hand, Hughes (1984: 588) reports that in England the average Crown Court jury trial in 1980 took 8.5 hours–not all that much shorter than the eleven-hour median trial in a sample of American criminal courts. See National Center for State Courts (1988: 9).

5. In Los Angeles County 48 percent of jurors who received jury duty notice in 1995 did not respond. In Dallas, Texas, the response rate ranges between 22 and 37 percent (Gerlin, 1995: B1).

6. A former prosecutor and defense lawyer writes: "The simple fact was that the evidence against most defendants was overwhelming. . . . Defendants who had little hope of winning at trial . . . correctly guessed that judges would usually reward of plea of guilty (even one entered without a bargain) with a greatly reduced sentence" (Lynch, 1994: 118). In Alaska, plea bargaining was forbidden by statute, but guilty pleas remained prevalent. One judge said, "Human nature doesn't want to engage in a fruitless act" (Rubinstein and White, 1979: 81).

7. But see Ramseyer and Rasmusen (1998).

8. As pointed out by William Pizzi (1999: 54), a leading American treatise on defense of criminal cases asserts that either before or after arrest, a client should always be advised to "say nothing at all to the police, tell them nothing under any circumstances." See Amsterdam (1988, vol. 5: 120).

9. Prior to California's 1994 enactment of a statewide three-strikes law mandating life imprisonment for a third felony conviction, about 90 percent of felony cases were resolved by guilty pleas, according to the state Legislative Analysts' Office; after the effective date of the three-strikes law, a majority of defendants in third-strike cases insisted on a jury trial (Butterfield, 1995: A1, A9; Bandow, 1995: A17). In Santa Clara County, California, the prosecutor refused to engage in plea bargaining. In consequence, 60 to 70 percent of felony cases went to trial. It became almost impossible to get a civil case trial in the overloaded county courthouse. In other California counties, prosecutors disregarded the clear words of the statute and engaged in plea bargaining, which cut the trial rate for three-strike cases to a third of the Santa Clara County level (Eisenberg, 1995: 50–58).

10. In Arizona, Lowenthal (1993: 82–83) discovered, prosecutors dismissed repetitive offender allegations in 76 percent of all cases in which such charges had been initially made, and dismissed dangerous felony enhancement charges 77 percent of the time, indicating those charges often are used as plea bargaining chips.

11. On the role of prosecutorial hierarchies in coordinating charging policies in France and the Netherlands, see Frase (1990: 560–563, 616) and Downes (1988: 15).

12. After a careful comparison of the available evidence, Richard Frase (1990: 639) concludes, "'Cooperation bargaining' has a relatively modest effect on sentencing in France." Compared to the United States, it entails modest concessions by prosecutors for modest degrees of cooperation. See also Thomas Weigend (1980: 409). In Germany many criminal cases referred by the police are disposed of via the *Strafbefehl* (penal order) by which the defendant can accept without trial a judgment of guilt, but the penalty is limited to a monetary fine. Unlike American plea bargaining, however, Weigend says (414), "neither side views the procedure as an

exchange of trial rights for a sentence discount" and "the German defendant is not punished for demanding trial." In minor cases, the German practice of conditional dismissal offers a dismissal and a monetary fine to defendants who decline trial, but unlike an American guilty plea, there is no criminal conviction (417–418).

13. German defendants who decline to contest penal orders are given lesser sentences, and those who confess at trial tend to be given lighter sentences; informing defendants of these options in advance might be considered a form of implicit plea bargaining. Langbein (1979b) forcefully distinguishes the implicit plea bargaining in the penal order cases from the outright bargaining and reductions in the legal charges that characterize American plea bargaining. Although German plea bargaining may be conducted in a more constrained manner than in the American version, by one estimate it affects about 20–30 percent of all trials in Germany (Hermann, 1992: 756; Frase and Weigend, 1995: 344–345).

14. A 1978 study of more than 400 lower court criminal trials in Lower Saxony indicated that the average trial length, when the defendant confessed (in whole or in part), was fifty minutes, and it was about seventy minutes when there was no confession (Weigend, 1980: 411).

15. Lay judges in Germany are elected by the local community and serve a term of four years, during which they must be available for a certain number of trial days per year. Hence they acquire some experience (Pizzi, 1999: 98). While they are clearly subordinate to the professional judges, surveys indicate that the German lay judges think the professionals are generally fair to them as well as to the defendants (Machura, 2000).

16. According to a study of nine urban trial courts in 1986–1987, jury selection averaged about one-third of total trial time. In Oakland, California, jury selection in the average robbery and aggravated assault case consumed more than eight hours. In the fastest criminal court in the study, in Elizabeth, New Jersey, jury selection averaged 20 percent of total trial time, or somewhat more than one hour (National Center for State Courts, 1988: 30, 40, 112). For a history of the legal changes that led to extended and adversarial jury selection processes, see Dennis Hale (2016: chapter 4).

17. In France the defendant who wishes to remain silent "must at least stand mute while the presiding judge poses questions suggesting the defendant's guilt. Moreover, French law does not forbid drawing adverse inferences from the defendant's silence" (Frase, 1990: 679). In Germany the court is precluded by law from drawing such a negative inference (Frase and Weigand, 1995: 343). American defendants have an absolute right not to take the witness stand, and "the exercise of this right [at least since the Supreme Court's 1965 decision in *Griffin v. California*] may not be the basis for adverse comment [to the jury] by the court or the prosecution" (Frase, 1990: 679).

18. The ability of lay judges in Germany to question witnesses, even though they often decline to do so (Machura, 2000), stands in marked distinction to the role of lay jurors in the United States, who are forced to sit mutely during the trial as well as during the legal instructions they belatedly receive from the judge. Any teacher knows that if the students don't ask questions, one can never be sure they understand the material. Little wonder that studies show that jurors in capital punishment

cases often misunderstand the judge's instructions (*San Francisco Chronicle,* 1995; Mansnerus, 1995; Garvey, Johnson, and Marcus, 2000).

19. Similarly, Frase notes (1990: 673) of French trials, "Judicial control of the taking of proof, combined with the practice of calling the defendant as first witness, allows the proof of guilt to focus only on the contested issues, thus improving the speed and quality of the guilt determination process." See also Peters (1992: 259, 285, 288).

20. For an account of the Dutch system, see also Pizzi (1999: 94–97).

21. The excesses of prosecutorial adversariness are reflected in the frequency with which unjust convictions unearthed by The Innocence Project (discussed in the Afterword) stem from evidence that prosecutors illegally withheld exculpatory evidence, as well as prosecutors' reluctance to dismiss cases even after DNA revelations of the defendants' innocence.

22. In the New Haven, Connecticut, lower criminal court studied by Feeley, any defendant who might initially have thought about demanding a trial to prove his or her innocence soon came to realize that it would take money and time—money for a bail bondsman and for an attorney (if the defendant was not indigent); several days away from work to confer with their lawyer and to appear in court; time rounding up defense witnesses. In Feeley's (1979: 9) sample of 1,640 cases, not a single defendant invoked their right to trial by jury. Instead, defendants chose a quick, lawyer-negotiated plea bargain; the usual sentence was a fine (usually less than a bail bond, a tenth the typical defense lawyer's fee) or a few days in jail, suspended because of the time already served between arrest and arraignment. For most defendants, the costs of the adversarial legal process would only exacerbate the punishment (241).

23. British criminal defendants and lawyers, surveys have indicated, regard magistrate's courts as more pro-police than Crown Courts (McConville, 1994). On the other hand, there is an acquittal rate of 22–24 percent (similar to that of U.S. juries), even though many cases involve strict liability minor offenses, and penalties are mild. Moreover, there is little evidence that defendants who insist on a magistrate's trial and are convicted are punished more harshly than those who plead guilty (Darbyshire, 1997a, 1997b). Darbyshire (1997b) does note, however, that in an increasingly racially diverse country, British magistrates are overwhelmingly white, disproportionately members of the Conservative Party, and rather old. In nonmetropolitan areas magistrates often are laymen and may not even have a law-trained clerk.

24. For a comparative description of American versus British recruitment of judges, see Atiyah and Summers (1987: chapter 12).

25. Some defense lawyers use the voir dire to eliminate alert, well-informed jurors and select the least capable and fair-minded ones in the pool. For a play-by-play description, see Adler (1994). In Dallas a prospective woman juror declined to answer some questions on a thirteen-page questionnaire handed her by the court—concerning her religion, income, political views, and memberships—on grounds that they were irrelevant to her ability to be an impartial juror. The judge held her in contempt, then sentenced her to three days in jail and a $200 fine; the sentence was upheld on appeal (Minow and Cate, 1994: A6).

26. In *Batson v. Kentucky* (1986) the U.S. Supreme Court condemned as unconstitutional peremptory challenges based on the race of the potential juror, although that in turn has led to much litigation and a complex body of precedent concerning the application of that principle in particular cases (Hale, 2016: 261–267).

27. "Constant objections stemming from a desire to overlook nothing are . . . not a feature of English procedure" (Hughes, 1984: 589–590).

28. To be sure, American appellate courts frequently employ a harmless error rule to avoid reversal for procedural error, but the large difference in trial practice, wherein American defense lawyers strive to build a record of procedural challenge rulings that may support an appeal, suggests there remain major differences in the two appellate processes.

29. British barristers, James Q. Wilson (1995) points out, can and often do represent the prosecution in a case one week and the defense the next. Nor do they have the same incentives as an ambitious American defense lawyer to seek lucrative, high-profile cases by building a reputation for superaggressive advocacy.

30. In early 1999 a team of *Chicago Tribune* reporters published a remarkable series of articles that detailed deception and other misbehavior by American prosecutors, who often went unpunished (Armstrong and Possley, 1999a; Possley and Armstrong, 1999b). According to Armstrong and Possley (1999a: 1C), "Since a 1963 Supreme Court decision designed to curb misconduct by prosecutors, at least 381 defendants nationally have had a homicide conviction thrown out because prosecutors concealed evidence suggesting innocence or presented evidence they knew to be false."

31. Police in England are instructed to warn suspects before they are questioned, "You do not have to say anything. But it may harm your defence if you do not mention something now which you later rely on in court."

32. In a carefully constructed sample survey, a majority of police officials, lawyers, and community leaders, as well as a majority of the public at large, chose the answer "a rich person usually gets treated better than a poor person in the American court system" rather than "almost every citizen can expect an equally fair trial" (McClosky and Brill, 1983: 150–151).

33. In 1992 almost 80 percent of state felony defendants were classified as indigent for purposes of obtaining state-provided defense counsel (Stuntz, 1997: 7).

34. In 2017, the American Civil Liberties Union filed a class action lawsuit against two South Carolina cities, asserting they systematically violated the rights of poor defendants who are jailed for misdemeanor offenses without meaningful access to legal representation. Tess Borden, a lawyer with the American Civil Liberties Union, told reporters that 139 of the state's 212 municipal courts have no public defenders available (Williams, 2017). As noted in Chapter 4, a study by the American Bar Association found that Louisiana has only one-fifth of the defense lawyers needed to provide adequate representation (*Economist*, 2017b).

35. Long before the O. J. Simpson case verdict, Langbein wrote (1995: 32–33), "Money is the defining element of our modern American criminal justice system. If Simpson walks, as most lawyers think he will, what will have decided the outcome is not that O. J. is black, but that he is rich. He can afford to buy what F. Lee Bailey, Alan Dershowitz, Johnnie Cochran and the others have to sell: the consultants on

jury packing, the obliging experts who will contradict the state's overpowering DNA and related evidence, and the defense lawyer's bag of tricks for sowing doubts, casting aspersions and coaching witnesses." See also Stephen Adler (1994) for an excellent and detailed journalistic account of the successful defense of Imelda Marcos.

36. See Citron (1991); Bright (1994: 1836–1837) ("Poor people accused of capital crimes are often defended by lawyers who lack the skills, resources, and commitment to handle such serious matters").

37. For a vivid example, see Thomas (1986: 1, 12).

38. Years later, I learned, Leonard was tried and convicted of six murders he committed in the course of two armed robberies, and then sentenced to death. On appeal, his lawyers argued that the trial court judge had erred in allowing the prosecution to enter into evidence a transcript of Leonard's "not guilty' statement during the pretrial hearing. The state supreme court rejected that argument. Thus both the prosecutors and the judge (and the California Supreme Court) ultimately were willing to treat Leonard's impromptu confession as legally relevant (Ofgang, 2007).

After his pretrial confession, the defense introduced the opinion of a psychiatrist who testified that Leonard was not mentally competent to stand trial because his confession had reflected a psychotic delusion: "a Christian path to speak the truth whenever the Holy Spirit touches" him, that had "more strength, validity and urgency than his rational understanding of the proceedings." The trial court, and a court-appointed psychiatrist, rejected that diagnosis, and that ruling also was upheld by the California Supreme Court (*People v. Leonard*, 2007, 14).

6. Adversarial Legalism and Civil Justice

1. See also Kessler (2017).

2. In 2009 on a trip to Glacier National Park in Montana, I ate in a restaurant in a nearby town: Columbia Falls. From residents I talked to there, I learned that the aluminum mill had *closed*. This reminds us of the sad truth that while civil litigation sometimes can remedy legal wrongs, it usually cannot change the underlying socioeconomic conditions, emotional clashes, or conflicting belief systems that generate legal disputes (Hazard, 1969).

3. Continental European legal systems, Langbein (1994: 2043) notes, also avert will litigation because substantive law statutes commonly guarantee children at least a minimum fraction of the parent's estate. And "in the English and Commonwealth systems, the so-called 'family provision' statutes empower the court of equity to make discretionary provision for children (and others) if the court determines that the testator disinherited them unfairly." The United States, in contrast, emphasizes testamentary freedom, including the parent's right to disinherit children. But ironically, an experienced trial lawyer wrote, "the average jury . . . is visited with a strong temptation to rewrite [the will] in accordance with the jury's idea of what is fair and right" (2043).

4. See, for example, *Watson v. Dingler* (1992); *In re Estate of Lamberson* (1981); *Newman v. Smith*, (1918).

5. In 2012, fewer than 2 percent of all civil case dispositions in federal courts occurred during or after jury trial (Galanter and Frozena, 2014, 117). The jury trial percentage in state courts, based on a fifteen-state study by the National Center for State Courts, was even lower. In the seventy-five most populous counties, there were 10,800 civil case jury trials in 2005, half the total in 1992.

6. The report of the Council on California Competitiveness (1992) displays a graph showing 281 *lawyers* per 100,000 population in the United States, 111 in Germany, and 82 in England and Wales. With respect to judges, in 1970 the United States provided 63 for every million citizens, compared to 81 in France, 93 in Sweden, 103 in Italy, and 213 in West Germany (Johnson and Drew, 1978: 8). In 1985 the United States had 94 judges per million population and West Germany then had 279 (Curran, 1986: 3; Clark, 1988: 1807).

7. German litigants are empowered to challenge the court's choice of a neutral expert witness for good cause. They also can comment on the court-appointed expert's report (to which the expert is asked to reply), and if they make an adequate argument, can ask the court to seek a second opinion from another expert (Langbein, 1985: 839–840).

8. In Los Angeles Superior Court the median civil case jury trial in 1984 took thirty hours; the median nonjury trial took ten hours (Kakalik et al., 1990, table D.6). In courts in nine urban counties in Northern California, Colorado, and New Jersey in 1986, the median jury trial (excluding day-of-trial pretrial motions) took 13.5 hours, and the median nonjury trial 5 hours. One might wonder if the nonjury trials were intrinsically less complex. The data do not say. But the Los Angeles data exclude very simple "short-cause" nonjury trials (those estimated before trial to require no more than one trial day), which suggests that the nonjury trial cases analyzed were not particularly simple. Indeed, the average (mean) Los Angeles nonjury trial took twenty-five hours (compared to thirty-six hours for the average jury trial), which suggests that nonjury trials often involved very complex cases (Kakalik et al., 1990, table D.6). The vast majority of civil trials in the United States are jury trials, as opposed to judge-only trials. (Daniels and Martin, 1995: 66).

9. In the late 1980s the average trial in the U.S. District Court in San Francisco took five days, but each year five to seven trials exceeded one month (Bilocki, 1989: 43–47). The mean length for a civil jury trial in Cook County, Illinois, in the period 1959–1979 was 3.8 days (Priest, 1993: 103, 115).

10. Summarizing recent studies, Dennis Hale (2016: 294) cites a National Center for State Courts report that nationwide in 2007, 9.4 percent of those summoned for jury duty failed to appear or received hardship exemptions. But in Los Angeles County in 2010, half the 3 million summonses sent out were ignored, and in South Florida that rate was even higher (294).

11. A study based on 1992 data from forty-five populous counties produced similar results: median time to jury verdict was 2.5 years, but 5.5 years in Chicago, 4.5 years in Alameda County, California, and over 4 years in Fairfield County, Connecticut (Heise, 2000: 835, 837).

12. The German social courts (*Sozialgerichte*) of first instance, for example, sit in panels designed to increase specialization. There usually are three judges, one professional and two lay judges. According to Timothy Jost (1998: 657–658), "In

disputes regarding insurance coverage, one of the lay judges represents insureds, and the other represents employers. In matters concerning the relationship between health insurance companies and insurance doctors, one of the lay judges represents the insurance companies, the other the doctors."

13. There are some specialized trial courts in the United States, including bankruptcy tribunals, family courts, and juvenile courts. Large cities may have special housing courts. And there are specialized administrative tribunals that deal with workers' compensation cases, federal tax cases, immigration cases, and patent appeals.

14. In France the new judge first takes a special two-year course in a national judge-training school (Meador, 1983: 20).

15. According to Langbein (1985: 850), "evaluations by senior judges pay particular regard to (1) a judge's effectiveness in conducting legal proceedings, including fact-gathering, and his treatment of witnesses and litigants; and (2) the quality of his opinions—his success in mastering and applying the law." The judge also receives an efficiency rating based on factors such as case disposition and reversal rates.

16. A survey of judges on the U.S. Court of Appeals in the 1960s found that four-fifths had been political activists at some point in their careers (Goldman, 1967). About three-quarters of the state supreme court judges during the 1900–1970 period reached the bench after having held another public office or after "a career closely involved with politics" (Kagan, Detlefsen, and Infelise, 1984: 378). Almost half joined the high court without having had any prior experience as a lower court judge (376).

17. See also MacCoun (1993: 137–180); Lempert (1993: 181–247); Vidmar (1993: 293); Vidmar and Rice (1993: 896).

18. More recent experimental studies also suggest modest differences between decision-making by judges and juries (MacCoun, 1993: 165–167; Sentell, 1991: 98–99). Defenders of the civil jury argue that the 20 percent judge-jury disagreement rate in the Kalven and Zeisel study is comparable to the rate of disagreement among experts of various kinds (e.g., scientists engaged in peer review) and comparable to the rate at which appeals courts reverse trial judges (Diamond, 1983; Clermont and Eisenberg, 1992). Nonetheless, an analysis of a large database of decisions by judges and juries (in different cases) found, after controlling for numerous variables likely to affect case outcomes, that juries make significantly larger money damage awards to injured plaintiffs than judges do, and juries are significantly more likely to find for plaintiffs in medical malpractice and product liability cases (Helland and Tabarrok, 2000). The authors also found that juries drawn from counties with higher poverty rates gave larger damage awards, controlling for other case factors, than juries in less poor counties or judges in poor counties.

19. Hensler (1985: 65) also reports that in Texas, a judge trying two asbestos-injury cases against the same defendant arranged for two separate juries to hear, at the same time, the same evidence relating to the defendant's liability. The juries then deliberated separately. They arrived at different verdicts. The same occurred in two related asbestos cases in Pennsylvania.

20. American trial and appellate court judges can and do set aside or reduce jury awards that strike them as unreasonably high, but they don't always do so and rarely do they raise "unreasonably low" verdicts. There are few legal standards to guide judges' decisions to reduce "unreasonably high" verdicts, and American judges, unlike their continental European counterparts, are not legally required to justify particular verdicts.

21. Daniels and Martin (1995: 75–77, table 3.2) combed through jury verdict reporters for eighty-two sites, covering 100 counties in sixteen states for the years 1988–1990. Seventeen of the eighty-two sites—including the entire states of Alaska and Idaho—had fewer than fifty civil case jury verdicts during the three-year period. Fewer than half of the sites—thirty-nine of eighty-two—had more than ten medical malpractice verdicts between 1988 and 1990, and only eleven states reported fifty or more (126). There were no products liability verdicts in eleven sites, and only twenty-two of eighty-two sites reported ten or more (171, table 5.2). Because these aggregate data fail to distinguish among different types of medical malpractice and products liability cases, the data tend to overstate the number of useful jury verdicts available to lawyers seeking to evaluate their client's claims. Daniels and Martin, who attack the comparison of the tort system with a lottery, thus concede that "jury verdicts, as a general proposition, are not predictable and uniform in the aggregate, if for no other reason than the lack of fungibility among the cases going to trial" (60).

22. In Evan Osborne's (1999: 193, 195) analysis, the overall correlation between attorneys' expectations and individual awards was .54 (and, in a regression analysis, $R_2 = .41$). That led Osborne to conclude that jury decisions are not "random events" (197) (as if any serious observer had ever argued that they were). Yet the statistics also indicate that attorney expectations explain only about half the variance in outcomes, which suggests a relatively high level of legal unpredictability, even for practitioners, in all types of civil cases.

23. More recently, uncertainty concerning judicial determination or negotiation of spousal support and child support payments in divorce cases has been substantially reduced by the adoption in many states of written guidelines based on a number of quantified factors. (Ellman and Ellman, 2008).

24. Two other flagmakers, neither of which had sold the flag, settled the claim by paying $14,000 and $1,500 respectively (Van de Putte, 1995: A14).

25. For similar empirical findings concerning the very low success rate of plaintiffs in employment discrimination claims, see Clermont and Schwab (2004).

26. Molot (1998: 992) notes that liberal American pleading rules, in which a lawyer need only state a claim and search for evidence later via pretrial discovery, also encourage the tactic of making and retaining weak legal claims, as does judicial reluctance to strike weak claims and defenses through early motions for partial summary judgment. As noted in the Afterword, two rulings by the Supreme Court in 2007 and 2009, applicable to the federal courts, empowered judges to dismiss complaints for failing to include more specific supporting facts; other Court rulings in the 1980s enhanced federal judges' authority to dispose of weak complaints or defenses via summary judgment rulings. Some states, too, have bolstered judges' capacity to resolve cases via summary judgment.

27. Most national legal systems have declined to follow the American lead, although some Canadian provinces and some Australian states have authorized class actions in mass tort cases (Flemming, 1994: 519–523). See also Coffee (2015: chapter 10) and Hensler (2016).

28. A study by Bryant Garth of all federal class actions in the Northern District of California from 1979 to 1984 found that in most cases plaintiffs' substantive justice claims were transformed into narrow procedural issues about notice and rights to be heard, providing few significant results for anyone except the lawyers (Garth, 1992: 237, 257).

29. Confronted with 12,359 individual lawsuits, filed in the wake of multimillion dollar verdicts for a few plaintiffs, Dow Corning and three other manufacturers of silicone breast-implants offered a $4.23 billion settlement, notwithstanding scientific studies that found no causal link between the implants and the plaintiffs' claimed immune system diseases (Coffee, 1995: 1405–1410; Angell, 1996). The settlement agreement later collapsed and Dow Corning filed for bankruptcy, only to settle remaining claims for $3.2 billion in 1998—even though by then the scientific evidence failing to find any causal relationship had become even more convincing (Bandow, 1998: A23; Kolata, 1998: A1; Bernstein, 1999).

30. Galanter and Kahill (1999: 1374).

31. In the Netherlands, until the late 1990s almost 60 percent of private households were entitled to legal aid assistance and court fee waivers (Blankenburg, 1994); reforms then reduced coverage to approximately 47 percent. Even in the aftermath of Thatcher-era cutbacks in legal aid, in 1990 about 37 percent of the British population was eligible for subsidized assistance from solicitors (Kritzer, 1996: 141). In the United States government-funded civil legal assistance is available to individuals below the poverty level and those with incomes between 100 and 125 percent of the poverty level; in 2000, 17 or 18 percent of households were covered (letter from Legal Services Corporation, November 2000).

32. In 1996 the federal government budget for the Legal Services Corporation was reduced from $400 million to $278 million (*New York Times,* 1996: A14; Gottlieb, 1996: A8; Pear, 1995: A1, A9).

33. Theodore Eisenberg, Geoffrey P. Miller, and Emily Sherwin (2008), using accessible corporate filings with the Securities and Exchange Commission, examined 164 negotiated contracts made among very large companies in the telecommunications, credit, and financial services industries, dealing with complex commitments in stock purchase agreements; credit and security agreements; and loan pooling and service agreements. The authors found that fewer than 10 percent of such contracts contained mandatory arbitration agreements. That suggests, they wrote, that large companies value litigation as the means for resolving large-stakes disputes with peers.

34. In September 1997 the securities industry discontinued mandatory arbitration of disputes with employees. Critics had charged that the pool of arbitrators was too closely linked with employers (Bales, 1998: 526).

35. In September 2016, the U.S. Health and Human Services Department issued a rule forbidding nursing homes that receive federal funding (as many do via Medicare and Medicaid) from requiring residents to resolve any disputes via arbitration

rather than seeking relief in court (Silver-Greenberg, 2016b). In 2017, that rule was repealed by the Trump administration.

7. The Tort Law System

1. Because the average mesothelioma victim dies one year after the disease has become manifest, the actual amounts paid to asbestos victims in the Netherlands are far less than the average tort recovery in the United States (Vinke and Wilthagen, 1992: 18).

2. To illustrate the difference, in a workers' compensation proceeding filed in 1968, Clarence Borel, the plaintiff in the Fifth Circuit case, had been awarded $13,081 (for lost wages and medical bills) "for injuries that amounted to a death sentence" (Barnes, 2011: 22). In his tort case, by contrast, he (or rather, his family) was awarded damages of $79,436. Borel had already died, still in his 50s.

3. As of 1984, asbestos claimants in the aggregate had received somewhat more than $235 million in damages. Their lawyers had earned $164 million. And the defendants had incurred more than $600 million in expenses (Kakalik et al., 1983: p. 39).

4. Thus "a disabled victim of [noncancerous] asbestosis will receive $50,000 under the Johns-Manville settlement but only between $5,800 and $7,500 [under the so-called *Georgine* class settlement with another coalition of manufacturers]" (Coffee, 1995: 1396). An appellate court later abrogated the *Georgine* settlement.

5. For an insightful, detailed analysis of how conflicting interests and ideas blocked congressional action to rationalize and improve compensation for asbestos victims, see Barnes, 2011. Barnes and Burke (2015) show how compensation programs propelled by adversarial legalism tend to generate a more complex, reform-slowing political process than government-funded, administratively-implemented compensation programs.

6. Barnes (2011: 42) reports that "In the Manville Trust, payments have dropped from 100 percent of liquidated value to 10 percent and now 5 percent."

7. By 2004, an estimated 730,000 individual claims for asbestos-related injuries had been filed in the United States, and the number was still growing (Carroll et al., 2005).

8. In New York City tort cases increased from less than 1 percent of all civil cases in 1870 to 3.6 percent in 1890, and then to almost 12 percent in 1910 (Bergstrom, 1992: 31–57). Bergstrom found that the increase in New York City tort suits reflected neither radical changes in the kinds of hazards that gave rise to the injuries in question nor changes in the law. The critical development, he concludes, was a shift in the attitudes of claimants and jurors—toward a greater willingness to perceive and impose responsibility for injury on others, particularly on the organizations that managed enterprises and technologies (chapter 7). For a similar increase in tort suits in Boston, see Robert Silverman (1981); and in St. Louis, Wayne McIntosh (1980–1981: 832, 836). Tort cases swelled from 5.7 percent of state supreme court cases in 1870–1880 to 16.4 percent in 1905–1935 (Kagan et al., 1977: 142).

9. The argument for enterprise liability, as in workers compensation law, is that it advances the goal of reducing the social costs of accidents in the most economically efficient way. Organized enterprises have greater capacity than individual customers to learn from experience and *prevent* injuries. They have greater capacity to bear the immediate costs, and under enterprise liability would have the incentive to build the cost of injuries arising from their business into the prices they charge, passing the cost of the business's goods or services on to those who demand them.

10. The avoidability standard means that "injuries are compensable if they would not have occurred in the hands *of a highly skilled and experienced physician in the relevant specialty.*" That standard is much more generous than the American negligence standard, which "compensates only those injuries resulting from care that fell below the customary standard of care that would be rendered by *a reasonable practitioner*" (Mello, Kachalia, Studdert, 2011: 4) (emphasis added).

11. In Sweden, for example, specialized no-fault plans for motor vehicle accidents, industrial injuries, medical malpractice, and adverse reactions to pharmaceuticals are said to have (1) reduced the incidence of arguments between accident victims and insurance companies over who caused the injury, (2) standardized the amounts awarded, and (3) diverted most disputes to a special board, whose informal but expeditious, expertise-based judgments rarely are appealed to the courts or to formal arbitration (Hellner, 1986; Oldertz, 1986).

12. In 2005, a New Zealand law adopted a new "treatment injury" standard, providing compensation for "a physical injury causally related to treatment by a registered health professional that is not a necessary part or ordinary consequence of the treatment" (Mello, Kachalia, and Studdert, 2011, 4). This comes fairly close to a true no-fault standard.

13. In addition to medical expenses and lost earnings, the New Zealand scheme originally allowed limited recoveries (up to about $18,000) for intangibles such as pain and suffering and loss of function; but in 1992 recoveries for pain and suffering were eliminated to reduce overall costs. Injured persons were, however, authorized to bring tort actions for damages not covered under the compensation scheme. The accident compensation system is funded by levies on employers and employees, a gasoline tax, and general revenues (Bell and O'Connell, 1997). If the Accident Commission determines that a negligent or inappropriate action occurred at the hands of a health care professional, it is supposed to communicate that information to the appropriate professional disciplinary body.

14. The Accident Commission rejects only a tiny proportion of the approximately 150,000 claims filed each year and judicial review proceedings are rare (Gellhorn, 1988: 194).

15. In 1990 in California's workers' compensation program, the litigation rate reached nearly 36 percent of claims (CWCI, 1991b). Direct litigation costs—fees for both sides' attorneys, forensic physicians, and so on—averaged over $7,000 per case in 1990; the average award for successful applicants was $11,879. See also CWCI (1991a); Frammolino (1988: 3).

16. Almost half of persons injured in *motor vehicle accidents* attempt to collect compensation from another party to the accident, pursuant to tort law. Yet only 3 of 100 *non-motor-vehicle accidents* lead to liability claims (Hensler et al., 1991). See also

the Wisconsin Civil Litigation Project, which surveyed households in five states. For every 1,000 potential tort cases, mostly involving personal injuries, 857 persons with grievances said they made claims against the alleged tortfeasor or an insurance company (about the same rate for most other kinds of legally cognizable grievances). Moreover, 57.9 percent of respondents with personal injury grievances saw a lawyer (much higher than the rate for most other kinds of grievances). But only 201 unresolved "disputes" emerged from the 857 grievances, and only 38 resulted in a lawsuit (Miller and Sarat, 1981: 544).

17. Health insurance or workers' compensation insurers can claim reimbursement for amounts paid to an injured person who subsequently obtains damages for the same expenses from the tortfeasor or his or her insurance company. In many cases, however, that leads to an additional adversarial, legalistic struggle.

18. See National Center for State Courts (1986); U.S. General Accounting Office (1988).

19. Annual TV advertising expenditures by lawyers, the Television Bureau of Advertising reports, grew from about $17 million in 1983 to over $100 million in 1991 (Geyelin, 1992).

20. According to the *New York Times,* 813 lawsuits were brought against tobacco companies in the period between 1954 and 1994. Of those suits, only twenty-three went to trial and the industry lost only twice; both losses were overturned on appeal (Collins, 1995).

21. The tobacco companies argued that there was no evidence that their denials had actually misled the smokers; that the state governments, knowing the risks, had allowed cigarettes to be marketed, while profiting from tobacco excise taxes; and, in a macabre vein, that even before taking tobacco tax revenues into account, government health care insurance programs actually *save* money on smokers, since they die earlier and with lower medical costs than nonsmokers (Viscusi, 1997: 27–32).

22. Ramseyer and Nakazato found that 80–95 percent of victims' families in fatal traffic accident cases file claims, and that in the ensuing settlements they "recover, on average, about 80–110 percent of the amount they would earn if they sued and won against a fully insured defendant" (Ramseyer and Nakazato, 1989: 280).

23. Daniel Foote (1995) provides an excellent account. The Tokyo traffic court judges, who led the movement, sought to create damage schedules that minimized the need for case-by-case examination (except for lost earnings) and sought to provide payments that did not vary according to the wealth or status of injured claimants, such as fixed sums for pain and suffering per month of hospitalization, and so on. They also worked out rules of thumb for assessing comparative fault in common accident scenarios. The judge-devised standards were disseminated, Foote points out, in a special 161-page issue of a mass circulation newspaper in 1975. Judges meet to reconcile divergent practices in courts in different cities. See also Ramsmeyer and Nakazato (1989: 269).

24. See Ramsmeyer and Nakazato (1989: 270): "Parties are far more likely to make similar estimates of the litigated outcome under the relatively clear and unified Japanese system than under the plastic and fragmented American one." The lesser degree of predictability in the United States leads to more litigation. Atiyah

and Summers (1987: 176) make a similar point: "The findings and awards of American juries are much less predictable than those of English judges, and unpredictability leads to uncertainty which naturally encourages more litigation and more appeals."

25. A California Department of Motor Vehicles official estimated in 1991 that of 18 million registered drivers, 4 to 6 million lower-income Californians—at least a quarter of all motorists—were driving without insurance (Wiebel, 1991).

26. See also Munch (1977: 38–39).

27. For a study indicating less consistency in punitive damages awards, see Sunstein, Kahnemann, and Schkade (1999).

28. The Harvard medical injury study, based on a careful review of hospital records in New York, discovered that fewer than one in three *serious* injuries apparently stemming from negligence led to a malpractice suit. See Harvard Medical Practice Study (1990).

29. According to an expert panel's review of over 1,000 claims against anesthesiologists, among plaintiffs who received *inadequate* care, one in five did not receive any compensation (Cheney et al., 1989).

30. In the same intensive review of claims against anesthesiologists cited in the preceding endnote, the expert panel concluded that 46 percent of the claimants had *not* received inadequate care. But of those, 42 percent received compensation—although not as much as those with comparable injuries for whom the care was found to be inadequate (Cheney et al., 1989: 1601–1602; Metzloff, 1993: 1181). A study of medical malpractice claims in Hawaii found that in 24 percent of the claims for which a screening panel deemed no liability, the claimant nevertheless filed suit. Of the fifty-one closed cases in that category, plaintiffs received some compensation in thirty cases (or 60 percent); and in ten cases, more than $100,000 (Metzloff, 1988: 209). See also Farber and White (1991: 203–204) (an expert panel review of 252 cases from one hospital found that of 95 cases found to involve *appropriate* care, 24 percent received some payment). See also Sloan and Van Wert (1991: 131–168).

31. See Bovbjerg et al. (1991: 15–16) (1980 malpractice verdicts were 6.5 times higher than reported auto accident verdicts; in a 1985 study, eleven times higher). See also Hammit et al. (1985: 754–755) (finding that "medical malpractice awards against doctors are almost 2.5 times as great as awards against other individuals in average case types, and awards against hospitals are 85 percent larger").

32. But see Vidmar (1993).

33. For other studies questioning tort law's effectiveness as a deterrent, see Schwartz (1994: 381–382); Laitin (1994); Abel (1990); Elliot (1989); Grady (1988: 305–306); Bruce (1984); Flemming (1984); O'Connell (1979); Dunlop (1975).

34. After reviewing a number of studies, Gary Schwartz (1994: 402) concluded that American malpractice law probably leads to "a substantial measure" of both the desirable and the excessive kinds of "defensive medicine." See also Mendelson and Rubin (1993) and Weiler (1991). In a study of a large urban hospital in Indiana, 34.5 percent of physicians responded that the threat of malpractice liability was a significant influence on the ordering of tests and procedures, and 29.3 percent said it was a major influence (McIntosh and Murray, 1994: 26). The researchers

estimated that legal liability added $450 in costs per patient admitted, of which defensive medicine, whereby doctors order unnecessary tests and procedures in order to avoid legal liability, contributed $327 or 3.9 percent of the of total medical costs per patient.

35. Compare Danzon (1991: 203) ("Informed observers believe that the elimination of liability [in New Zealand] has led to laxer standards of medical care") with Gellhorn (1988: 200) ("No study has shown that, as a consequence [of New Zealand's 1974 reform] the quality of medical service has suffered"). See also Brown (1985: 1002).

36. For example, in October 1997 a South Carolina jury handed down a $250 million punitive damages award against Chrysler Motors; the case involved serious injuries to a child in 1990, when he was thrown from a 1985 Plymouth minivan after an accident. The jury found Chrysler at fault for failure to put a stronger latch on the rear door. But Chrysler, under pressure from the National Highway Traffic Safety Agency, had strengthened the latches beginning in the 1995 model year, two years before the verdict, and had recalled earlier models for repairs (Geyelin, 1997).

37. Although all liability suits against manufacturers alleged that design or manufacturing defects led to the crashes, neither Federal Aviation Administration nor National Transport Safety Board investigations of 203 Beechcraft accidents that led to liability claims or lawsuits in the 1980s found that any were due to such defects. Pilot error was the predominant cause (Martin, 1991: 485). At best, Craig (1991: 457) finds that "some evidence suggests that liability litigation has improved the dissemination of information about flight safety, and that, arguably, has encouraged pilots to fly their planes more safely."

38. A spokesman for Cessna, once the leading American manufacturer of small aircraft, stated that the company had spent an average of $20 to $25 million annually on defending product liability suits–the same amount the company previously had spent on research and development of small aircraft (Weintraub, 1994a: D1). After the bill was passed, Cessna returned to the business of building small airplanes and announced plans to build 2,000 planes a year in the future (Bryant, 1995).

39. The risky clients, of course, go on to hire less prominent and perhaps more compliant accountants, presumably increasing the risk of fraud to the public.

40. Finally, after some companies were sued for not warning subsequent employers about a former employee's violent tendencies, a number of states passed laws providing employers with varying degrees of protection against defamation suits. Similarly, high school guidance counselors and college admissions offices complain that fear of litigation by parents has made high schools much more cautious about saying anything negative about students in letters of recommendation (Bronner, 1998).

41. See also Huber (1985); Kitch (1985); Lunzer (1985: 256).

42. Galanter (1998) emphasizes that McDonald's coffee was hotter than the standard in the trade; that the company had experienced some 700 prior claims, some of which it had settled; that McDonald's had rejected subsequent settlement proposals by the plaintiff's lawyer and by a court-appointed mediator that called

for a $225,000 payment; and that the parties eventually settled for approximately $600,000. From this system blame perspective, McDonald's is apparently to be faulted for not settling all cases regardless of the plaintiff's negligence.

43. At the extremes of the excess claims phenomena are occasional criminal enterprises, including one in New York City that, according to a well-sourced *New York Times* article, was "masterminded by organized crime figures from the former Soviet Union." In the scheme, "Staged or exaggerated car accidents were used to generate a tidal wave of 'patients.' Transportation companies then took the patients—often low-level criminals—to what in many instances were sham medical clinics, diagnostic testing offices, and acupuncture and physical therapy offices. Billing companies were created to collect money from insurers and management companies then siphoned the funds out to the scheme's operators. Some operators were so bold that they sued insurers that had stopped paying after they realized they were being defrauded" (Rashbaum et al., 2018).

44. The California State Automobile Association's guide on what to do in an accident unequivocally states, "Do not discuss the accident with anyone, sign anything (except a traffic ticket), accept blame, or blame anyone until you contact your insurance company" (CSAA, 1997: 12). See generally Wagatsuma and Rossett (1986). At an accident and injury seminar held for the public by lawyers and chiropractors in California, a lawyer told the audience that after an accident, "If you say you feel OK, I guarantee that little statement will come back to haunt you" (Rubinstein, 1997: C1).

45. Peter Pringle (1998), a British journalist, argues that in Britain the tobacco companies have been more forthcoming than in the United States because until very recently they were not threatened by lawsuits there.

46. As noted earlier, in 1986 Congress, while leaving claimants the option to bring a tort suit, enacted an enterprise liability law that enabled parents of children who suffered side effects from vaccines to recover substantial but not unlimited damages from the manufacturer without proving fault (Burke, 2002; Barnes & Burke, 2015). In 1987 the state of Virginia adopted a no-fault law that guarantees compensation for babies born with defects or who suffer injuries during or immediately after birth—even if the doctors, nurses, or hospitals have not been negligent (Sugarman, 1989: 109). Florida enacted a similar "bad baby law," but it allows for tort cases as well. The Florida compensation program has cut transactions costs compared to tort claims, but lawyers seem to have worked to restrict the program's visibility and use (Bovbjerg, Sloan, and Rankin, 1997). And in 2001 Congress created the September 11th Victim Compensation Fund, which provided economic compensation and limited pain-and-suffering payments to persons physically injured due to the terrorist attacks on the World Trade Center and the Pentagon and to the families of those killed. In contrast to tort law, claimants did not have to prove any entity (such as the airlines, the airports, etc.) at fault, or share their recovery with contingency-fee lawyers. The fund was administered, and disputes resolved, by a special master and the bureaucracy he established.

47. Mello, Kachalia, and Studdert (2011: 5–7) found that in the New Zealand, Sweden, and Denmark medical injury compensation systems, about 10 percent of injured patients file claims, compared to 2 to 3 percent in the negligence-based

U.S. tort system, and that claims in those countries are more likely to result in compensation, although in much smaller amounts than successful tort claims in the United States. "In 2009, the average compensation paid per claim was approximately US$20,000 in Sweden and US$40,000 in Denmark, compared to approximately $324,000 in the U.S." (7). In the three national systems studied, claims can be filed free of charge without the need for legal counsel. Primary care providers often assist in the preparation of claims. And claims are resolved in a fraction of the time that it takes to settle malpractice claims in the U.S. tort system.

48. Lipsen (1991: 248–249) wrote that in the mid-1980s to the early '90s forty-one states adopted tort law changes generally favorable to defendants. "The most popular changes include: revising the doctrine of joint and several liability (thirty-one states); modifying the collateral source rule (twenty states); altering common law treatment of punitive damages (twenty-five states); and establishing defenses for compliance with the 'state of the art' (eleven states), and government standards (nine states). Additionally, seventeen states have limited 'pain and suffering' damages."

49. In 1988, for example, Chief Justice Lucas wrote an opinion that overturned a 1979 decision that had facilitated injury victims' suits against insurance companies for "bad faith" resistance to compensation claims. Similarly, Lucas wrote an opinion limiting the damages employees can collect in unjust termination cases (Chiang, 1996b).

50. *BMW of North America v. Gore* (1996), *State Farm Mutual Insurance Co. v. Campbell* (2003). See also *Philip Morris USA v. Williams* (2007).

51. There was no comparable decline in cases brought on behalf of victims of negligent driving by tractor-trailer trucks, to which the medical malpractice damage cap did not apply and which typically do not confront the plaintiff's lawyer with such expensive case preparation expenses (Daniels and Martin, 2015: 212) Further evidence of the impact of damage caps is provided by Albert Yoon (2001), who compared medical malpractice litigation in Alabama and neighboring states. He found that after the Alabama legislature in 1987 capped on awards for noneconomic damages, average monetary recoveries by Alabama plaintiffs decreased by roughly $20,000 but increased by roughly double that amount after the Alabama Supreme Court ruled the cap unconstitutional in three decisions, 1991–1995.

8. Adversarial Legalism and the Welfare State

1. Constitution of Chile, 1925, article 10, no. 14. The Chilean Constitution also committed the state to apportion sufficient money for a national health care system (Couso, 1997).

2. For comparative statistics, see OECD, 2017. Under the 1935 National Labor Relations Act (NLRA), power to negotiate a favorable collective bargaining agreement flows to a union that manages to win an election among workers at a particular worksite. That workplace-by-workplace organizational structure often puts a unionized company at a competitive disadvantage vis-à-vis lower-wage non-union companies in the same industry—and gives employers incentives to resist

unionization. The 1947 Taft-Hartley Act, amending the NLRA, compounded those negative incentives for unionization by (1) outlawing secondary boycotts (an important union tool for organizing competing nonunion workplaces); and (2) authorizing states to enact right to work laws, under which employees in unionized workplaces may not be compelled to join a union or to pay union dues automatically (while generally receiving the same benefits as union members who contribute). Right to work laws were adopted by all the states in the low-wage Deep South, by many states in the Rocky Mountain West, and recently, by three states in the Midwest (for a current total of twenty-seven of the fifty states). Western European countries, in contrast, have labor laws that support a tradition of *national-level collective bargaining* between peak associations of employers and labor unions. This tends to level the competitive playing field among workplaces in the same industry, regardless of level of union membership (Kagan, 1990a).

3. In recent years, for example, political conservatives have successfully weakened the economic and political power of unions representing public sector employees. Republican governments in Wisconsin and Idaho severely restricted such unions' collective bargaining rights. In 2018, a 5:4 U.S. Supreme Court majority held that government workers covered by union contracts, but who had not joined the unions, could no longer be compelled by those contracts to pay fees (akin to union dues) to cover those costs (*Janus v. American Federation of State, County and Municipal Enterprises*, 2018).

4. The U.S. federal government compels governmentally subsidized hospitals to provide emergency care to all, including the uninsured. Major taxpayer-financed programs provide health insurance for the elderly (Medicare), the very poor (Medicaid), and the military (including veterans). Most government employees—federal, state, and local—receive statutorily mandated health benefits. Most large- and medium-sized businesses, universities, and other nonprofit organizations voluntarily provide employees health insurance as an employee benefit, although significant employee contributions increasingly are required. The 2010 Affordable Care Act (ACA) *required* employers with fifty or more employees to provide health care coverage. The ACA also expanded Medicaid programs to cover the near poor, although due to a Supreme Court ruling, conservative Republican state governments were authorized to choose not to contribute to and offer that expanded coverage, and those benefit increases were not approved by many conservative Republican state governments. Finally, the ACA required otherwise uninsured adults to buy health care policies through government-operated health insurance marketplaces and provided government subsidies to help pay for those premiums. The ACA remains politically controversial and vulnerable to repeal or crippling constraints by Republican political leaders.

5. In the early 1990s the lowest-paid decile (10 percent) of male employees in Western European countries earned almost 70 percent of the *median* wage in their countries; the lowest paid decile in the United States earned only 38 percent of the median wage. Richard Freeman (1994: 13) wrote, "I estimate that among men in the bottom decile, Americans earn roughly 45 percent of what Germans earn, 54 percent as much as Norwegians, half as much as Italians, and so on." These disparities reflect not only the higher minimum wage laws in Europe but

also the fact that a much larger proportion of European workers are covered by collective bargaining agreements than are American workers—which in turn stems in large measure from differences in American labor law (Freeman, 1994; Kagan, 1990a).

6. In recent years, facing persistent high unemployment, some European welfare states have curtailed some benefits. Nevertheless, an analysis by the Center on Budget and Policy Priorities indicates that a single parent of three in France, unemployed for several years, would receive $1,166 monthly in cash benefits from the government, whereas her counterpart in the United States would receive $767 in AFDC and food stamps (Whitney, 1998: A1).

7. In the United States, the inflation-adjusted real value of benefits from AFDC and TANF, the major welfare programs for poor mothers and children, has declined from its peak level in the early 1970s (Lieberman, 2005: 2). Legal changes in the mid-1990s limiting the duration of benefits and encouraging work, plus expansion of federal low income tax credit payments to working mothers, led to sharp reductions in the percentage of families on traditional welfare rolls (Halpern-Meekin et al, 2015) but heightened the inequality in benefits between the working poor and the worst off individuals and families (Lieberman, 2005: 3).

8. According to OECD data, in 2015 taxes in the United States (federal, state, and local combined) equaled 26.4 percent of GDP, while the OECD average was over 34 percent. German taxes were over 36 percent of GDP and in France, 45 percent (Porter, 2017a).

9. Jacob Hacker (2002) showed that in 1995, public social welfare expenditures in the United States equaled only 17.1 percent of GDP (as compared to 35–37 percent in Scandinavian countries, and 25–30 percent in Germany, the Netherlands, Italy, and the U.K.). However, private expenditures for the same purposes (often subsidized through tax deductions) were much higher in the United States, amounting to 8.3 percent of GDP, which narrows the U.S.–Western European difference in total social provision somewhat.

10. Since 2000, according OECD data, a number of countries—including Norway, the United Kingdom, Japan, and the Netherlands—have surpassed the United States in the percentage of young people obtaining a university degree (Hacker and Pierson, 2010: 29; Porter, 2014). In the United States, by 2014, state and local financing for public higher education, on a per student basis, had fallen by 30 percent over the preceding decade. Access to higher education has also become more unequal, as students have been forced to rely on loans to attend college. Again, relying on OECD data, Porter (2014: B8) reports that, "College enrollment after the first year is five times as high for high-income students as for low-income students" and those drop-outs (as well as graduates) often are saddled with very high debts. The absence of governmentally-provided early childcare is another obstacle for low-income mothers seeking higher education (Druckerman, 2016). Moreover, access to higher education is especially important in the United States, where "nearly 30 percent of Americans without a high school diploma live in poverty, compared to 5 percent with a college degree. . . . But in 28 other wealthy developed countries, a lack of a high school diploma increases the probability of poverty by less than 5 percent" (Shell, 2018).

11. OECD figures indicate that the United States spends a smaller proportion of gross domestic product on public pensions than any of the sixteen rich democracies studied except for Ireland and Australia. American public pensions (Social Security) are also less generous than most, replacing only 30 percent of the average wage, compared to over 50 percent in Sweden, France, Japan, New Zealand, and Belgium, and 39 percent or more in Italy, Germany, Austria, Denmark, and the Netherlands. Great Britain, like the United States, has a large privately provided pension system and a correspondingly less generous public system (*Economist*, 1996b: 105).

12. Recent journalistic analyses indicate that more than half of Americans below the poverty line must spend more than 50 percent of their income on housing, and millions pay up to 70 percent (*Economist*, 2018; Thrush, 2018).

13. Those page counts are conservative figures, arrived at by careful journalists (Giffey, 2012; O'Donnell and Akinnibi, 2013) who were justifiably skeptical of far larger page-counts publicized by opponents of the Affordable Care Act.

14. It is not easy for courts to deal with such complex policy and budgetary issues wisely. Sanders and Schoenbrod (2003) provide a detailed account of a class action, filed in mid-1979 against the huge, financially-pressed New York City school system. The plaintiffs charged that school administrators, in violation of the federal law, had been unconscionably slow in assessing which students needed special classes or services, and that they had engaged in racial and ethnic discrimination in their assessments. The lawsuit led to multiyear judicially-supervised consent decree, a highly contentious lawyer-dominated oversight system, rushed individual child assessments (in order to meet court-imposed deadlines), and massive expenditures that drained funds from the city's regular education system.

15. In a similar U.S.-German contrast, when U.S. officials suspect American physicians, hospitals, or HMOs of seeking excessive reimbursement, they often bring civil or criminal actions in general courts. In Germany those disputes are decided by special arbitration committees, staffed by representatives of the health care plans and the doctor's union, and its decisions are appealable to the social courts (Jost, 1998). In the United States legislatures and judges (rather than specialists as in Germany) end up trying to draw fine distinctions between justifiable and nonjustifiable medical services and between fraud and excusable error by providers, and then embed those distinctions in penal laws. Medical malpractice litigation has likewise become an important mechanism for regulating the efforts of managed care plans to constrain physicians' decisions about costly individual services for patients; hence American judges and juries make many decisions about which restrictions on provision are justifiable (Sage, 1999).

16. See Sugarman (1985a). This section draws extensively on Sugarman's account and analysis.

17. Illinois, California, New York, and Oregon, like Connecticut, had enacted rules curtailing benefits for AFDC mothers who declined to cooperate in identifying their children's fathers. Lower federal courts had ruled, in separate cases, that these states had violated federal law. In 1973 the Nixon administration's Department of Health, Education and Welfare (HEW), refusing to acquiesce in those courts' interpretation of the federal law, issued regulations stating that benefits *could*

be withheld. In a new case a U.S. District Court held that those HEW regulations conflicted with the federal statute. In March 1975 the Supreme Court affirmed that decision (Sugarman, 1985a: 405–406).

18. It is telling in this regard that the U.S. Fair Housing Act (1968), which did *not* provide federal officials with strong injunctive and other enforcement powers, and did *not* include fee shifting and monetary damage provisions that fostered private enforcement, was quite unsuccessful in deterring racial discrimination in the housing market in the 1960s, 1970s, and 1980s (Massey and Denton, 1993: chapter 7).

19. Citing several recent labor market studies, Lieberman (2005: 2) writes, "By 2002, nearly one-fourth of employed blacks held professional or managerial jobs (compared to 35 percent for non-Hispanic whites), more than three times the proportion in 1960. And despite decades of stagnation, the wage gap beween black and white workers remains historically small."

20. In a typical year in the 1970s, according to Mashaw (1983: 18), approximately 10,000 decisions by the Social Security Administration Appeals Council led to filings for judicial review in the federal courts.

21. *Dandridge v. Williams* (1970).

22. One prominent exception stems from late nineteenth or early twentieth century state constitutions that require states to provide public education for children. As discussed later in this chapter, many state courts, beginning in the 1970s, interpreted those provisions to require state governments to provide more financial aid for poorly funded local school districts.

23. For a striking comparison of poor urban neighborhoods in the United States and France, see Loic Wacquant (1995: 543–570). See also McLanahan and Garfinkel (1995) for an analysis indicating that the American welfare system has tended to promote greater dependency than France's and Sweden's more generous systems. One reason, they argue, is that American programs generally have failed to cover poor fathers. Another is that they provide fewer incentives for welfare recipients to seek and stay employed—partly because the United States doesn't provide guarantees of health care and other universal benefits for all families, employed or not, and partly because American governments have not provided generously subsidized child care.

24. The threat of wrongful termination or antidiscrimination lawsuits, as experienced by employers, is heightened by the atypical accounts of such cases in the press and in the literature put out by the U.S. Chamber of Commerce, defense lawyers' organizations, and human resources professional journals. Berrey, Nelson, and Nielsen (2017: 51–52) note that "national and local media coverage of employment cases report an overall plaintiff win-rate nearly three times the actual win-rate of 32%. Moroever . . . newspaper accounts of awards . . . have a median value of well over $1 million, [compared to] the actual median award of $150,000."

25. Berrey, Nelson, and Nielsen (2017: 47), summarizing a well-constructed nationwide survey by researchers at Rutgers University, note that 28 percent of African American workers said they had experienced workplace discrimination due to race in the past year, compared to 6 percent of white respondents. Of those who reported such unfair treatment, only 19 percent filed a complaint according

to company procedures, and only 3 percent said they sued the company or a co-worker. Suing might include filing a complaint with the federal Equal Employment Opportunity Commission or a state-level civil rights agency.

26. The Supreme Court's opinion encompassed two cases it considered at the same time. *Faragher v. City of Boca Raton* (1998); *Burlington Industries, Inc. v. Ellerth* (1998).

27. See generally Jackson (1985). This is not so in France, where local taxes on corporations contribute some 50 percent of municipal tax receipts, and local governments compete—as in the United States—to attract businesses (Levy, 1999: chapter 4).

28. The New Jersey legislation empowered suburbs to discharge their fair share obligation by subsidizing construction of low-income housing in older cities. The legislation also replaced lawsuits, a potent mechanism, with a less forceful state administrative system for determining each municipality's housing obligations.

29. On Louisville, see Wilkerson (1979: chapter 9). In Los Angeles a court order based on the state constitution created a massive busing plan, blending students from widely different communities in a huge county-wide school district. When the program was first instituted in 1978 for grades four through eight, one-way rides averaged almost fifty minutes. Massive numbers of students were withdrawn from the public schools. After busing was extended to other grades, white flight increased further, so that racial and ethnic integration did not really increase. Moreover, California voters in 1979 overwhelmingly voted for a ballot initiative prohibiting court-ordered busing except as a remedy for explicit violations of the federal constitution (Kagan, 1982).

30. In the wake of the New Jersey Supreme Court's *Robinson v. Cahill* decision in 1973, the Education Law Center challenged the state's school finance plans in court almost every year, resulting in no fewer than ten subsequent state supreme court decisions, each more detailed than its predecessor. One court order closed the state's public schools entirely until the legislature agreed to enact a state income tax to supplement the local property tax system. Another court order compelled the governor to raise the income tax, which led to his defeat in the next election Lehne, 1978). A 1997 New Jersey Supreme Court decision criticized the state's funding model for not providing enough money for security guards in urban schools (Goodnough, 1997).

31. There is considerable debate about how much spending differences matter in terms of educational performance. Spending in the United States in rich and poor districts alike is high in cross-national terms. In 1991 annual per-pupil expenditure for elementary and secondary schools in the United States averaged $5,780, compared to $1,768 in Belgium, $1,982 in Ireland, $2,450 in Spain, $3,559 in the United Kingdom, and $3,785 in France (Heise, 1995: 1743). On the correlation, or lack of it, between per-pupil expenditures and educational quality and achievement, see Hanushek (1989, 1994); Odden and Picus (1992: 277–281); Melnick (2016).

9. Adversarial Legalism and the Regulatory State

1. David Vogel (2012) makes the case that in recent decades, European risk control regulations, which earlier had been *less* stringent than their counterparts in the United States, now have become *more* stringent.

2. This distinctive characteristic of Japanese regulation has been analyzed by scholars in the United States and Japan. See, for example, Upham (1987); Haley (1986); Young (1984); Yamanouchi (1974).

3. Aoki and Cioffi (2000) note that the agency's chief of environmental enforcement later apologized in private to company officials for what he conceded was unfairly harsh treatment.

4. Aoki and Cioffi (2000: 53) acknowledge that "whereas the informal Japanese regulatory system appears to have been quite effective in the case of sophisticated, well-staffed companies like PREMCO, environmental contamination remains a serious problem in Japan," at least partly due to ineffective regulation of smaller and financially weak companies.

5. For example, John Dwyer and colleagues compared Ford Motor Company's experience with air pollution controls at its German and American assembly plants. German and American regulations, they noted, prescribed similar emissions levels for the pollutants produced during the vehicle painting process, and both required use of the best available control technology. The EPA's regulations, however, prescribed specific emission levels for each of three different coating processes, while the German regulations called for a single overall emission limit for the plant, which gives manufacturers more flexibility in adjusting production runs and processes and reduces monitoring and reporting requirements (Dwyer, Brooks, and Marco, 2000). See also Rose-Ackerman (1995).

6. American regulatory agencies also use administrative guidance to flesh out or supplement legally binding regulatory rules. Increasingly, they have used rules labeled "guidance" in order to bypass the slow, formal rule-making process and avoid the risk of judicial review or reversal (Farber, 2014; Melnick, 2018b). Research by Nicholas Parillo (2017) has found, however, that front-line American bureaucrats apply the guidance rules literally rather than flexibly, so as to reduce the risk of criticism for treating regulated entities inconsistently. And regulated entities often regard the guidance as binding, since that reduces the risk of legal trouble with the agency.

7. In an earlier publication on the density of legal rules, I wrote, "The U.S. water pollution regulations, for example, are 3.6 times as long as the U.S. Clean Water Act (and 4.5 times the length of Japan's water regulations). The total combined length of U.S. air and water pollution statutes and implementing regulations, according to Cooter and Ginsburg, 1996: 306) are 6.6 times as long as the Japanese statutes and regulations, and 14 times as long as the U.K.'s" (Kagan, 2010: 6).

8. In 1989, Braithwaite (1993: 23–24) reports, California and Texas imposed 1,800 and 1,700 administrative penalties respectively, although most states imposed fewer than 100. New Jersey suspended admissions on more than 130 occasions, Texas 218 times. In 1989, 53 nursing homes in the United States had their licenses revoked, and 130 were decertified for purposes of receiving vital Medicaid benefits.

9. Among the most prominent exceptions are the federal Occupational Safety and Health Act and the federal Mine Safety Act,, in which criminal convictions of individual corporate officials are treated as misdemeanors.

10. 33 U.S.C. §1319(c)(d); Cal. Water Code §§13385–13386.

11. In a 2010, according to Daniel Ulmann (2014), who studied federal legal actions for violations of environmental laws, the Justice Department filed 172 civil actions in court, compared to 111 criminal actions. These figures are dwarfed by the 1802 *administrative penalty* actions filed by the Environmental Protection Administration–actions taken by the agency itself, rather than referring the cases to the Department of Justice for civil actions or prosecutions in court. Similar ratios between administrative penalty actions, civil suits for damages, and criminal prosecutions were found by Jeremy Firestone (2003) in study of EPA enforcement cases, 1990–1997.

12. As of April 2015 British Petroleum had set aside $42 *billion* for fines, victim compensation, natural resource damages, and clean-up costs (*Economist*, 2015). That included $5.4 billion (as of July 2015) in civil damage awards to adversely affected businesses and individuals; $4 billion in criminal penalties; $5.5 billion in civil damages under the Clean Water Act; $7.1 billion under the National Resource Damage assessment law; and $6 billion in economic damages to state and local governments.

13. Similarly, small employers rarely are subjected to lawsuits by rejected minority job applicants; studies show that they often continue to discriminate against young black males (Pager, 2007; Pager and Western, 2005).

14. For a discussion of American business culture in this context, see Vogel (1986). According to Daniel Okimoto (1989: 158), government-business relations in Japan are "informal, close, cooperative, flexible, reciprocal, non-litigious, and long-term in orientation," while in the United States most business-government relations "can be characterized as formal, distant, rigid, suspicious, legalistic, narrow, and short-term oriented."

15. In some fields, regulations in some European nations impose *greater* delays and obstacles than do American regulations. For example, they often make it harder and slower to open a new business, a large discount store, to grow genetically modified agricultural products, and most significantly, to dismiss redundant employees.

16. After the 2016 election, Republicans controlled both the legislature and the governor's office in twenty-four states. Almost two-thirds of the states had Republican governors, and in almost two-thirds, both houses of the state legislature had Republican majorities.

17. It should be noted, however, that several politically liberal state governments in the United States have enacted fairly ambitious regulatory laws aimed at carbon emissions reduction. For a detailed journalistic account of the conservatives' political and legal efforts to halt governmental efforts to combat emission of greenhouse gases, see Davenport and Lipton (2017).

18. Thus in the 2009–2016 period, the Obama administration pushed important new statutes through Congress or issued new regulations aimed at controlling offshore oil drilling in deeper waters, improving food safety standards, increasing

reserve requirements and risk management obligations in major financial institutions, regulating home mortgage and other forms of consumer lending, compelling motor vehicle manufacturers to meet tougher fuel economy standards, preventing unfair treatment by private health insurance companies, pushing hospitals and physicians to curtail redundant medical procedures and hospital admissions, reducing carbon emissions from coal-burning electric utility plants, and more. Some of the Obama-era regulations may be successfully repealed by the Trump administration, but some probably will survive, while others may eventually be reenacted.

10. Economic Development, Environmental Protection, and Adversarial Legalism

1. I would like to thank Earl Finbar Murphy of the College of Law, Ohio State University, for calling Rosenthal's impressive book to my attention.

2. A 1790 French law states that the "judicial functions are and will remain forever separate from the administrative functions. The judges will not be allowed . . . to disturb in any manner whatsoever, the activities of the administrative corps, nor to summon before them administrators, concerning their functions" (Abraham, 1980: 272). On the decline of project-blocking litigation after the legal reforms of the French Revolution, see Rosenthal (1992: 52–53, 95–96, 119, 137, 179).

3. Andrew Savage (1995: 374) explained, "The Harbor is partially enclosed by islands and the coastline, and that, accompanied by the shallow depths of the Inner Harbor, results in only about seventeen percent of the Harbor's water being rejuvenated in any one tidal cycle. As a result, a substantial amount of the effluent discharged into the Harbor, as well as the pollution carried to the Harbor by the incoming rivers, simply stagnates in the Harbor waters and/or settles to its floor. In addition to the daily effluent discharges, until December 1991, Boston would release approximately 400,000 to 500,000 gallons (50 to 70 dry tons) of sludge into the Harbor daily. Sludge is composed of the greases and scum that have been skimmed off the top of the effluent and the heavier materials, including settleable solids and some suspended solids that settle to the bottom of the effluent. Duplicating the mistakes of the past, the MSS relied on discharging the sludge on the outgoing tide in the hope that it would reduce the amount of sludge in the Harbor. The discharge of the sludge resulted each day in a three-mile-long stream of sludge floating through Boston Harbor, dotted with grease balls and tampon applicators."

4. Garrity was quoted as saying "It is regrettable in terms of the vitality of democratic institutions that a judge has to kick ass to get the political branch to do what is in the public interest" (Dolin 2005: 122).

5. A legal analysis prepared by the Center for Law in the Public Interest, analyzing federal cases concerning the adequacy of environmental impact statements, conceded that there was very little encouraging precedent available (Detlefsen, 1994: 16).

6. Although most occupants of dwellings in the right-of-way had long since found new housing with the aid of federal relocation grants, the plaintiffs' argument was

that the freeway project had demolished 6,000 dwellings, that the housing stock of the communities had thereby been depleted, and that Caltrans was obligated to mitigate its adverse impact on the human environment.

7. An *Economist* article (1996a) pointed out that not only do cars in traffic jams cause three times the pollution of free-flowing traffic but that, "Hell is not other people, as [Jean Paul Sartre] claimed, it is other people in other cars in front of you, holding you up in a traffic jam."

8. Soundwalls alone, erected at the behest of municipalities along the route, cost $500,000 per mile (Trombley and Hebert, 1987a, 1987b).

9. Of the 113 mitigation projects listed by the Central Artery Environmental Oversight Committee, fewer than fifty were directly related to the project. The others, which sound worthy in and of themselves, included a study of the feasibility of water transportation to North Shore suburbs; improvements to the Lynn, Massachusetts, Central Square bus terminal and parking facilities; $150 million for the city of Cambridge; $80 million for a new park along the Charles River; a $5 million rat control program; and $5 million for restoring a long-graveled-over marsh in Revere, Massachusetts (Palmer, 1994).

10. In the 1976–1982 period, an average of fifty-six court cases were filed against the Nuclear Regulatory Commission *each year*, mostly alleging failure to follow procedural requirements concerning safety and siting (Delmas and Heiman, 2001). See generally Boyle (1998); Joppke (1993); Barkenbus (1984); Weingast (1980). The actuality or threat of litigation resulted in mounting delays in licensing processes for nuclear plants—from an average of twelve months for plants completed in 1960 to thirty-three months for those completed in 1973, and fifty-six months for 1981 plants (Chubb, 1989: 85). Chubb noted that in France, as in other countries, power plants "equivalent to American reactors in quality and safety . . . [were] built in much less time and at far lower cost" (75). Beginning in the early 1980s German courts issued rulings that sharply curtailed the role of courts in antinuclear litigation (Greve, 1989b: 212–213). The American courts did not.

11. 33 C.F.R. §320.4(a)(1).

12. For one relatively small dredging project in Boston Harbor in which no major controversy or litigation occurred, the cost of consulting contracts for environmental testing and report writing represented approximately 25 percent of the cost of the actual dredging and disposal (Kagan, 1990b: 112).

13. In principle, legal commands concerning interagency consultation will encourage true interagency collaboration and problem-solving. Sometimes that does occur, but more often busy bureaucrats simply communicate through memoranda forged within, not across, agencies. On the obstacles to interagency collaboration in an institutionally and legally fragmented system (and on ways in which those obstacles can be and sometimes have been surmounted), see Bardach (1998).

14. On some topics, however, Canadian and U.S. policy responses diverge. See Hoberg (1990).

15. The acronyms in the text have the following referents: CERCLA—Comprehensive Environmental Response, Compensation, and Liability Act of 1980;

FIFRA–Federal Insecticide, Fungicide, and Rodenticide Act; RCRA–Resource Conservation and Recovery Act; TSCA–Toxic Substances Control Act.

16. Cited in Schrecker (1992: 95–96).

Afterword

1. Plaintiffs' tort lawyers I have spoken with claim that these negative stereotypes about undeserving claimants and greedy lawyers now affect the attitudes of jurors–and probably many politicians as well. See also Burke (2002).

2. After the 2016 election, Republicans controlled both the legislature and the governor's office in twenty-four states. Almost two-thirds of the states had Republican governors, and in almost two-thirds, both houses of the state legislature had Republican majorities.

3. On the current U.S. Supreme Court, Chief Justice Roberts, Justice Thomas, and Justice Alito are affiliates of the conservative Federalist Society. So was the late Justice Scalia (Hollis-Brusky, 2015) and so is his 2017 replacement, Neil Gorsuch, as well as Justice Kennedy's 2019 replacement, Brett Kavanaugh.

4. Republican efforts to weaken the *private class action bar* in particular date back to the Reagan administration in the 1980s (Burbank and Farhang, 2014). And in the 1990s, according to Cioffi (2010: 104–105), congressional Republicans believed that "crippling the securities [law] plaintiffs' bar would deny the Democratic Party" the "substantial financial backing" that those attorneys contributed to Democrats' political campaign coffers–while also reinforcing support for Republicans among corporate managerial elites.

5. Omnibus Consolidated Rescissions and Appropriations Act of 1996, Pub. Law No. 104 Sec 504(a)(7), 110 Stat. 1321–53 (1996).

6. More specifically, Schlanger (2015, 153–154) writes, "The PLRA conditioned court access on prisoners' meticulously correct prior use of onerous and error-inviting prison grievance procedures. It increased filing fees, decreased attorneys' fees, and limited damages. It subjected injunctive settlements to scope limitations. . . . It made prison and jail population caps–previously common–far more difficult to obtain. And it put in place a rule inviting frequent relitigation of injunctive remedies, whether settled or litigated."

7. The federal Protection of Lawful Commerce in Arms Act (2005), however, does not block lawsuits based on negligent entrustment (e.g., sales to a person a dealer knew or had reason to know is mentally unstable) or suits based on injury from manufacturing or design defect, or based on other action for which gunmakers are directly responsible (Lytton, 2005b). As of 2005, "legislatures in thirty-two states, lobbied heavily by the NRA, [had] passed legislation granting the industry immunity from suit" (Lytton, 2005a: 3).

8. In that law, Congress also gave large institutional investors priority in serving as lead counsel in security fraud class actions, hoping thereby to squelch litigation brought by supposedly more self-interested plaintiffs' lawyers.

9. A 1998 amendment to Rule 23 of the Federal Rules made it easier to appeal lower court decisions on whether or not to certify an asserted class as appropriate

for a class action—a change that "substantially expanded the opportunities for the federal appellate courts, including the Supreme Court to control the course of class action jurisprudence. And control it they have, making certification more difficult and expensive" (Burbank and Farhang, 2017: 141).

10. The Burbank-Farhang database included "all bills that sought to amend federal law so as to (1) reduce the availability of attorneys' fees to plaintiffs or increase plaintiffs' liability for defendants' fees, (2) reduce the monetary damages that plaintiffs can recover, (3) reduce opportunities and incentives for class actions, (4) strengthen the operation of sanctions against counsel, and (5) strengthen the operation of offer of judgment rules" (Burbank and Farhang, 2017: 34).

11. Burbank and Farhang (2017: chapter 5) show that the court's decisions concerning *procedural issues* (in contrast to cases involving more dramatic substantive issues) generate only limited media coverage.

12. Burbank and Farhang (2017: 177) found that: "The Court's growing focus on business defendant Federal Rules cases since 2000 occurred at about the time (1998) that the Chamber of Commerce founded the Institute of Legal Reform, which focuses on such issues as class actions and discovery. It also corresponds to a surge in the Chamber's advocacy on private enforcement issues." The Chamber of Commerce, as well as two other conservative law reform organizations, regularly filed amicus briefs in a wide range of Supreme Court cases involving issues relevant to private law enforcement litigation (164).

13. *Celotex Corp. v. Catrett* (1986); *Anderson v. Liberty Lobby* (1986); *Matsushita Elec. Indus. Co. v. Zenith Radio Corp.* (1986).

14. *Bell Atlantic Corp. v. Twombly* (2007); *Ashcroft v. Iqbal* (2009).

15. *Buckhannon Board & Care Home v. West Virginia Dept of Health & Human Resources* (2001).

16. *Connick v. Thompson* (2011).

17. *United States v. Morrison* (2000).

18. *Alexander v. Sandoval,* (2001).

19. *Walmart Stores v. Dukes* (2011); *Amchem Products v Windsor* (1997).

20. The Court's rulings encouraging summary judgments, Sarah Staszak (2015: 105) asserts, "served to constrict access to the courts for minority groups and the poor pursuing civil rights claims—a major shift from the doctrinal and procedural innovations and goals of the rights revolution era." Similarly, a number of scholars, analyzing empirical data, conclude that the Court's rulings requiring plaintiffs' pleadings to contain specific facts supporting their legal claim (a departure from traditional notice pleading) have tended to block not only frivolous suits but also valid civil rights and consumer protection lawsuits, since plaintiffs often need pretrial discovery to obtain *detailed* information about defendants' behavior (Staszak, 2015: 113–114).

21. *Buckhannon Board & Care Home v. West Virginia Dept of Health & Human Resources* (2001).

22. Justice Ginsburg's dissenting opinion, which carefully reviews the evidence presented at trial, notes that "no fewer than five prosecutors" were involved in the Thompson cases; that they failed to disclose the exculpatory evidence "despite multiple opportunities, spanning nearly two decades, to set the record straight;"

that the nondisclosed evidence included a blood sample on one of the robbery victims that did not match defendant Thompson's, that Thompson was turned in by someone seeking a reward and prosecutors failed to turn over tapes of that conversation, and that an alleged eyewitness identification of the killer didn't match Thompson, a fact that was never shared with defense counsel.

23. A prosecutorial oversight coalition noted that the Texas prosecutorial error study doesn't begin to fully illustrate the scope of the problem. Almost all of the errors identified were of cases where defendants went to trial (only 3 percent of Texas criminal cases according to 2010 data) and had access to an attorney who raised the error on appeal. Courts declined to directly address the issue in many of the cases where the issue was raised. In the words of Stephen Saloom, policy director of the Innocence Project, which is affiliated with the Cardozo School of Law, "As best we can determine, most prosecutors' offices don't even have clear internal systems for preventing and reviewing misconduct. But perhaps even more alarming is that bar oversight entities tend not to act in the wake of even serious acts of misconduct" (Innocence Project (2012).

24. Changes in the Federal Rules of Civil Procedure have sought to reduce abusive pretrial discovery by creating limits on the number of interrogatories and pretrial depositions in each case, and in the length of depositions (subject to extension by judicial permission). But in cases that can result in large money damages, extensive nonabusive pretrial discovery tends to proceed apace.

25. In March 2013, British Petroleum (BP) agreed to settle lawsuits brought by more than 100,000 fishermen who lost work, cleanup workers who got sick, and others who claimed harm from the oil company's 2010 Gulf of Mexico offshore oil spill (*Economist*, 2015). The settlement had no cap for compensating the plaintiffs. BP estimated it would have to pay out about $7.8 billion. Earlier, on November 14, 2012, BP and the U.S. Department of Justice reached a settlement of criminal charges, under which BP agreed to pay $4.5 billion (Associated Press, 2012).

26. These figures exclude the roughly half of civil cases that were filed in small claims courts and other courts of restricted jurisdiction. National Center for State Courts (2012).

27. Two thirds of the civil cases in the National Center's study were contract cases. Almost two thirds of those were debt collection or landlord/tenant cases (National Center for State Courts, 2017).

28. The America Invents Act of 2011 created a Patent Trial and Appeal Board that (according to a patent lawyers at the Computer and Communications Industry Association) has provided an expeditious, relatively inexpensive way to challenge patent infringement claims of doubtful validity, saving companies more than $2 billion in legal fees alone (Porter, 2017a).

29. In *TC Heartland v Kraft Foods* (2017), a unanimous U.S. Supreme Court restricted patent trolls' ability to file cases in certain Texas courts, no matter where the defendant had been operating; juries in those courts had a record of remarkable favoritism toward patent trolls' claims (Fung, 2017).

30. Staszak (2015: 38) reports that, "In 2009 Public Citizen found that 80 percent of credit card companies (including all ten of the nation's largest), 70 percent of banks, and 90 percent of cell phone companies currently have mandatory arbitration clauses

in their contracts with consumers." Staszak adds that a "study of twenty-one major corporations found provisions for mandatory arbitration in 93 percent of their employment contracts" (39).

31. *AT&T Mobility LLC v. Concepcion* (2011). As Staszak (2015: 44) observes, these rulings give business corporations clear incentives to "use arbitration clauses to shorten statutes of limitations, restrict discovery, require confidentiality, waive . . . a variety of remedies, and contract with arbitrators sympathetic to their position as businesses."

32. Judith Resnik (2015, 2812) reports that in the 2009–2014 period about twenty-seven consumer claims a year were filed in the mandatory arbitration system established by AT&T Wireless. Resnik adds (2812–2813): "During that time period, the estimated number of AT&T Wireless customers rose from 85 million a year to 120 million people, and lawsuits filed by the federal government charged the company with a range of legal breaches, including systematic overcharging for extra services and insufficient payment of refunds when customers complained." In addition, the American Arbitration Association, the largest nonprofit provider of arbitration services averages less than 1,500 *consumer* arbitration cases annually.

33. In 2016, during the Obama administration, the federal government's Centers for Medicare and Medicaid Services adopted a regulation stipulating that nursing homes that receive federal funding—most of them—could no longer include mandatory arbitration clauses in their contracts. In July 2017 the same agency, with new Trump administration leadership, announced it would rescind the 2016 rule. That change has been opposed by seventeen state attorneys general, poised to sue the agency when the final rule is issued (Jaffe, 2017). In 2017, the Consumer Financial Protection Bureau, still with Obama-era leadership, banned banks, credit card issuers, and other financial institutions from requiring customers to sign away their rights to join class actions and submit potential disputes to private arbitration. The Republican Congress repealed that rule, with President Trump's signature (Lambert, 2017).

34. For example, coordinated civil fraud cases by AGs in twenty-seven states against scores of pharmaceutical companies resulted in settlements in which the defendants agreed to change a deceptive mode of pricing pharmaceutical sales to hospitals—a practice that had for years resulted in inflated reimbursement to those hospitals by federal Medicare and Medicaid programs, but which Congress had repeatedly failed to outlaw. To ensure that the drug firms would comply with the settlements, the AGs also insisted on further corporate integrity agreements under which the companies established new reporting systems, internal training in compliance, and independent monitoring systems. Ultimately, Congress wrote into the law the reforms embodied in the settlements of the AGs' court cases (Nolette, 2014).

35. The departments investigated include those in New York City, Los Angeles, Detroit, Cleveland, Washington, D.C., Seattle, Albuquerque, Cincinnati, and Newark N.J., as well as the smaller but recently infamous department in Ferguson, Missouri.

36. During the Trump administration, Attorney General Jeffrey Sessions announced that the Department of Justice would decline to launch these kinds of

investigations and seek consent decrees. But sooner or later, the department may well feel compelled to re-launch them in response to highly publicized incidents of flagrant rights violations by one local police department or another.

37. *Rasul v. Bush* (2004); *Boumedienne v. Bush* (2008).

38. *Hamdi v. Rumsfeld* (2004).

39. *District of Columbia v. Heller* (2008).

40. *McDonald v. Chicago* (2010).

41. In a number of states, courts have issued conflicting decisions on whether the newly established individual right to bear arms (*District of Columbia v. Heller*, 2008) trumps state and local laws that forbid people other than law enforcement officials from carrying loaded guns outside the home or that forbid carrying concealed weapons (Palazzolo, 2012). On the other hand, the *Heller* decision has encouraged conservative states to enact laws establishing the right to carry concealed firearms—in some cases, unconcealed weapons—in a wide variety of settings.

42. *Parents Involved in Community Schools v. Seattle School District No.1* (2007). Justice Kennedy, while agreeing with the four justice majority that the plans in question were unconstitutional, wrote a concurring opinion asserting that racial diversity, "avoiding racial isolation" and addressing "the problem of de facto resegregation in schooling" were "compelling interests" that a school district could constitutionally pursue as long as it did so through programs that were sufficiently "narrowly tailored."

43. *National Federation of Individual Businesses et al. v. Sebelius* (2012).

44. In October 2017, President Trump issued an executive order extending that exemption to any employer with a religious or moral objection to contraceptive products (Greenhouse, 2017). The legal validity of that exemption is likely to be challenged and perhaps decided in court.

45. *Citizens United v. Federal Election Commission* (2010).

46. *National Institute of Family and Life Advocates v. Becerra* (2018).

47. Kim Lane Scheppele, (2018), "How the Germans Do It," LawCourt-L, Listserv discussion, July 12, 2018, 1:57 p.m., https://list.umass.edu/mailman/listinfo/lawcourt-l.

48. In the first decade of the twenty-first century, state supreme courts in twenty-six states ruled on cases challenging the state's system for public school financing on grounds of unconstitutionally unequal funding across richer and poorer school districts or on grounds of the inadequacy of funding (in light of a state constitutional provision requiring provision of an adequate or suitable public education). In seventeen of those cases, plaintiffs won favorable court decisions, with partial victories in two others (Howard and Steigerwalt, 2012: 123–128). In the second decade of the century, after more conservative state governments cut back state funding for public schools, activists *intensified* litigation, arguing, based on detailed student performance data, that those states are violating their own constitutions by denying poorer children a quality education (Goldstein, 2018b).

49. Courts repeatedly have been asked to rule on the legitimacy and fairness of district lines that partisan state legislatures draw after each decennial census. Not infrequently, judges draw those new district lines themselves, with the aid of a special master whom the judge appoints.

50. In 1976, in *Buckley v. Valeo,* the Supreme Court decided that spending on political campaigns is constitutionally protected political speech. In that and numerous subsequent decisions—including the highly controversial 5–4 Supreme Court's *Citizens United* decision in 2010—courts have sharply limited efforts to regulate campaign spending, rulings that have deeply affected the nature of political campaigns (Ansolabehere, 2012).

References

Aarmson, David, C. Thomas Dienes, and Michael Musheno. (1978) "Changing the Public Drunkenness Laws: The Impact of Decriminalization." *Law & Soc'y Rev.* 12: 405.

Abel, Richard. (1987) "The Real Tort Crisis: Too Few Claims." *Ohio St. L.J.* 48: 443.

——. (1990) "A Critique of Torts." *UCLA L. Rev.* 37: 785.

Abraham, Henry. (1980) *The Judicial Process.* New York: Oxford University Press.

Abraham, Katherine, and Susan Houseman. (1993) *Job Security in America: Lessons from Germany.* Washington, D.C.: Brookings Institution.

Abraham, Kenneth S., and Lance Liebman. (1993) "Private Insurance, Social Insurance, and Tort Reform: Toward a New Vision of Compensation for Illness and Injury." *Colum. L. Rev.* 93: 75.

Adler, Stephen. (1994) *The Jury.* New York: Doubleday.

Aks, Judy, Anne Bloom, Michael McCann, and William Halton. (2000) "Hegemonic Tales and Subversive Statistics: A Twenty-Year Study of News Reporting about Civil Litigation." Paper presented at annual meeting of Law and Society Association, Miami Beach, Fla., May 26–29, 2000.

Albiston, Catherine, and Laura Beth Nielsen. (2007) "The Procedural Attack on Civil Rights: The Empirical Reality of Buckhannon for the Private Attorney General." *UCLA L. Rev.* 54: 1087–1134.

Alesina, Alberto, and Edward Glaeser. (2004) *Fighting Poverty in the US and Europe: A World of Difference.* Oxford: Oxford University Press.

Alexander, Janet Cooper. (1991) "Do the Merits Really Matter? A Study of Settlements in Securities Class Actions." *Stan. L. Rev.* 43: 497.

Alexander v. Sandoval. (2001) 532 U.S. 275.

Allen, Christopher. (1989) "Political Consequences of Change: The Chemical Industry." In *Industry and Politics in West Germany*, ed. Peter Katzenstein. Ithaca, N.Y.: Cornell University Press.

Alschuler, Albert N. (1983) "Implementing the Criminal Defendant's Right to Trial: Alternatives to the Plea Bargain System." *U. Chi. L. Rev.* 50: 931.

——. (1986) "Mediation with a Mugger: The Shortage of Adjudicative Services and the Need for a Two-Tier System in Civil Cases." *Harv. L. Rev.* 99: 1808.

——. (1990) "The Vanishing Civil Jury." *U. Chi. Legal F.* 1990: 1.

——. (1998) "Explaining the Public Wariness of Juries." *DePaul L. Rev.* 48: 407.

Alvarez, Lizette. (2014) "Florida Prosecutors Face Long Odds When Police Use Lethal Force." *New York Times,* September 4, 2014, A12.

Amchem Products v. Windsor. (1997) 21 U.S. 591.

American Law Institute. (1991) *Reporters' Study: Enterprise Responsibility for Personal Injury,* vol. 1. Philadelphia, Pa.: American Law Institute.

American Mining Congress v. EPA. (1987) 824 F.2d 1177, 1189 (D.C. Cir.).

Amsterdam, Anthony. (1988) *Trial Manual for the Defense of Criminal Cases,* 5th ed. Philadelphia, Pa.: American Law Institute-American Bar Association.

Anderson, Eugene, Irene Warshauer, and Adrienne Coffin. (1983) "The Asbestos Health Hazards Compensation Act: A Legislative Solution to a Litigation Crisis." *J. Legislation* 10: 25.

Anderson, Leigh, and Robert A. Kagan. (2000) "Adversarial Legalism and Trans-action Costs: The Industrial Flight Hypothesis Revisited." *Int'l Rev. Law & Econ.,* no. 20: 1–19.

Anderson v. Liberty Lobby. (1986) 477 U.S. 242.

Angell, Marcia. (1996) *Science on Trial: The Clash of Medical Evidence and the Law in the Breast Implant Cases.* New York: Norton.

Ansolabehere, Stephen. (2012) "Arizona Free Enterprise v Bennett and The Problem of Campaign Finance." *The Supreme Court Review* 2011, 39–80, University of Chicago Press.

Aoki, Kazumasu, and John Cioffi. (2000) "Poles Apart: Industrial Waste Management Regulation and Enforcement in the United States and Japan." In *Regulatory Encounters: Multinational Corporations and American Adversarial Legalism,* ed. Robert A. Kagan and Lee Axelrad. Berkeley: University of California Press.

Aoki, Kazumasu, Robert A. Kagan, and Lee Axelrad. (2000) "Industrial Effluent Control in the United States and Japan." In *Regulatory Encounters: Multinational Corporations and American Adversarial Legalism,* ed. Robert Kagan and Lee Axelrad. Berkeley: University of California Press.

Applebome, Peter. (1991) "Georgia Inmate Is Executed after 'Chaotic Legal Move.'" *New York Times,* September 26, 1991, A18.

Argersinger v. Hamlin. (1972) 407 U.S. 25.

Armstrong, Ken, and Maurice Possley. (1999a) "The Verdict: Dishonor." *Chicago Tribune,* January 10, 1999, 1C.

——. (1999b) "Break Rules: Be Promoted." *Chicago Tribune,* January 14, 1999, 1N.

Ashcroft v. Iqbal. (2009) 556 U.S. 662.

Associated Press. (2012) "BP Settles Gulf Oil Spill Lawsuits for $7.8 Billion," *U.S. News and World Report,* March 3, 2012. https://www.mlive.com/news/us-world/2012/03/bp_settles_gulf_oil_spill_laws.html.

Atiyah, P. S., and Robert S. Summers. (1987) *Form and Substance in Anglo-American Law: A Comparative Study of Legal Reasoning, Legal Theory, and Legal Institutions.* Oxford: Clarendon Press.

AT&T Mobility LLC v. Concepcion. (2011) 563 U.S. 321.

Aviram, Hadar (2015) *Cheap on Crime: Recession-Era Politics and the Transformation of American Punishment.* Berkeley: University of California Press.

Axelrad, Lee. (2000) "Investigation and Remediation of Contaminated Manufacturing Sites in the United States, the United Kingdom, and the Netherlands." In *Regulatory Encounters: Multinational Corporations and Adversarial Legalism*, ed. Robert A. Kagan and L. Axelrad. Berkeley: University of California Press.

Badaracco, Joseph L. (1985) *Loading the Dice: A Five Country Study of Vinyl Chloride Regulation*. Boston: Harvard Business School Press.

Bailis, Daniel, and Robert MacCoun. (1996) "Estimating Liability Risks with the Media as Your Guide: A Content Analysis of Media Coverage of Tort Litigation." *Law & Human Behavior* 20: 419.

Baldus, David, Catherine Grosso, George Woodworth, and Richard Newell (1983) "Comparative Review of Death Sentences: An Empirical Study of the Georgia Experience." *J. Crim. L. & Criminology* 74: 661.

Baldus, David, George Woodworth, and Charles Pulaski, Jr. (1990) *Equal Justice and the Death Penalty: A Legal and Empirical Analysis*. Boston: Northeastern University Press.

Baldwin, John, and Michael McConville. (1979) "Plea Bargaining and Plea Negotiation in England." *Law & Soc'y Rev.* 13: 287.

Bales, Richard. (1998) "Creating and Challenging Compulsory Arbitration Agreements." *Labor Law* 13: 511.

Bandow, Doug. (1995) "California's Three Strikes Law Strikes Out." *Wall Street J.*, April 19, 1995, A17.

———. (1998) "Many Torts Later, the Case against Implants Collapses." *Wall Street J.*, November 30, 1998, A23.

Bannon, Alicia, Mitali Nagrecha, and Rebekah Diller. (2010) *Criminal Justice Debt: A Barrier to Re-Entry*. New York: Brennan Center for Justice, NYU School of Law.

Bardach, Eugene. (1998) *Getting Agencies to Work Together: The Practice and Theory of Managerial Craftsmanship*. Washington, D.C.: Brookings Institution Press.

Bardach, Eugene, and Robert A. Kagan. (1982) *Going by the Book: The Problem of Regulatory Unreasonableness*. Philadelphia: Temple University Press.

Barkenbus, J. N. (1984) "Nuclear Power and Government Structure: The Divergent Paths of the United States and France." *Social Science Quarterly* 65: 37.

Barkow, Anthony, and Rachel Barkow, eds. (2011) *Prosecutors in the Boardroom: Using Criminal Law to Regulate*. New York: NYU Press.

Barnes, Jeb. (1997) "Bankrupt Bargain? Bankruptcy Reform and the Politics of Adversarial Legalism." *J.L. & Pol.* 13: 893.

———. (2004) *Overruled? Legislative Overrides, Pluralism, and Contemporary Court-Congress Relations*. Redwood City, Calif: University of Stanford Press.

———. (2011) *Dust Up: Asbestos Regulation and the Failure of Commonsense Policy Reform*. Washington, D.C.: Georgetown University Press.

Barnes, Jeb, and Thomas F. Burke. (2015) *How Policy Shapes Politics: Rights, Courts, Litigation and the Struggle Over Injury Compensation*. New York: Oxford University Press.

Barnett, Randy E. (1994) "Bad Trip: Drug Prohibition and the Weakness of Public Policy." *Yale L.J.* 103: 2593.

Baron, Roger M., and Ronald J. Baron. (1986) "The Penzoil-Texaco Dispute: An Independent Analysis." *Baylor L. Rev.* 38: 253.

Barstow, David. (2003) "A Trench Caves In; a Young Worker Is Dead. Is It a Crime? *New York Times,* December 21, 2003, Sec. 1, p. 1.

Bass, Jack. (1993) *Taming the Storm: The Life and Times of Judge Frank M. Johnson, Jr.* New York: Doubleday.

Bass, Sandra. (1997) "Blacks, Browns, and the Blues: Police and Minorities in California." *Public Affairs Report* 38: 1.

Bastings, Lincey, Ellen Mastenbroek, and Esther Versluis. (2017) "The Other Face of Eurolegalism: The Multifaceted Convergence of National Enforcement Styles." *Regulation & Governance* 11: 299–314.

Bates v. State Bar. (1977) 433 U.S. 350.

Batson v. Kentucky. (1986) 476 U.S. 79.

Baumgartner, Frank, Derek Epp, and Kelsey Shaub. (2018) *Suspect Citizens; What 20 Million Traffic Stops Tell Us About Policy and Race.* New York: Cambridge University Press.

Bayley, David. (1976) *Forces of Order: Police Behavior in Japan and the United States.* Berkeley: University of California Press.

——. (1979) "Police Function, Structure, and Control in Western Europe and North America: Comparative and Historical Studies." *Crime & Justice* 1: 109.

Bell Atlantic Corp. v. Twombly. (2007) 550 U.S. 544.

Bell, Peter, and Jeffrey O'Connell. (1997) *Accidental Justice: The Dilemmas of Tort Law.* New Haven, Conn.: Yale University Press.

Bellows, Randy. (1988) "Notes of a Public Defender." In *The Social Responsibilities of Lawyers,* ed. Philip B. Heyman and Lance Liebman. Westbury, N.Y.: Foundation Press.

Benedict, Roger. (1993) "Chevron: Political Risks for New Oil Ventures in U.S. Exceed Those in Former Soviet Union." *The Oil Daily,* April 12, 1993, 3.

Benner, Katie and Shaila Dewan (2019) "'Common, Cruel' Violence Met by Indifference." *New York Times,* April 4, A1.

Bennett, Daniel. (2017) *Defending Faith: The Politics of the Christian Conservative Legal Movement.* Lawrence: University of Kansas Press.

Berger, Eric (2011) "On Saving the Death Penalty: A Comment on Adam Gershowitz's Statewide Capital Punishment" *Vanderbilt L. Rev.* 64: 1–14.

Bergstrom, Randolph E. (1992) *Courting Danger: Injury and Law in New York City, 1870–1910.* Ithaca, N.Y.: Cornell University Press.

Berk, Richard, Harold Brackman, and Selma Lesser. (1977) *A Measure of Justice: An Empirical Study of Changes in the California Penal Code.* New York: Academic Press.

Bernstein, David. (1999) "The Breast Implant Fiasco." *Cal. L. Rev.* 87: 457.

Bernstein, Herbert. (1988) "Whose Advantage After All?: A Comment on the Comparison of Civil Justice Systems." *U.C. Davis L. Rev.* 21: 587.

Berrey, Ellen, Robert L. Nelson, and Laura Beth Nielsen. (2017) *Rights on Trial: How Workplace Discrimination Law Perpetuates Inequality.* Chicago: Chicago University Press.

Berton, Lee. (1995) "Big Accounting Firms Weed Out Risky Clients." *Wall Street J.,* June 26, 1995, B1.

Berton, Lee, and Joann Lublin. (1992) "Seeking Shelter: Partnership Structure Is Called in Question as Liability Risk Rises." *Wall Street J.,* June 10, 1992, A1.

Bignami, Francesca. (2011) "Cooperative Legalism and the Non-Americanization of European Regulatory Styles: The Case of Data Privacy." *Am. J. Comp. L.* 59: 411–461.

Bignami, Francesca, and R. Daniel Kelemen. (2018) "Kagan's Atlantic Crossing: Adversarial Legalism, Eurolegalism, and Cooperative Legalism in European Regulatory Style." In *Varieties of Legal Order: The Politics of Adversarial and Bureaucratic Legalism*, ed. Thomas Burke and Jeb Barnes. New York: Routledge.

Bilocki, Dennis. (1989) "A More Efficient Method of Jury Selection for Lengthy Trials." *Judicature* 73: 43.

Blabolil, Sandee, Ines Cho, Scott Haenni, and Joe Kuffler. (1997) "Environmental Crimes." *Am. Crim. L. Rev.* 34: 491.

Blankenburg, Erhard. (1994) "The Infrastructure for Avoiding Civil Litigation: Comparing Cultures of Legal Behavior in the Netherlands and West Germany." *Law & Soc'y Rev.* 28: 789.

Blankenburg, Erhard, and Freek Bruinsma. (1991) *Dutch Legal Culture*. Deventer, Netherlands: Kluwer.

Blumstein, James, Randall Bovbjerg, and Frank Sloan. (1990) "Beyond Tort Reform: Developing Better Tools for Assessing Damages for Personal Injury." *Yale J. on Reg.* 8: 171.

BMW of North America v. Gore. (1996) 517 U.S. 559.

Boden, Les, and David Wegman. (1978) "Increasing OSHA's Clout: Sixty Million New Inspectors." *Working Papers for a New Society* (May/June). Cambridge Mass.: Cambridge Policy Studies Institute.

Boggio, Andrea. (2013) *Compensating Asbestos Victims; Law and the Dark Side of Industrialization*. Surrey, England: Ashgate.

Bok, Derek. (1971) "Reflections on the Distinctive Character of American Labor Laws." *Harv. L. Rev.* 84: 1461.

Boland, Barbara, Catherine H. Conly, and Paul Mahanna. (1990) "The Prosecution of Felony Arrests, 1987." Washington, D.C.: U.S. Department of Justice, 91–97.

Bombaugh, Robert. (1971) "The Department of Transportation's Auto Insurance Study and Auto Accident Compensation Reform." *Colum. L. Rev.* 71: 207.

Bookspan, Phyllis. (1991) "Reworking the Warrant Requirement." *Vand. L. Rev.* 44: 473.

Boot, Max. (1996) "Stop Appeasing the Class Action Monster." *Wall Street J.,* May 8, 1996, A18.

Borel v. Fibreboard Products Corp (1973), 493 F. 2d 1076 (5th Cir.).

Bork, Diana Culp. (1996) "A Florida Judge Lets Junk Science into Her Courtroom." *Wall Street J.,* June 26, 1996, A15.

Boumedienne v. Bush. (2008) 553 U.S. 723.

Bovbjerg, Randall, Frank Sloan, and James Blumstein. (1989) "Valuing Life and Limb in Tort: Scheduling Pain and Suffering." *Nw. U. L. Rev.* 83: 980.

Bovbjerg, Randall, Frank Sloan, Avi Dor, and Chee Ruey Hsieh. (1991) "Juries and Justice: Are Malpractice and Other Personal Injuries Created Equal?" *Law & Contemp. Probs.* 54: 15.

Bovbjerg, Randall, Frank Sloan, and Peter Rankin. (1997) "Administrative Performance of 'No Fault' Compensation for Medical Injury." *Law & Contemp. Probs.* 60: 71.

Boyle, Elizabeth Heger. (1998) "Political Frames and Legal Activity: The Case of Nuclear Power in Four Countries." *Law & Soc'y Rev.* 32: 141.

Bradley, Craig. (1993) *The Failure of the Criminal Procedure Revolution.* Philadelphia: Pennsylvania University Press.

Braithwaite, John. (1985) *To Punish or Persuade: Enforcement of Coal Mine Safety.* Albany, N.Y.: SUNY Press.

——. (1993) "The Nursing Home Industry." In *Beyond the Law: Crime in Complex Organizations,* ed. Michael Tonry and Albert J. Reiss, Jr. Chicago: University of Chicago Press.

Braithwaite, John, John Walker, and Peter Grabosky. (1987) "An Enforcement Taxonomy of Regulatory Agencies." *Law & Pol'y* 9: 323–350.

Bratton, William, and Michael Wachter. (2012) "Reforming Securities Law Enforcement: Politics and Money at the Public/Private Divide." In *Regulatory Breakdown: The Crisis of Confidence in U.S. Regulation,* ed. Cary Coglianese. Philadelphia: University of Pennsylvania Press.

Braybrooke, David, and Charles E. Lindblom. (1963) *A Strategy of Decision.* New York: Free Press.

Brazil, Wayne. (1980) "'Views from the Front Lines' Observations by Chicago Lawyers about the System of Civil Discovery." *Am. Bar Foundation Research J.* 1980: 219.

——. (1990) "A Close Look at Three Court-Sponsored ADR Programs: Why They Exist, How They Operate, What They Deliver, and Whether They Threaten Important Values." *U. Chi. Legal F.* 1990: 303.

Brereton, David, and Jonathan D. Casper. (1981) "Does It Pay to Plead Guilty? Differential Sentencing and the Functioning of Criminal Courts." *Law & Soc'y Rev.* 16: 45.

Brickman, Lester. (1992) "The Asbestos Litigation Crisis: Is There a Need for an Administrative Alternative?" *Cardozo L. Rev.* 13: 1819.

Brickman, Lester, Michael Horowitz, and Jeffrey O'Connell. (1994) *Rethinking Contingency Fees.* New York: Manhattan Institute.

Brickman, Ronald, Sheila Jasanoff, and Thomas Ilgen. (1985) *Controlling Chemicals: The Politics of Regulation in Europe and the United States.* Ithaca, N.Y.: Cornell University Press.

Briffault, Richard. (1990) "Our Localism, Part I: The Structure of Local Government Law." *Colum. L. Rev.* 90: 1.

Bright, Stephen B. (1994) "Counsel for the Poor: The Death Sentence Not for the Worst Crime but for the Worst Lawyer." *Yale L.J.* 103: 1835.

Brill, Stephen. (1989) *"U.S. v. Int'l Brotherhood of Teamsters and SEC v. Drexel Lambert*: When the Government Goes Judge-Shopping." In *Trial by Jury.* New York: American Lawyer Press/Touchstone.

Broder, Ivy. (1986) "Characteristics of Million Dollar Awards: Jury Verdicts and Final Disbursements." *Justice System J.* 11: 349.

Brodkin, Evelyn, and Michael Lipsky. (1983) "Quality Control in AFDC as an Administrative Strategy." *Soc. Serv. Rev.* 57: 1.

Bronner, Ethan. (1998) "High Schools Fear Telling Colleges All about Johnny." *New York Times,* March 11, 1998, A1.

Brookings Institution. (1989) *Justice for All: Reducing Costs and Delay in Civil Litigation—Report of a Task Force.* Washington, D.C.: Brookings Institution.

Brown v. Board of Education of Topeka. (1954) 347 U.S. 483.

Brown, Craig. (1985) "Deterrence in Tort and No-Fault: The New Zealand Experience." *Cal. L. Rev.* 73: 976.

Brown v Plata. (2011) 563 U.S. 493.

Brown, Warren. (1988) "Surviving 'Creative Bankruptcy': As a Business Strategy Firms Find That It Exacts a Heavy Price." *Washington Post,* November 6, 1988, H1, H7.

Bruce, Christopher J. (1984) "The Deterrence Effects of Automobile Insurance and Tort Law: A Survey of the Empirical Literature." *Law & Pol'y* 6: 67.

Bryant, Adam. (1995) "Small Planes Are Coming Back." *New York Times,* March 19, 1995, F11(L).

Buckhannon Board & Care Home v. West Virginia Dept of Health & Human Resources. (2001) 532 U.S. 598.

Buckley v. Valeo (1976), 424 U.S. 1.

Burbank, Stephen, and Sean Farhang. (2014) "Litigation Reform: An Institutional Approach," *U. Pa. L. Rev.* 162: 1543.

———. (2017) *Rights and Retrenchment: The Counterrevolution against Federal Litigation.* New York: Cambridge University Press.

Bureau of Justice Statistics. (1991) *Jail Inmates, 1990.* Washington, D.C.: U.S. Department of Justice.

———. (1995) *Tort Cases in Large Counties.* Washington, D.C.: U.S. Department of Justice.

———. (2000) *Sourcebook of Criminal Justice Statistics.* Washington, D.C.: U.S. Department of Justice.

———. (2002). *National Crime Victimization Survey: Unbounded Data, 2002.* Washington, D.C.: United States Department of Justice.

Burke, Thomas F. (2002) *Lawyers, Lawsuits, and Legal Rights: The Battle over Litigation in American Society.* Berkeley: University of California Press.

Burlington Industries, Inc. v. Ellerth. (1998) 24 U.S. 742.

Burnep, Gregory. (2017) "Military Commissions and the War on Terror: A Separation of Powers Tug-of-War." *Polity* 49: 270–300.

Burwell v. Hobby Lobby Stores, Inc. (2014) 134 S. Ct. 2751.

Busch, Christopher, David Kirp, and Daniel Schoenholz. (1999) "Taming Adversarial Legalism." *NYU J. Legis. & Pub. Pol'y* 2: 179.

Bush v. Gore (1976) 531 U.S. 98.

Butterfield, Fox. (1995) "California Courts Clogging under Its 'Three Strikes' Law." *New York Times,* March 23, 1995, A1, A9.

———. (1998) "New Study Adds Evidence of Bias in Death Sentences." *New York Times,* June 7, 1998, 1, 22.

——. (2000a) "Racial Disparities Seen as Pervasive in Juvenile Justice." *New York Times,* April 26, 2000, A1.

——. (2000b) "Death Sentences Overturned in 2 of 3 Appeals." *New York Times,* June 12, 2000, A1.

Buzbee, William (2014) *Fighting Westway: Environmental Law, Citizen Activism, and the Regulatory War that Transformed New York City.* Ithaca, NY: Cornell University Press.

Caravelis, Cyndy, Ted Chiricos, and William Bales (2013). "Race, Ethnicity, Threat, and the Designation of Career Offenders." *Justice Quarterly* 30: 869–894.

Carleson v. Remillard. (1972) 406 U.S. 598.

Carré, Françoise and Chris Tilly. (2017) *Where Bad Jobs Are Better: Retail Jobs across Countries and Companies.* New York: Russell Sage.

Carrigan, Christopher, and Cary Coglianese. (2012) "Oversight in Hindsight: Assessing the U.S. Regulatory System in the Wake of Calamity." In *Regulatory Breakdown: The Crisis of Confidence in U.S. Regulation,* ed. Cary Coglianese. Philadelphia: University of Pennsylvania Press.

Carroll, Stephen, Allan Abrahamse, and Mary Vaiana. (1995) *The Costs of Excess Medical Claims for Automobile Personal Injuries.* Santa Monica, Calif.: RAND Institute for Civil Justice.

Carroll, Stephen, Deborah Hensler, Jennifer Gross, Elizabeth Sloss, Allan Abrahamse, and J. Scott Ashwood. (2005) *Asbestos Litigation.* Santa Monica, Calif.: RAND Institute for Civil Justice.

Casper, Gerhard, and Hans Zeisel. (1972) "Lay Judges in the German Criminal Courts." *J. Legal Stud.* 1: 135.

Casper, Jonathan. (1972) *American Criminal Justice: The Defendant's Perspective.* Englewood Cliffs, N.J.: Prentice Hall.

Celotex Corp. v. Catrett. (1986) 477 U.S. 317.

Central Intelligence Agency. (2017) "The World Factbook." https://www.cia.gov /library/publications/the-world-factbook.

Charkham, Johnathan P. (1994) *Keeping Good Company: A Study of Corporate Governance in Five Countries.* Oxford, U.K.: Clarendon Press.

Chase, Oscar. (1995) "Helping Jurors Determine Pain and Suffering Awards." *Hofstra L. Rev.* 23: 763.

Chen, Ming Hsu. (2014) "Governing by Guidance: Civil Rights Agencies and the Emergence of Language Rights in Schools and Workplaces." *Harv. C.R.-C.L. L. Rev.* 49: 201.

Cheney, Frederick W., Karen Posner, and Robert A. Caplan. (1989) "Standard of Care and Anesthesia Liability." *JAMA (Journal of the American Medical Association)* 261: 1599.

Chetty, Raj, David Grusky, Maximilian Hell, Nathaniel Hendren, Robert Manduca, and Jimmy Narang. (2017) "The Fading American Dream: Trends in Absolute Income Mobility since 1940." *Science* 356 (April 24, 2017): 398–406.

Chiang, Harriet. (1996a) "Dearth of Lawyers in Death Row Cases." *San Francisco Chronicle,* January 23, 1996, A1.

——. (1996b) "Lucas's Legacy–Order in the Court." *San Francisco Chronicle,* April 29, 1996, A1, A9.

Chin, Audrey, and Mark Peterson. (1985) *Deep Pockets, Empty Pockets: Who Wins in Cook County Jury Trials?* Santa Monica, Calif.: RAND Institute for Civil Justice.

Chingos, Matthew, and Kristi Blagg. (2017) *Do Poor Kids Get Their Fair Share of School Funding?* Urban Institute, May 2017. http://apps.urban.org/features/school -funding-do-poor-kids-get-fair-share.

Chinloy, Peter. (1989) *The Cost of Doing Business: Legal and Regulatory Issues in the United States and Abroad.* New York: Praeger.

Chubb, John E. (1989) "U.S. Energy Policy." In *Can the Government Govern?* ed. J. E. Chubb and Paul Peterson. Washington, D.C.: Brookings Institution.

Church, Thomas W., and Robert Nakamura. (1993) *Cleaning Up the Mess: Implementation Strategies in Superfund.* Washington, D.C.: Brookings Institution.

Cioffi, John (2010) *Public Law and Private Power: Corporate Governance Reform in the Age of Finance Capitalism.* Ithaca, N.Y.: Cornell University Press.

Citizens United v. Federal Election Commission. (2010) 558 U.S. 310.

Citron, Roger. (1991) "(Un)*Luckey v. Miller:* The Case for a Structural Injunction to Improve Indigent Defense Services." *Yale L.J.* 101: 481.

Civil Rights Cases. (1883) 109 U.S. 3.

Clark, David. (1988) "The Selection and Accountability of Judges in West Germany: Implementation of a Rechtstaat." *S. Cal. L. Rev.* 61: 1795.

——. (1990) "Civil Litigation Trends in Europe and Latin America since 1945." *Law & Society Rev.* 24: 549.

Clermont, Kevin, and Theodore Eisenberg. (1992) "Trial by Jury or Judge: Transcending Empiricism." *Cornell L. Rev.* 77: 1124–1177.

Clermont, Kevin, and Stewart Schwab. (2004) "How Employment Plaintiffs Fare in Federal Court." *J. Empirical Legal Stud.* 1: 429–458.

Coffee, John C., Jr. (1995) "Class Wars: The Dilemma of the Mass Tort Class Action." *Colum. L. Rev.* 95: 1343.

——. (2015) *Entrepreneurial Litigation: Its Rise, Fall and Future.* Cambridge, Mass.: Harvard University Press.

Coglianese, Cary. (1997) "Assessing Consensus: The Promise and Performance of Negotiated Rulemaking." *Duke L.J.* 46: 1255, 1296–1301, 1316, 1343–1349.

Cohen, Lauren, Umit Gurun, and Scott Duke Kaminers. (2016) "The Growing Problem of Patent Trolling." *Science* 352 (April): 521–22, 29.

Collins, Glenn. (1995) "A Tobacco Case's Legal Buccaneers." *New York Times,* March 6, 1995, D3.

Colvin, Alexander. (2015) "Mandatory Arbitration and Inequality of Justice in Employment." *Berkeley J. Emp. & Lab. L.* 35: 71–90.

Condlin, Robert. (1985) "'Cases on Both Sides': Patterns of Argument in Legal Dispute-Negotiation." *Md. L. Rev.* 44: 65.

Conlan, Timothy. (1985) *New Federalism; Intergovernmental Reform from Nixon to Reagan.* Washington, D.C.: Brookings Institution.

Conley, John M., and William M. O'Barr. (1987) "Fundamentals of Jurisprudence: An Ethnography of Judicial Decision Making in Informal Courts." *N. C. L. Rev.* 66: 467.

Connick v. Thompson. (2011) 563 U.S. 51.

Cooney, Mark. (1994) "Evidence as Partisanship." *Law & Soc'y Rev.* 28: 833.

Cooper, Alexia, and Erica Smith. (2011) *Homicide Trends in the United States, 1980–2008.* Washington, D.C.: U.S. Department of Justice, Bureau of Justice Statistics (November, 2011).

Cooter, Robert D., and Tom Ginsburg. (1996) "Comparative Judicial Discretion: An Empirical Test of Economic Models." *Int'l Rev. of Law & Econ.* 16: 295–313.

Coronado, Ramon. (1995) "'Thrill Killer' Suspect Stuns Courtroom: 'I am guilty.'" *Sacramento Bee,* September 14, 1995, 1.

Council on California Competitiveness. (1992) *California's Jobs and Future.* Sacramento: Council on California Competitiveness.

Couso, Javier. (1997) "Entrenching Economic Rights: The 'Economic' Constitution of Chile." Paper delivered at International Conference on Institutions, Markets, and Economic Performance, Utrecht University, Ultrecht, Netherlands, December 11–12, 1997.

Cowley, Stacy, and Jessica Silver-Greenberg. (2017) "Consumer Regulator to Step Down From Office He Opened." *New York Times,* November 16, 2017, B4.

Coyle, Marcia, Fred Strasser, and Marianne Lavell. (1990) "Fatal Defense: Trial and Error in the Nation's Death Belt." *National L.J.,* June 11, 1990, 30–44.

Craig, Andrew. (1991) "Product Liability and Safety in General Aviation." In *The Liability Maze,* ed. Peter Huber and Robert Litan. Washington, D.C.: Brookings Institution.

Crawford, Charles, Ted Chiricos, and Gary Kleck (1998). "Race, Racial Threat, and Sentencing of Habitual Offenders." *Criminology* 36: 481–511.

Croley, Steven. (2008) *Regulation and Public Interests: The Possibility of Good Regulatory Government.* Princeton, N.J.: Princeton University Press.

Cross, Frank, and Emerson Tiller. (1998) "Judicial Partisanship and Obedience to Legal Doctrine: Whistleblowing on the Federal Courts of Appeals," *Yale L.J.* 107: 2155–2176.

CSAA (California State Automobile Association). (1997) "What to Do in a Car Accident," *VIA* (the magazine of the CSAA) (November/December): 12.

Curran, Barbara A. (1986) *Supplement to the Lawyer Statistical Report: The U.S. Legal Profession in 1985.* Chicago: American Bar Foundation.

Curran, Barbara A., and Clara N. Carson. (1994). *The Lawyer Statistical Report: The U.S. Legal Profession in the 1990s.* Chicago: American Bar Foundation.

Curtis, W. Robert. (1986) "The Deinstitutionalization Story." *The Public Interest* (Fall): 34.

CWCI (California Workers' Compensation Institute). (1991a) "Research Notes: Workers' Compensation Litigation Costs, 1990." San Francisco: California Workers' Compensation Institute, September.

———. (1991b) "1991 Litigation Incidence." San Francisco: California Workers' Compensation Institute.

Damaska, Mirjan. (1975) "Structures of Authority and Comparative Criminal Procedure." *Yale L.J.* 84: 480.

———. (1986) *The Faces of Justice and State Authority: A Comparative Approach to the Legal Process.* New Haven, Conn.: Yale University Press.

——. (1990) "Reflections on American Constitutionalism." *Am. J. Comp. L.* 38: 421.

——. (1997a) "The Uncertain Fate of Evidentiary Transplants: Anglo-American and Continental Experiments." *Am. J. Comp. L.* 45: 839.

Dandridge v. Williams. 397 U.S. 471 (1970).

Daniels, Stephen, and Joanne Martin. (1995) *Civil Juries and the Politics of Reform.* Chicago: American Bar Foundation, Northwestern University Press.

——. (2010) "'It Is No Longer Viable from a Practical and Business Standpoint': Damage Caps, 'Hidden Victims,' and the Declining Interest in Medical Malpractice Cases." *International Journal of the Legal Profession,* 17: 59–82.

——. (2015) *Tort Reform, Plaintiffs' Lawyers, and Access to Justice.* Lawrence: University Press of Kansas.

Danzon, Patricia. (1984) "The Frequency and Severity of Medical Malpractice Claims." *J.L. & Econ.* 27: 115.

——. (1985) *Medical Malpractice: Theory, Evidence, and Public Policy.* Cambridge, Mass.: Harvard University Press.

——. (1990) "The 'Crisis' in Medical Malpractice: A Comparison of Trends in the United States, Canada, the United Kingdom and Australia." *Law, Medicine & Health Care* 18: 48.

——. (1991) "Malpractice Liability: Is the Grass on the Other Side Greener?" In *Tort Law and the Public Interest,* ed. Peter Schuck. New York: W. W. Norton.

Darbyshire, Penny. (1997a) "An Essay on the Importance and Neglect of the Magistracy." *Criminal L. Rev.* 1997: 627.

——. (1997b) "For the New Lord Chancellor–Some Causes for Concern about Magistrates." *Criminal L. Rev.* 1997: 861.

Daubert v. Merrell Dow Pharmaceuticals. (1993) 509 U.S. 579.

Davenport, Coral. (2018) "In the Trump Administration, Science Is Unwelcome. So Is Advice." *New York Times,* June 9, 2018. https://www.nytimes.com/2018/06/09/climate/trump-administration-science.html.

Davenport, Coral, and Eric Lipton. (2017) "How G.O.P. Shifted on Climate Science." *New York Times,* June 4, 2017, Sec 1, 1, 14–15.

Davidson, Al. (1990) *In the Wake of the Exxon Valdez.* San Francisco: Sierra Club Books.

Davidson, Roger. (1981) "Subcommittee Government: New Channels for Policy Making." In *The New Congress,* ed. Thomas Mann and Norman Ornstein. Washington, D.C.: American Enterprise Institute.

Davies, Thomas Y. (1983) "A Hard Look at What We Know (and Still Need to Learn) about the 'Costs' of the Exclusionary Rule." *Am. Bar Foundation Research J.* 1983: 611.

Davis, Bob, and Peter Gumbel. (1995) "Red Tape Traumas: To All U.S. Managers Upset by Regulations–Try Germany or Japan." *Wall Street J.,* December 14, 1995, A1.

Davis, Martha F. (1993) *Brutal Need: Lawyers and the Welfare Rights Movement.* New Haven, Conn.: Yale University Press.

Day, Patricia, and Rudolf Klein. (1987) "The Regulation of Nursing Homes: A Comparative Perspective." *Milbank Quarterly* 65: 303–334.

de Tocqueville, Alexis. (1835) *Democracy in America,* vol. 1. New York: Vintage Books.

Decker, Jefferson. (2016) *The Other Rights Revolution: Conservative Lawyers and the Remaking of American Government.* New York; Oxford University Press.

Deese, David A. (1982) "A Cross-National Perspective on the Politics of Nuclear Waste." In *The Politics of Nuclear Waste,* ed. E. William Colglazier. New York: Pergamon Press.

Delmas, Magali, and Bruce Heiman. (2001) "Government Credible Commitment in the French and American Nuclear Power Industries." *J. Pol'y Analysis & Mgmt.* 20 (3).

DelVecchio, Rick. (1997) "West Oakland Group Sues to Block Port Project." *San Francisco Chronicle,* October 7, 1997, A19.

Dertouzos, James, Elaine Holland, and Patricia Ebener. (1988) *The Legal and Economic Consequences of Wrongful Termination.* Santa Monica: RAND Institute for Civil Justice.

——. (1992) *The Legal and Economic Consequences of Wrongful Termination.* Santa Monica, Calif.: RAND Institute for Civil Justice.

Desmond, Matthew. (2016) *Evicted: Poverty and Profit in the American City.* New York: Penguin Random House.

Detlefsen, Robert. (1994) "The Role of Interest Groups in the Fashioning of Government Consent Decrees." Paper delivered annual meeting of Western Political Science Association, Albuquerque, N.M., March 1994.

——. (1995) "Government Consent Decrees and the Paradox of 'Consent': A Critical Case Study." *Justice System J.* 18: 13.

Dewan, Shaila. (2005) "Fighting Court by Court to End Judicial Policies That Fall Heavily on Poor." *New York Times,* October 25, 2015, A17.

——. (2015) "States Are Overturning Local Laws, Often at Behest of Industry." *New York Times,* February 24, 2015, A1, A12.

Dewees, Donald, and Michael Trebilcock. (1992) "The Efficacy of the Tort System and Its Alternatives: A Review of Empirical Evidence." *Osgoode Hall L.J.* 56.

Dewees, Donald, Michael Trebilcock, and Peter Coyte. (1991) "The Medical Malpractice Crisis: A Comparative Empirical Perspective." *Law & Contemp. Probs.* 54: 217–251.

Diamond, Shari. (1983) "Order in the Court: Consistency in Criminal Court Decisions." In *The Master Lecturers Series: Psychology and the Law,* vol. 2, ed. C. James Scheirer and Barbara L. Hammonds, 123–146. Washington, D.C.: American Psychological Association.

DiIulio, John J., Jr. (1990) *Courts, Corrections and the Constitution.* New York: Oxford University Press.

Dimento, Joseph. (1986) *Environmental Law and American Business: Dilemmas of Compliance.* New York: Plenum Press.

District of Columbia v. Heller. (2008) 554 U.S. 570.

Dodd, Lynda. (2015) "The Rights Revolution in the Age of Obama and Ferguson: Policing, the Rule of Law, and the Elusive Quest for Accountability." *Perspectives on Politics* 13: 657–679.

Doe v. Harder. (1970) 301 F. Supp. 302 (N.D. Conn.), appeal dismissed, 397 U.S. 902.

Doe v. Shapiro. (1969) 302 F. Supp. 761 (D. Conn.), appeal dismissed, 396 U.S. 488 (1970).

Dolin, Eric Jay. (2005) *Political Waters: The Long, Dirty, Contentious, Incredibly Expensive but Eventually Triumphant History of Boston Harbor—A Unique Environmental Success Story.* Amherst: University of Massachusetts Press.

Donohue, John J. III, and Daniel Ho. (2007) "The Impact of Damage Caps on Malpractice Claims: Randomization Inference with Difference-in-Differences." *J. Empirical Legal Stud.* 4: 69–102.

Douthwaite, Graham. (1988) *Jury Instructions on Damages in Tort Actions,* 2nd ed. Charlotesville, Va.: Michie Co.

Downes, David M. (1988) *Contrasts in Tolerance: Post War Penal Policy in the Netherlands and England and Wales.* Oxford: Clarendon Press.

Druckerman, Patricia. (2016) "The Panic of American Parenthood." *New York Times,* October 16, 2016, A21.

Dubber, Markus. (1997) "American Plea Bargaining, German Lay Judges, and the Crisis of Criminal Procedure." *Stan. L. Rev.* 49: 547.

Dudziak, Mary. (1988) "Desegregation as a Cold War Imperative." *Stan. L. Rev.* 41: 61.

Duffy, Tom, and Rolph Landis. (1988) "Workers Compensation in Switzerland." *NCCI Digest* 3: 31. New York: National Council on Compensation Insurance.

Dunlop, Bruce. (1975) "No-Fault Automobile Insurance and the Negligent Action: An Expensive Anomaly." *Osgoode Hall L. J.* 13: 439.

Dunworth, Terence, and Joel Rogers. (1996) "Corporations in Court: Big Business Litigation in U.S. Federal Courts." *Law & Soc. Inquiry* 21: 497.

Dwyer, John. (1990) "The Pathology of Symbolic Legislation." *Ecology L.Q.* 17: 233.

Dwyer, John, Richard Brooks, and Alan Marco. (2000) "The Air Pollution Permit Process for U.S. and German Automobile Assembly Plants." In *Regulatory Encounters: Multinational Corporations and American Adversarial Legalism,* ed. Robert A. Kagan and Lee Axelrad. Berkeley: University of California Press.

Eads, George, and Peter Reuter. (1984) "Designing Safer Products: Corporate Responses to Product Liability Law and Regulation." *J. Product Liability* 7: 263.

The Economist. (1990) "The Forest Service: Time for a Little Perestroika." March 10, 1990, 28.

——. (1992) "Twitching Millionaires." October 3, 1992, 29.

——. (1994) "Taxation." September 24, 1994, 112.

——. (1996a) "Crime in America." June 8, 1996, 23–25.

——. (1996b) "Pensions." November 30, 1996, 105.

——. (1997) "Thwack the Law." January 25, 1997, 46.

——. (1998) "Maternity Leave." February 28, 1998, 110.

——. (2014a) "The Slow Death of the Death Penalty." April 24, 2014. https://www.economist.com/united-states/2014/04/26/the-slow-death-of-the-death-penalty.

——. (2014b) "The Great Pot Experiment." July 12, 2014, 25–26.

——. (2014c) "Don't Shoot." December 13, 2014, 27.

——. (2015) "Double, Double, Oil and Trouble." April 18, 2015, 26.

——. (2017a) "Fat Tails: America's Governments Spend a Lot on Middle Income Earners and Little on the Poor." January 7, 2017, 21–22.

——. (2017b) "Gremlins and Phantoms," March 25, 2017, 25–26.

———. (2017c) "Reforming Taxes Will Not Be Easier than Abolishing Obamacare." March 30, 2017. https://www.economist.com/united-states/2017/03/30/reforming-taxes-will-not-be-easier-than-abolishing-obamacare.

———. (2017d) "Jail Break," May 27, 2017, 14.

———. (2017e) "Why America Still Executes People." June 12, 2017. https://www.economist.com/the-economist-explains/2017/06/12/why-america-still-executes-people.

———. (2017f) "Keeping the Wheels Turning." December 23, 2017, 30–40.

———. (2018) "In Praise of Gentrification." June 22, 2018, 23–24.

Edelman, Lauren. (2016) *Working Law: Courts, Corporations, and Symbolic Civil Rights.* Chicago: University of Chicago Press.

———. (2017) "What's the Goal of Sexual Harassment Training? Often, to Protect Employers." *Washington Post,* Nov. 17, 2017. https://www.washingtonpost.com/outlook/whats-the-point-of-sexual-harassment-training-often-to-protect-employers/2017/11/17/18.

Edelman, Lauren, Steven Abraham, and Howard Erlanger. (1992) "Professional Construction of Law: The Inflated Threat of Wrongful Discharge." *Law & Soc'y Rev.* 26: 47.

Edelman, Peter. (1988) "Japanese Product Standards as Non-Tariff Trade Barriers: When Regulatory Policy Becomes a Trade Issue." *Standard J. International Law* 24: 292.

Eisenberg, Ira. (1995) "Blind Justice." *San Francisco Focus* (September), 50–58.

Eisenberg, Theodore, Paula L. Hannaford-Agor, Michael Heise, Neil LaFountain, G. Thomas Munsterman, Brian Ostrom, and Martin T. Wells. (2006) "Juries, Judges, and Punitive Damages: Empirical Analyses Using the Civil Justice Survey of State Courts 1992, 1996, and 2001 Data." *J. Empirical Legal Stud.,* 3: 263–295.

Eisenberg, Theodore, and James Henderson, Jr. (1992) "Inside the Quiet Revolution in Products Liability." *UCLA L. Rev.* 39: 731.

Eisenberg, Theodore, John Goerdt, Brian Ostrom, and David Rottman. (1995) "Litigation Outcomes in State and Federal Court: A Statistical Portrait." Paper presented at annual meeting of the Law and Society Association, Toronto, June 2, 1995, later published in *Seattle U. L. Rev.,* 19: 433–453 (1996).

———. (1997) "The Predictability of Punitive Damages." *J. Legal Stud.* 26: 623.

Eisenstein, James, Roy B. Flemming, and Peter F. Nardulli. (1988) *The Contours of Justice: Communities and Their Courts.* Boston: Little, Brown.

Eisinger, Jesse. (2017) *The Chickenshit Club: Why the Justice Department Fails to Prosecute Executives.* New York: Simon & Schuster.

Elliot, Donald. (1989) "Why Punitive Damages Don't Deter Corporate Misconduct Effectively." *Ala. L. Rev.* 40: 1053.

Ellman, Ira Mark. (1991) "Inventing Family Law." *U.C. Davis L. Rev.* 32: 855.

Ellman, Ira and Tara Ellman. (2008) "The Theory of Child Support." *Harvard J. Legislation* 45: 107.

———. (2015) "'Frightening and High': The Supreme Court's Mistake about Sex Crime Statistics," *Constitutional Commentary* 30: 495.

Engel, David. (1984) "The Oven Bird's Song: Insiders, Outsiders, and Personal Injuries in an American Community." *Law & Soc'y Rev.* 18: 551.

Engstrom, David Freeman. (2013) "Agencies as Litigation Gatekeepers." *Yale L. Rev.* 2013: 616.

Epp, Charles R. (1998a) *The Rights Revolution: Lawyers, Activists and Supreme Courts in Comparative Perspective.* Chicago: University of Chicago Press.

———. (1998b) "Litigation Stories: Official Perceptions of Lawsuits against Local Governments." Paper presented at annual meeting of the Law and Society Association, Aspen, Colo., June 4–7, 1998.

———. (2009) *Making Rights Real: Activists, Bureaucrats, and the Creation of the Legalistic State.* Chicago: University of Chicago Press.

Epp, Charles, and Steven Maynard-Moody. (2014) "Driving While Black." *Washington Monthly,* 46, January/February 2014, 14.

Epp, Charles, Steven Maynard-Moody, and Donald Haider-Markel. (2014) *Pulled Over: How Police Stops Define Race and Citizenship.* Chicago: University of Chicago Press.

Erlanger, Howard, Elizabeth Chambliss, and Marygold Melli. (1987) "Participation and Flexibility in Informal Processes: Cautions from the Divorce Context." *Law & Soc'y Rev.* 21: 585.

Eskridge, William, Jr. (1991) "Overriding Supreme Court Statutory Interpretation Decisions." *Yale L.J.* 100: 331.

Esping-Anderson, Gosta. (1990) *The Three Worlds of Welfare Capitalism.* Princeton, N.J.: Princeton University Press.

Families, USA. (2000) *Go Directly to Work, Do Not Collect Health Insurance.* Washington, D.C.: Families, USA.

Faragher v. City of Boca Raton. (1988) 524 U.S. 775.

Farber, Daniel A. and Anne Joseph O'Connor. (2014) "The Lost World of Administrative Law." *Tex. L. Rev.* 92: 1137–1189.

Farber, Henry, and Michelle White. (1991) "Medical Malpractice: An Empirical Examination of the Litigation Process." *RAND J. Economics* 22: 199.

Farhang, Sean. (2010) *The Litigation State: Public Regulation and Private Lawsuits in the U.S.* Princeton, N.J.: Princeton University Press.

———. (2014) "Regulation, Litigation and Reform." In *The Politics of Major Policy Reform in Postwar America,* ed. Jeffrey Jenkins and Sidney Milkis. Cambridge: Cambridge University Press.

Fay v. Noia. (1963) 372 U.S. 391.

Feeley, Malcolm M. (1979) *The Process Is the Punishment: Handling Cases in a Lower Criminal Court.* New York: Russell Sage Foundation.

Feeley, Malcolm M., and Edward Rubin. (1998) *Judicial Policy Making and the Modern State: How the Courts Reformed America's Prisons.* New York: Cambridge University Press.

Feldman, Eric. (2000) "Blood Justice: Courts, Conflict, and Compensation in Japan, France, and the United States." *Law & Society Rev.* 34: 561.

Felker v. Turpin. (1996) 518 U.S. 651.

Feuer, Alan, and James McKinley Jr. (2017) "Rule Pushes Prosecutors to Disclose Evidence Favorable to Defense." *New York Times,* November 9, 2017, A18.

Fialka, John. (1998) "EPA Probers Find Big Flaws in Major Clean Air Effort." *Wall Street J.,* December 28, p. A16.

Fiorina, Morris. (1991) "Divided Government in the States." *PS: Political Science and Politics* (December), 646.

Fiorina, Morris P., and Samuel J. Abrams. (2009) *Disconnect: The Breakdown of Representation in American Politics.* Norman: University of Oklahoma Press.

Fiorino, Daniel. (1996) "Toward a New System of Environmental Regulation: The Case for an Industry Sector Approach." *Envtl. L.* 26: 457.

Firestone, Jeremy. (2003) "Enforcement of Pollution Laws and Regulations: An Analysis of Forum Choice," *Harv. Envtl. L. Rev.* 27: 105.

Fisher, Daniel. (2012) "Law Firm Hit with $429,000 Verdict over Faked Asbestos Suits." *Forbes,* December 21, 2012. https://www.forbes.com/sites/danielfisher /2012/12/21/law-firm-hit-with-429000-verdict-over-faked-asbestos-suits /#5b19b3212325.

Fisher, Stanley. (2000) "The Prosecutor's Ethical Duty to Seek Exculpatory Evidence in Police Hands: Lessons from England." *Fordham L. Rev.* 68: 101.

Fiss, Owen. (1984) "Against Settlement." *Yale L.J.* 93: 1073.

Flanagan, Robert J. (1987) *Labor Relations and the Litigation Explosion.* Washington, D.C.: Brookings Institution.

Flemming, John. (1984) "Is There a Future for Torts?" *La. L. Rev.* 44: 1193.

——. (1994) "Mass Torts." *Am. J. Comp. L.* 42: 507.

Fletcher, George P. (1994) "The Deliberators." Review of *We, the Jury* by Jeffrey Abramson. *New York Times Book Rev.,* December 11, 1994, 14–15.

Foote, Caleb. (1956) "Vagrancy-Type Law and Its Administration." *U. Pa. L. Rev.* 104: 603.

Foote, Daniel. (1992) "The Benevolent Paternalism of Japanese Criminal Justice." *Cal. L. Rev.* 80: 317.

——. (1995) "Resolution of Traffic Accident Disputes and Judicial Activism in Japan." *Law in Japan* 25: 19.

Foster, Sheila. (1998) "Justice from the Ground Up: Distributive Inequities, Grassroots Resistance, and the Transformative Politics of the Environmental Justice Movement." *Cal. L. Rev.* 86: 775.

Frammolino, Ralph. (1988) "Claims for Stress Devour Billions, Reformers Charge." *Los Angeles Times,* March 15, 1988, 3.

Frankel, Marvin. (1975) "The Search for Truth: An Umpireal View." *U. Pa. L. Rev.* 123: 1031.

Frase, Richard S. (1990) "Comparative Criminal Justice as a Guide to American Law Reform: How Do the French Do It, How Can We Find Out, and Why Should We Care?" *Cal. L. Rev.* 78: 545.

Frase, Richard S., and Thomas Weigend. (1995) "German Criminal Justice." *B. C. Int'l. & Comp. L. Rev.* 18: 317.

Freeman, Jody. (1997) "Collaborative Governance in the Administrative State." *UCLA L. Rev.* 45: 1.

Freeman, Richard B. (1994) "How Labor Fares in Advanced Economies: Lessons for the United States." In *Working under Different Rules,* ed. Richard B. Freeman. New York: Russell Sage Foundation.

Freeman, Richard B., and Lawrence Katz. (1994) "Rising Wage Inequality: The United States vs. Other Advanced Countries." In *Working under Different Rules,* ed. Richard Freeman. New York: Russell Sage Foundation.

Freyer, Roland G., Jr. (2016) *An Empirical Analysis of Racial Differences in Police Use of Force*. Cambridge, Mass.: National Bureau of Economic Research, working paper 22399, July. http://nber.org/papers/w22399.

Frieden, Bernard J. (1979) "The New Regulation Comes to Suburbia." *Public Interest* 55: 15.

Friedman, Lawrence M. (1973) *A History of American Law*. New York: Simon & Schuster.

——. (1978) "Civil Wrongs: Personal Injury Law in the Late 19th Century." *Am. Bar Foundation Research J.* 1978: 351.

——. (1979) "Plea Bargaining in Historical Perspective." *Law & Soc'y Rev.* 13: 257.

——. (1985) *Total Justice*. New York: Russell Sage Foundation.

——. (1986) "A Search for Seizure." *Law & Hist. Rev.* 4: 1.

——. (1993) *Crime and Punishment in American History*. New York: Basic Books.

Friedman, Lawrence M., Robert A. Kagan, Bliss Cartwright, and Stanton Wheeler. (1981) "State Supreme Courts: A Century of Style and Citation." *Stan. L. Rev.* 33: 773.

Friedman, Lawrence M., and Robert Percival. (1981) *The Roots of Justice: Crime and Punishment in Alameda County, California, 1870–1910*. Chapel Hill: University of North Carolina Press.

Friedman, Richard. (1998) "Anchors and Flotsam: Is Evidence Law 'Adrift'?" *Yale L. Rev.* 107: 1921.

Frymer, Paul. (2008) *Black and Blue: African Americans, the Labor Movement, and the Decline of the Democratic Party*. Princeton, N.J.: Princeton University Press.

Fukuyama, Francis. (2014) *Political Order and Political Decay: From the Industrial Revolution to the Globalization of Democracy*. New York: Farrar, Straus and Giroux.

Fulton, William. (1992) "The Gnatcatcher Follies." *Cal. Lawyer* (May): 42.

Fung, Brian. (2017) "The Supreme Court's Big Ruling on 'Patent Trolls.'" *Washington Post*, May 23, 2017. https://www.washingtonpost.com/news/the-switch/wp/2017/05/23/the-supreme-court-just-undercut-patent-trolls-in-a-big-way/?utm_term=.9232120a3e31.

Gaiter, Dorothy. (1996) "Eating Crow: How Shoney's, Belted by a Lawsuit, Found the Path to Diversity." *Wall Street J.*, April 16, 1996, A1, A11.

Galanter, Marc. (1974) "Why 'the Haves' Come Out Ahead: Speculations on the Limits of Legal Change." *Law & Soc'y Rev.* 9: 95.

——. (1983) "Reading the Landscape of Disputes: What We Know and Don't Know (and Think We Know) about Our Allegedly Contentious and Litigious Society." *UCLA L. Rev.* 31: 4.

——. (1992) "Law Abounding: Legislation around the North Atlantic." *Modern L. Rev.* 55: 1.

——. (1993) "The Regulatory Function of the Civil Jury." In *Verdict: Assessing the Civil Jury System*, ed. Robert Litan. Washington, D.C.: Brookings Institution.

——. (1998) "An Oil Strike in Hell: Contemporary Legends about the Justice System." *Ariz. L. Rev.* 40: 717.

Galanter, Marc, and Angela Frozena. (2014) "The Continuing Decline and Displacement of Trials in American Courts," *Daedalus,* Summer 2014: 115–128.

Galanter, Marc, and Mia Kahill. (1999) "Most Cases Settle: Judicial Promotion and Regulation of Settlement." *Stan. L. Rev.* 46: 1374.

Garoupa, Nino, and Jud Matthews. (2014) "Explaining Comparative Law of Administrative Review." *Am. J. of Comp. L.* 62: 133.

Garrett, Brandon. (2011) *Convicting the Innocent: Where Criminal Prosecutions Go Wrong.* Cambridge, Mass.: Harvard University Press.

——. (2014), *Too Big to Jail: How Prosecutors Compromise with Corporations.* Cambridge, Mass.: Belknap Press.

Garth, Bryant. (1992) "Power and Legal Artifice: The Federal Class Action." *Law & Soc'y Rev.* 26: 23.

——. (1993) "From Civil Litigation to Private Justice: Legal Practice at War with the Profession and Its Values." *Brook. L. Rev.* 59: 931.

Garvey, Stephen, Sheri Lynn Johnson, and Paul Marcus. (2000) "Correcting Deadly Confusion: Responding to Jury Inquiries in Capital Cases." *Cornell L. Rev.* 85: 627.

Gash, Alison. (2015) *Below the Radar: How Silence Can Save Civil Rights.* New York: Oxford University Press.

Gaylin, Willard. (1974) *Partial Justice: A Study in Bias in Sentencing.* New York: Knopf.

Geistfeld, Mark. (1995) "Placing a Price on Pain and Suffering: A Method for Helping Juries Determine Tort Damages for Nonmonetary Injuries." *Cal. L. Rev.* 83: 773.

Gelb, Joyce. (1989) *Feminism and Politics: A Comparative Perspective.* Berkeley: University of California Press.

Gellhorn, Walter. (1988) "Medical Malpractice Litigation (U.S.)–Medical Mishap Compensation (N.Z.)." *Cornell L. Rev.* 73: 170.

Gerlin, Andrea. (1994a) "Patent Lawyers Forgo Sure Fees on a Bet." *Wall Street J.,* June 24, 1994, B1.

——. (1994b) "A Matter of Degree: How a Jury Decided That a Coffee Spill Is Worth 2.9 Million." *Wall Street J.,* September 1, 1994, A1.

——. (1995) "Jury-Duty Scofflaws Try Patience of Courts." *Wall Street J.,* August 9, 1995, B1.

Geyelin, Milo. (1992) "Debate Intensifies over State Regulations that Restrict TV Advertising by Lawyers." *Wall Street J.,* August 31, 1991, B1.

——. (1997) "Costly Verdict: Why One Jury Dealt a Big Blow to Chrysler in Minivan-Latch Case." *Wall Street J.,* November 19, 1997, A1, A10.

Gibson, James. (1980) "Environmental Constraints on the Behavior of Judges: A Representational Model of Judicial Decision-Making." *Law & Soc'y Rev.* 14: 343.

Gideon v. Wainwright (1963) 372 *U.S.* 335.

Giffey, Tom. (2012) "Is 'Obamacare' Really That Long?" *Eau Clair Wisconsin Leader-Telegram,* July 17, 2012. https://www.leadertelegram.com/archives/is-obamacare-really-that-long/article_e92890ba-c93a-5276-b3d1-bfb44c06eaba.html.

Gifford, Donald G. (1991) "The American Tort Liability System." In *A Comparative Study of Liability Law and Compensation Schemes in Ten Countries and the United States,* ed. Werner Pfennigsdorf with D. G. Gifford. Oak Brook, Ill.: Insurance Research Council.

Gillman, Howard. (2002) "How Political Parties Can Use the Courts to Advance Their Agendas: Federal Courts in the United States, 1875–1891," *American Pol. Sci. Rev.* 96: 511–524.

Gilson, Ronald, and Robert Mnookin. (1994) "Disputing through Agents: Cooperation and Conflict between Lawyers in Litigation." *Colum. L. Rev.* 94: 509.

Ginsberg, Benjamin, and Martin Shefter. (1990) *Politics by Other Means: The Declining Importance of Elections in America.* New York: Basic Books.

Givelber, Daniel J., William Bowers, and Carolyn Blitch. (1984) *"Tarasoff:* Myth and Reality–An Empirical Study of Private Law in Action." *Wis. L. Rev.* 1984: 443.

Glaberson, William. (2000) "Court Rulings Curb Efforts to Rein in Judicial Races." *New York Times,* October 7, 2000, A8.

Glendon, Mary Ann. (1987) *Abortion and Divorce in Western Law.* Cambridge, Mass.: Harvard University Press.

Goerdt, John. (1991) "Explaining the Pace of Civil Case Litigation: The Latest Evidence from 37 Large Urban Trial Courts." *Justice System J.* 14: 289.

Goldberg v. Kelly. (1970) 397 U.S. 254.

Goldman, Eric. (1977) *Rendezvous with Destiny* [1952], rev. ed. New York: Vintage Books.

Goldman, Sheldon. (1967) "Judicial Appointments to the U.S. Courts of Appeal." *Wis. L. Rev.* 1967: 186.

Goldsmith, Barbara. (1987) *Johnson v. Johnson.* New York: Alfred Knopf.

Goldsmith, Jack. (2012) *Power and Constraint: The Accountable Presidency after 9/11* New York: W. W. Norton.

Goldstein, Amy. (2018a) "Opponents of Medicaid Work Requirement File Lawsuit to Try to Stop Kentucky Plan." *Washington Post,* January 24, 2018. https://www
.washingtonpost.com/national/health-science/opponents-of-medicaid-work
-requirement-file-lawsuit-to-try-to-stop-kentucky-plan/2018/01/24/e61d5bac-008c
-11e8-bb03-722769454f82_story.html?utm_term=.dd9ffb23856e.

Goldstein, Dana. (2018b) "Struggle to Fix Schools Drags States to Court." *New York Times,* August 21, 2018, A1.

Goodnough, Abby. (1997) "Court Rejects New Jersey School Plan." *New York Times,* May 15, 1997, A18.

Goodnough, Abby, and Kate Zarntke. (2017) "Under Trump, Rethinking How Doctors Charge." *New York Times,* November 12, 2017, A1, 13.

Goodwyn, Lawrence. (1978) *The Populist Moment: A Short History of the Agrarian Revolt in America.* New York: Oxford University Press.

Gornick, Janet, Marcia Meyers, and Katherine Ross. (1997) "Supporting the Employment of Mothers: Policy Variation across Fourteen Welfare States." *J. European Soc. Pol'y* 7: 126.

Gottlieb, Martin. (1996) "A Lawyer for the Poor Plans to Fight on His Own." *New York Times,* January 28, 1996, A8.

Gottschall, John. (1986) "Reagan's Appointments to the U.S. Courts of Appeals." *Judicature* (June/July), pp. 49–54.

Gould, William. (1984) *Japan's Reshaping of American Labor Law.* Cambridge, Mass.: MIT Press.

Graben, Sari, and Eric Biber. (2017) "Presidents, Parliaments and Legal Change; Quantifying the Effect of Political Systems on Comparative Environmental Law." *Va. Envtl. L.J.* 2017: 357.

Grady, Denise. (1996) "In One Country, Chronic Whiplash Is Uncompensated (and Unknown)." *New York Times,* May 7, 1996, B11.

Grady, Mark. (1988) "Why Are People Negligent? Technology, Nondurable Precautions and the Medical Malpractice Explosion." *Nw. U. L. Rev.* 82: 293.

Graham, John D. (1991) "Product Liability and Motor Vehicle Safety." In *The Liability Maze*, ed. Peter Huber and Robert Litan. Washington, D.C.: Brookings Institution.

Green, Michael. (1989) "The Inability of Offensive Collateral Estoppel to Fulfill Its Promise: An Examination of Estoppel in Asbestos Litigation." *Iowa L. Rev.* 70: 141.

Greene, Edith, and Brian Bornstein (2000) "Precious Little Guidance: Jury Instructions on Damages Awards." *Psychology, Public Policy & Law* 6: 743.

Greenhouse, Carol. (1986) *Praying for Justice: Faith, Order and Community in an American Town*. Ithaca, N.Y.: Cornell University Press.

Greenhouse, Linda. (2017) "On Contraception, It's Church Over State." *New York Times*, Sunday Review, October 15, 2017, 10.

Greve, Michael S. (1989a) "Environmentalism and Bounty Hunting." *Public Interest* 97: 15.

——. (1989b) "The Non-Reformation of Administrative Law: Standing to Sue and Public Interest Litigation in West German Environmental Law." *Cornell Int'l L.J.* 22: 197.

——. (1992) "Private Enforcement, Private Rewards: How Citizen Suits Became an Entitlement Program." In *Environmental Politics: Public Costs, Private Rewards*, ed. M. S. Greve and Fred Smith, Jr, eds. New York: Praeger.

Griffin v. California. (1965) 380 U.S. 609.

Griffin, Stephen. (1991) "Bringing the State into Constitutional Theory." *Law & Soc. Inquiry* 16: 659.

Griffiths, John. (1986) "What Do Dutch Lawyers Actually Do in Divorce Cases?" *Law & Soc'y Rev.* 20: 135.

Grinshteyn, Erin, and David Hemenway. (2016) "Violent Death Rates: The US Compared with Other High Income OECD Countries, 2010." *American Journal of Medicine,* no. 129: 266–273.

Gross, Samuel, and Kent Syverud. (1996) "Don't Try: Civil Jury Verdicts in a System Geared to Settlement." *UCLA L. Rev.* 44: 1.

Gunningham, Neil, Dorothy Thornton, and Robert A. Kagan. (2003) *Shades of Green: Business, Regulation, Environment.* Stanford, Calif.: Stanford University Press.

Gunnison, Robert B. (1993) "Nuclear Dump Plans for Mojave Are Halted." *San Francisco Chronicle,* November 25, 1993, A1, A21.

Hacker, Jacob. (2002) *The Divided Welfare State: The Battle Over Public and Private Social Benefits in the United States.* New York: Cambridge University Press.

——. (2005) "Inequality and Public Policy." In *Inequality and American Democracy: What We Know and What We Need to Learn,* ed. Lawrence R. Jacobs and Theda Skocpol. New York: Russell Sage Foundation.

Hacker, Jacob, and Paul Pierson. (2005) *Off Center: The Republican Revolution and the Erosion of American Democracy.* New Haven, Conn.: Yale University Press.

——. (2010) *Winner-Take-All Politics; How Washington Made the Rich Richer—and Turned Its Back on the Middle Class.* New York: Simon & Schuster.

——. (2016) *American Amnesia: How the War on Government Led Us To Forget What Made America Prosper.* New York: Simon & Schuster.

Hadfield, Gillian. (2014) "Innovating to Improve Access: Changing the Way Courts Regulate Legal Markets," *Daedalus*, Summer 2014: 83–95.

Hadfield, Gillian, and Jamie Heine. (2016) "Life in the Law-Thick World: The Legal Resource Landscape for Ordinary Americans." In *Beyond Elite Law: Access to Civil Justice in America*, ed. Samuel Estreicher and Joy Radice. New York: Cambridge University Press.

Haidt, Jonathan. (2012) *The Righteous Mind: Why Good People Are Divided by Politics and Religion*. New York: Vintage Books.

Haire, Susan, and Stefanie Lindquist. (1997) "Social Security Disability Cases in the U.S. Courts of Appeals." *Judicature* 80: 230.

Hakim, Danny, and William K. Rashbaum. (2017) "A Legal Thorn in the Side of an 'Aggressively Regressive' Trump." *New York Times*, December 27, A15.

Hall, Matthew. (2011) *The Nature of Supreme Court Power*. New York: Cambridge University Press.

Hale, Dennis. (2016) *The Jury in America: Triumph and Decline*. Lawrence: University Press of Kansas.

Haley, John. (1986) "Administrative Guidance versus Formal Regulation: Resolving the Paradox of Industrial Policy." In *Law and Trade Issues of the Japanese Economy*, Gary Saxonhouse and Kozo Yamamura. Seattle: University of Washington Press.

Halpern-Meekin, Sarah, Kathryn Edin, Laura Tach, and Jennifer Sykes. (2015) *It's Not Like I'm Poor: How Working Families Make Ends Meet in a Post-Welfare World*. Oakland: University of California Press.

Haltom, William, and Michael McCann. (2004) *Distorting the Law: Politics, Media, and the Litigation Crisis*. Chicago: University Chicago Press.

Hamdi v. Rumsfeld. (2004) 542 U.S. 507.

Hamlin, Rebecca. (2014) *Let Me Be A Refugee: Administrative Justice and the Politics of Asylum in the United States, Canada, and Australia*. New York: Oxford University Press.

Hammit, James K., Stephen Carroll, and Daniel Relles. (1985) "Tort Standards and Jury Decisions." *J. Legal Stud.* 14: 751.

Hanf, Kenneth, and Cor Smits. (1991) "Maintenance Dredging in the Port of Rotterdam: Trading Off Environmental Quality and Economic Development." Paper presented at annual meeting of Law and Society Association, Amsterdam, June 26–29, 1991.

Hans, Valerie, and William Lofquist. (1992) "Jurors' Judgments of Business Liability in Tort Cases: Implications for the Litigation Explosion Debate." *Law & Soc'y Rev.* 26: 85.

Hanson, Roger. (1992) *Indigent Defenders Get the Job Done and Done Well*. Williamsburg, Va.: National Center for State Courts.

Hanushek, Eric. (1989) "The Impact of Differential Expenditures on School Performance." *Education Researcher* 18: 45.

——. (1994) "Money Might Matter Somewhere: A Response to Hedges, Laine, and Greenwald." *Education Researcher* 23: 5.

Harris v. Alabama. (1995) 513 U.S. 504.

Harris, Alexes. (2016) *A Pound of Flesh: Monetary Sanctions as Punishment for Poor People*. New York: Russell Sage.

Harris, Lyle, and Mark Curriden. (1991) "McCleskey Is Executed for '78 Killing." *Atlanta Constitution,* September 25, 1991, A1, A13.

Harrison, Kathryn, and George Hoberg. (1991) "Setting the Environmental Agenda in Canada and the United States: The Cases of Dioxin and Radon." *Canadian J. Political Science* 24: 3.

Hartocollis, Anemona. (2017) "He Took on the Voting Rights Act and Won: Now He's Taking on Harvard." *New York Times,* November 17, 2017, A1.

Hartz, Louis. (1955) *The Liberal Tradition in America: An Interpretation of American Political Thought since the Revolution.* New York: Harcourt, Brace & World.

Harvard Medical Practice Study. (1990) *Patients, Doctors and Lawyers: Medical Injury, Malpractice Litigation, and Patient Compensation in New York.* Cambridge: Harvard University Press.

Hawley, Ellis. (1966) *The New Deal and the Problem of Monopoly.* Princeton, N.J.: Princeton University Press.

Hazard, Geoffrey. (1969) "Social Justice through Civil Justice." *U. Chi. L. Rev.* 36: 699.

Hazard, Geoffrey, and Michele Taruffo. (1993) *American Civil Procedure.* New Haven, Conn.: Yale University Press.

Hebert, Ray. (1972) "Class Action Lawsuit Hits Century Freeway." *Los Angeles Times,* February 18, 1972, 1.

——. (1986) "Century Freeway—When It's Born, an Era Will Die." *Los Angeles Times,* June 22, 1986, 4.

Heffernan, Richard, and Richard Lovely. (1991) "Evaluating the Fourth Amendment Exclusionary Rule: The Problem of Police Compliance with the Law." *Mich. J. L. Reform* 24: 537.

Heilbroner, David. (1990) *Rough Justice: Days and Nights of a Young D.A.* New York: Pantheon Books.

Heise, Michael. (1995) "State Constitutional Litigation, Educational Finance, and Legal Impact: An Empirical Analysis." *U. Cin. L. Rev.* 631: 735.

——. (2000) "Justice Delayed? An Empirical Analysis of Civil Case Disposition Time." *Case W. Res. L. Rev.* 50: 813.

Helland, Eric, and Alexander Tabarrok. (2000) "Runaway Judges? Selection Effects and the Jury." *J.L., Econ. & Org.* 16: 306–333.

Hellner, Jan. (1986) "Compensation for Personal Injury: The Swedish Alternative." *Am. J. Comp. L.* 34: 613.

Hensler, Deborah R. (1985) *Asbestos in the Courts.* Santa Monica, Calif.: RAND Institute for Civil Justice.

——. (1987) *Trends in Tort Litigation.* Santa Monica, Calif.: RAND Institute for Civil Justice.

——. (1990) "Court-Ordered Arbitration: An Alternative View." *U. Chi. Legal F.* 1990: 399.

——. (1991) *Compensation for Accidental Injuries in the United States.* Santa Monica, Calif.: RAND Institute for Civil Justice.

——. (2016) "Can Private Class Actions Enforce Regulations? Do They? Should They?" in Francesca Bignami and David Zaring, eds., *Comparative Law and Regulation: Understanding the Global Regulatory Process.* Cheltenham, U.K.: Edward Edgar.

Herbert, Bob. (1998) "Fighting Citizen Abuse." *New York Times,* June 21, 1998, 4, 15.

Hermann, Joachim. (1992) "Bargaining Justice–A Bargain for German Criminal Justice?" *U. Pitt. L. Rev.* 53: 755.

Hermann, Philip. (1962) "Predicting Verdicts in Personal Injury Cases." *Insurance L.J.* 475: 505.

Herrara v. Collins. (1993) 506 U.S. 390.

Heymann, Philip, and Lance Liebman. (1988) "No Fault, No Fee: The Legal Profession and Federal No-Fault Insurance Legislation." In *The Social Responsibilities of Lawyers.* Westbury, N.Y.: Foundation Press.

Hoberg, George. (1990) "Risk, Science and Politics: Alachlor Regulation in Canada and the United States." *Canadian J. Political Science* 23: 257.

———. (1991) "Sleeping with an Elephant: The American Influence on Canadian Environmental Regulation." *J. Pub. Pol'y* 11: 107.

———. (1993) "Environmental Policy: Alternative Styles." In *Governing Canada: State Institutions and Public Policy,* ed. Michael Atkinson. Toronto: Harcourt Brace Jovanovich Canada.

Hoebel, E. Adamson. (1964) *The Law of Primitive Man.* Cambridge, Mass.: Harvard University Press.

Holden, Benjamin, Laurie Cohen, and Eleena de Lisser. (1995) "Color Blinded? Race Seems to Play an Increasing Role in Many Jury Verdicts." *Wall Street J.,* October 4, 1995, A1.

Hollis-Brusky, Amanda. (2011) "Support Structures and Constitutional Change: Teles, Southworth, and the Conservative Legal Movement," *Law & Soc. Inquiry* 35: 516–536.

———. (2015) *Ideas with Consequences: The Federalist Society and the Conservative Counterrevolution.* New York: Oxford University Press.

Hollis-Brusky, Amanda, and Joshua Wilson. (2017) "Playing for the Rules: How and Why New Christian Right Public Interest Law Firms Invest in Secular Litigation." *Law & Pol'y* 39: 121–141.

Horwitz, Morton. (1977) *The Transformation of American Law, 1780–1860.* Cambridge, Mass.: Harvard University Press.

Howard, Christopher. (2007) *The Welfare State Nobody Knows.* Princeton, N.J.: Princeton University Press.

Howard, Philip. (2014) *The Rule of Nobody.* New York: W. W. Norton.

Howard, Robert, and Amy Steigerwalt. (2012) *Judging Law and Policy: Courts and Policymaking in the American Political System.* New York: Routledge.

Howlett, Michael. (1994) "The Judicialization of Canadian Environmental Policy, 1980–1990: Canada-U.S. Convergence?" *Canadian J. Political Science* 27: 99.

Huber, Peter W. (1985) "Safety and the Second Best: The Hazards of Public Risk Management in the Courts." *Colum. L. Rev.* 85: 277.

———. (1990) "Junk Science and the Jury." *U. Chi. Legal F.* 1990: 273.

———. (1997) "Easy Lawsuits Make Bad Medicine." *Forbes,* April 21, 1997, 166.

Hughes, Graham. (1984) "English Criminal Justice: Is It Better Than Ours?" *Ariz. L. Rev.* 26: 507.

Hulbert, Richard. (1997) "Comment on French Civil Procedure." *Am. J. Comparative Law* 45: 747.

Huntington, Samuel. (1981) *American Politics: The Promise of Disharmony*. Cambridge, Mass.: Belknap Press.

Huppes, Gjalt, and Robert A. Kagan. (1989) "Market-Oriented Regulation of Environmental Problems in the Netherlands." *Law & Policy* 11: 215.

Hurst, J. Willard. (1956) *Law and the Conditions of Freedom in Nineteenth Century United States*. Madison: University of Wisconsin Press.

——. (1964) *Law and Economic Growth: The Legal History of the Lumber Industry in Wisconsin, 1836–1915*. Madison: University of Wisconsin Law School.

Innocence Project. (2012) *New Research Illustrates Lack of Accountability for Prosecutors in Texas*. March 29, 2012. https://www.innocenceproject.org/new-research -illustrates-lack-of-accountability-for-prosecutors-in-texas/.

In re Estate of Lamberson. (1981) 407 So. 2d 358 (Fla. App., 5th Dist.).

Institute for Policy Integrity. (2019) *Irreplaceable: Why States Can't and Won't Make Up for Inadequate Federal Enforcement of Environmental Laws*. New York: New York University Law School (June, 6, 2017). https://policyintegrity.org/publications /detail/epa_enforcement.

——. (2019) *Roundup: Trump-Era Deregulation in the Courts*. New York: New York University Law School (April 22, 2019). https://policyintegrity.org/deregulation -roundup.

Jackson, Kenneth T. (1985) *Crabgrass Empire: The Suburbanization of the United States*. New York: Oxford University Press.

——. (1996) "America's Rush to Suburbia." *New York Times,* June 9, 1996, E15.

Jacob, Herbert. (1984) *The Frustration of Policy: Responses to Crime by American Cities*. Boston: Little, Brown.

Jacob, Herbert, Erhard Blankenburg, Herbert Kritzer, Doris Marie Provine, and Joseph Sanders. (1996) *Courts, Law and Politics in Comparative Perspective*. New Haven, Conn.: Yale University Press.

Jacobs, Margaret. (1994) "Arbitration Clauses Come under Scrutiny." *Wall Street J.,* December 22, 1994, B2.

——. (1997) "Prodding Unwed Dads to Admit Paternity." *Wall Street J.,* October 16, 1997, B1.

Jacobs, Margaret, and Michael Siconolfi. (1995) "Losing Battles: Investors Fare Poorly Fighting Wall Street–And May Do Worse." *Wall Street J.,* February 8, 1995, A1, A9.

Jaffe, Ina. (2017) "Under Trump Rule, Nursing Home Residents Will No Longer Be Able to Sue about Abuse." *National Public Radio,* Morning Edition, August 21, 2017.

James v. Valtierra. (1971) 402 U.S. 137.

Janovsky, Michael. (1996) "Suit Says Racial Bias Led to Clustering of Solid Waste Sites," *New York Times,* May 29, 1996, A15.

Janus v. American Federation of State, County, and Municipal Enterprises. (2018) 138 S. Ct. 2448.

Jasanoff, Sheila. (1986) *Risk Management and Political Culture*. New York: Russell Sage Foundation.

Jenkins, Jeffrey, and Sidney Milkis, eds. (2014) *The Politics of Major Policy Reform in Postwar America*. Cambridge: Cambridge University Press.

Jewell, Christopher. (2007) *Agents of the Welfare State: How Caseworkers Respond to Need in the United States, Germany, and Sweden.* New York: Palgrave Macmillan.

Johnson, David. (1998) "The Organization of Prosecution and the Possibility of Order." *Law & Soc'y Rev.* 32: 247.

Johnson, Earl, Jr., and Ann Barthelmes Drew. (1978) "This Nation Has Money for Everything–Except Its Courts." *Judges J.* (Summer): 10.

Joppke, Christian. (1993) *Mobilizing against Nuclear Power: A Comparison of Germany and the United States.* Berkeley: University of California Press.

Jost, Timothy Stoltzfus. (1998) "Health Care Rationing in the Courts: A Comparative Study." *Hastings International & Comparative L. Rev.* 21: 639.

Kagan, Robert A. (1978) *Regulatory Justice: Implementing a Wage Price Freeze.* New York: Russell Sage Foundation.

——. (1982) "What If Abe Fortas Had Been More Discreet?" In *What If? Explorations in Social-Science Fiction*, ed. Nelson W. Polsby. Lexington, Mass.: Lewis Publishing.

——. (1984) "Inside Administrative Law." *Colum. L. Rev.* 84: 816.

——. (1987) "Constitutional Litigation in the United States." In *Constitutional Courts in Comparison*, ed. Ralf Rogowski and Thomas Gawron. Gummersbach, West Germany: Theodor Huess Academie.

——. (1988) "What Makes Uncle Sammy Sue?" *Law & Soc'y Rev.* 21: 718.

——. (1990a) "How Much Does Law Matter? Labor Law, Competition, and Waterfront Labor Relations in Rotterdam and U.S. Ports." *Law & Soc'y Rev.* 24: 35.

——. (1990b) *Patterns of Port Development: Government, Intermodal Transportation, and Innovation in the United States, China and Hong Kong.* Berkeley, Calif.: Institute of Transportation Studies.

——. (1991) "The Dredging Dilemma: Economic Development and Environmental Protection in Oakland Harbor." *Coastal Management* 19: 313–341.

——. (1993) "Regulatory Enforcement." In *Handbook of Regulation and Administrative Law*, ed. David Rosenblum and Richard Schwartz. New York: Marcel Dekker.

——. (1994) "Do Lawyers Cause Adversarial Legalism?" *Law & Soc. Inquiry* 19: 1.

——. (1995) "What Socio-Legal Scholars Should Do When There Is Too Much Law to Study." *J. Law & Society* 22: 140.

——. (1997a) "Should Europe Worry about Adversarial Legalism?" *Oxford J. Legal Stud.* 17: 165.

——. (1997b) "Political and Legal Obstacles to Ecosystem Planning." *Environmental Law Quarterly* 24: 871.

——. (1999a) "Trying to Have It Both Ways: Local Discretion, Central Control, and Adversarial Legalism in American Environmental Regulation." *Ecology L. Q.* 25: 718.

——. (1999b) "Adversarial Legalism: Tamed or Still Wild?" *N.Y.U. J. Legis. Pub. Pol'y* 2: 101.

——. (2000a) "The Consequences of Adversarial Legalism." In *Regulatory Encounters: Multinational Corporations and American Adversarial Legalism*, ed. Robert A. Kagan and Lee Axelrad. Berkeley: University of California Press.

——. (2000b) "Introduction: Comparing National Styles of Regulation in Japan and the United States." *Law & Pol'y* 22: 225–244.

——. (2010) "Fragmented Political Structures and Fragmented Law." *Jus Politicum,* no. 4, Legal Science and Democracy. http://juspoliticum.com/article/Fragmented -Political-Structures-and-Fragmented-Law-213.html.

——. (2017) "Varieties of Bureaucratic Justice: Building on Mashaw's Typology." In *Administrative Law from the Inside Out: Essays on Themes in the Work of Jerry L. Mashaw,* ed. Nicholas Parillo. New York: Cambridge University Press.

Kagan, Robert A., and Lee Axelrad. (1997) "Adversarial Legalism: An International Perspective." In *Comparative Disadvantages? Social Regulations and the Global Economy,* ed. Pietro Nivola. Washington, D.C.: Brookings Institution.

Kagan, Robert A., and Lee Axelrad, eds. (2000) *Regulatory Encounters: Multinational Corporations and American Adversarial Legalism.* Berkeley: University of California Press.

Kagan, Robert, Bliss Cartwright, Lawrence M. Friedman, and Stanton Wheeler. (1977) "The Business of State Supreme Courts, 1870–1970." *Stan. L. Rev.* 30: 121.

Kagan, Robert A., Robert Detlefsen, and Bobby Infelise. (1984) "American State Supreme Court Justices, 1900–1970." *Am. Bar Foundation Research J.* 1984: 371.

Kagan, Robert A., Neil Gunningham, and Dorothy Thornton. (2011) "Fear, Duty, and Regulatory Compliance: Lessons from Three Research Projects." In *Explaining Compliance: Business Responses to Regulation,* ed. Christine Parker and Vibeke Nielsen, 37–55.Cheltenham, U.K. and Northhampton, Mass.: Edward Elgar.

Kagan, Robert A., and Todd Lochner. (1998) "Criminal Prosecution for Regulatory Offenses in the United States: Trends and Patterns in the Federal System." Paper prepared for Conference on Criminal Prosecution for Regulatory Offenses, Centre for Socio-Legal Studies, Oxford, England, September 1998.

Kagan, Robert A., and William Nelson. (2000) "The Politics of Tobacco Regulation in the United States." In *Regulatory Tobacco,* ed. Robert Rabin and Stephen Sugarman. New York: Oxford University Press.

Kagan, Robert A., and Robert Eli Rosen. (1985) "On the Social Significance of Large Law Firm Practice." *Stan. L. Rev.* 37: 399.

Kakalik, James S., Michael G. Shanley, William L. F. Felstiner, and Patricia A. Ebener. (1983) *Costs of Asbestos Litigation.* Santa Monica, Calif.: Institute for Civil Justice, RAND Corporation.

Kakalik, James S., Patricia A. Ebener, William L. F. Felstiner, Gus Haggstrom, Michael G. Shanley. (1984) *Variation in Asbestos Litigation Compensation Expenses.* Santa Monica, Calif.: Institute for Civil Justice, RAND Corporation.

Kakalik, James S., Molly Selvin, and Nicholas Pace. (1990) "A RAND Note: Strategies for Reducing Civil Delay in the Los Angeles Superior Court: Technical Appendixes." Santa Monica, Calif.: Institute for Civil Justice.

Kakalik, James S. and Nicholas M. Pace. (1986) *Costs and Compensation Paid in Tort Litigation.* Santa Monica, Calif.: Institute for Civil Justice, RAND Corporation.

Kalven, Harry. (1964) "The Dignity of the Civil Jury." *Va. L. Rev.* 50: 1055.

Kalven, Harry, and Hans Zeisel. (1966) *The American Jury.* Boston: Little, Brown.

Kamerman, Sheila B., and Alfred J. Kahn. (1988) "What Europe Does for Single-Parent Families." *Public Interest* 93: 70–86.

Kamin, Samuel. (1999) "The Death Penalty and the California Supreme Court." Ph.D. diss., University of California, Berkeley.

Kapiszewski, Diana, Gordon Silverstein, and Robert A. Kagan, eds. (2013) *Consequential Courts: Judicial Roles in Global Perspective.* New York: Cambridge University Press.

Kaplan, David. (1991) "New Rules on Death Row." *Newsweek,* April 29, 1991, 68.

Karpoff, Jonathan, John Lott, Jr., and Graeme Rankine. (1998) "Environmental Violations, Legal Penalties, and Reputation Costs." Working paper, University of Washington. http://faculty.washington.edu/karpoff/.

Katzenstein, Peter, ed. (1978) *Between Power and Plenty: Foreign Economic Policies of Advanced Industrial States.* Madison: University of Wisconsin Press.

Katzmann, Robert. (1995) "Making Sense of Congressional Intent: Statutory Interpretation and Welfare Policy." *Yale L.J.* 104: 2345.

Kawar, Leila. (2015) *Contesting Immigration Policy in Court: Legal Activism and Its Radiating Effects in the United States and France.* New York: Cambridge University Press.

Keck, Thomas M. (2014) *Judicial Politics in Polarized Times.* Chicago: University of Chicago Press.

Kelemen, R. Daniel. (1998) "Regulatory Federalism: The European Union in Comparative Perspective." Ph.D. diss., Stanford University.

——. (2011) *Eurolegalism: The Transformation of Law and Regulation in the European Union.* Cambridge, Mass: Harvard University Press.

Keller, Josh, and Adam Pearce. (2016) "This Small Indiana County Sends More People to Prison than San Francisco and Durham, N.C., Combined. Why?" *New York Times,* September 2, 2016, A1.

Kelman, Steven. (1981) *Regulating America, Regulating Sweden: A Comparative Study of Occupational Safety and Health Policy.* Cambridge, Mass.: MIT Press.

Kennedy, Eugene. (1985) *Defendant: A Psychiatrist on Trial for Medical Malpractice.* New York: Free Press.

Kessler, Amalia D. (2017) *Inventing American Exceptionalism: The Origins of American Adversarial Legal Culture, 1800–1877.* New Haven, Conn.: Yale University Press.

King v. Smith. (1968) 392 U.S. 309.

Kirk, David, and Andrew Papachristos. (2011) "Cultural Mechanisms and the Persistence of Neighborhood Violence." *American Journal of Sociology* 116: 1190–1233.

Kirp, David L. (1979) *Doing Good by Doing Little: Race and Schooling in Britain.* Berkeley: University of California Press.

——. (1982) "Professionalization as a Policy Choice: British Special Education in Comparative Perspective." *World Politics* 34: 137.

Kirp, David L., John Dwyer, and Larry Rosenthal. (1995) *Our Town: Race, Housing and the Soul of Suburbia.* New Brunswick, N.J.: Rutgers University Press.

Kitamura, Yoshinobu. (2000) "Regulatory Enforcement in Local Government in Japan." *Law & Pol'y* 22: 305–318.

Kitch, Edward. (1985) "Vaccines and Product Liability: A Case of Contagious Litigation." *Regulation* (May/June): 11.

Kniesner, Thomas, and John Leeth. (1991) "Improving Worker Safety." *Regulation,* Fall: 64–70.

Kolata, Gina. (1995) "Will the Lawyers Kill Off Norplant?" *New York Times,* May 28, 1995, Sec. 3, 1, 5.

——. (1998) "Panel Can't Link Implants to Any Diseases." *New York Times,* December 2, 1998, A1.

Krasner, Stephen. (1978) *Defending the National Interest.* Princeton, N.J.: Princeton University Press.

Kritzer, Herbert. (1990) *The Justice Broker: Lawyers and Ordinary Litigation.* New York: Oxford University Press.

——. (1991) "Propensity to Sue in England and the United States of America: Blaming and Claiming in Tort Cases." *J.L. Soc'y* 18: 400.

——. (1993) "The Politics of Redress: Controlling Access to the Court System in England." Paper presented to the annual meeting of the Law and Society Association, Chicago, May 27–30, 1993.

——. (1996) "Courts, Justice, and Politics in England." In *Courts, Law and Politics in Comparative Perspective,* by Herbert Jacob, Erhard Blankenburg, Herbert Kritzer, Doris Marie Provine, and Joseph Sanders. New Haven, Conn.: Yale University Press.

Krugman, Paul. (2018) "Why It Can Happen Here." *New York Times,* August 28, 2018, A22.

LaChance, Daniel. (2014) "What Will Doom the Death Penalty?" *New York Times,* September 9, 2014, A27.

LaFraniere, Sharon, Sarah Cohen, and Richard Oppel, Jr. (2015) "How Often Do Mass Shootings Occur?" *New York Times,* December 5, 2015, 1, 23.

LaFraniere, Sharon, and Andrew Lehren. (2015) "The Disproportionate Risks of Driving While Black," *New York Times,* October 25, 2015, A1.

Laitin, Howard. (1994) "'Good' Warnings, Bad Products, and Cognitive Limitations." *UCLA L. Rev.* 41: 1193.

Lambert, Lisa. (2017) "Trump Kills Class Action Rule against Banks, Lightening Wall Street Regulation." Reuters, November 1, 2017.

Lambert, Wade. (1995) "Costs of Settlements Reach Record in Suits against Directors, Officers." *Wall Street J.,* March 10, 1995, B6.

Lande, John. (1998) "Failing Faith in Litigation? A Survey of Business Lawyers' and Executives' Opinions." *Harv. J. Disp. Resol.* 3: 1.

Landes, William, and Richard Posner. (1975) "The Independent Judiciary in an Interest Group Perspective." *J.L. & Econ.* 18: 875.

Landy, Marc, and Martin Levin. (1995) "The New Politics of Public Policy." In *The New Politics of Public Policy.* Baltimore, Md.: Johns Hopkins Press.

Langan, Patricia, and Helen Grazadei. (1995) *Felony Sentences in State Courts, 1992.* Washington, D.C.: U.S. Department of Justice.

Langbein, John. (1979a) "Understanding the Short History of Plea Bargaining." *Law & Soc'y Rev.* 13: 261.

——. (1979b) "Land without Plea Bargaining: How the Germans Do It." *Mich. L. Rev.* 78: 204.

——. (1985) "The German Advantage in Civil Procedure." *U. Chi. L. Rev.* 52: 823.

——. (1994) "Will Contests." *Yale L.J.* 103: 2039.

——. (1995) "Money Talks, Clients Walk." *Newsweek,* April 17, 1995, 32–33.

Lasser, Michel de S.-O.-l'E. (2013) "The Judicial Dynamics of the French and European Fundamental Rights Revolution." In *Consequential Courts: Judicial Roles in Global Governance*, ed. Diana Kapiszewski, Gordon Silverstein, and Robert A. Kagan. New York: Cambridge University Press.

Law, David, and Mila Versteeg. (2012) "The Declining Influence of the United States Constitution." *N.Y.U. Law Rev.* 87: 762.

Lawrence, Susan. (1990) *The Poor in Court: The Legal Service Program and Supreme Court Decision Making.* Princeton, N.J.: Princeton University Press.

Lazarus, Richard. (1991) "The Tragedy of Distrust in the Implementation of Federal Environmental Law." *Law & Contemp. Probs.* 54: 311.

Lee, Louise. (1997) "Lots of Trouble: Courts Begin to Award Damages to Victims of Parking-Area Crime." *Wall Street J.,* April 23, 1997, A1.

Lee, Patrick. (1990) "Barrels of Losses at Point Arguello." *Los Angeles Times,* January 27, 1990, D1.

Leebron, David. (1989) "Final Moments: Damages for Pain and Suffering Prior to Death." *N.Y.U. L. Rev.* 64: 256.

Lehne, Richard. (1978) *The Quest for Justice: The Politics of School Finance Reform.* New York: Longman.

Lempert, Richard. (1993) "Civil Juries and Complex Cases." In *Verdict: Assessing the Civil Jury System*, ed. Robert Litan. Washington, D.C.: Brookings Institution.

Leo, Richard. (1996) "*Miranda*'s Revenge: Police Interrogation as a Confidence Game." *Law & Soc'y Rev.* 30: 259.

———. (2008) *Police Interrogation and American Justice.* Cambridge, Mass.: Harvard University Press.

Lester, Charles. (1992) "The Search for Dialogue in the Administrative State: The Politics, Policy, and Law of Offshore Oil Development." Ph.D. diss., University of California, Berkeley.

Levin, Martin. (1972) "Urban Politics and Judicial Behavior." *J. Legal Studies* 1: 193.

Levine, James. (1983) "Jury Toughness: The Impact of Conservatism on Criminal Court Verdicts." *Crime & Delinquency* 29: 71.

———. (1992) *Juries and Politics.* Pacific Grove, Calif.: Brooks/Cole.

Levy, Jonah. (1997) "Globalization, Liberalization, and National Capitalisms." *Structural Change & Economic Dynamics* 8: 87.

———. (1999) *Tocqueville's Revenge.* Cambridge, Mass.: Harvard University Press.

Lewin, Tamar. (1995) "Who Decides Who Will Die? Even within States, It Varies." *New York Times,* February 23, 1995, A1.

———. (1996) "U.S. Agency Wants the Pill Redefined." *New York Times,* July 1, 1996, A1, A10.

Lewis-Beck, Michael, and John Alford. (1980) "Can Government Regulate Safety?: The Coal Mine Example." *Am. Political Science Rev.,* no. 74: 745–755.

Liang, Bryan. (1997) "Assessing Medical Malpractice Jury Verdicts: A Case Study of an Anesthesiology Department." *Cornell J.L. & Pub. Pol'y* 7: 121.

Lieberman, Robert (2005) *Shaping Race Policy: The United States in Comparative Perspective.* Princeton, N.J.: Princeton University Press.

Lifsher, Mark. (1998) "EPA Urged to Move against Firm." *Wall Street J.,* June 17, A1, A4.

Lipsen, Linda. (1991) "The Evolution of Products Liability as a Federal Policy Issue." In *Tort Law and the Public Interest*, ed. Peter Schuck. New York: W. W. Norton.

Lipset, Seymour Martin. (1991) *Continental Divide: The Values and Institutions of the United States and Canada*. New York: Routledge.

———. (1996) *American Exceptionalism: A Double-Edged Sword*. New York: W. W. Norton.

Lipton, Eric, and Danielle Ivory. (2017) "E.P.A.'s Polluter Playbook Takes a Turn to Leniency." *New York Times,* December, 11, 2017, A1.

Litt, David, Jonathan Macey, Geoffrey Miller, and Edward Rubin. (1990) "Politics, Bureaucracies, and Financial Markets: Bank Entry into Commercial Paper Underwriting in the United States and Japan." *U. Pa. L. Rev.* 139: 369.

Lohr, Steve. (1995) "Vigorous Defense Stalls Injury Claims on Repetitive Strain." *New York Times,* May 28, 1995, 19.

Lopez, German. (2018) "The Growing Number of Lawsuits against Opioid Companies, Explained." *VOX,* May 18, 2018. https://www.vox.com/policy-and-politics/2017/6/7/15724054/opioid-epidemic-lawsuits-purdue-oxycontin.

Louis, Arthur. (1987) "The Reference Run-Around." *San Francisco Chronicle,* November 9, 1987, C1.

Lowenthal, Gary. (1993) "Mandatory Sentencing Laws: Undermining the Effectiveness of Determinate Sentencing Reform." *Cal. L. Rev.* 81: 61.

Lucas, Alaistair R. (1993) "Judicial Review of Environmental Assessment: Has the Federal Process Been Judicialized?" In *Law and Process in Environmental Management*, ed. Steven A. Kennett. Calgary: Canadian Institute of Resources Law.

Lucas, Charlotte-Anne. (1990) "Chevron's Albatross: Point Arguello Project a Multi-Billion-Dollar Disaster." *San Francisco Examiner,* February 4, 1990, D1, D16.

Lundqvist, Lennart J. (1980) *The Hare and the Tortoise: Clean Air Policies in the United States and Sweden*. Ann Arbor: University of Michigan Press.

Lunzer, Francesca. (1985) "Scared Shotless." *Forbes,* November 18, 1985, 256.

Lynch, David. (1994) "The Impropriety of Plea Agreements: A Tale of Two Counties." *Law & Soc. Inquiry* 19: 115.

Lynch, James. (1988) "A Comparison of Prison Use in England, Canada, West Germany and the United States." *J. Crim. L. & Criminology* 79: 180–217.

Lytton, Timothy. (2005a) "Introduction: An Overview of Lawsuits against the Gun Industry." In *Suing the Gun Industry: A Battle at the Crossroads of Gun Control and Mass Torts*. Ann Arbor: University of Michigan Press.

———. (2005b) "Afterword: Federal Gun Industry Immunity Legislation." In *Suing the Gun Industry: A Battle at the Crossroads of Gun Control and Mass Torts*. Ann Arbor: University of Michigan Press.

———. (2008) *Holding Bishops Accountable: How Lawsuits Helped the Catholic Church Confront Clergy Sexual Abuse*. Cambridge, Mass.: Harvard University Press.

Macaulay, Stewart. (1979) "Lawyers and Consumer Protection Laws." *Law & Soc'y Rev.* 14: 115.

MacCoun, Robert. (1993) "Decisionmaking by Civil Juries." In *Verdict: Assessing the Civil Jury System*, ed. Robert Litan. Washington, D.C.: Brookings Institution.

——. (1996) "Differential Treatment of Corporate Defendants by Juries: An Examination of the 'Deep Pockets' Hypothesis." *Law & Soc'y Rev.* 30: 121.

MacGillis, Alec. (2017) "Kushnerville." *New York Times Magazine.* May 26, 2017, 44.

Machura, Stefan. (2000) "Justice Evaluations by German Lay Assessors." Paper presented at annual meeting of Law and Society Association, Miami Beach, Fla., May 2000.

Mackay, Murray. (1991) "Liability, Safety, and Innovation in the Automotive Industry." In *The Liability Maze*, ed. Peter Huber and Robert Litan. Washington, D.C.: Brookings Institution.

Maltby, Lewis. (1994) "The Projected Impact of the Model Employment Termination Act." *Annals of the American Academy of Political & Social Science* 536: 103.

Manley, Howard. (1994) "Harsh Line Drawn on Crack Cocaine." *Columbus Dispatch,* July 24, 1994, A1, A14.

Mann, Kenneth. (1985) *Defending White Collar Crime.* New Haven, Conn.: Yale University Press.

Mansnerus, Laura. (1995) "Rewriting the Rules of the Jury System." *New York Times,* November 4, 1995, A7.

March, James, and Herbert Simon. (1958) *Organizations.* New York: John Wiley.

Marcus, Richard. (2014) "Civil Justice with Multiple Objectives." In *Goals of Civil Justice and Civil Procedure in Contemporary Judicial Systems*, ed. Alan Uzelac. New York: Springer.

Margolick, David. (1993) *Undue Influence: The Epic Battle for the Johnson & Johnson Fortune.* New York: William Morrow & Co.

——. (1994) "In a Death Penalty Case, the Defense Lawyer Is on Trial Himself, Accused of Incompetence and Worse." *New York Times,* June 3, 1994, B8.

Markesinis, Basil. (1990) "Litigation-Mania in England, Germany, and the USA: Are We So Very Different?" *Cambridge L.J.* 49: 233.

Marshall, Ineke. (1996) "How Exceptional Is the United States? Crime Trends in Europe and the U.S." *European J. Criminal Policy & Research* 4: 7–35.

Martin, Roger. (1991) "General Aviation Manufacturing: An Industry Under Siege." In *The Liability Maze*, ed. Peter Huber and Robert Litan. Washington, D.C.: Brookings Institution.

Mashaw, Jerry. (1971) "Welfare Reform and Local Administration of Aid to Families with Dependent Children in Virginia." *Va. L. Rev.* 57: 818.

——. (1983) *Bureaucratic Justice: Managing Social Security Disability Claims.* New Haven, Conn.: Yale University Press.

——. (2006) "The Story of Motor Vehicle Mfrs Ass'n of the US v. State Farm Mutual Automobile Ins. Co.: Law, Science and Politics in the Administrative State." In *Administrative Law Stories*, ed. Peter Strauss. New York: Foundation Press.

——. (2012) *Creating the Administrative Constitution; The Lost One Hundred Years of American Administrative Law.* New Haven, Conn.: Yale University Press.

Mashaw, Jerry L., and Daniel Harfst. (1987) "Regulation and Legal Culture: The Case of Motor Vehicle Safety." *Yale J. on Reg.* 4: 257–316.

——. (1991) *The Struggle for Auto Safety.* Cambridge, Mass.: Harvard University Press.

Massey, Douglas, and Nancy Denton. (1993) *American Apartheid: Segregation and the Making of the Underclass.* Cambridge, Mass.: Harvard University Press.

Masters, Jonathan. (2012) *U.S. Gun Policy: Global Comparisons.* New York: Council on Foreign Relations. https://www.cfr.org/backgrounder/us-gun-policy-global -comparisons.

Mastroianni, Luigi, Jr., Peter J. Donaldson, and Thomas T. Kane, eds. (1990) *Developing New Contraceptives: Obstacles and Opportunities.* Washington, D.C.: National Academy Press.

Mather, Lynn. (1998) "Theorizing about Trial Courts: Lawyers, Policymaking, and Tobacco Litigation." *Law & Soc. Inquiry* 23: 897.

Matsushita Elec. Indus. Co. v. Zenith Radio Corp. (1986) 475 U.S. 574.

Mauer, Marc. (2009) "The Changing Racial Dynamics of the War on Drugs." *Ethnicity and Race in a Changing World,* 1, 41–49. Washington, D.C.: The Sentencing Project.

Maxeiner, James. (1991) "The Expert in U.S. and German Patent Litigation." *IIC* 22: 595.

Mayhew, David. (1991) *Divided We Govern: Party Control, Lawmaking, and Investigations, 1946–1990.* New Haven, Conn.: Yale University Press.

Mayer, Jane. (2016) *Dark Money: The Hidden History of the Billionaires Behind the Rise of the Radical Right.* New York: Anchor Books.

McCann, Michael. (1986) *Taking Reform Seriously: Perspectives on Public Interest Liberalism.* Ithaca, N.Y.: Cornell University Press.

——. (1994) *Rights at Work: Law and the Politics of Pay Equity.* Chicago: University of Chicago Press.

——. (1999) "How the Supreme Court Matters in American Politics." In *The Supreme Court in American Politics: New Institutional Perspectives,* ed. Howard Gilman and Cornell Clayton. Lawrence: University Press of Kansas.

McCann, Michael, and William Haltom. (2018) "Seeing Through the Smoke: Adversarial Legalism and American Tobacco Politics." In *Varieties of Legal Order: The Politics of Adversarial and Bureaucratic Legalism,* ed. Thomas Burke and Jeb Barnes. New York: Routledge.

McCann, Michael, William Haltom, and S. Fisher. (2013) "Criminalizing Big Tobacco: Legal Mobilization and the Politics of Responsibility for Health Risks in the United States." *Law & Soc. Inquiry* 38: 288–321.

McCleskey v. Kemp. (1987) 481 U.S. 279.

McCleskey v. State. (1980) 263 S.E.2d 146 (Ga.), cert. denied, 449 U.S. 891.

McCleskey v. Zant. (1991) 499 U.S. 467.

McClosky, Herbert, and Alida Brill. (1983) *Dimensions of Tolerance: What Americans Believe about Civil Liberties.* New York: Russell Sage Foundation.

McConville, Michael. (1994) "An Error of Judgment." In *Criminal Justice in Crisis,* ed. M. McConville and Lee Bridges. Aldershot, England: E. Elgar.

McConville, Michael, and Chester Mirsky. (1986–1987) "Criminal Defense of the Poor in New York City." *N.Y.U. Rev. L. & Soc. Change* 15: 581.

McCoy, Candace. (2010) "How Civil Rights Lawsuits Improve American Policing." In *Holding Police Accountable,* ed. Candace McCoy. Washington, D.C.: Urban Institute Press.

McCreary, Scott. (1989) "Resolving Science-Intensive Public Policy Disputes: Lessons from the New York Bight Initiative." Ph.D. diss., Massachusetts Institute of Technology.

McDonald v. Chicago. (2010) 561 U.S. 3025.

McFate, Katherine. (1995) "Trampolines, Safety Nets, or Free Fall? Labor Market Policies and Social Assistance in the 1980s." In *Poverty, Inequality, and the Future of Social Policy: Western States in the New World Order*, ed. Katherine McFate, Roger Lawson, and William Julius Wilson. New York: Russell Sage Foundation.

McFate, Katherine, Roger Lawson, and William Julius Wilson, eds. (1995) *Poverty, Inequality, and the Future of Social Policy: Western States in the New World Order*. New York: Russell Sage Foundation.

McIntosh, David, and David Murray. (1994) *Medical Malpractice Liability: An Agenda for Reform*. Indianapolis, Ind.: Competitiveness Center of Hudson Institute.

McIntosh, Wayne. (1980–1981) "150 Years of Litigation and Dispute Settlement: A Court Tale." *Law & Soc'y Rev.* 15: 823.

McIntyre, Linda. (1987) *The Public Defender*. Chicago: University of Chicago Press.

McKinley, James, Jr. (1999) "Sugar Industry's Pivotal Role in Everglades Effort." *New York Times*, April 16, 1999, A1, A19.

McLanahan, Sara, and Irwin Garfinkel. (1995) "Single Mothers and Social Policy." In *Poverty, Inequality, and the Future of Social Policy: Western States in the New World Order*, ed. Katherine McFate, Roger Lawson, and William Julius Wilson. New York: Russell Sage Foundation.

McMahon, Kevin. (2000) "Constitutional Vision and Supreme Court Decisions: Roosevelt on Race." *Studies in American Political Development* 14: 20.

McMahon v. Bunn-O-Matic Corp. (1998) 150 F.3d 651 (7th Cir.).

McManus, Susan. (1993) "The Impact of Litigation on Municipalities." *Syracuse L. Rev.* 44: 833.

Meador, Daniel. (1983) "German Appellate Judges: Career Patterns and American-English Comparisons." *Judicature* 67: 16.

Meier, Barry. (1997) "In Fine Print, Customers Lose Ability to Sue." *New York Times*, March 10, 1997, A1.

Mello, Michelle, Allen Kachalia, and David Studdert. (2011) "Administrative Compensation for Medical Injuries: Lessons from Three Foreign Systems." *Issues in International Health Policy*, July 2011, publication no. 1517, vol 14.

Melnick, R. Shep. (1992) "Pollution Deadlines and the Coalition for Failure." In *Environmental Politics: Public Costs, Private Rewards*, ed. Michael Greve and Fred Smith. New York: Greenwood.

——. (1993) *Between the Lines: Interpreting Welfare Rights*. Washington, D.C.: Brookings Institution.

——. (1995) "Separation of Powers and the Strategy of Rights: The Expansion of Special Education." In *The New Politics of Public Policy*, Marc Landy and Martin Levin. Baltimore, Md.: Johns Hopkins Press.

——. (2014) "Courts and Agencies in the American Civil Rights State." In *The Politics of Major Policy Reform in Postwar America*, ed. Jeffrey Jenkins and Sidney Milkis. New York: Cambridge University Press.

——. (2016) "Civil Wrongs." *Education Next*. Winter, 30–36.

——. (2018a) "Adversarial Legalism, Civil Rights, and the Exceptional American State." In *Varieties of Legal Order: The Politics of Adversarial and Bureaucratic Legalism*, ed. Thomas Burke and Jeb Barnes. New York: Routledge.

——. (2018b) *The Transformation of Title IX: Regulating Gender Equality in Education.* Washington, D.C.: The Brookings Institution.

Meltzer, Judith, Rachel Molly Joseph, and Andy Shookhoff, eds. (2012) *For the Welfare of Children: Lessons Learned from Class Action Litigation.* Washington, D.C.: Center for the Study of Social Policy.

Mendeloff, John. (1987) *The Dilemma of Rulemaking for Toxic Substances.* Cambridge, Mass.: MIT Press.

Mendelson, David, and Robert Rubin. (1993) *Estimating the Costs of Defensive Medicine.* Fairfax, Va.: Lewin-VH1.

Meritor Savings Bank v. Vinson. (1986) 477 U.S. 57.

Merritt, Deborah, and Kathryn Barry. (1999) "Is the Tort System in Crisis? New Empirical Evidence." *Ohio St. L.J.* 60: 315.

Metzloff, Thomas. (1988) "Researching Litigation: The Medical Malpractice Example." *Law & Contemp. Probs.* 51: 199.

——. (1991) "Resolving Malpractice Disputes: Imaging the Jury's Shadow." *Law & Contemp. Probs.* 54: 43.

——. (1993) "Understanding the Malpractice Wars." Review of *Medical Malpractice on Trial* by Paul C. Weiler. *Harv. L. Rev.* 106: 1169.

Michael, Douglas. (1996) "Cooperative Implementation of Federal Regulations." *Yale J. on Reg.* 13: 535.

Milhaupt, Curtis, and Geoffrey Miller. (2000) "Regulatory Failure and the Collapse of Japan's Home Mortgage Lending Industry: A Legal and Economic Analysis" *Law & Pol'y* 22: 245–290.

Miller, Richard, and Austin Sarat. (1981) "Grievances, Claims and Disputes: Assessing the Adversary Culture." *Law & Soc'y Rev.* 15: 525.

Milliken v Bradley. (1974) 418 U.S. 717.

Minow, Newton, and Fred Cate. (1994) "Court Quiz Show: Grilling Jurors by Questionnaire." *Wall Street J.* October 12, 1994, A6.

Mnookin, Robert, and Robert Wilson. (1989) "Rational Bargaining and Market Efficiency: Understanding *Penzoil v. Texaco.*" *Va. L. Rev.* 75: 295.

Moe, Terry M. (1989) "The Politics of the Bureaucratic State." In *Can the Government Govern?* ed. John Chubb and Paul Peterson. Washington, D.C.: Brookings Institution.

Moller, Erik. (1996) *Trends in Jury Verdicts since 1985.* Santa Monica, Calif.: RAND Institute for Civil Justice.

Molot, Johnathan. (1998) "How Changes in the Legal Profession Reflect Changes in Legal Procedure." *Va. L. Rev.* 84: 955.

Monell v. Department of Social Services. (1978) 436 U.S. 658.

Monroe v. Pape. (1961) 365 U.S. 167.

Montgomery, Bill, and Mark Curriden. (1991) "Entire Process Barbaric: Lawyers Assail Execution." *Atlanta Constitution,* September 25, 1991, A6.

Motor Vehicles Manufacturers Association v. State Farm. (1983) 463 U.S. 29.

Mt. Laurel I: Southern Burlington County NAACP v. Township of Mt. Laurel. (1975) 67 N.J. 151, 33 A.2d 713.

Mt. Laurel II: Southern Burlington County NAACP v. Township of Mt. Laurel. (1983) 92 N.J. 158, 456 A.2d 390.

Mt. Laurel III: Hills Development Corp. v. Township of Bernards. (1986) 103 N.J. 1, 510 A.2d 621.

Muir, William K., Jr. (1973) *Law and Attitude Change.* Chicago: University of Chicago Press.

Munch, Patricia. (1977) *Costs and Benefits of the Torts System If Viewed as a Compensation System.* Santa Monica: RAND Institute for Civil Justice.

Myhre, Jonas. (1968) "Conviction without Trial in the United States and Norway: A Comparison." *Hous. L. Rev.* 5: 647.

Nardulli, Peter. (1983) "The Societal Cost of the Exclusionary Rule: An Empirical Assessment." *Am. Bar Foundation Research J.* 1983: 585.

National Academies of Sciences. (2017) *Designing Safety Regulations for High-Hazard Industries.* Washington, D.C.: National Academies Press.

National Center for State Courts. (1986) "A Preliminary Examination of Available Civil and Criminal Trend Data in State Trial Courts for 1978, 1981 and 1984." Williamsburg, Va.

———. (1988) "On Trial: The Length of Civil and Criminal Trials." Williamsburg, Va.

———. (1991) "State Court Caseload Statistics in 1989." Williamsburg, Va.

———. (2012) *Examining the Work of State Courts: An Analysis of 2010 State Court Caseloads Case Statistics Project.* http://www.courtstatistics.org/~/media/Microsites/Files /CSP/DATA%20PDF/CSP_DEC.ashx.

———. (2017) *Trends: Close Up, The Rise and Fall of State Court Caseloads.* Williamsburg, Va.

National Federation of Individual Businesses et al. v. Sebelius. (2012) 567 U.S 519, 132 Sup Ct. 2566.

National Institute of Family and Life Advocates v. Becerra. (2018) 585 U.S. 138 Sup Ct. 2361.

National Prison Project. (1990) "Status Report: State Prisons and the Courts." *Nat'l Prison Project J.* 22: 7.

National Research Council. (1985) *Dredging Coastal Ports: An Assessment of the Issues.* Washington, D.C.: National Academy Press.

Neal, David, and David L. Kirp. (1986) "The Allure of Legalization Reconsidered: The Case of Special Education." In *School Days, Rule Days: The Legalization and Regulation of Education,* ed. D. L. Kirp and Donald Jensen. New York: Falmer Press.

Nellis, Ashley. (2016) *The Color of Justice: Racial and Ethnic Disparity in State Prisons.* Washington D.C.: Sentencing Project.

Nelson, William. (1990) "Contract Litigation and the Elite Bar in New York City, 1960–1980." *Emory L. Rev.* 39: 413.

Nemetz, Peter N., W. T. Stanbury, and Fred Thompson. (1986) "Social Regulation in Canada: An Overview and Comparison with the American Model." *Policy Studies* 14: 580.

NERA. (2012) *Recent Trends in Securities Class Action Litigation.* Boston: National Economic and Research Associates. www.NERA.com.

Newman v. Smith. (1918) 82 So. 236 (Fla.); 79 Am. Jur. §§390–391 (New York: Lawyer Cooperative Publications, 1996 ed.).

New York Times. (1996) "Legal Services Survives, Barely." May 6, 1996, A14.

———. (2017) "An Innocent Man Who Imagined the World as It Should Be." October 6, 2017, A24.

Nielsen, Laura Beth. (1999) "Paying Workers or Paying Lawyers: Employee Termination Practices in the United States and Canada." *Law & Pol'y* 21: 247.

———. (2000) "Employee Termination Practices in the United States and Canada." In *Regulatory Encounters: Multinational Corporations and American Adversarial Legalism*, ed. Robert A. Kagan and Lee Axelrad. Berkeley: University of California Press.

Niemeijer, Bert. (1989) "Urban Land-Use and Building Control in the Netherlands: Flexible Decisions in a Rigid System." *Law & Pol'y* 11: 121–152.

Nolette, Paul. (2014) "Law Enforcement as Legal Mobilization: Reforming the Pharmaceutical Industry Through Government Litigation." *Law & Soc. Inquiry* 40: 123–151.

———. (2015) *Federalism on Trial: State Attorneys General and National Policymaking in Contemporary America*. Lawrence: University Press of Kansas.

Nonet, Philippe. (1969) *Administrative Justice*. New York: Russell Sage Foundation.

Nonet, Philippe, and Philip Selznick. (1978) *Law and Society in Transition: Toward Responsive Law*. New York: Harper Colophon.

Noonan, John T., Jr. (1993) "Horses of the Night: *Harris v Vasquez*." *Stan. L. Rev.* 45: 1011.

Novak, William. (2008) "The Myth of the Weak American State" *American Historical Review* 113: 752–772.

———. (2017) "Putting the 'Public' in Public Administration; The Rise of the Public Utility Idea." In *Administrative Law from the Inside Out: Essays on Themes in the Work of Jerry L. Mashaw*, ed. Nicholas Parillo. New York: Cambridge University Press.

Nutter, Franklin, and Keith Bateman. (1989) *The U.S. Tort System in the Era of the Global Economy*. Schaumberg, Ill.: Alliance of American Insurers.

O'Connell, Jeffrey. (1979) *The Lawsuit Lottery: Only the Lawyers Win*. New York: Free Press.

O'Connor, Karen, and Lee Epstein. (1985) "Bridging the Gap between Congress and the Supreme Court: Interest Groups and the Erosion of the American Rule Governing Awards of Attorneys' Fees." *Western Political Quarterly* 28: 238.

Odden, Allan, and Lawrence Picus. (1992) *School Finance: A Policy Perspective*. New York: McGraw Hill.

O'Donnell, Jayne, and Fola Akinnibi. (2013) "How Many Pages of Regulations are in the Affordable Care Act?" *USA Today,* October 25, 2013. https://www.usatoday.com/story/opinion/2013/10/23/affordable-care-act-pages-long/3174499/.

OECD (Organization for Economic Co-Operation and Development). (1986) *OECD Economic Surveys: Netherlands*. Paris: Organization for Economic Cooperation and Development.

———. (1987) *OECD Economic Surveys: Netherlands*. Paris: Organization for Economic Cooperation and Development.

———. (2005) *OECD Factbook 2005*. https://www.oecd-ilibrary.org/economics/oecd-factbook-2005_factbook-2005-en.

———. (2017) *Health at a Glance 2017: OECD Indicators*. OECD iLibrary. http://dx.doi.org/10.1787/health_glance-2017-en.

OECD Data. (2018) "Poverty Rate." OECD Data. https://data.oecd.org/inequality/poverty-rate.htm.

Ofgang, Kenneth (2007) "S.C. Upholds Death Sentence of Man Who Blurted 'I Am Guilty.'" *Metropolitan News-Enterprise*, May 18, 2007, 1. *Metnews.org.*

Okimoto, Daniel. (1989) *Between MITI and the Market: Japanese Industrial Policy for High Technology.* Stanford, Calif.: Stanford University Press.

Oldertz, Carl. (1986) "Security Insurance, Patient Insurance and Pharmaceutical Insurance in Sweden." *Am. J. Comp. L.* 34: 635.

Opatrny, Dennis. (1995) "Little Danger of Sudden Wealth in Suing the SFPD." *San Francisco Chronicle,* June 4, 1995, C1.

Orfield, Myron, Jr. (1987) "The Exclusionary Rule and Deterrence: An Empirical Study of Chicago Narcotics Officers." *U. Chi. L. Rev.* 54: 1016.

Ortiz v. Fibreboard Corp. (1999), 527 U.S. 815.

Osborne, Evan. (1999) "Courts as Casinos? An Empirical Investigation of Randomness and Efficiency in Civil Litigation." *J. Legal Stud.* 26: 187.

Osiel, Mark. (1990) "Lawyers as Monopolists and Entrepreneurs." Review of *Lawyer in Society*, ed. Richard Abel and Philip Lewis. *Harv. L. Rev.* 103: 2009.

Ostrom, Brian, Roger Hanson and Henry Daley. (1993) "So the Verdict Is In: What Happens Next?" *Justice System J.* 16: 97.

——. (1996) "A Step above Anecdote: A Profile of the Civil Jury in the 1990s." *Judicature* 79: 233.

Paduano, Anthony, and Clive Stafford-Smith. (1987) "Deathly Errors: Juror Misperceptions Concerning Parole in the Imposition of the Death Penalty." *Colum. Hum. Rts. L. Rev.* 18: 211.

Pager, Devah. (2007) *Marked: Race, Crime and Finding Work in an Era of Mass Incarceration.* Chicago: University of Chicago Press.

Pager, Devah, and Bruce Western. (2005) *Race at Work—Realities of Race and Criminal Record in the NYC Job Market.* New York: Schomburg Center for Research in Black Culture, New York Public Library.

Palazzolo, Joe. (2012) "Court Backs Loaded Guns in Public." *Wall Street J.*, December 12, 2012, A2.

Palmer, Emily, and Campbell Robertson. (2016) "Mississippi Fights to Keep Control of Its Child Welfare System." *New York Times,* January 18, 2016, A1.

Palmer, Thomas. (1994) "Commitments to Foes Raise Artery Price Tag." *Boston Globe,* September 14, 1994, 1, 6.

Pantuliano, Michael. (1993) "The US View of European Patent Litigation," *European Intellectual Property Review* 15: 307–311.

Papachristou v. City of Jacksonville. (1972) 405 U.S. 156.

Parents Involved in Community Schools v. Seattle School District No.1. (2007) 551 U.S. 701.

Parillo, Nicholas. (2017) *Federal Agency Guidance: An Institutional Perspective.* Washington, D.C.: Administrative Conference of the United States, October 12, 2017. https://www.acus.gov/report/agency-guidance-final-report.

Paris, Michael. (1998) "Legal Mobilization and the Rhetoric of Reform: School Finance Litigation in Kentucky, 1984–1990." Paper prepared for annual meeting of Law and Society Association, Aspen, Colo., June 3–7, 1998.

——. (2010) *Framing Equal Opportunity.* Redwood City, Calif: Stanford University Press.

Parloff, Roger. (1993) "False Confessions." *Am. Lawyer* (May), 58–62.

Paternoster, Raymond. (1991) *Capital Punishment in America.* New York: Lexington Books.

Pear, Robert. (1995) "As Welfare Overhaul Looms, Legal Aid for the Poor Diminishes." *New York Times,* September 5, 1995, A1, A9.

Peltason, Jack. (1961) *Fifty Eight Lonely Men: Southern Federal Judges and School Desegregation.* New York: Harcourt, Brace and World.

Penner, Bernard. (1992) "The Prosecutor and *Ex Parte* Communications." *National Environmental Enforcement J.* (May), 3.

People v. Leonard (2007) California Supreme Court. Docket no S054291, May 17, 2007. https://scocal.stanford.edu/opinion/people-v-leonard-33734.

Peoples, Steve. (2017) "States Escalate Legal Challenges against Trump." Associated Press, August 18, 2017. https://www2.bostonglobe.com/news/nation/2017/08/13 /state-attorneys-escalate-legal-fight-against-trump/4Y6RI5I0nsCSVkuLH64xbM /story.htm.

Peretti, Terri. (1999) *In Defense of a Political Court.* Princeton, N.J.: Princeton University Press.

Peters, Antonie. (1992) "Some Comparative Observations on the Criminal Process in Holland and Japan." *J. Japan-Netherlands Institute* 4: 247.

Peterson, Mark. (1987) *Civil Juries in the 1980s: Trends in Jury Trials and Verdicts in California and Cook County, Illinois.* Santa Monica, Calif.: RAND Institute of Civil Justice.

Peterson, Paul. (1995) *The Price of Federalism.* Washington, D.C.: Brookings Institution.

———. (1996) "Devolution's Price." *Yale Law & Pol'y Rev.* 14: 111.

Petzinger, Thomas. (1987) *Oil and Honor: The Texaco-Penzoil Wars.* New York: Putnam.

Philip Morris USA v. Williams. (2007) 549 U.S. 346.

Pinello, Daniel. (1999) "Linking Party to Judicial Ideology in American Courts: A Meta-Analysis." *Justice System J.* 20: 219.

Pitt, Harvey, and Karen Shapiro. (1990) "Securities Regulation by Enforcement: A Look Ahead at the Next Decade." *Yale J. on Reg.* 7: 149.

Pizzi, William. (1993) "Understanding Prosecutorial Discretion in the United States: The Limits of Comparative Criminal Procedure as an Instrument of Reform." *Ohio St. L.J.* 54: 1325.

———. (1999) *Trials without Truth.* New York: New York University Press.

Plotz, David. (1994) "Guilty! Guilty! Guilty!" *Washington City Paper,* March 25, 1994, 22–31.

Polinsky, A. Mitchell. (1997) "Are Punitive Damages Really Insignificant, Predictable, and Rational?" *J. Legal Stud.* 26: 663.

Polisar, Daniel, and Aaron Wildavsky. (1989) "From Individual to System Blame: A Cultural Analysis of Historical Change in the Law of Torts." *J. Policy History* 1: 129.

Pollock v. Farmers' Loan & Trust Co. (1895) 158 U.S. 601.

Polsby, Nelson. (1983) *The Consequences of Party Reform.* New York: Oxford University Press.

Porter, Eduardo. (2014) "Why Aid for College is Missing the Mark." *New York Times,* October 8, 2014, B1, B8.

———. (2017a) "Considering the True Cost of Keeping Taxes Lower," *New York Times,* November 15, 2017, B1, 4.

———. (2018) "American Exceptionalism Comes with a Social Cost." *New York Times,* May 30, 2018, B1.

Potter, Edward, and Ann Reesman. (1992) *Compensatory and Punitive Damages under Title VII–A Foreign Perspective.* Washington, D.C.: Employment Policy Foundation.

Priest, George L. (1985) "The Invention of Enterprise Liability: A Critical History of the Intellectual Foundations of Modern Tort Law." *J. Legal Stud.* 14: 461.

———. (1990) "The Role of the Civil Jury in a System of Private Litigation." *U. Chi. Legal F.* 1990: 161.

———. (1993) "Justifying the Civil Jury." In *Verdict: Assessing the Civil Jury System,* ed. Robert Litan. Washington, D.C.: Brookings Institution.

Pringle, Peter. (1998) *Cornered: Big Tobacco at the Bar of Justice.* New York: Henry Holt.

Privatera, John. (1992) "Using CERCLA's Natural Resource Damage Provision to Focus and Organize a State Environmental Penalty Case." *Nat'l Envtl Enforcement J.* (March).

Protess, Ben, and Jessica Silver-Greenberg. (2017) "Trump Era is Taming a Watchdog for Banks." *New York Times,* November 16, 2017, B1, 4.

Provine, Doris Marie. (1996) "Courts in the Political Process in France." In *Courts, Law and Politics in Comparative Perspective,* by Herbert Jacob, Erhard Blankenburg, Herbert Kritzer, Doris Marie Provine, and Joseph Sanders. New Haven, Conn.: Yale University Press.

PWC (Pricewaterhouse Coopers). (2017) *2017 Patent Litigation Study.* Boston: Pricewaterhouse Coopers.

Quam, Lois, Robert Dingwall, and Peter Fenn (1987) "Medical Malpractice in Perspective." *Br. Med. J.* 294: 1529, 1597.

Rabin, Robert. (1988) "Some Reflections on the Process of Tort Reform." *San Diego L. Rev.* 25: 13.

———. (1993) "Institutional and Historical Perspectives on Tobacco Tort Liability." In *Smoking Policy: Law, Politics, and Culture,* ed. Robert Rabin and Stephen Sugarman. New York: Oxford University Press.

Rabkin, Jeremy. (1980) "Office for Civil Rights." In *The Politics of Regulation,* ed. James Q. Wilson. New York: Basic Books.

———. (1989) *Judicial Compulsions: How Public Law Distorts Public Policy.* New York: Basic Books.

Ramji-Nogales, Jaya, Andrew Schoenholtz, and Philip G. Schrag. (2007) "Refugee Roulette: Disparities in Asylum Adjudication," *Stan. L. Rev.* 60: 295.

Ramseyer, J. Mark, and Minoru Nakazato. (1989) "The Rational Litigant: Settlement Amounts and Verdict Rates in Japan." *J. Legal Stud.* 18: 263.

Ramseyer, J. Mark, and Eric Rasmussen. (1998) "Why Is the Japanese Conviction Rate So High?" Discussion paper, John M. Olin Center for Law, Economics, and Business, Harvard Law School.

RAND Institute for Civil Justice. (1995) "How Big Is the Price Tag for Excess Auto Injury Claims?" *RAND Institute for Civil Justice Research Brief* (May), 1.

Ranney, Austin. (1983) "The President and His Party." In *Both Ends of the Avenue: The Presidency, the Executive Branch and Congress in the 1980s*, ed. Anthony King. Washington, D.C.: American Enterprise Institute.

Rasul v. Bush. (2004) 542 U.S. 466.

Rashbaum, William, Danny Hakim, Brian M. Rosenthal, Emily Flitter, and Jesse Drucker. (2018) "How Michael Cohen, Trump's Fixer, Built a Shadowy Business Empire." *New York Times*, May 5, 2018. https://www.nytimes.com/2018/05/05/business/michael-cohen-lawyer-trump.html.

Redelet, Michael, Hugo Adam Bedau, and Constance Putnam. (1992) *In Spite of Innocence: Erroneous Convictions in Capital Cases*. Boston: Northeastern University Press.

Redick, William P., Jr. (1993) "The Crisis in Representation of Tennessee Capital Cases." *Tenn. Bar J.* (March / April), 22.

Reed, Douglas. (1998) "Twenty Five Years after *Rodriguez*: School Finance Litigation and the Impact of the New Judicial Federalism." *Law & Soc'y Rev.* 32: 175.

——. (2001) *On Equal Terms: The Constitutional Politics of Educational Opportunity*. Princeton, NJ: Princeton University Press.

Rees, Joseph. (1988) *Reforming the Workplace: A Study of Self-Regulation in Occupational Safety*. Philadelphia: University of Pennsylvania Press.

Rehavi, M. Marit, and Sonja B. Starr. (2012) "Racial Disparity in Federal Criminal Charging and Its Sentencing Consequences." University of Michigan Law & Econ., Empirical Legal Studies Center Paper No. 12–002. http://dx.doi.org/10.2139/ssrn.1985377.

Reiner, Robert, and Malcolm Cross, eds. (1991) *Beyond Law and Order: Criminal Justice Policy and Politics into the 1990s*. London: Macmillan Academic and Professional LTD.

Reinhold, Robert. (1993) "Final Freeway Opens, Ending California Era." *New York Times,* October 14, 1993, A1.

Reitz, John C. (1990) "Why We Probably Cannot Adopt the German Advantage in Civil Procedure." *Iowa L. Rev.* 75: 987.

Resnik, Judith. (1982) "Managerial Judges." *Harv. L. Rev.* 96: 376.

——. (2015) "Diffusing Disputes and the Erasure of Rights," *Yale L.J.* 124: 2804.

Rhode, Deborah. (1999) "A Bad Press on Bad Lawyers: The Media Sees Research, Research Sees the Media." In *Social Science, Social Policy and the Law*, ed. Patricia Ewick, Robert A. Kagan, and Austin Sarat. New York: Russell Sage Foundation.

Robbins, Jim. (1998) "A Broken Pact and a $97 Million Payday." *New York Times,* April 19, 1998, Sec. 3, p. 1.

Robertson, Campbell, and Richard Fausset. (2015) "Southern Customs Yield to a New Age." *New York Times,* June 28, 2015, 1, 8.

Robinson v. Cahill. (1973) 62 N.J. 473.

Robles, Francis, and Shaila Dewan. (2015) "Skip Child Support. Go to Jail. Lose Job. Repeat." *New York Times*, April 19, 2015, A1.

Roe v. Norton. (1973) 365 F. Supp. 65 (D. Conn.), remanded, 422 U.S. 391 (1975).

Roe v. Wade. (1973) 410 U.S. 113.

Roe, Mark. (1991) "A Political Theory of American Corporate Finance." *Colum. L. Rev.* 91: 10.

Rogers, Joel. (1990) "Divide and Conquer: Further Reflections on the Distinctive Character of American Labor Laws." *Wis. L. Rev.* 1990: 1.

Roman, Andrew, and Mark Pikkov. (1990) "Public Interest Litigation in Canada." In *Into the Future: Environmental Law and Policy for the 1990s*, ed. Donna Tingley. Edmonton: Environmental Law Center.

Romano, Roberta. (1991) "The Shareholder Suit: Litigation without Foundation?" *J.L. Econ. & Org.* 7: 55.

Rosch, Joel. (1987) "Institutionalizing Mediation: The Evolution of the Civil Liberties Bureau in Japan." *Law & Soc'y Rev.* 21: 243.

Rose-Ackerman, Susan. (1995) *Controlling Environmental Policy: The Limits of Public Law in Germany and the United States.* New Haven, Conn.: Yale University Press.

Rosenberg, Gerald. (1991) *The Hollow Hope: Can Courts Bring About Social Change?* Chicago: University of Chicago Press.

Rosenthal, Douglas. (1974) *Lawyer and Client: Who's in Charge?* New York: Russell Sage Foundation.

Rosenthal, Jean-Laurent. (1992) *The Fruits of Revolution.* Los Angeles: UCLA Press.

Ross, H. Laurence, and James Foley. (1987) "Judicial Disobedience of the Mandate to Imprison Drunk Drivers." *Law & Soc'y Rev.* 21: 315.

Rothman, David J., and Sheila M. Rothman. (1984) *The Willowbrook Wars.* New York: Harper & Row.

Rothman, Stanley, and Stephen Powers. (1984) "Execution by Quota?" *Public Interest* (Summer), 3.

Rothwell, Jonathan. (2015) *Drug Offenders in American Prisons.* Washington. D.C.: Brookings Institution.

Rowland, C. K., and Robert A. Carp. (1983) "The Relative Effects of Maturation, Period, and Appointing President on District Judges' Policy Choice: A Cohort Analysis." *Political Behavior* 5: 109.

Rubin, Edward L. (1991) "Legislative Methodology: Some Lessons from the Truth-in-Lending Act." *Geo. L. Rev.* 80: 233.

———. (1997) "Discretion and Its Discontents." *Chi.-Kent L. Rev.* 72: 1299.

Rubinstein, Michael, and Teresa White. (1979) "Alaska's Ban on Plea Bargaining." *Law & Soc'y Rev.* 13: 367.

Rubinstein, Steve. (1997) "Driver's Education Takes a Warped Turn during an Accident." *San Francisco Chronicle,* February 19, 1997, C1.

Ruhl, J. B., James Salzman, Kai-Sheng Song, and Han Yu. (2002) "Environmental Compliance: Another Integrity Crisis or Too Many Rules?" *Natural Resources and Environment,* 17: 24–30.

Ruhlin, Charles. (2000) "Credit Card Collection and the Law: Germany and the United States." In *Regulatory Encounters: Multinational Corporations and American Adversarial Legalism*, ed. Robert A. Kagan and Lee Axelrad. Berkeley: University of California Press.

Rushin, Stephen. (2015) "Structural Reform Litigation in American Police Departments." *Minn L. Rev.* 99: 1343.

Sage, William. (1999) "Physicians as Advocates." *Houston L. Rev.* 35: 1529.

Saguy, Abigail. (2000) "Employment Discrimination or Sexual Violence?: Defining Sexual Harassment in American and French Law." *Law & Soc'y Rev.* 34 (40): 1091–1128.

Sakala, Leah. (2014) *Breaking Down Mass Incarceration in the 2010 Census: State-by-State Incarceration Rates by Race/Ethnicity.* Northhampton, Mass.: Prison Policy Initiative.

Saks, Michael J. (1992) "Do We Really Know Anything about the Behavior of the Tort Litigation System—And Why Not?" *Pa. L. Rev.* 140: 1147.

Sander, Richard, and E. Douglass Williams. (1989) "Why Are There So Many Lawyers? Perspectives on a Turbulent Market." *Law & Soc. Inquiry* 14: 431.

Sanders, Joseph. (1987) "The Meaning of the Law Explosion: On Friedman's *Total Justice.*" *Am. Bar Foundation Research J.* 1987: 601.

——. (1993) "From Science to Evidence: The Testimony on Causation in the Bendectin Cases." *Stan. L. Rev.* 42: 1.

———. (1996) "Courts and Law in Japan." In *Courts, Law and Politics in Comparative Perspective,* by Herbert Jacob, Erhard Blankenburg, Herbert Kritzer, Doris Marie Provine, and Joseph Sanders. New Haven, Conn.: Yale University Press.

——. (1998) "Scientifically Complex Cases, Trial by Jury, and the Erosion of Adversarial Processes." *DePaul L. Rev.* 48: 355.

Sanders, Joseph, and Craig Joyce. (1990) "'Off to the Races': The 1980s Tort Crisis and the Law Reform Process." *Houston L. Rev.* 27: 207.

Sandler, Ross, and David Schoenbrod. (2003) *Democracy by Decree: What Happens When Courts Run Government.* New Haven, Conn.: Yale University Press.

San Francisco Chronicle. (1995) "Jurors Found Predisposed to Death Penalty." February 2, 1995.

Sanger-Katz, Margot. (2019) "Struggling to Follow the Rules About Rules. *"New York Times,* January 23, 209, A18.

Sarat, Austin. (1990) "'The Law Is All Over': Power, Resistance and the Legal Consciousness of the Welfare Poor." *Yale J.L. & Human.* 2: 343.

Sarat, Austin, and William L. F. Felstiner. (1986) "Law and Strategy in the Divorce Lawyer's Office." *Law & Soc'y Rev.* 20: 93.

Savage, Andrew Thomas. (1995) "Boston Harbor: the Anatomy of a Court-Run Cleanup," *B. C. Envtl. L. Rev.* 22: 365.

Savelsberg, Joachim. (1994) "Knowledge, Domination, and Criminal Punishment." *Am. J. Sociology* 99: 911.

Scheiber, Harry N. (1969) *The Ohio Canal Era: Case Study of Government and the Economy, 1820–1861.* Athens, Ohio: Ohio University Press.

Scherer, Nancy, and Banks Miller. (2009) "The Federalist Society's Influence on the Federal Judiciary." *Political Research Quarterly* 62: 366–378.

Schkade, David, Cass Sunstein, and Daniel Kahneman. (2000) "Deliberating about Dollars: The Severity Shift." *Colum. L. Rev.* 2000: 1139–1175.

Schlanger, Margo. (2015) "Trends in Prisoner Litigation, as the PLRA Enters Adulthood." *UC Irvine L. Rev.* 5: 153–179.

Schmidt, William. (1994) "Silence May Speak against the Accused in Britain." *New York Times,* November 11, 1994, A17.

Schmitter, Philippe. (1979) "Still the Century of Corporatism?" In *Trends toward Corporatist Intermediation*, ed. Philippe Schmitter and Gerhard Lembruch. London: Sage.

Scholz, John T., and Feng Heng Wei. (1986) "Regulatory Enforcement in a Federalist System." *Am. Political Sci. Rev.* 80: 1249.

Schrecker, Ted. (1992) "Of Invisible Beasts and the Public Interest: Environmental Cases and the Judicial System." In *Canadian Environmental Policy: Ecosystems, Politics, and Process*, ed. Robert Boardman. Toronto: University of Oxford Press.

Schroeder, Elinor. (1986) "Legislative and Judicial Responses to the Inadequacy of Compensation for Occupational Disease." *Law & Contemp. Probs.* 49: 151.

Schuck, Peter. (1983) *Suing Government: Citizen Remedies for Official Wrongs*. New Haven, Conn.: Yale University Press.

——. (1992) "The Worst Should Go First: Deferral Registries in Asbestos Litigation." *Harv. L. Rev.* 15: 541.

——. (1993) "Mapping the Debate on Jury Reform." In *Verdict: Assessing the Civil Jury System*, ed. Robert Litan. Washington, D.C.: Brookings Institution.

——. (2000) *The Limits of the Law*. Boulder, Colo.: Westview Press.

——. (2014) *Why Government Fails So Often: And How It Can Do Better*. Princeton, N.J.: Princeton University Press.

Schwartz, Gary. (1991) "Product Liability and Medical Malpractice in Comparative Context." In *The Liability Maze*, ed. Peter Huber and Robert Litan. Washington, D.C.: Brookings Institution.

——. (1992) "The Beginning and the Possible End of the Rise of Modern American Tort Law." *Ga. L. Rev.* 26: 601.

——. (1994) "Reality in the Economic Analysis of Tort Law: Does Tort Law Really Deter?" *UCLA L. Rev.* 42: 263.

Schwartz, Richard D., and James Miller. (1964) "Legal Evolution and Social Complexity." *Am. J. Sociology* 70: 159.

Scruggs, Lyle A. (1998) "Sustaining Abundance: Environmental Performance in Advanced Societies." Ph.D. diss., Duke University.

——. (1999) "Institutions and Environmental Performance in Seventeen Western Democracies." *British J. Political Science* 29: 1–31.

Sebok Anthony. (2006) "Translating the Immeasurable: Thinking About Pain and Suffering Comparatively." *DePaul L. Rev.* 55, 379–398.

Selke, William. (1991) "A Comparison of Punishment Systems in Denmark and the United States." *Int'l. J. Comp. & Applied Criminal Justice* 15: 227.

Sellers, Jeffery M. (1995) "Litigation as a Local Political Resource: Courts in Controversies over Land Use in France, Germany and the United States." *Law & Soc'y Rev.* 29: 475.

Selvin, Molly, and Patricia A. Ebener. (1984) *Managing the Unmanageable: A History of Civil Delay in the Los Angeles Superior Court*. Santa Monica, Calif.: RAND Institute for Civil Justice.

Sentell, R. Perry. (1991) "The Georgia Jury and Negligence: The View from the Bench." *Ga. L. Rev.* 26: 85.

Serrano v. Priest. (1971) 487 P. 2d 1241 (Cal.).

Shanley, Michael, and Mark Peterson. (1983) *Comparative Justice: Civil Jury Verdicts in San Francisco and Cook Counties, 1959–1980*. Santa Monica, Calif.: RAND Institute for Civil Justice.

Shapiro v. Thompson. (1969) 394 U.S. 618.

Shapiro, Martin. (1988) *Who Guards the Guardians? Judicial Control of Administration*. Athens: University of Georgia Press.

Shear, Michael, Julie Hirschfeld Davis, Thomas Kaplan, and Robert Pear. (2018) "Federal Judge in California Halts Splitting of Migrant Families at Border." *New York Times,* June 27, 2018, A15.

Shear, Michael, Zolan Kanno-Youngs, and Maggie Haberman. (2019) "Policies May Include Return of Family Separations." *New York Times*, April 9, 2019, A1.Shefter, Martin. (1994) *Political Parties and the State: The American Historical Experience*. Princeton, N.J.: Princeton University Press.

Shelby County v. Holder. (2013) 570 U.S. 2.

Shell, Ellen Ruppel. (2018) "College May Not Be Worth It Anymore." *New York Times,* May 17, 2018, A23.

Sherman, Lawrence. (1992) "The Influence of Criminology on Criminal Law: Evaluating Arrests for Misdemeanor Domestic Violence." *J. Crim. L. & Criminology* 83: 1.

Shklar, Judith. (1964) *Legalism*. Cambridge, Mass.: Harvard University Press.

Shover, Neil, John Lynxwiler, Stephen Groce, and Donald Clelland. (1984) "Regional Variation in Regulatory Law Enforcement: The Surface Mining Control and Reclamation Act." In *Enforcing Regulation*, ed. Keith Hawkins and John Thomas. Boston: Kluwer-Nijhoff.

Siegel, Andrew M. (2006) "The Court against the Courts: Hostility to Litigation as an Organizing Theme in the Rehnquist Court's Jurisprudence." *Tex. L. Rev.* 84: 1097.

Silbey, Susan. (1984) "The Consequences of Responsive Regulation." In *Enforcing Regulation*, eds. Keith Hawkins and John Thomas. Boston : Kluwer-Nijhoff.

Silver-Greenberg, Jessica, and Michael Corkery. (2016a) "Start-Ups Turn to Arbitration in Workplace." *New York Times,* May 15, 2016, Sec. 1, 1, 4.

——. (2016b) "No Arbitration, U.S. Agency Tells Nursing Homes." *New York Times,* September 29, 2016, A6.

Silverman, Robert. (1981) *Law and Urban Growth: Civil Litigation in the Boston Trial Courts, 1880–1900*. Princeton, N.J.: Princeton University Press.

Silverstein, Gordon. (2009) *Law's Allure: How Law Shapes, Constrains, Saves, and Kills Politics*. New York: Cambridge University Press.

Simon, Herbert. (1957) *Administrative Behavior,* 2nd ed. New York: Macmillan.

Simon, Jonathan. (2014) *Mass Incarceration on Trial: A Remarkable Court Decision and the Future of Prisons in America*. New York: The New Press.

Simon, William H. (1983) "Legality, Bureaucracy, and Class in the Welfare System." *Yale L.J.* 92: 11.

Singer, Joseph. (2015) *No Freedom Without Regulation*. New Haven, Conn.: Yale University Press.

Skolnick, Jerome. (1998) "The Color of the Law." *The American Prospect* (July / August): 90, 94.

Skolnick, Jerome, and James Fyfe. (1993) *Above the Law: Police and the Excessive Use of Force.* New York: The Free Press.

Skowronek, Stephen. (1982) *Building a New American State: The Expansion of National Administrative Capacities, 1877–1920.* New York: Cambridge University Press.

Slaughter-House Cases. (1873) 83 U.S. (16 Wall.) 36.

Sloan, Frank A., and Chen Ruey Hsieh. (1990) "Variability in Medical Malpractice Payments: Is the Compensation System Fair?" *Law & Soc'y Rev.* 24: 997.

Sloan, Frank A., and Stephen S. Van Wert. (1991) "Cost and Compensation of Injuries in Medical Malpractice." *Law & Contemp. Probs.* 54: 131.

Sloane, Leonard. (1991) "Rising Fraud Worrying Car Insurers." *New York Times,* November 16, 1991, 15.

Smith, Charles. (2006) "Racial Profiling in Canada, the United States, and the United Kingdom." In *Racial Profiling in Canada,* ed. Carol Tator & Frances Henry, 55–91. Toronto: University of Toronto Press.

Smith, Mitch, and Matt Apuzzo. (2015) "Police in Cleveland Accept Tough Standards on Force." *New York Times,* May 27, 2015, A1, 13.

Smith, Robert J. (2012) "The Geography of the Death Penalty and its Ramifications." B.U. L. Rev. 92: 227–289.

Smith, Rogers. (1993) "Beyond Tocqueville, Myrdal, and Hartz: The Multiple Traditions in America." *Am. Political Science Rev.* 87: 549.

Smith, Stephen. (1989) *Call to Order: Floor Politics in the House and Senate.* Washington, D.C.: Brookings Institution.

Somaya, Deepak. (2000) "Obtaining and Protecting Patents in the United States, Europe and Japan." In *Regulatory Encounters: Multinational Corporations and American Adversarial Legalism,* ed. Robert Kagan and Lee Axelrad. Berkeley: University of California Press.

Songer, Donald. (1988) "Tort Reform in South Carolina: The Effect of Empirical Research on Elite Perceptions Concerning Jury Verdicts." *S.C. L. Rev.* 39: 585.

Soular, Lawrence. (1986) "A Study of Large Product Liability Claims Closed in 1985." Schaumberg, Ill.: Alliance of American Insurers.

Spangenberg, Robert, and Marea Beeman. (1995) "Indigent Defense Systems in the United States." *Law & Contemp. Probs.* (Winter): 31.

Speiser, Stuart. (1980) "How the Entrepreneurial Lawyer Changed the Rules of the Game." *Nat'l L.J.,* December 1.

Spivak, Peter, and Sujit Raman. (2008) "Regulating the 'New Regulators': Current Trends in Deferred Prosecution Agreements." *American Criminal Law Review* 45: 159.

Spohn, Cassia. (2000) "Thirty Years of Sentencing Reform: The Quest for a Racially Neutral Sentencing Process." In *Policies, Processes and Decisions of the Criminal Justice System.* Vol 3, 427–81.

Spohn, Cassia, John Gruhl and Susan Welch. (1987) "The Impact of the Ethnicity and Gender of Defendants on Prosecutors' Decisions to Reject or Dismiss Felony Charges." *Criminology* 25: 175–191.

Staszak, Sarah. (2015) *No Day in Court: Access to Justice, and the Politics of Judicial Retrenchment.* Oxford: Oxford University Press.

State Farm Mutual Insurance Co v. Campbell. (2003) 538 U.S. 408.

Steinmo, Sven. (1993) *Taxation and Democracy: Swedish, British and American Approaches to Financing the Modern State.* New Haven, Conn.: Yale University Press.

Stevenson, David, and David Studdert. (2003) "The Rise of Nursing Home Litigation: Findings from A National Survey of Attorneys." *Health Affairs* 22: 219–229.

Stewart, James B. (1983) *The Partners: Inside America's Most Powerful Law Firms.* New York: Simon & Schuster.

Stewart, Richard B. (1975) "The Reformation of Administrative Law." *Harvard L. Rev.* 88 : 1667–1813.

———. (1990) "Madison's Nightmare." *U. Chi. L. Rev.* 57: 335.

Stipp, David. (1991) "Interstate Highway Project in Boston May Face a Court Challenge with National Implications." *Wall Street J.,* June 25, 1991, A20.

———. (1993) "Dogma in Doubt: Extent of Lead's Risk to Kids, Need to Remove Paint." *Wall Street J.,* September 16, 1993, A1, 12.

Stone Sweet, Alec. (1999) "Judicialization and the Construction of Governance." *Comparative Political Studies* 31: 147–184.

———. (2000) *Governing With Judges: Constitutional Politics in Europe.* Oxford: Oxford University Press.

Strauss, Peter. (1987) "One Hundred Fifty Cases per Year: Some Implications of the Supreme Court's Limited Resources for Judicial Review of Agency Action." *Columbia L. Rev.* 87: 1093.

———. (2006) "Rulemaking in the Ages of Globalization and Information: What America Can Learn from Europe, and Vice Versa." *Columbia. J. Eur. L.* 12: 645.

Strum, Charles. (1993a) "U.S. Suspends Dredging Permit for Newark Bay." *New York Times,* January 27, 1993, B1.

———. (1993b) "U.S. Grants Permit for Dredging of Newark Bay Berths." *New York Times,* May 27, 1993, B7.

———. (1993c) "Judge Allows Dredging to Continue." *New York Times,* June 8, 1993, B5.

Studdert, David, and David Stevenson. (2004): "Nursing Home Litigation and Tort Reform: A Case for Exceptionalism," *The Gerontologist* 44: 588–595.

Studdert, David, Y. Tony Yang, and Michelle M. Mello. (2004) "Are Damages Caps Regressive? A Study of Malpractice Jury Verdicts in California," *Health Affairs* 2: 54.

Stuntz, William. (1997) "The Uneasy Relationship between Criminal Procedure and Criminal Justice." *Yale L.J.* 107: 1.

Suchman, Mark, and Mia Cahill. (1996) "The Hired Gun as Facilitator: Lawyers and the Suppression of Business Disputes in Silicon Valley." *Law & Soc. Inquiry* 21: 679.

Sugarman, Stephen D. (1985a) "Roe v. Norton." In *In the Interest of Children: Advocacy, Law Reform, and Public Policy,* ed. Robert Mnookin. New York: W. H. Freeman.

———. (1985b) "Doing Away with Tort Law." *Cal. L. Rev.* 73: 559.

———. (1989) *Doing Away with Personal Injury Law: New Compensation Mechanisms for Victims, Consumers, and Business.* New York: Quorum Books.

———. (1993a) *Pay at the Pump: Auto Insurance.* Berkeley: Institute of Governmental Studies Press.

——. (2006) "A Comparative Look at Pain and Suffering Awards." *DePaul L. Rev.* 55: 399–434.

Sullivan, John. (2000) "States and Cities Removing Prisons from Courts' Grip." *New York Times,* January 30, 2000, 1.

Summers, Robert, and Michele Taruffo. (1991) "Interpretation and Comparative Analysis." In *Interpreting Statutes: A Comparative Study,* ed. D. Neal McCormick and R. Summers. Aldershot: Dartmouth Publishing.

Sunstein, Cass. (1990) *After the Rights Revolution.* Cambridge, Mass.: Harvard University Press.

Sunstein, Cass, Daniel Kahnemann, and David Schkade. (1999) "Assessing Punitive Damages." *Yale L.J.* 107: 2071.

Swedlow, Brendan, Denise Kall, Zheng Zhou, James Hammitt, and Jonathan Wiener. (2009) "Theorizing and Generalizing about Risk Assessment and Regulation through Comparative Nested Analysis of Representative Cases." *Law & Po'y* 31: 252.

Sykes, Charles. (2017) "N.R.A. and G.O.P, Together Forever." *New York Times,* Sunday Review, October 8, 2017, 2.

Syverud, Kent. (1997) "ADR and the Decline of the American Civil Jury." *UCLA L. Rev.* 44: 1935.

Tach, Laura, and Kathryn Edin. (2017) "The Social Safety Net after Welfare Reform: Recent Developments and Consequences for Household Dynamics." *Annual Review of Sociology* 43: 541–561.

Talesh, Shauheen. (2012) "How Dispute Resolution System Design Matters: An Organizational Analysis of Dispute Resolution Structures and Consumer Lemon Laws." *Law & Soc'y Rev.* 46: 463.

Tanase, Takao. (1990) "The Management of Disputes: Automobile Accident Compensation in Japan." *Law & Soc'y Rev.* 24: 651.

Taragin, Mark, Laura Willett, Adam Wilczek, Richard Trout, and Jeffrey Carson. (1992) "The Influence of Standard of Care and Severity of Injury on the Resolution of Medical Malpractice Claims." *Annals of Internal Medicine* 117: 780.

Taylor, Serge. (1984) *Making Bureaucracies Think: The Environmental Impact Strategy of Administrative Reform.* Stanford, Calif.: Stanford University Press.

TC Heartland LLC v. Kraft Foods Group Brands LLC. (2017) 581 U.S. ___, 137 S. Ct. 1514.

Teff, Harvey. (1985) "Drug Approval in England and the United States." *Am. J. Comp. L.* 33: 567.

Teles, Steven. (2008) *The Rise of the Conservative Legal Movement.* Princeton, N.J.: Princeton University Press.

Tennessee v. Garner. (1985) 471 U.S. 1.

Thibaut, John, and Laurens Walker. (1978) "A Theory of Procedure." *Cal. L. Rev.* 66: 541.

Thomas, Jo. (1986) "Odds Heavily Favor Leniency for Drug Dealing in the City." *New York Times,* June 30, 1986, 1, 12.

Thornton, Dorothy, Robert A. Kagan, and Neil Gunningham. (2005) "General Deterrence and Corporate Environmental Behavior," *Law & Pol'y,* 27: 262.

——. (2009) "When Social Norms and Pressures Are Not Enough: Environmental Performance in the Trucking Industry." *Law & Society Review* 43: 405.

Thrush, Glenn. (2018) "Housing Crisis Grows as HUD Sits on the Sidelines." *New York Times,* July 28, 2018, A1.

Thurber, James. (1991) "Representation, Accountability, and Efficiency in Divided Party Control of Government." *PS: Political Science & Government* (December), 653.

Tonry, Michael. (1995) *Malign Neglect: Race, Crime and Punishment in America.* New York: Oxford University Press.

Tonry, Michael, and Richard Frase, eds. (2001) *Sentencing and Sanctions in Western Countries.* New York: Oxford University Press.

Topol, David. (1991) "Rethinking Who Is Left Holding the Nuclear Bag: The Legal and Policy Implications of *Nevada v. Watkins.*" *Utah L. Rev.* 4: 791.

Tort Policy Working Group. (1986) *Report on the Causes, Extent, and Policy Implications of the Current Crisis in Insurance Availability and Affordability.* Washington, D.C.: Government Printing Office.

Townsend v. Swank. (1971) 404 U.S. 282.

Trombley, William, and Ray Hebert. (1987a) "Litigation, Confusion: Road Paved with Good Intentions." *Los Angeles Times,* December 27, 1987, 1.

——. (1987b) "Bold Housing Program Develops Big Problems." *Los Angeles Times,* December 28, 1987, 1.

Trubek, David, Austin Sarat, William Felstiner, Herbert Kritzer, and Joel Grossman. (1983) "The Costs of Ordinary Litigation." *UCLA L. Rev.* 31: 72.

Tyack, David, and Aaron Benavot. (1985) "Courts and Public Schools: Education Litigation in Historical Perspective." *Law & Soc'y Rev.* 19: 339.

Uhlman, Thomas M., and Darlene Walker. (1979) "'He Takes Some of My Time, I Take Some of His': An Analysis of Sentencing Patterns in Jury Cases." *Law & Soc'y Rev.* 14: 323.

Uhlmann, David. (2014) "Prosecutorial Discretion and Environmental Crime." *Harv. Envtl. L. Rev.* 38: 159–216.

United States v. Morrison. (2000). 529 U.S. 598.

Upham, Frank. (1987) *Law and Social Change in Postwar Japan.* Cambridge, Mass.: Harvard University Press.

Ursin, Edmund. (1981) "Judicial Creativity and Tort Law." *Geo. Wash. L. Rev.* 49: 229.

U.S. Advisory Commission on Intergovernmental Relations. (1992) *Intergovernmental Decisionmaking for Environmental Protection and Public Works.* Washington, D.C.: Government Printing Office.

U.S. Army Corps of Engineers. (1992a) *Appendix D: Finding of No Significant Impact and Environmental Assessment, Oakland Inner Harbor—38-Foot Separable Element of the Oakland Harbor Navigation Improvement Project.* San Francisco: U.S. Army Corps of Engineers.

U.S. General Accounting Office. (1988) "Product Liability: Extent of 'Litigation Explosion' in Federal Courts Questioned." Washington, D.C.: GAO.

U.S. v. Cruikshank. (1876) 92 U.S. 542.

U.S. v. Harris. (1882) 106 U.S. 629.

Utz, Pamela. (1978) *Settling the Facts: Discretion and Negotiation in Criminal Court.* Lexington, Mass.: Lexington Books.

Vallinder, Torbjorn. (1995) "When the Courts Go Marching In." In *The Global Expansion of Judicial Power*, ed. C. Neal Tate and T. Vallinder. New York: New York University Press.

Van Cleve, Nicole Gonzalez. (2016) *Crook County: Racism and Injustice in America's Largest Criminal Court.* Stanford, Calif.: Stanford Law Books (Stanford University Press).

Vandenberg, Michael. (2003) "Beyond Elegance: A Testable Typology of Social Norms in Corporate Environmental Compliance." *Stan. Envtl, L.J.* 22: 55.

Van de Putte, Pete. (1995) "A Red, White and Blue Mess." *Wall Street J.,* April 27, 1995, A14.

Van Kessel, Gordon. (1992) "Adversary Excesses in the American Criminal Trial." *Notre Dame L. Rev.* 67: 403.

Verhovek, Sam Howe. (1995) "Across the U.S., Executions Are Neither Swift Nor Cheap." *New York Times,* February 22, 1995, A1, A13.

——. (1999) "Across 10 Years, Exxon Valdez Casts a Shadow." *New York Times,* March 6, 1999, A1.

Verweij, Marco. (2001) "Why Is the River Rhine Cleaner than the Great Lakes (Despite Looser Regulation)?" *Law & Soc'y Rev.* 34, 1007.

Veterans and Agent Orange: Update 1996. (1996) Institute of Medicine, Washington, D.C.: National Academy Press. https://doi.org/10.17226/5203.

Vidmar, Neil. (1993) "Empirical Evidence on the 'Deep Pockets' Hypothesis: Jury Awards for Pain and Suffering in Medical Malpractice Cases." *Duke L.J.* 43: 217.

Vidmar, Neil, Felicia Gross, and Mary Rose. (1998) "Jury Awards for Medical Malpractice and Post-Verdict Adjustments of Those Awards." *DePaul L. Rev.* 48: 265.

Vidmar, Neil, and Jeffrey Rice. (1993) "Assessments of Noneconomic Damage Awards in Medical Malpractice: A Comparison of Juries with Legal Professionals." *Iowa L. Rev.* 78: 883.

Village of Arlington Heights v. Metropolitan Housing Development Corp. (1977) 429 U.S. 252.

Vinke, Harriet, and Ton Wilthagen. (1992) "The Nonmobilization of Law by Asbestos Victims in the Netherlands: Social Insurance versus Tort-Based Compensation." Amsterdam, Netherlands: Hugo Sinzheimer Institute, University of Amsterdam.

Viscusi, Kip. (1990) "Do Smokers Underestimate Risks?" *J. Political Economy* 98: 125.

——. (1992) *Smoking: Making the Risky Decision.* New York: Oxford University Press.

——. (1997) "From Cash Crop to Cash Cow." *Regulation* (Summer): 27.

Vlasic, Bill. (2017) "VW's Criminal Case Ends, but Not without a Scolding." *New York Times,* April 22, 2017, B5.

Vogel, David. (1978) *Lobbying the Corporation: Citizen Challenges to Business Authority.* New York: Basic Books.

——. (1986) *National Styles of Regulation: Environmental Policy in Great Britain and the United States.* Ithaca, N.Y.: Cornell University Press.

——. (1989) *Fluctuating Fortunes: The Political Power of Business in America.* New York: Basic Books.

——. (1990) "Consumer Protection and Protectionism in Japan." Paper presented at annual meeting of American Political Science Association, August 30–September 2, 1990, San Francisco, Calif.

——. (1996) *Kindred Strangers: The Uneasy Relationship between Politics and Business in America.* Princeton, N.J.: Princeton University Press.

——. (2005) *The Market for Virtue: The Potential and Limits of Corporate Social Responsibility.* Washington, D.C.: The Brookings Institution.

——. (2012) *The Politics of Precaution: Regulating Health, Safety and Environmental Risks in Europe and the United States.* Princeton, N.J.: Princeton University Press.

——. (2017) *California Greenin': How the Golden State Became an Environmental Leader.* Princeton, N.J.: Princeton University Press.

Wacquant, Loic. (1995) "The Comparative Structure and Experience of Urban Exclusion: 'Race,' Class, and Space in Chicago and Paris." In *Poverty, Inequality, and the Future of Social Policy,* ed. Katherine McFate, Roger Lawson, and William Julius Wilson. New York: Russell Sage Foundation.

Wagatsuma, Hiroshi, and Arthur Rossett. (1986) "The Implications of Apology: Law and Culture in Japan and the U.S." *Law & Soc'y Rev.* 20: 461.

Wagner, Peter, and Alison Walsh. (2017) *States of Incarceration: The Global Context.* Northhampton, Mass.: Prison Policy Initiative.

Walker, Samuel. (1993) *Taming the System: The Control of Discretion in Criminal Justice, 1950–1990.* New York: Oxford University Press.

Wallace, David. (1995) *Environmental Policy and Industrial Innovation: Strategies in Europe, the U.S., and Japan.* London: Royal Institute of International Affairs, Earthscan Publications, Ltd.

Wall Street Journal. (1993) "Crass Action." April 1, 1993, A14.

Walmart Stores v. Dukes. (2011) 131 Sup Ct. 2541.

Washington Post. (1991) "Judge Endorses $1 Billion Exxon Valdez Settlement." October 9, 1991, A4.

Wasserman, Howard. (2012) "The Roberts Court and the Civil Procedure Revival." *Rev. Litig.* 31: 313–351.

Watson v. Dingler. (1992) 831 S.W.2d 834 (Tex. App., Houston 14th Dis.).

Weber, Edward. (1998) *Pluralism by the Rules: Conflict and Cooperation in Environmental Regulation.* Washington, D.C.: Georgetown University Press.

Weigend, Thomas. (1980) "Continental Cures for American Ailments: European Criminal Procedure as a Model for Law Reform." *Crime & Justice* 2: 381–428.

Weiler, Paul C. (1991) *Medical Malpractice on Trial.* Cambridge, Mass.: Harvard University Press.

Weingast, Barry. (1980) "Congress, Regulation, and the Decline of Nuclear Power." *Public Pol'y* 28: 232.

Weintraub, Richard. (1994a) "Waiting on the Fields of Flight." *Washington Post,* June 7, 1994, D1.

Weir, Margaret. (1995) "The Politics of Racial Isolation in Europe and America." In *Classifying by Race,* ed. Paul E. Peterson. Princeton, N.J.: Princeton University Press.

Weiss, Debra Cassens (2018) "9th Circuit Keeps DACA in Place, Says Decision to End Program is Likely 'Arbitrary and Capricious'." *ABA Journal Daily News,* November 8, 2018.

Weisburd, David. (1999) "Good for What Purpose? Social Science, Race, and Proportionality Review in New Jersey." In *Social Science, Social Policy, and the Law,* ed. Patrick Ewick, Robert Kagan, and Austin Sarat. New York: Russell Sage Foundation.

Welles, Holly, and Kirsten Engel. (2000) "A Comparative Study of Solid Waste Landfill Regulation: Case Studies from the United States, the United Kingdom, and the Netherlands." In *Regulatory Encounters: Multinational Corporations and American Adversarial Legalism,* ed. Robert A. Kagan and Lee Axelrad. Berkeley: University of California Press.

Welsh, Wayne. (1992) "The Dynamics of Jail Reform Litigation: A Comparative Analysis of Litigation in California Counties." *Law & Soc'y Rev.* 26: 591.

Wessel, Ann E., and Marc J. Hershman. (1988) "Mitigation: Compensating the Environment for Unavoidable Harm." In *Urban Port and Harbor Management,* ed. M. J. Hershman. New York: Taylor & Francis.

Whelan, Jeanne, and Sara Randazzo. (2018) "Florida and Texas Are Among Latest States to Sue Opioid Painkiller Companies." *Wall Street J.,* May 15, 2018.

White, Richard. (2011) *Railroaded: Transcontinentals and The Making of Modern America.* New York: W. W. Norton.

White, Welsh S. (1987) "Patterns in Capital Punishment." *Cal. L. Rev.* 75: 2165.

Whitman, James Q. (2003) *Harsh Justice: Criminal Punishment and the Widening Divide between America and Europe.* New York: Oxford University Press.

Whitney, Craig. (1998) "French Jobless Find the World Is Harsher." *New York Times,* March 19, 1998, A1.

Wiebel, Tom. (1991) "Automobile Insurance: Identification of Issues and Possible Solutions." Sacramento: Department of Motor Vehicles (testimony).

Wiener, Jonathan. (2007) "Whose Precaution After All? A Comment on the Comparison and Evolution of Risk Regulatory Systems." *J. Comp. & Int'l L.* 13: 214.

Wildavsky, Aaron. (1990) "A World of Difference—The Public Philosophies and Political Behaviors of Rival American Cultures." In *The New American Political System,* 2nd ed., ed. Anthony King. Washington, D.C.: AEI Press.

Wilensky, Harold. (1965) "Problems and Prospects of the Welfare State." In *Industrial Society and Social Welfare,* ed. H. Wilensky and Charles Lebaux. New York: Free Press.

——. (1975) *The Welfare State and Equality: Structural and Ideological Roots of Public Expenditures.* Berkeley: University of California Press.

——. (1976) *The "New Corporatism," Centralization, and the Welfare State.* Beverly Hills, Calif.: Sage Publications.

——. (1983) *Political Legitimacy and Consensus: Missing Variables in the Assessment of Social Policy.* Berkeley: Institute of Industrial Relations.

——. (2002) *Rich Democracies: Political Economy, Public Policy, and Performance* Berkeley: University of California Press.

Wiley, Jerry. (1981) "The Impact of Judicial Decisions on Professional Conduct: An Empirical Study." *S. Cal. L. Rev.* 55: 345.

Wilkerson, J. Harvie, III. (1979) *From Brown to Bakke: The Supreme Court and School Integration, 1954–1978*. New York: Oxford University Press.

Williams, C. Arthur. (1991) *An International Comparison of Workers Compensation*. Boston: Kluwer Academic Publishers.

Williams, Gerald. (1983) *Legal Negotiation and Settlement*. St. Paul, Minn.: West Publishing.

Williams, Timothy. (2017) "In South Carolina, No Money And No Lawyer Often Mean Jail Time for Minor Crimes." *"New York Times,* October 13 2017, A10.

Wilson, Graham. (1985) *The Politics of Safety and Health*. Oxford: Clarendon Press.

Wilson, James Q. (1968) *Varieties of Police Behavior*. Cambridge, Mass.: Harvard University Press.

——. (1980) *The Politics of Regulation*. New York: Basic Books.

——. (1989) *Bureaucracy*. New York: Basic Books.

——. (1994) "What to Do about Crime?" *Commentary* (September), 25–34.

——. (1995) "Reforming Criminal Trials." *Wall Street J.,* November 20, 1995, op-ed.

——. (1997) "Criminal Justice in England and America." *Public Interest* (Winter), 3.

Winter, Ralph K. (1992) "Forward: In Defense of Discovery Reform." *Brook. L. Rev.* 58: 263.

Witt, John Fabian. (2007) *Patriots and Cosmopolitans: Hidden Histories of American Law*. Cambridge, Mass.: Harvard University Press.

Wokutch, Richard E. (1992) *Worker Protection, Japanese Style: Occupational Safety and Health in the Auto Industry*. Ithaca, N.Y.: ILR Press.

Wolchover, David. (1989) "Should Judges Sum Up on the Facts?" *Criminal L. Rev.* 1989: 781.

Wold, Jon, and John Culver. (1987) "The Defeat of the California Justices." *Judicature* (April/May): 323.

Woo, Junda. (1993) "Legal Beat: Business Finds Suits on Security Hard to Defend." *Wall Street J.,* September 1, 1993, B1.

Wood, B. Dan, and Richard Waterman. (1991) "The Dynamics of Political Control of the Bureaucracy." *Am. Political Science Rev.* 85: 801.

Woodard, Colin. (2011) *American Nations: A History of the Eleven Rival Regional Cultures of North America*. New York: Penguin Books.

Workers Compensation Research Institute. (1988) "Reducing Litigation." *WCRI Research Brief,* 4.

Yamanouchi, Kazuo. (1974) "Administrative Guidance and the Rule of Law." *Law in Japan* 7: 22.

Yeazell, Steven. (1994) "The Misunderstood Consequences of Modern Court Process." *Wis. L. Rev.* 1994: 631.

Yoon, Albert. (2001) "Damage Caps and Civil Litigation: An Empirical Study of Medical Malpractice Litigation in the South." *Am. Law & Econ. Rev.* 3: 199–227.

Young, Michael. (1984) "Judicial Review of Administrative Guidance: Governmentally Encouraged Consensual Dispute Resolution in Japan." *Colum. L. Rev.* 84: 923.

Zehnder, Egon. (1987) "The Litigious Society: Is It Hampering Creativity, Innovation and Our Ability to Compete?" *Corporate Issues Monitor* 23, 1.

Zimmerman, Adam. (2011) "Distributing Justice." *N.Y.U. L. Rev.* 86: 500.

Zimring, Frank. (2017) *When Police Kill*. Cambridge, Mass.: Harvard University Press.

Zimring, Frank, and Gordon Hawkins. (1986) *Capital Punishment and the American Agenda*. Cambridge: Cambridge University Press.

———. (1997) *Crime Is Not the Problem: Lethal Violence in America*. New York: Oxford University Press.

Index